Introductory Accounting
Exercise Workbook
Combo Edition

755 Practice Questions and Business Cases
Pertaining to Financial Accounting,
Management Accounting
and Financial Audit

L Castelluzzo

Preface

This book provides the reader with an opportunity to practice the double entry system of accounting, managerial accounting, finance, audit, and full cycle accounting.

Financial Accounting 200 Multiple Choice
Financial Accounting 200 Non-Multiple Choice
Managerial Accounting Key Performance Indicating Metrics 200 Business Cases
Financial Audit 150 Multiple Choice
Financial Accounting 1 Year Full Cycle from Transactions to Financial Statements 5 Cases

The solutions are provided for each question, along with an explanation, so that the student will be able to pinpoint exactly where any errors may have been made.

These financial accounting questions pertain to fictitious companies with revenues from services and sales. They include sales revenue, sales returns, various expenses, capital purchases, depreciation, dividend payouts, unearned revenue, and prepaid expenses. There are also practice questions for business loans, which include the posting of interest expense as well as the principal portion of the loan repayment.

The businesses cases involve the calculation revenue, cost of sales, wages, salaries, overhead, depreciation of buildings, depreciation of equipment, and a high-level effective tax rate. The quantitative analysis involves the calculation of gross margin, labor costs, fixed costs, net income, EBITDA, the tax effect, cash flow, and break-even sales quantity.

The 5 full cycle cases are each presented as a list of transactions for a full yearly cycle, and then the reader can then prepare a full set of journal entries, as well as a general ledger, trial balance, balance sheet, income statement, statement of retained earnings, and cash flow statement. These comprehensive accounting cases cover fictitious start-up companies with revenues from services and sales, as well as sales returns, various expenses, capital purchases, depreciation, shareholder investment and dividends, unearned revenue, prepaid expenses, the year-end closing entry to book the income statement accounts to retained earnings. Each case also includes a business loan, along with the loan amortization schedule which allows the student to practice posting journal entries for interest expense and loan repayments.

This book does not teach the theory, but instead, it is intended to allow students to practice what they have learned in their introductory accounting, managerial accounting, and audit courses.

Financial Accounting

Types of Accounts

Debits are represented by "DR" and credits are represented by "CR".

Asset accounts represent money or any other items that the company owns or something which will provide the company with a future benefit. When assets are increased, they are debited. When assets are decreased, they are credited.

Liability accounts represent money or any other amounts that the company does not own. When liabilities are increased, they are credited. When liabilities are decreased, they are debited.

Revenue accounts represent amounts that the company has earned from their regular operations. When revenues are increased, they are credited. When revenues are decreased, they are debited.

Expense accounts represent amounts that the company has spent through the course of their regular operations. When expenses are increased, they are debited. When expenses are decreased, they are credited.

Contra accounts represent a reduction to an account, which is tracked separately. Examples of contra accounts are sales returns, allowance for doubtful accounts, and accumulated depreciation on the property plant & equipment accounts. Debits and credits to contra accounts are posted in a reverse manner, when compared to the account to which they apply.

The following is a guide for how these entries are posted.

Sell services:
DR Accounts Receivable
  CR Sales

Buy inventory:
DR Inventory
  CR Accounts Payable

Sell inventory:
DR Accounts Receivable
  CR Sales Revenue
DR Cost of Goods Sold
  CR Inventory

Sales are returned:
DR Sales Returns
  CR Accounts Receivable
DR Inventory
  CR Cost of Goods Sold

Pay rent:
DR Rent Expense
  CR Accounts Payable

Pay employees:
DR Wages Expense
  CR Accounts Payable

Cash is received from accounts receivable for sales:
DR Cash
  CR Accounts Receivable

Cash is paid to settle amounts owing in accounts payable for purchases:
DR Accounts Payable
  CR Cash

When it is estimated that an amount might not be collectible:
DR Bad Debt Expense
  CR Allowance for Doubtful Accounts

When it is confirmed that an amount will not be collectible:
DR Allowance for Doubtful Accounts
  CR Accounts Receivable

Buy equipment that will be used by the business for more than one year:
DR Equipment
  CR Accounts Payable

Depreciate equipment for the portion of the useful life that has passed:
DR Depreciation Expense
  CR Accumulated Depreciation

Buy a building :
DR Building
  CR Cash

Depreciate building for the portion of the useful life that has passed:
DR Depreciation Expense
  CR Accumulated Depreciation

Receive a loan that is to be repaid over the course of more than one year:
DR Cash
  CR Note Payable

Payment is made to repay a long-term loan
DR Interest Expense
DR Note Payable
  CR Cash

Pay upfront for expenses that will be incurred in the future:
DR Prepaid Expense
  CR Accounts Payable
* NOTE: Prepaid Expense is an asset account because it represents a future benefit whereby the company will receive goods/services in the future.

Amortize a prepaid expense as it is incurred:
DR Expense
  CR Prepaid Expense

Receive upfront payment goods/services that will be provided in the future:
DR Cash
  CR Unearned Revenue

Provide the goods/services that had been paid for upfront beforehand:
DR Unearned Revenue*
  CR Revenue
* NOTE: Unearned Revenue is a liability account because it represents an obligation to provide goods/services in the future.

Pay a dividend to a shareholder:
DR Retained Earnings
  CR Cash

Financial Accounting Multiple Choice Questions

1 Pharma Drug Company Ltd. sells several different types of medications. This month, Pharma Drug Company Ltd. accepted 22000 batches of pills which were returned by customers. These products had been marked up by 35% and they had originally been bought at a per-unit cost of $2700.
   A) DR Sales Returns $3,510
       DR Inventory $2,700
            CR Accounts Receivable $3,510
            CR Cost of Goods Sold $2,700
   B) DR Accounts Receivable $80,190,000
       DR Accounts Receivable $59,400,000
            CR Sales Returns $80,190,000
            CR Inventory $59,400,000
   C) DR Accounts Receivable $3,510
       DR Accounts Receivable $2,700
            CR Sales Returns $3,510
            CR Inventory $2,700
   D) DR Sales Returns $80,190,000
       DR Inventory $59,400,000
            CR Accounts Receivable $80,190,000
            CR Cost of Goods Sold $59,400,000

2 A to Z Event Guru Ltd sells several different types of start-to-finish event planning services for large gatherings. Today, A to Z Event Guru Ltd has paid cash to their supplier to fully pay off their account payable balance, which was $76000.
   A) DR Accounts Payable $76,000
            CR Cash $76,000
   B) DR Cash $6,333
            CR Accounts Payable $6,333
   C) DR Cash $76,000
            CR Accounts Payable $76,000
   D) DR Accounts Payable $6,333
            CR Cash $6,333

3 Sprike Inc offers their customers a wide range of athletic apparel. This December, Sprike Inc recognized 1 year of depreciation on equipment which had a total useful life of 10 years, and which had originally cost $260000.
   A) DR Accumulated Depreciation $26,000
            CR Depreciation expense $26,000
   B) DR Depreciation expense $26,000
            CR Accumulated Depreciation $26,000
   C) DR Depreciation expense $260,000
            CR Accumulated Depreciation $260,000
   D) DR Accumulated Depreciation $260,000
            CR Depreciation expense $260,000

4   Pharma Drug Company Ltd. is a privately-held corporation which focuses on their niche of premium medications. Today Pharma Drug Company Ltd. sold 29400 batches of pills which had a 30% mark-up. They had originally been bought from their suppliers for a unit cost of $2340.

    A)   DR Sales $3,042
       DR Sales $2,340
           CR Accounts Receivable $3,042
           CR Cost of Goods Sold $2,340
    B)   DR Accounts Receivable $3,042
       DR Cost of Goods Sold $2,340
           CR Sales $3,042
           CR Inventory $2,340
    C)   DR Accounts Receivable $89,434,800
       DR Cost of Goods Sold $68,796,000
           CR Sales $89,434,800
           CR Inventory $68,796,000
    D)   DR Sales $89,434,800
       DR Sales $68,796,000
           CR Accounts Receivable $89,434,800
           CR Cost of Goods Sold $68,796,000

5   Mount Tessory Academy is a company which offers their customers a wide selection of private school education. This week, Mount Tessory Academy paid each of the 2790 staff members their bi-weekly wages, which per person had a cost of $2600.

    A)   DR Accounts Payable $7,254,000
           CR Wage expense $7,254,000
    B)   DR Wage expense $7,254,000
           CR Accounts Payable $7,254,000
    C)   DR Wage expense $2,600
           CR Accounts Payable $2,600
    D)   DR Accounts Payable $2,600
           CR Wage expense $2,600

6   A to Z Event Guru Ltd sells several different types of start-to-finish event planning services for large gatherings. Today A to Z Event Guru Ltd signed up for a loan with a 5% interest rate, and so the bank immediately transferred cash to the company in the amount of $103000.

    A)   DR Loan Payable $103,000
           CR Cash $103,000
    B)   DR Cash $103,000
           CR Loan Payable $103,000
    C)   DR Cash $5,150
           CR Loan Payable $5,150
    D)   DR Loan Payable $5,150
           CR Cash $5,150

7   Sprike Inc is a company which offers their customers a wide selection of athletic apparel. Today, Sprike Inc received an upfront payment for 1510 batches of athletic t-shirts which will be provided to the customer 6 months from now. The payment for each was $1600.

A)   DR Unearned Revenue $1,600
          CR Cash $1,600

B)   DR Cash $1,600
          CR Unearned Revenue $1,600

C)   DR Cash $2,416,000
          CR Unearned Revenue $2,416,000

D)   DR Unearned Revenue $2,416,000
          CR Cash $2,416,000

8   Club Disco is a company which offers their customers a wide selection of dance venue rentals for large family gatherings. This month, Club Disco must amortize 1 month worth of utility bills which they had prepaid at the beginning of the year. The amount that they had paid upfront for the year was $45600.

A)   DR Prepaid Expense $3,800
          CR Utilities expense $3,800

B)   DR Utilities expense $3,800
          CR Prepaid Expense $3,800

C)   DR Utilities expense $45,600
          CR Prepaid Expense $45,600

D)   DR Prepaid Expense $45,600
          CR Utilities expense $45,600

9   NBG Media Corporation is a corporation which sells broadcasting services for advertising agencies. This month, NBG Media Corporation paid for 1 month of rent for their company's office space. Each month, the rent owing was $9000.

A)   DR Accounts Payable $108,000
          CR Rent expense $108,000

B)   DR Rent expense $108,000
          CR Accounts Payable $108,000

C)   DR Rent expense $9,000
          CR Accounts Payable $9,000

D)   DR Accounts Payable $9,000
          CR Rent expense $9,000

10   AC&C Ltd. is a privately-held corporation which focuses on their niche of premium cell phone plans. This month, AC&C Ltd. must amortize 1 month worth of utility bills which they had prepaid at the beginning of the year. The amount that they had paid upfront for the year was $37200.

A)   DR Prepaid Expense $3,100
          CR Utilities expense $3,100

B)   DR Utilities expense $3,100
          CR Prepaid Expense $3,100

C)   DR Utilities expense $37,200
          CR Prepaid Expense $37,200

D)   DR Prepaid Expense $37,200
          CR Utilities expense $37,200

11   Pharma Drug Company Ltd. sells several different types of medications. This month, Pharma Drug Company Ltd. accepted 14800 batches of pills which were returned by customers. These products had been marked up by 35% and they had originally been bought at a per-unit cost of $1600.
  A)   DR Sales Returns $2,080
          DR Inventory $1,600
                  CR Accounts Receivable $2,080
                  CR Cost of Goods Sold $1,600
  B)   DR Accounts Receivable $31,968,000
          DR Accounts Receivable $23,680,000
                  CR Sales Returns $31,968,000
                  CR Inventory $23,680,000
  C)   DR Accounts Receivable $2,080
          DR Accounts Receivable $1,600
                  CR Sales Returns $2,080
                  CR Inventory $1,600
  D)   DR Sales Returns $31,968,000
          DR Inventory $23,680,000
                  CR Accounts Receivable $31,968,000
                  CR Cost of Goods Sold $23,680,000

12   Pharma Drug Company Ltd. is a company which offers their customers a wide selection of medications. This week, Pharma Drug Company Ltd. purchased 2000 batches of pills which were placed into the warehouse, and which had a per unit cost of $2700.
  A)   DR Accounts Payable $5,400,000
                  CR Inventory $5,400,000
  B)   DR Inventory $5,400,000
                  CR Accounts Payable $5,400,000
  C)   DR Inventory $2,700
                  CR Accounts Payable $2,700
  D)   DR Accounts Payable $2,700
                  CR Inventory $2,700

13   Fairway Malls offers their customers a wide range of retail spaces in their shopping centers. Today, Fairway Malls has paid cash to their supplier to fully pay off their account payable balance, which was $8000.
  A)   DR Accounts Payable $0,667
                  CR Cash $0,667
  B)   DR Cash $8,000
                  CR Accounts Payable $8,000
  C)   DR Cash $0,667
                  CR Accounts Payable $0,667
  D)   DR Accounts Payable $8,000
                  CR Cash $8,000

14   Hogtown Records sells several different types of audio services for local musicians to record their music albums. This December, Hogtown Records recognized 1 year of depreciation on equipment which had a total useful life of 10 years, and which had originally cost $130000.
- A) DR Accumulated Depreciation $130,000
    CR Depreciation expense $130,000
- B) DR Depreciation expense $130,000
    CR Accumulated Depreciation $130,000
- C) DR Depreciation expense $13,000
    CR Accumulated Depreciation $13,000
- D) DR Accumulated Depreciation $13,000
    CR Depreciation expense $13,000

15   Mr. Mop provides their customers with household cleaners. This month, Mr. Mop has estimated that 15% of the accounts receivable might not end up being collectable, based on past experience. The accounts receivable will need to be adjusted from its current balance of $106000.
- A) DR Bad Debt expense $106,000
    CR Allowance for Doubtful Accounts $106,000
- B) DR Allowance for Doubtful Accounts $15,900
    CR Bad Debt expense $15,900
- C) DR Allowance for Doubtful Accounts $106,000
    CR Bad Debt expense $106,000
- D) DR Bad Debt expense $15,900
    CR Allowance for Doubtful Accounts $15,900

16   Payday Now is an organization which specializes in providing their customers with short-term loan arrangements. This December, Payday Now recognized 1 year of depreciation on a building which had a total useful life of 25 years, and which had originally been bought for $84000.
- A) DR Depreciation expense $84,000
    CR Accumulated Depreciation $84,000
- B) DR Accumulated Depreciation $3,360
    CR Depreciation expense $3,360
- C) DR Accumulated Depreciation $84,000
    CR Depreciation expense $84,000
- D) DR Depreciation expense $3,360
    CR Accumulated Depreciation $3,360

17   NY Fitness is a corporation which sells gym memberships for professional sports teams. This January, NY Fitness has made an advance payment to cover the next 12 months of utility bills, which have a monthly cost of $1100.
- A) DR Cash $1,100
    CR Prepaid Expense $1,100
- B) DR Prepaid Expense $1,100
    CR Cash $1,100
- C) DR Prepaid Expense $13,200
    CR Cash $13,200
- D) DR Cash $13,200
    CR Prepaid Expense $13,200

18   AC&C Ltd. is a market leader that is well-known for their brand of cell phone plans. This month, AC&C Ltd. must amortize 1 month worth of utility bills which they had prepaid at the beginning of the year. The amount that they had paid upfront for the year was $32400.
   A)   DR Utilities expense $32,400
             CR Prepaid Expense $32,400
   B)   DR Prepaid Expense $2,700
             CR Utilities expense $2,700
   C)   DR Prepaid Expense $32,400
             CR Utilities expense $32,400
   D)   DR Utilities expense $2,700
             CR Prepaid Expense $2,700

19   Payday Now is a market leader that is well-known for their brand of short-term loan arrangements. Today Payday Now signed up for a loan with a 5% interest rate, and so the bank immediately transferred cash to the company in the amount of $39000.
   A)   DR Cash $39,000
             CR Loan Payable $39,000
   B)   DR Loan Payable $1,950
             CR Cash $1,950
   C)   DR Loan Payable $39,000
             CR Cash $39,000
   D)   DR Cash $1,950
             CR Loan Payable $1,950

20   Kola-Nut Ltd provides their customers with soft drinks. Today Kola-Nut Ltd sold 35800 batches of soda bottles which had a 30% mark-up. They had originally been bought from their suppliers for a unit cost of $1950.
   A)   DR Accounts Receivable $2,535
         DR Cost of Goods Sold $1,950
             CR Sales $2,535
             CR Inventory $1,950
   B)   DR Sales $90,753,000
         DR Sales $69,810,000
             CR Accounts Receivable $90,753,000
             CR Cost of Goods Sold $69,810,000
   C)   DR Sales $2,535
         DR Sales $1,950
             CR Accounts Receivable $2,535
             CR Cost of Goods Sold $1,950
   D)   DR Accounts Receivable $90,753,000
         DR Cost of Goods Sold $69,810,000
             CR Sales $90,753,000
             CR Inventory $69,810,000

21 Mr. Mop is an organization which specializes in providing their customers with household cleaners. This month, Mr. Mop accepted 18900 tons of cleaning solution which were returned by customers. These products had been marked up by 35% and they had originally been bought at a per-unit cost of $2000.
   A)   DR Sales Returns $51,030,000
        DR Inventory $37,800,000
             CR Accounts Receivable $51,030,000
             CR Cost of Goods Sold $37,800,000
   B)   DR Accounts Receivable $2,600
        DR Accounts Receivable $2,000
             CR Sales Returns $2,600
             CR Inventory $2,000
   C)   DR Accounts Receivable $51,030,000
        DR Accounts Receivable $37,800,000
             CR Sales Returns $51,030,000
             CR Inventory $37,800,000
   D)   DR Sales Returns $2,600
        DR Inventory $2,000
             CR Accounts Receivable $2,600
             CR Cost of Goods Sold $2,000

22 AC&C Ltd. is a privately-held corporation which focuses on their niche of premium cell phone plans. This December, AC&C Ltd. recognized 1 year of depreciation on equipment which had a total useful life of 10 years, and which had originally cost $90000.
   A)   DR Depreciation expense $9,000
             CR Accumulated Depreciation $9,000
   B)   DR Accumulated Depreciation $90,000
             CR Depreciation expense $90,000
   C)   DR Accumulated Depreciation $9,000
             CR Depreciation expense $9,000
   D)   DR Depreciation expense $90,000
             CR Accumulated Depreciation $90,000

23 Air America sells various global flights. Air America has just provided 1600 large orders which had been paid for in advance last year. Each order was in the amount of $1700.
   A)   DR Sales $1,700
             CR Unearned Revenue $1,700
   B)   DR Unearned Revenue $1,700
             CR Sales $1,700
   C)   DR Unearned Revenue $2,720,000
             CR Sales $2,720,000
   D)   DR Sales $2,720,000
             CR Unearned Revenue $2,720,000

24 Payday Now offers their customers a wide range of short-term loan arrangements. Today, Payday Now bought equipment which has a 5 year useful life, and which had a cost of $15000.
A) DR Equipment $3,000
     CR Accounts Payable $3,000
B) DR Accounts Payable $15,000
     CR Equipment $15,000
C) DR Accounts Payable $3,000
     CR Equipment $3,000
D) DR Equipment $15,000
     CR Accounts Payable $15,000

25 Air America provides their customers with global flights. Today Air America signed up for a loan with a 5% interest rate, and so the bank immediately transferred cash to the company in the amount of $58000.
A) DR Cash $2,900
     CR Loan Payable $2,900
B) DR Loan Payable $58,000
     CR Cash $58,000
C) DR Loan Payable $2,900
     CR Cash $2,900
D) DR Cash $58,000
     CR Loan Payable $58,000

26 Paytech Ltd offers their customers a wide range of payroll transaction processing services. This month, Paytech Ltd paid for 1 month of rent for their company's office space. Each month, the rent owing was $14000.
A) DR Accounts Payable $14,000
     CR Rent expense $14,000
B) DR Rent expense $14,000
     CR Accounts Payable $14,000
C) DR Rent expense $168,000
     CR Accounts Payable $168,000
D) DR Accounts Payable $168,000
     CR Rent expense $168,000

27 Mount Tessory Academy is a market leader that is well-known for their brand of private school education. This month, Mount Tessory Academy has estimated that 15% of the accounts receivable might not end up being collectable, based on past experience. The accounts receivable will need to be adjusted from its current balance of $53000.
A) DR Bad Debt expense $7,950
     CR Allowance for Doubtful Accounts $7,950
B) DR Allowance for Doubtful Accounts $53,000
     CR Bad Debt expense $53,000
C) DR Allowance for Doubtful Accounts $7,950
     CR Bad Debt expense $7,950
D) DR Bad Debt expense $53,000
     CR Allowance for Doubtful Accounts $53,000

17

28   Mount Tessory Academy provides their customers with private school education. This month, Mount Tessory Academy must amortize 1 month worth of utility bills which they had prepaid at the beginning of the year. The amount that they had paid upfront for the year was $26400.
    A)   DR Utilities expense $26,400
                    CR Prepaid Expense $26,400
    B)   DR Prepaid Expense $2,200
                    CR Utilities expense $2,200
    C)   DR Prepaid Expense $26,400
                    CR Utilities expense $26,400
    D)   DR Utilities expense $2,200
                    CR Prepaid Expense $2,200

29   NY Fitness is an organization which specializes in providing their customers with gym memberships for professional sports teams. This year, NY Fitness has provided 2200 team memberships each of which earned revenues of $1530.
    A)   DR Accounts Receivable $3,366,000
                    CR Sales $3,366,000
    B)   DR Sales $1,530
                    CR Accounts Receivable $1,530
    C)   DR Sales $3,366,000
                    CR Accounts Receivable $3,366,000
    D)   DR Accounts Receivable $1,530
                    CR Sales $1,530

30   Jameson & Jameson is an organization which specializes in providing their customers with soap products. Today, Jameson & Jameson received an upfront payment for 5540 truckloads of bars of soap which will be provided to the customer 6 months from now. The payment for each was $1700.
    A)   DR Unearned Revenue $9,418,000
                    CR Cash $9,418,000
    B)   DR Cash $9,418,000
                    CR Unearned Revenue $9,418,000
    C)   DR Cash $1,700
                    CR Unearned Revenue $1,700
    D)   DR Unearned Revenue $1,700
                    CR Cash $1,700

31   A to Z Event Guru Ltd sells various start-to-finish event planning services for large gatherings. This week, A to Z Event Guru Ltd paid each of the 2910 staff members their bi-weekly wages, which per person had a cost of $2600.
    A)   DR Wage expense $2,600
                    CR Accounts Payable $2,600
    B)   DR Accounts Payable $7,566,000
                    CR Wage expense $7,566,000
    C)   DR Accounts Payable $2,600
                    CR Wage expense $2,600
    D)   DR Wage expense $7,566,000
                    CR Accounts Payable $7,566,000

32 Grand Convention Ltd is a market leader that is well-known for their brand of banquet hall rentals for corporate meetings. This December, Grand Convention Ltd has paid each of the company's 2400 owners an annual dividend in the amount of $26000.
   A)   DR Retained Earnings $26,000
            CR Cash $26,000
   B)   DR Cash $62,400,000
            CR Retained Earnings $62,400,000
   C)   DR Cash $26,000
            CR Retained Earnings $26,000
   D)   DR Retained Earnings $62,400,000
            CR Cash $62,400,000

33 Grand Convention Ltd is a company which offers their customers a wide selection of banquet hall rentals for corporate meetings. This December, Grand Convention Ltd has paid each of the company's 1000 owners an annual dividend in the amount of $13000.
   A)   DR Cash $13,000,000
            CR Retained Earnings $13,000,000
   B)   DR Retained Earnings $13,000,000
            CR Cash $13,000,000
   C)   DR Retained Earnings $13,000
            CR Cash $13,000
   D)   DR Cash $13,000
            CR Retained Earnings $13,000

34 Kola-Nut Ltd is an organization which specializes in providing their customers with soft drinks. Today Kola-Nut Ltd sold 43400 batches of soda bottles which had a 30% mark-up. They had originally been bought from their suppliers for a unit cost of $2310.
   A)   DR Accounts Receivable $130,330,200
         DR Cost of Goods Sold $100,254,000
            CR Sales $130,330,200
            CR Inventory $100,254,000
   B)   DR Sales $3,003
         DR Sales $2,310
            CR Accounts Receivable $3,003
            CR Cost of Goods Sold $2,310
   C)   DR Sales $130,330,200
         DR Sales $100,254,000
            CR Accounts Receivable $130,330,200
            CR Cost of Goods Sold $100,254,000
   D)   DR Accounts Receivable $3,003
         DR Cost of Goods Sold $2,310
            CR Sales $3,003
            CR Inventory $2,310

35 Fairway Malls sells several different types of retail spaces in their shopping centers. This December, Fairway Malls has paid each of the company's 2100 owners an annual dividend in the amount of $23000.
    A)   DR Retained Earnings $48,300,000
              CR Cash $48,300,000
    B)   DR Cash $23,000
              CR Retained Earnings $23,000
    C)   DR Cash $48,300,000
              CR Retained Earnings $48,300,000
    D)   DR Retained Earnings $23,000
              CR Cash $23,000

36 NBG Media Corporation is an organization which specializes in providing their customers with broadcasting services for advertising agencies. This month, NBG Media Corporation made 1 monthly loan repayment towards their long-term note payable. The interest portion was 60% of the payment. The total amount paid in cash was $15000.
    A)   DR Interest Expense $9,000
              DR Loan Payable $6,000
              CR Cash $15,000
    B)   DR Cash $15,000
              CR Interest Expense $6,000
              CR Loan Payable $9,000
    C)   DR Cash $15,000
              CR Interest Expense $9,000
              CR Loan Payable $6,000
    D)   DR Interest Expense $6,000
              DR Loan Payable $9,000
              CR Cash $15,000

37 Hogtown Records offers their customers a wide range of audio services for local musicians to record their music albums. This month, Hogtown Records paid for 1 month of rent for their company's office space. Each month, the rent owing was $10000.
    A)   DR Accounts Payable $120,000
              CR Rent expense $120,000
    B)   DR Rent expense $120,000
              CR Accounts Payable $120,000
    C)   DR Rent expense $10,000
              CR Accounts Payable $10,000
    D)   DR Accounts Payable $10,000
              CR Rent expense $10,000

38 David & Johnson provides their customers with legal services. This month, David & Johnson paid for 1 month of rent for their company's office space. Each month, the rent owing was $20000.
    A) DR Accounts Payable $20,000
            CR Rent expense $20,000
    B) DR Rent expense $20,000
            CR Accounts Payable $20,000
    C) DR Rent expense $240,000
            CR Accounts Payable $240,000
    D) DR Accounts Payable $240,000
            CR Rent expense $240,000

39 Mr. Mop is an organization which specializes in providing their customers with household cleaners. This month, Mr. Mop paid for 1 month of rent for the warehouse room, which has a monthly cost of $1000.
    A) DR Accounts Payable $1,000
            CR Rent expense $1,000
    B) DR Rent expense $1,000
            CR Accounts Payable $1,000
    C) DR Rent expense $12,000
            CR Accounts Payable $12,000
    D) DR Accounts Payable $12,000
            CR Rent expense $12,000

40 Comedy 253 is a privately-held corporation which focuses on their niche of premium live performances of stand-up comedy. This year, Comedy 253 has provided 1500 shows each of which earned revenues of $2440.
    A) DR Sales $3,660,000
            CR Accounts Receivable $3,660,000
    B) DR Accounts Receivable $3,660,000
            CR Sales $3,660,000
    C) DR Accounts Receivable $2,440
            CR Sales $2,440
    D) DR Sales $2,440
            CR Accounts Receivable $2,440

41 Paytech Ltd sells various payroll transaction processing services. This month, Paytech Ltd must amortize 1 month worth of utility bills which they had prepaid at the beginning of the year. The amount that they had paid upfront for the year was $12000.
    A) DR Prepaid Expense $1,000
            CR Utilities expense $1,000
    B) DR Utilities expense $1,000
            CR Prepaid Expense $1,000
    C) DR Utilities expense $12,000
            CR Prepaid Expense $12,000
    D) DR Prepaid Expense $12,000
            CR Utilities expense $12,000

42   Pharma Drug Company Ltd. offers their customers a wide range of medications. This week, Pharma Drug Company Ltd. purchased 2250 batches of pills which were placed into the warehouse, and which had a per unit cost of $1100.
A)   DR Inventory $2,475,000
            CR Accounts Payable $2,475,000
B)   DR Accounts Payable $1,100
            CR Inventory $1,100
C)   DR Accounts Payable $2,475,000
            CR Inventory $2,475,000
D)   DR Inventory $1,100
            CR Accounts Payable $1,100

43   A to Z Event Guru Ltd is a privately-held corporation which focuses on their niche of premium start-to-finish event planning services for large gatherings. This December, A to Z Event Guru Ltd recognized 1 year of depreciation on equipment which had a total useful life of 10 years, and which had originally cost $220000.
A)   DR Depreciation expense $220,000
            CR Accumulated Depreciation $220,000
B)   DR Accumulated Depreciation $22,000
            CR Depreciation expense $22,000
C)   DR Accumulated Depreciation $220,000
            CR Depreciation expense $220,000
D)   DR Depreciation expense $22,000
            CR Accumulated Depreciation $22,000

44   Kola-Nut Ltd offers their customers a wide range of soft drinks. Today Kola-Nut Ltd sold 45800 batches of soda bottles which had a 30% mark-up. They had originally been bought from their suppliers for a unit cost of $2920.
A)   DR Sales $173,856,800
      DR Sales $133,736,000
            CR Accounts Receivable $173,856,800
            CR Cost of Goods Sold $133,736,000
B)   DR Accounts Receivable $173,856,800
      DR Cost of Goods Sold $133,736,000
            CR Sales $173,856,800
            CR Inventory $133,736,000
C)   DR Accounts Receivable $3,796
      DR Cost of Goods Sold $2,920
            CR Sales $3,796
            CR Inventory $2,920
D)   DR Sales $3,796
      DR Sales $2,920
            CR Accounts Receivable $3,796
            CR Cost of Goods Sold $2,920

45   Jameson & Jameson is a company which offers their customers a wide selection of soap products. This month, Jameson & Jameson accepted 22700 truckloads of bars of soap which were returned by customers. These products had been marked up by 35% and they had originally been bought at a per-unit cost of $1500.

    A)   DR Accounts Receivable $45,967,500
            DR Accounts Receivable $34,050,000
                CR Sales Returns $45,967,500
                CR Inventory $34,050,000

    B)   DR Sales Returns $45,967,500
            DR Inventory $34,050,000
                CR Accounts Receivable $45,967,500
                CR Cost of Goods Sold $34,050,000

    C)   DR Sales Returns $1,950
            DR Inventory $1,500
                CR Accounts Receivable $1,950
                CR Cost of Goods Sold $1,500

    D)   DR Accounts Receivable $1,950
            DR Accounts Receivable $1,500
                CR Sales Returns $1,950
                CR Inventory $1,500

46   McGerald's is an organization which specializes in providing their customers with fast food meals. Today, McGerald's bought equipment which has a 5 year useful life, and which had a cost of $25000.

    A)   DR Accounts Payable $5,000
                CR Equipment $5,000

    B)   DR Equipment $5,000
                CR Accounts Payable $5,000

    C)   DR Equipment $25,000
                CR Accounts Payable $25,000

    D)   DR Accounts Payable $25,000
                CR Equipment $25,000

47   Mount Tessory Academy sells several different types of private school education. This January, Mount Tessory Academy has made an advance payment to cover the next 12 months of utility bills, which have a monthly cost of $1300.

    A)   DR Prepaid Expense $15,600
                CR Cash $15,600

    B)   DR Cash $1,300
                CR Prepaid Expense $1,300

    C)   DR Cash $15,600
                CR Prepaid Expense $15,600

    D)   DR Prepaid Expense $1,300
                CR Cash $1,300

48   Sprike Inc is a corporation which sells athletic apparel. This December, Sprike Inc recognized 1 year of depreciation on equipment which had a total useful life of 10 years, and which had originally cost $240000.
   A)   DR Accumulated Depreciation $24,000
            CR Depreciation expense $24,000
   B)   DR Depreciation expense $24,000
            CR Accumulated Depreciation $24,000
   C)   DR Depreciation expense $240,000
            CR Accumulated Depreciation $240,000
   D)   DR Accumulated Depreciation $240,000
            CR Depreciation expense $240,000

49   AC&C Ltd. is a market leader that is well-known for their brand of cell phone plans. This year, AC&C Ltd. has provided 1700 monthly cell phone service each of which earned revenues of $1680.
   A)   DR Sales $2,856,000
            CR Accounts Receivable $2,856,000
   B)   DR Accounts Receivable $2,856,000
            CR Sales $2,856,000
   C)   DR Accounts Receivable $1,680
            CR Sales $1,680
   D)   DR Sales $1,680
            CR Accounts Receivable $1,680

50   Mr. Mop is a company which offers their customers a wide selection of household cleaners. This month, Mr. Mop paid for 1 month of rent for the warehouse room, which has a monthly costs of $2200.
   A)   DR Rent expense $2,200
            CR Accounts Payable $2,200
   B)   DR Accounts Payable $26,400
            CR Rent expense $26,400
   C)   DR Accounts Payable $2,200
            CR Rent expense $2,200
   D)   DR Rent expense $26,400
            CR Accounts Payable $26,400

51 Mr. Mop is a corporation which sells household cleaners. This month, Mr. Mop accepted 26900 tons of cleaning solution which were returned by customers. These products had been marked up by 35% and they had originally been bought at a per-unit cost of $2700.

A) DR Sales Returns $98,050,500
DR Inventory $72,630,000
    CR Accounts Receivable $98,050,500
    CR Cost of Goods Sold $72,630,000

B) DR Accounts Receivable $3,510
DR Accounts Receivable $2,700
    CR Sales Returns $3,510
    CR Inventory $2,700

C) DR Accounts Receivable $98,050,500
DR Accounts Receivable $72,630,000
    CR Sales Returns $98,050,500
    CR Inventory $72,630,000

D) DR Sales Returns $3,510
DR Inventory $2,700
    CR Accounts Receivable $3,510
    CR Cost of Goods Sold $2,700

52 Mr. Mop offers their customers a wide range of household cleaners. Today, Mr. Mop received an upfront payment for 3260 tons of cleaning solution which will be provided to the customer 6 months from now. The payment for each was $1200.

A) DR Cash $1,200
    CR Unearned Revenue $1,200

B) DR Unearned Revenue $3,912,000
    CR Cash $3,912,000

C) DR Unearned Revenue $1,200
    CR Cash $1,200

D) DR Cash $3,912,000
    CR Unearned Revenue $3,912,000

53 Pharma Drug Company Ltd. is a company which offers their customers a wide selection of medications. This month, Pharma Drug Company Ltd. paid for 1 month of rent for the warehouse room, which has a monthly costs of $1000.

A) DR Rent expense $12,000
    CR Accounts Payable $12,000

B) DR Accounts Payable $1,000
    CR Rent expense $1,000

C) DR Accounts Payable $12,000
    CR Rent expense $12,000

D) DR Rent expense $1,000
    CR Accounts Payable $1,000

54   Sprike Inc is a market leader that is well-known for their brand of athletic apparel. This
      week, Sprike Inc purchased 1460 batches of athletic t-shirts which were placed into the
      warehouse, and which had a per unit cost of $1700.
      A)   DR Inventory $1,700
                  CR Accounts Payable $1,700
      B)   DR Accounts Payable $2,482,000
                  CR Inventory $2,482,000
      C)   DR Accounts Payable $1,700
                  CR Inventory $1,700
      D)   DR Inventory $2,482,000
                  CR Accounts Payable $2,482,000

55   AC&C Ltd. offers their customers a wide range of cell phone plans. This week, AC&C Ltd.
      paid each of the 1220 staff members their bi-weekly wages, which per person had a cost of
      $1000.
      A)   DR Accounts Payable $1,220,000
                  CR Wage expense $1,220,000
      B)   DR Wage expense $1,220,000
                  CR Accounts Payable $1,220,000
      C)   DR Wage expense $1,000
                  CR Accounts Payable $1,000
      D)   DR Accounts Payable $1,000
                  CR Wage expense $1,000

56   Jameson & Jameson is a market leader that is well-known for their brand of soap products.
      Today Jameson & Jameson sold 28600 truckloads of bars of soap which had a 30% mark-
      up. They had originally been bought from their suppliers for a unit cost of $2670.
      A)   DR Sales $99,270,600
            DR Sales $76,362,000
                  CR Accounts Receivable $99,270,600
                  CR Cost of Goods Sold $76,362,000
      B)   DR Accounts Receivable $99,270,600
            DR Cost of Goods Sold $76,362,000
                  CR Sales $99,270,600
                  CR Inventory $76,362,000
      C)   DR Accounts Receivable $3,471
            DR Cost of Goods Sold $2,670
                  CR Sales $3,471
                  CR Inventory $2,670
      D)   DR Sales $3,471
            DR Sales $2,670
                  CR Accounts Receivable $3,471
                  CR Cost of Goods Sold $2,670

57 Mr. Mop is a corporation which sells household cleaners. Today Mr. Mop signed up for a loan with a 5% interest rate, and so the bank immediately transferred cash to the company in the amount of $30000.

    A)   DR Cash $30,000
            CR Loan Payable $30,000
    B)   DR Loan Payable $1,500
            CR Cash $1,500
    C)   DR Loan Payable $30,000
            CR Cash $30,000
    D)   DR Cash $1,500
            CR Loan Payable $1,500

58 AC&C Ltd. is a corporation which sells cell phone plans. Today, AC&C Ltd. received payment upfront for 2200 large orders which will not be provided until early next year. Each order was in the amount of $2500.

    A)   DR Unearned Revenue $2,500
            CR Cash $2,500
    B)   DR Cash $2,500
            CR Unearned Revenue $2,500
    C)   DR Cash $5,500,000
            CR Unearned Revenue $5,500,000
    D)   DR Unearned Revenue $5,500,000
            CR Cash $5,500,000

59 Comedy 253 is a privately-held corporation which focuses on their niche of premium live performances of stand-up comedy. This month, Comedy 253 has estimated that 30% of the accounts receivable might not end up being collectable, based on past experience. The accounts receivable will need to be adjusted from its current balance of $101000.

    A)   DR Allowance for Doubtful Accounts $30,300
            CR Bad Debt expense $30,300
    B)   DR Bad Debt expense $30,300
            CR Allowance for Doubtful Accounts $30,300
    C)   DR Bad Debt expense $101,000
            CR Allowance for Doubtful Accounts $101,000
    D)   DR Allowance for Doubtful Accounts $101,000
            CR Bad Debt expense $101,000

60 Fairway Malls provides their customers with retail spaces in their shopping centers. Today Fairway Malls signed up for a loan with a 5% interest rate, and so the bank immediately transferred cash to the company in the amount of $36000.

    A)   DR Loan Payable $1,800
            CR Cash $1,800
    B)   DR Cash $1,800
            CR Loan Payable $1,800
    C)   DR Cash $36,000
            CR Loan Payable $36,000
    D)   DR Loan Payable $36,000
            CR Cash $36,000

61 LA Met Theatre Company is a company which offers their customers a wide selection of live theatrical performances. Today LA Met Theatre Company signed up for a loan with a 5% interest rate, and so the bank immediately transferred cash to the company in the amount of $74000.
   A)   DR Cash $3,700
               CR Loan Payable $3,700
   B)   DR Loan Payable $74,000
               CR Cash $74,000
   C)   DR Loan Payable $3,700
               CR Cash $3,700
   D)   DR Cash $74,000
               CR Loan Payable $74,000

62 Kola-Nut Ltd is a corporation which sells soft drinks. Today, Kola-Nut Ltd bought equipment which has a 5 year useful life, and which had a cost of $18000.
   A)   DR Equipment $3,600
               CR Accounts Payable $3,600
   B)   DR Accounts Payable $18,000
               CR Equipment $18,000
   C)   DR Accounts Payable $3,600
               CR Equipment $3,600
   D)   DR Equipment $18,000
               CR Accounts Payable $18,000

63 Mr. Mop offers their customers a wide range of household cleaners. Today, Mr. Mop received an upfront payment for 3010 tons of cleaning solution which will be provided to the customer 6 months from now. The payment for each was $2400.
   A)   DR Cash $7,224,000
               CR Unearned Revenue $7,224,000
   B)   DR Unearned Revenue $2,400
               CR Cash $2,400
   C)   DR Unearned Revenue $7,224,000
               CR Cash $7,224,000
   D)   DR Cash $2,400
               CR Unearned Revenue $2,400

64 Kola-Nut Ltd sells several different types of soft drinks. Today, Kola-Nut Ltd has paid cash to their supplier to fully pay off their account payable balance, which was $41000.
   A)   DR Accounts Payable $41,000
               CR Cash $41,000
   B)   DR Cash $3,417
               CR Accounts Payable $3,417
   C)   DR Cash $41,000
               CR Accounts Payable $41,000
   D)   DR Accounts Payable $3,417
               CR Cash $3,417

65 Sprike Inc is a corporation which sells athletic apparel. This month, Sprike Inc paid for 1 month of rent for the warehouse room, which has a monthly costs of $1000.
A) DR Accounts Payable $1,000
   CR Rent expense $1,000
B) DR Rent expense $1,000
   CR Accounts Payable $1,000
C) DR Rent expense $12,000
   CR Accounts Payable $12,000
D) DR Accounts Payable $12,000
   CR Rent expense $12,000

66 Mr. Mop is a market leader that is well-known for their brand of household cleaners. This month, Mr. Mop accepted 17300 tons of cleaning solution which were returned by customers. These products had been marked up by 35% and they had originally been bought at a per-unit cost of $2800.
A) DR Sales Returns $65,394,000
   DR Inventory $48,440,000
      CR Accounts Receivable $65,394,000
      CR Cost of Goods Sold $48,440,000
B) DR Accounts Receivable $3,640
   DR Accounts Receivable $2,800
      CR Sales Returns $3,640
      CR Inventory $2,800
C) DR Accounts Receivable $65,394,000
   DR Accounts Receivable $48,440,000
      CR Sales Returns $65,394,000
      CR Inventory $48,440,000
D) DR Sales Returns $3,640
   DR Inventory $2,800
      CR Accounts Receivable $3,640
      CR Cost of Goods Sold $2,800

67 NY Fitness is a company which offers their customers a wide selection of gym memberships for professional sports teams. Today, NY Fitness has paid cash to their supplier to fully pay off their account payable balance, which was $72000.
A) DR Cash $72,000
   CR Accounts Payable $72,000
B) DR Accounts Payable $72,000
   CR Cash $72,000
C) DR Accounts Payable $6,000
   CR Cash $6,000
D) DR Cash $6,000
   CR Accounts Payable $6,000

68   AC&C Ltd. is a privately-held corporation which focuses on their niche of premium cell phone plans. This week, AC&C Ltd. paid each of the 1370 staff members their bi-weekly wages, which per person had a cost of $1800.
  A)   DR Wage expense $2,466,000
            CR Accounts Payable $2,466,000
  B)   DR Accounts Payable $1,800
            CR Wage expense $1,800
  C)   DR Accounts Payable $2,466,000
            CR Wage expense $2,466,000
  D)   DR Wage expense $1,800
            CR Accounts Payable $1,800

69   Cirque du Lune sells various circus performances. This month, Cirque du Lune must amortize 1 month worth of utility bills which they had prepaid at the beginning of the year. The amount that they had paid upfront for the year was $12000.
  A)   DR Prepaid Expense $1,000
            CR Utilities expense $1,000
  B)   DR Utilities expense $1,000
            CR Prepaid Expense $1,000
  C)   DR Utilities expense $12,000
            CR Prepaid Expense $12,000
  D)   DR Prepaid Expense $12,000
            CR Utilities expense $12,000

70   A to Z Event Guru Ltd sells several different types of start-to-finish event planning services for large gatherings. Today, A to Z Event Guru Ltd has paid cash to their supplier to fully pay off their account payable balance, which was $14000.
  A)   DR Cash $14,000
            CR Accounts Payable $14,000
  B)   DR Accounts Payable $14,000
            CR Cash $14,000
  C)   DR Accounts Payable $1,167
            CR Cash $1,167
  D)   DR Cash $1,167
            CR Accounts Payable $1,167

71 Jameson & Jameson provides their customers with soap products. This month, Jameson & Jameson accepted 9100 truckloads of bars of soap which were returned by customers. These products had been marked up by 35% and they had originally been bought at a per-unit cost of $1500.

- A) DR Accounts Receivable $1,950
     DR Accounts Receivable $1,500
         CR Sales Returns $1,950
         CR Inventory $1,500
- B) DR Sales Returns $1,950
     DR Inventory $1,500
         CR Accounts Receivable $1,950
         CR Cost of Goods Sold $1,500
- C) DR Sales Returns $18,427,500
     DR Inventory $13,650,000
         CR Accounts Receivable $18,427,500
         CR Cost of Goods Sold $13,650,000
- D) DR Accounts Receivable $18,427,500
     DR Accounts Receivable $13,650,000
         CR Sales Returns $18,427,500
         CR Inventory $13,650,000

72 A to Z Event Guru Ltd is a corporation which sells start-to-finish event planning services for large gatherings. This year, A to Z Event Guru Ltd has provided 1000 events each of which earned revenues of $1500.

- A) DR Sales $1,500,000
         CR Accounts Receivable $1,500,000
- B) DR Accounts Receivable $1,500,000
         CR Sales $1,500,000
- C) DR Accounts Receivable $1,500
         CR Sales $1,500
- D) DR Sales $1,500
         CR Accounts Receivable $1,500

73 NY Fitness is an organization which specializes in providing their customers with gym memberships for professional sports teams. This month, NY Fitness has estimated that 10% of the accounts receivable might not end up being collectable, based on past experience. The accounts receivable will need to be adjusted from its current balance of $58000.

- A) DR Bad Debt expense $58,000
         CR Allowance for Doubtful Accounts $58,000
- B) DR Allowance for Doubtful Accounts $5,800
         CR Bad Debt expense $5,800
- C) DR Allowance for Doubtful Accounts $58,000
         CR Bad Debt expense $58,000
- D) DR Bad Debt expense $5,800
         CR Allowance for Doubtful Accounts $5,800

74   Cirque du Lune sells several different types of circus performances. This month, Cirque du Lune paid for 1 month of rent for their company's office space. Each month, the rent owing was $16000.
    A)   DR Rent expense $192,000
            CR Accounts Payable $192,000
    B)   DR Accounts Payable $16,000
            CR Rent expense $16,000
    C)   DR Accounts Payable $192,000
            CR Rent expense $192,000
    D)   DR Rent expense $16,000
            CR Accounts Payable $16,000

75   David & Johnson is a company which offers their customers a wide selection of legal services. This year, David & Johnson has provided 1900 billable hours each of which earned revenues of $2060.
    A)   DR Sales $2,060
            CR Accounts Receivable $2,060
    B)   DR Accounts Receivable $2,060
            CR Sales $2,060
    C)   DR Accounts Receivable $3,914,000
            CR Sales $3,914,000
    D)   DR Sales $3,914,000
            CR Accounts Receivable $3,914,000

76   Fairway Malls is a corporation which sells retail spaces in their shopping centers. This December, Fairway Malls recognized 1 year of depreciation on a building which had a total useful life of 25 years, and which had originally been bought for $869000.
    A)   DR Accumulated Depreciation $869,000
            CR Depreciation expense $869,000
    B)   DR Depreciation expense $869,000
            CR Accumulated Depreciation $869,000
    C)   DR Depreciation expense $34,760
            CR Accumulated Depreciation $34,760
    D)   DR Accumulated Depreciation $34,760
            CR Depreciation expense $34,760

77   Jameson & Jameson is an organization which specializes in providing their customers with soap products. Today, Jameson & Jameson received an upfront payment for 3000 truckloads of bars of soap which will be provided to the customer 6 months from now. The payment for each was $1900.
    A)   DR Unearned Revenue $5,700,000
            CR Cash $5,700,000
    B)   DR Cash $5,700,000
            CR Unearned Revenue $5,700,000
    C)   DR Cash $1,900
            CR Unearned Revenue $1,900
    D)   DR Unearned Revenue $1,900
            CR Cash $1,900

78 Toyonda sells various cars. This month, Toyonda must amortize 1 month worth of utility bills which they had prepaid at the beginning of the year. The amount that they had paid upfront for the year was $25200.
- A) DR Prepaid Expense $2,100
  - CR Utilities expense $2,100
- B) DR Utilities expense $2,100
  - CR Prepaid Expense $2,100
- C) DR Utilities expense $25,200
  - CR Prepaid Expense $25,200
- D) DR Prepaid Expense $25,200
  - CR Utilities expense $25,200

79 Air America is an organization which specializes in providing their customers with global flights. Today, Air America bought equipment which has a 5 year useful life, and which had a cost of $24000.
- A) DR Accounts Payable $24,000
  - CR Equipment $24,000
- B) DR Equipment $24,000
  - CR Accounts Payable $24,000
- C) DR Equipment $4,800
  - CR Accounts Payable $4,800
- D) DR Accounts Payable $4,800
  - CR Equipment $4,800

80 Mr. Mop is a company which offers their customers a wide selection of household cleaners. This week, Mr. Mop purchased 3190 tons of cleaning solution which were placed into the warehouse, and which had a per unit cost of $1900.
- A) DR Inventory $1,900
  - CR Accounts Payable $1,900
- B) DR Accounts Payable $6,061,000
  - CR Inventory $6,061,000
- C) DR Accounts Payable $1,900
  - CR Inventory $1,900
- D) DR Inventory $6,061,000
  - CR Accounts Payable $6,061,000

81   Sprike Inc offers their customers a wide range of athletic apparel. Today Sprike Inc sold
        40800 batches of athletic t-shirts which had a 30% mark-up. They had originally been
        bought from their suppliers for a unit cost of $1370.
    A)   DR Accounts Receivable $72,664,800
        DR Cost of Goods Sold $55,896,000
            CR Sales $72,664,800
            CR Inventory $55,896,000
    B)   DR Sales $1,781
        DR Sales $1,370
            CR Accounts Receivable $1,781
            CR Cost of Goods Sold $1,370
    C)   DR Sales $72,664,800
        DR Sales $55,896,000
            CR Accounts Receivable $72,664,800
            CR Cost of Goods Sold $55,896,000
    D)   DR Accounts Receivable $1,781
        DR Cost of Goods Sold $1,370
            CR Sales $1,781
            CR Inventory $1,370

82   Pharma Drug Company Ltd. is a company which offers their customers a wide selection of
        medications. This month, Pharma Drug Company Ltd. accepted 23100 batches of pills
        which were returned by customers. These products had been marked up by 35% and they
        had originally been bought at a per-unit cost of $1000.
    A)   DR Sales Returns $1,300
        DR Inventory $1,000
            CR Accounts Receivable $1,300
            CR Cost of Goods Sold $1,000
    B)   DR Accounts Receivable $31,185,000
        DR Accounts Receivable $23,100,000
            CR Sales Returns $31,185,000
            CR Inventory $23,100,000
    C)   DR Accounts Receivable $1,300
        DR Accounts Receivable $1,000
            CR Sales Returns $1,300
            CR Inventory $1,000
    D)   DR Sales Returns $31,185,000
        DR Inventory $23,100,000
            CR Accounts Receivable $31,185,000
            CR Cost of Goods Sold $23,100,000

83   Toyonda offers their customers a wide range of cars. Today, Toyonda bought equipment which has a 5 year useful life, and which had a cost of $12000.
    A)   DR Accounts Payable $12,000
            CR Equipment $12,000
    B)   DR Equipment $12,000
            CR Accounts Payable $12,000
    C)   DR Equipment $2,400
            CR Accounts Payable $2,400
    D)   DR Accounts Payable $2,400
            CR Equipment $2,400

84   Pharma Drug Company Ltd. is a privately-held corporation which focuses on their niche of premium medications. This January, Pharma Drug Company Ltd. has made an advance payment to cover the next 12 months of utility bills, which have a monthly cost of $2700.
    A)   DR Prepaid Expense $2,700
            CR Cash $2,700
    B)   DR Cash $32,400
            CR Prepaid Expense $32,400
    C)   DR Cash $2,700
            CR Prepaid Expense $2,700
    D)   DR Prepaid Expense $32,400
            CR Cash $32,400

85   Mr. Mop sells several different types of household cleaners. Today, Mr. Mop bought equipment which has a 5 year useful life, and which had a cost of $9000.
    A)   DR Equipment $1,800
            CR Accounts Payable $1,800
    B)   DR Accounts Payable $9,000
             CR Equipment $9,000
    C)   DR Accounts Payable $1,800
             CR Equipment $1,800
    D)   DR Equipment $9,000
            CR Accounts Payable $9,000

86   Jameson & Jameson offers their customers a wide range of soap products. This month, Jameson & Jameson paid for 1 month of rent for the warehouse room, which has a monthly costs of $1900.
    A)   DR Accounts Payable $22,800
            CR Rent expense $22,800
    B)   DR Rent expense $22,800
            CR Accounts Payable $22,800
    C)   DR Rent expense $1,900
            CR Accounts Payable $1,900
    D)   DR Accounts Payable $1,900
            CR Rent expense $1,900

87   Mr. Mop is a privately-held corporation which focuses on their niche of premium household cleaners. This month, Mr. Mop accepted 9200 tons of cleaning solution which were returned by customers. These products had been marked up by 35% and they had originally been bought at a per-unit cost of $2700.

   A)   DR Sales Returns $3,510
         DR Inventory $2,700
              CR Accounts Receivable $3,510
              CR Cost of Goods Sold $2,700
   B)   DR Accounts Receivable $33,534,000
         DR Accounts Receivable $24,840,000
              CR Sales Returns $33,534,000
              CR Inventory $24,840,000
   C)   DR Accounts Receivable $3,510
         DR Accounts Receivable $2,700
              CR Sales Returns $3,510
              CR Inventory $2,700
   D)   DR Sales Returns $33,534,000
         DR Inventory $24,840,000
              CR Accounts Receivable $33,534,000
              CR Cost of Goods Sold $24,840,000

88   Air America is a corporation which sells global flights. Air America has just provided 1100 large orders which had been paid for in advance last year. Each order was in the amount of $2300.

   A)   DR Sales $2,530,000
              CR Unearned Revenue $2,530,000
   B)   DR Unearned Revenue $2,530,000
              CR Sales $2,530,000
   C)   DR Unearned Revenue $2,300
              CR Sales $2,300
   D)   DR Sales $2,300
              CR Unearned Revenue $2,300

89   Cirque du Lune is an organization which specializes in providing their customers with circus performances. Cirque du Lune has just received a cash payment for the full amount that this customer owed to the company for all of their purchases to date. The outstanding balance which has now been paid was $13000.

   A)   DR Accounts Receivable $13,000
              CR Cash $13,000
   B)   DR Cash $13,000
              CR Accounts Receivable $13,000
   C)   DR Cash $1,083
              CR Accounts Receivable $1,083
   D)   DR Accounts Receivable $1,083
              CR Cash $1,083

90 McGerald's offers their customers a wide range of fast food meals. This week, McGerald's paid each of the 3210 staff members their bi-weekly wages, which per person had a cost of $2100.

    A)   DR Wage expense $2,100
                CR Accounts Payable $2,100
    B)   DR Accounts Payable $6,741,000
                CR Wage expense $6,741,000
    C)   DR Accounts Payable $2,100
                CR Wage expense $2,100
    D)   DR Wage expense $6,741,000
                CR Accounts Payable $6,741,000

91 LA Met Theatre Company offers their customers a wide range of live theatrical performances. Today LA Met Theatre Company signed up for a loan with a 5% interest rate, and so the bank immediately transferred cash to the company in the amount of $41000.

    A)   DR Loan Payable $41,000
                CR Cash $41,000
    B)   DR Cash $41,000
                CR Loan Payable $41,000
    C)   DR Cash $2,050
                CR Loan Payable $2,050
    D)   DR Loan Payable $2,050
                CR Cash $2,050

92 Sprike Inc is an organization which specializes in providing their customers with athletic apparel. Today, Sprike Inc received an upfront payment for 3350 batches of athletic t-shirts which will be provided to the customer 6 months from now. The payment for each was $1600.

    A)   DR Cash $5,360,000
                CR Unearned Revenue $5,360,000
    B)   DR Unearned Revenue $1,600
                CR Cash $1,600
    C)   DR Unearned Revenue $5,360,000
                CR Cash $5,360,000
    D)   DR Cash $1,600
                CR Unearned Revenue $1,600

93   Mr. Mop provides their customers with household cleaners. Today Mr. Mop sold 23900 tons of cleaning solution which had a 30% mark-up. They had originally been bought from their suppliers for a unit cost of $2330.
    A)   DR Accounts Receivable $3,029
        DR Cost of Goods Sold $2,330
            CR Sales $3,029
            CR Inventory $2,330
    B)   DR Sales $72,393,100
        DR Sales $55,687,000
            CR Accounts Receivable $72,393,100
            CR Cost of Goods Sold $55,687,000
    C)   DR Sales $3,029
        DR Sales $2,330
            CR Accounts Receivable $3,029
            CR Cost of Goods Sold $2,330
    D)   DR Accounts Receivable $72,393,100
        DR Cost of Goods Sold $55,687,000
            CR Sales $72,393,100
            CR Inventory $55,687,000

94   Fairway Malls is a market leader that is well-known for their brand of retail spaces in their shopping centers. Today Fairway Malls signed up for a loan with a 5% interest rate, and so the bank immediately transferred cash to the company in the amount of $94000.
    A)   DR Cash $4,700
            CR Loan Payable $4,700
    B)   DR Loan Payable $94,000
            CR Cash $94,000
    C)   DR Loan Payable $4,700
            CR Cash $4,700
    D)   DR Cash $94,000
            CR Loan Payable $94,000

95   Comedy 253 offers their customers a wide range of live performances of stand-up comedy. Comedy 253 has just received a cash payment for the full amount that this customer owed to the company for all of their purchases to date. The outstanding balance which has now been paid was $36000.
    A)   DR Accounts Receivable $3,000
            CR Cash $3,000
    B)   DR Cash $3,000
            CR Accounts Receivable $3,000
    C)   DR Cash $36,000
            CR Accounts Receivable $36,000
    D)   DR Accounts Receivable $36,000
            CR Cash $36,000

96 Jameson & Jameson is an organization which specializes in providing their customers with soap products. This December, Jameson & Jameson recognized 1 year of depreciation on equipment which had a total useful life of 10 years, and which had originally cost $260000.
   A) DR Accumulated Depreciation $260,000
           CR Depreciation expense $260,000
   B) DR Depreciation expense $260,000
           CR Accumulated Depreciation $260,000
   C) DR Depreciation expense $26,000
           CR Accumulated Depreciation $26,000
   D) DR Accumulated Depreciation $26,000
           CR Depreciation expense $26,000

97 Air America is a company which offers their customers a wide selection of global flights. Air America has just received a cash payment for the full amount that this customer owed to the company for all of their purchases to date. The outstanding balance which has now been paid was $83000.
   A) DR Accounts Receivable $83,000
           CR Cash $83,000
   B) DR Cash $83,000
           CR Accounts Receivable $83,000
   C) DR Cash $6,917
           CR Accounts Receivable $6,917
   D) DR Accounts Receivable $6,917
           CR Cash $6,917

98 Hogtown Records sells several different types of audio services for local musicians to record their music albums. This December, Hogtown Records recognized 1 year of depreciation on equipment which had a total useful life of 10 years, and which had originally cost $210000.
   A) DR Depreciation expense $210,000
           CR Accumulated Depreciation $210,000
   B) DR Accumulated Depreciation $21,000
           CR Depreciation expense $21,000
   C) DR Accumulated Depreciation $210,000
           CR Depreciation expense $210,000
   D) DR Depreciation expense $21,000
           CR Accumulated Depreciation $21,000

99 Payday Now sells several different types of short-term loan arrangements. This December, Payday Now recognized 1 year of depreciation on equipment which had a total useful life of 10 years, and which had originally cost $80000.
   A) DR Accumulated Depreciation $80,000
           CR Depreciation expense $80,000
   B) DR Depreciation expense $80,000
           CR Accumulated Depreciation $80,000
   C) DR Depreciation expense $8,000
           CR Accumulated Depreciation $8,000
   D) DR Accumulated Depreciation $8,000
           CR Depreciation expense $8,000

100 Paytech Ltd is a privately-held corporation which focuses on their niche of premium payroll transaction processing services. This December, Paytech Ltd recognized 1 year of depreciation on equipment which had a total useful life of 10 years, and which had originally cost $120000.
- A) DR Accumulated Depreciation $12,000
   CR Depreciation expense $12,000
- B) DR Depreciation expense $12,000
   CR Accumulated Depreciation $12,000
- C) DR Depreciation expense $120,000
   CR Accumulated Depreciation $120,000
- D) DR Accumulated Depreciation $120,000
   CR Depreciation expense $120,000

101 McGerald's offers their customers a wide range of fast food meals. Today, McGerald's received payment upfront for 1000 large orders which will not be provided until early next year. Each order was in the amount of $1400.
- A) DR Cash $1,400
   CR Unearned Revenue $1,400
- B) DR Unearned Revenue $1,400,000
   CR Cash $1,400,000
- C) DR Unearned Revenue $1,400
   CR Cash $1,400
- D) DR Cash $1,400,000
   CR Unearned Revenue $1,400,000

102 McGerald's is an organization which specializes in providing their customers with fast food meals. This week, McGerald's paid each of the 3870 staff members their bi-weekly wages, which per person had a cost of $1500.
- A) DR Accounts Payable $5,805,000
   CR Wage expense $5,805,000
- B) DR Wage expense $5,805,000
   CR Accounts Payable $5,805,000
- C) DR Wage expense $1,500
   CR Accounts Payable $1,500
- D) DR Accounts Payable $1,500
   CR Wage expense $1,500

103 Kola-Nut Ltd provides their customers with soft drinks. Today, Kola-Nut Ltd has paid cash to their supplier to fully pay off their account payable balance, which was $66000.
- A) DR Cash $5,500
   CR Accounts Payable $5,500
- B) DR Accounts Payable $5,500
   CR Cash $5,500
- C) DR Accounts Payable $66,000
   CR Cash $66,000
- D) DR Cash $66,000
   CR Accounts Payable $66,000

104 Club Disco is a company which offers their customers a wide selection of dance venue rentals for large family gatherings. This January, Club Disco has made an advance payment to cover the next 12 months of utility bills, which have a monthly cost of $2300.
   A)   DR Cash $2,300
              CR Prepaid Expense $2,300
   B)   DR Prepaid Expense $2,300
              CR Cash $2,300
   C)   DR Prepaid Expense $27,600
              CR Cash $27,600
   D)   DR Cash $27,600
              CR Prepaid Expense $27,600

105 Mount Tessory Academy provides their customers with private school education. This December, Mount Tessory Academy recognized 1 year of depreciation on equipment which had a total useful life of 10 years, and which had originally cost $140000.
   A)   DR Accumulated Depreciation $14,000
              CR Depreciation expense $14,000
   B)   DR Depreciation expense $14,000
              CR Accumulated Depreciation $14,000
   C)   DR Depreciation expense $140,000
              CR Accumulated Depreciation $140,000
   D)   DR Accumulated Depreciation $140,000
              CR Depreciation expense $140,000

106 Toyonda offers their customers a wide range of cars. This month, Toyonda paid for 1 month of rent for their company's office space. Each month, the rent owing was $19000.
   A)   DR Accounts Payable $19,000
              CR Rent expense $19,000
   B)   DR Rent expense $19,000
              CR Accounts Payable $19,000
   C)   DR Rent expense $228,000
              CR Accounts Payable $228,000
   D)   DR Accounts Payable $228,000
              CR Rent expense $228,000

107 LA Met Theatre Company sells several different types of live theatrical performances. Today, LA Met Theatre Company received payment upfront for 1700 large orders which will not be provided until early next year. Each order was in the amount of $1200.
   A)   DR Cash $1,200
              CR Unearned Revenue $1,200
   B)   DR Unearned Revenue $2,040,000
              CR Cash $2,040,000
   C)   DR Unearned Revenue $1,200
              CR Cash $1,200
   D)   DR Cash $2,040,000
              CR Unearned Revenue $2,040,000

41

108 LA Met Theatre Company provides their customers with live theatrical performances. This December, LA Met Theatre Company recognized 1 year of depreciation on equipment which had a total useful life of 10 years, and which had originally cost $80000.
   A) DR Depreciation expense $8,000
          CR Accumulated Depreciation $8,000
   B) DR Accumulated Depreciation $80,000
          CR Depreciation expense $80,000
   C) DR Accumulated Depreciation $8,000
          CR Depreciation expense $8,000
   D) DR Depreciation expense $80,000
          CR Accumulated Depreciation $80,000

109 AC&C Ltd. is a corporation which sells cell phone plans. Today, AC&C Ltd. bought equipment which has a 5 year useful life, and which had a cost of $21000.
   A) DR Equipment $4,200
          CR Accounts Payable $4,200
   B) DR Accounts Payable $21,000
          CR Equipment $21,000
   C) DR Accounts Payable $4,200
          CR Equipment $4,200
   D) DR Equipment $21,000
          CR Accounts Payable $21,000

110 Comedy 253 provides their customers with live performances of stand-up comedy. This month, Comedy 253 has estimated that 30% of the accounts receivable might not end up being collectable, based on past experience. The accounts receivable will need to be adjusted from its current balance of $97000.
   A) DR Allowance for Doubtful Accounts $29,100
          CR Bad Debt expense $29,100
   B) DR Bad Debt expense $29,100
          CR Allowance for Doubtful Accounts $29,100
   C) DR Bad Debt expense $97,000
          CR Allowance for Doubtful Accounts $97,000
   D) DR Allowance for Doubtful Accounts $97,000
          CR Bad Debt expense $97,000

111 Mr. Mop is a market leader that is well-known for their brand of household cleaners. Today, Mr. Mop received an upfront payment for 1240 tons of cleaning solution which will be provided to the customer 6 months from now. The payment for each was $2600.
   A) DR Unearned Revenue $2,600
          CR Cash $2,600
   B) DR Cash $2,600
          CR Unearned Revenue $2,600
   C) DR Cash $3,224,000
          CR Unearned Revenue $3,224,000
   D) DR Unearned Revenue $3,224,000
          CR Cash $3,224,000

112 David & Johnson sells several different types of legal services. This week, David & Johnson paid each of the 3870 staff members their bi-weekly wages, which per person had a cost of $2700.
- A) DR Wage expense $2,700
    - CR Accounts Payable $2,700
- B) DR Accounts Payable $10,449,000
    - CR Wage expense $10,449,000
- C) DR Accounts Payable $2,700
    - CR Wage expense $2,700
- D) DR Wage expense $10,449,000
    - CR Accounts Payable $10,449,000

113 Sprike Inc is an organization which specializes in providing their customers with athletic apparel. This week, Sprike Inc purchased 3930 batches of athletic t-shirts which were placed into the warehouse, and which had a per unit cost of $2200.
- A) DR Inventory $2,200
    - CR Accounts Payable $2,200
- B) DR Accounts Payable $8,646,000
    - CR Inventory $8,646,000
- C) DR Accounts Payable $2,200
    - CR Inventory $2,200
- D) DR Inventory $8,646,000
    - CR Accounts Payable $8,646,000

114 Sprike Inc is an organization which specializes in providing their customers with athletic apparel. This month, Sprike Inc paid for 1 month of rent for the warehouse room, which has a monthly costs of $1700.
- A) DR Accounts Payable $1,700
    - CR Rent expense $1,700
- B) DR Rent expense $1,700
    - CR Accounts Payable $1,700
- C) DR Rent expense $20,400
    - CR Accounts Payable $20,400
- D) DR Accounts Payable $20,400
    - CR Rent expense $20,400

115 NBG Media Corporation sells several different types of broadcasting services for advertising agencies. NBG Media Corporation has just received a cash payment for the full amount that this customer owed to the company for all of their purchases to date. The outstanding balance which has now been paid was $86000.
- A) DR Cash $7,167
    - CR Accounts Receivable $7,167
- B) DR Accounts Receivable $86,000
    - CR Cash $86,000
- C) DR Accounts Receivable $7,167
    - CR Cash $7,167
- D) DR Cash $86,000
    - CR Accounts Receivable $86,000

116 Pharma Drug Company Ltd. is a privately-held corporation which focuses on their niche of premium medications. Today Pharma Drug Company Ltd. sold 17900 batches of pills which had a 30% mark-up. They had originally been bought from their suppliers for a unit cost of $2610.
   A)   DR Accounts Receivable $60,734,700
        DR Cost of Goods Sold $46,719,000
            CR Sales $60,734,700
            CR Inventory $46,719,000
   B)   DR Sales $3,393
        DR Sales $2,610
            CR Accounts Receivable $3,393
            CR Cost of Goods Sold $2,610
   C)   DR Sales $60,734,700
        DR Sales $46,719,000
            CR Accounts Receivable $60,734,700
            CR Cost of Goods Sold $46,719,000
   D)   DR Accounts Receivable $3,393
        DR Cost of Goods Sold $2,610
            CR Sales $3,393
            CR Inventory $2,610

117 Grand Convention Ltd is a market leader that is well-known for their brand of banquet hall rentals for corporate meetings. This month, Grand Convention Ltd has estimated that 20% of the accounts receivable might not end up being collectable, based on past experience. The accounts receivable will need to be adjusted from its current balance of $55000.
   A)   DR Allowance for Doubtful Accounts $55,000
            CR Bad Debt expense $55,000
   B)   DR Bad Debt expense $55,000
            CR Allowance for Doubtful Accounts $55,000
   C)   DR Bad Debt expense $11,000
            CR Allowance for Doubtful Accounts $11,000
   D)   DR Allowance for Doubtful Accounts $11,000
            CR Bad Debt expense $11,000

118 NBG Media Corporation is a company which offers their customers a wide selection of broadcasting services for advertising agencies. Today, NBG Media Corporation bought equipment which has a 5 year useful life, and which had a cost of $18000.
   A)   DR Accounts Payable $3,600
            CR Equipment $3,600
   B)   DR Equipment $3,600
            CR Accounts Payable $3,600
   C)   DR Equipment $18,000
            CR Accounts Payable $18,000
   D)   DR Accounts Payable $18,000
            CR Equipment $18,000

119 NY Fitness is a market leader that is well-known for their brand of gym memberships for professional sports teams. NY Fitness has just provided 1800 large orders which had been paid for in advance last year. Each order was in the amount of $1100.
    A)   DR Sales $1,100
                CR Unearned Revenue $1,100
    B)   DR Unearned Revenue $1,100
                CR Sales $1,100
    C)   DR Unearned Revenue $1,980,000
                CR Sales $1,980,000
    D)   DR Sales $1,980,000
                CR Unearned Revenue $1,980,000

120 Jameson & Jameson offers their customers a wide range of soap products. This month, Jameson & Jameson paid for 1 month of rent for the warehouse room, which has a monthly costs of $2200.
    A)   DR Accounts Payable $26,400
                CR Rent expense $26,400
    B)   DR Rent expense $26,400
                CR Accounts Payable $26,400
    C)   DR Rent expense $2,200
                CR Accounts Payable $2,200
    D)   DR Accounts Payable $2,200
                CR Rent expense $2,200

121 David & Johnson sells several different types of legal services. This December, David & Johnson has paid each of the company's 2400 owners an annual dividend in the amount of $16000.
    A)   DR Cash $38,400,000
                CR Retained Earnings $38,400,000
    B)   DR Retained Earnings $38,400,000
                CR Cash $38,400,000
    C)   DR Retained Earnings $16,000
                CR Cash $16,000
    D)   DR Cash $16,000
                CR Retained Earnings $16,000

122 McGerald's is an organization which specializes in providing their customers with fast food meals. This month, McGerald's must amortize 1 month worth of utility bills which they had prepaid at the beginning of the year. The amount that they had paid upfront for the year was $24000.
    A)   DR Prepaid Expense $2,000
                CR Utilities expense $2,000
    B)   DR Utilities expense $2,000
                CR Prepaid Expense $2,000
    C)   DR Utilities expense $24,000
                CR Prepaid Expense $24,000
    D)   DR Prepaid Expense $24,000
                CR Utilities expense $24,000

123 NY Fitness provides their customers with gym memberships for professional sports teams. Today, NY Fitness received payment upfront for 1900 large orders which will not be provided until early next year. Each order was in the amount of $1700.
- A) DR Cash $1,700
    CR Unearned Revenue $1,700
- B) DR Unearned Revenue $3,230,000
    CR Cash $3,230,000
- C) DR Unearned Revenue $1,700
    CR Cash $1,700
- D) DR Cash $3,230,000
    CR Unearned Revenue $3,230,000

124 AC&C Ltd. is a company which offers their customers a wide selection of cell phone plans. This month, AC&C Ltd. must amortize 1 month worth of utility bills which they had prepaid at the beginning of the year. The amount that they had paid upfront for the year was $44400.
- A) DR Prepaid Expense $3,700
    CR Utilities expense $3,700
- B) DR Utilities expense $3,700
    CR Prepaid Expense $3,700
- C) DR Utilities expense $44,400
    CR Prepaid Expense $44,400
- D) DR Prepaid Expense $44,400
    CR Utilities expense $44,400

125 Club Disco is a company which offers their customers a wide selection of dance venue rentals for large family gatherings. Club Disco has just purchased a building using cash, which has an expected useful life of 30 years, and which had a total cost of $498000.
- A) DR Cash $16,600
    CR Building $16,600
- B) DR Building $16,600
    CR Cash $16,600
- C) DR Building $498,000
    CR Cash $498,000
- D) DR Cash $498,000
    CR Building $498,000

126 Kola-Nut Ltd sells several different types of soft drinks. This month, Kola-Nut Ltd accepted 26400 batches of soda bottles which were returned by customers. These products had been marked up by 35% and they had originally been bought at a per-unit cost of $2300.

A) DR Accounts Receivable $2,990
DR Accounts Receivable $2,300
   CR Sales Returns $2,990
   CR Inventory $2,300

B) DR Sales Returns $2,990
DR Inventory $2,300
   CR Accounts Receivable $2,990
   CR Cost of Goods Sold $2,300

C) DR Sales Returns $81,972,000
DR Inventory $60,720,000
   CR Accounts Receivable $81,972,000
   CR Cost of Goods Sold $60,720,000

D) DR Accounts Receivable $81,972,000
DR Accounts Receivable $60,720,000
   CR Sales Returns $81,972,000
   CR Inventory $60,720,000

127 Jameson & Jameson is a corporation which sells soap products. This month, Jameson & Jameson paid for 1 month of rent for the warehouse room, which has a monthly costs of $2600.

A) DR Accounts Payable $2,600
   CR Rent expense $2,600

B) DR Rent expense $2,600
   CR Accounts Payable $2,600

C) DR Rent expense $31,200
   CR Accounts Payable $31,200

D) DR Accounts Payable $31,200
   CR Rent expense $31,200

128 LA Met Theatre Company provides their customers with live theatrical performances. Today, LA Met Theatre Company bought equipment which has a 5 year useful life, and which had a cost of $12000.

A) DR Accounts Payable $12,000
   CR Equipment $12,000

B) DR Equipment $12,000
   CR Accounts Payable $12,000

C) DR Equipment $2,400
   CR Accounts Payable $2,400

D) DR Accounts Payable $2,400
   CR Equipment $2,400

129 McGerald's is a market leader that is well-known for their brand of fast food meals. Today McGerald's signed up for a loan with a 5% interest rate, and so the bank immediately transferred cash to the company in the amount of $89000.

A)   DR Loan Payable $4,450
            CR Cash $4,450
B)   DR Cash $4,450
            CR Loan Payable $4,450
C)   DR Cash $89,000
            CR Loan Payable $89,000
D)   DR Loan Payable $89,000
            CR Cash $89,000

130 LA Met Theatre Company is a company which offers their customers a wide selection of live theatrical performances. This month, LA Met Theatre Company has estimated that 10% of the accounts receivable might not end up being collectable, based on past experience. The accounts receivable will need to be adjusted from its current balance of $30000.

A)   DR Allowance for Doubtful Accounts $30,000
            CR Bad Debt expense $30,000
B)   DR Bad Debt expense $30,000
            CR Allowance for Doubtful Accounts $30,000
C)   DR Bad Debt expense $3,000
            CR Allowance for Doubtful Accounts $3,000
D)   DR Allowance for Doubtful Accounts $3,000
            CR Bad Debt expense $3,000

131 Sprike Inc is an organization which specializes in providing their customers with athletic apparel. Today, Sprike Inc received an upfront payment for 4750 batches of athletic t-shirts which will be provided to the customer 6 months from now. The payment for each was $1000.

A)   DR Cash $1,000
            CR Unearned Revenue $1,000
B)   DR Unearned Revenue $4,750,000
            CR Cash $4,750,000
C)   DR Unearned Revenue $1,000
            CR Cash $1,000
D)   DR Cash $4,750,000
            CR Unearned Revenue $4,750,000

132 Grand Convention Ltd is a corporation which sells banquet hall rentals for corporate meetings. Today, Grand Convention Ltd has paid cash to their supplier to fully pay off their account payable balance, which was $86000.

A)   DR Accounts Payable $7,167
            CR Cash $7,167
B)   DR Cash $86,000
            CR Accounts Payable $86,000
C)   DR Cash $7,167
            CR Accounts Payable $7,167
D)   DR Accounts Payable $86,000
            CR Cash $86,000

133 Pharma Drug Company Ltd. is a market leader that is well-known for their brand of medications. Today, Pharma Drug Company Ltd. received an upfront payment for 4610 batches of pills which will be provided to the customer 6 months from now. The payment for each was $2000.
- A) DR Unearned Revenue $2,000
    - CR Cash $2,000
- B) DR Cash $2,000
    - CR Unearned Revenue $2,000
- C) DR Cash $9,220,000
    - CR Unearned Revenue $9,220,000
- D) DR Unearned Revenue $9,220,000
    - CR Cash $9,220,000

134 Kola-Nut Ltd offers their customers a wide range of soft drinks. Today, Kola-Nut Ltd bought equipment which has a 5 year useful life, and which had a cost of $20000.
- A) DR Accounts Payable $20,000
    - CR Equipment $20,000
- B) DR Equipment $20,000
    - CR Accounts Payable $20,000
- C) DR Equipment $4,000
    - CR Accounts Payable $4,000
- D) DR Accounts Payable $4,000
    - CR Equipment $4,000

135 Mr. Mop sells several different types of household cleaners. This December, Mr. Mop recognized 1 year of depreciation on a building which had a total useful life of 25 years, and which had originally been bought for $32000.
- A) DR Depreciation expense $32,000
    - CR Accumulated Depreciation $32,000
- B) DR Accumulated Depreciation $1,280
    - CR Depreciation expense $1,280
- C) DR Accumulated Depreciation $32,000
    - CR Depreciation expense $32,000
- D) DR Depreciation expense $1,280
    - CR Accumulated Depreciation $1,280

136 David & Johnson is an organization which specializes in providing their customers with legal services. David & Johnson has just provided 1800 large orders which had been paid for in advance last year. Each order was in the amount of $1800.
- A) DR Sales $3,240,000
    - CR Unearned Revenue $3,240,000
- B) DR Unearned Revenue $3,240,000
    - CR Sales $3,240,000
- C) DR Unearned Revenue $1,800
    - CR Sales $1,800
- D) DR Sales $1,800
    - CR Unearned Revenue $1,800

137 Fairway Malls is a corporation which sells retail spaces in their shopping centers. This December, Fairway Malls recognized 1 year of depreciation on a building which had a total useful life of 25 years, and which had originally been bought for $405000.
- A) DR Depreciation expense $405,000
  - CR Accumulated Depreciation $405,000
- B) DR Accumulated Depreciation $16,200
  - CR Depreciation expense $16,200
- C) DR Accumulated Depreciation $405,000
  - CR Depreciation expense $405,000
- D) DR Depreciation expense $16,200
  - CR Accumulated Depreciation $16,200

138 Jameson & Jameson is a privately-held corporation which focuses on their niche of premium soap products. This week, Jameson & Jameson purchased 1630 truckloads of bars of soap which were placed into the warehouse, and which had a per unit cost of $1600.
- A) DR Inventory $1,600
  - CR Accounts Payable $1,600
- B) DR Accounts Payable $2,608,000
  - CR Inventory $2,608,000
- C) DR Accounts Payable $1,600
  - CR Inventory $1,600
- D) DR Inventory $2,608,000
  - CR Accounts Payable $2,608,000

139 Kola-Nut Ltd is a privately-held corporation which focuses on their niche of premium soft drinks. This month, Kola-Nut Ltd accepted 9300 batches of soda bottles which were returned by customers. These products had been marked up by 35% and they had originally been bought at a per-unit cost of $2600.
- A) DR Accounts Receivable $3,380
  - DR Accounts Receivable $2,600
  - CR Sales Returns $3,380
  - CR Inventory $2,600
- B) DR Sales Returns $3,380
  - DR Inventory $2,600
  - CR Accounts Receivable $3,380
  - CR Cost of Goods Sold $2,600
- C) DR Sales Returns $32,643,000
  - DR Inventory $24,180,000
  - CR Accounts Receivable $32,643,000
  - CR Cost of Goods Sold $24,180,000
- D) DR Accounts Receivable $32,643,000
  - DR Accounts Receivable $24,180,000
  - CR Sales Returns $32,643,000
  - CR Inventory $24,180,000

140 Jameson & Jameson is a market leader that is well-known for their brand of soap products. Today Jameson & Jameson sold 31900 truckloads of bars of soap which had a 30% mark-up. They had originally been bought from their suppliers for a unit cost of $2960.

    A)   DR Sales $122,751,200
            DR Sales $94,424,000
                CR Accounts Receivable $122,751,200
                CR Cost of Goods Sold $94,424,000

    B)   DR Accounts Receivable $122,751,200
            DR Cost of Goods Sold $94,424,000
                CR Sales $122,751,200
                CR Inventory $94,424,000

    C)   DR Accounts Receivable $3,848
            DR Cost of Goods Sold $2,960
                CR Sales $3,848
                CR Inventory $2,960

    D)   DR Sales $3,848
            DR Sales $2,960
                CR Accounts Receivable $3,848
                CR Cost of Goods Sold $2,960

141 Pharma Drug Company Ltd. sells several different types of medications. Pharma Drug Company Ltd. has just received a cash payment for the full amount that this customer owed to the company for all of their purchases to date. The outstanding balance which has now been paid was $45000.

    A)   DR Cash $3,750
                CR Accounts Receivable $3,750

    B)   DR Accounts Receivable $45,000
                CR Cash $45,000

    C)   DR Accounts Receivable $3,750
                CR Cash $3,750

    D)   DR Cash $45,000
                CR Accounts Receivable $45,000

142 Fairway Malls sells several different types of retail spaces in their shopping centers. Today, Fairway Malls bought equipment which has a 5 year useful life, and which had a cost of $23000.

    A)   DR Accounts Payable $23,000
                CR Equipment $23,000

    B)   DR Equipment $23,000
                CR Accounts Payable $23,000

    C)   DR Equipment $4,600
                CR Accounts Payable $4,600

    D)   DR Accounts Payable $4,600
                CR Equipment $4,600

143 Air America is a privately-held corporation which focuses on their niche of premium global flights. This month, Air America has estimated that 5% of the accounts receivable might not end up being collectable, based on past experience. The accounts receivable will need to be adjusted from its current balance of $52000.
  A) DR Allowance for Doubtful Accounts $52,000
       CR Bad Debt expense $52,000
  B) DR Bad Debt expense $52,000
       CR Allowance for Doubtful Accounts $52,000
  C) DR Bad Debt expense $2,600
       CR Allowance for Doubtful Accounts $2,600
  D) DR Allowance for Doubtful Accounts $2,600
       CR Bad Debt expense $2,600

144 NBG Media Corporation sells various broadcasting services for advertising agencies. This month, NBG Media Corporation made 1 monthly loan repayment towards their long-term note payable. The interest portion was 60% of the payment. The total amount paid in cash was $15000.
  A) DR Cash $15,000
       CR Interest Expense $6,000
       CR Loan Payable $9,000
  B) DR Interest Expense $6,000
       DR Loan Payable $9,000
       CR Cash $15,000
  C) DR Interest Expense $9,000
       DR Loan Payable $6,000
       CR Cash $15,000
  D) DR Cash $15,000
       CR Interest Expense $9,000
       CR Loan Payable $6,000

145 Toyonda is a corporation which sells cars. Today, Toyonda bought equipment which has a 5 year useful life, and which had a cost of $21000.
  A) DR Equipment $4,200
       CR Accounts Payable $4,200
  B) DR Accounts Payable $21,000
       CR Equipment $21,000
  C) DR Accounts Payable $4,200
       CR Equipment $4,200
  D) DR Equipment $21,000
       CR Accounts Payable $21,000

146 Mr. Mop offers their customers a wide range of household cleaners. Today, Mr. Mop bought equipment which has a 5 year useful life, and which had a cost of $12000.
   A)   DR Equipment $2,400
                CR Accounts Payable $2,400
   B)   DR Accounts Payable $12,000
                CR Equipment $12,000
   C)   DR Accounts Payable $2,400
                CR Equipment $2,400
   D)   DR Equipment $12,000
                CR Accounts Payable $12,000

147 Pharma Drug Company Ltd. is a privately-held corporation which focuses on their niche of premium medications. This month, Pharma Drug Company Ltd. must amortize 1 month worth of utility bills which they had prepaid at the beginning of the year. The amount that they had paid upfront for the year was $21600.
   A)   DR Utilities expense $1,800
                CR Prepaid Expense $1,800
   B)   DR Prepaid Expense $21,600
                CR Utilities expense $21,600
   C)   DR Prepaid Expense $1,800
                CR Utilities expense $1,800
   D)   DR Utilities expense $21,600
                CR Prepaid Expense $21,600

148 Payday Now is a corporation which sells short-term loan arrangements. This month, Payday Now has estimated that 10% of the accounts receivable might not end up being collectable, based on past experience. The accounts receivable will need to be adjusted from its current balance of $51000.
   A)   DR Bad Debt expense $51,000
                CR Allowance for Doubtful Accounts $51,000
   B)   DR Allowance for Doubtful Accounts $5,100
                CR Bad Debt expense $5,100
   C)   DR Allowance for Doubtful Accounts $51,000
                CR Bad Debt expense $51,000
   D)   DR Bad Debt expense $5,100
                CR Allowance for Doubtful Accounts $5,100

149 Comedy 253 offers their customers a wide range of live performances of stand-up comedy. Comedy 253 has just provided 1300 large orders which had been paid for in advance last year. Each order was in the amount of $1700.
   A)   DR Sales $1,700
                CR Unearned Revenue $1,700
   B)   DR Unearned Revenue $1,700
                CR Sales $1,700
   C)   DR Unearned Revenue $2,210,000
                CR Sales $2,210,000
   D)   DR Sales $2,210,000
                CR Unearned Revenue $2,210,000

150 A to Z Event Guru Ltd sells various start-to-finish event planning services for large gatherings. This month, A to Z Event Guru Ltd made 1 monthly loan repayment towards their long-term note payable. The interest portion was 60% of the payment. The total amount paid in cash was $19000.

A)   DR Cash $19,000
          CR Interest Expense $11,400
          CR Loan Payable $7,600

B)   DR Interest Expense $11,400
     DR Loan Payable $7,600
          CR Cash $19,000

C)   DR Interest Expense $7,600
     DR Loan Payable $11,400
          CR Cash $19,000

D)   DR Cash $19,000
          CR Interest Expense $7,600
          CR Loan Payable $11,400

151 LA Met Theatre Company is a market leader that is well-known for their brand of live theatrical performances. LA Met Theatre Company has just purchased a building using cash, which has an expected useful life of 30 years, and which had a total cost of $891000.

A)   DR Building $29,700
          CR Cash $29,700

B)   DR Cash $891,000
          CR Building $891,000

C)   DR Cash $29,700
          CR Building $29,700

D)   DR Building $891,000
          CR Cash $891,000

152 Pharma Drug Company Ltd. is a corporation which sells medications. Today, Pharma Drug Company Ltd. received an upfront payment for 4960 batches of pills which will be provided to the customer 6 months from now. The payment for each was $1000.

A)   DR Cash $4,960,000
          CR Unearned Revenue $4,960,000

B)   DR Unearned Revenue $1,000
          CR Cash $1,000

C)   DR Unearned Revenue $4,960,000
          CR Cash $4,960,000

D)   DR Cash $1,000
          CR Unearned Revenue $1,000

153 Club Disco provides their customers with dance venue rentals for large family gatherings. This year, Club Disco has provided 1500 evening rentals each of which earned revenues of $2280.

A)   DR Accounts Receivable $2,280
         CR Sales $2,280
B)   DR Sales $3,420,000
         CR Accounts Receivable $3,420,000
C)   DR Sales $2,280
         CR Accounts Receivable $2,280
D)   DR Accounts Receivable $3,420,000
         CR Sales $3,420,000

154 AC&C Ltd. is a privately-held corporation which focuses on their niche of premium cell phone plans. AC&C Ltd. has just received a cash payment for the full amount that this customer owed to the company for all of their purchases to date. The outstanding balance which has now been paid was $29000.

A)   DR Cash $2,417
         CR Accounts Receivable $2,417
B)   DR Accounts Receivable $29,000
         CR Cash $29,000
C)   DR Accounts Receivable $2,417
         CR Cash $2,417
D)   DR Cash $29,000
         CR Accounts Receivable $29,000

155 Kola-Nut Ltd sells various soft drinks. Today, Kola-Nut Ltd has paid cash to their supplier to fully pay off their account payable balance, which was $56000.

A)   DR Accounts Payable $4,667
         CR Cash $4,667
B)   DR Cash $56,000
         CR Accounts Payable $56,000
C)   DR Cash $4,667
         CR Accounts Payable $4,667
D)   DR Accounts Payable $56,000
         CR Cash $56,000

156 Fairway Malls is an organization which specializes in providing their customers with retail spaces in their shopping centers. This month, Fairway Malls has estimated that 15% of the accounts receivable might not end up being collectable, based on past experience. The accounts receivable will need to be adjusted from its current balance of $81000.

A)   DR Allowance for Doubtful Accounts $12,150
         CR Bad Debt expense $12,150
B)   DR Bad Debt expense $12,150
         CR Allowance for Doubtful Accounts $12,150
C)   DR Bad Debt expense $81,000
         CR Allowance for Doubtful Accounts $81,000
D)   DR Allowance for Doubtful Accounts $81,000
         CR Bad Debt expense $81,000

157 Club Disco provides their customers with dance venue rentals for large family gatherings. Today, Club Disco bought equipment which has a 5 year useful life, and which had a cost of $23000.
A) DR Equipment $4,600
        CR Accounts Payable $4,600
B) DR Accounts Payable $23,000
        CR Equipment $23,000
C) DR Accounts Payable $4,600
        CR Equipment $4,600
D) DR Equipment $23,000
        CR Accounts Payable $23,000

158 Jameson & Jameson is a corporation which sells soap products. This month, Jameson & Jameson made 1 monthly loan repayment towards their long-term note payable. The interest portion was 60% of the payment. The total amount paid in cash was $8000.
A) DR Cash $8,000
        CR Interest Expense $4,800
        CR Loan Payable $3,200
B) DR Interest Expense $4,800
    DR Loan Payable $3,200
        CR Cash $8,000
C) DR Interest Expense $3,200
    DR Loan Payable $4,800
        CR Cash $8,000
D) DR Cash $8,000
        CR Interest Expense $3,200
        CR Loan Payable $4,800

159 Cirque du Lune is a corporation which sells circus performances. Cirque du Lune has just received a cash payment for the full amount that this customer owed to the company for all of their purchases to date. The outstanding balance which has now been paid was $90000.
A) DR Accounts Receivable $7,500
        CR Cash $7,500
B) DR Cash $7,500
        CR Accounts Receivable $7,500
C) DR Cash $90,000
        CR Accounts Receivable $90,000
D) DR Accounts Receivable $90,000
        CR Cash $90,000

160 Comedy 253 is a corporation which sells live performances of stand-up comedy. This year, Comedy 253 has provided 1000 shows each of which earned revenues of $1580.
A) DR Sales $1,580
        CR Accounts Receivable $1,580
B) DR Accounts Receivable $1,580
        CR Sales $1,580
C) DR Accounts Receivable $1,580,000
        CR Sales $1,580,000
D) DR Sales $1,580,000
        CR Accounts Receivable $1,580,000

161 Club Disco is a company which offers their customers a wide selection of dance venue rentals for large family gatherings. This December, Club Disco has paid each of the company's 1200 owners an annual dividend in the amount of $12000.
   A) DR Cash $12,000
           CR Retained Earnings $12,000
   B) DR Retained Earnings $12,000
           CR Cash $12,000
   C) DR Retained Earnings $14,400,000
           CR Cash $14,400,000
   D) DR Cash $14,400,000
           CR Retained Earnings $14,400,000

162 Cirque du Lune is a market leader that is well-known for their brand of circus performances. Cirque du Lune has just provided 1300 large orders which had been paid for in advance last year. Each order was in the amount of $1200.
   A) DR Unearned Revenue $1,200
           CR Sales $1,200
   B) DR Sales $1,560,000
           CR Unearned Revenue $1,560,000
   C) DR Sales $1,200
           CR Unearned Revenue $1,200
   D) DR Unearned Revenue $1,560,000
           CR Sales $1,560,000

163 LA Met Theatre Company provides their customers with live theatrical performances. LA Met Theatre Company has just purchased a building using cash, which has an expected useful life of 30 years, and which had a total cost of $943000.
   A) DR Cash $943,000
           CR Building $943,000
   B) DR Building $943,000
           CR Cash $943,000
   C) DR Building $31,433
           CR Cash $31,433
   D) DR Cash $31,433
           CR Building $31,433

164   Sprike Inc sells various athletic apparel. Today Sprike Inc sold 30000 batches of athletic t-shirts which had a 30% mark-up. They had originally been bought from their suppliers for a unit cost of $1070.
    A)   DR Accounts Receivable $1,391
           DR Cost of Goods Sold $1,070
                 CR Sales $1,391
                 CR Inventory $1,070
    B)   DR Sales $41,730,000
           DR Sales $32,100,000
                 CR Accounts Receivable $41,730,000
                 CR Cost of Goods Sold $32,100,000
    C)   DR Sales $1,391
           DR Sales $1,070
                 CR Accounts Receivable $1,391
                 CR Cost of Goods Sold $1,070
    D)   DR Accounts Receivable $41,730,000
           DR Cost of Goods Sold $32,100,000
                 CR Sales $41,730,000
                 CR Inventory $32,100,000

165   Jameson & Jameson provides their customers with soap products. This December, Jameson & Jameson recognized 1 year of depreciation on a building which had a total useful life of 25 years, and which had originally been bought for $258000.
    A)   DR Accumulated Depreciation $10,320
                 CR Depreciation expense $10,320
    B)   DR Depreciation expense $10,320
                 CR Accumulated Depreciation $10,320
    C)   DR Depreciation expense $258,000
                 CR Accumulated Depreciation $258,000
    D)   DR Accumulated Depreciation $258,000
                 CR Depreciation expense $258,000

166   A to Z Event Guru Ltd sells several different types of start-to-finish event planning services for large gatherings. A to Z Event Guru Ltd has just provided 2000 large orders which had been paid for in advance last year. Each order was in the amount of $1600.
    A)   DR Unearned Revenue $1,600
                 CR Sales $1,600
    B)   DR Sales $3,200,000
                 CR Unearned Revenue $3,200,000
    C)   DR Sales $1,600
                 CR Unearned Revenue $1,600
    D)   DR Unearned Revenue $3,200,000
                 CR Sales $3,200,000

167 A to Z Event Guru Ltd sells various start-to-finish event planning services for large gatherings. This year, A to Z Event Guru Ltd has provided 2100 events each of which earned revenues of $2140.
    A)   DR Sales $2,140
           CR Accounts Receivable $2,140
    B)   DR Accounts Receivable $2,140
           CR Sales $2,140
    C)   DR Accounts Receivable $4,494,000
           CR Sales $4,494,000
    D)   DR Sales $4,494,000
           CR Accounts Receivable $4,494,000

168 Air America is a market leader that is well-known for their brand of global flights. This December, Air America recognized 1 year of depreciation on a building which had a total useful life of 25 years, and which had originally been bought for $420000.
    A)   DR Depreciation expense $420,000
           CR Accumulated Depreciation $420,000
    B)   DR Accumulated Depreciation $16,800
           CR Depreciation expense $16,800
    C)   DR Accumulated Depreciation $420,000
           CR Depreciation expense $420,000
    D)   DR Depreciation expense $16,800
           CR Accumulated Depreciation $16,800

169 Payday Now provides their customers with short-term loan arrangements. Payday Now has just purchased a building using cash, which has an expected useful life of 30 years, and which had a total cost of $907000.
    A)   DR Cash $30,233
           CR Building $30,233
    B)   DR Building $30,233
           CR Cash $30,233
    C)   DR Building $907,000
           CR Cash $907,000
    D)   DR Cash $907,000
           CR Building $907,000

170 Jameson & Jameson provides their customers with soap products. This month, Jameson & Jameson paid for 1 month of rent for their company's office space. Each month, the rent owing was $23000.
    A)   DR Rent expense $276,000
           CR Accounts Payable $276,000
    B)   DR Accounts Payable $23,000
           CR Rent expense $23,000
    C)   DR Accounts Payable $276,000
           CR Rent expense $276,000
    D)   DR Rent expense $23,000
           CR Accounts Payable $23,000

171 Mr. Mop is a privately-held corporation which focuses on their niche of premium household cleaners. This month, Mr. Mop paid for 1 month of rent for their company's office space. Each month, the rent owing was $25000.
- A) DR Accounts Payable $300,000
  - CR Rent expense $300,000
- B) DR Rent expense $300,000
  - CR Accounts Payable $300,000
- C) DR Rent expense $25,000
  - CR Accounts Payable $25,000
- D) DR Accounts Payable $25,000
  - CR Rent expense $25,000

172 Mr. Mop is a privately-held corporation which focuses on their niche of premium household cleaners. Today, Mr. Mop received an upfront payment for 2470 tons of cleaning solution which will be provided to the customer 6 months from now. The payment for each was $1100.
- A) DR Cash $1,100
  - CR Unearned Revenue $1,100
- B) DR Unearned Revenue $2,717,000
  - CR Cash $2,717,000
- C) DR Unearned Revenue $1,100
  - CR Cash $1,100
- D) DR Cash $2,717,000
  - CR Unearned Revenue $2,717,000

173 Mr. Mop is a corporation which sells household cleaners. This week, Mr. Mop purchased 1020 tons of cleaning solution which were placed into the warehouse, and which had a per unit cost of $1600.
- A) DR Accounts Payable $1,632,000
  - CR Inventory $1,632,000
- B) DR Inventory $1,632,000
  - CR Accounts Payable $1,632,000
- C) DR Inventory $1,600
  - CR Accounts Payable $1,600
- D) DR Accounts Payable $1,600
  - CR Inventory $1,600

174 Sprike Inc provides their customers with athletic apparel. This month, Sprike Inc paid for 1 month of rent for the warehouse room, which has a monthly costs of $2800.
- A) DR Accounts Payable $33,600
  - CR Rent expense $33,600
- B) DR Rent expense $33,600
  - CR Accounts Payable $33,600
- C) DR Rent expense $2,800
  - CR Accounts Payable $2,800
- D) DR Accounts Payable $2,800
  - CR Rent expense $2,800

175 Kola-Nut Ltd is a company which offers their customers a wide selection of soft drinks. This month, Kola-Nut Ltd accepted 1700 batches of soda bottles which were returned by customers. These products had been marked up by 35% and they had originally been bought at a per-unit cost of $2800.
- A) DR Accounts Receivable $6,426,000
     DR Accounts Receivable $4,760,000
        CR Sales Returns $6,426,000
        CR Inventory $4,760,000
- B) DR Sales Returns $6,426,000
     DR Inventory $4,760,000
        CR Accounts Receivable $6,426,000
        CR Cost of Goods Sold $4,760,000
- C) DR Sales Returns $3,640
     DR Inventory $2,800
        CR Accounts Receivable $3,640
        CR Cost of Goods Sold $2,800
- D) DR Accounts Receivable $3,640
     DR Accounts Receivable $2,800
        CR Sales Returns $3,640
        CR Inventory $2,800

176 Payday Now is a privately-held corporation which focuses on their niche of premium short-term loan arrangements. Today, Payday Now received payment upfront for 1200 large orders which will not be provided until early next year. Each order was in the amount of $1700.
- A) DR Cash $1,700
        CR Unearned Revenue $1,700
- B) DR Unearned Revenue $2,040,000
        CR Cash $2,040,000
- C) DR Unearned Revenue $1,700
        CR Cash $1,700
- D) DR Cash $2,040,000
        CR Unearned Revenue $2,040,000

177 Mr. Mop sells several different types of household cleaners. This January, Mr. Mop has made an advance payment to cover the next 12 months of utility bills, which have a monthly cost of $1100.
- A) DR Cash $13,200
        CR Prepaid Expense $13,200
- B) DR Prepaid Expense $13,200
        CR Cash $13,200
- C) DR Prepaid Expense $1,100
        CR Cash $1,100
- D) DR Cash $1,100
        CR Prepaid Expense $1,100

178 Cirque du Lune sells several different types of circus performances. Cirque du Lune has just provided 2100 large orders which had been paid for in advance last year. Each order was in the amount of $2500.
 A)   DR Unearned Revenue $2,500
        CR Sales $2,500
 B)   DR Sales $5,250,000
        CR Unearned Revenue $5,250,000
 C)   DR Sales $2,500
        CR Unearned Revenue $2,500
 D)   DR Unearned Revenue $5,250,000
        CR Sales $5,250,000

179 Jameson & Jameson provides their customers with soap products. Today, Jameson & Jameson received an upfront payment for 5710 truckloads of bars of soap which will be provided to the customer 6 months from now. The payment for each was $2100.
 A)   DR Unearned Revenue $2,100
        CR Cash $2,100
 B)   DR Cash $2,100
        CR Unearned Revenue $2,100
 C)   DR Cash $11,991,000
        CR Unearned Revenue $11,991,000
 D)   DR Unearned Revenue $11,991,000
        CR Cash $11,991,000

180 Paytech Ltd is a market leader that is well-known for their brand of payroll transaction processing services. This month, Paytech Ltd paid for 1 month of rent for their company's office space. Each month, the rent owing was $24000.
 A)   DR Accounts Payable $24,000
        CR Rent expense $24,000
 B)   DR Rent expense $24,000
        CR Accounts Payable $24,000
 C)   DR Rent expense $288,000
        CR Accounts Payable $288,000
 D)   DR Accounts Payable $288,000
        CR Rent expense $288,000

181 LA Met Theatre Company is a corporation which sells live theatrical performances. Today, LA Met Theatre Company bought equipment which has a 5 year useful life, and which had a cost of $26000.
 A)   DR Accounts Payable $26,000
        CR Equipment $26,000
 B)   DR Equipment $26,000
        CR Accounts Payable $26,000
 C)   DR Equipment $5,200
        CR Accounts Payable $5,200
 D)   DR Accounts Payable $5,200
        CR Equipment $5,200

182 Cirque du Lune is a corporation which sells circus performances. This December, Cirque du Lune has paid each of the company's 2100 owners an annual dividend in the amount of $10000.
    A)   DR Retained Earnings $10,000
            CR Cash $10,000
    B)   DR Cash $21,000,000
            CR Retained Earnings $21,000,000
    C)   DR Cash $10,000
            CR Retained Earnings $10,000
    D)   DR Retained Earnings $21,000,000
            CR Cash $21,000,000

183 Sprike Inc provides their customers with athletic apparel. This month, Sprike Inc accepted 26300 batches of athletic t-shirts which were returned by customers. These products had been marked up by 35% and they had originally been bought at a per-unit cost of $2600.
    A)   DR Sales Returns $3,380
            DR Inventory $2,600
            CR Accounts Receivable $3,380
            CR Cost of Goods Sold $2,600
    B)   DR Accounts Receivable $92,313,000
            DR Accounts Receivable $68,380,000
            CR Sales Returns $92,313,000
            CR Inventory $68,380,000
    C)   DR Accounts Receivable $3,380
            DR Accounts Receivable $2,600
            CR Sales Returns $3,380
            CR Inventory $2,600
    D)   DR Sales Returns $92,313,000
            DR Inventory $68,380,000
            CR Accounts Receivable $92,313,000
            CR Cost of Goods Sold $68,380,000

184 Payday Now is a market leader that is well-known for their brand of short-term loan arrangements. Today, Payday Now bought equipment which has a 5 year useful life, and which had a cost of $12000.
    A)   DR Accounts Payable $12,000
            CR Equipment $12,000
    B)   DR Equipment $12,000
            CR Accounts Payable $12,000
    C)   DR Equipment $2,400
            CR Accounts Payable $2,400
    D)   DR Accounts Payable $2,400
            CR Equipment $2,400

185 Air America is a corporation which sells global flights. This December, Air America recognized 1 year of depreciation on equipment which had a total useful life of 10 years, and which had originally cost $160000.
   A) DR Accumulated Depreciation $16,000
              CR Depreciation expense $16,000
   B) DR Depreciation expense $16,000
              CR Accumulated Depreciation $16,000
   C) DR Depreciation expense $160,000
              CR Accumulated Depreciation $160,000
   D) DR Accumulated Depreciation $160,000
              CR Depreciation expense $160,000

186 Sprike Inc sells several different types of athletic apparel. Sprike Inc has just received a cash payment for the full amount that this customer owed to the company for all of their purchases to date. The outstanding balance which has now been paid was $19000.
   A) DR Cash $1,583
              CR Accounts Receivable $1,583
   B) DR Accounts Receivable $19,000
              CR Cash $19,000
   C) DR Accounts Receivable $1,583
              CR Cash $1,583
   D) DR Cash $19,000
              CR Accounts Receivable $19,000

187 Jameson & Jameson offers their customers a wide range of soap products. This week, Jameson & Jameson purchased 5200 truckloads of bars of soap which were placed into the warehouse, and which had a per unit cost of $1800.
   A) DR Inventory $1,800
              CR Accounts Payable $1,800
   B) DR Accounts Payable $9,360,000
              CR Inventory $9,360,000
   C) DR Accounts Payable $1,800
              CR Inventory $1,800
   D) DR Inventory $9,360,000
              CR Accounts Payable $9,360,000

188 LA Met Theatre Company is an organization which specializes in providing their customers with live theatrical performances. LA Met Theatre Company has just received a cash payment for the full amount that this customer owed to the company for all of their purchases to date. The outstanding balance which has now been paid was $60000.
   A) DR Accounts Receivable $60,000
              CR Cash $60,000
   B) DR Cash $60,000
              CR Accounts Receivable $60,000
   C) DR Cash $5,000
              CR Accounts Receivable $5,000
   D) DR Accounts Receivable $5,000
              CR Cash $5,000

189 Pharma Drug Company Ltd. is a company which offers their customers a wide selection of medications. This December, Pharma Drug Company Ltd. recognized 1 year of depreciation on a building which had a total useful life of 25 years, and which had originally been bought for $374000.
- A) DR Accumulated Depreciation $14,960
  - CR Depreciation expense $14,960
- B) DR Depreciation expense $14,960
  - CR Accumulated Depreciation $14,960
- C) DR Depreciation expense $374,000
  - CR Accumulated Depreciation $374,000
- D) DR Accumulated Depreciation $374,000
  - CR Depreciation expense $374,000

190 Mount Tessory Academy is a company which offers their customers a wide selection of private school education. This December, Mount Tessory Academy recognized 1 year of depreciation on a building which had a total useful life of 25 years, and which had originally been bought for $637000.
- A) DR Depreciation expense $637,000
  - CR Accumulated Depreciation $637,000
- B) DR Accumulated Depreciation $25,480
  - CR Depreciation expense $25,480
- C) DR Accumulated Depreciation $637,000
  - CR Depreciation expense $637,000
- D) DR Depreciation expense $25,480
  - CR Accumulated Depreciation $25,480

191 A to Z Event Guru Ltd is a privately-held corporation which focuses on their niche of premium start-to-finish event planning services for large gatherings. This December, A to Z Event Guru Ltd recognized 1 year of depreciation on a building which had a total useful life of 25 years, and which had originally been bought for $793000.
- A) DR Depreciation expense $793,000
  - CR Accumulated Depreciation $793,000
- B) DR Accumulated Depreciation $31,720
  - CR Depreciation expense $31,720
- C) DR Accumulated Depreciation $793,000
  - CR Depreciation expense $793,000
- D) DR Depreciation expense $31,720
  - CR Accumulated Depreciation $31,720

192 David & Johnson is an organization which specializes in providing their customers with legal services. Today, David & Johnson has paid cash to their supplier to fully pay off their account payable balance, which was $21000.
- A) DR Accounts Payable $1,750
  - CR Cash $1,750
- B) DR Cash $21,000
  - CR Accounts Payable $21,000
- C) DR Cash $1,750
  - CR Accounts Payable $1,750
- D) DR Accounts Payable $21,000
  - CR Cash $21,000

193 Hogtown Records sells various audio services for local musicians to record their music albums. Hogtown Records has just purchased a building using cash, which has an expected useful life of 30 years, and which had a total cost of $72000.
- A) DR Cash $2,400
    CR Building $2,400
- B) DR Building $2,400
    CR Cash $2,400
- C) DR Building $72,000
    CR Cash $72,000
- D) DR Cash $72,000
    CR Building $72,000

194 A to Z Event Guru Ltd is a privately-held corporation which focuses on their niche of premium start-to-finish event planning services for large gatherings. Today, A to Z Event Guru Ltd has paid cash to their supplier to fully pay off their account payable balance, which was $94000.
- A) DR Cash $7,833
    CR Accounts Payable $7,833
- B) DR Accounts Payable $7,833
    CR Cash $7,833
- C) DR Accounts Payable $94,000
    CR Cash $94,000
- D) DR Cash $94,000
    CR Accounts Payable $94,000

195 Mr. Mop is an organization which specializes in providing their customers with household cleaners. This month, Mr. Mop accepted 18900 tons of cleaning solution which were returned by customers. These products had been marked up by 35% and they had originally been bought at a per-unit cost of $2700.
- A) DR Accounts Receivable $68,890,500
    DR Accounts Receivable $51,030,000
        CR Sales Returns $68,890,500
        CR Inventory $51,030,000
- B) DR Sales Returns $68,890,500
    DR Inventory $51,030,000
        CR Accounts Receivable $68,890,500
        CR Cost of Goods Sold $51,030,000
- C) DR Sales Returns $3,510
    DR Inventory $2,700
        CR Accounts Receivable $3,510
        CR Cost of Goods Sold $2,700
- D) DR Accounts Receivable $3,510
    DR Accounts Receivable $2,700
        CR Sales Returns $3,510
        CR Inventory $2,700

196   Air America is a company which offers their customers a wide selection of global flights. This month, Air America must amortize 1 month worth of utility bills which they had prepaid at the beginning of the year. The amount that they had paid upfront for the year was $34800.
    A)   DR Utilities expense $34,800
                CR Prepaid Expense $34,800
    B)   DR Prepaid Expense $2,900
                CR Utilities expense $2,900
    C)   DR Prepaid Expense $34,800
                CR Utilities expense $34,800
    D)   DR Utilities expense $2,900
                CR Prepaid Expense $2,900

197   Mount Tessory Academy is a company which offers their customers a wide selection of private school education. Today, Mount Tessory Academy bought equipment which has a 5 year useful life, and which had a cost of $9000.
    A)   DR Equipment $1,800
                CR Accounts Payable $1,800
    B)   DR Accounts Payable $9,000
                CR Equipment $9,000
    C)   DR Accounts Payable $1,800
                CR Equipment $1,800
    D)   DR Equipment $9,000
                CR Accounts Payable $9,000

198   Mr. Mop provides their customers with household cleaners. This month, Mr. Mop paid for 1 month of rent for the warehouse room, which has a monthly costs of $1800.
    A)   DR Rent expense $21,600
                CR Accounts Payable $21,600
    B)   DR Accounts Payable $1,800
                CR Rent expense $1,800
    C)   DR Accounts Payable $21,600
                CR Rent expense $21,600
    D)   DR Rent expense $1,800
                CR Accounts Payable $1,800

199   Paytech Ltd is a corporation which sells payroll transaction processing services. Today, Paytech Ltd bought equipment which has a 5 year useful life, and which had a cost of $11000.
    A)   DR Equipment $11,000
                CR Accounts Payable $11,000
    B)   DR Accounts Payable $2,200
                CR Equipment $2,200
    C)   DR Accounts Payable $11,000
                CR Equipment $11,000
    D)   DR Equipment $2,200
                CR Accounts Payable $2,200

200   Sprike Inc offers their customers a wide range of athletic apparel. This week, Sprike Inc purchased 5750 batches of athletic t-shirts which were placed into the warehouse, and which had a per unit cost of $2600.
    A)   DR Accounts Payable $14,950,000
            CR Inventory $14,950,000
    B)   DR Inventory $14,950,000
            CR Accounts Payable $14,950,000
    C)   DR Inventory $2,600
            CR Accounts Payable $2,600
    D)   DR Accounts Payable $2,600
            CR Inventory $2,600

Financial Accounting Non-Multiple Choice Questions

1   Pharma Drug Company Ltd. sells various medications. Today, Pharma Drug Company Ltd. received an upfront payment for 2700 batches of pills which will be provided to the customer 6 months from now. The payment for each was $2000.

2   AC&C Ltd. is a corporation which sells cell phone plans. AC&C Ltd. has just received a cash payment for the full amount that this customer owed to the company for all of their purchases to date. The outstanding balance which has now been paid was $77000.

3   Sprike Inc provides their customers with athletic apparel. This month, Sprike Inc paid for 1 month of rent for their company's office space. Each month, the rent owing was $10000.

4   McGerald's is an organization which specializes in providing their customers with fast food meals. This December, McGerald's recognized 1 year of depreciation on a building which had a total useful life of 25 years, and which had originally been bought for $46000.

5   McGerald's is a market leader that is well-known for their brand of fast food meals. Today, McGerald's has paid cash to their supplier to fully pay off their account payable balance, which was $80000.

6   LA Met Theatre Company is an organization which specializes in providing their customers with live theatrical performances. This month, LA Met Theatre Company paid for 1 month of rent for their company's office space. Each month, the rent owing was $12000.

7   Pharma Drug Company Ltd. is a privately-held corporation which focuses on their niche of premium medications. Today Pharma Drug Company Ltd. sold 12100 batches of pills which had a 30% mark-up. They had originally been bought from their suppliers for a unit cost of $1630.

8   Air America is a market leader that is well-known for their brand of global flights. This December, Air America recognized 1 year of depreciation on equipment which had a total useful life of 10 years, and which had originally cost $170000.

9   NY Fitness sells several different types of gym memberships for professional sports teams. This month, NY Fitness paid for 1 month of rent for their company's office space. Each month, the rent owing was $26000.

10 NBG Media Corporation offers their customers a wide range of broadcasting services for advertising agencies. This month, NBG Media Corporation must amortize 1 month worth of utility bills which they had prepaid at the beginning of the year. The amount that they had paid upfront for the year was $45600.

11 Pharma Drug Company Ltd. offers their customers a wide range of medications. This month, Pharma Drug Company Ltd. accepted 14300 batches of pills which were returned by customers. These products had been marked up by 35% and they had originally been bought at a per-unit cost of $1600.

12   Mr. Mop offers their customers a wide range of household cleaners. This month, Mr. Mop paid for 1 month of rent for their company's office space. Each month, the rent owing was $16000.

13   Grand Convention Ltd is a corporation which sells banquet hall rentals for corporate meetings. This year, Grand Convention Ltd has provided 2100 corporate events each of which earned revenues of $2240.

14   Club Disco is a privately-held corporation which focuses on their niche of premium dance venue rentals for large family gatherings. This December, Club Disco recognized 1 year of depreciation on equipment which had a total useful life of 10 years, and which had originally cost $180000.

15   Club Disco is a corporation which sells dance venue rentals for large family gatherings. Today, Club Disco received payment upfront for 1000 large orders which will not be provided until early next year. Each order was in the amount of $1400.

16   Kola-Nut Ltd is a corporation which sells soft drinks. This week, Kola-Nut Ltd purchased 1400 batches of soda bottles which were placed into the warehouse, and which had a per unit cost of $2800.

17   Jameson & Jameson provides their customers with soap products. This January, Jameson & Jameson has made an advance payment to cover the next 12 months of utility bills, which have a monthly cost of $1300.

18   Mr. Mop offers their customers a wide range of household cleaners. This month, Mr. Mop must amortize 1 month worth of utility bills which they had prepaid at the beginning of the year. The amount that they had paid upfront for the year was $19200.

19   David & Johnson offers their customers a wide range of legal services. Today, David & Johnson received payment upfront for 1600 large orders which will not be provided until early next year. Each order was in the amount of $1500.

20   Kola-Nut Ltd provides their customers with soft drinks. This December, Kola-Nut Ltd recognized 1 year of depreciation on a building which had a total useful life of 25 years, and which had originally been bought for $215000.

21   David & Johnson provides their customers with legal services. This month, David & Johnson paid for 1 month of rent for their company's office space. Each month, the rent owing was $25000.

22   A to Z Event Guru Ltd sells several different types of start-to-finish event planning services for large gatherings. This December, A to Z Event Guru Ltd recognized 1 year of depreciation on a building which had a total useful life of 25 years, and which had originally been bought for $314000.

23   Pharma Drug Company Ltd. is a company which offers their customers a wide selection of medications. This month, Pharma Drug Company Ltd. has estimated that 20% of the accounts receivable might not end up being collectable, based on past experience. The accounts receivable will need to be adjusted from its current balance of $102000.

24   Mount Tessory Academy is a company which offers their customers a wide selection of private school education. This December, Mount Tessory Academy recognized 1 year of depreciation on a building which had a total useful life of 25 years, and which had originally been bought for $219000.

25   Fairway Malls is an organization which specializes in providing their customers with retail spaces in their shopping centers. This month, Fairway Malls paid 1 monthly loan repayment towards their long-term note payable. The interest portion was 60% of the payment. The total amount paid in cash was $26000.

26   Air America offers their customers a wide range of global flights. This December, Air America has paid each of the company's 1900 owners an annual dividend in the amount of $12000.

27   Toyonda sells several different types of cars. This December, Toyonda recognized 1 year of depreciation on a building which had a total useful life of 25 years, and which had originally been bought for $385000.

28   Mr. Mop sells various household cleaners. Today, Mr. Mop bought equipment which has a 5 year useful life, and which had a cost of $22000.

29   Kola-Nut Ltd is an organization which specializes in providing their customers with soft drinks. Today Kola-Nut Ltd signed up for a loan with a 5% interest rate, and so the bank immediately transferred cash to the company in the amount of $32000.

30   A to Z Event Guru Ltd is a corporation which sells start-to-finish event planning services for large gatherings. Today A to Z Event Guru Ltd signed up for a loan with a 5% interest rate, and so the bank immediately transferred cash to the company in the amount of $77000.

31   Kola-Nut Ltd is a corporation which sells soft drinks. This week, Kola-Nut Ltd purchased 4630 batches of soda bottles which were placed into the warehouse, and which had a per unit cost of $2700.

32   Fairway Malls provides their customers with retail spaces in their shopping centers. This month, Fairway Malls must amortize 1 month worth of utility bills which they had prepaid at the beginning of the year. The amount that they had paid upfront for the year was $13200.

33   NBG Media Corporation provides their customers with broadcasting services for advertising agencies. Today, NBG Media Corporation bought equipment which has a 5 year useful life, and which had a cost of $15000.

34   Pharma Drug Company Ltd. is a company which offers their customers a wide selection of medications. Today, Pharma Drug Company Ltd. received an upfront payment for 3360 batches of pills which will be provided to the customer 6 months from now. The payment for each was $2800.

35   NBG Media Corporation is a privately-held corporation which focuses on their niche of premium broadcasting services for advertising agencies. This December, NBG Media Corporation recognized 1 year of depreciation on a building which had a total useful life of 25 years, and which had originally been bought for $845000.

36   Mr. Mop offers their customers a wide range of household cleaners. This month, Mr. Mop paid for 1 month of rent for their company's office space. Each month, the rent owing was $8000.

37   Sprike Inc is a privately-held corporation which focuses on their niche of premium athletic apparel. This month, Sprike Inc paid for 1 month of rent for the warehouse room, which has a monthly costs of $2300.

38   NY Fitness offers their customers a wide range of gym memberships for professional sports teams. This December, NY Fitness recognized 1 year of depreciation on a building which had a total useful life of 25 years, and which had originally been bought for $158000.

39   Cirque du Lune sells several different types of circus performances. This year, Cirque du Lune has provided 2000 shows each of which earned revenues of $1360.

40   Mr. Mop provides their customers with household cleaners. This month, Mr. Mop paid for 1 month of rent for their company's office space. Each month, the rent owing was $8000.

41   Jameson & Jameson offers their customers a wide range of soap products. Today Jameson & Jameson sold 41900 truckloads of bars of soap which had a 30% mark-up. They had originally been bought from their suppliers for a unit cost of $1670.

42   Cirque du Lune is a privately-held corporation which focuses on their niche of premium circus performances. This year, Cirque du Lune has provided 1000 shows each of which earned revenues of $2910.

43   Fairway Malls provides their customers with retail spaces in their shopping centers. Today Fairway Malls signed up for a loan with a 5% interest rate, and so the bank immediately transferred cash to the company in the amount of $102000.

44   Pharma Drug Company Ltd. is a company which offers their customers a wide selection of medications. This week, Pharma Drug Company Ltd. purchased 4260 batches of pills which were placed into the warehouse, and which had a per unit cost of $2200.

45   AC&C Ltd. sells various cell phone plans. AC&C Ltd. has just provided 1900 large orders which had been paid for in advance last year. Each order was in the amount of $1000.

46   Mr. Mop sells various household cleaners. Today, Mr. Mop received an upfront payment for 1120 tons of cleaning solution which will be provided to the customer 6 months from now. The payment for each was $1000.

47   Grand Convention Ltd sells several different types of banquet hall rentals for corporate meetings. Grand Convention Ltd has just purchased a building using cash, which has an expected useful life of 30 years, and which had a total cost of $424000.

48   Jameson & Jameson is a corporation which sells soap products. This week, Jameson & Jameson purchased 1470 truckloads of bars of soap which were placed into the warehouse, and which had a per unit cost of $1400.

49   NY Fitness is an organization which specializes in providing their customers with gym memberships for professional sports teams. This year, NY Fitness has provided 2300 team memberships each of which earned revenues of $1690.

50   Pharma Drug Company Ltd. is a privately-held corporation which focuses on their niche of premium medications. Today, Pharma Drug Company Ltd. received an upfront payment for 2260 batches of pills which will be provided to the customer 6 months from now. The payment for each was $2600.

51   David & Johnson is a privately-held corporation which focuses on their niche of premium legal services. Today, David & Johnson received payment upfront for 2300 large orders which will not be provided until early next year. Each order was in the amount of $1700.

52   AC&C Ltd. provides their customers with cell phone plans. This year, AC&C Ltd. has provided 1600 monthly cell phone service each of which earned revenues of $2800.

53   NY Fitness is a market leader that is well-known for their brand of gym memberships for professional sports teams. Today, NY Fitness received payment upfront for 2300 large orders which will not be provided until early next year. Each order was in the amount of $2100.

54   AC&C Ltd. is a market leader that is well-known for their brand of cell phone plans. Today, AC&C Ltd. has paid cash to their supplier to fully pay off their account payable balance, which was $18000.

55   Toyonda sells various cars. This January, Toyonda has made an advance payment to cover the next 12 months of utility bills, which have a monthly cost of $2200.

56   Pharma Drug Company Ltd. is a corporation which sells medications. This week, Pharma Drug Company Ltd. purchased 4580 batches of pills which were placed into the warehouse, and which had a per unit cost of $1100.

57   Comedy 253 offers their customers a wide range of live performances of stand-up comedy. Today, Comedy 253 bought equipment which has a 5 year useful life, and which had a cost of $18000.

58   Grand Convention Ltd is a market leader that is well-known for their brand of banquet hall rentals for corporate meetings. This month, Grand Convention Ltd has estimated that 15% of the accounts receivable might not end up being collectable, based on past experience. The accounts receivable will need to be adjusted from its current balance of $85000.

59   Grand Convention Ltd provides their customers with banquet hall rentals for corporate meetings. This month, Grand Convention Ltd must amortize 1 month worth of utility bills which they had prepaid at the beginning of the year. The amount that they had paid upfront for the year was $37200.

60   Kola-Nut Ltd sells several different types of soft drinks. This month, Kola-Nut Ltd accepted 18400 batches of soda bottles which were returned by customers. These products had been marked up by 35% and they had originally been bought at a per-unit cost of $1300.

61   Cirque du Lune offers their customers a wide range of circus performances. This month, Cirque du Lune has estimated that 25% of the accounts receivable might not end up being collectable, based on past experience. The accounts receivable will need to be adjusted from its current balance of $48000.

62   Club Disco is a privately-held corporation which focuses on their niche of premium dance venue rentals for large family gatherings. This December, Club Disco recognized 1 year of depreciation on equipment which had a total useful life of 10 years, and which had originally cost $180000.

63   Pharma Drug Company Ltd. provides their customers with medications. This month, Pharma Drug Company Ltd. has estimated that 25% of the accounts receivable might not end up being collectable, based on past experience. The accounts receivable will need to be adjusted from its current balance of $89000.

64   Hogtown Records sells several different types of audio services for local musicians to record their music albums. This January, Hogtown Records has made an advance payment to cover the next 12 months of utility bills, which have a monthly cost of $1000.

65   Comedy 253 is a privately-held corporation which focuses on their niche of premium live performances of stand-up comedy. Comedy 253 has just received a cash payment for the full amount that this customer owed to the company for all of their purchases to date. The outstanding balance which has now been paid was $91000.

66   Kola-Nut Ltd is a corporation which sells soft drinks. Today Kola-Nut Ltd sold 4600 batches of soda bottles which had a 30% mark-up. They had originally been bought from their suppliers for a unit cost of $2520.

67   Payday Now is a privately-held corporation which focuses on their niche of premium short-term loan arrangements. Today, Payday Now received payment upfront for 1800 large orders which will not be provided until early next year. Each order was in the amount of $2700.

68   AC&C Ltd. is a privately-held corporation which focuses on their niche of premium cell phone plans. This month, AC&C Ltd. must amortize 1 month worth of utility bills which they had prepaid at the beginning of the year. The amount that they had paid upfront for the year was $19200.

69   Payday Now is a privately-held corporation which focuses on their niche of premium short-term loan arrangements. This January, Payday Now has made an advance payment to cover the next 12 months of utility bills, which have a monthly cost of $1000.

70   NBG Media Corporation sells several different types of broadcasting services for advertising agencies. NBG Media Corporation has just received a cash payment for the full amount that this customer owed to the company for all of their purchases to date. The outstanding balance which has now been paid was $35000.

71   Kola-Nut Ltd sells several different types of soft drinks. This month, Kola-Nut Ltd paid 1 monthly loan repayment towards their long-term note payable. The interest portion was 60% of the payment. The total amount paid in cash was $19000.

72   Hogtown Records provides their customers with audio services for local musicians to record their music albums. This month, Hogtown Records paid for 1 month of rent for their company's office space. Each month, the rent owing was $21000.

73   Toyonda provides their customers with cars. Today, Toyonda bought equipment which has a 5 year useful life, and which had a cost of $20000.

74   Payday Now is a corporation which sells short-term loan arrangements. This January, Payday Now has made an advance payment to cover the next 12 months of utility bills, which have a monthly cost of $1200.

75   Hogtown Records is a corporation which sells audio services for local musicians to record their music albums. Hogtown Records has just purchased a building using cash, which has an expected useful life of 30 years, and which had a total cost of $469000.

76   Air America is a privately-held corporation which focuses on their niche of premium global flights. This January, Air America has made an advance payment to cover the next 12 months of utility bills, which have a monthly cost of $2700.

77   Air America sells various global flights. This month, Air America has estimated that 10% of the accounts receivable might not end up being collectable, based on past experience. The accounts receivable will need to be adjusted from its current balance of $28000.

78   Pharma Drug Company Ltd. is a market leader that is well-known for their brand of medications. This January, Pharma Drug Company Ltd. has made an advance payment to cover the next 12 months of utility bills, which have a monthly cost of $1100.

79   Mr. Mop sells various household cleaners. This month, Mr. Mop accepted 3000 tons of cleaning solution which were returned by customers. These products had been marked up by 35% and they had originally been bought at a per-unit cost of $2100.

80   Sprike Inc is an organization which specializes in providing their customers with athletic apparel. This month, Sprike Inc paid for 1 month of rent for the warehouse room, which has a monthly costs of $1500.

81   Pharma Drug Company Ltd. is a corporation which sells medications. Today, Pharma Drug Company Ltd. received an upfront payment for 1590 batches of pills which will be provided to the customer 6 months from now. The payment for each was $2100.

82   Grand Convention Ltd sells several different types of banquet hall rentals for corporate meetings. This month, Grand Convention Ltd paid 1 monthly loan repayment towards their long-term note payable. The interest portion was 60% of the payment. The total amount paid in cash was $18000.

83   Jameson & Jameson is a company which offers their customers a wide selection of soap products. This month, Jameson & Jameson paid for 1 month of rent for the warehouse room, which has a monthly costs of $1900.

84 Payday Now is a company which offers their customers a wide selection of short-term loan arrangements. This month, Payday Now has estimated that 10% of the accounts receivable might not end up being collectable, based on past experience. The accounts receivable will need to be adjusted from its current balance of $100000.

85 Mr. Mop is an organization which specializes in providing their customers with household cleaners. This month, Mr. Mop paid for 1 month of rent for the warehouse room, which has a monthly costs of $2500.

86 Air America is an organization which specializes in providing their customers with global flights. Air America has just received a cash payment for the full amount that this customer owed to the company for all of their purchases to date. The outstanding balance which has now been paid was $39000.

87 Comedy 253 offers their customers a wide range of live performances of stand-up comedy. Today, Comedy 253 has paid cash to their supplier to fully pay off their account payable balance, which was $65000.

88 AC&C Ltd. offers their customers a wide range of cell phone plans. AC&C Ltd. has just received a cash payment for the full amount that this customer owed to the company for all of their purchases to date. The outstanding balance which has now been paid was $35000.

89 A to Z Event Guru Ltd offers their customers a wide range of start-to-finish event planning services for large gatherings. This December, A to Z Event Guru Ltd recognized 1 year of depreciation on equipment which had a total useful life of 10 years, and which had originally cost $110000.

90 Grand Convention Ltd is a company which offers their customers a wide selection of banquet hall rentals for corporate meetings. Today Grand Convention Ltd signed up for a loan with a 5% interest rate, and so the bank immediately transferred cash to the company in the amount of $70000.

91 Hogtown Records sells several different types of audio services for local musicians to record their music albums. This December, Hogtown Records has paid each of the company's 2400 owners an annual dividend in the amount of $8000.

92 Fairway Malls offers their customers a wide range of retail spaces in their shopping centers. This January, Fairway Malls has made an advance payment to cover the next 12 months of utility bills, which have a monthly cost of $1000.

93 Fairway Malls sells various retail spaces in their shopping centers. This December, Fairway Malls recognized 1 year of depreciation on a building which had a total useful life of 25 years, and which had originally been bought for $636000.

94 Club Disco provides their customers with dance venue rentals for large family gatherings. This month, Club Disco must amortize 1 month worth of utility bills which they had prepaid at the beginning of the year. The amount that they had paid upfront for the year was $14400.

95 NBG Media Corporation is a corporation which sells broadcasting services for advertising agencies. This month, NBG Media Corporation paid for 1 month of rent for their company's office space. Each month, the rent owing was $11000.

96 NY Fitness is an organization which specializes in providing their customers with gym memberships for professional sports teams. This December, NY Fitness recognized 1 year of depreciation on a building which had a total useful life of 25 years, and which had originally been bought for $587000.

97 Comedy 253 is an organization which specializes in providing their customers with live performances of stand-up comedy. This month, Comedy 253 paid 1 monthly loan repayment towards their long-term note payable. The interest portion was 60% of the payment. The total amount paid in cash was $17000.

98 Kola-Nut Ltd is an organization which specializes in providing their customers with soft drinks. Today, Kola-Nut Ltd received an upfront payment for 2610 batches of soda bottles which will be provided to the customer 6 months from now. The payment for each was $1100.

99 David & Johnson is a company which offers their customers a wide selection of legal services. David & Johnson has just purchased a building using cash, which has an expected useful life of 30 years, and which had a total cost of $908000.

100 Mount Tessory Academy provides their customers with private school education. This year, Mount Tessory Academy has provided 2000 annual tuition memberships each of which earned revenues of $2030.

101 Paytech Ltd is a market leader that is well-known for their brand of payroll transaction processing services. This December, Paytech Ltd recognized 1 year of depreciation on equipment which had a total useful life of 10 years, and which had originally cost $110000.

102 Mount Tessory Academy is a corporation which sells private school education. This December, Mount Tessory Academy has paid each of the company's 1100 owners an annual dividend in the amount of $9000.

103 Pharma Drug Company Ltd. is a company which offers their customers a wide selection of medications. Today, Pharma Drug Company Ltd. received an upfront payment for 3650 batches of pills which will be provided to the customer 6 months from now. The payment for each was $1400.

104 Sprike Inc is a corporation which sells athletic apparel. Today, Sprike Inc received an upfront payment for 1790 batches of athletic t-shirts which will be provided to the customer 6 months from now. The payment for each was $2500.

105 Sprike Inc sells various athletic apparel. This January, Sprike Inc has made an advance payment to cover the next 12 months of utility bills, which have a monthly cost of $1500.

106 Mount Tessory Academy offers their customers a wide range of private school education. Today, Mount Tessory Academy has paid cash to their supplier to fully pay off their account payable balance, which was $96000.

107   Pharma Drug Company Ltd. is a privately-held corporation which focuses on their niche of premium medications. This month, Pharma Drug Company Ltd. accepted 5900 batches of pills which were returned by customers. These products had been marked up by 35% and they had originally been bought at a per-unit cost of $1400.

108   LA Met Theatre Company is a privately-held corporation which focuses on their niche of premium live theatrical performances. Today LA Met Theatre Company signed up for a loan with a 5% interest rate, and so the bank immediately transferred cash to the company in the amount of $104000.

109   Fairway Malls sells various retail spaces in their shopping centers. This December, Fairway Malls recognized 1 year of depreciation on equipment which had a total useful life of 10 years, and which had originally cost $210000.

110   Mr. Mop is a privately-held corporation which focuses on their niche of premium household cleaners. This month, Mr. Mop paid for 1 month of rent for the warehouse room, which has a monthly costs of $1700.

111   A to Z Event Guru Ltd offers their customers a wide range of start-to-finish event planning services for large gatherings. Today, A to Z Event Guru Ltd has paid cash to their supplier to fully pay off their account payable balance, which was $72000.

112   Mr. Mop is a privately-held corporation which focuses on their niche of premium household cleaners. Today Mr. Mop sold 41300 tons of cleaning solution which had a 30% mark-up. They had originally been bought from their suppliers for a unit cost of $2960.

113   Kola-Nut Ltd is a privately-held corporation which focuses on their niche of premium soft drinks. Today, Kola-Nut Ltd received an upfront payment for 3040 batches of soda bottles which will be provided to the customer 6 months from now. The payment for each was $1200.

114   NY Fitness is an organization which specializes in providing their customers with gym memberships for professional sports teams. NY Fitness has just received a cash payment for the full amount that this customer owed to the company for all of their purchases to date. The outstanding balance which has now been paid was $71000.

115   Fairway Malls offers their customers a wide range of retail spaces in their shopping centers. Fairway Malls has just purchased a building using cash, which has an expected useful life of 30 years, and which had a total cost of $831000.

116   McGerald's sells several different types of fast food meals. Today McGerald's signed up for a loan with a 5% interest rate, and so the bank immediately transferred cash to the company in the amount of $34000.

117   Sprike Inc offers their customers a wide range of athletic apparel. Today, Sprike Inc bought equipment which has a 5 year useful life, and which had a cost of $15000.

118   Jameson & Jameson sells several different types of soap products. Jameson & Jameson has just purchased a building using cash, which has an expected useful life of 30 years, and which had a total cost of $912000.

119   Jameson & Jameson is a company which offers their customers a wide selection of soap products. This week, Jameson & Jameson purchased 4460 truckloads of bars of soap which were placed into the warehouse, and which had a per unit cost of $2300.

120   Club Disco offers their customers a wide range of dance venue rentals for large family gatherings. This year, Club Disco has provided 1800 evening rentals each of which earned revenues of $2520.

121   Pharma Drug Company Ltd. is an organization which specializes in providing their customers with medications. This month, Pharma Drug Company Ltd. has estimated that 5% of the accounts receivable might not end up being collectable, based on past experience. The accounts receivable will need to be adjusted from its current balance of $77000.

122   Mr. Mop is a corporation which sells household cleaners. This week, Mr. Mop purchased 3430 tons of cleaning solution which were placed into the warehouse, and which had a per unit cost of $1900.

123   Hogtown Records sells several different types of audio services for local musicians to record their music albums. This month, Hogtown Records must amortize 1 month worth of utility bills which they had prepaid at the beginning of the year. The amount that they had paid upfront for the year was $44400.

124   Kola-Nut Ltd is a corporation which sells soft drinks. Today, Kola-Nut Ltd has paid cash to their supplier to fully pay off their account payable balance, which was $64000.

125   Jameson & Jameson provides their customers with soap products. This month, Jameson & Jameson accepted 17700 truckloads of bars of soap which were returned by customers. These products had been marked up by 35% and they had originally been bought at a per-unit cost of $1300.

126   Mr. Mop offers their customers a wide range of household cleaners. This month, Mr. Mop must amortize 1 month worth of utility bills which they had prepaid at the beginning of the year. The amount that they had paid upfront for the year was $13200.

127   Fairway Malls sells several different types of retail spaces in their shopping centers. This month, Fairway Malls has estimated that 5% of the accounts receivable might not end up being collectable, based on past experience. The accounts receivable will need to be adjusted from its current balance of $74000.

128   AC&C Ltd. is a company which offers their customers a wide selection of cell phone plans. This month, AC&C Ltd. paid for 1 month of rent for their company's office space. Each month, the rent owing was $18000.

129   NBG Media Corporation offers their customers a wide range of broadcasting services for advertising agencies. This month, NBG Media Corporation paid 1 monthly loan repayment towards their long-term note payable. The interest portion was 60% of the payment. The total amount paid in cash was $26000.

130   David & Johnson sells several different types of legal services. Today, David & Johnson received payment upfront for 2300 large orders which will not be provided until early next year. Each order was in the amount of $2100.

131   Club Disco sells various dance venue rentals for large family gatherings. Club Disco has just provided 1400 large orders which had been paid for in advance last year. Each order was in the amount of $2400.

132   Kola-Nut Ltd sells various soft drinks. This month, Kola-Nut Ltd paid for 1 month of rent for the warehouse room, which has a monthly costs of $1200.

133   McGerald's sells various fast food meals. This month, McGerald's has estimated that 10% of the accounts receivable might not end up being collectable, based on past experience. The accounts receivable will need to be adjusted from its current balance of $82000.

134   Pharma Drug Company Ltd. offers their customers a wide range of medications. This month, Pharma Drug Company Ltd. paid 1 monthly loan repayment towards their long-term note payable. The interest portion was 60% of the payment. The total amount paid in cash was $17000.

135   McGerald's sells various fast food meals. Today McGerald's signed up for a loan with a 5% interest rate, and so the bank immediately transferred cash to the company in the amount of $27000.

136   Mount Tessory Academy is a market leader that is well-known for their brand of private school education. This month, Mount Tessory Academy must amortize 1 month worth of utility bills which they had prepaid at the beginning of the year. The amount that they had paid upfront for the year was $18000.

137   Comedy 253 is a privately-held corporation which focuses on their niche of premium live performances of stand-up comedy. Comedy 253 has just provided 1600 large orders which had been paid for in advance last year. Each order was in the amount of $2700.

138   Air America is a privately-held corporation which focuses on their niche of premium global flights. This December, Air America has paid each of the company's 1500 owners an annual dividend in the amount of $16000.

139   Grand Convention Ltd is a privately-held corporation which focuses on their niche of premium banquet hall rentals for corporate meetings. This December, Grand Convention Ltd has paid each of the company's 1200 owners an annual dividend in the amount of $22000.

140   NY Fitness is a market leader that is well-known for their brand of gym memberships for professional sports teams. This month, NY Fitness must amortize 1 month worth of utility bills which they had prepaid at the beginning of the year. The amount that they had paid upfront for the year was $40800.

141   Payday Now offers their customers a wide range of short-term loan arrangements. This month, Payday Now must amortize 1 month worth of utility bills which they had prepaid at the beginning of the year. The amount that they had paid upfront for the year was $13200.

142 Jameson & Jameson sells various soap products. This month, Jameson & Jameson must amortize 1 month worth of utility bills which they had prepaid at the beginning of the year. The amount that they had paid upfront for the year was $39600.

143 Mount Tessory Academy sells various private school education. Today Mount Tessory Academy signed up for a loan with a 5% interest rate, and so the bank immediately transferred cash to the company in the amount of $57000.

144 LA Met Theatre Company is an organization which specializes in providing their customers with live theatrical performances. Today LA Met Theatre Company signed up for a loan with a 5% interest rate, and so the bank immediately transferred cash to the company in the amount of $37000.

145 NY Fitness offers their customers a wide range of gym memberships for professional sports teams. This January, NY Fitness has made an advance payment to cover the next 12 months of utility bills, which have a monthly cost of $2700.

146 LA Met Theatre Company is a market leader that is well-known for their brand of live theatrical performances. Today, LA Met Theatre Company bought equipment which has a 5 year useful life, and which had a cost of $12000.

147 NBG Media Corporation offers their customers a wide range of broadcasting services for advertising agencies. Today, NBG Media Corporation has paid cash to their supplier to fully pay off their account payable balance, which was $45000.

148 Fairway Malls is a corporation which sells retail spaces in their shopping centers. Today, Fairway Malls received payment upfront for 1900 large orders which will not be provided until early next year. Each order was in the amount of $2800.

149 NY Fitness is a market leader that is well-known for their brand of gym memberships for professional sports teams. This January, NY Fitness has made an advance payment to cover the next 12 months of utility bills, which have a monthly cost of $1300.

150 LA Met Theatre Company is a corporation which sells live theatrical performances. This December, LA Met Theatre Company recognized 1 year of depreciation on equipment which had a total useful life of 10 years, and which had originally cost $220000.

151 Club Disco offers their customers a wide range of dance venue rentals for large family gatherings. This December, Club Disco recognized 1 year of depreciation on a building which had a total useful life of 25 years, and which had originally been bought for $437000.

152 NY Fitness sells various gym memberships for professional sports teams. Today, NY Fitness received payment upfront for 1500 large orders which will not be provided until early next year. Each order was in the amount of $2300.

153 Grand Convention Ltd is a market leader that is well-known for their brand of banquet hall rentals for corporate meetings. This week, Grand Convention Ltd paid each of the 3810 staff members their bi-weekly wages, which per person had a cost of $2600.

154   Jameson & Jameson is a corporation which sells soap products. This month, Jameson & Jameson accepted 17000 truckloads of bars of soap which were returned by customers. These products had been marked up by 35% and they had originally been bought at a per-unit cost of $1400.

155   Jameson & Jameson offers their customers a wide range of soap products. This December, Jameson & Jameson has paid each of the company's 1700 owners an annual dividend in the amount of $18000.

156   AC&C Ltd. sells several different types of cell phone plans. Today AC&C Ltd. signed up for a loan with a 5% interest rate, and so the bank immediately transferred cash to the company in the amount of $75000.

157   Kola-Nut Ltd offers their customers a wide range of soft drinks. This month, Kola-Nut Ltd paid for 1 month of rent for the warehouse room, which has a monthly costs of $1800.

158   A to Z Event Guru Ltd is a corporation which sells start-to-finish event planning services for large gatherings. This week, A to Z Event Guru Ltd paid each of the 3350 staff members their bi-weekly wages, which per person had a cost of $1300.

159   Comedy 253 provides their customers with live performances of stand-up comedy. Comedy 253 has just received a cash payment for the full amount that this customer owed to the company for all of their purchases to date. The outstanding balance which has now been paid was $15000.

160   NY Fitness is an organization which specializes in providing their customers with gym memberships for professional sports teams. This month, NY Fitness paid for 1 month of rent for their company's office space. Each month, the rent owing was $12000.

161   Mr. Mop is a corporation which sells household cleaners. This month, Mr. Mop accepted 20700 tons of cleaning solution which were returned by customers. These products had been marked up by 35% and they had originally been bought at a per-unit cost of $2700.

162   Jameson & Jameson is an organization which specializes in providing their customers with soap products. This month, Jameson & Jameson paid for 1 month of rent for the warehouse room, which has a monthly costs of $1200.

163   LA Met Theatre Company provides their customers with live theatrical performances. This week, LA Met Theatre Company paid each of the 2150 staff members their bi-weekly wages, which per person had a cost of $2200.

164   Kola-Nut Ltd offers their customers a wide range of soft drinks. This month, Kola-Nut Ltd accepted 24900 batches of soda bottles which were returned by customers. These products had been marked up by 35% and they had originally been bought at a per-unit cost of $2100.

165   Comedy 253 is a company which offers their customers a wide selection of live performances of stand-up comedy. Comedy 253 has just purchased a building using cash, which has an expected useful life of 30 years, and which had a total cost of $644000.

166   Payday Now offers their customers a wide range of short-term loan arrangements. Payday Now has just provided 1000 large orders which had been paid for in advance last year. Each order was in the amount of $2000.

167   Jameson & Jameson is a market leader that is well-known for their brand of soap products. This December, Jameson & Jameson recognized 1 year of depreciation on equipment which had a total useful life of 10 years, and which had originally cost $190000.

168   Sprike Inc is a corporation which sells athletic apparel. Today, Sprike Inc received an upfront payment for 3540 batches of athletic t-shirts which will be provided to the customer 6 months from now. The payment for each was $2600.

169   Air America is an organization which specializes in providing their customers with global flights. This month, Air America paid 1 monthly loan repayment towards their long-term note payable. The interest portion was 60% of the payment. The total amount paid in cash was $22000.

170   Toyonda sells several different types of cars. This month, Toyonda paid 1 monthly loan repayment towards their long-term note payable. The interest portion was 60% of the payment. The total amount paid in cash was $16000.

171   Mr. Mop offers their customers a wide range of household cleaners. This month, Mr. Mop accepted 2800 tons of cleaning solution which were returned by customers. These products had been marked up by 35% and they had originally been bought at a per-unit cost of $1300.

172   David & Johnson is a market leader that is well-known for their brand of legal services. This month, David & Johnson paid 1 monthly loan repayment towards their long-term note payable. The interest portion was 60% of the payment. The total amount paid in cash was $13000.

173   Air America is a market leader that is well-known for their brand of global flights. This January, Air America has made an advance payment to cover the next 12 months of utility bills, which have a monthly cost of $1600.

174   McGerald's is a market leader that is well-known for their brand of fast food meals. McGerald's has just provided 1900 large orders which had been paid for in advance last year. Each order was in the amount of $2800.

175   Comedy 253 is an organization which specializes in providing their customers with live performances of stand-up comedy. This month, Comedy 253 must amortize 1 month worth of utility bills which they had prepaid at the beginning of the year. The amount that they had paid upfront for the year was $32400.

176   Mount Tessory Academy offers their customers a wide range of private school education. Today, Mount Tessory Academy has paid cash to their supplier to fully pay off their account payable balance, which was $80000.

177   Pharma Drug Company Ltd. sells various medications. This month, Pharma Drug Company Ltd. paid for 1 month of rent for the warehouse room, which has a monthly costs of $2100.

178 Cirque du Lune is an organization which specializes in providing their customers with circus performances. This December, Cirque du Lune recognized 1 year of depreciation on a building which had a total useful life of 25 years, and which had originally been bought for $770000.

179 Mr. Mop is a privately-held corporation which focuses on their niche of premium household cleaners. Mr. Mop has just received a cash payment for the full amount that this customer owed to the company for all of their purchases to date. The outstanding balance which has now been paid was $82000.

180 Kola-Nut Ltd is an organization which specializes in providing their customers with soft drinks. Today, Kola-Nut Ltd received an upfront payment for 1090 batches of soda bottles which will be provided to the customer 6 months from now. The payment for each was $1900.

181 Pharma Drug Company Ltd. offers their customers a wide range of medications. This month, Pharma Drug Company Ltd. must amortize 1 month worth of utility bills which they had prepaid at the beginning of the year. The amount that they had paid upfront for the year was $22800.

182 Jameson & Jameson is a privately-held corporation which focuses on their niche of premium soap products. This week, Jameson & Jameson purchased 3670 truckloads of bars of soap which were placed into the warehouse, and which had a per unit cost of $1500.

183 NY Fitness is a corporation which sells gym memberships for professional sports teams. Today NY Fitness signed up for a loan with a 5% interest rate, and so the bank immediately transferred cash to the company in the amount of $42000.

184 Kola-Nut Ltd is a company which offers their customers a wide selection of soft drinks. Today Kola-Nut Ltd signed up for a loan with a 5% interest rate, and so the bank immediately transferred cash to the company in the amount of $111000.

185 Pharma Drug Company Ltd. provides their customers with medications. Today Pharma Drug Company Ltd. signed up for a loan with a 5% interest rate, and so the bank immediately transferred cash to the company in the amount of $111000.

186 Grand Convention Ltd is a market leader that is well-known for their brand of banquet hall rentals for corporate meetings. This December, Grand Convention Ltd recognized 1 year of depreciation on equipment which had a total useful life of 10 years, and which had originally cost $110000.

187 Fairway Malls sells various retail spaces in their shopping centers. Today, Fairway Malls received payment upfront for 2000 large orders which will not be provided until early next year. Each order was in the amount of $2200.

188 Sprike Inc provides their customers with athletic apparel. Today Sprike Inc sold 29900 batches of athletic t-shirts which had a 30% mark-up. They had originally been bought from their suppliers for a unit cost of $1190.

189 Jameson & Jameson offers their customers a wide range of soap products. This month, Jameson & Jameson paid for 1 month of rent for the warehouse room, which has a monthly costs of $2100.

190 Kola-Nut Ltd is a privately-held corporation which focuses on their niche of premium soft drinks. This month, Kola-Nut Ltd paid for 1 month of rent for the warehouse room, which has a monthly costs of $1900.

191 Toyonda offers their customers a wide range of cars. This January, Toyonda has made an advance payment to cover the next 12 months of utility bills, which have a monthly cost of $2200.

192 Mr. Mop provides their customers with household cleaners. This week, Mr. Mop purchased 2010 tons of cleaning solution which were placed into the warehouse, and which had a per unit cost of $1200.

193 Toyonda is a market leader that is well-known for their brand of cars. Today, Toyonda bought equipment which has a 5 year useful life, and which had a cost of $20000.

194 Fairway Malls sells several different types of retail spaces in their shopping centers. This month, Fairway Malls has estimated that 20% of the accounts receivable might not end up being collectable, based on past experience. The accounts receivable will need to be adjusted from its current balance of $73000.

195 AC&C Ltd. sells various cell phone plans. This January, AC&C Ltd. has made an advance payment to cover the next 12 months of utility bills, which have a monthly cost of $1500.

196 Kola-Nut Ltd is a corporation which sells soft drinks. Today, Kola-Nut Ltd has paid cash to their supplier to fully pay off their account payable balance, which was $57000.

197 A to Z Event Guru Ltd is a corporation which sells start-to-finish event planning services for large gatherings. This month, A to Z Event Guru Ltd paid 1 monthly loan repayment towards their long-term note payable. The interest portion was 60% of the payment. The total amount paid in cash was $19000.

198 Club Disco is an organization which specializes in providing their customers with dance venue rentals for large family gatherings. This December, Club Disco has paid each of the company's 1300 owners an annual dividend in the amount of $8000.

199 Cirque du Lune is a market leader that is well-known for their brand of circus performances. Today, Cirque du Lune received payment upfront for 1100 large orders which will not be provided until early next year. Each order was in the amount of $1300.

200 McGerald's sells several different types of fast food meals. Today, McGerald's received payment upfront for 1900 large orders which will not be provided until early next year. Each order was in the amount of $2400.

Managerial Accounting Key Performance Indicating Metrics

Gross Margin
= [Gross Profit] ÷ [Revenue]

Labor Costs
= [(Wage x Headcount x Hours/week x 50 weeks per year)] + [Salaries]

Fixed Costs
= [Salaries] + [Overhead expenses] + [Depreciation]

Net Income
= [(Revenues) - (Cost of Sales)] - [Total Labor Costs] - [Overhead] - [Depreciation]

EBITDA
= [(Revenues) - (Cost of Goods Sold)] - [Total Labor Costs] - [Overhead]

Tax Expense
= (Net Income excluding depreciation) x Effective tax rate

Cash flow
= (Net Income excluding depreciation) - Tax

Break-even quantity
= { [Total Labor Costs] + [Overhead] + [Depreciation] } ÷ (Gross Profit per Unit)

1   Grand Convention Ltd is a company which offers their customers a wide selection of banquet hall rentals for corporate meetings. Last year, they sold 19,815 wedding ceremonies, 15,415 corporate events, and 4,495 convention events. Each of the wedding ceremonies sells for $19,800 and they cost the company $600. The per-unit cost incurred for the corporate events is $600 and they sell for $30,600 each. Each of the convention events are priced at $9,000, and the cost incurred by the company is $200.
       There are 40 full-time employees who earn $24 per hour and work 18 hours per week. The company also employs 24 temporary contract workers for 11 hours per week, and pays them $12 per hour. Aside from the hourly staff members, there is a chief operating officer who earns an annual salary of $18,000 and the senior manager is paid $8,000 per year. HVAC expenses are the main overhead expense, which costs $520,000 per year. The building was originally bought for $1,300,000, and it has a useful life of 108 years, and the equipment, which had cost the company $650,000 has a useful life of 72 years. This company's effective tax rate is 32%. Calculate the monthly tax expense.

2   Fairway Malls offers their customers a wide range of retail spaces in their shopping centers. Last year, they sold 24,060 monthly retail space rentals, 12,160 monthly anchor store rentals, and 3,995 monthly food court rentals. Each of the monthly retail space rentals sells for $24,000 and they cost the company $1,200. The per-unit cost incurred for the monthly anchor store rentals is $1,300 and they sell for $36,000 each. Each of the monthly food court rentals are priced at $12,000, and the cost incurred by the company is $400.
       There are 50 permanent full-time staff who earn $27 per hour and work 23 hours per week. The company also employs 27 part-time employees for 14 hours per week, and pays them $13 per hour. Aside from the hourly staff members, there is a director who earns an annual salary of $20,000 and the manager is paid $9,000 per year. Janitorial services are the main overhead expense, which costs $580,000 per year. The building was originally bought for $1,450,000, and it has a useful life of 120 years, and the equipment, which had cost the company $725,000 has a useful life of 80 years. This company's effective tax rate is 33%. Calculate the monthly cash flow.

3   Fairway Malls provides their customers with retail spaces in their shopping centers. Last year, they sold 28,033 monthly retail space rentals, 8,133 monthly anchor store rentals, and 3,195 monthly food court rentals. Each of the monthly retail space rentals sells for $28,000 and they cost the company $3,500. The per-unit cost incurred for the monthly anchor store rentals is $3,600 and they sell for $40,000 each. Each of the monthly food court rentals are priced at $16,000, and the cost incurred by the company is $900.
       There are 70 senior employees who earn $33 per hour and work 33 hours per week. The company also employs 33 student interns for 20 hours per week, and pays them $15 per hour. Aside from the hourly staff members, there is a senior manager who earns an annual salary of $24,000 and the bookkeeper is paid $11,000 per year. Utilities are the main overhead expense, which costs $700,000 per year. The building was originally bought for $1,750,000, and it has a useful life of 120 years, and the equipment, which had cost the company $875,000 has a useful life of 80 years. This company's effective tax rate is 35%. Calculate the monthly cash flow.

4   Mount Tessory Academy sells various private school education. Last year, they sold 21,670 annual kindergarten memberships, 3,370 annual elementary school tuition memberships, and 1,595 annual pre-school memberships. Each of the annual kindergarten memberships sells for $21,600 and they cost the company $13,900. The per-unit cost incurred for the annual elementary school tuition memberships is $14,000 and they sell for $28,800 each. Each of the annual pre-school memberships are priced at $14,400, and the cost incurred by the company is $2,700.

          There are 110 full-timers who earn $45 per hour and work 53 hours per week. The company also employs 45 seasonal employees for 32 hours per week, and pays them $19 per hour. Aside from the hourly staff members, there is a supervisor who earns an annual salary of $32,000 and the receptionist is paid $15,000 per year. Insurance costs are the main overhead expense, which costs $940,000 per year. The building was originally bought for $2,350,000, and it has a useful life of 72 years, and the equipment, which had cost the company $1,175,000 has a useful life of 48 years. This company's effective tax rate is 39%. Calculate the monthly net income before tax.

5   NY Fitness sells various gym memberships for professional sports teams. Last year, they sold 23,424 premium baseball team memberships, 3,591 deluxe football team memberships, and 1,728 soccer team memberships. Each of the premium baseball team memberships sells for $23,400 and they cost the company $13,900. The per-unit cost incurred for the deluxe football team memberships is $14,000 and they sell for $31,200 each. Each of the soccer team memberships are priced at $15,600, and the cost incurred by the company is $2,700.

          There are 110 full-timers who earn $45 per hour and work 53 hours per week. The company also employs 45 seasonal employees for 32 hours per week, and pays them $19 per hour. Aside from the hourly staff members, there is a supervisor who earns an annual salary of $32,000 and the receptionist is paid $15,000 per year. Insurance costs are the main overhead expense, which costs $940,000 per year. The building was originally bought for $2,350,000, and it has a useful life of 78 years, and the equipment, which had cost the company $1,175,000 has a useful life of 52 years. This company's effective tax rate is 39%. Calculate the annual EBITDA.

6   Sprike Inc sells several different types of athletic apparel. Last year, they sold 1,071 batches of yoga pants, 1,771 batches of track suits, and 395 batches of athletic t-shirts. Each of the batches of yoga pants sells for $1,000 and they cost the company $200. The per-unit cost incurred for the batches of track suits is $200 and they sell for $1,600 each. Each of the batches of athletic t-shirts are priced at $400, and the cost incurred by the company is $100.

          There are 30 full-time employees who earn $21 per hour and work 13 hours per week. The company also employs 21 temporary contract workers for 8 hours per week, and pays them $11 per hour. Aside from the hourly staff members, there is a chief operating officer who earns an annual salary of $16,000 and the senior manager is paid $7,000 per year. HVAC expenses are the main overhead expense, which costs $460,000 per year. The building was originally bought for $1,150,000, and it has a useful life of 6 years, and the equipment, which had cost the company $575,000 has a useful life of 4 years. This company's effective tax rate is 31%. Calculate the gross margin.

7   Paytech Ltd is a company which offers their customers a wide selection of payroll transaction processing services. Last year, they sold 23,164 monthly subscriptions, 18,014 annual subscriptions, and 5,245 temporary coverage contracts. Each of the monthly subscriptions sells for $23,100 and they cost the company $600. The per-unit cost incurred for the annual subscriptions is $600 and they sell for $35,700 each. Each of the temporary coverage contracts are priced at $10,500, and the cost incurred by the company is $200.

There are 40 full-time employees who earn $24 per hour and work 18 hours per week. The company also employs 24 temporary contract workers for 11 hours per week, and pays them $12 per hour. Aside from the hourly staff members, there is a chief operating officer who earns an annual salary of $18,000 and the senior manager is paid $8,000 per year. HVAC expenses are the main overhead expense, which costs $520,000 per year. The building was originally bought for $1,300,000, and it has a useful life of 126 years, and the equipment, which had cost the company $650,000 has a useful life of 84 years. This company's effective tax rate is 32%. Calculate the annual cash flow.

8   LA Met Theatre Company offers their customers a wide range of live theatrical performances. Last year, they sold 18,012 premium monthly memberships, 9,112 platinum annual memberships, and 2,995 student memberships. Each of the premium monthly memberships sells for $18,000 and they cost the company $1,200. The per-unit cost incurred for the platinum annual memberships is $1,300 and they sell for $27,000 each. Each of the student memberships are priced at $9,000, and the cost incurred by the company is $400.

There are 50 permanent full-time staff who earn $27 per hour and work 23 hours per week. The company also employs 27 part-time employees for 14 hours per week, and pays them $13 per hour. Aside from the hourly staff members, there is a director who earns an annual salary of $20,000 and the manager is paid $9,000 per year. Janitorial services are the main overhead expense, which costs $580,000 per year. The building was originally bought for $1,450,000, and it has a useful life of 90 years, and the equipment, which had cost the company $725,000 has a useful life of 60 years. This company's effective tax rate is 33%. Calculate the annual EBITDA.

9   Fairway Malls sells various retail spaces in their shopping centers. Last year, they sold 36,033 monthly retail space rentals, 5,466 monthly anchor store rentals, and 2,662 monthly food court rentals. Each of the monthly retail space rentals sells for $36,000 and they cost the company $13,900. The per-unit cost incurred for the monthly anchor store rentals is $14,000 and they sell for $48,000 each. Each of the monthly food court rentals are priced at $24,000, and the cost incurred by the company is $2,700.

There are 110 full-timers who earn $45 per hour and work 53 hours per week. The company also employs 45 seasonal employees for 32 hours per week, and pays them $19 per hour. Aside from the hourly staff members, there is a supervisor who earns an annual salary of $32,000 and the receptionist is paid $15,000 per year. Insurance costs are the main overhead expense, which costs $940,000 per year. The building was originally bought for $2,350,000, and it has a useful life of 120 years, and the equipment, which had cost the company $1,175,000 has a useful life of 80 years. This company's effective tax rate is 39%. Calculate the monthly cash flow.

10   AC&C Ltd. sells various cell phone plans. Last year, they sold 18,011 annual unlimited talk and text plans, 2,778 annual unlimited voice and data plans, and 1,328 annual prepaid wireless phone cards. Each of the annual unlimited talk and text plans sells for $18,000 and they cost the company $13,900. The per-unit cost incurred for the annual unlimited voice and data plans is $14,000 and they sell for $24,000 each. Each of the annual prepaid wireless phone cards are priced at $12,000, and the cost incurred by the company is $2,700.

        There are 110 full-timers who earn $45 per hour and work 53 hours per week. The company also employs 45 seasonal employees for 32 hours per week, and pays them $19 per hour. Aside from the hourly staff members, there is a supervisor who earns an annual salary of $32,000 and the receptionist is paid $15,000 per year. Insurance costs are the main overhead expense, which costs $940,000 per year. The building was originally bought for $2,350,000, and it has a useful life of 60 years, and the equipment, which had cost the company $1,175,000 has a useful life of 40 years. This company's effective tax rate is 39%. Calculate the monthly net income before tax.

11   NY Fitness is a privately-held corporation which focuses on their niche of premium gym memberships for professional sports teams. Last year, they sold 22,140 premium baseball team memberships, 3,878 deluxe football team memberships, and 1,783 soccer team memberships. Each of the premium baseball team memberships sells for $22,100 and they cost the company $10,400. The per-unit cost incurred for the deluxe football team memberships is $10,600 and they sell for $29,900 each. Each of the soccer team memberships are priced at $14,300, and the cost incurred by the company is $2,200.

        There are 100 union workers who earn $42 per hour and work 48 hours per week. The company also employs 42 non-union workers for 29 hours per week, and pays them $18 per hour. Aside from the hourly staff members, there is a president who earns an annual salary of $30,000 and the vice-president is paid $14,000 per year. Employee assistance services are the main overhead expense, which costs $880,000 per year. The building was originally bought for $2,200,000, and it has a useful life of 78 years, and the equipment, which had cost the company $1,100,000 has a useful life of 52 years. This company's effective tax rate is 38%. Calculate the annual EBITDA.

12   Comedy 253 is an organization which specializes in providing their customers with live performances of stand-up comedy. Last year, they sold 24,078 week-end comedy festivals, 5,778 private events, and 2,395 week-day comedy events. Each of the week-end comedy festivals sells for $24,000 and they cost the company $5,300. The per-unit cost incurred for the private events is $5,400 and they sell for $33,600 each. Each of the week-day comedy events are priced at $14,400, and the cost incurred by the company is $1,300.

        There are 80 senior employees who earn $36 per hour and work 38 hours per week. The company also employs 36 student interns for 23 hours per week, and pays them $16 per hour. Aside from the hourly staff members, there is a senior manager who earns an annual salary of $26,000 and the bookkeeper is paid $12,000 per year. Utilities are the main overhead expense, which costs $760,000 per year. The building was originally bought for $1,900,000, and it has a useful life of 96 years, and the equipment, which had cost the company $950,000 has a useful life of 64 years. This company's effective tax rate is 36%. Calculate the monthly tax expense.

13   Hogtown Records is a corporation which sells audio services for local musicians who would like to record their music. Last year, they sold 24,768 singles CDs, 9,193 full albums on LP, and 3,320 individual song recordings. Each of the singles CDs sells for $24,700 and they cost the company $2,200. The per-unit cost incurred for the full albums on LP is $2,200 and they sell for $36,100 each. Each of the individual song recordings are priced at $13,300, and the cost incurred by the company is $600.

There are 60 permanent full-time staff who earn $30 per hour and work 28 hours per week. The company also employs 30 part-time employees for 17 hours per week, and pays them $14 per hour. Aside from the hourly staff members, there is a director who earns an annual salary of $22,000 and the manager is paid $10,000 per year. Janitorial services are the main overhead expense, which costs $640,000 per year. The building was originally bought for $1,600,000, and it has a useful life of 114 years, and the equipment, which had cost the company $800,000 has a useful life of 76 years. This company's effective tax rate is 34%. Calculate the annual cash flow.

14   AC&C Ltd. is an organization which specializes in providing their customers with cell phone plans. Last year, they sold 15,085 annual unlimited talk and text plans, 3,685 annual unlimited voice and data plans, and 1,495 annual prepaid wireless phone cards. Each of the annual unlimited talk and text plans sells for $15,000 and they cost the company $5,300. The per-unit cost incurred for the annual unlimited voice and data plans is $5,400 and they sell for $21,000 each. Each of the annual prepaid wireless phone cards are priced at $9,000, and the cost incurred by the company is $1,300.

There are 80 senior employees who earn $36 per hour and work 38 hours per week. The company also employs 36 student interns for 23 hours per week, and pays them $16 per hour. Aside from the hourly staff members, there is a senior manager who earns an annual salary of $26,000 and the bookkeeper is paid $12,000 per year. Utilities are the main overhead expense, which costs $760,000 per year. The building was originally bought for $1,900,000, and it has a useful life of 60 years, and the equipment, which had cost the company $950,000 has a useful life of 40 years. This company's effective tax rate is 36%. Calculate the monthly net income before tax.

15   Paytech Ltd offers their customers a wide range of payroll transaction processing services. Last year, they sold 25,223 monthly subscriptions, 12,723 annual subscriptions, and 4,195 temporary coverage contracts. Each of the monthly subscriptions sells for $25,200 and they cost the company $1,200. The per-unit cost incurred for the annual subscriptions is $1,300 and they sell for $37,800 each. Each of the temporary coverage contracts are priced at $12,600, and the cost incurred by the company is $400.

There are 50 permanent full-time staff who earn $27 per hour and work 23 hours per week. The company also employs 27 part-time employees for 14 hours per week, and pays them $13 per hour. Aside from the hourly staff members, there is a director who earns an annual salary of $20,000 and the manager is paid $9,000 per year. Janitorial services are the main overhead expense, which costs $580,000 per year. The building was originally bought for $1,450,000, and it has a useful life of 126 years, and the equipment, which had cost the company $725,000 has a useful life of 84 years. This company's effective tax rate is 33%. Calculate the annual cash flow.

16   LA Met Theatre Company is a company which offers their customers a wide selection of live theatrical performances. Last year, they sold 16,568 premium monthly memberships, 12,918 platinum annual memberships, and 3,745 student memberships. Each of the premium monthly memberships sells for $16,500 and they cost the company $600. The per-unit cost incurred for the platinum annual memberships is $600 and they sell for $25,500 each. Each of the student memberships are priced at $7,500, and the cost incurred by the company is $200.

There are 40 full-time employees who earn $24 per hour and work 18 hours per week. The company also employs 24 temporary contract workers for 11 hours per week, and pays them $12 per hour. Aside from the hourly staff members, there is a chief operating officer who earns an annual salary of $18,000 and the senior manager is paid $8,000 per year. HVAC expenses are the main overhead expense, which costs $520,000 per year. The building was originally bought for $1,300,000, and it has a useful life of 90 years, and the equipment, which had cost the company $650,000 has a useful life of 60 years. This company's effective tax rate is 32%. Calculate the annual EBITDA.

17   NY Fitness is a corporation which sells gym memberships for professional sports teams. Last year, they sold 16,921 premium baseball team memberships, 6,296 deluxe football team memberships, and 2,270 soccer team memberships. Each of the premium baseball team memberships sells for $16,900 and they cost the company $2,200. The per-unit cost incurred for the deluxe football team memberships is $2,200 and they sell for $24,700 each. Each of the soccer team memberships are priced at $9,100, and the cost incurred by the company is $600.

There are 60 permanent full-time staff who earn $30 per hour and work 28 hours per week. The company also employs 30 part-time employees for 17 hours per week, and pays them $14 per hour. Aside from the hourly staff members, there is a director who earns an annual salary of $22,000 and the manager is paid $10,000 per year. Janitorial services are the main overhead expense, which costs $640,000 per year. The building was originally bought for $1,600,000, and it has a useful life of 78 years, and the equipment, which had cost the company $800,000 has a useful life of 52 years. This company's effective tax rate is 34%. Calculate the annual EBITDA.

18   Payday Now provides their customers with short-term loan arrangements. Last year, they sold 15,470 lines of credit, 4,570 payday loans, and 1,755 prepaid credit cards. Each of the lines of credit sells for $15,400 and they cost the company $3,500. The per-unit cost incurred for the payday loans is $3,600 and they sell for $22,000 each. Each of the prepaid credit cards are priced at $8,800, and the cost incurred by the company is $900.

There are 70 senior employees who earn $33 per hour and work 33 hours per week. The company also employs 33 student interns for 20 hours per week, and pays them $15 per hour. Aside from the hourly staff members, there is a senior manager who earns an annual salary of $24,000 and the bookkeeper is paid $11,000 per year. Utilities are the main overhead expense, which costs $700,000 per year. The building was originally bought for $1,750,000, and it has a useful life of 66 years, and the equipment, which had cost the company $875,000 has a useful life of 44 years. This company's effective tax rate is 35%. Calculate the annual net income before tax.

19   AC&C Ltd. is a corporation which sells cell phone plans. Last year, they sold 13,082 annual unlimited talk and text plans, 4,932 annual unlimited voice and data plans, and 1,745 annual prepaid wireless phone cards. Each of the annual unlimited talk and text plans sells for $13,000 and they cost the company $2,200. The per-unit cost incurred for the annual unlimited voice and data plans is $2,200 and they sell for $19,000 each. Each of the annual prepaid wireless phone cards are priced at $7,000, and the cost incurred by the company is $600.

There are 60 permanent full-time staff who earn $30 per hour and work 28 hours per week. The company also employs 30 part-time employees for 17 hours per week, and pays them $14 per hour. Aside from the hourly staff members, there is a director who earns an annual salary of $22,000 and the manager is paid $10,000 per year. Janitorial services are the main overhead expense, which costs $640,000 per year. The building was originally bought for $1,600,000, and it has a useful life of 60 years, and the equipment, which had cost the company $800,000 has a useful life of 40 years. This company's effective tax rate is 34%. Calculate the monthly net income before tax.

20   Paytech Ltd sells various payroll transaction processing services. Last year, they sold 37,807 monthly subscriptions, 5,707 annual subscriptions, and 2,795 temporary coverage contracts. Each of the monthly subscriptions sells for $37,800 and they cost the company $13,900. The per-unit cost incurred for the annual subscriptions is $14,000 and they sell for $50,400 each. Each of the temporary coverage contracts are priced at $25,200, and the cost incurred by the company is $2,700.

There are 110 full-timers who earn $45 per hour and work 53 hours per week. The company also employs 45 seasonal employees for 32 hours per week, and pays them $19 per hour. Aside from the hourly staff members, there is a supervisor who earns an annual salary of $32,000 and the receptionist is paid $15,000 per year. Insurance costs are the main overhead expense, which costs $940,000 per year. The building was originally bought for $2,350,000, and it has a useful life of 126 years, and the equipment, which had cost the company $1,175,000 has a useful life of 84 years. This company's effective tax rate is 39%. Calculate the annual cash flow.

21   Hogtown Records sells various audio services for local musicians who would like to record their music. Last year, they sold 34,291 singles CDs, 5,258 full albums on LP, and 2,528 individual song recordings. Each of the singles CDs sells for $34,200 and they cost the company $13,900. The per-unit cost incurred for the full albums on LP is $14,000 and they sell for $45,600 each. Each of the individual song recordings are priced at $22,800, and the cost incurred by the company is $2,700.

There are 110 full-timers who earn $45 per hour and work 53 hours per week. The company also employs 45 seasonal employees for 32 hours per week, and pays them $19 per hour. Aside from the hourly staff members, there is a supervisor who earns an annual salary of $32,000 and the receptionist is paid $15,000 per year. Insurance costs are the main overhead expense, which costs $940,000 per year. The building was originally bought for $2,350,000, and it has a useful life of 114 years, and the equipment, which had cost the company $1,175,000 has a useful life of 76 years. This company's effective tax rate is 39%. Calculate the annual cash flow.

22   Mount Tessory Academy sells several different types of private school education. Last year, they sold 12,007 annual kindergarten memberships, 19,307 annual elementary school tuition memberships, and 4,795 annual pre-school memberships. Each of the annual kindergarten memberships sells for $12,000 and they cost the company $200. The per-unit cost incurred for the annual elementary school tuition memberships is $200 and they sell for $19,200 each. Each of the annual pre-school memberships are priced at $4,800, and the cost incurred by the company is $100.

          There are 30 full-time employees who earn $21 per hour and work 13 hours per week. The company also employs 21 temporary contract workers for 8 hours per week, and pays them $11 per hour. Aside from the hourly staff members, there is a chief operating officer who earns an annual salary of $16,000 and the senior manager is paid $7,000 per year. HVAC expenses are the main overhead expense, which costs $460,000 per year. The building was originally bought for $1,150,000, and it has a useful life of 72 years, and the equipment, which had cost the company $575,000 has a useful life of 48 years. This company's effective tax rate is 31%. Calculate the monthly net income before tax.

23   Paytech Ltd is a company which offers their customers a wide selection of payroll transaction processing services. Last year, they sold 23,154 monthly subscriptions, 18,004 annual subscriptions, and 5,245 temporary coverage contracts. Each of the monthly subscriptions sells for $23,100 and they cost the company $600. The per-unit cost incurred for the annual subscriptions is $600 and they sell for $35,700 each. Each of the temporary coverage contracts are priced at $10,500, and the cost incurred by the company is $200.

          There are 40 full-time employees who earn $24 per hour and work 18 hours per week. The company also employs 24 temporary contract workers for 11 hours per week, and pays them $12 per hour. Aside from the hourly staff members, there is a chief operating officer who earns an annual salary of $18,000 and the senior manager is paid $8,000 per year. HVAC expenses are the main overhead expense, which costs $520,000 per year. The building was originally bought for $1,300,000, and it has a useful life of 126 years, and the equipment, which had cost the company $650,000 has a useful life of 84 years. This company's effective tax rate is 32%. Calculate the annual cash flow.

24   Club Disco is a corporation which sells dance venue rentals for large family gatherings. Last year, they sold 22,163 week-end party rentals, 8,238 holiday rentals, and 2,970 evening rentals. Each of the week-end party rentals sells for $22,100 and they cost the company $2,200. The per-unit cost incurred for the holiday rentals is $2,200 and they sell for $32,300 each. Each of the evening rentals are priced at $11,900, and the cost incurred by the company is $600.

          There are 60 permanent full-time staff who earn $30 per hour and work 28 hours per week. The company also employs 30 part-time employees for 17 hours per week, and pays them $14 per hour. Aside from the hourly staff members, there is a director who earns an annual salary of $22,000 and the manager is paid $10,000 per year. Janitorial services are the main overhead expense, which costs $640,000 per year. The building was originally bought for $1,600,000, and it has a useful life of 102 years, and the equipment, which had cost the company $800,000 has a useful life of 68 years. This company's effective tax rate is 34%. Calculate the annual tax expense.

25	Cirque du Lune sells various circus performances. Last year, they sold 26,659 monthly shows, 3,659 holiday special performances, and 1,815 performances at schools. Each of the monthly shows sells for $26,600 and they cost the company $18,000. The per-unit cost incurred for the holiday special performances is $18,200 and they sell for $35,000 each. Each of the performances at schools are priced at $18,200, and the cost incurred by the company is $3,300.

There are 120 full-timers who earn $48 per hour and work 58 hours per week. The company also employs 48 seasonal employees for 35 hours per week, and pays them $20 per hour. Aside from the hourly staff members, there is a supervisor who earns an annual salary of $34,000 and the receptionist is paid $16,000 per year. Insurance costs are the main overhead expense, which costs $1,000,000 per year. The building was originally bought for $2,500,000, and it has a useful life of 84 years, and the equipment, which had cost the company $1,250,000 has a useful life of 56 years. This company's effective tax rate is 40%. Calculate the monthly EBITDA.

26	Paytech Ltd is an organization which specializes in providing their customers with payroll transaction processing services. Last year, they sold 31,580 monthly subscriptions, 7,530 annual subscriptions, and 3,145 temporary coverage contracts. Each of the monthly subscriptions sells for $31,500 and they cost the company $5,300. The per-unit cost incurred for the annual subscriptions is $5,400 and they sell for $44,100 each. Each of the temporary coverage contracts are priced at $18,900, and the cost incurred by the company is $1,300.

There are 80 senior employees who earn $36 per hour and work 38 hours per week. The company also employs 36 student interns for 23 hours per week, and pays them $16 per hour. Aside from the hourly staff members, there is a senior manager who earns an annual salary of $26,000 and the bookkeeper is paid $12,000 per year. Utilities are the main overhead expense, which costs $760,000 per year. The building was originally bought for $1,900,000, and it has a useful life of 126 years, and the equipment, which had cost the company $950,000 has a useful life of 84 years. This company's effective tax rate is 36%. Calculate the annual cash flow.

27	Mount Tessory Academy is an organization which specializes in providing their customers with private school education. Last year, they sold 18,076 annual kindergarten memberships, 4,376 annual elementary school tuition memberships, and 1,795 annual pre-school memberships. Each of the annual kindergarten memberships sells for $18,000 and they cost the company $5,300. The per-unit cost incurred for the annual elementary school tuition memberships is $5,400 and they sell for $25,200 each. Each of the annual pre-school memberships are priced at $10,800, and the cost incurred by the company is $1,300.

There are 80 senior employees who earn $36 per hour and work 38 hours per week. The company also employs 36 student interns for 23 hours per week, and pays them $16 per hour. Aside from the hourly staff members, there is a senior manager who earns an annual salary of $26,000 and the bookkeeper is paid $12,000 per year. Utilities are the main overhead expense, which costs $760,000 per year. The building was originally bought for $1,900,000, and it has a useful life of 72 years, and the equipment, which had cost the company $950,000 has a useful life of 48 years. This company's effective tax rate is 36%. Calculate the monthly net income before tax.

28   Jameson & Jameson is a corporation which sells soap products. Last year, they sold 3,907 truckloads of shampoo bottles, 1,532 truckloads of toothpaste, and 520 truckloads of bars of soap. Each of the truckloads of shampoo bottles sells for $3,900 and they cost the company $2,200. The per-unit cost incurred for the truckloads of toothpaste is $2,200 and they sell for $5,700 each. Each of the truckloads of bars of soap are priced at $2,100, and the cost incurred by the company is $600.

        There are 60 permanent full-time staff who earn $30 per hour and work 28 hours per week. The company also employs 30 part-time employees for 17 hours per week, and pays them $14 per hour. Aside from the hourly staff members, there is a director who earns an annual salary of $22,000 and the manager is paid $10,000 per year. Janitorial services are the main overhead expense, which costs $640,000 per year. The building was originally bought for $1,600,000, and it has a useful life of 18 years, and the equipment, which had cost the company $800,000 has a useful life of 12 years. This company's effective tax rate is 34%. Calculate the gross margin.

29   AC&C Ltd. is a market leader that is well-known for their brand of cell phone plans. Last year, they sold 16,091 annual unlimited talk and text plans, 3,334 annual unlimited voice and data plans, and 1,424 annual prepaid wireless phone cards. Each of the annual unlimited talk and text plans sells for $16,000 and they cost the company $7,600. The per-unit cost incurred for the annual unlimited voice and data plans is $7,700 and they sell for $22,000 each. Each of the annual prepaid wireless phone cards are priced at $10,000, and the cost incurred by the company is $1,700.

        There are 90 union workers who earn $39 per hour and work 43 hours per week. The company also employs 39 non-union workers for 26 hours per week, and pays them $17 per hour. Aside from the hourly staff members, there is a president who earns an annual salary of $28,000 and the vice-president is paid $13,000 per year. Employee assistance services are the main overhead expense, which costs $820,000 per year. The building was originally bought for $2,050,000, and it has a useful life of 60 years, and the equipment, which had cost the company $1,025,000 has a useful life of 40 years. This company's effective tax rate is 37%. Calculate the monthly net income before tax.

30   NY Fitness sells several different types of gym memberships for professional sports teams. Last year, they sold 13,028 premium baseball team memberships, 20,928 deluxe football team memberships, and 5,195 soccer team memberships. Each of the premium baseball team memberships sells for $13,000 and they cost the company $200. The per-unit cost incurred for the deluxe football team memberships is $200 and they sell for $20,800 each. Each of the soccer team memberships are priced at $5,200, and the cost incurred by the company is $100.

        There are 30 full-time employees who earn $21 per hour and work 13 hours per week. The company also employs 21 temporary contract workers for 8 hours per week, and pays them $11 per hour. Aside from the hourly staff members, there is a chief operating officer who earns an annual salary of $16,000 and the senior manager is paid $7,000 per year. HVAC expenses are the main overhead expense, which costs $460,000 per year. The building was originally bought for $1,150,000, and it has a useful life of 78 years, and the equipment, which had cost the company $575,000 has a useful life of 52 years. This company's effective tax rate is 31%. Calculate the annual EBITDA.

31   Hogtown Records sells various audio services for local musicians who would like to record their music. Last year, they sold 34,225 singles CDs, 5,192 full albums on LP, and 2,528 individual song recordings. Each of the singles CDs sells for $34,200 and they cost the company $13,900. The per-unit cost incurred for the full albums on LP is $14,000 and they sell for $45,600 each. Each of the individual song recordings are priced at $22,800, and the cost incurred by the company is $2,700.

        There are 110 full-timers who earn $45 per hour and work 53 hours per week. The company also employs 45 seasonal employees for 32 hours per week, and pays them $19 per hour. Aside from the hourly staff members, there is a supervisor who earns an annual salary of $32,000 and the receptionist is paid $15,000 per year. Insurance costs are the main overhead expense, which costs $940,000 per year. The building was originally bought for $2,350,000, and it has a useful life of 114 years, and the equipment, which had cost the company $1,175,000 has a useful life of 76 years. This company's effective tax rate is 39%. Calculate the annual cash flow.

32   Paytech Ltd is a company which offers their customers a wide selection of payroll transaction processing services. Last year, they sold 23,170 monthly subscriptions, 18,020 annual subscriptions, and 5,245 temporary coverage contracts. Each of the monthly subscriptions sells for $23,100 and they cost the company $600. The per-unit cost incurred for the annual subscriptions is $600 and they sell for $35,700 each. Each of the temporary coverage contracts are priced at $10,500, and the cost incurred by the company is $200.

        There are 40 full-time employees who earn $24 per hour and work 18 hours per week. The company also employs 24 temporary contract workers for 11 hours per week, and pays them $12 per hour. Aside from the hourly staff members, there is a chief operating officer who earns an annual salary of $18,000 and the senior manager is paid $8,000 per year. HVAC expenses are the main overhead expense, which costs $520,000 per year. The building was originally bought for $1,300,000, and it has a useful life of 126 years, and the equipment, which had cost the company $650,000 has a useful life of 84 years. This company's effective tax rate is 32%. Calculate the annual cash flow.

33   Payday Now sells various short-term loan arrangements. Last year, they sold 20,955 lines of credit, 2,905 payday loans, and 1,425 prepaid credit cards. Each of the lines of credit sells for $20,900 and they cost the company $18,000. The per-unit cost incurred for the payday loans is $18,200 and they sell for $27,500 each. Each of the prepaid credit cards are priced at $14,300, and the cost incurred by the company is $3,300.

        There are 120 full-timers who earn $48 per hour and work 58 hours per week. The company also employs 48 seasonal employees for 35 hours per week, and pays them $20 per hour. Aside from the hourly staff members, there is a supervisor who earns an annual salary of $34,000 and the receptionist is paid $16,000 per year. Insurance costs are the main overhead expense, which costs $1,000,000 per year. The building was originally bought for $2,500,000, and it has a useful life of 66 years, and the equipment, which had cost the company $1,250,000 has a useful life of 44 years. This company's effective tax rate is 40%. Calculate the annual net income before tax.

34   LA Met Theatre Company is an organization which specializes in providing their customers with live theatrical performances. Last year, they sold 22,592 premium monthly memberships, 5,442 platinum annual memberships, and 2,245 student memberships. Each of the premium monthly memberships sells for $22,500 and they cost the company $5,300. The per-unit cost incurred for the platinum annual memberships is $5,400 and they sell for $31,500 each. Each of the student memberships are priced at $13,500, and the cost incurred by the company is $1,300.

There are 80 senior employees who earn $36 per hour and work 38 hours per week. The company also employs 36 student interns for 23 hours per week, and pays them $16 per hour. Aside from the hourly staff members, there is a senior manager who earns an annual salary of $26,000 and the bookkeeper is paid $12,000 per year. Utilities are the main overhead expense, which costs $760,000 per year. The building was originally bought for $1,900,000, and it has a useful life of 90 years, and the equipment, which had cost the company $950,000 has a useful life of 60 years. This company's effective tax rate is 36%. Calculate the annual EBITDA.

35   Club Disco is a corporation which sells dance venue rentals for large family gatherings. Last year, they sold 22,103 week-end party rentals, 8,178 holiday rentals, and 2,970 evening rentals. Each of the week-end party rentals sells for $22,100 and they cost the company $2,200. The per-unit cost incurred for the holiday rentals is $2,200 and they sell for $32,300 each. Each of the evening rentals are priced at $11,900, and the cost incurred by the company is $600.

There are 60 permanent full-time staff who earn $30 per hour and work 28 hours per week. The company also employs 30 part-time employees for 17 hours per week, and pays them $14 per hour. Aside from the hourly staff members, there is a director who earns an annual salary of $22,000 and the manager is paid $10,000 per year. Janitorial services are the main overhead expense, which costs $640,000 per year. The building was originally bought for $1,600,000, and it has a useful life of 102 years, and the equipment, which had cost the company $800,000 has a useful life of 68 years. This company's effective tax rate is 34%. Calculate the annual tax expense.

36   LA Met Theatre Company sells several different types of live theatrical performances. Last year, they sold 15,052 premium monthly memberships, 24,152 platinum annual memberships, and 5,995 student memberships. Each of the premium monthly memberships sells for $15,000 and they cost the company $200. The per-unit cost incurred for the platinum annual memberships is $200 and they sell for $24,000 each. Each of the student memberships are priced at $6,000, and the cost incurred by the company is $100.

There are 30 full-time employees who earn $21 per hour and work 13 hours per week. The company also employs 21 temporary contract workers for 8 hours per week, and pays them $11 per hour. Aside from the hourly staff members, there is a chief operating officer who earns an annual salary of $16,000 and the senior manager is paid $7,000 per year. HVAC expenses are the main overhead expense, which costs $460,000 per year. The building was originally bought for $1,150,000, and it has a useful life of 90 years, and the equipment, which had cost the company $575,000 has a useful life of 60 years. This company's effective tax rate is 31%. Calculate the annual EBITDA.

37   AC&C Ltd. provides their customers with cell phone plans. Last year, they sold 14,091 annual unlimited talk and text plans, 4,191 annual unlimited voice and data plans, and 1,595 annual prepaid wireless phone cards. Each of the annual unlimited talk and text plans sells for $14,000 and they cost the company $3,500. The per-unit cost incurred for the annual unlimited voice and data plans is $3,600 and they sell for $20,000 each. Each of the annual prepaid wireless phone cards are priced at $8,000, and the cost incurred by the company is $900.

There are 70 senior employees who earn $33 per hour and work 33 hours per week. The company also employs 33 student interns for 20 hours per week, and pays them $15 per hour. Aside from the hourly staff members, there is a senior manager who earns an annual salary of $24,000 and the bookkeeper is paid $11,000 per year. Utilities are the main overhead expense, which costs $700,000 per year. The building was originally bought for $1,750,000, and it has a useful life of 60 years, and the equipment, which had cost the company $875,000 has a useful life of 40 years. This company's effective tax rate is 35%. Calculate the monthly net income before tax.

38   LA Met Theatre Company is a market leader that is well-known for their brand of live theatrical performances. Last year, they sold 24,088 premium monthly memberships, 4,902 platinum annual memberships, and 2,138 student memberships. Each of the premium monthly memberships sells for $24,000 and they cost the company $7,600. The per-unit cost incurred for the platinum annual memberships is $7,700 and they sell for $33,000 each. Each of the student memberships are priced at $15,000, and the cost incurred by the company is $1,700.

There are 90 union workers who earn $39 per hour and work 43 hours per week. The company also employs 39 non-union workers for 26 hours per week, and pays them $17 per hour. Aside from the hourly staff members, there is a president who earns an annual salary of $28,000 and the vice-president is paid $13,000 per year. Employee assistance services are the main overhead expense, which costs $820,000 per year. The building was originally bought for $2,050,000, and it has a useful life of 90 years, and the equipment, which had cost the company $1,025,000 has a useful life of 60 years. This company's effective tax rate is 37%. Calculate the annual EBITDA.

39   Club Disco sells various dance venue rentals for large family gatherings. Last year, they sold 32,379 week-end party rentals, 4,429 holiday rentals, and 2,205 evening rentals. Each of the week-end party rentals sells for $32,300 and they cost the company $18,000. The per-unit cost incurred for the holiday rentals is $18,200 and they sell for $42,500 each. Each of the evening rentals are priced at $22,100, and the cost incurred by the company is $3,300.

There are 120 full-timers who earn $48 per hour and work 58 hours per week. The company also employs 48 seasonal employees for 35 hours per week, and pays them $20 per hour. Aside from the hourly staff members, there is a supervisor who earns an annual salary of $34,000 and the receptionist is paid $16,000 per year. Insurance costs are the main overhead expense, which costs $1,000,000 per year. The building was originally bought for $2,500,000, and it has a useful life of 102 years, and the equipment, which had cost the company $1,250,000 has a useful life of 68 years. This company's effective tax rate is 40%. Calculate the annual tax expense.

40   Mount Tessory Academy is a privately-held corporation which focuses on their niche of premium private school education. Last year, they sold 20,430 annual kindergarten memberships, 3,580 annual elementary school tuition memberships, and 1,645 annual pre-school memberships. Each of the annual kindergarten memberships sells for $20,400 and they cost the company $10,400. The per-unit cost incurred for the annual elementary school tuition memberships is $10,600 and they sell for $27,600 each. Each of the annual pre-school memberships are priced at $13,200, and the cost incurred by the company is $2,200.

        There are 100 union workers who earn $42 per hour and work 48 hours per week. The company also employs 42 non-union workers for 29 hours per week, and pays them $18 per hour. Aside from the hourly staff members, there is a president who earns an annual salary of $30,000 and the vice-president is paid $14,000 per year. Employee assistance services are the main overhead expense, which costs $880,000 per year. The building was originally bought for $2,200,000, and it has a useful life of 72 years, and the equipment, which had cost the company $1,100,000 has a useful life of 48 years. This company's effective tax rate is 38%. Calculate the monthly net income before tax.

41   Hogtown Records provides their customers with audio services for local musicians who would like to record their music. Last year, they sold 26,699 singles CDs, 7,799 full albums on LP, and 3,035 individual song recordings. Each of the singles CDs sells for $26,600 and they cost the company $3,500. The per-unit cost incurred for the full albums on LP is $3,600 and they sell for $38,000 each. Each of the individual song recordings are priced at $15,200, and the cost incurred by the company is $900.

        There are 70 senior employees who earn $33 per hour and work 33 hours per week. The company also employs 33 student interns for 20 hours per week, and pays them $15 per hour. Aside from the hourly staff members, there is a senior manager who earns an annual salary of $24,000 and the bookkeeper is paid $11,000 per year. Utilities are the main overhead expense, which costs $700,000 per year. The building was originally bought for $1,750,000, and it has a useful life of 114 years, and the equipment, which had cost the company $875,000 has a useful life of 76 years. This company's effective tax rate is 35%. Calculate the annual cash flow.

42   Hogtown Records is a market leader that is well-known for their brand of audio services for local musicians who would like to record their music. Last year, they sold 30,449 singles CDs, 6,120 full albums on LP, and 2,709 individual song recordings. Each of the singles CDs sells for $30,400 and they cost the company $7,600. The per-unit cost incurred for the full albums on LP is $7,700 and they sell for $41,800 each. Each of the individual song recordings are priced at $19,000, and the cost incurred by the company is $1,700.

        There are 90 union workers who earn $39 per hour and work 43 hours per week. The company also employs 39 non-union workers for 26 hours per week, and pays them $17 per hour. Aside from the hourly staff members, there is a president who earns an annual salary of $28,000 and the vice-president is paid $13,000 per year. Employee assistance services are the main overhead expense, which costs $820,000 per year. The building was originally bought for $2,050,000, and it has a useful life of 114 years, and the equipment, which had cost the company $1,025,000 has a useful life of 76 years. This company's effective tax rate is 37%. Calculate the annual cash flow.

43   Mount Tessory Academy sells several different types of private school education. Last year, they sold 12,064 annual kindergarten memberships, 19,364 annual elementary school tuition memberships, and 4,795 annual pre-school memberships. Each of the annual kindergarten memberships sells for $12,000 and they cost the company $200. The per-unit cost incurred for the annual elementary school tuition memberships is $200 and they sell for $19,200 each. Each of the annual pre-school memberships are priced at $4,800, and the cost incurred by the company is $100.

           There are 30 full-time employees who earn $21 per hour and work 13 hours per week. The company also employs 21 temporary contract workers for 8 hours per week, and pays them $11 per hour. Aside from the hourly staff members, there is a chief operating officer who earns an annual salary of $16,000 and the senior manager is paid $7,000 per year. HVAC expenses are the main overhead expense, which costs $460,000 per year. The building was originally bought for $1,150,000, and it has a useful life of 72 years, and the equipment, which had cost the company $575,000 has a useful life of 48 years. This company's effective tax rate is 31%. Calculate the monthly net income before tax.

44   Comedy 253 is an organization which specializes in providing their customers with live performances of stand-up comedy. Last year, they sold 24,067 week-end comedy festivals, 5,767 private events, and 2,395 week-day comedy events. Each of the week-end comedy festivals sells for $24,000 and they cost the company $5,300. The per-unit cost incurred for the private events is $5,400 and they sell for $33,600 each. Each of the week-day comedy events are priced at $14,400, and the cost incurred by the company is $1,300.

           There are 80 senior employees who earn $36 per hour and work 38 hours per week. The company also employs 36 student interns for 23 hours per week, and pays them $16 per hour. Aside from the hourly staff members, there is a senior manager who earns an annual salary of $26,000 and the bookkeeper is paid $12,000 per year. Utilities are the main overhead expense, which costs $760,000 per year. The building was originally bought for $1,900,000, and it has a useful life of 96 years, and the equipment, which had cost the company $950,000 has a useful life of 64 years. This company's effective tax rate is 36%. Calculate the monthly tax expense.

45   Mount Tessory Academy is a corporation which sells private school education. Last year, they sold 15,689 annual kindergarten memberships, 5,889 annual elementary school tuition memberships, and 2,095 annual pre-school memberships. Each of the annual kindergarten memberships sells for $15,600 and they cost the company $2,200. The per-unit cost incurred for the annual elementary school tuition memberships is $2,200 and they sell for $22,800 each. Each of the annual pre-school memberships are priced at $8,400, and the cost incurred by the company is $600.

           There are 60 permanent full-time staff who earn $30 per hour and work 28 hours per week. The company also employs 30 part-time employees for 17 hours per week, and pays them $14 per hour. Aside from the hourly staff members, there is a director who earns an annual salary of $22,000 and the manager is paid $10,000 per year. Janitorial services are the main overhead expense, which costs $640,000 per year. The building was originally bought for $1,600,000, and it has a useful life of 72 years, and the equipment, which had cost the company $800,000 has a useful life of 48 years. This company's effective tax rate is 34%. Calculate the monthly net income before tax.

46   NY Fitness is a corporation which sells gym memberships for professional sports teams. Last year, they sold 16,972 premium baseball team memberships, 6,347 deluxe football team memberships, and 2,270 soccer team memberships. Each of the premium baseball team memberships sells for $16,900 and they cost the company $2,200. The per-unit cost incurred for the deluxe football team memberships is $2,200 and they sell for $24,700 each. Each of the soccer team memberships are priced at $9,100, and the cost incurred by the company is $600.

There are 60 permanent full-time staff who earn $30 per hour and work 28 hours per week. The company also employs 30 part-time employees for 17 hours per week, and pays them $14 per hour. Aside from the hourly staff members, there is a director who earns an annual salary of $22,000 and the manager is paid $10,000 per year. Janitorial services are the main overhead expense, which costs $640,000 per year. The building was originally bought for $1,600,000, and it has a useful life of 78 years, and the equipment, which had cost the company $800,000 has a useful life of 52 years. This company's effective tax rate is 34%. Calculate the annual EBITDA.

47   Paytech Ltd is a company which offers their customers a wide selection of payroll transaction processing services. Last year, they sold 23,106 monthly subscriptions, 17,956 annual subscriptions, and 5,245 temporary coverage contracts. Each of the monthly subscriptions sells for $23,100 and they cost the company $600. The per-unit cost incurred for the annual subscriptions is $600 and they sell for $35,700 each. Each of the temporary coverage contracts are priced at $10,500, and the cost incurred by the company is $200.

There are 40 full-time employees who earn $24 per hour and work 18 hours per week. The company also employs 24 temporary contract workers for 11 hours per week, and pays them $12 per hour. Aside from the hourly staff members, there is a chief operating officer who earns an annual salary of $18,000 and the senior manager is paid $8,000 per year. HVAC expenses are the main overhead expense, which costs $520,000 per year. The building was originally bought for $1,300,000, and it has a useful life of 126 years, and the equipment, which had cost the company $650,000 has a useful life of 84 years. This company's effective tax rate is 32%. Calculate the annual cash flow.

48   Paytech Ltd sells several different types of payroll transaction processing services. Last year, they sold 21,025 monthly subscriptions, 33,725 annual subscriptions, and 8,395 temporary coverage contracts. Each of the monthly subscriptions sells for $21,000 and they cost the company $200. The per-unit cost incurred for the annual subscriptions is $200 and they sell for $33,600 each. Each of the temporary coverage contracts are priced at $8,400, and the cost incurred by the company is $100.

There are 30 full-time employees who earn $21 per hour and work 13 hours per week. The company also employs 21 temporary contract workers for 8 hours per week, and pays them $11 per hour. Aside from the hourly staff members, there is a chief operating officer who earns an annual salary of $16,000 and the senior manager is paid $7,000 per year. HVAC expenses are the main overhead expense, which costs $460,000 per year. The building was originally bought for $1,150,000, and it has a useful life of 126 years, and the equipment, which had cost the company $575,000 has a useful life of 84 years. This company's effective tax rate is 31%. Calculate the annual cash flow.

49   Mount Tessory Academy provides their customers with private school education. Last year, they sold 16,887 annual kindergarten memberships, 4,987 annual elementary school tuition memberships, and 1,915 annual pre-school memberships. Each of the annual kindergarten memberships sells for $16,800 and they cost the company $3,500. The per-unit cost incurred for the annual elementary school tuition memberships is $3,600 and they sell for $24,000 each. Each of the annual pre-school memberships are priced at $9,600, and the cost incurred by the company is $900.

There are 70 senior employees who earn $33 per hour and work 33 hours per week. The company also employs 33 student interns for 20 hours per week, and pays them $15 per hour. Aside from the hourly staff members, there is a senior manager who earns an annual salary of $24,000 and the bookkeeper is paid $11,000 per year. Utilities are the main overhead expense, which costs $700,000 per year. The building was originally bought for $1,750,000, and it has a useful life of 72 years, and the equipment, which had cost the company $875,000 has a useful life of 48 years. This company's effective tax rate is 35%. Calculate the monthly net income before tax.

50   Mount Tessory Academy is an organization which specializes in providing their customers with private school education. Last year, they sold 18,054 annual kindergarten memberships, 4,354 annual elementary school tuition memberships, and 1,795 annual pre-school memberships. Each of the annual kindergarten memberships sells for $18,000 and they cost the company $5,300. The per-unit cost incurred for the annual elementary school tuition memberships is $5,400 and they sell for $25,200 each. Each of the annual pre-school memberships are priced at $10,800, and the cost incurred by the company is $1,300.

There are 80 senior employees who earn $36 per hour and work 38 hours per week. The company also employs 36 student interns for 23 hours per week, and pays them $16 per hour. Aside from the hourly staff members, there is a senior manager who earns an annual salary of $26,000 and the bookkeeper is paid $12,000 per year. Utilities are the main overhead expense, which costs $760,000 per year. The building was originally bought for $1,900,000, and it has a useful life of 72 years, and the equipment, which had cost the company $950,000 has a useful life of 48 years. This company's effective tax rate is 36%. Calculate the monthly net income before tax.

51   Hogtown Records is a corporation which sells audio services for local musicians who would like to record their music. Last year, they sold 24,726 singles CDs, 9,151 full albums on LP, and 3,320 individual song recordings. Each of the singles CDs sells for $24,700 and they cost the company $2,200. The per-unit cost incurred for the full albums on LP is $2,200 and they sell for $36,100 each. Each of the individual song recordings are priced at $13,300, and the cost incurred by the company is $600.

There are 60 permanent full-time staff who earn $30 per hour and work 28 hours per week. The company also employs 30 part-time employees for 17 hours per week, and pays them $14 per hour. Aside from the hourly staff members, there is a director who earns an annual salary of $22,000 and the manager is paid $10,000 per year. Janitorial services are the main overhead expense, which costs $640,000 per year. The building was originally bought for $1,600,000, and it has a useful life of 114 years, and the equipment, which had cost the company $800,000 has a useful life of 76 years. This company's effective tax rate is 34%. Calculate the annual cash flow.

52   Payday Now is an organization which specializes in providing their customers with short-term loan arrangements. Last year, they sold 16,589 lines of credit, 4,039 payday loans, and 1,645 prepaid credit cards. Each of the lines of credit sells for $16,500 and they cost the company $5,300. The per-unit cost incurred for the payday loans is $5,400 and they sell for $23,100 each. Each of the prepaid credit cards are priced at $9,900, and the cost incurred by the company is $1,300.

There are 80 senior employees who earn $36 per hour and work 38 hours per week. The company also employs 36 student interns for 23 hours per week, and pays them $16 per hour. Aside from the hourly staff members, there is a senior manager who earns an annual salary of $26,000 and the bookkeeper is paid $12,000 per year. Utilities are the main overhead expense, which costs $760,000 per year. The building was originally bought for $1,900,000, and it has a useful life of 66 years, and the equipment, which had cost the company $950,000 has a useful life of 44 years. This company's effective tax rate is 36%. Calculate the annual net income before tax.

53   Fairway Malls is a company which offers their customers a wide selection of retail spaces in their shopping centers. Last year, they sold 22,046 monthly retail space rentals, 17,146 monthly anchor store rentals, and 4,995 monthly food court rentals. Each of the monthly retail space rentals sells for $22,000 and they cost the company $600. The per-unit cost incurred for the monthly anchor store rentals is $600 and they sell for $34,000 each. Each of the monthly food court rentals are priced at $10,000, and the cost incurred by the company is $200.

There are 40 full-time employees who earn $24 per hour and work 18 hours per week. The company also employs 24 temporary contract workers for 11 hours per week, and pays them $12 per hour. Aside from the hourly staff members, there is a chief operating officer who earns an annual salary of $18,000 and the senior manager is paid $8,000 per year. HVAC expenses are the main overhead expense, which costs $520,000 per year. The building was originally bought for $1,300,000, and it has a useful life of 120 years, and the equipment, which had cost the company $650,000 has a useful life of 80 years. This company's effective tax rate is 32%. Calculate the monthly cash flow.

54   Hogtown Records sells various audio services for local musicians who would like to record their music. Last year, they sold 34,273 singles CDs, 5,240 full albums on LP, and 2,528 individual song recordings. Each of the singles CDs sells for $34,200 and they cost the company $13,900. The per-unit cost incurred for the full albums on LP is $14,000 and they sell for $45,600 each. Each of the individual song recordings are priced at $22,800, and the cost incurred by the company is $2,700.

There are 110 full-timers who earn $45 per hour and work 53 hours per week. The company also employs 45 seasonal employees for 32 hours per week, and pays them $19 per hour. Aside from the hourly staff members, there is a supervisor who earns an annual salary of $32,000 and the receptionist is paid $15,000 per year. Insurance costs are the main overhead expense, which costs $940,000 per year. The building was originally bought for $2,350,000, and it has a useful life of 114 years, and the equipment, which had cost the company $1,175,000 has a useful life of 76 years. This company's effective tax rate is 39%. Calculate the annual cash flow.

55   Payday Now is a corporation which sells short-term loan arrangements. Last year, they sold 14,396 lines of credit, 5,421 payday loans, and 1,920 prepaid credit cards. Each of the lines of credit sells for $14,300 and they cost the company $2,200. The per-unit cost incurred for the payday loans is $2,200 and they sell for $20,900 each. Each of the prepaid credit cards are priced at $7,700, and the cost incurred by the company is $600.

There are 60 permanent full-time staff who earn $30 per hour and work 28 hours per week. The company also employs 30 part-time employees for 17 hours per week, and pays them $14 per hour. Aside from the hourly staff members, there is a director who earns an annual salary of $22,000 and the manager is paid $10,000 per year. Janitorial services are the main overhead expense, which costs $640,000 per year. The building was originally bought for $1,600,000, and it has a useful life of 66 years, and the equipment, which had cost the company $800,000 has a useful life of 44 years. This company's effective tax rate is 34%. Calculate the annual net income before tax.

56   Jameson & Jameson offers their customers a wide range of soap products. Last year, they sold 3,648 truckloads of shampoo bottles, 1,948 truckloads of toothpaste, and 595 truckloads of bars of soap. Each of the truckloads of shampoo bottles sells for $3,600 and they cost the company $1,200. The per-unit cost incurred for the truckloads of toothpaste is $1,300 and they sell for $5,400 each. Each of the truckloads of bars of soap are priced at $1,800, and the cost incurred by the company is $400.

There are 50 permanent full-time staff who earn $27 per hour and work 23 hours per week. The company also employs 27 part-time employees for 14 hours per week, and pays them $13 per hour. Aside from the hourly staff members, there is a director who earns an annual salary of $20,000 and the manager is paid $9,000 per year. Janitorial services are the main overhead expense, which costs $580,000 per year. The building was originally bought for $1,450,000, and it has a useful life of 18 years, and the equipment, which had cost the company $725,000 has a useful life of 12 years. This company's effective tax rate is 33%. Calculate the gross margin.

57   Payday Now is a market leader that is well-known for their brand of short-term loan arrangements. Last year, they sold 17,657 lines of credit, 3,614 payday loans, and 1,566 prepaid credit cards. Each of the lines of credit sells for $17,600 and they cost the company $7,600. The per-unit cost incurred for the payday loans is $7,700 and they sell for $24,200 each. Each of the prepaid credit cards are priced at $11,000, and the cost incurred by the company is $1,700.

There are 90 union workers who earn $39 per hour and work 43 hours per week. The company also employs 39 non-union workers for 26 hours per week, and pays them $17 per hour. Aside from the hourly staff members, there is a president who earns an annual salary of $28,000 and the vice-president is paid $13,000 per year. Employee assistance services are the main overhead expense, which costs $820,000 per year. The building was originally bought for $2,050,000, and it has a useful life of 66 years, and the equipment, which had cost the company $1,025,000 has a useful life of 44 years. This company's effective tax rate is 37%. Calculate the annual net income before tax.

58   Comedy 253 sells several different types of live performances of stand-up comedy. Last year, they sold 16,005 week-end comedy festivals, 25,705 private events, and 6,395 week-day comedy events. Each of the week-end comedy festivals sells for $16,000 and they cost the company $200. The per-unit cost incurred for the private events is $200 and they sell for $25,600 each. Each of the week-day comedy events are priced at $6,400, and the cost incurred by the company is $100.

          There are 30 full-time employees who earn $21 per hour and work 13 hours per week. The company also employs 21 temporary contract workers for 8 hours per week, and pays them $11 per hour. Aside from the hourly staff members, there is a chief operating officer who earns an annual salary of $16,000 and the senior manager is paid $7,000 per year. HVAC expenses are the main overhead expense, which costs $460,000 per year. The building was originally bought for $1,150,000, and it has a useful life of 96 years, and the equipment, which had cost the company $575,000 has a useful life of 64 years. This company's effective tax rate is 31%. Calculate the monthly tax expense.

59   Fairway Malls is a privately-held corporation which focuses on their niche of premium retail spaces in their shopping centers. Last year, they sold 34,049 monthly retail space rentals, 5,899 monthly anchor store rentals, and 2,745 monthly food court rentals. Each of the monthly retail space rentals sells for $34,000 and they cost the company $10,400. The per-unit cost incurred for the monthly anchor store rentals is $10,600 and they sell for $46,000 each. Each of the monthly food court rentals are priced at $22,000, and the cost incurred by the company is $2,200.

          There are 100 union workers who earn $42 per hour and work 48 hours per week. The company also employs 42 non-union workers for 29 hours per week, and pays them $18 per hour. Aside from the hourly staff members, there is a president who earns an annual salary of $30,000 and the vice-president is paid $14,000 per year. Employee assistance services are the main overhead expense, which costs $880,000 per year. The building was originally bought for $2,200,000, and it has a useful life of 120 years, and the equipment, which had cost the company $1,100,000 has a useful life of 80 years. This company's effective tax rate is 38%. Calculate the monthly cash flow.

60   Grand Convention Ltd sells various banquet hall rentals for corporate meetings. Last year, they sold 34,291 wedding ceremonies, 4,691 corporate events, and 2,335 convention events. Each of the wedding ceremonies sells for $34,200 and they cost the company $18,000. The per-unit cost incurred for the corporate events is $18,200 and they sell for $45,000 each. Each of the convention events are priced at $23,400, and the cost incurred by the company is $3,300.

          There are 120 full-timers who earn $48 per hour and work 58 hours per week. The company also employs 48 seasonal employees for 35 hours per week, and pays them $20 per hour. Aside from the hourly staff members, there is a supervisor who earns an annual salary of $34,000 and the receptionist is paid $16,000 per year. Insurance costs are the main overhead expense, which costs $1,000,000 per year. The building was originally bought for $2,500,000, and it has a useful life of 108 years, and the equipment, which had cost the company $1,250,000 has a useful life of 72 years. This company's effective tax rate is 40%. Calculate the monthly tax expense.

61	Kola-Nut Ltd sells several different types of bottled beverages. Last year, they sold 2,042 batches of fruit juice, 3,342 batches of energy drinks, and 795 batches of soda bottles. Each of the batches of fruit juice sells for $2,000 and they cost the company $200. The per-unit cost incurred for the batches of energy drinks is $200 and they sell for $3,200 each. Each of the batches of soda bottles are priced at $800, and the cost incurred by the company is $100.

There are 30 full-time employees who earn $21 per hour and work 13 hours per week. The company also employs 21 temporary contract workers for 8 hours per week, and pays them $11 per hour. Aside from the hourly staff members, there is a chief operating officer who earns an annual salary of $16,000 and the senior manager is paid $7,000 per year. HVAC expenses are the main overhead expense, which costs $460,000 per year. The building was originally bought for $1,150,000, and it has a useful life of 12 years, and the equipment, which had cost the company $575,000 has a useful life of 8 years. This company's effective tax rate is 31%. Calculate the gross margin.

62	AC&C Ltd. provides their customers with cell phone plans. Last year, they sold 14,020 annual unlimited talk and text plans, 4,120 annual unlimited voice and data plans, and 1,595 annual prepaid wireless phone cards. Each of the annual unlimited talk and text plans sells for $14,000 and they cost the company $3,500. The per-unit cost incurred for the annual unlimited voice and data plans is $3,600 and they sell for $20,000 each. Each of the annual prepaid wireless phone cards are priced at $8,000, and the cost incurred by the company is $900.

There are 70 senior employees who earn $33 per hour and work 33 hours per week. The company also employs 33 student interns for 20 hours per week, and pays them $15 per hour. Aside from the hourly staff members, there is a senior manager who earns an annual salary of $24,000 and the bookkeeper is paid $11,000 per year. Utilities are the main overhead expense, which costs $700,000 per year. The building was originally bought for $1,750,000, and it has a useful life of 60 years, and the equipment, which had cost the company $875,000 has a useful life of 40 years. This company's effective tax rate is 35%. Calculate the monthly net income before tax.

63	Mount Tessory Academy is an organization which specializes in providing their customers with private school education. Last year, they sold 18,091 annual kindergarten memberships, 4,391 annual elementary school tuition memberships, and 1,795 annual pre-school memberships. Each of the annual kindergarten memberships sells for $18,000 and they cost the company $5,300. The per-unit cost incurred for the annual elementary school tuition memberships is $5,400 and they sell for $25,200 each. Each of the annual pre-school memberships are priced at $10,800, and the cost incurred by the company is $1,300.

There are 80 senior employees who earn $36 per hour and work 38 hours per week. The company also employs 36 student interns for 23 hours per week, and pays them $16 per hour. Aside from the hourly staff members, there is a senior manager who earns an annual salary of $26,000 and the bookkeeper is paid $12,000 per year. Utilities are the main overhead expense, which costs $760,000 per year. The building was originally bought for $1,900,000, and it has a useful life of 72 years, and the equipment, which had cost the company $950,000 has a useful life of 48 years. This company's effective tax rate is 36%. Calculate the monthly net income before tax.

64   Payday Now is an organization which specializes in providing their customers with short-term loan arrangements. Last year, they sold 16,566 lines of credit, 4,016 payday loans, and 1,645 prepaid credit cards. Each of the lines of credit sells for $16,500 and they cost the company $5,300. The per-unit cost incurred for the payday loans is $5,400 and they sell for $23,100 each. Each of the prepaid credit cards are priced at $9,900, and the cost incurred by the company is $1,300.

        There are 80 senior employees who earn $36 per hour and work 38 hours per week. The company also employs 36 student interns for 23 hours per week, and pays them $16 per hour. Aside from the hourly staff members, there is a senior manager who earns an annual salary of $26,000 and the bookkeeper is paid $12,000 per year. Utilities are the main overhead expense, which costs $760,000 per year. The building was originally bought for $1,900,000, and it has a useful life of 66 years, and the equipment, which had cost the company $950,000 has a useful life of 44 years. This company's effective tax rate is 36%. Calculate the annual net income before tax.

65   Comedy 253 is a company which offers their customers a wide selection of live performances of stand-up comedy. Last year, they sold 17,676 week-end comedy festivals, 13,776 private events, and 3,995 week-day comedy events. Each of the week-end comedy festivals sells for $17,600 and they cost the company $600. The per-unit cost incurred for the private events is $600 and they sell for $27,200 each. Each of the week-day comedy events are priced at $8,000, and the cost incurred by the company is $200.

        There are 40 full-time employees who earn $24 per hour and work 18 hours per week. The company also employs 24 temporary contract workers for 11 hours per week, and pays them $12 per hour. Aside from the hourly staff members, there is a chief operating officer who earns an annual salary of $18,000 and the senior manager is paid $8,000 per year. HVAC expenses are the main overhead expense, which costs $520,000 per year. The building was originally bought for $1,300,000, and it has a useful life of 96 years, and the equipment, which had cost the company $650,000 has a useful life of 64 years. This company's effective tax rate is 32%. Calculate the monthly tax expense.

66   Grand Convention Ltd provides their customers with banquet hall rentals for corporate meetings. Last year, they sold 25,256 wedding ceremonies, 7,356 corporate events, and 2,875 convention events. Each of the wedding ceremonies sells for $25,200 and they cost the company $3,500. The per-unit cost incurred for the corporate events is $3,600 and they sell for $36,000 each. Each of the convention events are priced at $14,400, and the cost incurred by the company is $900.

        There are 70 senior employees who earn $33 per hour and work 33 hours per week. The company also employs 33 student interns for 20 hours per week, and pays them $15 per hour. Aside from the hourly staff members, there is a senior manager who earns an annual salary of $24,000 and the bookkeeper is paid $11,000 per year. Utilities are the main overhead expense, which costs $700,000 per year. The building was originally bought for $1,750,000, and it has a useful life of 108 years, and the equipment, which had cost the company $875,000 has a useful life of 72 years. This company's effective tax rate is 35%. Calculate the monthly tax expense.

67   NY Fitness is an organization which specializes in providing their customers with gym memberships for professional sports teams. Last year, they sold 19,537 premium baseball team memberships, 4,687 deluxe football team memberships, and 1,945 soccer team memberships. Each of the premium baseball team memberships sells for $19,500 and they cost the company $5,300. The per-unit cost incurred for the deluxe football team memberships is $5,400 and they sell for $27,300 each. Each of the soccer team memberships are priced at $11,700, and the cost incurred by the company is $1,300.

There are 80 senior employees who earn $36 per hour and work 38 hours per week. The company also employs 36 student interns for 23 hours per week, and pays them $16 per hour. Aside from the hourly staff members, there is a senior manager who earns an annual salary of $26,000 and the bookkeeper is paid $12,000 per year. Utilities are the main overhead expense, which costs $760,000 per year. The building was originally bought for $1,900,000, and it has a useful life of 78 years, and the equipment, which had cost the company $950,000 has a useful life of 52 years. This company's effective tax rate is 36%. Calculate the annual EBITDA.

68   Fairway Malls is a company which offers their customers a wide selection of retail spaces in their shopping centers. Last year, they sold 22,002 monthly retail space rentals, 17,102 monthly anchor store rentals, and 4,995 monthly food court rentals. Each of the monthly retail space rentals sells for $22,000 and they cost the company $600. The per-unit cost incurred for the monthly anchor store rentals is $600 and they sell for $34,000 each. Each of the monthly food court rentals are priced at $10,000, and the cost incurred by the company is $200.

There are 40 full-time employees who earn $24 per hour and work 18 hours per week. The company also employs 24 temporary contract workers for 11 hours per week, and pays them $12 per hour. Aside from the hourly staff members, there is a chief operating officer who earns an annual salary of $18,000 and the senior manager is paid $8,000 per year. HVAC expenses are the main overhead expense, which costs $520,000 per year. The building was originally bought for $1,300,000, and it has a useful life of 120 years, and the equipment, which had cost the company $650,000 has a useful life of 80 years. This company's effective tax rate is 32%. Calculate the monthly cash flow.

69   Mount Tessory Academy offers their customers a wide range of private school education. Last year, they sold 14,425 annual kindergarten memberships, 7,325 annual elementary school tuition memberships, and 2,395 annual pre-school memberships. Each of the annual kindergarten memberships sells for $14,400 and they cost the company $1,200. The per-unit cost incurred for the annual elementary school tuition memberships is $1,300 and they sell for $21,600 each. Each of the annual pre-school memberships are priced at $7,200, and the cost incurred by the company is $400.

There are 50 permanent full-time staff who earn $27 per hour and work 23 hours per week. The company also employs 27 part-time employees for 14 hours per week, and pays them $13 per hour. Aside from the hourly staff members, there is a director who earns an annual salary of $20,000 and the manager is paid $9,000 per year. Janitorial services are the main overhead expense, which costs $580,000 per year. The building was originally bought for $1,450,000, and it has a useful life of 72 years, and the equipment, which had cost the company $725,000 has a useful life of 48 years. This company's effective tax rate is 33%. Calculate the monthly net income before tax.

70   Jameson & Jameson is a corporation which sells soap products. Last year, they sold 3,991 truckloads of shampoo bottles, 1,616 truckloads of toothpaste, and 520 truckloads of bars of soap. Each of the truckloads of shampoo bottles sells for $3,900 and they cost the company $2,200. The per-unit cost incurred for the truckloads of toothpaste is $2,200 and they sell for $5,700 each. Each of the truckloads of bars of soap are priced at $2,100, and the cost incurred by the company is $600.

There are 60 permanent full-time staff who earn $30 per hour and work 28 hours per week. The company also employs 30 part-time employees for 17 hours per week, and pays them $14 per hour. Aside from the hourly staff members, there is a director who earns an annual salary of $22,000 and the manager is paid $10,000 per year. Janitorial services are the main overhead expense, which costs $640,000 per year. The building was originally bought for $1,600,000, and it has a useful life of 18 years, and the equipment, which had cost the company $800,000 has a useful life of 12 years. This company's effective tax rate is 34%. Calculate the gross margin.

71   Mount Tessory Academy is an organization which specializes in providing their customers with private school education. Last year, they sold 18,028 annual kindergarten memberships, 4,328 annual elementary school tuition memberships, and 1,795 annual pre-school memberships. Each of the annual kindergarten memberships sells for $18,000 and they cost the company $5,300. The per-unit cost incurred for the annual elementary school tuition memberships is $5,400 and they sell for $25,200 each. Each of the annual pre-school memberships are priced at $10,800, and the cost incurred by the company is $1,300.

There are 80 senior employees who earn $36 per hour and work 38 hours per week. The company also employs 36 student interns for 23 hours per week, and pays them $16 per hour. Aside from the hourly staff members, there is a senior manager who earns an annual salary of $26,000 and the bookkeeper is paid $12,000 per year. Utilities are the main overhead expense, which costs $760,000 per year. The building was originally bought for $1,900,000, and it has a useful life of 72 years, and the equipment, which had cost the company $950,000 has a useful life of 48 years. This company's effective tax rate is 36%. Calculate the monthly net income before tax.

72   Club Disco is a company which offers their customers a wide selection of dance venue rentals for large family gatherings. Last year, they sold 18,729 week-end party rentals, 14,579 holiday rentals, and 4,245 evening rentals. Each of the week-end party rentals sells for $18,700 and they cost the company $600. The per-unit cost incurred for the holiday rentals is $600 and they sell for $28,900 each. Each of the evening rentals are priced at $8,500, and the cost incurred by the company is $200.

There are 40 full-time employees who earn $24 per hour and work 18 hours per week. The company also employs 24 temporary contract workers for 11 hours per week, and pays them $12 per hour. Aside from the hourly staff members, there is a chief operating officer who earns an annual salary of $18,000 and the senior manager is paid $8,000 per year. HVAC expenses are the main overhead expense, which costs $520,000 per year. The building was originally bought for $1,300,000, and it has a useful life of 102 years, and the equipment, which had cost the company $650,000 has a useful life of 68 years. This company's effective tax rate is 32%. Calculate the annual tax expense.

73   AC&C Ltd. offers their customers a wide range of cell phone plans. Last year, they sold 12,020 annual unlimited talk and text plans, 6,120 annual unlimited voice and data plans, and 1,995 annual prepaid wireless phone cards. Each of the annual unlimited talk and text plans sells for $12,000 and they cost the company $1,200. The per-unit cost incurred for the annual unlimited voice and data plans is $1,300 and they sell for $18,000 each. Each of the annual prepaid wireless phone cards are priced at $6,000, and the cost incurred by the company is $400.
        There are 50 permanent full-time staff who earn $27 per hour and work 23 hours per week. The company also employs 27 part-time employees for 14 hours per week, and pays them $13 per hour. Aside from the hourly staff members, there is a director who earns an annual salary of $20,000 and the manager is paid $9,000 per year. Janitorial services are the main overhead expense, which costs $580,000 per year. The building was originally bought for $1,450,000, and it has a useful life of 60 years, and the equipment, which had cost the company $725,000 has a useful life of 40 years. This company's effective tax rate is 33%. Calculate the monthly net income before tax.

74   Fairway Malls is a corporation which sells retail spaces in their shopping centers. Last year, they sold 26,075 monthly retail space rentals, 9,675 monthly anchor store rentals, and 3,495 monthly food court rentals. Each of the monthly retail space rentals sells for $26,000 and they cost the company $2,200. The per-unit cost incurred for the monthly anchor store rentals is $2,200 and they sell for $38,000 each. Each of the monthly food court rentals are priced at $14,000, and the cost incurred by the company is $600.
        There are 60 permanent full-time staff who earn $30 per hour and work 28 hours per week. The company also employs 30 part-time employees for 17 hours per week, and pays them $14 per hour. Aside from the hourly staff members, there is a director who earns an annual salary of $22,000 and the manager is paid $10,000 per year. Janitorial services are the main overhead expense, which costs $640,000 per year. The building was originally bought for $1,600,000, and it has a useful life of 120 years, and the equipment, which had cost the company $800,000 has a useful life of 80 years. This company's effective tax rate is 34%. Calculate the monthly cash flow.

75   NY Fitness is a corporation which sells gym memberships for professional sports teams. Last year, they sold 16,985 premium baseball team memberships, 6,360 deluxe football team memberships, and 2,270 soccer team memberships. Each of the premium baseball team memberships sells for $16,900 and they cost the company $2,200. The per-unit cost incurred for the deluxe football team memberships is $2,200 and they sell for $24,700 each. Each of the soccer team memberships are priced at $9,100, and the cost incurred by the company is $600.
        There are 60 permanent full-time staff who earn $30 per hour and work 28 hours per week. The company also employs 30 part-time employees for 17 hours per week, and pays them $14 per hour. Aside from the hourly staff members, there is a director who earns an annual salary of $22,000 and the manager is paid $10,000 per year. Janitorial services are the main overhead expense, which costs $640,000 per year. The building was originally bought for $1,600,000, and it has a useful life of 78 years, and the equipment, which had cost the company $800,000 has a useful life of 52 years. This company's effective tax rate is 34%. Calculate the annual EBITDA.

76   LA Met Theatre Company is a market leader that is well-known for their brand of live theatrical performances. Last year, they sold 24,036 premium monthly memberships, 4,850 platinum annual memberships, and 2,138 student memberships. Each of the premium monthly memberships sells for $24,000 and they cost the company $7,600. The per-unit cost incurred for the platinum annual memberships is $7,700 and they sell for $33,000 each. Each of the student memberships are priced at $15,000, and the cost incurred by the company is $1,700.

         There are 90 union workers who earn $39 per hour and work 43 hours per week. The company also employs 39 non-union workers for 26 hours per week, and pays them $17 per hour. Aside from the hourly staff members, there is a president who earns an annual salary of $28,000 and the vice-president is paid $13,000 per year. Employee assistance services are the main overhead expense, which costs $820,000 per year. The building was originally bought for $2,050,000, and it has a useful life of 90 years, and the equipment, which had cost the company $1,025,000 has a useful life of 60 years. This company's effective tax rate is 37%. Calculate the annual EBITDA.

77   Hogtown Records sells various audio services for local musicians who would like to record their music. Last year, they sold 34,278 singles CDs, 5,245 full albums on LP, and 2,528 individual song recordings. Each of the singles CDs sells for $34,200 and they cost the company $13,900. The per-unit cost incurred for the full albums on LP is $14,000 and they sell for $45,600 each. Each of the individual song recordings are priced at $22,800, and the cost incurred by the company is $2,700.

         There are 110 full-timers who earn $45 per hour and work 53 hours per week. The company also employs 45 seasonal employees for 32 hours per week, and pays them $19 per hour. Aside from the hourly staff members, there is a supervisor who earns an annual salary of $32,000 and the receptionist is paid $15,000 per year. Insurance costs are the main overhead expense, which costs $940,000 per year. The building was originally bought for $2,350,000, and it has a useful life of 114 years, and the equipment, which had cost the company $1,175,000 has a useful life of 76 years. This company's effective tax rate is 39%. Calculate the annual cash flow.

78   Cirque du Lune sells various circus performances. Last year, they sold 26,634 monthly shows, 3,634 holiday special performances, and 1,815 performances at schools. Each of the monthly shows sells for $26,600 and they cost the company $18,000. The per-unit cost incurred for the holiday special performances is $18,200 and they sell for $35,000 each. Each of the performances at schools are priced at $18,200, and the cost incurred by the company is $3,300.

         There are 120 full-timers who earn $48 per hour and work 58 hours per week. The company also employs 48 seasonal employees for 35 hours per week, and pays them $20 per hour. Aside from the hourly staff members, there is a supervisor who earns an annual salary of $34,000 and the receptionist is paid $16,000 per year. Insurance costs are the main overhead expense, which costs $1,000,000 per year. The building was originally bought for $2,500,000, and it has a useful life of 84 years, and the equipment, which had cost the company $1,250,000 has a useful life of 56 years. This company's effective tax rate is 40%. Calculate the monthly EBITDA.

79   Cirque du Lune sells various circus performances. Last year, they sold 26,656 monthly shows, 3,656 holiday special performances, and 1,815 performances at schools. Each of the monthly shows sells for $26,600 and they cost the company $18,000. The per-unit cost incurred for the holiday special performances is $18,200 and they sell for $35,000 each. Each of the performances at schools are priced at $18,200, and the cost incurred by the company is $3,300.

There are 120 full-timers who earn $48 per hour and work 58 hours per week. The company also employs 48 seasonal employees for 35 hours per week, and pays them $20 per hour. Aside from the hourly staff members, there is a supervisor who earns an annual salary of $34,000 and the receptionist is paid $16,000 per year. Insurance costs are the main overhead expense, which costs $1,000,000 per year. The building was originally bought for $2,500,000, and it has a useful life of 84 years, and the equipment, which had cost the company $1,250,000 has a useful life of 56 years. This company's effective tax rate is 40%. Calculate the monthly EBITDA.

80   Grand Convention Ltd is a privately-held corporation which focuses on their niche of premium banquet hall rentals for corporate meetings. Last year, they sold 30,627 wedding ceremonies, 5,302 corporate events, and 2,470 convention events. Each of the wedding ceremonies sells for $30,600 and they cost the company $10,400. The per-unit cost incurred for the corporate events is $10,600 and they sell for $41,400 each. Each of the convention events are priced at $19,800, and the cost incurred by the company is $2,200.

There are 100 union workers who earn $42 per hour and work 48 hours per week. The company also employs 42 non-union workers for 29 hours per week, and pays them $18 per hour. Aside from the hourly staff members, there is a president who earns an annual salary of $30,000 and the vice-president is paid $14,000 per year. Employee assistance services are the main overhead expense, which costs $880,000 per year. The building was originally bought for $2,200,000, and it has a useful life of 108 years, and the equipment, which had cost the company $1,100,000 has a useful life of 72 years. This company's effective tax rate is 38%. Calculate the monthly tax expense.

81   AC&C Ltd. offers their customers a wide range of cell phone plans. Last year, they sold 12,066 annual unlimited talk and text plans, 6,166 annual unlimited voice and data plans, and 1,995 annual prepaid wireless phone cards. Each of the annual unlimited talk and text plans sells for $12,000 and they cost the company $1,200. The per-unit cost incurred for the annual unlimited voice and data plans is $1,300 and they sell for $18,000 each. Each of the annual prepaid wireless phone cards are priced at $6,000, and the cost incurred by the company is $400.

There are 50 permanent full-time staff who earn $27 per hour and work 23 hours per week. The company also employs 27 part-time employees for 14 hours per week, and pays them $13 per hour. Aside from the hourly staff members, there is a director who earns an annual salary of $20,000 and the manager is paid $9,000 per year. Janitorial services are the main overhead expense, which costs $580,000 per year. The building was originally bought for $1,450,000, and it has a useful life of 60 years, and the equipment, which had cost the company $725,000 has a useful life of 40 years. This company's effective tax rate is 33%. Calculate the monthly net income before tax.

82   AC&C Ltd. is a privately-held corporation which focuses on their niche of premium cell phone plans. Last year, they sold 17,076 annual unlimited talk and text plans, 3,051 annual unlimited voice and data plans, and 1,370 annual prepaid wireless phone cards. Each of the annual unlimited talk and text plans sells for $17,000 and they cost the company $10,400. The per-unit cost incurred for the annual unlimited voice and data plans is $10,600 and they sell for $23,000 each. Each of the annual prepaid wireless phone cards are priced at $11,000, and the cost incurred by the company is $2,200.

        There are 100 union workers who earn $42 per hour and work 48 hours per week. The company also employs 42 non-union workers for 29 hours per week, and pays them $18 per hour. Aside from the hourly staff members, there is a president who earns an annual salary of $30,000 and the vice-president is paid $14,000 per year. Employee assistance services are the main overhead expense, which costs $880,000 per year. The building was originally bought for $2,200,000, and it has a useful life of 60 years, and the equipment, which had cost the company $1,100,000 has a useful life of 40 years. This company's effective tax rate is 38%. Calculate the monthly net income before tax.

83   Payday Now is an organization which specializes in providing their customers with short-term loan arrangements. Last year, they sold 16,556 lines of credit, 4,006 payday loans, and 1,645 prepaid credit cards. Each of the lines of credit sells for $16,500 and they cost the company $5,300. The per-unit cost incurred for the payday loans is $5,400 and they sell for $23,100 each. Each of the prepaid credit cards are priced at $9,900, and the cost incurred by the company is $1,300.

        There are 80 senior employees who earn $36 per hour and work 38 hours per week. The company also employs 36 student interns for 23 hours per week, and pays them $16 per hour. Aside from the hourly staff members, there is a senior manager who earns an annual salary of $26,000 and the bookkeeper is paid $12,000 per year. Utilities are the main overhead expense, which costs $760,000 per year. The building was originally bought for $1,900,000, and it has a useful life of 66 years, and the equipment, which had cost the company $950,000 has a useful life of 44 years. This company's effective tax rate is 36%. Calculate the annual net income before tax.

84   LA Met Theatre Company is a corporation which sells live theatrical performances. Last year, they sold 19,597 premium monthly memberships, 7,322 platinum annual memberships, and 2,620 student memberships. Each of the premium monthly memberships sells for $19,500 and they cost the company $2,200. The per-unit cost incurred for the platinum annual memberships is $2,200 and they sell for $28,500 each. Each of the student memberships are priced at $10,500, and the cost incurred by the company is $600.

        There are 60 permanent full-time staff who earn $30 per hour and work 28 hours per week. The company also employs 30 part-time employees for 17 hours per week, and pays them $14 per hour. Aside from the hourly staff members, there is a director who earns an annual salary of $22,000 and the manager is paid $10,000 per year. Janitorial services are the main overhead expense, which costs $640,000 per year. The building was originally bought for $1,600,000, and it has a useful life of 90 years, and the equipment, which had cost the company $800,000 has a useful life of 60 years. This company's effective tax rate is 34%. Calculate the annual EBITDA.

85   Fairway Malls is an organization which specializes in providing their customers with retail spaces in their shopping centers. Last year, they sold 30,090 monthly retail space rentals, 7,190 monthly anchor store rentals, and 2,995 monthly food court rentals. Each of the monthly retail space rentals sells for $30,000 and they cost the company $5,300. The per-unit cost incurred for the monthly anchor store rentals is $5,400 and they sell for $42,000 each. Each of the monthly food court rentals are priced at $18,000, and the cost incurred by the company is $1,300.

There are 80 senior employees who earn $36 per hour and work 38 hours per week. The company also employs 36 student interns for 23 hours per week, and pays them $16 per hour. Aside from the hourly staff members, there is a senior manager who earns an annual salary of $26,000 and the bookkeeper is paid $12,000 per year. Utilities are the main overhead expense, which costs $760,000 per year. The building was originally bought for $1,900,000, and it has a useful life of 120 years, and the equipment, which had cost the company $950,000 has a useful life of 80 years. This company's effective tax rate is 36%. Calculate the monthly cash flow.

86   Kola-Nut Ltd offers their customers a wide range of bottled beverages. Last year, they sold 2,442 batches of fruit juice, 1,342 batches of energy drinks, and 395 batches of soda bottles. Each of the batches of fruit juice sells for $2,400 and they cost the company $1,200. The per-unit cost incurred for the batches of energy drinks is $1,300 and they sell for $3,600 each. Each of the batches of soda bottles are priced at $1,200, and the cost incurred by the company is $400.

There are 50 permanent full-time staff who earn $27 per hour and work 23 hours per week. The company also employs 27 part-time employees for 14 hours per week, and pays them $13 per hour. Aside from the hourly staff members, there is a director who earns an annual salary of $20,000 and the manager is paid $9,000 per year. Janitorial services are the main overhead expense, which costs $580,000 per year. The building was originally bought for $1,450,000, and it has a useful life of 12 years, and the equipment, which had cost the company $725,000 has a useful life of 8 years. This company's effective tax rate is 33%. Calculate the gross margin.

87   NY Fitness is an organization which specializes in providing their customers with gym memberships for professional sports teams. Last year, they sold 19,541 premium baseball team memberships, 4,691 deluxe football team memberships, and 1,945 soccer team memberships. Each of the premium baseball team memberships sells for $19,500 and they cost the company $5,300. The per-unit cost incurred for the deluxe football team memberships is $5,400 and they sell for $27,300 each. Each of the soccer team memberships are priced at $11,700, and the cost incurred by the company is $1,300.

There are 80 senior employees who earn $36 per hour and work 38 hours per week. The company also employs 36 student interns for 23 hours per week, and pays them $16 per hour. Aside from the hourly staff members, there is a senior manager who earns an annual salary of $26,000 and the bookkeeper is paid $12,000 per year. Utilities are the main overhead expense, which costs $760,000 per year. The building was originally bought for $1,900,000, and it has a useful life of 78 years, and the equipment, which had cost the company $950,000 has a useful life of 52 years. This company's effective tax rate is 36%. Calculate the annual EBITDA.

88   LA Met Theatre Company sells various live theatrical performances. Last year, they sold 27,056 premium monthly memberships, 4,156 platinum annual memberships, and 1,995 student memberships. Each of the premium monthly memberships sells for $27,000 and they cost the company $13,900. The per-unit cost incurred for the platinum annual memberships is $14,000 and they sell for $36,000 each. Each of the student memberships are priced at $18,000, and the cost incurred by the company is $2,700.

There are 110 full-timers who earn $45 per hour and work 53 hours per week. The company also employs 45 seasonal employees for 32 hours per week, and pays them $19 per hour. Aside from the hourly staff members, there is a supervisor who earns an annual salary of $32,000 and the receptionist is paid $15,000 per year. Insurance costs are the main overhead expense, which costs $940,000 per year. The building was originally bought for $2,350,000, and it has a useful life of 90 years, and the equipment, which had cost the company $1,175,000 has a useful life of 60 years. This company's effective tax rate is 39%. Calculate the annual EBITDA.

89   Paytech Ltd is a privately-held corporation which focuses on their niche of premium payroll transaction processing services. Last year, they sold 35,741 monthly subscriptions, 6,179 annual subscriptions, and 2,883 temporary coverage contracts. Each of the monthly subscriptions sells for $35,700 and they cost the company $10,400. The per-unit cost incurred for the annual subscriptions is $10,600 and they sell for $48,300 each. Each of the temporary coverage contracts are priced at $23,100, and the cost incurred by the company is $2,200.

There are 100 union workers who earn $42 per hour and work 48 hours per week. The company also employs 42 non-union workers for 29 hours per week, and pays them $18 per hour. Aside from the hourly staff members, there is a president who earns an annual salary of $30,000 and the vice-president is paid $14,000 per year. Employee assistance services are the main overhead expense, which costs $880,000 per year. The building was originally bought for $2,200,000, and it has a useful life of 126 years, and the equipment, which had cost the company $1,100,000 has a useful life of 84 years. This company's effective tax rate is 38%. Calculate the annual cash flow.

90   Comedy 253 provides their customers with live performances of stand-up comedy. Last year, they sold 22,491 week-end comedy festivals, 6,591 private events, and 2,555 week-day comedy events. Each of the week-end comedy festivals sells for $22,400 and they cost the company $3,500. The per-unit cost incurred for the private events is $3,600 and they sell for $32,000 each. Each of the week-day comedy events are priced at $12,800, and the cost incurred by the company is $900.

There are 70 senior employees who earn $33 per hour and work 33 hours per week. The company also employs 33 student interns for 20 hours per week, and pays them $15 per hour. Aside from the hourly staff members, there is a senior manager who earns an annual salary of $24,000 and the bookkeeper is paid $11,000 per year. Utilities are the main overhead expense, which costs $700,000 per year. The building was originally bought for $1,750,000, and it has a useful life of 96 years, and the equipment, which had cost the company $875,000 has a useful life of 64 years. This company's effective tax rate is 35%. Calculate the monthly tax expense.

91   Hogtown Records provides their customers with audio services for local musicians who would like to record their music. Last year, they sold 26,626 singles CDs, 7,726 full albums on LP, and 3,035 individual song recordings. Each of the singles CDs sells for $26,600 and they cost the company $3,500. The per-unit cost incurred for the full albums on LP is $3,600 and they sell for $38,000 each. Each of the individual song recordings are priced at $15,200, and the cost incurred by the company is $900.

          There are 70 senior employees who earn $33 per hour and work 33 hours per week. The company also employs 33 student interns for 20 hours per week, and pays them $15 per hour. Aside from the hourly staff members, there is a senior manager who earns an annual salary of $24,000 and the bookkeeper is paid $11,000 per year. Utilities are the main overhead expense, which costs $700,000 per year. The building was originally bought for $1,750,000, and it has a useful life of 114 years, and the equipment, which had cost the company $875,000 has a useful life of 76 years. This company's effective tax rate is 35%. Calculate the annual cash flow.

92   NY Fitness is a market leader that is well-known for their brand of gym memberships for professional sports teams. Last year, they sold 20,891 premium baseball team memberships, 4,277 deluxe football team memberships, and 1,852 soccer team memberships. Each of the premium baseball team memberships sells for $20,800 and they cost the company $7,600. The per-unit cost incurred for the deluxe football team memberships is $7,700 and they sell for $28,600 each. Each of the soccer team memberships are priced at $13,000, and the cost incurred by the company is $1,700.

          There are 90 union workers who earn $39 per hour and work 43 hours per week. The company also employs 39 non-union workers for 26 hours per week, and pays them $17 per hour. Aside from the hourly staff members, there is a president who earns an annual salary of $28,000 and the vice-president is paid $13,000 per year. Employee assistance services are the main overhead expense, which costs $820,000 per year. The building was originally bought for $2,050,000, and it has a useful life of 78 years, and the equipment, which had cost the company $1,025,000 has a useful life of 52 years. This company's effective tax rate is 37%. Calculate the annual EBITDA.

93   AC&C Ltd. is a privately-held corporation which focuses on their niche of premium cell phone plans. Last year, they sold 17,028 annual unlimited talk and text plans, 3,003 annual unlimited voice and data plans, and 1,370 annual prepaid wireless phone cards. Each of the annual unlimited talk and text plans sells for $17,000 and they cost the company $10,400. The per-unit cost incurred for the annual unlimited voice and data plans is $10,600 and they sell for $23,000 each. Each of the annual prepaid wireless phone cards are priced at $11,000, and the cost incurred by the company is $2,200.

          There are 100 union workers who earn $42 per hour and work 48 hours per week. The company also employs 42 non-union workers for 29 hours per week, and pays them $18 per hour. Aside from the hourly staff members, there is a president who earns an annual salary of $30,000 and the vice-president is paid $14,000 per year. Employee assistance services are the main overhead expense, which costs $880,000 per year. The building was originally bought for $2,200,000, and it has a useful life of 60 years, and the equipment, which had cost the company $1,100,000 has a useful life of 40 years. This company's effective tax rate is 38%. Calculate the monthly net income before tax.

94   Hogtown Records is a company which offers their customers a wide selection of audio services for local musicians who would like to record their music. Last year, they sold 20,993 singles CDs, 16,343 full albums on LP, and 4,745 individual song recordings. Each of the singles CDs sells for $20,900 and they cost the company $600. The per-unit cost incurred for the full albums on LP is $600 and they sell for $32,300 each. Each of the individual song recordings are priced at $9,500, and the cost incurred by the company is $200.

          There are 40 full-time employees who earn $24 per hour and work 18 hours per week. The company also employs 24 temporary contract workers for 11 hours per week, and pays them $12 per hour. Aside from the hourly staff members, there is a chief operating officer who earns an annual salary of $18,000 and the senior manager is paid $8,000 per year. HVAC expenses are the main overhead expense, which costs $520,000 per year. The building was originally bought for $1,300,000, and it has a useful life of 114 years, and the equipment, which had cost the company $650,000 has a useful life of 76 years. This company's effective tax rate is 32%. Calculate the annual cash flow.

95   Paytech Ltd sells several different types of payroll transaction processing services. Last year, they sold 21,079 monthly subscriptions, 33,779 annual subscriptions, and 8,395 temporary coverage contracts. Each of the monthly subscriptions sells for $21,000 and they cost the company $200. The per-unit cost incurred for the annual subscriptions is $200 and they sell for $33,600 each. Each of the temporary coverage contracts are priced at $8,400, and the cost incurred by the company is $100.

          There are 30 full-time employees who earn $21 per hour and work 13 hours per week. The company also employs 21 temporary contract workers for 8 hours per week, and pays them $11 per hour. Aside from the hourly staff members, there is a chief operating officer who earns an annual salary of $16,000 and the senior manager is paid $7,000 per year. HVAC expenses are the main overhead expense, which costs $460,000 per year. The building was originally bought for $1,150,000, and it has a useful life of 126 years, and the equipment, which had cost the company $575,000 has a useful life of 84 years. This company's effective tax rate is 31%. Calculate the annual cash flow.

96   Fairway Malls sells various retail spaces in their shopping centers. Last year, they sold 36,095 monthly retail space rentals, 5,528 monthly anchor store rentals, and 2,662 monthly food court rentals. Each of the monthly retail space rentals sells for $36,000 and they cost the company $13,900. The per-unit cost incurred for the monthly anchor store rentals is $14,000 and they sell for $48,000 each. Each of the monthly food court rentals are priced at $24,000, and the cost incurred by the company is $2,700.

          There are 110 full-timers who earn $45 per hour and work 53 hours per week. The company also employs 45 seasonal employees for 32 hours per week, and pays them $19 per hour. Aside from the hourly staff members, there is a supervisor who earns an annual salary of $32,000 and the receptionist is paid $15,000 per year. Insurance costs are the main overhead expense, which costs $940,000 per year. The building was originally bought for $2,350,000, and it has a useful life of 120 years, and the equipment, which had cost the company $1,175,000 has a useful life of 80 years. This company's effective tax rate is 39%. Calculate the monthly cash flow.

97   Kola-Nut Ltd sells several different types of bottled beverages. Last year, they sold 2,059 batches of fruit juice, 3,359 batches of energy drinks, and 795 batches of soda bottles. Each of the batches of fruit juice sells for $2,000 and they cost the company $200. The per-unit cost incurred for the batches of energy drinks is $200 and they sell for $3,200 each. Each of the batches of soda bottles are priced at $800, and the cost incurred by the company is $100.

          There are 30 full-time employees who earn $21 per hour and work 13 hours per week. The company also employs 21 temporary contract workers for 8 hours per week, and pays them $11 per hour. Aside from the hourly staff members, there is a chief operating officer who earns an annual salary of $16,000 and the senior manager is paid $7,000 per year. HVAC expenses are the main overhead expense, which costs $460,000 per year. The building was originally bought for $1,150,000, and it has a useful life of 12 years, and the equipment, which had cost the company $575,000 has a useful life of 8 years. This company's effective tax rate is 31%. Calculate the gross margin.

98   NY Fitness is a privately-held corporation which focuses on their niche of premium gym memberships for professional sports teams. Last year, they sold 22,107 premium baseball team memberships, 3,845 deluxe football team memberships, and 1,783 soccer team memberships. Each of the premium baseball team memberships sells for $22,100 and they cost the company $10,400. The per-unit cost incurred for the deluxe football team memberships is $10,600 and they sell for $29,900 each. Each of the soccer team memberships are priced at $14,300, and the cost incurred by the company is $2,200.

          There are 100 union workers who earn $42 per hour and work 48 hours per week. The company also employs 42 non-union workers for 29 hours per week, and pays them $18 per hour. Aside from the hourly staff members, there is a president who earns an annual salary of $30,000 and the vice-president is paid $14,000 per year. Employee assistance services are the main overhead expense, which costs $880,000 per year. The building was originally bought for $2,200,000, and it has a useful life of 78 years, and the equipment, which had cost the company $1,100,000 has a useful life of 52 years. This company's effective tax rate is 38%. Calculate the annual EBITDA.

99   Mount Tessory Academy provides their customers with private school education. Last year, they sold 16,803 annual kindergarten memberships, 4,903 annual elementary school tuition memberships, and 1,915 annual pre-school memberships. Each of the annual kindergarten memberships sells for $16,800 and they cost the company $3,500. The per-unit cost incurred for the annual elementary school tuition memberships is $3,600 and they sell for $24,000 each. Each of the annual pre-school memberships are priced at $9,600, and the cost incurred by the company is $900.

          There are 70 senior employees who earn $33 per hour and work 33 hours per week. The company also employs 33 student interns for 20 hours per week, and pays them $15 per hour. Aside from the hourly staff members, there is a senior manager who earns an annual salary of $24,000 and the bookkeeper is paid $11,000 per year. Utilities are the main overhead expense, which costs $700,000 per year. The building was originally bought for $1,750,000, and it has a useful life of 72 years, and the equipment, which had cost the company $875,000 has a useful life of 48 years. This company's effective tax rate is 35%. Calculate the monthly net income before tax.

100   Mount Tessory Academy is a company which offers their customers a wide selection of private school education. Last year, they sold 13,206 annual kindergarten memberships, 10,306 annual elementary school tuition memberships, and 2,995 annual pre-school memberships. Each of the annual kindergarten memberships sells for $13,200 and they cost the company $600. The per-unit cost incurred for the annual elementary school tuition memberships is $600 and they sell for $20,400 each. Each of the annual pre-school memberships are priced at $6,000, and the cost incurred by the company is $200.

       There are 40 full-time employees who earn $24 per hour and work 18 hours per week. The company also employs 24 temporary contract workers for 11 hours per week, and pays them $12 per hour. Aside from the hourly staff members, there is a chief operating officer who earns an annual salary of $18,000 and the senior manager is paid $8,000 per year. HVAC expenses are the main overhead expense, which costs $520,000 per year. The building was originally bought for $1,300,000, and it has a useful life of 72 years, and the equipment, which had cost the company $650,000 has a useful life of 48 years. This company's effective tax rate is 32%. Calculate the monthly net income before tax.

101   LA Met Theatre Company sells several different types of live theatrical performances. Last year, they sold 15,066 premium monthly memberships, 24,166 platinum annual memberships, and 5,995 student memberships. Each of the premium monthly memberships sells for $15,000 and they cost the company $200. The per-unit cost incurred for the platinum annual memberships is $200 and they sell for $24,000 each. Each of the student memberships are priced at $6,000, and the cost incurred by the company is $100.

       There are 30 full-time employees who earn $21 per hour and work 13 hours per week. The company also employs 21 temporary contract workers for 8 hours per week, and pays them $11 per hour. Aside from the hourly staff members, there is a chief operating officer who earns an annual salary of $16,000 and the senior manager is paid $7,000 per year. HVAC expenses are the main overhead expense, which costs $460,000 per year. The building was originally bought for $1,150,000, and it has a useful life of 90 years, and the equipment, which had cost the company $575,000 has a useful life of 60 years. This company's effective tax rate is 31%. Calculate the annual EBITDA.

102   Grand Convention Ltd is a corporation which sells banquet hall rentals for corporate meetings. Last year, they sold 23,476 wedding ceremonies, 8,726 corporate events, and 3,145 convention events. Each of the wedding ceremonies sells for $23,400 and they cost the company $2,200. The per-unit cost incurred for the corporate events is $2,200 and they sell for $34,200 each. Each of the convention events are priced at $12,600, and the cost incurred by the company is $600.

       There are 60 permanent full-time staff who earn $30 per hour and work 28 hours per week. The company also employs 30 part-time employees for 17 hours per week, and pays them $14 per hour. Aside from the hourly staff members, there is a director who earns an annual salary of $22,000 and the manager is paid $10,000 per year. Janitorial services are the main overhead expense, which costs $640,000 per year. The building was originally bought for $1,600,000, and it has a useful life of 108 years, and the equipment, which had cost the company $800,000 has a useful life of 72 years. This company's effective tax rate is 34%. Calculate the monthly tax expense.

103   Payday Now is a corporation which sells short-term loan arrangements. Last year, they sold 14,355 lines of credit, 5,380 payday loans, and 1,920 prepaid credit cards. Each of the lines of credit sells for $14,300 and they cost the company $2,200. The per-unit cost incurred for the payday loans is $2,200 and they sell for $20,900 each. Each of the prepaid credit cards are priced at $7,700, and the cost incurred by the company is $600.

        There are 60 permanent full-time staff who earn $30 per hour and work 28 hours per week. The company also employs 30 part-time employees for 17 hours per week, and pays them $14 per hour. Aside from the hourly staff members, there is a director who earns an annual salary of $22,000 and the manager is paid $10,000 per year. Janitorial services are the main overhead expense, which costs $640,000 per year. The building was originally bought for $1,600,000, and it has a useful life of 66 years, and the equipment, which had cost the company $800,000 has a useful life of 44 years. This company's effective tax rate is 34%. Calculate the annual net income before tax.

104   Fairway Malls is a privately-held corporation which focuses on their niche of premium retail spaces in their shopping centers. Last year, they sold 34,022 monthly retail space rentals, 5,872 monthly anchor store rentals, and 2,745 monthly food court rentals. Each of the monthly retail space rentals sells for $34,000 and they cost the company $10,400. The per-unit cost incurred for the monthly anchor store rentals is $10,600 and they sell for $46,000 each. Each of the monthly food court rentals are priced at $22,000, and the cost incurred by the company is $2,200.

        There are 100 union workers who earn $42 per hour and work 48 hours per week. The company also employs 42 non-union workers for 29 hours per week, and pays them $18 per hour. Aside from the hourly staff members, there is a president who earns an annual salary of $30,000 and the vice-president is paid $14,000 per year. Employee assistance services are the main overhead expense, which costs $880,000 per year. The building was originally bought for $2,200,000, and it has a useful life of 120 years, and the equipment, which had cost the company $1,100,000 has a useful life of 80 years. This company's effective tax rate is 38%. Calculate the monthly cash flow.

105   Comedy 253 is a privately-held corporation which focuses on their niche of premium live performances of stand-up comedy. Last year, they sold 27,269 week-end comedy festivals, 4,769 private events, and 2,195 week-day comedy events. Each of the week-end comedy festivals sells for $27,200 and they cost the company $10,400. The per-unit cost incurred for the private events is $10,600 and they sell for $36,800 each. Each of the week-day comedy events are priced at $17,600, and the cost incurred by the company is $2,200.

        There are 100 union workers who earn $42 per hour and work 48 hours per week. The company also employs 42 non-union workers for 29 hours per week, and pays them $18 per hour. Aside from the hourly staff members, there is a president who earns an annual salary of $30,000 and the vice-president is paid $14,000 per year. Employee assistance services are the main overhead expense, which costs $880,000 per year. The building was originally bought for $2,200,000, and it has a useful life of 96 years, and the equipment, which had cost the company $1,100,000 has a useful life of 64 years. This company's effective tax rate is 38%. Calculate the monthly tax expense.

106   Club Disco provides their customers with dance venue rentals for large family gatherings. Last year, they sold 23,816 week-end party rentals, 6,916 holiday rentals, and 2,715 evening rentals. Each of the week-end party rentals sells for $23,800 and they cost the company $3,500. The per-unit cost incurred for the holiday rentals is $3,600 and they sell for $34,000 each. Each of the evening rentals are priced at $13,600, and the cost incurred by the company is $900.

        There are 70 senior employees who earn $33 per hour and work 33 hours per week. The company also employs 33 student interns for 20 hours per week, and pays them $15 per hour. Aside from the hourly staff members, there is a senior manager who earns an annual salary of $24,000 and the bookkeeper is paid $11,000 per year. Utilities are the main overhead expense, which costs $700,000 per year. The building was originally bought for $1,750,000, and it has a useful life of 102 years, and the equipment, which had cost the company $875,000 has a useful life of 68 years. This company's effective tax rate is 35%. Calculate the annual tax expense.

107   NY Fitness is a market leader that is well-known for their brand of gym memberships for professional sports teams. Last year, they sold 20,818 premium baseball team memberships, 4,204 deluxe football team memberships, and 1,852 soccer team memberships. Each of the premium baseball team memberships sells for $20,800 and they cost the company $7,600. The per-unit cost incurred for the deluxe football team memberships is $7,700 and they sell for $28,600 each. Each of the soccer team memberships are priced at $13,000, and the cost incurred by the company is $1,700.

        There are 90 union workers who earn $39 per hour and work 43 hours per week. The company also employs 39 non-union workers for 26 hours per week, and pays them $17 per hour. Aside from the hourly staff members, there is a president who earns an annual salary of $28,000 and the vice-president is paid $13,000 per year. Employee assistance services are the main overhead expense, which costs $820,000 per year. The building was originally bought for $2,050,000, and it has a useful life of 78 years, and the equipment, which had cost the company $1,025,000 has a useful life of 52 years. This company's effective tax rate is 37%. Calculate the annual EBITDA.

108   NY Fitness offers their customers a wide range of gym memberships for professional sports teams. Last year, they sold 15,644 premium baseball team memberships, 7,944 deluxe football team memberships, and 2,595 soccer team memberships. Each of the premium baseball team memberships sells for $15,600 and they cost the company $1,200. The per-unit cost incurred for the deluxe football team memberships is $1,300 and they sell for $23,400 each. Each of the soccer team memberships are priced at $7,800, and the cost incurred by the company is $400.

        There are 50 permanent full-time staff who earn $27 per hour and work 23 hours per week. The company also employs 27 part-time employees for 14 hours per week, and pays them $13 per hour. Aside from the hourly staff members, there is a director who earns an annual salary of $20,000 and the manager is paid $9,000 per year. Janitorial services are the main overhead expense, which costs $580,000 per year. The building was originally bought for $1,450,000, and it has a useful life of 78 years, and the equipment, which had cost the company $725,000 has a useful life of 52 years. This company's effective tax rate is 33%. Calculate the annual EBITDA.

109   Club Disco offers their customers a wide range of dance venue rentals for large family gatherings. Last year, they sold 20,489 week-end party rentals, 10,389 holiday rentals, and 3,395 evening rentals. Each of the week-end party rentals sells for $20,400 and they cost the company $1,200. The per-unit cost incurred for the holiday rentals is $1,300 and they sell for $30,600 each. Each of the evening rentals are priced at $10,200, and the cost incurred by the company is $400.

        There are 50 permanent full-time staff who earn $27 per hour and work 23 hours per week. The company also employs 27 part-time employees for 14 hours per week, and pays them $13 per hour. Aside from the hourly staff members, there is a director who earns an annual salary of $20,000 and the manager is paid $9,000 per year. Janitorial services are the main overhead expense, which costs $580,000 per year. The building was originally bought for $1,450,000, and it has a useful life of 102 years, and the equipment, which had cost the company $725,000 has a useful life of 68 years. This company's effective tax rate is 33%. Calculate the annual tax expense.

110   Cirque du Lune is a corporation which sells circus performances. Last year, they sold 18,255 monthly shows, 6,805 holiday special performances, and 2,445 performances at schools. Each of the monthly shows sells for $18,200 and they cost the company $2,200. The per-unit cost incurred for the holiday special performances is $2,200 and they sell for $26,600 each. Each of the performances at schools are priced at $9,800, and the cost incurred by the company is $600.

        There are 60 permanent full-time staff who earn $30 per hour and work 28 hours per week. The company also employs 30 part-time employees for 17 hours per week, and pays them $14 per hour. Aside from the hourly staff members, there is a director who earns an annual salary of $22,000 and the manager is paid $10,000 per year. Janitorial services are the main overhead expense, which costs $640,000 per year. The building was originally bought for $1,600,000, and it has a useful life of 84 years, and the equipment, which had cost the company $800,000 has a useful life of 56 years. This company's effective tax rate is 34%. Calculate the monthly EBITDA.

111   Paytech Ltd provides their customers with payroll transaction processing services. Last year, they sold 29,453 monthly subscriptions, 8,553 annual subscriptions, and 3,355 temporary coverage contracts. Each of the monthly subscriptions sells for $29,400 and they cost the company $3,500. The per-unit cost incurred for the annual subscriptions is $3,600 and they sell for $42,000 each. Each of the temporary coverage contracts are priced at $16,800, and the cost incurred by the company is $900.

        There are 70 senior employees who earn $33 per hour and work 33 hours per week. The company also employs 33 student interns for 20 hours per week, and pays them $15 per hour. Aside from the hourly staff members, there is a senior manager who earns an annual salary of $24,000 and the bookkeeper is paid $11,000 per year. Utilities are the main overhead expense, which costs $700,000 per year. The building was originally bought for $1,750,000, and it has a useful life of 126 years, and the equipment, which had cost the company $875,000 has a useful life of 84 years. This company's effective tax rate is 35%. Calculate the annual cash flow.

112   Comedy 253 is a corporation which sells live performances of stand-up comedy. Last year, they sold 20,877 week-end comedy festivals, 7,777 private events, and 2,795 week-day comedy events. Each of the week-end comedy festivals sells for $20,800 and they cost the company $2,200. The per-unit cost incurred for the private events is $2,200 and they sell for $30,400 each. Each of the week-day comedy events are priced at $11,200, and the cost incurred by the company is $600.

    There are 60 permanent full-time staff who earn $30 per hour and work 28 hours per week. The company also employs 30 part-time employees for 17 hours per week, and pays them $14 per hour. Aside from the hourly staff members, there is a director who earns an annual salary of $22,000 and the manager is paid $10,000 per year. Janitorial services are the main overhead expense, which costs $640,000 per year. The building was originally bought for $1,600,000, and it has a useful life of 96 years, and the equipment, which had cost the company $800,000 has a useful life of 64 years. This company's effective tax rate is 34%. Calculate the monthly tax expense.

113   Paytech Ltd offers their customers a wide range of payroll transaction processing services. Last year, they sold 25,255 monthly subscriptions, 12,755 annual subscriptions, and 4,195 temporary coverage contracts. Each of the monthly subscriptions sells for $25,200 and they cost the company $1,200. The per-unit cost incurred for the annual subscriptions is $1,300 and they sell for $37,800 each. Each of the temporary coverage contracts are priced at $12,600, and the cost incurred by the company is $400.

    There are 50 permanent full-time staff who earn $27 per hour and work 23 hours per week. The company also employs 27 part-time employees for 14 hours per week, and pays them $13 per hour. Aside from the hourly staff members, there is a director who earns an annual salary of $20,000 and the manager is paid $9,000 per year. Janitorial services are the main overhead expense, which costs $580,000 per year. The building was originally bought for $1,450,000, and it has a useful life of 126 years, and the equipment, which had cost the company $725,000 has a useful life of 84 years. This company's effective tax rate is 33%. Calculate the annual cash flow.

114   Fairway Malls is an organization which specializes in providing their customers with retail spaces in their shopping centers. Last year, they sold 30,042 monthly retail space rentals, 7,142 monthly anchor store rentals, and 2,995 monthly food court rentals. Each of the monthly retail space rentals sells for $30,000 and they cost the company $5,300. The per-unit cost incurred for the monthly anchor store rentals is $5,400 and they sell for $42,000 each. Each of the monthly food court rentals are priced at $18,000, and the cost incurred by the company is $1,300.

    There are 80 senior employees who earn $36 per hour and work 38 hours per week. The company also employs 36 student interns for 23 hours per week, and pays them $16 per hour. Aside from the hourly staff members, there is a senior manager who earns an annual salary of $26,000 and the bookkeeper is paid $12,000 per year. Utilities are the main overhead expense, which costs $760,000 per year. The building was originally bought for $1,900,000, and it has a useful life of 120 years, and the equipment, which had cost the company $950,000 has a useful life of 80 years. This company's effective tax rate is 36%. Calculate the monthly cash flow.

115   Cirque du Lune sells various circus performances. Last year, they sold 25,289 monthly shows, 3,922 holiday special performances, and 1,862 performances at schools. Each of the monthly shows sells for $25,200 and they cost the company $13,900. The per-unit cost incurred for the holiday special performances is $14,000 and they sell for $33,600 each. Each of the performances at schools are priced at $16,800, and the cost incurred by the company is $2,700.

There are 110 full-timers who earn $45 per hour and work 53 hours per week. The company also employs 45 seasonal employees for 32 hours per week, and pays them $19 per hour. Aside from the hourly staff members, there is a supervisor who earns an annual salary of $32,000 and the receptionist is paid $15,000 per year. Insurance costs are the main overhead expense, which costs $940,000 per year. The building was originally bought for $2,350,000, and it has a useful life of 84 years, and the equipment, which had cost the company $1,175,000 has a useful life of 56 years. This company's effective tax rate is 39%. Calculate the monthly EBITDA.

116   Paytech Ltd is a privately-held corporation which focuses on their niche of premium payroll transaction processing services. Last year, they sold 35,748 monthly subscriptions, 6,186 annual subscriptions, and 2,883 temporary coverage contracts. Each of the monthly subscriptions sells for $35,700 and they cost the company $10,400. The per-unit cost incurred for the annual subscriptions is $10,600 and they sell for $48,300 each. Each of the temporary coverage contracts are priced at $23,100, and the cost incurred by the company is $2,200.

There are 100 union workers who earn $42 per hour and work 48 hours per week. The company also employs 42 non-union workers for 29 hours per week, and pays them $18 per hour. Aside from the hourly staff members, there is a president who earns an annual salary of $30,000 and the vice-president is paid $14,000 per year. Employee assistance services are the main overhead expense, which costs $880,000 per year. The building was originally bought for $2,200,000, and it has a useful life of 126 years, and the equipment, which had cost the company $1,100,000 has a useful life of 84 years. This company's effective tax rate is 38%. Calculate the annual cash flow.

117   Cirque du Lune provides their customers with circus performances. Last year, they sold 19,685 monthly shows, 5,785 holiday special performances, and 2,235 performances at schools. Each of the monthly shows sells for $19,600 and they cost the company $3,500. The per-unit cost incurred for the holiday special performances is $3,600 and they sell for $28,000 each. Each of the performances at schools are priced at $11,200, and the cost incurred by the company is $900.

There are 70 senior employees who earn $33 per hour and work 33 hours per week. The company also employs 33 student interns for 20 hours per week, and pays them $15 per hour. Aside from the hourly staff members, there is a senior manager who earns an annual salary of $24,000 and the bookkeeper is paid $11,000 per year. Utilities are the main overhead expense, which costs $700,000 per year. The building was originally bought for $1,750,000, and it has a useful life of 84 years, and the equipment, which had cost the company $875,000 has a useful life of 56 years. This company's effective tax rate is 35%. Calculate the monthly EBITDA.

118   Comedy 253 sells various live performances of stand-up comedy. Last year, they sold 28,881 week-end comedy festivals, 4,448 private events, and 2,128 week-day comedy events. Each of the week-end comedy festivals sells for $28,800 and they cost the company $13,900. The per-unit cost incurred for the private events is $14,000 and they sell for $38,400 each. Each of the week-day comedy events are priced at $19,200, and the cost incurred by the company is $2,700.

There are 110 full-timers who earn $45 per hour and work 53 hours per week. The company also employs 45 seasonal employees for 32 hours per week, and pays them $19 per hour. Aside from the hourly staff members, there is a supervisor who earns an annual salary of $32,000 and the receptionist is paid $15,000 per year. Insurance costs are the main overhead expense, which costs $940,000 per year. The building was originally bought for $2,350,000, and it has a useful life of 96 years, and the equipment, which had cost the company $1,175,000 has a useful life of 64 years. This company's effective tax rate is 39%. Calculate the monthly tax expense.

119   Jameson & Jameson is a company which offers their customers a wide selection of soap products. Last year, they sold 3,376 truckloads of shampoo bottles, 2,726 truckloads of toothpaste, and 745 truckloads of bars of soap. Each of the truckloads of shampoo bottles sells for $3,300 and they cost the company $600. The per-unit cost incurred for the truckloads of toothpaste is $600 and they sell for $5,100 each. Each of the truckloads of bars of soap are priced at $1,500, and the cost incurred by the company is $200.

There are 40 full-time employees who earn $24 per hour and work 18 hours per week. The company also employs 24 temporary contract workers for 11 hours per week, and pays them $12 per hour. Aside from the hourly staff members, there is a chief operating officer who earns an annual salary of $18,000 and the senior manager is paid $8,000 per year. HVAC expenses are the main overhead expense, which costs $520,000 per year. The building was originally bought for $1,300,000, and it has a useful life of 18 years, and the equipment, which had cost the company $650,000 has a useful life of 12 years. This company's effective tax rate is 32%. Calculate the gross margin.

120   Hogtown Records is an organization which specializes in providing their customers with audio services for local musicians who would like to record their music. Last year, they sold 28,586 singles CDs, 6,836 full albums on LP, and 2,845 individual song recordings. Each of the singles CDs sells for $28,500 and they cost the company $5,300. The per-unit cost incurred for the full albums on LP is $5,400 and they sell for $39,900 each. Each of the individual song recordings are priced at $17,100, and the cost incurred by the company is $1,300.

There are 80 senior employees who earn $36 per hour and work 38 hours per week. The company also employs 36 student interns for 23 hours per week, and pays them $16 per hour. Aside from the hourly staff members, there is a senior manager who earns an annual salary of $26,000 and the bookkeeper is paid $12,000 per year. Utilities are the main overhead expense, which costs $760,000 per year. The building was originally bought for $1,900,000, and it has a useful life of 114 years, and the equipment, which had cost the company $950,000 has a useful life of 76 years. This company's effective tax rate is 36%. Calculate the annual cash flow.

121   Grand Convention Ltd is a privately-held corporation which focuses on their niche of premium banquet hall rentals for corporate meetings. Last year, they sold 30,697 wedding ceremonies, 5,372 corporate events, and 2,470 convention events. Each of the wedding ceremonies sells for $30,600 and they cost the company $10,400. The per-unit cost incurred for the corporate events is $10,600 and they sell for $41,400 each. Each of the convention events are priced at $19,800, and the cost incurred by the company is $2,200.

        There are 100 union workers who earn $42 per hour and work 48 hours per week. The company also employs 42 non-union workers for 29 hours per week, and pays them $18 per hour. Aside from the hourly staff members, there is a president who earns an annual salary of $30,000 and the vice-president is paid $14,000 per year. Employee assistance services are the main overhead expense, which costs $880,000 per year. The building was originally bought for $2,200,000, and it has a useful life of 108 years, and the equipment, which had cost the company $1,100,000 has a useful life of 72 years. This company's effective tax rate is 38%. Calculate the monthly tax expense.

122   Comedy 253 is a market leader that is well-known for their brand of live performances of stand-up comedy. Last year, they sold 25,638 week-end comedy festivals, 5,167 private events, and 2,281 week-day comedy events. Each of the week-end comedy festivals sells for $25,600 and they cost the company $7,600. The per-unit cost incurred for the private events is $7,700 and they sell for $35,200 each. Each of the week-day comedy events are priced at $16,000, and the cost incurred by the company is $1,700.

        There are 90 union workers who earn $39 per hour and work 43 hours per week. The company also employs 39 non-union workers for 26 hours per week, and pays them $17 per hour. Aside from the hourly staff members, there is a president who earns an annual salary of $28,000 and the vice-president is paid $13,000 per year. Employee assistance services are the main overhead expense, which costs $820,000 per year. The building was originally bought for $2,050,000, and it has a useful life of 96 years, and the equipment, which had cost the company $1,025,000 has a useful life of 64 years. This company's effective tax rate is 37%. Calculate the monthly tax expense.

123   AC&C Ltd. is a corporation which sells cell phone plans. Last year, they sold 13,094 annual unlimited talk and text plans, 4,944 annual unlimited voice and data plans, and 1,745 annual prepaid wireless phone cards. Each of the annual unlimited talk and text plans sells for $13,000 and they cost the company $2,200. The per-unit cost incurred for the annual unlimited voice and data plans is $2,200 and they sell for $19,000 each. Each of the annual prepaid wireless phone cards are priced at $7,000, and the cost incurred by the company is $600.

        There are 60 permanent full-time staff who earn $30 per hour and work 28 hours per week. The company also employs 30 part-time employees for 17 hours per week, and pays them $14 per hour. Aside from the hourly staff members, there is a director who earns an annual salary of $22,000 and the manager is paid $10,000 per year. Janitorial services are the main overhead expense, which costs $640,000 per year. The building was originally bought for $1,600,000, and it has a useful life of 60 years, and the equipment, which had cost the company $800,000 has a useful life of 40 years. This company's effective tax rate is 34%. Calculate the monthly net income before tax.

124   NY Fitness is a corporation which sells gym memberships for professional
sports teams. Last year, they sold 16,936 premium baseball team memberships, 6,311
deluxe football team memberships, and 2,270 soccer team memberships. Each of the
premium baseball team memberships sells for $16,900 and they cost the company
$2,200. The per-unit cost incurred for the deluxe football team memberships is $2,200
and they sell for $24,700 each. Each of the soccer team memberships are priced at
$9,100, and the cost incurred by the company is $600.
           There are 60 permanent full-time staff who earn $30 per hour and work 28 hours
per week. The company also employs 30 part-time employees for 17 hours per week,
and pays them $14 per hour. Aside from the hourly staff members, there is a director who
earns an annual salary of $22,000 and the manager is paid $10,000 per year. Janitorial
services are the main overhead expense, which costs $640,000 per year. The building
was originally bought for $1,600,000, and it has a useful life of 78 years, and the
equipment, which had cost the company $800,000 has a useful life of 52 years. This
company's effective tax rate is 34%. Calculate the annual EBITDA.

125   Comedy 253 is a company which offers their customers a wide selection of live
performances of stand-up comedy. Last year, they sold 17,692 week-end comedy
festivals, 13,792 private events, and 3,995 week-day comedy events. Each of the week-
end comedy festivals sells for $17,600 and they cost the company $600. The per-unit
cost incurred for the private events is $600 and they sell for $27,200 each. Each of the
week-day comedy events are priced at $8,000, and the cost incurred by the company is
$200.
           There are 40 full-time employees who earn $24 per hour and work 18 hours per
week. The company also employs 24 temporary contract workers for 11 hours per week,
and pays them $12 per hour. Aside from the hourly staff members, there is a chief
operating officer who earns an annual salary of $18,000 and the senior manager is paid
$8,000 per year. HVAC expenses are the main overhead expense, which costs $520,000
per year. The building was originally bought for $1,300,000, and it has a useful life of 96
years, and the equipment, which had cost the company $650,000 has a useful life of 64
years. This company's effective tax rate is 32%. Calculate the monthly tax expense.

126   Paytech Ltd is a company which offers their customers a wide selection of
payroll transaction processing services. Last year, they sold 23,133 monthly
subscriptions, 17,983 annual subscriptions, and 5,245 temporary coverage contracts.
Each of the monthly subscriptions sells for $23,100 and they cost the company $600. The
per-unit cost incurred for the annual subscriptions is $600 and they sell for $35,700 each.
Each of the temporary coverage contracts are priced at $10,500, and the cost incurred by
the company is $200.
           There are 40 full-time employees who earn $24 per hour and work 18 hours per
week. The company also employs 24 temporary contract workers for 11 hours per week,
and pays them $12 per hour. Aside from the hourly staff members, there is a chief
operating officer who earns an annual salary of $18,000 and the senior manager is paid
$8,000 per year. HVAC expenses are the main overhead expense, which costs $520,000
per year. The building was originally bought for $1,300,000, and it has a useful life of 126
years, and the equipment, which had cost the company $650,000 has a useful life of 84
years. This company's effective tax rate is 32%. Calculate the annual cash flow.

127   Grand Convention Ltd is a market leader that is well-known for their brand of banquet hall rentals for corporate meetings. Last year, they sold 28,875 wedding ceremonies, 5,832 corporate events, and 2,566 convention events. Each of the wedding ceremonies sells for $28,800 and they cost the company $7,600. The per-unit cost incurred for the corporate events is $7,700 and they sell for $39,600 each. Each of the convention events are priced at $18,000, and the cost incurred by the company is $1,700.

        There are 90 union workers who earn $39 per hour and work 43 hours per week. The company also employs 39 non-union workers for 26 hours per week, and pays them $17 per hour. Aside from the hourly staff members, there is a president who earns an annual salary of $28,000 and the vice-president is paid $13,000 per year. Employee assistance services are the main overhead expense, which costs $820,000 per year. The building was originally bought for $2,050,000, and it has a useful life of 108 years, and the equipment, which had cost the company $1,025,000 has a useful life of 72 years. This company's effective tax rate is 37%. Calculate the monthly tax expense.

128   AC&C Ltd. is a company which offers their customers a wide selection of cell phone plans. Last year, they sold 11,042 annual unlimited talk and text plans, 8,642 annual unlimited voice and data plans, and 2,495 annual prepaid wireless phone cards. Each of the annual unlimited talk and text plans sells for $11,000 and they cost the company $600. The per-unit cost incurred for the annual unlimited voice and data plans is $600 and they sell for $17,000 each. Each of the annual prepaid wireless phone cards are priced at $5,000, and the cost incurred by the company is $200.

        There are 40 full-time employees who earn $24 per hour and work 18 hours per week. The company also employs 24 temporary contract workers for 11 hours per week, and pays them $12 per hour. Aside from the hourly staff members, there is a chief operating officer who earns an annual salary of $18,000 and the senior manager is paid $8,000 per year. HVAC expenses are the main overhead expense, which costs $520,000 per year. The building was originally bought for $1,300,000, and it has a useful life of 60 years, and the equipment, which had cost the company $650,000 has a useful life of 40 years. This company's effective tax rate is 32%. Calculate the monthly net income before tax.

129   NY Fitness is a privately-held corporation which focuses on their niche of premium gym memberships for professional sports teams. Last year, they sold 22,145 premium baseball team memberships, 3,883 deluxe football team memberships, and 1,783 soccer team memberships. Each of the premium baseball team memberships sells for $22,100 and they cost the company $10,400. The per-unit cost incurred for the deluxe football team memberships is $10,600 and they sell for $29,900 each. Each of the soccer team memberships are priced at $14,300, and the cost incurred by the company is $2,200.

        There are 100 union workers who earn $42 per hour and work 48 hours per week. The company also employs 42 non-union workers for 29 hours per week, and pays them $18 per hour. Aside from the hourly staff members, there is a president who earns an annual salary of $30,000 and the vice-president is paid $14,000 per year. Employee assistance services are the main overhead expense, which costs $880,000 per year. The building was originally bought for $2,200,000, and it has a useful life of 78 years, and the equipment, which had cost the company $1,100,000 has a useful life of 52 years. This company's effective tax rate is 38%. Calculate the annual EBITDA.

130   Hogtown Records is a privately-held corporation which focuses on their niche of premium audio services for local musicians who would like to record their music. Last year, they sold 32,349 singles CDs, 5,612 full albums on LP, and 2,608 individual song recordings. Each of the singles CDs sells for $32,300 and they cost the company $10,400. The per-unit cost incurred for the full albums on LP is $10,600 and they sell for $43,700 each. Each of the individual song recordings are priced at $20,900, and the cost incurred by the company is $2,200.

      There are 100 union workers who earn $42 per hour and work 48 hours per week. The company also employs 42 non-union workers for 29 hours per week, and pays them $18 per hour. Aside from the hourly staff members, there is a president who earns an annual salary of $30,000 and the vice-president is paid $14,000 per year. Employee assistance services are the main overhead expense, which costs $880,000 per year. The building was originally bought for $2,200,000, and it has a useful life of 114 years, and the equipment, which had cost the company $1,100,000 has a useful life of 76 years. This company's effective tax rate is 38%. Calculate the annual cash flow.

131   Payday Now offers their customers a wide range of short-term loan arrangements. Last year, they sold 13,261 lines of credit, 6,761 payday loans, and 2,195 prepaid credit cards. Each of the lines of credit sells for $13,200 and they cost the company $1,200. The per-unit cost incurred for the payday loans is $1,300 and they sell for $19,800 each. Each of the prepaid credit cards are priced at $6,600, and the cost incurred by the company is $400.

      There are 50 permanent full-time staff who earn $27 per hour and work 23 hours per week. The company also employs 27 part-time employees for 14 hours per week, and pays them $13 per hour. Aside from the hourly staff members, there is a director who earns an annual salary of $20,000 and the manager is paid $9,000 per year. Janitorial services are the main overhead expense, which costs $580,000 per year. The building was originally bought for $1,450,000, and it has a useful life of 66 years, and the equipment, which had cost the company $725,000 has a useful life of 44 years. This company's effective tax rate is 33%. Calculate the annual net income before tax.

132   Comedy 253 is a market leader that is well-known for their brand of live performances of stand-up comedy. Last year, they sold 25,640 week-end comedy festivals, 5,169 private events, and 2,281 week-day comedy events. Each of the week-end comedy festivals sells for $25,600 and they cost the company $7,600. The per-unit cost incurred for the private events is $7,700 and they sell for $35,200 each. Each of the week-day comedy events are priced at $16,000, and the cost incurred by the company is $1,700.

      There are 90 union workers who earn $39 per hour and work 43 hours per week. The company also employs 39 non-union workers for 26 hours per week, and pays them $17 per hour. Aside from the hourly staff members, there is a president who earns an annual salary of $28,000 and the vice-president is paid $13,000 per year. Employee assistance services are the main overhead expense, which costs $820,000 per year. The building was originally bought for $2,050,000, and it has a useful life of 96 years, and the equipment, which had cost the company $1,025,000 has a useful life of 64 years. This company's effective tax rate is 37%. Calculate the monthly tax expense.

133   LA Met Theatre Company provides their customers with live theatrical performances. Last year, they sold 21,047 premium monthly memberships, 6,147 platinum annual memberships, and 2,395 student memberships. Each of the premium monthly memberships sells for $21,000 and they cost the company $3,500. The per-unit cost incurred for the platinum annual memberships is $3,600 and they sell for $30,000 each. Each of the student memberships are priced at $12,000, and the cost incurred by the company is $900.

          There are 70 senior employees who earn $33 per hour and work 33 hours per week. The company also employs 33 student interns for 20 hours per week, and pays them $15 per hour. Aside from the hourly staff members, there is a senior manager who earns an annual salary of $24,000 and the bookkeeper is paid $11,000 per year. Utilities are the main overhead expense, which costs $700,000 per year. The building was originally bought for $1,750,000, and it has a useful life of 90 years, and the equipment, which had cost the company $875,000 has a useful life of 60 years. This company's effective tax rate is 35%. Calculate the annual EBITDA.

134   Payday Now is a market leader that is well-known for their brand of short-term loan arrangements. Last year, they sold 17,613 lines of credit, 3,570 payday loans, and 1,566 prepaid credit cards. Each of the lines of credit sells for $17,600 and they cost the company $7,600. The per-unit cost incurred for the payday loans is $7,700 and they sell for $24,200 each. Each of the prepaid credit cards are priced at $11,000, and the cost incurred by the company is $1,700.

          There are 90 union workers who earn $39 per hour and work 43 hours per week. The company also employs 39 non-union workers for 26 hours per week, and pays them $17 per hour. Aside from the hourly staff members, there is a president who earns an annual salary of $28,000 and the vice-president is paid $13,000 per year. Employee assistance services are the main overhead expense, which costs $820,000 per year. The building was originally bought for $2,050,000, and it has a useful life of 66 years, and the equipment, which had cost the company $1,025,000 has a useful life of 44 years. This company's effective tax rate is 37%. Calculate the annual net income before tax.

135   Fairway Malls is an organization which specializes in providing their customers with retail spaces in their shopping centers. Last year, they sold 30,018 monthly retail space rentals, 7,118 monthly anchor store rentals, and 2,995 monthly food court rentals. Each of the monthly retail space rentals sells for $30,000 and they cost the company $5,300. The per-unit cost incurred for the monthly anchor store rentals is $5,400 and they sell for $42,000 each. Each of the monthly food court rentals are priced at $18,000, and the cost incurred by the company is $1,300.

          There are 80 senior employees who earn $36 per hour and work 38 hours per week. The company also employs 36 student interns for 23 hours per week, and pays them $16 per hour. Aside from the hourly staff members, there is a senior manager who earns an annual salary of $26,000 and the bookkeeper is paid $12,000 per year. Utilities are the main overhead expense, which costs $760,000 per year. The building was originally bought for $1,900,000, and it has a useful life of 120 years, and the equipment, which had cost the company $950,000 has a useful life of 80 years. This company's effective tax rate is 36%. Calculate the monthly cash flow.

136   LA Met Theatre Company provides their customers with live theatrical performances. Last year, they sold 21,078 premium monthly memberships, 6,178 platinum annual memberships, and 2,395 student memberships. Each of the premium monthly memberships sells for $21,000 and they cost the company $3,500. The per-unit cost incurred for the platinum annual memberships is $3,600 and they sell for $30,000 each. Each of the student memberships are priced at $12,000, and the cost incurred by the company is $900.

There are 70 senior employees who earn $33 per hour and work 33 hours per week. The company also employs 33 student interns for 20 hours per week, and pays them $15 per hour. Aside from the hourly staff members, there is a senior manager who earns an annual salary of $24,000 and the bookkeeper is paid $11,000 per year. Utilities are the main overhead expense, which costs $700,000 per year. The building was originally bought for $1,750,000, and it has a useful life of 90 years, and the equipment, which had cost the company $875,000 has a useful life of 60 years. This company's effective tax rate is 35%. Calculate the annual EBITDA.

137   Cirque du Lune sells various circus performances. Last year, they sold 26,605 monthly shows, 3,605 holiday special performances, and 1,815 performances at schools. Each of the monthly shows sells for $26,600 and they cost the company $18,000. The per-unit cost incurred for the holiday special performances is $18,200 and they sell for $35,000 each. Each of the performances at schools are priced at $18,200, and the cost incurred by the company is $3,300.

There are 120 full-timers who earn $48 per hour and work 58 hours per week. The company also employs 48 seasonal employees for 35 hours per week, and pays them $20 per hour. Aside from the hourly staff members, there is a supervisor who earns an annual salary of $34,000 and the receptionist is paid $16,000 per year. Insurance costs are the main overhead expense, which costs $1,000,000 per year. The building was originally bought for $2,500,000, and it has a useful life of 84 years, and the equipment, which had cost the company $1,250,000 has a useful life of 56 years. This company's effective tax rate is 40%. Calculate the monthly EBITDA.

138   Payday Now is a privately-held corporation which focuses on their niche of premium short-term loan arrangements. Last year, they sold 18,772 lines of credit, 3,335 payday loans, and 1,508 prepaid credit cards. Each of the lines of credit sells for $18,700 and they cost the company $10,400. The per-unit cost incurred for the payday loans is $10,600 and they sell for $25,300 each. Each of the prepaid credit cards are priced at $12,100, and the cost incurred by the company is $2,200.

There are 100 union workers who earn $42 per hour and work 48 hours per week. The company also employs 42 non-union workers for 29 hours per week, and pays them $18 per hour. Aside from the hourly staff members, there is a president who earns an annual salary of $30,000 and the vice-president is paid $14,000 per year. Employee assistance services are the main overhead expense, which costs $880,000 per year. The building was originally bought for $2,200,000, and it has a useful life of 66 years, and the equipment, which had cost the company $1,100,000 has a useful life of 44 years. This company's effective tax rate is 38%. Calculate the annual net income before tax.

139   Fairway Malls offers their customers a wide range of retail spaces in their shopping centers. Last year, they sold 24,040 monthly retail space rentals, 12,140 monthly anchor store rentals, and 3,995 monthly food court rentals. Each of the monthly retail space rentals sells for $24,000 and they cost the company $1,200. The per-unit cost incurred for the monthly anchor store rentals is $1,300 and they sell for $36,000 each. Each of the monthly food court rentals are priced at $12,000, and the cost incurred by the company is $400.

There are 50 permanent full-time staff who earn $27 per hour and work 23 hours per week. The company also employs 27 part-time employees for 14 hours per week, and pays them $13 per hour. Aside from the hourly staff members, there is a director who earns an annual salary of $20,000 and the manager is paid $9,000 per year. Janitorial services are the main overhead expense, which costs $580,000 per year. The building was originally bought for $1,450,000, and it has a useful life of 120 years, and the equipment, which had cost the company $725,000 has a useful life of 80 years. This company's effective tax rate is 33%. Calculate the monthly cash flow.

140   AC&C Ltd. offers their customers a wide range of cell phone plans. Last year, they sold 12,057 annual unlimited talk and text plans, 6,157 annual unlimited voice and data plans, and 1,995 annual prepaid wireless phone cards. Each of the annual unlimited talk and text plans sells for $12,000 and they cost the company $1,200. The per-unit cost incurred for the annual unlimited voice and data plans is $1,300 and they sell for $18,000 each. Each of the annual prepaid wireless phone cards are priced at $6,000, and the cost incurred by the company is $400.

There are 50 permanent full-time staff who earn $27 per hour and work 23 hours per week. The company also employs 27 part-time employees for 14 hours per week, and pays them $13 per hour. Aside from the hourly staff members, there is a director who earns an annual salary of $20,000 and the manager is paid $9,000 per year. Janitorial services are the main overhead expense, which costs $580,000 per year. The building was originally bought for $1,450,000, and it has a useful life of 60 years, and the equipment, which had cost the company $725,000 has a useful life of 40 years. This company's effective tax rate is 33%. Calculate the monthly net income before tax.

141   Paytech Ltd offers their customers a wide range of payroll transaction processing services. Last year, they sold 25,263 monthly subscriptions, 12,763 annual subscriptions, and 4,195 temporary coverage contracts. Each of the monthly subscriptions sells for $25,200 and they cost the company $1,200. The per-unit cost incurred for the annual subscriptions is $1,300 and they sell for $37,800 each. Each of the temporary coverage contracts are priced at $12,600, and the cost incurred by the company is $400.

There are 50 permanent full-time staff who earn $27 per hour and work 23 hours per week. The company also employs 27 part-time employees for 14 hours per week, and pays them $13 per hour. Aside from the hourly staff members, there is a director who earns an annual salary of $20,000 and the manager is paid $9,000 per year. Janitorial services are the main overhead expense, which costs $580,000 per year. The building was originally bought for $1,450,000, and it has a useful life of 126 years, and the equipment, which had cost the company $725,000 has a useful life of 84 years. This company's effective tax rate is 33%. Calculate the annual cash flow.

142   NY Fitness is a corporation which sells gym memberships for professional sports teams. Last year, they sold 16,967 premium baseball team memberships, 6,342 deluxe football team memberships, and 2,270 soccer team memberships. Each of the premium baseball team memberships sells for $16,900 and they cost the company $2,200. The per-unit cost incurred for the deluxe football team memberships is $2,200 and they sell for $24,700 each. Each of the soccer team memberships are priced at $9,100, and the cost incurred by the company is $600.

        There are 60 permanent full-time staff who earn $30 per hour and work 28 hours per week. The company also employs 30 part-time employees for 17 hours per week, and pays them $14 per hour. Aside from the hourly staff members, there is a director who earns an annual salary of $22,000 and the manager is paid $10,000 per year. Janitorial services are the main overhead expense, which costs $640,000 per year. The building was originally bought for $1,600,000, and it has a useful life of 78 years, and the equipment, which had cost the company $800,000 has a useful life of 52 years. This company's effective tax rate is 34%. Calculate the annual EBITDA.

143   Club Disco sells various dance venue rentals for large family gatherings. Last year, they sold 30,653 week-end party rentals, 4,686 holiday rentals, and 2,262 evening rentals. Each of the week-end party rentals sells for $30,600 and they cost the company $13,900. The per-unit cost incurred for the holiday rentals is $14,000 and they sell for $40,800 each. Each of the evening rentals are priced at $20,400, and the cost incurred by the company is $2,700.

        There are 110 full-timers who earn $45 per hour and work 53 hours per week. The company also employs 45 seasonal employees for 32 hours per week, and pays them $19 per hour. Aside from the hourly staff members, there is a supervisor who earns an annual salary of $32,000 and the receptionist is paid $15,000 per year. Insurance costs are the main overhead expense, which costs $940,000 per year. The building was originally bought for $2,350,000, and it has a useful life of 102 years, and the equipment, which had cost the company $1,175,000 has a useful life of 68 years. This company's effective tax rate is 39%. Calculate the annual tax expense.

144   Fairway Malls is an organization which specializes in providing their customers with retail spaces in their shopping centers. Last year, they sold 30,027 monthly retail space rentals, 7,127 monthly anchor store rentals, and 2,995 monthly food court rentals. Each of the monthly retail space rentals sells for $30,000 and they cost the company $5,300. The per-unit cost incurred for the monthly anchor store rentals is $5,400 and they sell for $42,000 each. Each of the monthly food court rentals are priced at $18,000, and the cost incurred by the company is $1,300.

        There are 80 senior employees who earn $36 per hour and work 38 hours per week. The company also employs 36 student interns for 23 hours per week, and pays them $16 per hour. Aside from the hourly staff members, there is a senior manager who earns an annual salary of $26,000 and the bookkeeper is paid $12,000 per year. Utilities are the main overhead expense, which costs $760,000 per year. The building was originally bought for $1,900,000, and it has a useful life of 120 years, and the equipment, which had cost the company $950,000 has a useful life of 80 years. This company's effective tax rate is 36%. Calculate the monthly cash flow.

145   Grand Convention Ltd is a market leader that is well-known for their brand of banquet hall rentals for corporate meetings. Last year, they sold 28,843 wedding ceremonies, 5,800 corporate events, and 2,566 convention events. Each of the wedding ceremonies sells for $28,800 and they cost the company $7,600. The per-unit cost incurred for the corporate events is $7,700 and they sell for $39,600 each. Each of the convention events are priced at $18,000, and the cost incurred by the company is $1,700.

        There are 90 union workers who earn $39 per hour and work 43 hours per week. The company also employs 39 non-union workers for 26 hours per week, and pays them $17 per hour. Aside from the hourly staff members, there is a president who earns an annual salary of $28,000 and the vice-president is paid $13,000 per year. Employee assistance services are the main overhead expense, which costs $820,000 per year. The building was originally bought for $2,050,000, and it has a useful life of 108 years, and the equipment, which had cost the company $1,025,000 has a useful life of 72 years. This company's effective tax rate is 37%. Calculate the monthly tax expense.

146   Comedy 253 sells several different types of live performances of stand-up comedy. Last year, they sold 16,033 week-end comedy festivals, 25,733 private events, and 6,395 week-day comedy events. Each of the week-end comedy festivals sells for $16,000 and they cost the company $200. The per-unit cost incurred for the private events is $200 and they sell for $25,600 each. Each of the week-day comedy events are priced at $6,400, and the cost incurred by the company is $100.

        There are 30 full-time employees who earn $21 per hour and work 13 hours per week. The company also employs 21 temporary contract workers for 8 hours per week, and pays them $11 per hour. Aside from the hourly staff members, there is a chief operating officer who earns an annual salary of $16,000 and the senior manager is paid $7,000 per year. HVAC expenses are the main overhead expense, which costs $460,000 per year. The building was originally bought for $1,150,000, and it has a useful life of 96 years, and the equipment, which had cost the company $575,000 has a useful life of 64 years. This company's effective tax rate is 31%. Calculate the monthly tax expense.

147   Cirque du Lune is an organization which specializes in providing their customers with circus performances. Last year, they sold 21,072 monthly shows, 5,072 holiday special performances, and 2,095 performances at schools. Each of the monthly shows sells for $21,000 and they cost the company $5,300. The per-unit cost incurred for the holiday special performances is $5,400 and they sell for $29,400 each. Each of the performances at schools are priced at $12,600, and the cost incurred by the company is $1,300.

        There are 80 senior employees who earn $36 per hour and work 38 hours per week. The company also employs 36 student interns for 23 hours per week, and pays them $16 per hour. Aside from the hourly staff members, there is a senior manager who earns an annual salary of $26,000 and the bookkeeper is paid $12,000 per year. Utilities are the main overhead expense, which costs $760,000 per year. The building was originally bought for $1,900,000, and it has a useful life of 84 years, and the equipment, which had cost the company $950,000 has a useful life of 56 years. This company's effective tax rate is 36%. Calculate the monthly EBITDA.

148   Payday Now offers their customers a wide range of short-term loan arrangements. Last year, they sold 13,248 lines of credit, 6,748 payday loans, and 2,195 prepaid credit cards. Each of the lines of credit sells for $13,200 and they cost the company $1,200. The per-unit cost incurred for the payday loans is $1,300 and they sell for $19,800 each. Each of the prepaid credit cards are priced at $6,600, and the cost incurred by the company is $400.

       There are 50 permanent full-time staff who earn $27 per hour and work 23 hours per week. The company also employs 27 part-time employees for 14 hours per week, and pays them $13 per hour. Aside from the hourly staff members, there is a director who earns an annual salary of $20,000 and the manager is paid $9,000 per year. Janitorial services are the main overhead expense, which costs $580,000 per year. The building was originally bought for $1,450,000, and it has a useful life of 66 years, and the equipment, which had cost the company $725,000 has a useful life of 44 years. This company's effective tax rate is 33%. Calculate the annual net income before tax.

149   AC&C Ltd. is a privately-held corporation which focuses on their niche of premium cell phone plans. Last year, they sold 17,034 annual unlimited talk and text plans, 3,009 annual unlimited voice and data plans, and 1,370 annual prepaid wireless phone cards. Each of the annual unlimited talk and text plans sells for $17,000 and they cost the company $10,400. The per-unit cost incurred for the annual unlimited voice and data plans is $10,600 and they sell for $23,000 each. Each of the annual prepaid wireless phone cards are priced at $11,000, and the cost incurred by the company is $2,200.

       There are 100 union workers who earn $42 per hour and work 48 hours per week. The company also employs 42 non-union workers for 29 hours per week, and pays them $18 per hour. Aside from the hourly staff members, there is a president who earns an annual salary of $30,000 and the vice-president is paid $14,000 per year. Employee assistance services are the main overhead expense, which costs $880,000 per year. The building was originally bought for $2,200,000, and it has a useful life of 60 years, and the equipment, which had cost the company $1,100,000 has a useful life of 40 years. This company's effective tax rate is 38%. Calculate the monthly net income before tax.

150   Paytech Ltd is a corporation which sells payroll transaction processing services. Last year, they sold 27,392 monthly subscriptions, 10,167 annual subscriptions, and 3,670 temporary coverage contracts. Each of the monthly subscriptions sells for $27,300 and they cost the company $2,200. The per-unit cost incurred for the annual subscriptions is $2,200 and they sell for $39,900 each. Each of the temporary coverage contracts are priced at $14,700, and the cost incurred by the company is $600.

       There are 60 permanent full-time staff who earn $30 per hour and work 28 hours per week. The company also employs 30 part-time employees for 17 hours per week, and pays them $14 per hour. Aside from the hourly staff members, there is a director who earns an annual salary of $22,000 and the manager is paid $10,000 per year. Janitorial services are the main overhead expense, which costs $640,000 per year. The building was originally bought for $1,600,000, and it has a useful life of 126 years, and the equipment, which had cost the company $800,000 has a useful life of 84 years. This company's effective tax rate is 34%. Calculate the annual cash flow.

151   NY Fitness is a market leader that is well-known for their brand of gym memberships for professional sports teams. Last year, they sold 20,814 premium baseball team memberships, 4,200 deluxe football team memberships, and 1,852 soccer team memberships. Each of the premium baseball team memberships sells for $20,800 and they cost the company $7,600. The per-unit cost incurred for the deluxe football team memberships is $7,700 and they sell for $28,600 each. Each of the soccer team memberships are priced at $13,000, and the cost incurred by the company is $1,700.

There are 90 union workers who earn $39 per hour and work 43 hours per week. The company also employs 39 non-union workers for 26 hours per week, and pays them $17 per hour. Aside from the hourly staff members, there is a president who earns an annual salary of $28,000 and the vice-president is paid $13,000 per year. Employee assistance services are the main overhead expense, which costs $820,000 per year. The building was originally bought for $2,050,000, and it has a useful life of 78 years, and the equipment, which had cost the company $1,025,000 has a useful life of 52 years. This company's effective tax rate is 37%. Calculate the annual EBITDA.

152   Jameson & Jameson provides their customers with soap products. Last year, they sold 4,225 truckloads of shampoo bottles, 1,325 truckloads of toothpaste, and 475 truckloads of bars of soap. Each of the truckloads of shampoo bottles sells for $4,200 and they cost the company $3,500. The per-unit cost incurred for the truckloads of toothpaste is $3,600 and they sell for $6,000 each. Each of the truckloads of bars of soap are priced at $2,400, and the cost incurred by the company is $900.

There are 70 senior employees who earn $33 per hour and work 33 hours per week. The company also employs 33 student interns for 20 hours per week, and pays them $15 per hour. Aside from the hourly staff members, there is a senior manager who earns an annual salary of $24,000 and the bookkeeper is paid $11,000 per year. Utilities are the main overhead expense, which costs $700,000 per year. The building was originally bought for $1,750,000, and it has a useful life of 18 years, and the equipment, which had cost the company $875,000 has a useful life of 12 years. This company's effective tax rate is 35%. Calculate the gross margin.

153   Hogtown Records offers their customers a wide range of audio services for local musicians who would like to record their music. Last year, they sold 22,805 singles CDs, 11,505 full albums on LP, and 3,795 individual song recordings. Each of the singles CDs sells for $22,800 and they cost the company $1,200. The per-unit cost incurred for the full albums on LP is $1,300 and they sell for $34,200 each. Each of the individual song recordings are priced at $11,400, and the cost incurred by the company is $400.

There are 50 permanent full-time staff who earn $27 per hour and work 23 hours per week. The company also employs 27 part-time employees for 14 hours per week, and pays them $13 per hour. Aside from the hourly staff members, there is a director who earns an annual salary of $20,000 and the manager is paid $9,000 per year. Janitorial services are the main overhead expense, which costs $580,000 per year. The building was originally bought for $1,450,000, and it has a useful life of 114 years, and the equipment, which had cost the company $725,000 has a useful life of 76 years. This company's effective tax rate is 33%. Calculate the annual cash flow.

154   Mount Tessory Academy is a corporation which sells private school education. Last year, they sold 15,682 annual kindergarten memberships, 5,882 annual elementary school tuition memberships, and 2,095 annual pre-school memberships. Each of the annual kindergarten memberships sells for $15,600 and they cost the company $2,200. The per-unit cost incurred for the annual elementary school tuition memberships is $2,200 and they sell for $22,800 each. Each of the annual pre-school memberships are priced at $8,400, and the cost incurred by the company is $600.

There are 60 permanent full-time staff who earn $30 per hour and work 28 hours per week. The company also employs 30 part-time employees for 17 hours per week, and pays them $14 per hour. Aside from the hourly staff members, there is a director who earns an annual salary of $22,000 and the manager is paid $10,000 per year. Janitorial services are the main overhead expense, which costs $640,000 per year. The building was originally bought for $1,600,000, and it has a useful life of 72 years, and the equipment, which had cost the company $800,000 has a useful life of 48 years. This company's effective tax rate is 34%. Calculate the monthly net income before tax.

155   LA Met Theatre Company is an organization which specializes in providing their customers with live theatrical performances. Last year, they sold 22,511 premium monthly memberships, 5,361 platinum annual memberships, and 2,245 student memberships. Each of the premium monthly memberships sells for $22,500 and they cost the company $5,300. The per-unit cost incurred for the platinum annual memberships is $5,400 and they sell for $31,500 each. Each of the student memberships are priced at $13,500, and the cost incurred by the company is $1,300.

There are 80 senior employees who earn $36 per hour and work 38 hours per week. The company also employs 36 student interns for 23 hours per week, and pays them $16 per hour. Aside from the hourly staff members, there is a senior manager who earns an annual salary of $26,000 and the bookkeeper is paid $12,000 per year. Utilities are the main overhead expense, which costs $760,000 per year. The building was originally bought for $1,900,000, and it has a useful life of 90 years, and the equipment, which had cost the company $950,000 has a useful life of 60 years. This company's effective tax rate is 36%. Calculate the annual EBITDA.

156   Paytech Ltd is a corporation which sells payroll transaction processing services. Last year, they sold 27,356 monthly subscriptions, 10,131 annual subscriptions, and 3,670 temporary coverage contracts. Each of the monthly subscriptions sells for $27,300 and they cost the company $2,200. The per-unit cost incurred for the annual subscriptions is $2,200 and they sell for $39,900 each. Each of the temporary coverage contracts are priced at $14,700, and the cost incurred by the company is $600.

There are 60 permanent full-time staff who earn $30 per hour and work 28 hours per week. The company also employs 30 part-time employees for 17 hours per week, and pays them $14 per hour. Aside from the hourly staff members, there is a director who earns an annual salary of $22,000 and the manager is paid $10,000 per year. Janitorial services are the main overhead expense, which costs $640,000 per year. The building was originally bought for $1,600,000, and it has a useful life of 126 years, and the equipment, which had cost the company $800,000 has a useful life of 84 years. This company's effective tax rate is 34%. Calculate the annual cash flow.

157   Comedy 253 sells several different types of live performances of stand-up comedy. Last year, they sold 16,095 week-end comedy festivals, 25,795 private events, and 6,395 week-day comedy events. Each of the week-end comedy festivals sells for $16,000 and they cost the company $200. The per-unit cost incurred for the private events is $200 and they sell for $25,600 each. Each of the week-day comedy events are priced at $6,400, and the cost incurred by the company is $100.

There are 30 full-time employees who earn $21 per hour and work 13 hours per week. The company also employs 21 temporary contract workers for 8 hours per week, and pays them $11 per hour. Aside from the hourly staff members, there is a chief operating officer who earns an annual salary of $16,000 and the senior manager is paid $7,000 per year. HVAC expenses are the main overhead expense, which costs $460,000 per year. The building was originally bought for $1,150,000, and it has a useful life of 96 years, and the equipment, which had cost the company $575,000 has a useful life of 64 years. This company's effective tax rate is 31%. Calculate the monthly tax expense.

158   LA Met Theatre Company offers their customers a wide range of live theatrical performances. Last year, they sold 18,019 premium monthly memberships, 9,119 platinum annual memberships, and 2,995 student memberships. Each of the premium monthly memberships sells for $18,000 and they cost the company $1,200. The per-unit cost incurred for the platinum annual memberships is $1,300 and they sell for $27,000 each. Each of the student memberships are priced at $9,000, and the cost incurred by the company is $400.

There are 50 permanent full-time staff who earn $27 per hour and work 23 hours per week. The company also employs 27 part-time employees for 14 hours per week, and pays them $13 per hour. Aside from the hourly staff members, there is a director who earns an annual salary of $20,000 and the manager is paid $9,000 per year. Janitorial services are the main overhead expense, which costs $580,000 per year. The building was originally bought for $1,450,000, and it has a useful life of 90 years, and the equipment, which had cost the company $725,000 has a useful life of 60 years. This company's effective tax rate is 33%. Calculate the annual EBITDA.

159   Payday Now is a company which offers their customers a wide selection of short-term loan arrangements. Last year, they sold 12,170 lines of credit, 9,520 payday loans, and 2,745 prepaid credit cards. Each of the lines of credit sells for $12,100 and they cost the company $600. The per-unit cost incurred for the payday loans is $600 and they sell for $18,700 each. Each of the prepaid credit cards are priced at $5,500, and the cost incurred by the company is $200.

There are 40 full-time employees who earn $24 per hour and work 18 hours per week. The company also employs 24 temporary contract workers for 11 hours per week, and pays them $12 per hour. Aside from the hourly staff members, there is a chief operating officer who earns an annual salary of $18,000 and the senior manager is paid $8,000 per year. HVAC expenses are the main overhead expense, which costs $520,000 per year. The building was originally bought for $1,300,000, and it has a useful life of 66 years, and the equipment, which had cost the company $650,000 has a useful life of 44 years. This company's effective tax rate is 32%. Calculate the annual net income before tax.

160   Payday Now sells various short-term loan arrangements. Last year, they sold 19,840 lines of credit, 3,073 payday loans, and 1,462 prepaid credit cards. Each of the lines of credit sells for $19,800 and they cost the company $13,900. The per-unit cost incurred for the payday loans is $14,000 and they sell for $26,400 each. Each of the prepaid credit cards are priced at $13,200, and the cost incurred by the company is $2,700.

There are 110 full-timers who earn $45 per hour and work 53 hours per week. The company also employs 45 seasonal employees for 32 hours per week, and pays them $19 per hour. Aside from the hourly staff members, there is a supervisor who earns an annual salary of $32,000 and the receptionist is paid $15,000 per year. Insurance costs are the main overhead expense, which costs $940,000 per year. The building was originally bought for $2,350,000, and it has a useful life of 66 years, and the equipment, which had cost the company $1,175,000 has a useful life of 44 years. This company's effective tax rate is 39%. Calculate the annual net income before tax.

161   Payday Now is a privately-held corporation which focuses on their niche of premium short-term loan arrangements. Last year, they sold 18,750 lines of credit, 3,313 payday loans, and 1,508 prepaid credit cards. Each of the lines of credit sells for $18,700 and they cost the company $10,400. The per-unit cost incurred for the payday loans is $10,600 and they sell for $25,300 each. Each of the prepaid credit cards are priced at $12,100, and the cost incurred by the company is $2,200.

There are 100 union workers who earn $42 per hour and work 48 hours per week. The company also employs 42 non-union workers for 29 hours per week, and pays them $18 per hour. Aside from the hourly staff members, there is a president who earns an annual salary of $30,000 and the vice-president is paid $14,000 per year. Employee assistance services are the main overhead expense, which costs $880,000 per year. The building was originally bought for $2,200,000, and it has a useful life of 66 years, and the equipment, which had cost the company $1,100,000 has a useful life of 44 years. This company's effective tax rate is 38%. Calculate the annual net income before tax.

162   Comedy 253 is a corporation which sells live performances of stand-up comedy. Last year, they sold 20,872 week-end comedy festivals, 7,772 private events, and 2,795 week-day comedy events. Each of the week-end comedy festivals sells for $20,800 and they cost the company $2,200. The per-unit cost incurred for the private events is $2,200 and they sell for $30,400 each. Each of the week-day comedy events are priced at $11,200, and the cost incurred by the company is $600.

There are 60 permanent full-time staff who earn $30 per hour and work 28 hours per week. The company also employs 30 part-time employees for 17 hours per week, and pays them $14 per hour. Aside from the hourly staff members, there is a director who earns an annual salary of $22,000 and the manager is paid $10,000 per year. Janitorial services are the main overhead expense, which costs $640,000 per year. The building was originally bought for $1,600,000, and it has a useful life of 96 years, and the equipment, which had cost the company $800,000 has a useful life of 64 years. This company's effective tax rate is 34%. Calculate the monthly tax expense.

163   Fairway Malls is a privately-held corporation which focuses on their niche of premium retail spaces in their shopping centers. Last year, they sold 34,046 monthly retail space rentals, 5,896 monthly anchor store rentals, and 2,745 monthly food court rentals. Each of the monthly retail space rentals sells for $34,000 and they cost the company $10,400. The per-unit cost incurred for the monthly anchor store rentals is $10,600 and they sell for $46,000 each. Each of the monthly food court rentals are priced at $22,000, and the cost incurred by the company is $2,200.

There are 100 union workers who earn $42 per hour and work 48 hours per week. The company also employs 42 non-union workers for 29 hours per week, and pays them $18 per hour. Aside from the hourly staff members, there is a president who earns an annual salary of $30,000 and the vice-president is paid $14,000 per year. Employee assistance services are the main overhead expense, which costs $880,000 per year. The building was originally bought for $2,200,000, and it has a useful life of 120 years, and the equipment, which had cost the company $1,100,000 has a useful life of 80 years. This company's effective tax rate is 38%. Calculate the monthly cash flow.

164   NY Fitness is an organization which specializes in providing their customers with gym memberships for professional sports teams. Last year, they sold 19,588 premium baseball team memberships, 4,738 deluxe football team memberships, and 1,945 soccer team memberships. Each of the premium baseball team memberships sells for $19,500 and they cost the company $5,300. The per-unit cost incurred for the deluxe football team memberships is $5,400 and they sell for $27,300 each. Each of the soccer team memberships are priced at $11,700, and the cost incurred by the company is $1,300.

There are 80 senior employees who earn $36 per hour and work 38 hours per week. The company also employs 36 student interns for 23 hours per week, and pays them $16 per hour. Aside from the hourly staff members, there is a senior manager who earns an annual salary of $26,000 and the bookkeeper is paid $12,000 per year. Utilities are the main overhead expense, which costs $760,000 per year. The building was originally bought for $1,900,000, and it has a useful life of 78 years, and the equipment, which had cost the company $950,000 has a useful life of 52 years. This company's effective tax rate is 36%. Calculate the annual EBITDA.

165   Paytech Ltd provides their customers with payroll transaction processing services. Last year, they sold 29,497 monthly subscriptions, 8,597 annual subscriptions, and 3,355 temporary coverage contracts. Each of the monthly subscriptions sells for $29,400 and they cost the company $3,500. The per-unit cost incurred for the annual subscriptions is $3,600 and they sell for $42,000 each. Each of the temporary coverage contracts are priced at $16,800, and the cost incurred by the company is $900.

There are 70 senior employees who earn $33 per hour and work 33 hours per week. The company also employs 33 student interns for 20 hours per week, and pays them $15 per hour. Aside from the hourly staff members, there is a senior manager who earns an annual salary of $24,000 and the bookkeeper is paid $11,000 per year. Utilities are the main overhead expense, which costs $700,000 per year. The building was originally bought for $1,750,000, and it has a useful life of 126 years, and the equipment, which had cost the company $875,000 has a useful life of 84 years. This company's effective tax rate is 35%. Calculate the annual cash flow.

166   Fairway Malls is a company which offers their customers a wide selection of retail spaces in their shopping centers. Last year, they sold 22,023 monthly retail space rentals, 17,123 monthly anchor store rentals, and 4,995 monthly food court rentals. Each of the monthly retail space rentals sells for $22,000 and they cost the company $600. The per-unit cost incurred for the monthly anchor store rentals is $600 and they sell for $34,000 each. Each of the monthly food court rentals are priced at $10,000, and the cost incurred by the company is $200.

There are 40 full-time employees who earn $24 per hour and work 18 hours per week. The company also employs 24 temporary contract workers for 11 hours per week, and pays them $12 per hour. Aside from the hourly staff members, there is a chief operating officer who earns an annual salary of $18,000 and the senior manager is paid $8,000 per year. HVAC expenses are the main overhead expense, which costs $520,000 per year. The building was originally bought for $1,300,000, and it has a useful life of 120 years, and the equipment, which had cost the company $650,000 has a useful life of 80 years. This company's effective tax rate is 32%. Calculate the monthly cash flow.

167   Mount Tessory Academy sells various private school education. Last year, they sold 22,854 annual kindergarten memberships, 3,154 annual elementary school tuition memberships, and 1,555 annual pre-school memberships. Each of the annual kindergarten memberships sells for $22,800 and they cost the company $18,000. The per-unit cost incurred for the annual elementary school tuition memberships is $18,200 and they sell for $30,000 each. Each of the annual pre-school memberships are priced at $15,600, and the cost incurred by the company is $3,300.

There are 120 full-timers who earn $48 per hour and work 58 hours per week. The company also employs 48 seasonal employees for 35 hours per week, and pays them $20 per hour. Aside from the hourly staff members, there is a supervisor who earns an annual salary of $34,000 and the receptionist is paid $16,000 per year. Insurance costs are the main overhead expense, which costs $1,000,000 per year. The building was originally bought for $2,500,000, and it has a useful life of 72 years, and the equipment, which had cost the company $1,250,000 has a useful life of 48 years. This company's effective tax rate is 40%. Calculate the monthly net income before tax.

168   Fairway Malls is a corporation which sells retail spaces in their shopping centers. Last year, they sold 26,013 monthly retail space rentals, 9,613 monthly anchor store rentals, and 3,495 monthly food court rentals. Each of the monthly retail space rentals sells for $26,000 and they cost the company $2,200. The per-unit cost incurred for the monthly anchor store rentals is $2,200 and they sell for $38,000 each. Each of the monthly food court rentals are priced at $14,000, and the cost incurred by the company is $600.

There are 60 permanent full-time staff who earn $30 per hour and work 28 hours per week. The company also employs 30 part-time employees for 17 hours per week, and pays them $14 per hour. Aside from the hourly staff members, there is a director who earns an annual salary of $22,000 and the manager is paid $10,000 per year. Janitorial services are the main overhead expense, which costs $640,000 per year. The building was originally bought for $1,600,000, and it has a useful life of 120 years, and the equipment, which had cost the company $800,000 has a useful life of 80 years. This company's effective tax rate is 34%. Calculate the monthly cash flow.

169   Club Disco is a corporation which sells dance venue rentals for large family gatherings. Last year, they sold 22,154 week-end party rentals, 8,229 holiday rentals, and 2,970 evening rentals. Each of the week-end party rentals sells for $22,100 and they cost the company $2,200. The per-unit cost incurred for the holiday rentals is $2,200 and they sell for $32,300 each. Each of the evening rentals are priced at $11,900, and the cost incurred by the company is $600.

         There are 60 permanent full-time staff who earn $30 per hour and work 28 hours per week. The company also employs 30 part-time employees for 17 hours per week, and pays them $14 per hour. Aside from the hourly staff members, there is a director who earns an annual salary of $22,000 and the manager is paid $10,000 per year. Janitorial services are the main overhead expense, which costs $640,000 per year. The building was originally bought for $1,600,000, and it has a useful life of 102 years, and the equipment, which had cost the company $800,000 has a useful life of 68 years. This company's effective tax rate is 34%. Calculate the annual tax expense.

170   Mount Tessory Academy is an organization which specializes in providing their customers with private school education. Last year, they sold 18,003 annual kindergarten memberships, 4,303 annual elementary school tuition memberships, and 1,795 annual pre-school memberships. Each of the annual kindergarten memberships sells for $18,000 and they cost the company $5,300. The per-unit cost incurred for the annual elementary school tuition memberships is $5,400 and they sell for $25,200 each. Each of the annual pre-school memberships are priced at $10,800, and the cost incurred by the company is $1,300.

         There are 80 senior employees who earn $36 per hour and work 38 hours per week. The company also employs 36 student interns for 23 hours per week, and pays them $16 per hour. Aside from the hourly staff members, there is a senior manager who earns an annual salary of $26,000 and the bookkeeper is paid $12,000 per year. Utilities are the main overhead expense, which costs $760,000 per year. The building was originally bought for $1,900,000, and it has a useful life of 72 years, and the equipment, which had cost the company $950,000 has a useful life of 48 years. This company's effective tax rate is 36%. Calculate the monthly net income before tax.

171   Sprike Inc sells several different types of athletic apparel. Last year, they sold 1,021 batches of yoga pants, 1,721 batches of track suits, and 395 batches of athletic t-shirts. Each of the batches of yoga pants sells for $1,000 and they cost the company $200. The per-unit cost incurred for the batches of track suits is $200 and they sell for $1,600 each. Each of the batches of athletic t-shirts are priced at $400, and the cost incurred by the company is $100.

         There are 30 full-time employees who earn $21 per hour and work 13 hours per week. The company also employs 21 temporary contract workers for 8 hours per week, and pays them $11 per hour. Aside from the hourly staff members, there is a chief operating officer who earns an annual salary of $16,000 and the senior manager is paid $7,000 per year. HVAC expenses are the main overhead expense, which costs $460,000 per year. The building was originally bought for $1,150,000, and it has a useful life of 6 years, and the equipment, which had cost the company $575,000 has a useful life of 4 years. This company's effective tax rate is 31%. Calculate the gross margin.

172   Hogtown Records offers their customers a wide range of audio services for local musicians who would like to record their music. Last year, they sold 22,803 singles CDs, 11,503 full albums on LP, and 3,795 individual song recordings. Each of the singles CDs sells for $22,800 and they cost the company $1,200. The per-unit cost incurred for the full albums on LP is $1,300 and they sell for $34,200 each. Each of the individual song recordings are priced at $11,400, and the cost incurred by the company is $400.
              There are 50 permanent full-time staff who earn $27 per hour and work 23 hours per week. The company also employs 27 part-time employees for 14 hours per week, and pays them $13 per hour. Aside from the hourly staff members, there is a director who earns an annual salary of $20,000 and the manager is paid $9,000 per year. Janitorial services are the main overhead expense, which costs $580,000 per year. The building was originally bought for $1,450,000, and it has a useful life of 114 years, and the equipment, which had cost the company $725,000 has a useful life of 76 years. This company's effective tax rate is 33%. Calculate the annual cash flow.

173   LA Met Theatre Company sells various live theatrical performances. Last year, they sold 27,038 premium monthly memberships, 4,138 platinum annual memberships, and 1,995 student memberships. Each of the premium monthly memberships sells for $27,000 and they cost the company $13,900. The per-unit cost incurred for the platinum annual memberships is $14,000 and they sell for $36,000 each. Each of the student memberships are priced at $18,000, and the cost incurred by the company is $2,700.
              There are 110 full-timers who earn $45 per hour and work 53 hours per week. The company also employs 45 seasonal employees for 32 hours per week, and pays them $19 per hour. Aside from the hourly staff members, there is a supervisor who earns an annual salary of $32,000 and the receptionist is paid $15,000 per year. Insurance costs are the main overhead expense, which costs $940,000 per year. The building was originally bought for $2,350,000, and it has a useful life of 90 years, and the equipment, which had cost the company $1,175,000 has a useful life of 60 years. This company's effective tax rate is 39%. Calculate the annual EBITDA.

174   Payday Now sells several different types of short-term loan arrangements. Last year, they sold 11,090 lines of credit, 17,790 payday loans, and 4,395 prepaid credit cards. Each of the lines of credit sells for $11,000 and they cost the company $200. The per-unit cost incurred for the payday loans is $200 and they sell for $17,600 each. Each of the prepaid credit cards are priced at $4,400, and the cost incurred by the company is $100.
              There are 30 full-time employees who earn $21 per hour and work 13 hours per week. The company also employs 21 temporary contract workers for 8 hours per week, and pays them $11 per hour. Aside from the hourly staff members, there is a chief operating officer who earns an annual salary of $16,000 and the senior manager is paid $7,000 per year. HVAC expenses are the main overhead expense, which costs $460,000 per year. The building was originally bought for $1,150,000, and it has a useful life of 66 years, and the equipment, which had cost the company $575,000 has a useful life of 44 years. This company's effective tax rate is 31%. Calculate the annual net income before tax.

175   Payday Now provides their customers with short-term loan arrangements. Last year, they sold 15,496 lines of credit, 4,596 payday loans, and 1,755 prepaid credit cards. Each of the lines of credit sells for $15,400 and they cost the company $3,500. The per-unit cost incurred for the payday loans is $3,600 and they sell for $22,000 each. Each of the prepaid credit cards are priced at $8,800, and the cost incurred by the company is $900.

There are 70 senior employees who earn $33 per hour and work 33 hours per week. The company also employs 33 student interns for 20 hours per week, and pays them $15 per hour. Aside from the hourly staff members, there is a senior manager who earns an annual salary of $24,000 and the bookkeeper is paid $11,000 per year. Utilities are the main overhead expense, which costs $700,000 per year. The building was originally bought for $1,750,000, and it has a useful life of 66 years, and the equipment, which had cost the company $875,000 has a useful life of 44 years. This company's effective tax rate is 35%. Calculate the annual net income before tax.

176   Club Disco sells various dance venue rentals for large family gatherings. Last year, they sold 30,697 week-end party rentals, 4,730 holiday rentals, and 2,262 evening rentals. Each of the week-end party rentals sells for $30,600 and they cost the company $13,900. The per-unit cost incurred for the holiday rentals is $14,000 and they sell for $40,800 each. Each of the evening rentals are priced at $20,400, and the cost incurred by the company is $2,700.

There are 110 full-timers who earn $45 per hour and work 53 hours per week. The company also employs 45 seasonal employees for 32 hours per week, and pays them $19 per hour. Aside from the hourly staff members, there is a supervisor who earns an annual salary of $32,000 and the receptionist is paid $15,000 per year. Insurance costs are the main overhead expense, which costs $940,000 per year. The building was originally bought for $2,350,000, and it has a useful life of 102 years, and the equipment, which had cost the company $1,175,000 has a useful life of 68 years. This company's effective tax rate is 39%. Calculate the annual tax expense.

177   AC&C Ltd. provides their customers with cell phone plans. Last year, they sold 14,034 annual unlimited talk and text plans, 4,134 annual unlimited voice and data plans, and 1,595 annual prepaid wireless phone cards. Each of the annual unlimited talk and text plans sells for $14,000 and they cost the company $3,500. The per-unit cost incurred for the annual unlimited voice and data plans is $3,600 and they sell for $20,000 each. Each of the annual prepaid wireless phone cards are priced at $8,000, and the cost incurred by the company is $900.

There are 70 senior employees who earn $33 per hour and work 33 hours per week. The company also employs 33 student interns for 20 hours per week, and pays them $15 per hour. Aside from the hourly staff members, there is a senior manager who earns an annual salary of $24,000 and the bookkeeper is paid $11,000 per year. Utilities are the main overhead expense, which costs $700,000 per year. The building was originally bought for $1,750,000, and it has a useful life of 60 years, and the equipment, which had cost the company $875,000 has a useful life of 40 years. This company's effective tax rate is 35%. Calculate the monthly net income before tax.

178   Fairway Malls is a market leader that is well-known for their brand of retail spaces in their shopping centers. Last year, they sold 32,015 monthly retail space rentals, 6,401 monthly anchor store rentals, and 2,852 monthly food court rentals. Each of the monthly retail space rentals sells for $32,000 and they cost the company $7,600. The per-unit cost incurred for the monthly anchor store rentals is $7,700 and they sell for $44,000 each. Each of the monthly food court rentals are priced at $20,000, and the cost incurred by the company is $1,700.

There are 90 union workers who earn $39 per hour and work 43 hours per week. The company also employs 39 non-union workers for 26 hours per week, and pays them $17 per hour. Aside from the hourly staff members, there is a president who earns an annual salary of $28,000 and the vice-president is paid $13,000 per year. Employee assistance services are the main overhead expense, which costs $820,000 per year. The building was originally bought for $2,050,000, and it has a useful life of 120 years, and the equipment, which had cost the company $1,025,000 has a useful life of 80 years. This company's effective tax rate is 37%. Calculate the monthly cash flow.

179   LA Met Theatre Company is a company which offers their customers a wide selection of live theatrical performances. Last year, they sold 16,523 premium monthly memberships, 12,873 platinum annual memberships, and 3,745 student memberships. Each of the premium monthly memberships sells for $16,500 and they cost the company $600. The per-unit cost incurred for the platinum annual memberships is $600 and they sell for $25,500 each. Each of the student memberships are priced at $7,500, and the cost incurred by the company is $200.

There are 40 full-time employees who earn $24 per hour and work 18 hours per week. The company also employs 24 temporary contract workers for 11 hours per week, and pays them $12 per hour. Aside from the hourly staff members, there is a chief operating officer who earns an annual salary of $18,000 and the senior manager is paid $8,000 per year. HVAC expenses are the main overhead expense, which costs $520,000 per year. The building was originally bought for $1,300,000, and it has a useful life of 90 years, and the equipment, which had cost the company $650,000 has a useful life of 60 years. This company's effective tax rate is 32%. Calculate the annual EBITDA.

180   Mount Tessory Academy provides their customers with private school education. Last year, they sold 16,855 annual kindergarten memberships, 4,955 annual elementary school tuition memberships, and 1,915 annual pre-school memberships. Each of the annual kindergarten memberships sells for $16,800 and they cost the company $3,500. The per-unit cost incurred for the annual elementary school tuition memberships is $3,600 and they sell for $24,000 each. Each of the annual pre-school memberships are priced at $9,600, and the cost incurred by the company is $900.

There are 70 senior employees who earn $33 per hour and work 33 hours per week. The company also employs 33 student interns for 20 hours per week, and pays them $15 per hour. Aside from the hourly staff members, there is a senior manager who earns an annual salary of $24,000 and the bookkeeper is paid $11,000 per year. Utilities are the main overhead expense, which costs $700,000 per year. The building was originally bought for $1,750,000, and it has a useful life of 72 years, and the equipment, which had cost the company $875,000 has a useful life of 48 years. This company's effective tax rate is 35%. Calculate the monthly net income before tax.

181   Comedy 253 sells various live performances of stand-up comedy. Last year, they sold 30,475 week-end comedy festivals, 4,175 private events, and 2,075 week-day comedy events. Each of the week-end comedy festivals sells for $30,400 and they cost the company $18,000. The per-unit cost incurred for the private events is $18,200 and they sell for $40,000 each. Each of the week-day comedy events are priced at $20,800, and the cost incurred by the company is $3,300.

There are 120 full-timers who earn $48 per hour and work 58 hours per week. The company also employs 48 seasonal employees for 35 hours per week, and pays them $20 per hour. Aside from the hourly staff members, there is a supervisor who earns an annual salary of $34,000 and the receptionist is paid $16,000 per year. Insurance costs are the main overhead expense, which costs $1,000,000 per year. The building was originally bought for $2,500,000, and it has a useful life of 96 years, and the equipment, which had cost the company $1,250,000 has a useful life of 64 years. This company's effective tax rate is 40%. Calculate the monthly tax expense.

182   Kola-Nut Ltd is a company which offers their customers a wide selection of bottled beverages. Last year, they sold 2,226 batches of fruit juice, 1,826 batches of energy drinks, and 495 batches of soda bottles. Each of the batches of fruit juice sells for $2,200 and they cost the company $600. The per-unit cost incurred for the batches of energy drinks is $600 and they sell for $3,400 each. Each of the batches of soda bottles are priced at $1,000, and the cost incurred by the company is $200.

There are 40 full-time employees who earn $24 per hour and work 18 hours per week. The company also employs 24 temporary contract workers for 11 hours per week, and pays them $12 per hour. Aside from the hourly staff members, there is a chief operating officer who earns an annual salary of $18,000 and the senior manager is paid $8,000 per year. HVAC expenses are the main overhead expense, which costs $520,000 per year. The building was originally bought for $1,300,000, and it has a useful life of 12 years, and the equipment, which had cost the company $650,000 has a useful life of 8 years. This company's effective tax rate is 32%. Calculate the gross margin.

183   LA Met Theatre Company is a market leader that is well-known for their brand of live theatrical performances. Last year, they sold 24,061 premium monthly memberships, 4,875 platinum annual memberships, and 2,138 student memberships. Each of the premium monthly memberships sells for $24,000 and they cost the company $7,600. The per-unit cost incurred for the platinum annual memberships is $7,700 and they sell for $33,000 each. Each of the student memberships are priced at $15,000, and the cost incurred by the company is $1,700.

There are 90 union workers who earn $39 per hour and work 43 hours per week. The company also employs 39 non-union workers for 26 hours per week, and pays them $17 per hour. Aside from the hourly staff members, there is a president who earns an annual salary of $28,000 and the vice-president is paid $13,000 per year. Employee assistance services are the main overhead expense, which costs $820,000 per year. The building was originally bought for $2,050,000, and it has a useful life of 90 years, and the equipment, which had cost the company $1,025,000 has a useful life of 60 years. This company's effective tax rate is 37%. Calculate the annual EBITDA.

184   Club Disco is a company which offers their customers a wide selection of dance venue rentals for large family gatherings. Last year, they sold 18,744 week-end party rentals, 14,594 holiday rentals, and 4,245 evening rentals. Each of the week-end party rentals sells for $18,700 and they cost the company $600. The per-unit cost incurred for the holiday rentals is $600 and they sell for $28,900 each. Each of the evening rentals are priced at $8,500, and the cost incurred by the company is $200.

        There are 40 full-time employees who earn $24 per hour and work 18 hours per week. The company also employs 24 temporary contract workers for 11 hours per week, and pays them $12 per hour. Aside from the hourly staff members, there is a chief operating officer who earns an annual salary of $18,000 and the senior manager is paid $8,000 per year. HVAC expenses are the main overhead expense, which costs $520,000 per year. The building was originally bought for $1,300,000, and it has a useful life of 102 years, and the equipment, which had cost the company $650,000 has a useful life of 68 years. This company's effective tax rate is 32%. Calculate the annual tax expense.

185   Payday Now is an organization which specializes in providing their customers with short-term loan arrangements. Last year, they sold 16,557 lines of credit, 4,007 payday loans, and 1,645 prepaid credit cards. Each of the lines of credit sells for $16,500 and they cost the company $5,300. The per-unit cost incurred for the payday loans is $5,400 and they sell for $23,100 each. Each of the prepaid credit cards are priced at $9,900, and the cost incurred by the company is $1,300.

        There are 80 senior employees who earn $36 per hour and work 38 hours per week. The company also employs 36 student interns for 23 hours per week, and pays them $16 per hour. Aside from the hourly staff members, there is a senior manager who earns an annual salary of $26,000 and the bookkeeper is paid $12,000 per year. Utilities are the main overhead expense, which costs $760,000 per year. The building was originally bought for $1,900,000, and it has a useful life of 66 years, and the equipment, which had cost the company $950,000 has a useful life of 44 years. This company's effective tax rate is 36%. Calculate the annual net income before tax.

186   Hogtown Records is a privately-held corporation which focuses on their niche of premium audio services for local musicians who would like to record their music. Last year, they sold 32,359 singles CDs, 5,622 full albums on LP, and 2,608 individual song recordings. Each of the singles CDs sells for $32,300 and they cost the company $10,400. The per-unit cost incurred for the full albums on LP is $10,600 and they sell for $43,700 each. Each of the individual song recordings are priced at $20,900, and the cost incurred by the company is $2,200.

        There are 100 union workers who earn $42 per hour and work 48 hours per week. The company also employs 42 non-union workers for 29 hours per week, and pays them $18 per hour. Aside from the hourly staff members, there is a president who earns an annual salary of $30,000 and the vice-president is paid $14,000 per year. Employee assistance services are the main overhead expense, which costs $880,000 per year. The building was originally bought for $2,200,000, and it has a useful life of 114 years, and the equipment, which had cost the company $1,100,000 has a useful life of 76 years. This company's effective tax rate is 38%. Calculate the annual cash flow.

187		Comedy 253 is a corporation which sells live performances of stand-up comedy. Last year, they sold 20,861 week-end comedy festivals, 7,761 private events, and 2,795 week-day comedy events. Each of the week-end comedy festivals sells for $20,800 and they cost the company $2,200. The per-unit cost incurred for the private events is $2,200 and they sell for $30,400 each. Each of the week-day comedy events are priced at $11,200, and the cost incurred by the company is $600.

There are 60 permanent full-time staff who earn $30 per hour and work 28 hours per week. The company also employs 30 part-time employees for 17 hours per week, and pays them $14 per hour. Aside from the hourly staff members, there is a director who earns an annual salary of $22,000 and the manager is paid $10,000 per year. Janitorial services are the main overhead expense, which costs $640,000 per year. The building was originally bought for $1,600,000, and it has a useful life of 96 years, and the equipment, which had cost the company $800,000 has a useful life of 64 years. This company's effective tax rate is 34%. Calculate the monthly tax expense.

188		Paytech Ltd sells various payroll transaction processing services. Last year, they sold 37,848 monthly subscriptions, 5,748 annual subscriptions, and 2,795 temporary coverage contracts. Each of the monthly subscriptions sells for $37,800 and they cost the company $13,900. The per-unit cost incurred for the annual subscriptions is $14,000 and they sell for $50,400 each. Each of the temporary coverage contracts are priced at $25,200, and the cost incurred by the company is $2,700.

There are 110 full-timers who earn $45 per hour and work 53 hours per week. The company also employs 45 seasonal employees for 32 hours per week, and pays them $19 per hour. Aside from the hourly staff members, there is a supervisor who earns an annual salary of $32,000 and the receptionist is paid $15,000 per year. Insurance costs are the main overhead expense, which costs $940,000 per year. The building was originally bought for $2,350,000, and it has a useful life of 126 years, and the equipment, which had cost the company $1,175,000 has a useful life of 84 years. This company's effective tax rate is 39%. Calculate the annual cash flow.

189		Fairway Malls is a corporation which sells retail spaces in their shopping centers. Last year, they sold 26,034 monthly retail space rentals, 9,634 monthly anchor store rentals, and 3,495 monthly food court rentals. Each of the monthly retail space rentals sells for $26,000 and they cost the company $2,200. The per-unit cost incurred for the monthly anchor store rentals is $2,200 and they sell for $38,000 each. Each of the monthly food court rentals are priced at $14,000, and the cost incurred by the company is $600.

There are 60 permanent full-time staff who earn $30 per hour and work 28 hours per week. The company also employs 30 part-time employees for 17 hours per week, and pays them $14 per hour. Aside from the hourly staff members, there is a director who earns an annual salary of $22,000 and the manager is paid $10,000 per year. Janitorial services are the main overhead expense, which costs $640,000 per year. The building was originally bought for $1,600,000, and it has a useful life of 120 years, and the equipment, which had cost the company $800,000 has a useful life of 80 years. This company's effective tax rate is 34%. Calculate the monthly cash flow.

190   Cirque du Lune is a corporation which sells circus performances. Last year, they sold 18,210 monthly shows, 6,760 holiday special performances, and 2,445 performances at schools. Each of the monthly shows sells for $18,200 and they cost the company $2,200. The per-unit cost incurred for the holiday special performances is $2,200 and they sell for $26,600 each. Each of the performances at schools are priced at $9,800, and the cost incurred by the company is $600.

        There are 60 permanent full-time staff who earn $30 per hour and work 28 hours per week. The company also employs 30 part-time employees for 17 hours per week, and pays them $14 per hour. Aside from the hourly staff members, there is a director who earns an annual salary of $22,000 and the manager is paid $10,000 per year. Janitorial services are the main overhead expense, which costs $640,000 per year. The building was originally bought for $1,600,000, and it has a useful life of 84 years, and the equipment, which had cost the company $800,000 has a useful life of 56 years. This company's effective tax rate is 34%. Calculate the monthly EBITDA.

191   Cirque du Lune is a market leader that is well-known for their brand of circus performances. Last year, they sold 22,440 monthly shows, 4,540 holiday special performances, and 1,995 performances at schools. Each of the monthly shows sells for $22,400 and they cost the company $7,600. The per-unit cost incurred for the holiday special performances is $7,700 and they sell for $30,800 each. Each of the performances at schools are priced at $14,000, and the cost incurred by the company is $1,700.

        There are 90 union workers who earn $39 per hour and work 43 hours per week. The company also employs 39 non-union workers for 26 hours per week, and pays them $17 per hour. Aside from the hourly staff members, there is a president who earns an annual salary of $28,000 and the vice-president is paid $13,000 per year. Employee assistance services are the main overhead expense, which costs $820,000 per year. The building was originally bought for $2,050,000, and it has a useful life of 84 years, and the equipment, which had cost the company $1,025,000 has a useful life of 56 years. This company's effective tax rate is 37%. Calculate the monthly EBITDA.

192   Jameson & Jameson is a company which offers their customers a wide selection of soap products. Last year, they sold 3,379 truckloads of shampoo bottles, 2,729 truckloads of toothpaste, and 745 truckloads of bars of soap. Each of the truckloads of shampoo bottles sells for $3,300 and they cost the company $600. The per-unit cost incurred for the truckloads of toothpaste is $600 and they sell for $5,100 each. Each of the truckloads of bars of soap are priced at $1,500, and the cost incurred by the company is $200.

        There are 40 full-time employees who earn $24 per hour and work 18 hours per week. The company also employs 24 temporary contract workers for 11 hours per week, and pays them $12 per hour. Aside from the hourly staff members, there is a chief operating officer who earns an annual salary of $18,000 and the senior manager is paid $8,000 per year. HVAC expenses are the main overhead expense, which costs $520,000 per year. The building was originally bought for $1,300,000, and it has a useful life of 18 years, and the equipment, which had cost the company $650,000 has a useful life of 12 years. This company's effective tax rate is 32%. Calculate the gross margin.

193   AC&C Ltd. is a company which offers their customers a wide selection of cell phone plans. Last year, they sold 11,096 annual unlimited talk and text plans, 8,696 annual unlimited voice and data plans, and 2,495 annual prepaid wireless phone cards. Each of the annual unlimited talk and text plans sells for $11,000 and they cost the company $600. The per-unit cost incurred for the annual unlimited voice and data plans is $600 and they sell for $17,000 each. Each of the annual prepaid wireless phone cards are priced at $5,000, and the cost incurred by the company is $200.

        There are 40 full-time employees who earn $24 per hour and work 18 hours per week. The company also employs 24 temporary contract workers for 11 hours per week, and pays them $12 per hour. Aside from the hourly staff members, there is a chief operating officer who earns an annual salary of $18,000 and the senior manager is paid $8,000 per year. HVAC expenses are the main overhead expense, which costs $520,000 per year. The building was originally bought for $1,300,000, and it has a useful life of 60 years, and the equipment, which had cost the company $650,000 has a useful life of 40 years. This company's effective tax rate is 32%. Calculate the monthly net income before tax.

194   Paytech Ltd offers their customers a wide range of payroll transaction processing services. Last year, they sold 25,257 monthly subscriptions, 12,757 annual subscriptions, and 4,195 temporary coverage contracts. Each of the monthly subscriptions sells for $25,200 and they cost the company $1,200. The per-unit cost incurred for the annual subscriptions is $1,300 and they sell for $37,800 each. Each of the temporary coverage contracts are priced at $12,600, and the cost incurred by the company is $400.

        There are 50 permanent full-time staff who earn $27 per hour and work 23 hours per week. The company also employs 27 part-time employees for 14 hours per week, and pays them $13 per hour. Aside from the hourly staff members, there is a director who earns an annual salary of $20,000 and the manager is paid $9,000 per year. Janitorial services are the main overhead expense, which costs $580,000 per year. The building was originally bought for $1,450,000, and it has a useful life of 126 years, and the equipment, which had cost the company $725,000 has a useful life of 84 years. This company's effective tax rate is 33%. Calculate the annual cash flow.

195   Grand Convention Ltd is a company which offers their customers a wide selection of banquet hall rentals for corporate meetings. Last year, they sold 19,872 wedding ceremonies, 15,472 corporate events, and 4,495 convention events. Each of the wedding ceremonies sells for $19,800 and they cost the company $600. The per-unit cost incurred for the corporate events is $600 and they sell for $30,600 each. Each of the convention events are priced at $9,000, and the cost incurred by the company is $200.

        There are 40 full-time employees who earn $24 per hour and work 18 hours per week. The company also employs 24 temporary contract workers for 11 hours per week, and pays them $12 per hour. Aside from the hourly staff members, there is a chief operating officer who earns an annual salary of $18,000 and the senior manager is paid $8,000 per year. HVAC expenses are the main overhead expense, which costs $520,000 per year. The building was originally bought for $1,300,000, and it has a useful life of 108 years, and the equipment, which had cost the company $650,000 has a useful life of 72 years. This company's effective tax rate is 32%. Calculate the monthly tax expense.

196   Fairway Malls is a company which offers their customers a wide selection of retail spaces in their shopping centers. Last year, they sold 22,034 monthly retail space rentals, 17,134 monthly anchor store rentals, and 4,995 monthly food court rentals. Each of the monthly retail space rentals sells for $22,000 and they cost the company $600. The per-unit cost incurred for the monthly anchor store rentals is $600 and they sell for $34,000 each. Each of the monthly food court rentals are priced at $10,000, and the cost incurred by the company is $200.

There are 40 full-time employees who earn $24 per hour and work 18 hours per week. The company also employs 24 temporary contract workers for 11 hours per week, and pays them $12 per hour. Aside from the hourly staff members, there is a chief operating officer who earns an annual salary of $18,000 and the senior manager is paid $8,000 per year. HVAC expenses are the main overhead expense, which costs $520,000 per year. The building was originally bought for $1,300,000, and it has a useful life of 120 years, and the equipment, which had cost the company $650,000 has a useful life of 80 years. This company's effective tax rate is 32%. Calculate the monthly cash flow.

197   Cirque du Lune is a privately-held corporation which focuses on their niche of premium circus performances. Last year, they sold 23,805 monthly shows, 4,130 holiday special performances, and 1,920 performances at schools. Each of the monthly shows sells for $23,800 and they cost the company $10,400. The per-unit cost incurred for the holiday special performances is $10,600 and they sell for $32,200 each. Each of the performances at schools are priced at $15,400, and the cost incurred by the company is $2,200.

There are 100 union workers who earn $42 per hour and work 48 hours per week. The company also employs 42 non-union workers for 29 hours per week, and pays them $18 per hour. Aside from the hourly staff members, there is a president who earns an annual salary of $30,000 and the vice-president is paid $14,000 per year. Employee assistance services are the main overhead expense, which costs $880,000 per year. The building was originally bought for $2,200,000, and it has a useful life of 84 years, and the equipment, which had cost the company $1,100,000 has a useful life of 56 years. This company's effective tax rate is 38%. Calculate the monthly EBITDA.

198   Payday Now provides their customers with short-term loan arrangements. Last year, they sold 15,414 lines of credit, 4,514 payday loans, and 1,755 prepaid credit cards. Each of the lines of credit sells for $15,400 and they cost the company $3,500. The per-unit cost incurred for the payday loans is $3,600 and they sell for $22,000 each. Each of the prepaid credit cards are priced at $8,800, and the cost incurred by the company is $900.

There are 70 senior employees who earn $33 per hour and work 33 hours per week. The company also employs 33 student interns for 20 hours per week, and pays them $15 per hour. Aside from the hourly staff members, there is a senior manager who earns an annual salary of $24,000 and the bookkeeper is paid $11,000 per year. Utilities are the main overhead expense, which costs $700,000 per year. The building was originally bought for $1,750,000, and it has a useful life of 66 years, and the equipment, which had cost the company $875,000 has a useful life of 44 years. This company's effective tax rate is 35%. Calculate the annual net income before tax.

199   Paytech Ltd provides their customers with payroll transaction processing services. Last year, they sold 29,491 monthly subscriptions, 8,591 annual subscriptions, and 3,355 temporary coverage contracts. Each of the monthly subscriptions sells for $29,400 and they cost the company $3,500. The per-unit cost incurred for the annual subscriptions is $3,600 and they sell for $42,000 each. Each of the temporary coverage contracts are priced at $16,800, and the cost incurred by the company is $900.

There are 70 senior employees who earn $33 per hour and work 33 hours per week. The company also employs 33 student interns for 20 hours per week, and pays them $15 per hour. Aside from the hourly staff members, there is a senior manager who earns an annual salary of $24,000 and the bookkeeper is paid $11,000 per year. Utilities are the main overhead expense, which costs $700,000 per year. The building was originally bought for $1,750,000, and it has a useful life of 126 years, and the equipment, which had cost the company $875,000 has a useful life of 84 years. This company's effective tax rate is 35%. Calculate the annual cash flow.

200   Mount Tessory Academy sells various private school education. Last year, they sold 21,677 annual kindergarten memberships, 3,377 annual elementary school tuition memberships, and 1,595 annual pre-school memberships. Each of the annual kindergarten memberships sells for $21,600 and they cost the company $13,900. The per-unit cost incurred for the annual elementary school tuition memberships is $14,000 and they sell for $28,800 each. Each of the annual pre-school memberships are priced at $14,400, and the cost incurred by the company is $2,700.

There are 110 full-timers who earn $45 per hour and work 53 hours per week. The company also employs 45 seasonal employees for 32 hours per week, and pays them $19 per hour. Aside from the hourly staff members, there is a supervisor who earns an annual salary of $32,000 and the receptionist is paid $15,000 per year. Insurance costs are the main overhead expense, which costs $940,000 per year. The building was originally bought for $2,350,000, and it has a useful life of 72 years, and the equipment, which had cost the company $1,175,000 has a useful life of 48 years. This company's effective tax rate is 39%. Calculate the monthly net income before tax.

Financial Audit

Inherent risk is the likelihood that there will be a financial misstatement that is not caused by the lack of an internal control.

Detection risk is the probability that there will be a financial misstatement that is not found by the audit procedures.

Audit risk is the probability that an auditor will incorrectly issue an unqualified audit report when there is a material misstatement.

Control risk is the probability that there will be a material misstatement that will not be prevented by an internal control.

When control risk is high, the auditors will reduce their reliance on internal control testing, and increase their reliance on substantive testing. Detection risk decreases as more reliance is placed substantive testing.

Audit Risk = Inherent Risk x Control Risk x Detection Risk

Detection Risk = Audit Risk / (Control Risk x Inherent Risk)

1   What assertion is being tested by the following audit procedure? Perform analytics by
      calculating if Inventory Turnover has increased or decreased
      (a) Cut-off
      (b) Accuracy
      (c) Valuation
      (d) Existence

2   The audit client has increased the headcount of the accounting department in the past
      year.. Which of the following statements is true?
      (a) Inherent risk has increased
      (b) Detection risk has increased
      (c) Inherent risk has decreased

3   Which audit procedure can be used to test for the Cut-off of Expenses?
      (a) Vouch a sample of purchase orders and invoices from the first and last month of the
      fiscal year.
      (b) Perform an inventory count and indicate which items have been in stock for longer
      than one year
      (c) Check the price that would be incurred to obtain a similar asset from the market
      (d) Send confirmations to customers that have balances owing

4   If inherent risk is high, control risk is low and audit risk is medium, what is detection risk,
      according to the risk categorization table in the appendix?
      (a) medium
      (b) high
      (c) high

5   If inherent risk is low, control risk is low and detection risk is medium, what is audit risk,
      according to the risk categorization table in the appendix?
      (a) high
      (b) low
      (c) medium

6   If inherent risk is high, control risk is medium and detection risk is high, what is audit risk,
      according to the risk categorization table in the appendix?
      (a) medium
      (b) high
      (c) low

7   Which audit procedure can be used to test for the Valuation of Inventory?
      (a) Perform an inventory count and compare results to a list of inventory
      (b) Perform an inventory count on items that were selected from a list of inventory
      (c) Perform an inventory count on items that are held on consignment
      (d) Perform an inventory count and indicate which items have been in stock for longer
      than one year

8   If control risk increases, how can the audit procedures be adjusted in order to maintain the same level of audit risk?
(a) substantive testing can be decreased which will increase detection risk
(b) substantive testing can be decreased which will decrease detection risk
(c) substantive testing can be increased which will decrease detection risk
(d) inherent risk can be decreased which will increase detection risk

9   What assertion is being tested by the following audit procedure? Transactions that comprise the final balance are checked against the originating documents
(a) Valuation
(b) Rights
(c) Accuracy
(d) Classification

10   Which audit procedure can be used to test for the Completeness of Inventory?
(a) Perform an inventory count and compare results to a list of inventory
(b) Perform an inventory count on items that were selected from a list of inventory
(c) Perform an inventory count on items that are held on consignment
(d) Perform an inventory count and indicate which items have been in stock for longer than one year

11   The financial institution has begun to invest in derivative investments which involve complex contractual arrangements.. Which of the following statements is true?
(a) Inherent risk has decreased
(b) Inherent risk has increased
(c) Inherent risk has remained unchanged

12   If inherent risk is medium, control risk is medium and audit risk is medium, what is detection risk, according to the risk categorization table in the appendix?
(a) medium
(b) high
(c) high

13   The company has experienced a decrease in accounts receivable, which used to require significant estimations in order to quantify the amounts that were collectible.. Which of the following statements is true?
(a) Inherent risk has increased
(b) Inherent risk has decreased
(c) Control risk has increased

14   What assertion is being tested by the following audit procedure? Perform an inventory count on items that were selected from a list of inventory
(a) Accuracy
(b) Existence
(c) Occurrence
(d) Valuation

15 The media organization has sold all of its largest license agreements and goodwill assets. .
    Which of the following statements is true?
    (a) Inherent risk has increased
    (b) Detection risk has decreased
    (c) Inherent risk has decreased

16 If inherent risk is low, control risk is medium and audit risk is low, what is detection risk,
    according to the risk categorization table in the appendix?
    (a) high
    (b) low
    (c) medium

17 If inherent risk is medium, control risk is low and audit risk is low, what is detection risk,
    according to the risk categorization table in the appendix?
    (a) high
    (b) medium
    (c) low

18 If inherent risk is medium, control risk is high and detection risk is low, what is audit risk,
    according to the risk categorization table in the appendix?
    (a) medium
    (b) high
    (c) high

19 If control risk increases, then this will cause
    (a) detection risk to decrease
    (b) detection risk to increase
    (c) inherent risk to increase
    (d) inherent risk to decrease

20 If inherent risk is high, control risk is low and audit risk is medium-high, what is detection
    risk, according to the risk categorization table in the appendix?
    (a) medium
    (b) high
    (c) low

21 What assertion is being tested by the following audit procedure? Check third party
    documentation to verify that the amount is owing.
    (a) Accuracy
    (b) Rights
    (c) Occurrence
    (d) Valuation

22 Which audit procedure can be used to test for the Valuation of Assets?
    (a) Test a sample of customer transactions to see if they appear in the billing system
    (b) Check the price that would be incurred to obtain a similar asset from the market
    (c) Send confirmations to customers that have balances owing
    (d) Send confirmations to the organizations to whom the outstanding balances are
    owing

23   If inherent risk is low, control risk is high and detection risk is low, what is audit risk, according to the risk categorization table in the appendix?
(a) medium-high
(b) medium
(c) medium-low

24   What assertion is being tested by the following audit procedure? Vouch a sample of customer transactions from the first and last month of the fiscal year.
(a) Valuation
(b) Rights
(c) Classification
(d) Cut-off

25   If inherent risk is low, control risk is medium and detection risk is low, what is audit risk, according to the risk categorization table in the appendix?
(a) high
(b) low
(c) medium

26   During internal control testing, several major control weaknesses that were noted during last year's audit have been mitigated by adding additional internal controls.. Which of the following statements is true?
(a) Detection risk has decreased
(b) Detection risk has increased
(c) Inherent risk has remained unchanged

27   What assertion is being tested by the following audit procedure? Vouch accounting records to the underlying third party documentation
(a) Cut-off
(b) Accuracy
(c) Rights
(d) Existence

28   Which audit procedure can be used to test for the Completeness of Expenses?
(a) Send confirmations to customers that have balances owing
(b) Check the price that would be incurred to obtain a similar asset from the market
(c) Perform an inventory count and compare results to a list of inventory
(d) Perform a reasonability analysis.

29   Which audit procedure can be used to test for the Existence of Inventory?
(a) Perform an inventory count and compare results to a list of inventory
(b) Perform an inventory count on items that were selected from a list of inventory
(c) Perform an inventory count on items that are held on consignment
(d) Perform an inventory count and indicate which items have been in stock for longer than one year

30   During internal control testing, several major control weaknesses were discovered by the internal audit team.. Which of the following statements is true?
(a) Detection risk has decreased
(b) Detection risk has increased
(c) Inherent risk has remained unchanged

31   Which audit procedure can be used to test for the Rights of Assets?
       (a) Test a sample of customer transactions to see if they appear in the billing system
       (b) Send confirmations to customers that have balances owing
       (c) Vouch accounting records to the underlying third party documentation
       (d) Perform analytics by calculating if Day Sales Inventory has increased or decreased

32   If inherent risk is low, control risk is medium and audit risk is medium-low, what is detection
       risk, according to the risk categorization table in the appendix?
       (a) low
       (b) high
       (c) medium

33   Which audit procedure can be used to test for the Existence of Liabilities?
       (a) Perform substantive analytics by calculating the number of units that were sold and
       multiplying by the average per unit sales price for each category of products that are sold.
       (b) Send confirmations to the organizations to whom the outstanding balances are
       owing
       (c) Check third party documentation to verify that the amount is owing.
       (d) Send confirmations to customers that have balances owing

34   If inherent risk is medium, control risk is high and audit risk is medium, what is detection
       risk, according to the risk categorization table in the appendix?
       (a) high
       (b) low
       (c) medium

35   If inherent risk is medium, control risk is low and detection risk is low, what is audit risk,
       according to the risk categorization table in the appendix?
       (a) high
       (b) medium
       (c) low

36   The media organization has purchased smaller media agencies which includes the
       purchase of very costly licenses and goodwill assets. . Which of the following statements
       is true?
       (a) Inherent risk has increased
       (b) Inherent risk has decreased
       (c) Detection risk has decreased

37   What assertion is being tested by the following audit procedure? Perform substantive
       analytics by calculating the number of units that were sold and multiplying by the average
       per unit sales price for each category of products that are sold.
       (a) Valuation
       (b) Rights
       (c) Accuracy
       (d) Classification

38   If inherent risk is high, control risk is high and audit risk is medium-high, what is detection risk, according to the risk categorization table in the appendix?
    (a) high
    (b) low
    (c) medium

39   If inherent risk is medium, control risk is high and detection risk is high, what is audit risk, according to the risk categorization table in the appendix?
    (a) medium
    (b) low
    (c) high

40   The company's information system which was fully implemented two years ago has continued to be used in the past year.. Which of the following statements is true?
    (a) Control risk has decreased
    (b) Inherent risk has increased
    (c) Control risk has decreased

41   If inherent risk is high, control risk is medium and detection risk is medium, what is audit risk, according to the risk categorization table in the appendix?
    (a) medium-low
    (b) medium-high
    (c) medium

42   What assertion is being tested by the following audit procedure? Send confirmations to the organizations to whom the outstanding balances are owing
    (a) Accuracy
    (b) Existence
    (c) Occurrence
    (d) Valuation

43   What assertion is being tested by the following audit procedure? Perform a reasonability analysis by comparing the accounting records to the bank account, and by reconciling the cash flow.
    (a) Valuation
    (b) Rights
    (c) Completeness
    (d) Classification

44   Within the past year, the level of debt that is owed by the organization has remained low, which is consistent with prior years.. Which of the following statements is true?
    (a) Inherent risk has increased
    (b) Inherent risk has decreased
    (c) Inherent risk has remained unchanged

45   If control risk decreases, how can the audit procedures be adjusted in order to maintain the same level of audit risk?
    (a) substantive testing can be increased which will decrease detection risk
    (b) substantive testing can be increased which will increase detection risk
    (c) inherent risk can be increased which will decrease detection risk
    (d) substantive testing can be decreased which will increase detection risk

46   What assertion is being tested by the following audit procedure? Perform an inventory
      count and indicate which items have been in stock for longer than one year
      (a) Accuracy
      (b) Valuation
      (c) Occurrence
      (d) Existence

47   The internal audit reports reveal that mitigating controls have been added and have
      succeeded in preventing theft of company assets for the past three years. . Which of the
      following statements is true?
      (a) Inherent risk has decreased
      (b) Inherent risk has increased
      (c) Inherent risk has remained unchanged

48   The company has experienced an increase in accounts receivable, which involves
      estimations to quantify the amounts that are likely to be collectible.. Which of the
      following statements is true?
      (a) Inherent risk has decreased
      (b) Inherent risk has increased
      (c) Inherent risk has remained unchanged

49   If inherent risk is low, control risk is low and detection risk is low, what is audit risk,
      according to the risk categorization table in the appendix?
      (a) high
      (b) medium
      (c) low

50   If inherent risk is high, control risk is low and detection risk is high, what is audit risk,
      according to the risk categorization table in the appendix?
      (a) medium-low
      (b) medium-high
      (c) medium

51   If inherent risk is high, control risk is medium and audit risk is medium, what is detection
      risk, according to the risk categorization table in the appendix?
      (a) high
      (b) medium
      (c) low

52   What assertion is being tested by the following audit procedure? Vouch accounting records
      to the underlying third party purchase order and invoice
      (a) Valuation
      (b) Rights
      (c) Accuracy
      (d) Classification

53   The audit client has reduced the headcount in the accounting department in the past year..
      Which of the following statements is true?
      (a) Inherent risk has decreased
      (b) Inherent risk has remained unchanged
      (c) Inherent risk has increased

54   If inherent risk is medium, control risk is medium and audit risk is medium-low, what is
      detection risk, according to the risk categorization table in the appendix?
      (a) low
      (b) medium
      (c) medium

55   If inherent risk increases, how can the audit procedures be adjusted in order to maintain the
      same level of audit risk?
      (a) substantive testing can be decreased which will increase detection risk
      (b) substantive testing can be increased which will decrease detection risk
      (c) substantive testing can be decreased which will decrease detection risk
      (d) control risk can be decreased which will increase detection risk

56   Which audit procedure can be used to test for the Existence of Accounts Receivable?
      (a) Test a sample of customer transactions to see if they appear in the billing system
      (b) Send confirmations to customers that have balances owing
      (c) Vouch the accounting records by physically locating and examining the assets that
      are recorded in the ledger.
      (d) Perform analytics by calculating if Day Sales Inventory has increased or decreased

57   Which audit procedure can be used to test for the Completeness of Revenues?
      (a) Send confirmations to customers that have balances owing
      (b) Perform analytics by calculating if Day Sales Inventory has increased or decreased
      (c) Perform analytics by calculating if Inventory Turnover has increased or decreased
      (d) Perform a reasonability analysis by comparing the accounting records to the bank
      account, and by reconciling the cash flow.

58   The economy is currently experiencing a downturn, however this audit client is exhibiting
      record high profits.. Which of the following statements is true?
      (a) Inherent risk has increased
      (b) Inherent risk has decreased
      (c) Inherent risk has remained unchanged

59   If inherent risk decreases, how can the audit procedures be adjusted in order to maintain
      the same level of audit risk?
      (a) substantive testing can be decreased which will increase detection risk
      (b) substantive testing can be increased which will decrease detection risk
      (c) substantive testing can be increased which will increase detection risk
      (d) control risk can be increased which will decrease detection risk

60   Which audit procedure can be used to test for the Valuation of Liabilities?
      (a) Perform substantive analytics by calculating the number of units that were sold and
      multiplying by the average per unit sales price for each category of products that are sold.
      (b) Send confirmations to the organizations to whom the outstanding balances are
      owing
      (c) Perform reasonability checks using substantive analytics
      (d) Vouch a sample of purchase orders and invoices from the first and last month of the
      fiscal year.

61   If inherent risk is low, control risk is high and audit risk is medium-high, what is detection risk, according to the risk categorization table in the appendix?
      (a) medium
      (b) high
      (c) low

62   If control risk increases, then this will cause
      (a) substantive testing to increase
      (b) substantive testing to decrease
      (c) inherent risk to increase
      (d) inherent risk to decrease

63   Management has decided to cancel the profit sharing plan which paid a bonus to staff members based on the company's performance. Which of the following statements is true?
      (a) Inherent risk has increased
      (b) Inherent risk has remained unchanged
      (c) Inherent risk has decreased

64   Which audit procedure can be used to test for the Accuracy of Expenses?
      (a) Perform substantive analytics by calculating the number of units that were sold and multiplying by the average per unit sales price for each category of products that are sold.
      (b) Send confirmations to the organizations to whom the outstanding balances are owing
      (c) Transactions that comprise the final balance are checked against the originating documents
      (d) Vouch a sample of purchase orders and invoices from the first and last month of the fiscal year.

65   Which audit procedure can be used to test for the Valuation of Accounts Receivable?
      (a) Perform analytics by calculating if Inventory Turnover has increased or decreased
      (b) Test a sample of customer transactions to see if they appear in the billing system
      (c) Send confirmations to customers that have balances owing
      (d) Perform an inventory count and indicate which items have been in stock for longer than one year

66   What assertion is being tested by the following audit procedure? Send confirmations to customers that have balances owing
      (a) Classification
      (b) Cut-off
      (c) Existence
      (d) Rights

67   The company's information system has been changed in the past year. Which of the following statements is true?
      (a) Audit risk has increased
      (b) Audit risk has remained unchanged
      (c) Audit risk has decreased

68   If inherent risk is medium, control risk is high and audit risk is medium-high, what is
      detection risk, according to the risk categorization table in the appendix?
      (a) low
      (b) high
      (c) medium

69   If inherent risk is high, control risk is high and audit risk is high, what is detection risk,
      according to the risk categorization table in the appendix?
      (a) low
      (b) medium
      (c) high

70   Which audit procedure can be used to test for the Valuation of Accounts Receivable?
      (a) Test a sample of customer transactions to see if they appear in the billing system
      (b) Perform analytics by calculating if Day Sales Inventory has increased or decreased
      (c) Send confirmations to customers that have balances owing
      (d) Perform an inventory count and indicate which items have been in stock for longer
      than one year

71   What assertion is being tested by the following audit procedure? Observe that inventory is
      not moved and missed during inventory count
      (a) Accuracy
      (b) Completeness
      (c) Occurrence
      (d) Valuation

72   Which audit procedure can be used to test for the Rights of Liabilities?
      (a) Perform substantive analytics by calculating the number of units that were sold and
      multiplying by the average per unit sales price for each category of products that are sold.
      (b) Check third party documentation to verify that the amount is owing.
      (c) Perform reasonability checks using substantive analytics
      (d) Perform an inventory count and indicate which items have been in stock for longer
      than one year

73   If inherent risk is low, control risk is medium and audit risk is medium, what is detection risk,
      according to the risk categorization table in the appendix?
      (a) medium
      (b) high
      (c) low

74   If substantive testing increases, then this will cause
      (a) detection risk to decrease
      (b) detection risk to increase
      (c) inherent risk to increase
      (d) inherent risk to decrease

75   If inherent risk is medium, control risk is medium and detection risk is low, what is audit risk,
      according to the risk categorization table in the appendix?
      (a) medium-high
      (b) medium-low
      (c) low

76   If inherent risk is medium, control risk is medium and detection risk is high, what is audit
      risk, according to the risk categorization table in the appendix?
      (a) medium-low
      (b) medium-high
      (c) medium

77   If inherent risk is medium, control risk is low and audit risk is medium, what is detection risk,
      according to the risk categorization table in the appendix?
      (a) high
      (b) low
      (c) low

78   If inherent risk is medium, control risk is low and detection risk is medium, what is audit risk,
      according to the risk categorization table in the appendix?
      (a) medium-high
      (b) medium-low
      (c) low

79   Within the past year, the level of debt that is owed by the organization has increased
      significantly.. Which of the following statements is true?
      (a) Inherent risk has decreased
      (b) Control risk has decreased
      (c) Inherent risk has increased

80   During internal control testing, several major control weaknesses that were noted during
      last year's audit have been mitigated by adding additional internal controls.. Which of the
      following statements is true?
      (a) Control risk has increased
      (b) Control risk has increased
      (c) Inherent risk has decreased

81   If inherent risk is high, control risk is low and detection risk is medium, what is audit risk,
      according to the risk categorization table in the appendix?
      (a) low
      (b) medium
      (c) high

82   Which audit procedure can be used to test for the Accuracy of Revenues?
      (a) Vouch a sample of purchase orders and invoices from the first and last month of the
      fiscal year.
      (b) Check the price that would be incurred to obtain a similar asset from the market
      (c) Send confirmations to the organizations to whom the outstanding balances are
      owing
      (d) Perform substantive analytics by calculating the number of units that were sold and
      multiplying by the average per unit sales price for each category of products that are sold.

83   If inherent risk decreases, then this will cause
      (a) audit risk to increase
      (b) audit risk to decrease
      (c) control risk to decrease
      (d) control risk to increase

84   If inherent risk is low, control risk is high and detection risk is high, what is audit risk, according to the risk categorization table in the appendix?
      (a) medium-low
      (b) medium-high
      (c) medium

85   Management has decided to begin paying a bonus to staff members based on the company's performance. Which of the following statements is true?
      (a) Inherent risk has decreased
      (b) Inherent risk has increased
      (c) Inherent risk has remained unchanged

86   What assertion is being tested by the following audit procedure? Check the price that would be incurred to obtain a similar asset from the market
      (a) Classification
      (b) Cut-off
      (c) Existence
      (d) Valuation

87   If inherent risk is low, control risk is high and audit risk is medium-low, what is detection risk, according to the risk categorization table in the appendix?
      (a) high
      (b) medium
      (c) low

88   What assertion is being tested by the following audit procedure? Perform an inventory count and compare results to a list of inventory
      (a) Classification
      (b) Cut-off
      (c) Existence
      (d) Completeness

89   The economy is currently experiencing a downturn, and this audit client has been affected, as noted by the decrease in net income.. Which of the following statements is true?
      (a) Inherent risk has increased
      (b) Inherent risk has decreased
      (c) Inherent risk has remained unchanged

90   What assertion is being tested by the following audit procedure? Vouch the accounting records by physically locating and examining the assets that are recorded in the ledger.
      (a) Cut-off
      (b) Accuracy
      (c) Existence
      (d) Rights

91   If inherent risk is medium, control risk is medium and detection risk is medium, what is audit risk, according to the risk categorization table in the appendix?
      (a) medium
      (b) high
      (c) high

92 During internal control testing, several major control weaknesses were discovered by the internal audit team.. Which of the following statements is true?
(a) Control risk has increased
(b) Inherent risk has decreased
(c) Control risk has decreased

93 Which audit procedure can be used to test for the Completeness of Accounts Receivable?
(a) Test a sample of customer transactions to see if they appear in the billing system
(b) Send confirmations to customers that have balances owing
(c) Perform an inventory count on items that were selected from a list of inventory
(d) Perform analytics by calculating if Day Sales Inventory has increased or decreased

94 Which audit procedure can be used to test for the Accuracy of Expenses?
(a) Perform substantive analytics by calculating the number of units that were sold and multiplying by the average per unit sales price for each category of products that are sold.
(b) Send confirmations to the organizations to whom the outstanding balances are owing
(c) Vouch accounting records to the underlying third party purchase order and invoice
(d) Vouch a sample of purchase orders and invoices from the first and last month of the fiscal year.

95 The company's information system has been changed in the past year. Which of the following statements is true?
(a) Control risk has decreased
(b) Control risk has increased
(c) Inherent risk has decreased

96 If inherent risk is high, control risk is low and detection risk is low, what is audit risk, according to the risk categorization table in the appendix?
(a) medium-high
(b) medium-low
(c) low

97 In the past year, the audit client finished repaying a contractual debt arrangement which required that their debt was to be repaid in full if certain key financial performance ratios were not maintained. . Which of the following statements is true?
(a) Inherent risk has increased
(b) Inherent risk
(c) Inherent risk has remained unchanged

98 If inherent risk is low, control risk is low and audit risk is medium-low, what is detection risk, according to the risk categorization table in the appendix?
(a) medium
(b) low
(c) high

99 What assertion is being tested by the following audit procedure? Perform a reasonability analysis.
  (a) Rights
  (b) Completeness
  (c) Existence
  (d) Cut-off

100 If control risk decreases, then this will cause
  (a) detection risk to decrease
  (b) inherent risk to decrease
  (c) detection risk to increase
  (d) inherent risk to increase

101 What assertion is being tested by the following audit procedure? Send confirmations to the organizations to whom the outstanding balances are owing
  (a) Classification
  (b) Cut-off
  (c) Existence
  (d) Valuation

102 If inherent risk is high, control risk is medium and audit risk is high, what is detection risk, according to the risk categorization table in the appendix?
  (a) medium
  (b) low
  (c) high

103 What assertion is being tested by the following audit procedure? Send confirmations to customers that have balances owing
  (a) Accuracy
  (b) Existence
  (c) Occurrence
  (d) Valuation

104 Which audit procedure can be used to test for the Existence of Inventory?
  (a) Perform an inventory count and compare results to a list of inventory
  (b) Perform an inventory count on items that are held on consignment
  (c) Perform an inventory count and indicate which items have been in stock for longer than one year
  (d) Observe that inventory is not moved and double-counted during inventory count

105 In the past year, the audit client has signed a contractual agreement which requires that their debt must be repaid in full if certain key financial performance ratios are not maintained. . Which of the following statements is true?
  (a) Inherent risk has increased
  (b) Inherent risk has remained unchanged
  (c) Inherent risk has increased

106 Which audit procedure can be used to test for the Accuracy of Revenues?
(a) Vouch a sample of customer transactions from the first and last month of the fiscal year.
(b) Check the price that would be incurred to obtain a similar asset from the market
(c) Vouch accounting records to the underlying third party documentation
(d) Send confirmations to the organizations to whom the outstanding balances are owing

107 What assertion is being tested by the following audit procedure? Perform an inventory count on items that are held on consignment
(a) Rights
(b) Occurrence
(c) Accuracy
(d) Valuation

108 If control risk decreases, then this will cause
(a) substantive testing to increase
(b) inherent risk to decrease
(c) inherent risk to increase
(d) substantive testing to decrease

109 Which audit procedure can be used to test for the Existence of Assets?
(a) Vouch the accounting records by physically locating and examining the assets that are recorded in the ledger.
(b) Test a sample of customer transactions to see if they appear in the billing system
(c) Send confirmations to customers that have balances owing
(d) Perform analytics by calculating if Day Sales Inventory has increased or decreased

110 The internal audit reports reveal that some employees were found to have stolen company assets in the past year. . Which of the following statements is true?
(a) Inherent risk has decreased
(b) Control risk has decreased
(c) Inherent risk has increased

111 What assertion is being tested by the following audit procedure? Vouch a sample of purchase orders and invoices from the first and last month of the fiscal year.
(a) Rights
(b) Cut-off
(c) Existence
(d) Classification

112 If inherent risk is low, control risk is low and audit risk is low, what is detection risk, according to the risk categorization table in the appendix?
(a) high
(b) medium
(c) low

113 If inherent risk is medium, control risk is low and audit risk is medium-low, what is detection risk, according to the risk categorization table in the appendix?
(a) medium
(b) high
(c) high

114 What assertion is being tested by the following audit procedure? Vouch a sample of the accounting records to the third-party delivery documents.
(a) Existence
(b) Valuation
(c) Classification
(d) Occurrence

115 Which audit procedure can be used to test for the Rights of Accounts Receivable?
(a) Test a sample of customer transactions to see if they appear in the billing system
(b) Send confirmations to customers that have balances owing
(c) Perform an inventory count on items that are held on consignment
(d) Perform analytics by calculating if Day Sales Inventory has increased or decreased

116 What assertion is being tested by the following audit procedure? Vouch accounting records to the underlying third party documentation
(a) Accuracy
(b) Existence
(c) Rights
(d) Cut-off

117 Which audit procedure can be used to test for the Cut-off of Revenues?
(a) Perform an inventory count and indicate which items have been in stock for longer than one year
(b) Vouch a sample of customer transactions from the first and last month of the fiscal year.
(c) Check the price that would be incurred to obtain a similar asset from the market
(d) Send confirmations to the organizations to whom the outstanding balances are owing

118 What assertion is being tested by the following audit procedure? Perform analytics by calculating if Day Sales Inventory has increased or decreased
(a) Accuracy
(b) Valuation
(c) Occurrence
(d) Existence

119 If inherent risk is high, control risk is low and audit risk is medium-low, what is detection risk, according to the risk categorization table in the appendix?
(a) high
(b) low
(c) medium

120 If inherent risk is low, control risk is medium and detection risk is high, what is audit risk, according to the risk categorization table in the appendix?
(a) medium
(b) high
(c) high

121 Which audit procedure can be used to test for the Occurrence of Revenues?
(a) Send confirmations to customers that have balances owing
(b) Perform analytics by calculating if Day Sales Inventory has increased or decreased
(c) Perform analytics by calculating if Inventory Turnover has increased or decreased
(d) Vouch a sample of the accounting records to the third-party delivery documents.

122 If inherent risk is low, control risk is low and detection risk is high, what is audit risk, according to the risk categorization table in the appendix?
(a) medium-high
(b) medium-low
(c) low

123 What assertion is being tested by the following audit procedure? Test a sample of customer transactions to see if they appear in the billing system
(a) Cut-off
(b) Accuracy
(c) Completeness
(d) Existence

124 Which audit procedure can be used to test for the Completeness of Revenues?
(a) Vouch a sample of customer transactions from the first and last month of the fiscal year.
(b) Vouch a sample of purchase orders and invoices from the first and last month of the fiscal year.
(c) Perform reasonability checks using substantive analytics
(d) Send confirmations to the organizations to whom the outstanding balances are owing

125 What assertion is being tested by the following audit procedure? Perform reasonability checks using substantive analytics
(a) Valuation
(b) Rights
(c) Completeness
(d) Classification

126 Which audit procedure can be used to test for the Rights of Inventory?
(a) Perform an inventory count and compare results to a list of inventory
(b) Perform an inventory count on items that were selected from a list of inventory
(c) Perform an inventory count on items that are held on consignment
(d) Perform an inventory count and indicate which items have been in stock for longer than one year

127   If inherent risk is medium, control risk is low and detection risk is high, what is audit risk, according to the risk categorization table in the appendix?
      (a) low
      (b) high
      (c) medium

128   If inherent risk is low, control risk is high and audit risk is medium, what is detection risk, according to the risk categorization table in the appendix?
      (a) low
      (b) high
      (c) medium

129   The client has added discontinued their line of diamonds from their collections of fashion accessories. . Which of the following statements is true?
      (a) Inherent risk has increased
      (b) Inherent risk has decreased
      (c) Detection risk has increased

130   If inherent risk is medium, control risk is high and audit risk is high, what is detection risk, according to the risk categorization table in the appendix?
      (a) medium
      (b) low
      (c) high

131   If inherent risk is low, control risk is low and audit risk is low, what is detection risk, according to the risk categorization table in the appendix?
      (a) low
      (b) high
      (c) medium

132   What assertion is being tested by the following audit procedure? Observe that inventory is not moved and double-counted during inventory count
      (a) Cut-off
      (b) Accuracy
      (c) Existence
      (d) Rights

133   If inherent risk increases, then this will cause
      (a) audit risk to decrease
      (b) control risk to increase
      (c) control risk to decrease
      (d) audit risk to increase

134   If inherent risk is low, control risk is medium and detection risk is medium, what is audit risk, according to the risk categorization table in the appendix?
      (a) medium-high
      (b) medium
      (c) medium-low

135 If inherent risk is high, control risk is medium and detection risk is low, what is audit risk, according to the risk categorization table in the appendix?
(a) low
(b) high
(c) medium

136 The financial institution has sold all of its in derivative investments which had been arranged with complex contractual arrangements.. Which of the following statements is true?
(a) Inherent risk has decreased
(b) Inherent risk has increased
(c) Inherent risk has remained unchanged

137 If inherent risk is medium, control risk is medium and audit risk is medium-high, what is detection risk, according to the risk categorization table in the appendix?
(a) high
(b) low
(c) low

138 The company's information system which was fully implemented two years ago has continued to be used in the past year.. Which of the following statements is true?
(a) Detection risk has decreased
(b) Inherent risk has remained unchanged
(c) Detection risk has increased

139 The company's information system which was fully implemented two years ago has continued to be used in the past year.. Which of the following statements is true?
(a) Audit risk has remained unchanged
(b) Audit risk has decreased
(c) Audit risk has increased

140 If inherent risk is high, control risk is high and detection risk is medium, what is audit risk, according to the risk categorization table in the appendix?
(a) medium
(b) high
(c) low

141 Upon accepting a new client, the auditor has contacted the previous auditors and found that the client had no disagreements with the auditors.. Which of the following statements is true?
(a) Inherent risk has increased
(b) Inherent risk has decreased
(c) Control risk has increased

142 What assertion is being tested by the following audit procedure? Transactions that comprise the final balance are checked against the originating documents
(a) Rights
(b) Completeness
(c) Existence
(d) Cut-off

143   If inherent risk is high, control risk is medium and audit risk is medium-high, what is detection risk, according to the risk categorization table in the appendix?
(a) medium
(b) high
(c) high

144   If inherent risk is high, control risk is high and audit risk is high, what is detection risk, according to the risk categorization table in the appendix?
(a) medium
(b) high
(c) low

145   Which audit procedure can be used to test for the Occurrence of Expenses?
(a) Send confirmations to customers that have balances owing
(b) Perform analytics by calculating if Day Sales Inventory has increased or decreased
(c) Vouch accounting records to the underlying third party purchase order and invoice
(d) Perform analytics by calculating if Inventory Turnover has increased or decreased

146   What assertion is being tested by the following audit procedure? Vouch accounting records to the underlying third party purchase order and invoice
(a) Occurrence
(b) Existence
(c) Rights
(d) Accuracy

147   Upon accepting a new client, the auditor has contacted the previous auditors and found that the client had significant disagreements with the auditors, which lead the client to seek out a different audit firm.. Which of the following statements is true?
(a) Inherent risk has decreased
(b) Inherent risk has increased
(c) Control risk has decreased

148   The client has added genuine diamonds to their collections of fashion accessories. . Which of the following statements is true?
(a) Inherent risk has decreased
(b) Inherent risk has increased
(c) Detection risk has decreased

149   If substantive testing decreases, then this will cause
(a) detection risk to decrease
(b) inherent risk to decrease
(c) detection risk to increase
(d) inherent risk to increase

150   If inherent risk is high, control risk is high and detection risk is low, what is audit risk, according to the risk categorization table in the appendix?
(a) medium-low
(b) medium-high
(c) medium

FULL CYCLE ACCOUNTING CASES

A Brief Review...
How Financial Statements are Prepared

The financial statements are composed primarily of the balance sheet and income statement. A Balance Sheet displays a snapshot of all assets, liabilities, and shareholders' equity as of a certain point in time, which is often the end of a calendar year.
An Income Statement displays all revenues and expenses over the course of an extended period of time, which is often from the beginning to the end of a calendar year.

Types of Accounts

Debits are represented by "DR" and credits are represented by "CR".

Asset accounts represent money or any other items that the company owns or something which will provide the company with a future benefit. When assets are increased, they are debited. When assets are decreased, they are credited.

Liability accounts represent money or any other amounts that the company does not own. When liabilities are increased, they are credited. When liabilities are decreased, they are debited.

Revenue accounts represent amounts that the company has earned from their regular operations. When revenues are increased, they are credited. When revenues are decreased, they are debited.

Expense accounts represent amounts that the company has spent in the course of their regular operations. When expenses are increased, they are debited. When expenses are decreased, they are credited.

Contra accounts represent a reduction to an account that is tracked separately. Examples of contra accounts are sales returns, allowance for doubtful accounts, and accumulated depreciation on the property plant & equipment accounts. Debits and credits to contra accounts are posted in a reverse manner, in comparison to the account to which they apply.

For each transaction, the General Journal and General Ledger are updated. After both are completed for the full year, the total net balances from each account in the general ledger are summarized in a trial balance.

Journal Entries are posted to the General Journal as follows:

Transaction #1
Date
Description
DR Account $XXX.XX
    CR Account $XXX.XX

Journal Entries are posted to the General Ledger as follows:

Asset Account "A"
DR Transaction Date $XXX.XX
DR Transaction Date $XXX.XX
DR Transaction Date $XXX.XX
CR Transaction Date $XXX.XX

Liability Account "B"
CR Transaction Date $XXX.XX
CR Transaction Date $XXX.XX

Equity Account "C"
CR Transaction Date $XXX.XX
CR Transaction Date $XXX.XX

Revenue Account "D"
CR Transaction Date $XXX.XX
CR Transaction Date $XXX.XX

Expense Account "E"
DR Transaction Date $XXX.XX
DR Transaction Date $XXX.XX

At the end of the calendar year, each of the account totals is placed into the trial balance, which summarizes the transactions before they are summarized further in the financial statements.

This can be displayed by showing each account's debit or credit position, or alternatively, a positive amount signifies a debit balance, whereas a negative amount, shown in brackets, signifies a credit amount.

This trial balance is then summarized further by grouping the information into the balance sheet, income statement, statement of retained earnings, and cash flow statement.

The following section includes transactions which affect the following accounts:

Cash
Accounts Receivable
Allowance for Doubtful Accounts
Inventory
Equipment
Accumulated Depreciation: Eqmt
Building
Accumulated Depreciation: Bldg
Prepaid Expense
Accounts Payable
Business Loan
Unearned Revenue
Retained Earnings
Owner's Equity
Service Revenue
Sales Revenue
Sales Returns
Cost of Goods Sold
Salaries Expense
Rent Expense
Bad Debt Expense
Depreciation Expense
Insurance Expense
Interest Expense

Case #1

Date	Amount	Transaction
01/01	0.00	Started new business. All Accounts are nil.
01/05	1,356,364.00	Bought inventory
01/08	4,069,092.00	Sold services
01/10	1,627,636.80	Sold all inventory
01/24	32,552.74	2% of Sales were returned
02/01	339,091.00	Paid Rent for the current month
02/05	1,627,636.80	Bought inventory
02/08	4,069,092.00	Sold services
02/10	2,278,691.52	Sold all inventory
02/15	813,818.40	Paid employees
02/24	45,573.83	2% of Sales were returned
02/27	598,319.29	Allowance for Doubtful Accounts is estimated to be 5% of accounts receivable balance
02/30	813,818.40	Paid employees
03/01	339,091.00	Paid Rent for the current month
03/05	2,034,546.00	Bought inventory
03/08	4,069,092.00	Sold services
03/10	2,848,364.40	Sold all inventory
03/15	813,818.40	Paid employees
03/24	56,967.29	2% of Sales were returned
03/26	8,138,184.00	Settle all accounts payable
03/27	941,343.74	Allowance for Doubtful Accounts is estimated to be 5% of accounts receivable balance
03/28	17,885,531.12	Received cash from 95% of accts receivable
03/29	1,539,663.03	Recognized bad debt expense for all amounts in Allowance for Doubtful Accounts
03/30	813,818.40	Paid employees
04/01	339,091.00	Paid Rent for the current month
04/05	2,441,455.20	Bought inventory
04/06	8,138,184.00	Bought equipment 5yr life
04/08	4,069,092.00	Sold services
04/10	3,418,037.28	Sold all inventory
04/15	813,818.40	Paid employees
04/24	68,360.75	2% of Sales were returned
04/26	12,546,367.00	Settle all accounts payable
04/27	341,022.46	Allowance for Doubtful Accounts is estimated to be 5% of accounts receivable balance
04/28	6,479,426.78	Received cash from 95% of accts receivable
04/29	341,022.46	Recognized bad debt expense for all amounts in Allowance for Doubtful Accounts
04/30	813,818.40	Paid employees
05/01	339,091.00	Paid Rent for the current month
05/05	2,848,364.40	Bought inventory
05/06	135,636.40	Depreciate equipment for 1 month
05/08	4,069,092.00	Sold services
05/10	3,987,710.16	Sold all inventory
05/15	813,818.40	Paid employees
05/24	79,754.20	2% of Sales were returned
05/26	4,815,092.20	Settle all accounts payable

05/27	398,852.40	Allowance for Doubtful Accounts is estimated to be 5% of accounts receivable balance
05/28	7,578,195.56	Received cash from 95% of accts receivable
05/29	398,852.40	Recognized bad debt expense for all amounts in Allowance for Doubtful Accounts
05/30	813,818.40	Paid employees
06/01	339,091.00	Paid Rent for the current month
06/03	101,727,300.00	Received a business loan for building payable monthly 5yr term @5%
06/04	101,727,300.00	Bought building 20yr life
06/05	3,255,273.60	Bought inventory
06/06	135,636.40	Depreciate equipment for 1 month
06/08	4,069,092.00	Sold services
06/10	4,557,383.04	Sold all inventory
06/15	813,818.40	Paid employees
06/24	91,147.66	2% of Sales were returned
06/26	5,222,001.40	Settle all accounts payable
06/27	426,766.37	Allowance for Doubtful Accounts is estimated to be 5% of accounts receivable balance
06/28	8,108,561.01	Received cash from 95% of accts receivable
06/29	426,766.37	Recognized bad debt expense for all amounts in Allowance for Doubtful Accounts
06/30	813,818.40	Paid employees
07/01	20,345,460.00	Owner invested cash into the business
07/02	423,863.75	Paid 1 month of interest per Loan Amortization Schedule
07/03	1,495,855.90	Paid principal portion based on Loan Amortization Schedule
07/04	423,863.75	Depreciate building for 1 month
07/05	3,662,182.80	Bought inventory
07/06	135,636.40	Depreciate equipment for 1 month
07/08	4,069,092.00	Sold services
07/10	5,127,055.92	Sold all inventory
07/15	813,818.40	Paid employees
07/24	102,541.12	2% of Sales were returned
07/26	5,289,819.60	Settle all accounts payable
07/27	454,680.34	Allowance for Doubtful Accounts is estimated to be 5% of accounts receivable balance
07/28	8,638,926.46	Received cash from 95% of accts receivable
07/29	454,680.34	Recognized bad debt expense for all amounts in Allowance for Doubtful Accounts
07/30	813,818.40	Paid employees
08/02	417,631.02	Paid 1 month of interest per Loan Amortization Schedule
08/03	1,502,088.63	Paid principal portion based on Loan Amortization Schedule
08/04	423,863.75	Depreciate building for 1 month
08/05	4,069,092.00	Bought inventory
08/06	135,636.40	Depreciate equipment for 1 month
08/08	4,069,092.00	Sold services
08/10	5,696,728.80	Sold all inventory
08/11	4,882,910.40	Prepaid for 12 months of insurance
08/15	813,818.40	Paid employees
08/24	113,934.58	2% of Sales were returned
08/26	10,579,639.20	Settle all accounts payable
08/27	482,594.31	Allowance for Doubtful Accounts is estimated to be 5% of accounts receivable balance
08/28	9,169,291.91	Received cash from 95% of accts receivable
08/29	482,594.31	Recognized bad debt expense for all amounts in Allowance for Doubtful Accounts

08/30	813,818.40	Paid employees
09/02	411,372.31	Paid 1 month of interest per Loan Amortization Schedule
09/03	1,508,347.33	Paid principal portion based on Loan Amortization Schedule
09/04	423,863.75	Depreciate building for 1 month
09/05	4,476,001.20	Bought inventory
09/06	135,636.40	Depreciate equipment for 1 month
09/08	4,069,092.00	Sold services
09/10	6,266,401.68	Sold all inventory
09/11	406,909.20	Amortize prepaid insurance for 1 month
09/15	813,818.40	Paid employees
09/24	125,328.03	2% of Sales were returned
09/26	6,103,638.00	Settle all accounts payable
09/27	510,508.28	Allowance for Doubtful Accounts is estimated to be 5% of accounts receivable balance
09/28	9,699,657.37	Received cash from 95% of accts receivable
09/29	510,508.28	Recognized bad debt expense for all amounts in Allowance for Doubtful Accounts
09/30	813,818.40	Paid employees
10/02	405,087.53	Paid 1 month of interest per Loan Amortization Schedule
10/03	1,514,632.11	Paid principal portion based on Loan Amortization Schedule
10/04	423,863.75	Depreciate building for 1 month
10/05	4,882,910.40	Bought inventory
10/06	135,636.40	Depreciate equipment for 1 month
10/08	4,069,092.00	Sold services
10/10	6,836,074.56	Sold all inventory
10/11	406,909.20	Amortize prepaid insurance for 1 month
10/13	16,276,368.00	Received upfront payment for a large project to be fulfilled next month
10/15	813,818.40	Paid employees
10/24	136,721.49	2% of Sales were returned
10/26	6,510,547.20	Settle all accounts payable
10/27	538,422.25	Allowance for Doubtful Accounts is estimated to be 5% of accounts receivable balance
10/28	10,230,022.82	Received cash from 95% of accts receivable
10/29	538,422.25	Recognized bad debt expense for all amounts in Allowance for Doubtful Accounts
10/30	813,818.40	Paid employees
11/02	398,776.57	Paid 1 month of interest per Loan Amortization Schedule
11/03	1,520,943.08	Paid principal portion based on Loan Amortization Schedule
11/04	423,863.75	Depreciate building for 1 month
11/05	5,289,819.60	Bought inventory
11/06	135,636.40	Depreciate equipment for 1 month
11/08	4,069,092.00	Sold services
11/10	7,405,747.44	Sold all inventory
11/11	406,909.20	Amortize prepaid insurance for 1 month
11/13	16,276,368.00	Provide the services for the large sale that was paid up front last month
11/15	813,818.40	Paid employees
11/20	4,069,092.00	Paid a dividend to the owner
11/24	148,114.95	2% of Sales were returned
11/26	6,917,456.40	Settle all accounts payable
11/27	566,336.22	Allowance for Doubtful Accounts is estimated to be 5% of accounts receivable balance
11/28	10,760,388.27	Received cash from 95% of accts receivable
11/29	566,336.22	Recognized bad debt expense for all amounts in Allowance for Doubtful Accounts

11/30	813,818.40	Paid employees
12/02	392,439.30	Paid 1 month of interest per Loan Amortization Schedule
12/03	1,527,280.34	Paid principal portion based on Loan Amortization Schedule
12/04	423,863.75	Depreciate building for 1 month
12/05	5,696,728.80	Bought inventory
12/06	135,636.40	Depreciate equipment for 1 month
12/08	4,069,092.00	Sold services
12/10	7,975,420.32	Sold all inventory
12/11	406,909.20	Amortize prepaid insurance for 1 month
12/15	813,818.40	Paid employees
12/24	159,508.41	2% of Sales were returned
12/26	7,324,365.60	Settle all accounts payable
12/27	594,250.20	Allowance for Doubtful Accounts is estimated to be 5% of accounts receivable balance
12/28	11,290,753.71	Received cash from 95% of accts receivable
12/29	594,250.20	Recognized bad debt expense for all amounts in Allowance for Doubtful Accounts
12/30	813,818.40	Paid employees
12/31	48,139,294.96	Closing entry to post all revenues and expenses to retained earnings

Loan Amortization Schedule

	60months		5%		

Month	Payment	Interest	Principal	Balance
				101,727,300.00
1	1,919,719.65	423,863.75	1,495,855.90	100,231,444.10
2	1,919,719.65	417,631.02	1,502,088.63	98,729,355.47
3	1,919,719.65	411,372.31	1,508,347.33	97,221,008.14
4	1,919,719.65	405,087.53	1,514,632.11	95,706,376.03
5	1,919,719.65	398,776.57	1,520,943.08	94,185,432.95
6	1,919,719.65	392,439.30	1,527,280.34	92,658,152.61
7	1,919,719.65	386,075.64	1,533,644.01	91,124,508.60
8	1,919,719.65	379,685.45	1,540,034.19	89,584,474.40
9	1,919,719.65	373,268.64	1,546,451.00	88,038,023.40
10	1,919,719.65	366,825.10	1,552,894.55	86,485,128.85
11	1,919,719.65	360,354.70	1,559,364.94	84,925,763.91
12	1,919,719.65	353,857.35	1,565,862.30	83,359,901.61
13	1,919,719.65	347,332.92	1,572,386.72	81,787,514.89
14	1,919,719.65	340,781.31	1,578,938.33	80,208,576.56
15	1,919,719.65	334,202.40	1,585,517.24	78,623,059.31
16	1,919,719.65	327,596.08	1,592,123.57	77,030,935.75
17	1,919,719.65	320,962.23	1,598,757.41	75,432,178.33
18	1,919,719.65	314,300.74	1,605,418.90	73,826,759.43
19	1,919,719.65	307,611.50	1,612,108.15	72,214,651.28
20	1,919,719.65	300,894.38	1,618,825.27	70,595,826.01
21	1,919,719.65	294,149.28	1,625,570.37	68,970,255.64
22	1,919,719.65	287,376.07	1,632,343.58	67,337,912.06
23	1,919,719.65	280,574.63	1,639,145.01	65,698,767.05
24	1,919,719.65	273,744.86	1,645,974.78	64,052,792.27
25	1,919,719.65	266,886.63	1,652,833.01	62,399,959.25
26	1,919,719.65	259,999.83	1,659,719.82	60,740,239.44
27	1,919,719.65	253,084.33	1,666,635.32	59,073,604.12
28	1,919,719.65	246,140.02	1,673,579.63	57,400,024.49
29	1,919,719.65	239,166.77	1,680,552.88	55,719,471.62
30	1,919,719.65	232,164.47	1,687,555.18	54,031,916.44
31	1,919,719.65	225,132.99	1,694,586.66	52,337,329.77
32	1,919,719.65	218,072.21	1,701,647.44	50,635,682.34
33	1,919,719.65	210,982.01	1,708,737.64	48,926,944.70
34	1,919,719.65	203,862.27	1,715,857.38	47,211,087.32
35	1,919,719.65	196,712.86	1,723,006.78	45,488,080.54
36	1,919,719.65	189,533.67	1,730,185.98	43,757,894.56
37	1,919,719.65	182,324.56	1,737,395.09	42,020,499.48
38	1,919,719.65	175,085.41	1,744,634.23	40,275,865.24
39	1,919,719.65	167,816.11	1,751,903.54	38,523,961.70
40	1,919,719.65	160,516.51	1,759,203.14	36,764,758.56
41	1,919,719.65	153,186.49	1,766,533.15	34,998,225.41
42	1,919,719.65	145,825.94	1,773,893.71	33,224,331.71
43	1,919,719.65	138,434.72	1,781,284.93	31,443,046.77
44	1,919,719.65	131,012.69	1,788,706.95	29,654,339.82
45	1,919,719.65	123,559.75	1,796,159.90	27,858,179.93
46	1,919,719.65	116,075.75	1,803,643.90	26,054,536.03
47	1,919,719.65	108,560.57	1,811,159.08	24,243,376.95
48	1,919,719.65	101,014.07	1,818,705.58	22,424,671.37
49	1,919,719.65	93,436.13	1,826,283.52	20,598,387.86
50	1,919,719.65	85,826.62	1,833,893.03	18,764,494.83
51	1,919,719.65	78,185.40	1,841,534.25	16,922,960.58
52	1,919,719.65	70,512.34	1,849,207.31	15,073,753.27
53	1,919,719.65	62,807.31	1,856,912.34	13,216,840.93
54	1,919,719.65	55,070.17	1,864,649.48	11,352,191.45
55	1,919,719.65	47,300.80	1,872,418.85	9,479,772.60
56	1,919,719.65	39,499.05	1,880,220.59	7,599,552.01
57	1,919,719.65	31,664.80	1,888,054.85	5,711,497.16
58	1,919,719.65	23,797.90	1,895,921.74	3,815,575.42
59	1,919,719.65	15,898.23	1,903,821.42	1,911,754.00
60	1,919,719.65	7,965.64	1,911,754.00	0.00

Case #2

Date	Amount	Transaction
01/01	0.00	Started new business. All Accounts are nil.
01/05	1,532,691.00	Bought inventory
01/08	4,598,073.00	Sold services
01/10	1,839,229.20	Sold all inventory
01/24	36,784.58	2% of Sales were returned
02/01	383,172.75	Paid Rent for the current month
02/05	1,839,229.20	Bought inventory
02/08	4,598,073.00	Sold services
02/10	2,574,920.88	Sold all inventory
02/15	919,614.60	Paid employees
02/24	51,498.42	2% of Sales were returned
02/27	676,100.65	Allowance for Doubtful Accounts is estimated to be 5% of accounts receivable balance
02/30	919,614.60	Paid employees
03/01	383,172.75	Paid Rent for the current month
03/05	2,299,036.50	Bought inventory
03/08	4,598,073.00	Sold services
03/10	3,218,651.10	Sold all inventory
03/15	919,614.60	Paid employees
03/24	64,373.02	2% of Sales were returned
03/26	9,196,146.00	Settle all accounts payable
03/27	1,063,718.21	Allowance for Doubtful Accounts is estimated to be 5% of accounts receivable balance
03/28	20,210,645.95	Received cash from 95% of accts receivable
03/29	1,739,818.86	Recognized bad debt expense for all amounts in Allowance for Doubtful Accounts
03/30	919,614.60	Paid employees
04/01	383,172.75	Paid Rent for the current month
04/05	2,758,843.80	Bought inventory
04/06	9,196,146.00	Bought equipment 5yr life
04/08	4,598,073.00	Sold services
04/10	3,862,381.32	Sold all inventory
04/15	919,614.60	Paid employees
04/24	77,247.63	2% of Sales were returned
04/26	14,177,391.75	Settle all accounts payable
04/27	385,355.30	Allowance for Doubtful Accounts is estimated to be 5% of accounts receivable balance
04/28	7,321,750.74	Received cash from 95% of accts receivable
04/29	385,355.30	Recognized bad debt expense for all amounts in Allowance for Doubtful Accounts
04/30	919,614.60	Paid employees
05/01	383,172.75	Paid Rent for the current month
05/05	3,218,651.10	Bought inventory
05/06	153,269.10	Depreciate equipment for 1 month
05/08	4,598,073.00	Sold services

05/10	4,506,111.54	Sold all inventory
05/15	919,614.60	Paid employees
05/24	90,122.23	2% of Sales were returned
05/26	5,441,053.05	Settle all accounts payable
05/27	450,703.12	Allowance for Doubtful Accounts is estimated to be 5% of accounts receivable balance
05/28	8,563,359.19	Received cash from 95% of accts receivable
05/29	450,703.12	Recognized bad debt expense for all amounts in Allowance for Doubtful Accounts
05/30	919,614.60	Paid employees
06/01	383,172.75	Paid Rent for the current month
06/03	114,951,825.00	Received a business loan for building payable monthly 5yr term @5%
06/04	114,951,825.00	Bought building 20yr life
06/05	3,678,458.40	Bought inventory
06/06	153,269.10	Depreciate equipment for 1 month
06/08	4,598,073.00	Sold services
06/10	5,149,841.76	Sold all inventory
06/15	919,614.60	Paid employees
06/24	102,996.84	2% of Sales were returned
06/26	5,900,860.35	Settle all accounts payable
06/27	482,245.90	Allowance for Doubtful Accounts is estimated to be 5% of accounts receivable balance
06/28	9,162,672.02	Received cash from 95% of accts receivable
06/29	482,245.90	Recognized bad debt expense for all amounts in Allowance for Doubtful Accounts
06/30	919,614.60	Paid employees
07/01	22,990,365.00	Owner invested cash into the business
07/02	478,965.94	Paid 1 month of interest per Loan Amortization Schedule
07/03	1,690,316.81	Paid principal portion based on Loan Amortization Schedule
07/04	478,965.94	Depreciate building for 1 month
07/05	4,138,265.70	Bought inventory
07/06	153,269.10	Depreciate equipment for 1 month
07/08	4,598,073.00	Sold services
07/10	5,793,571.98	Sold all inventory
07/15	919,614.60	Paid employees
07/24	115,871.44	2% of Sales were returned
07/26	5,977,494.90	Settle all accounts payable
07/27	513,788.68	Allowance for Doubtful Accounts is estimated to be 5% of accounts receivable balance
07/28	9,761,984.86	Received cash from 95% of accts receivable
07/29	513,788.68	Recognized bad debt expense for all amounts in Allowance for Doubtful Accounts
07/30	919,614.60	Paid employees
08/02	471,922.95	Paid 1 month of interest per Loan Amortization Schedule
08/03	1,697,359.80	Paid principal portion based on Loan Amortization Schedule
08/04	478,965.94	Depreciate building for 1 month
08/05	4,598,073.00	Bought inventory
08/06	153,269.10	Depreciate equipment for 1 month
08/08	4,598,073.00	Sold services

08/10	6,437,302.20	Sold all inventory
08/11	5,517,687.60	Prepaid for 12 months of insurance
08/15	919,614.60	Paid employees
08/24	128,746.04	2% of Sales were returned
08/26	11,954,989.80	Settle all accounts payable
08/27	545,331.46	Allowance for Doubtful Accounts is estimated to be 5% of accounts receivable balance
08/28	10,361,297.70	Received cash from 95% of accts receivable
08/29	545,331.46	Recognized bad debt expense for all amounts in Allowance for Doubtful Accounts
08/30	919,614.60	Paid employees
09/02	464,850.62	Paid 1 month of interest per Loan Amortization Schedule
09/03	1,704,432.13	Paid principal portion based on Loan Amortization Schedule
09/04	478,965.94	Depreciate building for 1 month
09/05	5,057,880.30	Bought inventory
09/06	153,269.10	Depreciate equipment for 1 month
09/08	4,598,073.00	Sold services
09/10	7,081,032.42	Sold all inventory
09/11	459,807.30	Amortize prepaid insurance for 1 month
09/15	919,614.60	Paid employees
09/24	141,620.65	2% of Sales were returned
09/26	6,897,109.50	Settle all accounts payable
09/27	576,874.24	Allowance for Doubtful Accounts is estimated to be 5% of accounts receivable balance
09/28	10,960,610.53	Received cash from 95% of accts receivable
09/29	576,874.24	Recognized bad debt expense for all amounts in Allowance for Doubtful Accounts
09/30	919,614.60	Paid employees
10/02	457,748.82	Paid 1 month of interest per Loan Amortization Schedule
10/03	1,711,533.93	Paid principal portion based on Loan Amortization Schedule
10/04	478,965.94	Depreciate building for 1 month
10/05	5,517,687.60	Bought inventory
10/06	153,269.10	Depreciate equipment for 1 month
10/08	4,598,073.00	Sold services
10/10	7,724,762.64	Sold all inventory
10/11	459,807.30	Amortize prepaid insurance for 1 month
10/13	18,392,292.00	Received upfront payment for a large project to be fulfilled next month
10/15	919,614.60	Paid employees
10/24	154,495.25	2% of Sales were returned
10/26	7,356,916.80	Settle all accounts payable
10/27	608,417.02	Allowance for Doubtful Accounts is estimated to be 5% of accounts receivable balance
10/28	11,559,923.37	Received cash from 95% of accts receivable
10/29	608,417.02	Recognized bad debt expense for all amounts in Allowance for Doubtful Accounts
10/30	919,614.60	Paid employees
11/02	450,617.43	Paid 1 month of interest per Loan Amortization Schedule
11/03	1,718,665.32	Paid principal portion based on Loan Amortization Schedule
11/04	478,965.94	Depreciate building for 1 month

11/05	5,977,494.90	Bought inventory
11/06	153,269.10	Depreciate equipment for 1 month
11/08	4,598,073.00	Sold services
11/10	8,368,492.86	Sold all inventory
11/11	459,807.30	Amortize prepaid insurance for 1 month
11/13	18,392,292.00	Provide the services for the large sale that was paid up front last month
11/15	919,614.60	Paid employees
11/20	4,598,073.00	Paid a dividend to the owner
11/24	167,369.86	2% of Sales were returned
11/26	7,816,724.10	Settle all accounts payable
11/27	639,959.80	Allowance for Doubtful Accounts is estimated to be 5% of accounts receivable balance
11/28	12,159,236.20	Received cash from 95% of accts receivable
11/29	639,959.80	Recognized bad debt expense for all amounts in Allowance for Doubtful Accounts
11/30	919,614.60	Paid employees
12/02	443,456.32	Paid 1 month of interest per Loan Amortization Schedule
12/03	1,725,826.43	Paid principal portion based on Loan Amortization Schedule
12/04	478,965.94	Depreciate building for 1 month
12/05	6,437,302.20	Bought inventory
12/06	153,269.10	Depreciate equipment for 1 month
12/08	4,598,073.00	Sold services
12/10	9,012,223.08	Sold all inventory
12/11	459,807.30	Amortize prepaid insurance for 1 month
12/15	919,614.60	Paid employees
12/24	180,244.46	2% of Sales were returned
12/26	8,276,531.40	Settle all accounts payable
12/27	671,502.58	Allowance for Doubtful Accounts is estimated to be 5% of accounts receivable balance
12/28	12,758,549.04	Received cash from 95% of accts receivable
12/29	671,502.58	Recognized bad debt expense for all amounts in Allowance for Doubtful Accounts
12/30	919,614.60	Paid employees
12/31	54,397,391.91	Closing entry to post all revenues and expenses to retained earnings

Loan Amortization Schedule

60months		5%		
Month	Payment	Interest	Principal	Balance
				114,951,825.00
1	2,169,282.75	478,965.94	1,690,316.81	113,261,508.19
2	2,169,282.75	471,922.95	1,697,359.80	111,564,148.39
3	2,169,282.75	464,850.62	1,704,432.13	109,859,716.26
4	2,169,282.75	457,748.82	1,711,533.93	108,148,182.33
5	2,169,282.75	450,617.43	1,718,665.32	106,429,517.01
6	2,169,282.75	443,456.32	1,725,826.43	104,703,690.59
7	2,169,282.75	436,265.38	1,733,017.37	102,970,673.22
8	2,169,282.75	429,044.47	1,740,238.28	101,230,434.94
9	2,169,282.75	421,793.48	1,747,489.27	99,482,945.67
10	2,169,282.75	414,512.27	1,754,770.47	97,728,175.20
11	2,169,282.75	407,200.73	1,762,082.02	95,966,093.18
12	2,169,282.75	399,858.72	1,769,424.03	94,196,669.16
13	2,169,282.75	392,486.12	1,776,796.63	92,419,872.53
14	2,169,282.75	385,082.80	1,784,199.95	90,635,672.59
15	2,169,282.75	377,648.64	1,791,634.11	88,844,038.47
16	2,169,282.75	370,183.49	1,799,099.25	87,044,939.22
17	2,169,282.75	362,687.25	1,806,595.50	85,238,343.72
18	2,169,282.75	355,159.77	1,814,122.98	83,424,220.74
19	2,169,282.75	347,600.92	1,821,681.83	81,602,538.91
20	2,169,282.75	340,010.58	1,829,272.17	79,773,266.74
21	2,169,282.75	332,388.61	1,836,894.14	77,936,372.61
22	2,169,282.75	324,734.89	1,844,547.86	76,091,824.74
23	2,169,282.75	317,049.27	1,852,233.48	74,239,591.27
24	2,169,282.75	309,331.63	1,859,951.12	72,379,640.15
25	2,169,282.75	301,581.83	1,867,700.91	70,511,939.24
26	2,169,282.75	293,799.75	1,875,483.00	68,636,456.24
27	2,169,282.75	285,985.23	1,883,297.51	66,753,158.72
28	2,169,282.75	278,138.16	1,891,144.59	64,862,014.14
29	2,169,282.75	270,258.39	1,899,024.36	62,962,989.78
30	2,169,282.75	262,345.79	1,906,936.96	61,056,052.82
31	2,169,282.75	254,400.22	1,914,882.53	59,141,170.30
32	2,169,282.75	246,421.54	1,922,861.20	57,218,309.09
33	2,169,282.75	238,409.62	1,930,873.13	55,287,435.97
34	2,169,282.75	230,364.32	1,938,918.43	53,348,517.54
35	2,169,282.75	222,285.49	1,946,997.26	51,401,520.28
36	2,169,282.75	214,173.00	1,955,109.75	49,446,410.53
37	2,169,282.75	206,026.71	1,963,256.04	47,483,154.49
38	2,169,282.75	197,846.48	1,971,436.27	45,511,718.22
39	2,169,282.75	189,632.16	1,979,650.59	43,532,067.64
40	2,169,282.75	181,383.62	1,987,899.13	41,544,168.50
41	2,169,282.75	173,100.70	1,996,182.05	39,547,986.46
42	2,169,282.75	164,783.28	2,004,499.47	37,543,486.99
43	2,169,282.75	156,431.20	2,012,851.55	35,530,635.44
44	2,169,282.75	148,044.31	2,021,238.43	33,509,397.00
45	2,169,282.75	139,622.49	2,029,660.26	31,479,736.74
46	2,169,282.75	131,165.57	2,038,117.18	29,441,619.57
47	2,169,282.75	122,673.41	2,046,609.33	27,395,010.23
48	2,169,282.75	114,145.88	2,055,136.87	25,339,873.36
49	2,169,282.75	105,582.81	2,063,699.94	23,276,173.42
50	2,169,282.75	96,984.06	2,072,298.69	21,203,874.73
51	2,169,282.75	88,349.48	2,080,933.27	19,122,941.46
52	2,169,282.75	79,678.92	2,089,603.82	17,033,337.64
53	2,169,282.75	70,972.24	2,098,310.51	14,935,027.13
54	2,169,282.75	62,229.28	2,107,053.47	12,827,973.66
55	2,169,282.75	53,449.89	2,115,832.86	10,712,140.80
56	2,169,282.75	44,633.92	2,124,648.83	8,587,491.98
57	2,169,282.75	35,781.22	2,133,501.53	6,453,990.44
58	2,169,282.75	26,891.63	2,142,391.12	4,311,599.32
59	2,169,282.75	17,965.00	2,151,317.75	2,160,281.57
60	2,169,282.75	9,001.17	2,160,281.57	0.00

Case #3

Date	Amount	Transaction
01/01	0.00	Started new business. All Accounts are nil.
01/05	1,731,941.00	Bought inventory
01/08	5,195,823.00	Sold services
01/10	2,078,329.20	Sold all inventory
01/24	41,566.58	2% of Sales were returned
02/01	432,985.25	Paid Rent for the current month
02/05	2,078,329.20	Bought inventory
02/08	5,195,823.00	Sold services
02/10	2,909,660.88	Sold all inventory
02/15	1,039,164.60	Paid employees
02/24	58,193.22	2% of Sales were returned
02/27	763,993.81	Allowance for Doubtful Accounts is estimated to be 5% of accounts receivable balance
02/30	1,039,164.60	Paid employees
03/01	432,985.25	Paid Rent for the current month
03/05	2,597,911.50	Bought inventory
03/08	5,195,823.00	Sold services
03/10	3,637,076.10	Sold all inventory
03/15	1,039,164.60	Paid employees
03/24	72,741.52	2% of Sales were returned
03/26	10,391,646.00	Settle all accounts payable
03/27	1,202,001.69	Allowance for Doubtful Accounts is estimated to be 5% of accounts receivable balance
03/28	22,838,032.17	Received cash from 95% of accts receivable
03/29	1,965,995.50	Recognized bad debt expense for all amounts in Allowance for Doubtful Accounts
03/30	1,039,164.60	Paid employees
04/01	432,985.25	Paid Rent for the current month
04/05	3,117,493.80	Bought inventory
04/06	10,391,646.00	Bought equipment 5yr life
04/08	5,195,823.00	Sold services
04/10	4,364,491.32	Sold all inventory
04/15	1,039,164.60	Paid employees
04/24	87,289.83	2% of Sales were returned
04/26	16,020,454.25	Settle all accounts payable
04/27	435,451.53	Allowance for Doubtful Accounts is estimated to be 5% of accounts receivable balance
04/28	8,273,579.15	Received cash from 95% of accts receivable
04/29	435,451.53	Recognized bad debt expense for all amounts in Allowance for Doubtful Accounts
04/30	1,039,164.60	Paid employees
05/01	432,985.25	Paid Rent for the current month
05/05	3,637,076.10	Bought inventory
05/06	173,194.10	Depreciate equipment for 1 month
05/08	5,195,823.00	Sold services
05/10	5,091,906.54	Sold all inventory
05/15	1,039,164.60	Paid employees
05/24	101,838.13	2% of Sales were returned
05/26	6,148,390.55	Settle all accounts payable

05/27	509,294.57	Allowance for Doubtful Accounts is estimated to be 5% of accounts receivable balance
05/28	9,676,596.84	Received cash from 95% of accts receivable
05/29	509,294.57	Recognized bad debt expense for all amounts in Allowance for Doubtful Accounts
05/30	1,039,164.60	Paid employees
06/01	432,985.25	Paid Rent for the current month
06/03	129,895,575.00	Received a business loan for building payable monthly 5yr term @5%
06/04	129,895,575.00	Bought building 20yr life
06/05	4,156,658.40	Bought inventory
06/06	173,194.10	Depreciate equipment for 1 month
06/08	5,195,823.00	Sold services
06/10	5,819,321.76	Sold all inventory
06/15	1,039,164.60	Paid employees
06/24	116,386.44	2% of Sales were returned
06/26	6,667,972.85	Settle all accounts payable
06/27	544,937.92	Allowance for Doubtful Accounts is estimated to be 5% of accounts receivable balance
06/28	10,353,820.40	Received cash from 95% of accts receivable
06/29	544,937.92	Recognized bad debt expense for all amounts in Allowance for Doubtful Accounts
06/30	1,039,164.60	Paid employees
07/01	25,979,115.00	Owner invested cash into the business
07/02	541,231.56	Paid 1 month of interest per Loan Amortization Schedule
07/03	1,910,058.18	Paid principal portion based on Loan Amortization Schedule
07/04	541,231.56	Depreciate building for 1 month
07/05	4,676,240.70	Bought inventory
07/06	173,194.10	Depreciate equipment for 1 month
07/08	5,195,823.00	Sold services
07/10	6,546,736.98	Sold all inventory
07/15	1,039,164.60	Paid employees
07/24	130,934.74	2% of Sales were returned
07/26	6,754,569.90	Settle all accounts payable
07/27	580,581.26	Allowance for Doubtful Accounts is estimated to be 5% of accounts receivable balance
07/28	11,031,043.98	Received cash from 95% of accts receivable
07/29	580,581.26	Recognized bad debt expense for all amounts in Allowance for Doubtful Accounts
07/30	1,039,164.60	Paid employees
08/02	533,272.99	Paid 1 month of interest per Loan Amortization Schedule
08/03	1,918,016.76	Paid principal portion based on Loan Amortization Schedule
08/04	541,231.56	Depreciate building for 1 month
08/05	5,195,823.00	Bought inventory
08/06	173,194.10	Depreciate equipment for 1 month
08/08	5,195,823.00	Sold services
08/10	7,274,152.20	Sold all inventory
08/11	6,234,987.60	Prepaid for 12 months of insurance
08/15	1,039,164.60	Paid employees
08/24	145,483.04	2% of Sales were returned
08/26	13,509,139.80	Settle all accounts payable
08/27	616,224.61	Allowance for Doubtful Accounts is estimated to be 5% of accounts receivable balance
08/28	11,708,267.55	Received cash from 95% of accts receivable
08/29	616,224.61	Recognized bad debt expense for all amounts in Allowance for Doubtful Accounts

08/30	1,039,164.60	Paid employees
09/02	525,281.25	Paid 1 month of interest per Loan Amortization Schedule
09/03	1,926,008.49	Paid principal portion based on Loan Amortization Schedule
09/04	541,231.56	Depreciate building for 1 month
09/05	5,715,405.30	Bought inventory
09/06	173,194.10	Depreciate equipment for 1 month
09/08	5,195,823.00	Sold services
09/10	8,001,567.42	Sold all inventory
09/11	519,582.30	Amortize prepaid insurance for 1 month
09/15	1,039,164.60	Paid employees
09/24	160,031.35	2% of Sales were returned
09/26	7,793,734.50	Settle all accounts payable
09/27	651,867.95	Allowance for Doubtful Accounts is estimated to be 5% of accounts receivable balance
09/28	12,385,491.12	Received cash from 95% of accts receivable
09/29	651,867.95	Recognized bad debt expense for all amounts in Allowance for Doubtful Accounts
09/30	1,039,164.60	Paid employees
10/02	517,256.21	Paid 1 month of interest per Loan Amortization Schedule
10/03	1,934,033.53	Paid principal portion based on Loan Amortization Schedule
10/04	541,231.56	Depreciate building for 1 month
10/05	6,234,987.60	Bought inventory
10/06	173,194.10	Depreciate equipment for 1 month
10/08	5,195,823.00	Sold services
10/10	8,728,982.64	Sold all inventory
10/11	519,582.30	Amortize prepaid insurance for 1 month
10/13	20,783,292.00	Received upfront payment for a large project to be fulfilled next month
10/15	1,039,164.60	Paid employees
10/24	174,579.65	2% of Sales were returned
10/26	8,313,316.80	Settle all accounts payable
10/27	687,511.30	Allowance for Doubtful Accounts is estimated to be 5% of accounts receivable balance
10/28	13,062,714.69	Received cash from 95% of accts receivable
10/29	687,511.30	Recognized bad debt expense for all amounts in Allowance for Doubtful Accounts
10/30	1,039,164.60	Paid employees
11/02	509,197.74	Paid 1 month of interest per Loan Amortization Schedule
11/03	1,942,092.00	Paid principal portion based on Loan Amortization Schedule
11/04	541,231.56	Depreciate building for 1 month
11/05	6,754,569.90	Bought inventory
11/06	173,194.10	Depreciate equipment for 1 month
11/08	5,195,823.00	Sold services
11/10	9,456,397.86	Sold all inventory
11/11	519,582.30	Amortize prepaid insurance for 1 month
11/13	20,783,292.00	Provide the services for the large sale that was paid up front last month
11/15	1,039,164.60	Paid employees
11/20	5,195,823.00	Paid a dividend to the owner
11/24	189,127.96	2% of Sales were returned
11/26	8,832,899.10	Settle all accounts payable
11/27	723,154.65	Allowance for Doubtful Accounts is estimated to be 5% of accounts receivable balance
11/28	13,739,938.26	Received cash from 95% of accts receivable
11/29	723,154.65	Recognized bad debt expense for all amounts in Allowance for Doubtful Accounts

11/30	1,039,164.60	Paid employees
12/02	501,105.69	Paid 1 month of interest per Loan Amortization Schedule
12/03	1,950,184.05	Paid principal portion based on Loan Amortization Schedule
12/04	541,231.56	Depreciate building for 1 month
12/05	7,274,152.20	Bought inventory
12/06	173,194.10	Depreciate equipment for 1 month
12/08	5,195,823.00	Sold services
12/10	10,183,813.08	Sold all inventory
12/11	519,582.30	Amortize prepaid insurance for 1 month
12/15	1,039,164.60	Paid employees
12/24	203,676.26	2% of Sales were returned
12/26	9,352,481.40	Settle all accounts payable
12/27	758,797.99	Allowance for Doubtful Accounts is estimated to be 5% of accounts receivable balance
12/28	14,417,161.82	Received cash from 95% of accts receivable
12/29	758,797.99	Recognized bad debt expense for all amounts in Allowance for Doubtful Accounts
12/30	1,039,164.60	Paid employees
12/31	61,469,058.96	Closing entry to post all revenues and expenses to retained earnings

Loan Amortization Schedule

	60months	5%		
Month	Payment	Interest	Principal	Balance
				129,895,575.00
1	2,451,289.75	541,231.56	1,910,058.18	127,985,516.82
2	2,451,289.75	533,272.99	1,918,016.76	126,067,500.06
3	2,451,289.75	525,281.25	1,926,008.49	124,141,491.56
4	2,451,289.75	517,256.21	1,934,033.53	122,207,458.03
5	2,451,289.75	509,197.74	1,942,092.00	120,265,366.03
6	2,451,289.75	501,105.69	1,950,184.05	118,315,181.98
7	2,451,289.75	492,979.92	1,958,309.82	116,356,872.16
8	2,451,289.75	484,820.30	1,966,469.44	114,390,402.71
9	2,451,289.75	476,626.68	1,974,663.07	112,415,739.65
10	2,451,289.75	468,398.92	1,982,890.83	110,432,848.82
11	2,451,289.75	460,136.87	1,991,152.88	108,441,695.94
12	2,451,289.75	451,840.40	1,999,449.35	106,442,246.59
13	2,451,289.75	443,509.36	2,007,780.38	104,434,466.21
14	2,451,289.75	435,143.61	2,016,146.14	102,418,320.07
15	2,451,289.75	426,743.00	2,024,546.74	100,393,773.33
16	2,451,289.75	418,307.39	2,032,982.36	98,360,790.97
17	2,451,289.75	409,836.63	2,041,453.12	96,319,337.86
18	2,451,289.75	401,330.57	2,049,959.17	94,269,378.69
19	2,451,289.75	392,789.08	2,058,500.67	92,210,878.02
20	2,451,289.75	384,211.99	2,067,077.75	90,143,800.27
21	2,451,289.75	375,599.17	2,075,690.58	88,068,109.69
22	2,451,289.75	366,950.46	2,084,339.29	85,983,770.40
23	2,451,289.75	358,265.71	2,093,024.04	83,890,746.37
24	2,451,289.75	349,544.78	2,101,744.97	81,789,001.40
25	2,451,289.75	340,787.51	2,110,502.24	79,678,499.16
26	2,451,289.75	331,993.75	2,119,296.00	77,559,203.16
27	2,451,289.75	323,163.35	2,128,126.40	75,431,076.76
28	2,451,289.75	314,296.15	2,136,993.59	73,294,083.17
29	2,451,289.75	305,392.01	2,145,897.73	71,148,185.44
30	2,451,289.75	296,450.77	2,154,838.97	68,993,346.46
31	2,451,289.75	287,472.28	2,163,817.47	66,829,529.00
32	2,451,289.75	278,456.37	2,172,833.37	64,656,695.62
33	2,451,289.75	269,402.90	2,181,886.85	62,474,808.77
34	2,451,289.75	260,311.70	2,190,978.04	60,283,830.73
35	2,451,289.75	251,182.63	2,200,107.12	58,083,723.62
36	2,451,289.75	242,015.52	2,209,274.23	55,874,449.39
37	2,451,289.75	232,810.21	2,218,479.54	53,655,969.85
38	2,451,289.75	223,566.54	2,227,723.20	51,428,246.64
39	2,451,289.75	214,284.36	2,237,005.38	49,191,241.26
40	2,451,289.75	204,963.51	2,246,326.24	46,944,915.02
41	2,451,289.75	195,603.81	2,255,685.93	44,689,229.08
42	2,451,289.75	186,205.12	2,265,084.62	42,424,144.46
43	2,451,289.75	176,767.27	2,274,522.48	40,149,621.98
44	2,451,289.75	167,290.09	2,283,999.65	37,865,622.33
45	2,451,289.75	157,773.43	2,293,516.32	35,572,106.01
46	2,451,289.75	148,217.11	2,303,072.64	33,269,033.38
47	2,451,289.75	138,620.97	2,312,668.77	30,956,364.60
48	2,451,289.75	128,984.85	2,322,304.89	28,634,059.71
49	2,451,289.75	119,308.58	2,331,981.16	26,302,078.55
50	2,451,289.75	109,591.99	2,341,697.75	23,960,380.80
51	2,451,289.75	99,834.92	2,351,454.83	21,608,925.97
52	2,451,289.75	90,037.19	2,361,252.55	19,247,673.42
53	2,451,289.75	80,198.64	2,371,091.11	16,876,582.31
54	2,451,289.75	70,319.09	2,380,970.65	14,495,611.66
55	2,451,289.75	60,398.38	2,390,891.36	12,104,720.30
56	2,451,289.75	50,436.33	2,400,853.41	9,703,866.89
57	2,451,289.75	40,432.78	2,410,856.97	7,293,009.92
58	2,451,289.75	30,387.54	2,420,902.20	4,872,107.71
59	2,451,289.75	20,300.45	2,430,989.30	2,441,118.42
60	2,451,289.75	10,171.33	2,441,118.42	0.00

Case #4

Date	Amount	Transaction
01/01	0.00	Started new business. All Accounts are nil.
01/05	1,957,093.00	Bought inventory
01/08	5,871,279.00	Sold services
01/10	2,348,511.60	Sold all inventory
01/24	46,970.23	2% of Sales were returned
02/01	489,273.25	Paid Rent for the current month
02/05	2,348,511.60	Bought inventory
02/08	5,871,279.00	Sold services
02/10	3,287,916.24	Sold all inventory
02/15	1,174,255.80	Paid employees
02/24	65,758.32	2% of Sales were returned
02/27	863,312.86	Allowance for Doubtful Accounts is estimated to be 5% of accounts receivable balance
02/30	1,174,255.80	Paid employees
03/01	489,273.25	Paid Rent for the current month
03/05	2,935,639.50	Bought inventory
03/08	5,871,279.00	Sold services
03/10	4,109,895.30	Sold all inventory
03/15	1,174,255.80	Paid employees
03/24	82,197.91	2% of Sales were returned
03/26	11,742,558.00	Settle all accounts payable
03/27	1,358,261.68	Allowance for Doubtful Accounts is estimated to be 5% of accounts receivable balance
03/28	25,806,972.00	Received cash from 95% of accts receivable
03/29	2,221,574.54	Recognized bad debt expense for all amounts in Allowance for Doubtful Accounts
03/30	1,174,255.80	Paid employees
04/01	489,273.25	Paid Rent for the current month
04/05	3,522,767.40	Bought inventory
04/06	11,742,558.00	Bought equipment 5yr life
04/08	5,871,279.00	Sold services
04/10	4,931,874.36	Sold all inventory
04/15	1,174,255.80	Paid employees
04/24	98,637.49	2% of Sales were returned
04/26	18,103,110.25	Settle all accounts payable
04/27	492,060.15	Allowance for Doubtful Accounts is estimated to be 5% of accounts receivable balance
04/28	9,349,142.86	Received cash from 95% of accts receivable
04/29	492,060.15	Recognized bad debt expense for all amounts in Allowance for Doubtful Accounts
04/30	1,174,255.80	Paid employees
05/01	489,273.25	Paid Rent for the current month
05/05	4,109,895.30	Bought inventory
05/06	195,709.30	Depreciate equipment for 1 month
05/08	5,871,279.00	Sold services
05/10	5,753,853.42	Sold all inventory
05/15	1,174,255.80	Paid employees
05/24	115,077.07	2% of Sales were returned
05/26	6,947,680.15	Settle all accounts payable
05/27	575,502.77	Allowance for Doubtful Accounts is estimated to be 5% of accounts receivable balance

05/28	10,934,552.58	Received cash from 95% of accts receivable
05/29	575,502.77	Recognized bad debt expense for all amounts in Allowance for Doubtful Accounts
05/30	1,174,255.80	Paid employees
06/01	489,273.25	Paid Rent for the current month
06/03	146,781,975.00	Received a business loan for building payable monthly 5yr term @5%
06/04	146,781,975.00	Bought building 20yr life
06/05	4,697,023.20	Bought inventory
06/06	195,709.30	Depreciate equipment for 1 month
06/08	5,871,279.00	Sold services
06/10	6,575,832.48	Sold all inventory
06/15	1,174,255.80	Paid employees
06/24	131,516.65	2% of Sales were returned
06/26	7,534,808.05	Settle all accounts payable
06/27	615,779.74	Allowance for Doubtful Accounts is estimated to be 5% of accounts receivable balance
06/28	11,699,815.09	Received cash from 95% of accts receivable
06/29	615,779.74	Recognized bad debt expense for all amounts in Allowance for Doubtful Accounts
06/30	1,174,255.80	Paid employees
07/01	29,356,395.00	Owner invested cash into the business
07/02	611,591.56	Paid 1 month of interest per Loan Amortization Schedule
07/03	2,158,365.38	Paid principal portion based on Loan Amortization Schedule
07/04	611,591.56	Depreciate building for 1 month
07/05	5,284,151.10	Bought inventory
07/06	195,709.30	Depreciate equipment for 1 month
07/08	5,871,279.00	Sold services
07/10	7,397,811.54	Sold all inventory
07/15	1,174,255.80	Paid employees
07/24	147,956.23	2% of Sales were returned
07/26	7,632,662.70	Settle all accounts payable
07/27	656,056.72	Allowance for Doubtful Accounts is estimated to be 5% of accounts receivable balance
07/28	12,465,077.59	Received cash from 95% of accts receivable
07/29	656,056.72	Recognized bad debt expense for all amounts in Allowance for Doubtful Accounts
07/30	1,174,255.80	Paid employees
08/02	602,598.37	Paid 1 month of interest per Loan Amortization Schedule
08/03	2,167,358.57	Paid principal portion based on Loan Amortization Schedule
08/04	611,591.56	Depreciate building for 1 month
08/05	5,871,279.00	Bought inventory
08/06	195,709.30	Depreciate equipment for 1 month
08/08	5,871,279.00	Sold services
08/10	8,219,790.60	Sold all inventory
08/11	7,045,534.80	Prepaid for 12 months of insurance
08/15	1,174,255.80	Paid employees
08/24	164,395.81	2% of Sales were returned
08/26	15,265,325.40	Settle all accounts payable
08/27	696,333.69	Allowance for Doubtful Accounts is estimated to be 5% of accounts receivable balance
08/28	13,230,340.10	Received cash from 95% of accts receivable
08/29	696,333.69	Recognized bad debt expense for all amounts in Allowance for Doubtful Accounts
08/30	1,174,255.80	Paid employees
09/02	593,567.71	Paid 1 month of interest per Loan Amortization Schedule

09/03	2,176,389.23	Paid principal portion based on Loan Amortization Schedule
09/04	611,591.56	Depreciate building for 1 month
09/05	6,458,406.90	Bought inventory
09/06	195,709.30	Depreciate equipment for 1 month
09/08	5,871,279.00	Sold services
09/10	9,041,769.66	Sold all inventory
09/11	587,127.90	Amortize prepaid insurance for 1 month
09/15	1,174,255.80	Paid employees
09/24	180,835.39	2% of Sales were returned
09/26	8,806,918.50	Settle all accounts payable
09/27	736,610.66	Allowance for Doubtful Accounts is estimated to be 5% of accounts receivable balance
09/28	13,995,602.61	Received cash from 95% of accts receivable
09/29	736,610.66	Recognized bad debt expense for all amounts in Allowance for Doubtful Accounts
09/30	1,174,255.80	Paid employees
10/02	584,499.42	Paid 1 month of interest per Loan Amortization Schedule
10/03	2,185,457.52	Paid principal portion based on Loan Amortization Schedule
10/04	611,591.56	Depreciate building for 1 month
10/05	7,045,534.80	Bought inventory
10/06	195,709.30	Depreciate equipment for 1 month
10/08	5,871,279.00	Sold services
10/10	9,863,748.72	Sold all inventory
10/11	587,127.90	Amortize prepaid insurance for 1 month
10/13	23,485,116.00	Received upfront payment for a large project to be fulfilled next month
10/15	1,174,255.80	Paid employees
10/24	197,274.97	2% of Sales were returned
10/26	9,394,046.40	Settle all accounts payable
10/27	776,887.64	Allowance for Doubtful Accounts is estimated to be 5% of accounts receivable balance
10/28	14,760,865.11	Received cash from 95% of accts receivable
10/29	776,887.64	Recognized bad debt expense for all amounts in Allowance for Doubtful Accounts
10/30	1,174,255.80	Paid employees
11/02	575,393.35	Paid 1 month of interest per Loan Amortization Schedule
11/03	2,194,563.59	Paid principal portion based on Loan Amortization Schedule
11/04	611,591.56	Depreciate building for 1 month
11/05	7,632,662.70	Bought inventory
11/06	195,709.30	Depreciate equipment for 1 month
11/08	5,871,279.00	Sold services
11/10	10,685,727.78	Sold all inventory
11/11	587,127.90	Amortize prepaid insurance for 1 month
11/13	23,485,116.00	Provide the services for the large sale that was paid up front last month
11/15	1,174,255.80	Paid employees
11/20	5,871,279.00	Paid a dividend to the owner
11/24	213,714.56	2% of Sales were returned
11/26	9,981,174.30	Settle all accounts payable
11/27	817,164.61	Allowance for Doubtful Accounts is estimated to be 5% of accounts receivable balance
11/28	15,526,127.61	Received cash from 95% of accts receivable
11/29	817,164.61	Recognized bad debt expense for all amounts in Allowance for Doubtful Accounts
11/30	1,174,255.80	Paid employees
12/02	566,249.34	Paid 1 month of interest per Loan Amortization Schedule

12/03	2,203,707.61	Paid principal portion based on Loan Amortization Schedule
12/04	611,591.56	Depreciate building for 1 month
12/05	8,219,790.60	Bought inventory
12/06	195,709.30	Depreciate equipment for 1 month
12/08	5,871,279.00	Sold services
12/10	11,507,706.84	Sold all inventory
12/11	587,127.90	Amortize prepaid insurance for 1 month
12/15	1,174,255.80	Paid employees
12/24	230,154.14	2% of Sales were returned
12/26	10,568,302.20	Settle all accounts payable
12/27	857,441.59	Allowance for Doubtful Accounts is estimated to be 5% of accounts receivable balance
12/28	16,291,390.12	Received cash from 95% of accts receivable
12/29	857,441.59	Recognized bad debt expense for all amounts in Allowance for Doubtful Accounts
12/30	1,174,255.80	Paid employees
12/31	69,460,024.91	Closing entry to post all revenues and expenses to retained earnings

Loan Amortization Schedule

60months		5%		
Month	Payment	Interest	Principal	Balance
				146,781,975.00
1	2,769,956.94	611,591.56	2,158,365.38	144,623,609.62
2	2,769,956.94	602,598.37	2,167,358.57	142,456,251.05
3	2,769,956.94	593,567.71	2,176,389.23	140,279,861.81
4	2,769,956.94	584,499.42	2,185,457.52	138,094,404.29
5	2,769,956.94	575,393.35	2,194,563.59	135,899,840.70
6	2,769,956.94	566,249.34	2,203,707.61	133,696,133.09
7	2,769,956.94	557,067.22	2,212,889.72	131,483,243.37
8	2,769,956.94	547,846.85	2,222,110.10	129,261,133.27
9	2,769,956.94	538,588.06	2,231,368.89	127,029,764.38
10	2,769,956.94	529,290.68	2,240,666.26	124,789,098.12
11	2,769,956.94	519,954.58	2,250,002.37	122,539,095.75
12	2,769,956.94	510,579.57	2,259,377.38	120,279,718.37
13	2,769,956.94	501,165.49	2,268,791.45	118,010,926.92
14	2,769,956.94	491,712.20	2,278,244.75	115,732,682.17
15	2,769,956.94	482,219.51	2,287,737.44	113,444,944.73
16	2,769,956.94	472,687.27	2,297,269.68	111,147,675.06
17	2,769,956.94	463,115.31	2,306,841.63	108,840,833.43
18	2,769,956.94	453,503.47	2,316,453.47	106,524,379.95
19	2,769,956.94	443,851.58	2,326,105.36	104,198,274.59
20	2,769,956.94	434,159.48	2,335,797.47	101,862,477.12
21	2,769,956.94	424,426.99	2,345,529.96	99,516,947.17
22	2,769,956.94	414,653.95	2,355,303.00	97,161,644.17
23	2,769,956.94	404,840.18	2,365,116.76	94,796,527.41
24	2,769,956.94	394,985.53	2,374,971.41	92,421,555.99
25	2,769,956.94	385,089.82	2,384,867.13	90,036,688.87
26	2,769,956.94	375,152.87	2,394,804.07	87,641,884.79
27	2,769,956.94	365,174.52	2,404,782.42	85,237,102.37
28	2,769,956.94	355,154.59	2,414,802.35	82,822,300.01
29	2,769,956.94	345,092.92	2,424,864.03	80,397,435.99
30	2,769,956.94	334,989.32	2,434,967.63	77,962,468.36
31	2,769,956.94	324,843.62	2,445,113.33	75,517,355.03
32	2,769,956.94	314,655.65	2,455,301.30	73,062,053.73
33	2,769,956.94	304,425.22	2,465,531.72	70,596,522.01
34	2,769,956.94	294,152.18	2,475,804.77	68,120,717.24
35	2,769,956.94	283,836.32	2,486,120.62	65,634,596.62
36	2,769,956.94	273,477.49	2,496,479.46	63,138,117.16
37	2,769,956.94	263,075.49	2,506,881.46	60,631,235.70
38	2,769,956.94	252,630.15	2,517,326.80	58,113,908.91
39	2,769,956.94	242,141.29	2,527,815.66	55,586,093.25
40	2,769,956.94	231,608.72	2,538,348.22	53,047,745.03
41	2,769,956.94	221,032.27	2,548,924.67	50,498,820.35
42	2,769,956.94	210,411.75	2,559,545.19	47,939,275.16
43	2,769,956.94	199,746.98	2,570,209.97	45,369,065.19
44	2,769,956.94	189,037.77	2,580,919.17	42,788,146.02
45	2,769,956.94	178,283.94	2,591,673.00	40,196,473.02
46	2,769,956.94	167,485.30	2,602,471.64	37,594,001.38
47	2,769,956.94	156,641.67	2,613,315.27	34,980,686.10
48	2,769,956.94	145,752.86	2,624,204.09	32,356,482.02
49	2,769,956.94	134,818.68	2,635,138.27	29,721,343.75
50	2,769,956.94	123,838.93	2,646,118.01	27,075,225.73
51	2,769,956.94	112,813.44	2,657,143.50	24,418,082.23
52	2,769,956.94	101,742.01	2,668,214.94	21,749,867.29
53	2,769,956.94	90,624.45	2,679,332.50	19,070,534.80
54	2,769,956.94	79,460.56	2,690,496.38	16,380,038.41
55	2,769,956.94	68,250.16	2,701,706.78	13,678,331.63
56	2,769,956.94	56,993.05	2,712,963.90	10,965,367.73
57	2,769,956.94	45,689.03	2,724,267.91	8,241,099.82
58	2,769,956.94	34,337.92	2,735,619.03	5,505,480.79
59	2,769,956.94	22,939.50	2,747,017.44	2,758,463.35
60	2,769,956.94	11,493.60	2,758,463.35	0.00

197

Case #5

Date	Amount	Transaction
01/01	0.00	Started new business. All Accounts are nil.
01/05	2,211,515.00	Bought inventory
01/08	6,634,545.00	Sold services
01/10	2,653,818.00	Sold all inventory
01/24	53,076.36	2% of Sales were returned
02/01	552,878.75	Paid Rent for the current month
02/05	2,653,818.00	Bought inventory
02/08	6,634,545.00	Sold services
02/10	3,715,345.20	Sold all inventory
02/15	1,326,909.00	Paid employees
02/24	74,306.90	2% of Sales were returned
02/27	975,543.50	Allowance for Doubtful Accounts is estimated to be 5% of accounts receivable balance
02/30	1,326,909.00	Paid employees
03/01	552,878.75	Paid Rent for the current month
03/05	3,317,272.50	Bought inventory
03/08	6,634,545.00	Sold services
03/10	4,644,181.50	Sold all inventory
03/15	1,326,909.00	Paid employees
03/24	92,883.63	2% of Sales were returned
03/26	13,269,090.00	Settle all accounts payable
03/27	1,534,835.64	Allowance for Doubtful Accounts is estimated to be 5% of accounts receivable balance
03/28	29,161,877.17	Received cash from 95% of accts receivable
03/29	2,510,379.14	Recognized bad debt expense for all amounts in Allowance for Doubtful Accounts
03/30	1,326,909.00	Paid employees
04/01	552,878.75	Paid Rent for the current month
04/05	3,980,727.00	Bought inventory
04/06	13,269,090.00	Bought equipment 5yr life
04/08	6,634,545.00	Sold services
04/10	5,573,017.80	Sold all inventory
04/15	1,326,909.00	Paid employees
04/24	111,460.36	2% of Sales were returned
04/26	20,456,513.75	Settle all accounts payable
04/27	556,027.95	Allowance for Doubtful Accounts is estimated to be 5% of accounts receivable balance
04/28	10,564,530.99	Received cash from 95% of accts receivable
04/29	556,027.95	Recognized bad debt expense for all amounts in Allowance for Doubtful Accounts
04/30	1,326,909.00	Paid employees
05/01	552,878.75	Paid Rent for the current month
05/05	4,644,181.50	Bought inventory
05/06	221,151.50	Depreciate equipment for 1 month
05/08	6,634,545.00	Sold services
05/10	6,501,854.10	Sold all inventory
05/15	1,326,909.00	Paid employees
05/24	130,037.08	2% of Sales were returned
05/26	7,850,878.25	Settle all accounts payable
05/27	650,318.10	Allowance for Doubtful Accounts is estimated to be 5% of accounts receivable balance

Date	Amount	Description
05/28	12,356,043.92	Received cash from 95% of accts receivable
05/29	650,318.10	Recognized bad debt expense for all amounts in Allowance for Doubtful Accounts
05/30	1,326,909.00	Paid employees
06/01	552,878.75	Paid Rent for the current month
06/03	165,863,625.00	Received a business loan for building payable monthly 5yr term @5%
06/04	165,863,625.00	Bought building 20yr life
06/05	5,307,636.00	Bought inventory
06/06	221,151.50	Depreciate equipment for 1 month
06/08	6,634,545.00	Sold services
06/10	7,430,690.40	Sold all inventory
06/15	1,326,909.00	Paid employees
06/24	148,613.81	2% of Sales were returned
06/26	8,514,332.75	Settle all accounts payable
06/27	695,831.08	Allowance for Doubtful Accounts is estimated to be 5% of accounts receivable balance
06/28	13,220,790.51	Received cash from 95% of accts receivable
06/29	695,831.08	Recognized bad debt expense for all amounts in Allowance for Doubtful Accounts
06/30	1,326,909.00	Paid employees
07/01	33,172,725.00	Owner invested cash into the business
07/02	691,098.44	Paid 1 month of interest per Loan Amortization Schedule
07/03	2,438,952.78	Paid principal portion based on Loan Amortization Schedule
07/04	691,098.44	Depreciate building for 1 month
07/05	5,971,090.50	Bought inventory
07/06	221,151.50	Depreciate equipment for 1 month
07/08	6,634,545.00	Sold services
07/10	8,359,526.70	Sold all inventory
07/15	1,326,909.00	Paid employees
07/24	167,190.53	2% of Sales were returned
07/26	8,624,908.50	Settle all accounts payable
07/27	741,344.06	Allowance for Doubtful Accounts is estimated to be 5% of accounts receivable balance
07/28	14,085,537.11	Received cash from 95% of accts receivable
07/29	741,344.06	Recognized bad debt expense for all amounts in Allowance for Doubtful Accounts
07/30	1,326,909.00	Paid employees
08/02	680,936.13	Paid 1 month of interest per Loan Amortization Schedule
08/03	2,449,115.09	Paid principal portion based on Loan Amortization Schedule
08/04	691,098.44	Depreciate building for 1 month
08/05	6,634,545.00	Bought inventory
08/06	221,151.50	Depreciate equipment for 1 month
08/08	6,634,545.00	Sold services
08/10	9,288,363.00	Sold all inventory
08/11	7,961,454.00	Prepaid for 12 months of insurance
08/15	1,326,909.00	Paid employees
08/24	185,767.26	2% of Sales were returned
08/26	17,249,817.00	Settle all accounts payable
08/27	786,857.04	Allowance for Doubtful Accounts is estimated to be 5% of accounts receivable balance
08/28	14,950,283.70	Received cash from 95% of accts receivable
08/29	786,857.04	Recognized bad debt expense for all amounts in Allowance for Doubtful Accounts
08/30	1,326,909.00	Paid employees
09/02	670,731.49	Paid 1 month of interest per Loan Amortization Schedule

09/03	2,459,319.73	Paid principal portion based on Loan Amortization Schedule
09/04	691,098.44	Depreciate building for 1 month
09/05	7,297,999.50	Bought inventory
09/06	221,151.50	Depreciate equipment for 1 month
09/08	6,634,545.00	Sold services
09/10	10,217,199.30	Sold all inventory
09/11	663,454.50	Amortize prepaid insurance for 1 month
09/15	1,326,909.00	Paid employees
09/24	204,343.99	2% of Sales were returned
09/26	9,951,817.50	Settle all accounts payable
09/27	832,370.02	Allowance for Doubtful Accounts is estimated to be 5% of accounts receivable balance
09/28	15,815,030.29	Received cash from 95% of accts receivable
09/29	832,370.02	Recognized bad debt expense for all amounts in Allowance for Doubtful Accounts
09/30	1,326,909.00	Paid employees
10/02	660,484.32	Paid 1 month of interest per Loan Amortization Schedule
10/03	2,469,566.90	Paid principal portion based on Loan Amortization Schedule
10/04	691,098.44	Depreciate building for 1 month
10/05	7,961,454.00	Bought inventory
10/06	221,151.50	Depreciate equipment for 1 month
10/08	6,634,545.00	Sold services
10/10	11,146,035.60	Sold all inventory
10/11	663,454.50	Amortize prepaid insurance for 1 month
10/13	26,538,180.00	Received upfront payment for a large project to be fulfilled next month
10/15	1,326,909.00	Paid employees
10/24	222,920.71	2% of Sales were returned
10/26	10,615,272.00	Settle all accounts payable
10/27	877,882.99	Allowance for Doubtful Accounts is estimated to be 5% of accounts receivable balance
10/28	16,679,776.90	Received cash from 95% of accts receivable
10/29	877,882.99	Recognized bad debt expense for all amounts in Allowance for Doubtful Accounts
10/30	1,326,909.00	Paid employees
11/02	650,194.46	Paid 1 month of interest per Loan Amortization Schedule
11/03	2,479,856.76	Paid principal portion based on Loan Amortization Schedule
11/04	691,098.44	Depreciate building for 1 month
11/05	8,624,908.50	Bought inventory
11/06	221,151.50	Depreciate equipment for 1 month
11/08	6,634,545.00	Sold services
11/10	12,074,871.90	Sold all inventory
11/11	663,454.50	Amortize prepaid insurance for 1 month
11/13	26,538,180.00	Provide the services for the large sale that was paid up front last month
11/15	1,326,909.00	Paid employees
11/20	6,634,545.00	Paid a dividend to the owner
11/24	241,497.44	2% of Sales were returned
11/26	11,278,726.50	Settle all accounts payable
11/27	923,395.97	Allowance for Doubtful Accounts is estimated to be 5% of accounts receivable balance
11/28	17,544,523.49	Received cash from 95% of accts receivable
11/29	923,395.97	Recognized bad debt expense for all amounts in Allowance for Doubtful Accounts
11/30	1,326,909.00	Paid employees
12/02	639,861.72	Paid 1 month of interest per Loan Amortization Schedule

12/03	2,490,189.50	Paid principal portion based on Loan Amortization Schedule
12/04	691,098.44	Depreciate building for 1 month
12/05	9,288,363.00	Bought inventory
12/06	221,151.50	Depreciate equipment for 1 month
12/08	6,634,545.00	Sold services
12/10	13,003,708.20	Sold all inventory
12/11	663,454.50	Amortize prepaid insurance for 1 month
12/15	1,326,909.00	Paid employees
12/24	260,074.16	2% of Sales were returned
12/26	11,942,181.00	Settle all accounts payable
12/27	968,908.95	Allowance for Doubtful Accounts is estimated to be 5% of accounts receivable balance
12/28	18,409,270.09	Received cash from 95% of accts receivable
12/29	968,908.95	Recognized bad debt expense for all amounts in Allowance for Doubtful Accounts
12/30	1,326,909.00	Paid employees
12/31	78,489,824.92	Closing entry to post all revenues and expenses to retained earnings

Loan Amortization Schedule

	60months	5%		
Month	Payment	Interest	Principal	Balance
				165,863,625.00
1	3,130,051.22	691,098.44	2,438,952.78	163,424,672.22
2	3,130,051.22	680,936.13	2,449,115.09	160,975,557.13
3	3,130,051.22	670,731.49	2,459,319.73	158,516,237.40
4	3,130,051.22	660,484.32	2,469,566.90	156,046,670.50
5	3,130,051.22	650,194.46	2,479,856.76	153,566,813.74
6	3,130,051.22	639,861.72	2,490,189.50	151,076,624.24
7	3,130,051.22	629,485.93	2,500,565.29	148,576,058.96
8	3,130,051.22	619,066.91	2,510,984.31	146,065,074.65
9	3,130,051.22	608,604.48	2,521,446.74	143,543,627.91
10	3,130,051.22	598,098.45	2,531,952.77	141,011,675.14
11	3,130,051.22	587,548.65	2,542,502.57	138,469,172.56
12	3,130,051.22	576,954.89	2,553,096.33	135,916,076.23
13	3,130,051.22	566,316.98	2,563,734.24	133,352,341.99
14	3,130,051.22	555,634.76	2,574,416.46	130,777,925.53
15	3,130,051.22	544,908.02	2,585,143.20	128,192,782.33
16	3,130,051.22	534,136.59	2,595,914.63	125,596,867.70
17	3,130,051.22	523,320.28	2,606,730.94	122,990,136.77
18	3,130,051.22	512,458.90	2,617,592.32	120,372,544.45
19	3,130,051.22	501,552.27	2,628,498.95	117,744,045.50
20	3,130,051.22	490,600.19	2,639,451.03	115,104,594.47
21	3,130,051.22	479,602.48	2,650,448.74	112,454,145.72
22	3,130,051.22	468,558.94	2,661,492.28	109,792,653.44
23	3,130,051.22	457,469.39	2,672,581.83	107,120,071.61
24	3,130,051.22	446,333.63	2,683,717.59	104,436,354.02
25	3,130,051.22	435,151.48	2,694,899.75	101,741,454.28
26	3,130,051.22	423,922.73	2,706,128.49	99,035,325.78
27	3,130,051.22	412,647.19	2,717,404.03	96,317,921.75
28	3,130,051.22	401,324.67	2,728,726.55	93,589,195.21
29	3,130,051.22	389,954.98	2,740,096.24	90,849,098.97
30	3,130,051.22	378,537.91	2,751,513.31	88,097,585.66
31	3,130,051.22	367,073.27	2,762,977.95	85,334,607.71
32	3,130,051.22	355,560.87	2,774,490.35	82,560,117.36
33	3,130,051.22	344,000.49	2,786,050.73	79,774,066.63
34	3,130,051.22	332,391.94	2,797,659.28	76,976,407.35
35	3,130,051.22	320,735.03	2,809,316.19	74,167,091.16
36	3,130,051.22	309,029.55	2,821,021.67	71,346,069.49
37	3,130,051.22	297,275.29	2,832,775.93	68,513,293.56
38	3,130,051.22	285,472.06	2,844,579.16	65,668,714.39
39	3,130,051.22	273,619.64	2,856,431.58	62,812,282.81
40	3,130,051.22	261,717.85	2,868,333.38	59,943,949.44
41	3,130,051.22	249,766.46	2,880,284.76	57,063,664.67
42	3,130,051.22	237,765.27	2,892,285.95	54,171,378.72
43	3,130,051.22	225,714.08	2,904,337.14	51,267,041.58
44	3,130,051.22	213,612.67	2,916,438.55	48,350,603.03
45	3,130,051.22	201,460.85	2,928,590.37	45,422,012.66
46	3,130,051.22	189,258.39	2,940,792.83	42,481,219.83
47	3,130,051.22	177,005.08	2,953,046.14	39,528,173.69
48	3,130,051.22	164,700.72	2,965,350.50	36,562,823.19
49	3,130,051.22	152,345.10	2,977,706.12	33,585,117.07
50	3,130,051.22	139,937.99	2,990,113.23	30,595,003.83
51	3,130,051.22	127,479.18	3,002,572.04	27,592,431.80
52	3,130,051.22	114,968.47	3,015,082.75	24,577,349.04
53	3,130,051.22	102,405.62	3,027,645.60	21,549,703.44
54	3,130,051.22	89,790.43	3,040,260.79	18,509,442.65
55	3,130,051.22	77,122.68	3,052,928.54	15,456,514.11
56	3,130,051.22	64,402.14	3,065,649.08	12,390,865.03
57	3,130,051.22	51,628.60	3,078,422.62	9,312,442.42
58	3,130,051.22	38,801.84	3,091,249.38	6,221,193.04
59	3,130,051.22	25,921.64	3,104,129.58	3,117,063.46
60	3,130,051.22	12,987.76	3,117,063.46	0.00

SOLUTIONS

FINANCIAL ACCOUNTING MULTIPLE CHOICE SOLUTIONS

1   Pharma Drug Company Ltd. sells several different types of medications. This month, Pharma Drug Company Ltd. accepted 22000 batches of pills which were returned by customers. These products had been marked up by 35% and they had originally been bought at a per-unit cost of $2700.

D)   DR Sales Returns $80,190,000
DR Inventory $59,400,000
          CR Accounts Receivable $80,190,000
          CR Cost of Goods Sold $59,400,000

This transaction increases the sales returns (contra-revenue) account, and the inventory (asset) account. The accounts receivable (asset) account and the cost of goods sold (expense) account have both decreased. 22000 batches of pills x $2,700 = $59,400,000. The 35% markup applies to the sales returns and accounts receivable amounts, i.e. $59,400,000 x 1.35 = $80,190,000

2   A to Z Event Guru Ltd sells several different types of start-to-finish event planning services for large gatherings. Today, A to Z Event Guru Ltd has paid cash to their supplier to fully pay off their account payable balance, which was $76000.

A)   DR Accounts Payable $76,000
          CR Cash $76,000

The accounts payable (liability) and cash (asset) accounts have both increased by $76,000.

3   Sprike Inc offers their customers a wide range of athletic apparel. This December, Sprike Inc recognized 1 year of depreciation on equipment which had a total useful life of 10 years, and which had originally cost $260000.

B)   DR Depreciation expense $26,000
          CR Accumulated Depreciation $26,000

The depreciation (expense) account and the accumulated depreciation (contra-asset) accounts have both increased by: $260,000 divided by 10 years = $26,000 depreciation per year.

4   Pharma Drug Company Ltd. is a privately-held corporation which focuses on their niche of premium medications. Today Pharma Drug Company Ltd. sold 29400 batches of pills which had a 30% mark-up. They had originally been bought from their suppliers for a unit cost of $2340.

C)   DR Accounts Receivable $89,434,800
          DR Cost of Goods Sold $68,796,000
          CR Sales $89,434,800
          CR Inventory $68,796,000

This transaction increases the accounts receivable (asset) account, the sales (revenue) account, and the cost of goods sold (expense) account. The inventory (asset) account has decreased. 29400 batches of pills x $2,340 = $68,796,000. The 30% markup applies to the sales and accounts receivable amounts, i.e. $68,796,000 x 1.30 = $89,434,800

5   Mount Tessory Academy is a company which offers their customers a wide selection of private school education. This week, Mount Tessory Academy paid each of the 2790 staff members their bi-weekly wages, which per person had a cost of $2600.

        B)   DR Wage expense $7,254,000
                  CR Accounts Payable $7,254,000

The wage (expense) and the accounts payable (liability) accounts have both increased by: 2790 staff members x $2,600 = $7,254,000

6   A to Z Event Guru Ltd sells several different types of start-to-finish event planning services for large gatherings. Today A to Z Event Guru Ltd signed up for a loan with a 5% interest rate, and so the bank immediately transferred cash to the company in the amount of $103000.

        B)   DR Cash $103,000
                  CR Loan Payable $103,000

The cash (asset) and the loan payable (liability) accounts have both increased by: $103,000. The interest rate does not affect this initial accounting entry, but it will be used for the calculation of interest expense when repayments are made in the future toward this loan.

7   Sprike Inc is a company which offers their customers a wide selection of athletic apparel. Today, Sprike Inc received an upfront payment for 1510 batches of athletic t-shirts which will be provided to the customer 6 months from now. The payment for each was $1600.

        C)   DR Cash $2,416,000
                  CR Unearned Revenue $2,416,000

The cash (asset) and the unearned revenue (liability) accounts have both increased by: 1510 batches of athletic t-shirts x $1,600 = $2,416,000

8   Club Disco is a company which offers their customers a wide selection of dance venue rentals for large family gatherings. This month, Club Disco must amortize 1 month worth of utility bills which they had prepaid at the beginning of the year. The amount that they had paid upfront for the year was $45600.

        B)   DR Utilities expense $3,800
                  CR Prepaid Expense $3,800

The utilities (expense) account has increased and the prepaid expense (asset) account has decreased by: $45,600 for the year, divided by 12 months = $3,800

9   NBG Media Corporation is a corporation which sells broadcasting services for advertising agencies. This month, NBG Media Corporation paid for 1 month of rent for their company's office space. Each month, the rent owing was $9000.

        C)   DR Rent expense $9,000
                  CR Accounts Payable $9,000

The rent (expense) and the accounts payable (liability) accounts are both increased by one month's worth of rent, which is $9,000.

10   AC&C Ltd. is a privately-held corporation which focuses on their niche of premium cell phone plans. This month, AC&C Ltd. must amortize 1 month worth of utility bills which they had prepaid at the beginning of the year. The amount that they had paid upfront for the year was $37200.

        B)   DR Utilities expense $3,100

                    CR Prepaid Expense $3,100

The utilities (expense) account has increased and the prepaid expense (asset) account has decreased by: $37,200 for the year, divided by 12 months = $3,100

11   Pharma Drug Company Ltd. sells several different types of medications. This month, Pharma Drug Company Ltd. accepted 14800 batches of pills which were returned by customers. These products had been marked up by 35% and they had originally been bought at a per-unit cost of $1600.

        D)   DR Sales Returns $31,968,000

                  DR Inventory $23,680,000

                    CR Accounts Receivable $31,968,000

                    CR Cost of Goods Sold $23,680,000

This transaction increases the sales returns (contra-revenue) account, and the inventory (asset) account. The accounts receivable (asset) account and the cost of goods sold (expense) account have both decreased. 14800 batches of pills x $1,600 = $23,680,000. The 35% markup applies to the sales returns and accounts receivable amounts, i.e. $23,680,000 x 1.35 = $31,968,000

12   Pharma Drug Company Ltd. is a company which offers their customers a wide selection of medications. This week, Pharma Drug Company Ltd. purchased 2000 batches of pills which were placed into the warehouse, and which had a per unit cost of $2700.

        B)   DR Inventory $5,400,000

                    CR Accounts Payable $5,400,000

There was an increase in the inventory (asset) account, and also an increase in the accounts payable (liability) account. 2000 batches of pills x $2,700 = $5,400,000

13   Fairway Malls offers their customers a wide range of retail spaces in their shopping centers. Today, Fairway Malls has paid cash to their supplier to fully pay off their account payable balance, which was $8000.

        D)   DR Accounts Payable $8,000

                    CR Cash $8,000

The accounts payable (liability) and cash (asset) accounts have both increased by $8,000.

14   Hogtown Records sells several different types of audio services for local musicians to record their music albums. This December, Hogtown Records recognized 1 year of depreciation on equipment which had a total useful life of 10 years, and which had originally cost $130000.

        C)   DR Depreciation expense $13,000

                    CR Accumulated Depreciation $13,000

The depreciation (expense) account and the accumulated depreciation (contra-asset) accounts have both increased by: $130,000 divided by 10 years = $13,000 depreciation per year.

15   Mr. Mop provides their customers with household cleaners. This month, Mr. Mop has estimated that 15% of the accounts receivable might not end up being collectable, based on past experience. The accounts receivable will need to be adjusted from its current balance of $106000.

           D)   DR Bad Debt expense $15,900
                        CR Allowance for Doubtful Accounts $15,900

The bad debts (expense) and the allowance for doubtful accounts (contra-asset) have both increased by: 15% x $106,000 = $15,900

16   Payday Now is an organization which specializes in providing their customers with short-term loan arrangements. This December, Payday Now recognized 1 year of depreciation on a building which had a total useful life of 25 years, and which had originally been bought for $84000.

           D)   DR Depreciation expense $3,360
                        CR Accumulated Depreciation $3,360

The depreciation (expense) account and the accumulated depreciation (contra-asset) accounts have both increased by: $84,000 divided by 25 years = $3,360 depreciation per year.

17   NY Fitness is a corporation which sells gym memberships for professional sports teams. This January, NY Fitness has made an advance payment to cover the next 12 months of utility bills, which have a monthly cost of $1100.

           C)   DR Prepaid Expense $13,200
                        CR Cash $13,200

The prepaid expense (asset) account has increased, and the cash (asset) account has decreased by: 12 months x $1,100 per month = $13,200 for the year.

18   AC&C Ltd. is a market leader that is well-known for their brand of cell phone plans. This month, AC&C Ltd. must amortize 1 month worth of utility bills which they had prepaid at the beginning of the year. The amount that they had paid upfront for the year was $32400.

           D)   DR Utilities expense $2,700
                        CR Prepaid Expense $2,700

The utilities (expense) account has increased and the prepaid expense (asset) account has decreased by: $32,400 for the year, divided by 12 months = $2,700

19   Payday Now is a market leader that is well-known for their brand of short-term loan arrangements. Today Payday Now signed up for a loan with a 5% interest rate, and so the bank immediately transferred cash to the company in the amount of $39000.

           A)   DR Cash $39,000
                        CR Loan Payable $39,000

The cash (asset) and the loan payable (liability) accounts have both increased by: $39,000. The interest rate does not affect this initial accounting entry, but it will be used for the calculation of interest expense when repayments are made in the future toward this loan.

20   Kola-Nut Ltd provides their customers with soft drinks. Today Kola-Nut Ltd sold 35800 batches of soda bottles which had a 30% mark-up. They had originally been bought from their suppliers for a unit cost of $1950.

D)   DR Accounts Receivable $90,753,000
DR Cost of Goods Sold $69,810,000
    CR Sales $90,753,000
    CR Inventory $69,810,000

This transaction increases the accounts receivable (asset) account, the sales (revenue) account, and the cost of goods sold (expense) account. The inventory (asset) account has decreased. 35800 batches of soda bottles x $1,950 = $69,810,000. The 30% markup applies to the sales and accounts receivable amounts, i.e. $69,810,000 x 1.30 = $90,753,000

21   Mr. Mop is an organization which specializes in providing their customers with household cleaners. This month, Mr. Mop accepted 18900 tons of cleaning solution which were returned by customers. These products had been marked up by 35% and they had originally been bought at a per-unit cost of $2000.

A)   DR Sales Returns $51,030,000
DR Inventory $37,800,000
    CR Accounts Receivable $51,030,000
    CR Cost of Goods Sold $37,800,000

This transaction increases the sales returns (contra-revenue) account, and the inventory (asset) account. The accounts receivable (asset) account and the cost of goods sold (expense) account have both decreased. 18900 tons of cleaning solution x $2,000 = $37,800,000. The 35% markup applies to the sales returns and accounts receivable amounts, i.e. $37,800,000 x 1.35 = $51,030,000

22   AC&C Ltd. is a privately-held corporation which focuses on their niche of premium cell phone plans. This December, AC&C Ltd. recognized 1 year of depreciation on equipment which had a total useful life of 10 years, and which had originally cost $90000.

A)   DR Depreciation expense $9,000
    CR Accumulated Depreciation $9,000

The depreciation (expense) account and the accumulated depreciation (contra-asset) accounts have both increased by: $90,000 divided by 10 years = $9,000 depreciation per year.

23   Air America sells various global flights. Air America has just provided 1600 large orders which had been paid for in advance last year. Each order was in the amount of $1700.

C)   DR Unearned Revenue $2,720,000
    CR Sales $2,720,000

The unearned revenue (liability) account has decreased and the and the sales (revenue) account has increased by: 1600 large orders x $1,700 = $2,720,000

24 Payday Now offers their customers a wide range of short-term loan arrangements. Today, Payday Now bought equipment which has a 5 year useful life, and which had a cost of $15000.

    D)   DR Equipment $15,000
                  CR Accounts Payable $15,000

The equipment (asset) and the accounts payable (liability) accounts have both increased by: $15,000. The useful life does not affect this original accounting entry, but it will be used to calculate depreciation of the asset in the future.

25 Air America provides their customers with global flights. Today Air America signed up for a loan with a 5% interest rate, and so the bank immediately transferred cash to the company in the amount of $58000.

    D)   DR Cash $58,000
                  CR Loan Payable $58,000

The cash (asset) and the loan payable (liability) accounts have both increased by: $58,000. The interest rate does not affect this initial accounting entry, but it will be used for the calculation of interest expense when repayments are made in the future toward this loan.

26 Paytech Ltd offers their customers a wide range of payroll transaction processing services. This month, Paytech Ltd paid for 1 month of rent for their company's office space. Each month, the rent owing was $14000.

    B)   DR Rent expense $14,000
                  CR Accounts Payable $14,000

The rent (expense) and the accounts payable (liability) accounts are both increased by one month's worth of rent, which is $14,000.

27 Mount Tessory Academy is a market leader that is well-known for their brand of private school education. This month, Mount Tessory Academy has estimated that 15% of the accounts receivable might not end up being collectable, based on past experience. The accounts receivable will need to be adjusted from its current balance of $53000.

    A)   DR Bad Debt expense $7,950
                  CR Allowance for Doubtful Accounts $7,950

The bad debts (expense) and the allowance for doubtful accounts (contra-asset) have both increased by: 15% x $53,000 = $7,950

28 Mount Tessory Academy provides their customers with private school education. This month, Mount Tessory Academy must amortize 1 month worth of utility bills which they had prepaid at the beginning of the year. The amount that they had paid upfront for the year was $26400.

    D)   DR Utilities expense $2,200
                  CR Prepaid Expense $2,200

The utilities (expense) account has increased and the prepaid expense (asset) account has decreased by: $26,400 for the year, divided by 12 months = $2,200

29   NY Fitness is an organization which specializes in providing their customers with gym memberships for professional sports teams. This year, NY Fitness has provided 2200 team memberships each of which earned revenues of $1530.
        A)   DR Accounts Receivable $3,366,000
                CR Sales $3,366,000
The accounts receivable (asset) and the sales (revenue) accounts have both increased by: 2200 team memberships x $1,530 = $3,366,000

30   Jameson & Jameson is an organization which specializes in providing their customers with soap products. Today, Jameson & Jameson received an upfront payment for 5540 truckloads of bars of soap which will be provided to the customer 6 months from now. The payment for each was $1700.
        B)   DR Cash $9,418,000
                CR Unearned Revenue $9,418,000
The cash (asset) and the unearned revenue (liability) accounts have both increased by: 5540 truckloads of bars of soap x $1,700 = $9,418,000

31   A to Z Event Guru Ltd sells various start-to-finish event planning services for large gatherings. This week, A to Z Event Guru Ltd paid each of the 2910 staff members their bi-weekly wages, which per person had a cost of $2600.
        D)   DR Wage expense $7,566,000
                CR Accounts Payable $7,566,000
The wage (expense) and the accounts payable (liability) accounts have both increased by: 2910 staff members x $2,600 = $7,566,000

32   Grand Convention Ltd is a market leader that is well-known for their brand of banquet hall rentals for corporate meetings. This December, Grand Convention Ltd has paid each of the company's 2400 owners an annual dividend in the amount of $26000.
        D)   DR Retained Earnings $62,400,000
                CR Cash $62,400,000
The retained earnings (equity) and the cash accounts have both decreased by: 2400 owners x $26,000 = $62,400,000

33   Grand Convention Ltd is a company which offers their customers a wide selection of banquet hall rentals for corporate meetings. This December, Grand Convention Ltd has paid each of the company's 1000 owners an annual dividend in the amount of $13000.
        B)   DR Retained Earnings $13,000,000
                CR Cash $13,000,000
The retained earnings (equity) and the cash accounts have both decreased by: 1000 owners x $13,000 = $13,000,000

34   Kola-Nut Ltd is an organization which specializes in providing their customers with soft drinks. Today Kola-Nut Ltd sold 43400 batches of soda bottles which had a 30% mark-up. They had originally been bought from their suppliers for a unit cost of $2310.

A)   DR Accounts Receivable $130,330,200
       DR Cost of Goods Sold $100,254,000
              CR Sales $130,330,200
              CR Inventory $100,254,000

This transaction increases the accounts receivable (asset) account, the sales (revenue) account, and the cost of goods sold (expense) account. The inventory (asset) account has decreased. 43400 batches of soda bottles x $2,310 = $100,254,000. The 30% markup applies to the sales and accounts receivable amounts, i.e. $100,254,000 x 1.30 = $130,330,200

35   Fairway Malls sells several different types of retail spaces in their shopping centers. This December, Fairway Malls has paid each of the company's 2100 owners an annual dividend in the amount of $23000.

A)   DR Retained Earnings $48,300,000
              CR Cash $48,300,000

The retained earnings (equity) and the cash accounts have both decreased by: 2100 owners x $23,000 = $48,300,000

36   NBG Media Corporation is an organization which specializes in providing their customers with broadcasting services for advertising agencies. This month, NBG Media Corporation made 1 monthly loan repayment towards their long-term note payable. The interest portion was 60% of the payment. The total amount paid in cash was $15000.

A)   DR Interest Expense $9,000
       DR Loan Payable $6,000
              CR Cash $15,000

The interest (expense) account has increased by $15,000 x 0.6 = $9,000. The loan payable (liability) has decreased by $15,000 x 0.4 = $6,000. The cash (asset) account has decreased by the full amount of the payment, which is $15,000

37   Hogtown Records offers their customers a wide range of audio services for local musicians to record their music albums. This month, Hogtown Records paid for 1 month of rent for their company's office space. Each month, the rent owing was $10000.

C)   DR Rent expense $10,000
              CR Accounts Payable $10,000

The rent (expense) and the accounts payable (liability) accounts are both increased by one month's worth of rent, which is $10,000.

38   David & Johnson provides their customers with legal services. This month, David & Johnson paid for 1 month of rent for their company's office space. Each month, the rent owing was $20000.

B)   DR Rent expense $20,000
              CR Accounts Payable $20,000

The rent (expense) and the accounts payable (liability) accounts are both increased by one month's worth of rent, which is $20,000.

39   Mr. Mop is an organization which specializes in providing their customers with household cleaners. This month, Mr. Mop paid for 1 month of rent for the warehouse room, which has a monthly costs of $1000.

B)   DR Rent expense $1,000
            CR Accounts Payable $1,000

The rent (expense) and the accounts payable (liability) accounts are both increased by one month's worth of rent, which is $1,000.

40   Comedy 253 is a privately-held corporation which focuses on their niche of premium live performances of stand-up comedy. This year, Comedy 253 has provided 1500 shows each of which earned revenues of $2440.

B)   DR Accounts Receivable $3,660,000
            CR Sales $3,660,000

The accounts receivable (asset) and the sales (revenue) accounts have both increased by: 1500 shows x $2,440 = $3,660,000

41   Paytech Ltd sells various payroll transaction processing services. This month, Paytech Ltd must amortize 1 month worth of utility bills which they had prepaid at the beginning of the year. The amount that they had paid upfront for the year was $12000.

B)   DR Utilities expense $1,000
            CR Prepaid Expense $1,000

The utilities (expense) account has increased and the prepaid expense (asset) account has decreased by: $12,000 for the year, divided by 12 months = $1,000

42   Pharma Drug Company Ltd. offers their customers a wide range of medications. This week, Pharma Drug Company Ltd. purchased 2250 batches of pills which were placed into the warehouse, and which had a per unit cost of $1100.

A)   DR Inventory $2,475,000
            CR Accounts Payable $2,475,000

There was an increase in the inventory (asset) account, and also an increase in the accounts payable (liability) account. 2250 batches of pills x $1,100 = $2,475,000

43   A to Z Event Guru Ltd is a privately-held corporation which focuses on their niche of premium start-to-finish event planning services for large gatherings. This December, A to Z Event Guru Ltd recognized 1 year of depreciation on equipment which had a total useful life of 10 years, and which had originally cost $220000.

D)   DR Depreciation expense $22,000
            CR Accumulated Depreciation $22,000

The depreciation (expense) account and the accumulated depreciation (contra-asset) accounts have both increased by: $220,000 divided by 10 years = $22,000 depreciation per year.

44   Kola-Nut Ltd offers their customers a wide range of soft drinks. Today Kola-Nut Ltd sold 45800 batches of soda bottles which had a 30% mark-up. They had originally been bought from their suppliers for a unit cost of $2920.

        B)   DR Accounts Receivable $173,856,800
            DR Cost of Goods Sold $133,736,000
                CR Sales $173,856,800
                CR Inventory $133,736,000

This transaction increases the accounts receivable (asset) account, the sales (revenue) account, and the cost of goods sold (expense) account. The inventory (asset) account has decreased. 45800 batches of soda bottles x $2,920 = $133,736,000. The 30% markup applies to the sales and accounts receivable amounts, i.e. $133,736,000 x 1.30 = $173,856,800

45   Jameson & Jameson is a company which offers their customers a wide selection of soap products. This month, Jameson & Jameson accepted 22700 truckloads of bars of soap which were returned by customers. These products had been marked up by 35% and they had originally been bought at a per-unit cost of $1500.

        B)   DR Sales Returns $45,967,500
            DR Inventory $34,050,000
                CR Accounts Receivable $45,967,500
                CR Cost of Goods Sold $34,050,000

This transaction increases the sales returns (contra-revenue) account, and the inventory (asset) account. The accounts receivable (asset) account and the cost of goods sold (expense) account have both decreased. 22700 truckloads of bars of soap x $1,500 = $34,050,000. The 35% markup applies to the sales returns and accounts receivable amounts, i.e. $34,050,000 x 1.35 = $45,967,500

46   McGerald's is an organization which specializes in providing their customers with fast food meals. Today, McGerald's bought equipment which has a 5 year useful life, and which had a cost of $25000.

        C)   DR Equipment $25,000
                CR Accounts Payable $25,000

The equipment (asset) and the accounts payable (liability) accounts have both increased by: $25,000. The useful life does not affect this original accounting entry, but it will be used to calculate depreciation of the asset in the future.

47   Mount Tessory Academy sells several different types of private school education. This January, Mount Tessory Academy has made an advance payment to cover the next 12 months of utility bills, which have a monthly cost of $1300.

        A)   DR Prepaid Expense $15,600
                CR Cash $15,600

The prepaid expense (asset) account has increased, and the cash (asset) account has decreased by: 12 months x $1,300 per month = $15,600 for the year.

48 Sprike Inc is a corporation which sells athletic apparel. This December, Sprike Inc recognized 1 year of depreciation on equipment which had a total useful life of 10 years, and which had originally cost $240000.

B)   DR Depreciation expense $24,000
            CR Accumulated Depreciation $24,000

The depreciation (expense) account and the accumulated depreciation (contra-asset) accounts have both increased by: $240,000 divided by 10 years = $24,000 depreciation per year.

49 AC&C Ltd. is a market leader that is well-known for their brand of cell phone plans. This year, AC&C Ltd. has provided 1700 monthly cell phone service each of which earned revenues of $1680.

B)   DR Accounts Receivable $2,856,000
            CR Sales $2,856,000

The accounts receivable (asset) and the sales (revenue) accounts have both increased by: 1700 monthly cell phone service x $1,680 = $2,856,000

50 Mr. Mop is a company which offers their customers a wide selection of household cleaners. This month, Mr. Mop paid for 1 month of rent for the warehouse room, which has a monthly costs of $2200.

A)   DR Rent expense $2,200
            CR Accounts Payable $2,200

The rent (expense) and the accounts payable (liability) accounts are both increased by one month's worth of rent, which is $2,200.

51 Mr. Mop is a corporation which sells household cleaners. This month, Mr. Mop accepted 26900 tons of cleaning solution which were returned by customers. These products had been marked up by 35% and they had originally been bought at a per-unit cost of $2700.

A)   DR Sales Returns $98,050,500
            DR Inventory $72,630,000
                CR Accounts Receivable $98,050,500
                CR Cost of Goods Sold $72,630,000

This transaction increases the sales returns (contra-revenue) account, and the inventory (asset) account. The accounts receivable (asset) account and the cost of goods sold (expense) account have both decreased. 26900 tons of cleaning solution x $2,700 = $72,630,000. The 35% markup applies to the sales returns and accounts receivable amounts, i.e. $72,630,000 x 1.35 = $98,050,500

52 Mr. Mop offers their customers a wide range of household cleaners. Today, Mr. Mop received an upfront payment for 3260 tons of cleaning solution which will be provided to the customer 6 months from now. The payment for each was $1200.

D)   DR Cash $3,912,000
            CR Unearned Revenue $3,912,000

The cash (asset) and the unearned revenue (liability) accounts have both increased by: 3260 tons of cleaning solution x $1,200 = $3,912,000

53   Pharma Drug Company Ltd. is a company which offers their customers a wide selection of medications. This month, Pharma Drug Company Ltd. paid for 1 month of rent for the warehouse room, which has a monthly costs of $1000.

        D)   DR Rent expense $1,000
                  CR Accounts Payable $1,000

The rent (expense) and the accounts payable (liability) accounts are both increased by one month's worth of rent, which is $1,000.

54   Sprike Inc is a market leader that is well-known for their brand of athletic apparel. This week, Sprike Inc purchased 1460 batches of athletic t-shirts which were placed into the warehouse, and which had a per unit cost of $1700.

        D)   DR Inventory $2,482,000
                  CR Accounts Payable $2,482,000

There was an increase in the inventory (asset) account, and also an increase in the accounts payable (liability) account. 1460 batches of athletic t-shirts x $1,700 = $2,482,000

55   AC&C Ltd. offers their customers a wide range of cell phone plans. This week, AC&C Ltd. paid each of the 1220 staff members their bi-weekly wages, which per person had a cost of $1000.

        B)   DR Wage expense $1,220,000
                  CR Accounts Payable $1,220,000

The wage (expense) and the accounts payable (liability) accounts have both increased by: 1220 staff members x $1,000 = $1,220,000

56   Jameson & Jameson is a market leader that is well-known for their brand of soap products. Today Jameson & Jameson sold 28600 truckloads of bars of soap which had a 30% mark-up. They had originally been bought from their suppliers for a unit cost of $2670.

        B)   DR Accounts Receivable $99,270,600
                  DR Cost of Goods Sold $76,362,000
                     CR Sales $99,270,600
                     CR Inventory $76,362,000

This transaction increases the accounts receivable (asset) account, the sales (revenue) account, and the cost of goods sold (expense) account. The inventory (asset) account has decreased. 28600 truckloads of bars of soap x $2,670 = $76,362,000. The 30% markup applies to the sales and accounts receivable amounts, i.e. $76,362,000 x 1.30 = $99,270,600

57   Mr. Mop is a corporation which sells household cleaners. Today Mr. Mop signed up for a loan with a 5% interest rate, and so the bank immediately transferred cash to the company in the amount of $30000.

        A)   DR Cash $30,000
                  CR Loan Payable $30,000

The cash (asset) and the loan payable (liability) accounts have both increased by: $30,000. The interest rate does not affect this initial accounting entry, but it will be used for the calculation of interest expense when repayments are made in the future toward this loan.

58   AC&C Ltd. is a corporation which sells cell phone plans. Today, AC&C Ltd. received payment upfront for 2200 large orders which will not be provided until early next year. Each order was in the amount of $2500.

          C)   DR Cash $5,500,000
                     CR Unearned Revenue $5,500,000

The cash (asset) and the unearned revenue (liability) accounts have both increased by: 2200 large orders x $2,500 = $5,500,000

59   Comedy 253 is a privately-held corporation which focuses on their niche of premium live performances of stand-up comedy. This month, Comedy 253 has estimated that 30% of the accounts receivable might not end up being collectable, based on past experience. The accounts receivable will need to be adjusted from its current balance of $101000.

          B)   DR Bad Debt expense $30,300
                     CR Allowance for Doubtful Accounts $30,300

The bad debts (expense) and the allowance for doubtful accounts (contra-asset) have both increased by: 30% x $101,000 = $30,300

60   Fairway Malls provides their customers with retail spaces in their shopping centers. Today Fairway Malls signed up for a loan with a 5% interest rate, and so the bank immediately transferred cash to the company in the amount of $36000.

          C)   DR Cash $36,000
                     CR Loan Payable $36,000

The cash (asset) and the loan payable (liability) accounts have both increased by: $36,000. The interest rate does not affect this initial accounting entry, but it will be used for the calculation of interest expense when repayments are made in the future toward this loan.

61   LA Met Theatre Company is a company which offers their customers a wide selection of live theatrical performances. Today LA Met Theatre Company signed up for a loan with a 5% interest rate, and so the bank immediately transferred cash to the company in the amount of $74000.

          D)   DR Cash $74,000
                     CR Loan Payable $74,000

The cash (asset) and the loan payable (liability) accounts have both increased by: $74,000. The interest rate does not affect this initial accounting entry, but it will be used for the calculation of interest expense when repayments are made in the future toward this loan.

62   Kola-Nut Ltd is a corporation which sells soft drinks. Today, Kola-Nut Ltd bought equipment which has a 5 year useful life, and which had a cost of $18000.

          D)   DR Equipment $18,000
                     CR Accounts Payable $18,000

The equipment (asset) and the accounts payable (liability) accounts have both increased by: $18,000. The useful life does not affect this original accounting entry, but it will be used to calculate depreciation of the asset in the future.

63   Mr. Mop offers their customers a wide range of household cleaners. Today, Mr. Mop received an upfront payment for 3010 tons of cleaning solution which will be provided to the customer 6 months from now. The payment for each was $2400.

A)   DR Cash $7,224,000
        CR Unearned Revenue $7,224,000

The cash (asset) and the unearned revenue (liability) accounts have both increased by: 3010 tons of cleaning solution x $2,400 = $7,224,000

64   Kola-Nut Ltd sells several different types of soft drinks. Today, Kola-Nut Ltd has paid cash to their supplier to fully pay off their account payable balance, which was $41000.

A)   DR Accounts Payable $41,000
        CR Cash $41,000

The accounts payable (liability) and cash (asset) accounts have both increased by $41,000.

65   Sprike Inc is a corporation which sells athletic apparel. This month, Sprike Inc paid for 1 month of rent for the warehouse room, which has a monthly costs of $1000.

B)   DR Rent expense $1,000
        CR Accounts Payable $1,000

The rent (expense) and the accounts payable (liability) accounts are both increased by one month's worth of rent, which is $1,000.

66   Mr. Mop is a market leader that is well-known for their brand of household cleaners. This month, Mr. Mop accepted 17300 tons of cleaning solution which were returned by customers. These products had been marked up by 35% and they had originally been bought at a per-unit cost of $2800.

A)   DR Sales Returns $65,394,000
        DR Inventory $48,440,000
            CR Accounts Receivable $65,394,000
            CR Cost of Goods Sold $48,440,000

This transaction increases the sales returns (contra-revenue) account, and the inventory (asset) account. The accounts receivable (asset) account and the cost of goods sold (expense) account have both decreased. 17300 tons of cleaning solution x $2,800 = $48,440,000. The 35% markup applies to the sales returns and accounts receivable amounts, i.e. $48,440,000 x 1.35 = $65,394,000

67   NY Fitness is a company which offers their customers a wide selection of gym memberships for professional sports teams. Today, NY Fitness has paid cash to their supplier to fully pay off their account payable balance, which was $72000.

B)   DR Accounts Payable $72,000
        CR Cash $72,000

The accounts payable (liability) and cash (asset) accounts have both increased by $72,000.

68 AC&C Ltd. is a privately-held corporation which focuses on their niche of premium cell phone plans. This week, AC&C Ltd. paid each of the 1370 staff members their bi-weekly wages, which per person had a cost of $1800.

A) DR Wage expense $2,466,000
        CR Accounts Payable $2,466,000

The wage (expense) and the accounts payable (liability) accounts have both increased by: 1370 staff members x $1,800 = $2,466,000

69 Cirque du Lune sells various circus performances. This month, Cirque du Lune must amortize 1 month worth of utility bills which they had prepaid at the beginning of the year. The amount that they had paid upfront for the year was $12000.

B) DR Utilities expense $1,000
        CR Prepaid Expense $1,000

The utilities (expense) account has increased and the prepaid expense (asset) account has decreased by: $12,000 for the year, divided by 12 months = $1,000

70 A to Z Event Guru Ltd sells several different types of start-to-finish event planning services for large gatherings. Today, A to Z Event Guru Ltd has paid cash to their supplier to fully pay off their account payable balance, which was $14000.

B) DR Accounts Payable $14,000
        CR Cash $14,000

The accounts payable (liability) and cash (asset) accounts have both increased by $14,000.

71 Jameson & Jameson provides their customers with soap products. This month, Jameson & Jameson accepted 9100 truckloads of bars of soap which were returned by customers. These products had been marked up by 35% and they had originally been bought at a per-unit cost of $1500.

C) DR Sales Returns $18,427,500
        DR Inventory $13,650,000
            CR Accounts Receivable $18,427,500
            CR Cost of Goods Sold $13,650,000

This transaction increases the sales returns (contra-revenue) account, and the inventory (asset) account. The accounts receivable (asset) account and the cost of goods sold (expense) account have both decreased. 9100 truckloads of bars of soap x $1,500 = $13,650,000. The 35% markup applies to the sales returns and accounts receivable amounts, i.e. $13,650,000 x 1.35 = $18,427,500

72 A to Z Event Guru Ltd is a corporation which sells start-to-finish event planning services for large gatherings. This year, A to Z Event Guru Ltd has provided 1000 events each of which earned revenues of $1500.

B) DR Accounts Receivable $1,500,000
        CR Sales $1,500,000

The accounts receivable (asset) and the sales (revenue) accounts have both increased by: 1000 events x $1,500 = $1,500,000

73   NY Fitness is an organization which specializes in providing their customers with gym memberships for professional sports teams. This month, NY Fitness has estimated that 10% of the accounts receivable might not end up being collectable, based on past experience. The accounts receivable will need to be adjusted from its current balance of $58000.

        D)   DR Bad Debt expense $5,800
                    CR Allowance for Doubtful Accounts $5,800

The bad debts (expense) and the allowance for doubtful accounts (contra-asset) have both increased by: 10% x $58,000 = $5,800

74   Cirque du Lune sells several different types of circus performances. This month, Cirque du Lune paid for 1 month of rent for their company's office space. Each month, the rent owing was $16000.

        D)   DR Rent expense $16,000
                    CR Accounts Payable $16,000

The rent (expense) and the accounts payable (liability) accounts are both increased by one month's worth of rent, which is $16,000.

75   David & Johnson is a company which offers their customers a wide selection of legal services. This year, David & Johnson has provided 1900 billable hours each of which earned revenues of $2060.

        C)   DR Accounts Receivable $3,914,000
                    CR Sales $3,914,000

The accounts receivable (asset) and the sales (revenue) accounts have both increased by: 1900 billable hours x $2,060 = $3,914,000

76   Fairway Malls is a corporation which sells retail spaces in their shopping centers. This December, Fairway Malls recognized 1 year of depreciation on a building which had a total useful life of 25 years, and which had originally been bought for $869000.

        C)   DR Depreciation expense $34,760
                    CR Accumulated Depreciation $34,760

The depreciation (expense) account and the accumulated depreciation (contra-asset) accounts have both increased by: $869,000 divided by 25 years = $34,760 depreciation per year.

77   Jameson & Jameson is an organization which specializes in providing their customers with soap products. Today, Jameson & Jameson received an upfront payment for 3000 truckloads of bars of soap which will be provided to the customer 6 months from now. The payment for each was $1900.

        B)   DR Cash $5,700,000
                    CR Unearned Revenue $5,700,000

The cash (asset) and the unearned revenue (liability) accounts have both increased by: 3000 truckloads of bars of soap x $1,900 = $5,700,000

78   Toyonda sells various cars. This month, Toyonda must amortize 1 month worth of utility
bills which they had prepaid at the beginning of the year. The amount that they had paid
upfront for the year was $25200.

    B)   DR Utilities expense $2,100
                CR Prepaid Expense $2,100

The utilities (expense) account has increased and the prepaid expense (asset) account
has decreased by: $25,200 for the year, divided by 12 months = $2,100

79   Air America is an organization which specializes in providing their customers with global
flights. Today, Air America bought equipment which has a 5 year useful life, and which
had a cost of $24000.

    B)   DR Equipment $24,000
                CR Accounts Payable $24,000

The equipment (asset) and the accounts payable (liability) accounts have both increased
by: $24,000. The useful life does not affect this original accounting entry, but it will be
used to calculate depreciation of the asset in the future.

80   Mr. Mop is a company which offers their customers a wide selection of household
cleaners. This week, Mr. Mop purchased 3190 tons of cleaning solution which were
placed into the warehouse, and which had a per unit cost of $1900.

    D)   DR Inventory $6,061,000
                CR Accounts Payable $6,061,000

There was an increase in the inventory (asset) account, and also an increase in the
accounts payable (liability) account. 3190 tons of cleaning solution x $1,900 = $6,061,000

81   Sprike Inc offers their customers a wide range of athletic apparel. Today Sprike Inc sold
40800 batches of athletic t-shirts which had a 30% mark-up. They had originally been
bought from their suppliers for a unit cost of $1370.

    A)   DR Accounts Receivable $72,664,800
                DR Cost of Goods Sold $55,896,000
                    CR Sales $72,664,800
                    CR Inventory $55,896,000

This transaction increases the accounts receivable (asset) account, the sales (revenue)
account, and the cost of goods sold (expense) account. The inventory (asset) account
has decreased. 40800 batches of athletic t-shirts x $1,370 = $55,896,000. The 30%
markup applies to the sales and accounts receivable amounts, i.e. $55,896,000 x 1.30 =
$72,664,800

82   Pharma Drug Company Ltd. is a company which offers their customers a wide selection of medications. This month, Pharma Drug Company Ltd. accepted 23100 batches of pills which were returned by customers. These products had been marked up by 35% and they had originally been bought at a per-unit cost of $1000.

D)   DR Sales Returns $31,185,000
      DR Inventory $23,100,000
             CR Accounts Receivable $31,185,000
             CR Cost of Goods Sold $23,100,000

This transaction increases the sales returns (contra-revenue) account, and the inventory (asset) account. The accounts receivable (asset) account and the cost of goods sold (expense) account have both decreased. 23100 batches of pills x $1,000 = $23,100,000. The 35% markup applies to the sales returns and accounts receivable amounts, i.e. $23,100,000 x 1.35 = $31,185,000

83   Toyonda offers their customers a wide range of cars. Today, Toyonda bought equipment which has a 5 year useful life, and which had a cost of $12000.

B)   DR Equipment $12,000
             CR Accounts Payable $12,000

The equipment (asset) and the accounts payable (liability) accounts have both increased by: $12,000. The useful life does not affect this original accounting entry, but it will be used to calculate depreciation of the asset in the future.

84   Pharma Drug Company Ltd. is a privately-held corporation which focuses on their niche of premium medications. This January, Pharma Drug Company Ltd. has made an advance payment to cover the next 12 months of utility bills, which have a monthly cost of $2700.

D)   DR Prepaid Expense $32,400
             CR Cash $32,400

The prepaid expense (asset) account has increased, and the cash (asset) account has decreased by: 12 months x $2,700 per month = $32,400 for the year.

85   Mr. Mop sells several different types of household cleaners. Today, Mr. Mop bought equipment which has a 5 year useful life, and which had a cost of $9000.

D)   DR Equipment $9,000
             CR Accounts Payable $9,000

The equipment (asset) and the accounts payable (liability) accounts have both increased by: $9,000. The useful life does not affect this original accounting entry, but it will be used to calculate depreciation of the asset in the future.

86   Jameson & Jameson offers their customers a wide range of soap products. This month, Jameson & Jameson paid for 1 month of rent for the warehouse room, which has a monthly costs of $1900.

C)   DR Rent expense $1,900
             CR Accounts Payable $1,900

The rent (expense) and the accounts payable (liability) accounts are both increased by one month's worth of rent, which is $1,900.

87   Mr. Mop is a privately-held corporation which focuses on their niche of premium
      household cleaners. This month, Mr. Mop accepted 9200 tons of cleaning solution which
      were returned by customers. These products had been marked up by 35% and they had
      originally been bought at a per-unit cost of $2700.
                D)   DR Sales Returns $33,534,000
                        DR Inventory $24,840,000
                            CR Accounts Receivable $33,534,000
                            CR Cost of Goods Sold $24,840,000
      This transaction increases the sales returns (contra-revenue) account, and the inventory
      (asset) account. The accounts receivable (asset) account and the cost of goods sold
      (expense) account have both decreased. 9200 tons of cleaning solution x $2,700 =
      $24,840,000. The 35% markup applies to the sales returns and accounts receivable
      amounts, i.e. $24,840,000 x 1.35 = $33,534,000

88   Air America is a corporation which sells global flights. Air America has just provided 1100
      large orders which had been paid for in advance last year. Each order was in the amount
      of $2300.
                B)   DR Unearned Revenue $2,530,000
                            CR Sales $2,530,000
      The unearned revenue (liability) account has decreased and the and the sales (revenue)
      account has increased by: 1100 large orders x $2,300 = $2,530,000

89   Cirque du Lune is an organization which specializes in providing their customers with
      circus performances. Cirque du Lune has just received a cash payment for the full
      amount that this customer owed to the company for all of their purchases to date. The
      outstanding balance which has now been paid was $13000.
                B)   DR Cash $13,000
                            CR Accounts Receivable $13,000
      The cash (asset) account has increased, and the accounts receivable (asset) account
      has decreased by $13,000.

90   McGerald's offers their customers a wide range of fast food meals. This week,
      McGerald's paid each of the 3210 staff members their bi-weekly wages, which per person
      had a cost of $2100.
                D)   DR Wage expense $6,741,000
                            CR Accounts Payable $6,741,000
      The wage (expense) and the accounts payable (liability) accounts have both increased
      by: 3210 staff members x $2,100 = $6,741,000

91   LA Met Theatre Company offers their customers a wide range of live theatrical
      performances. Today LA Met Theatre Company signed up for a loan with a 5% interest
      rate, and so the bank immediately transferred cash to the company in the amount of
      $41000.

                B)   DR Cash $41,000
                            CR Loan Payable $41,000
      The cash (asset) and the loan payable (liability) accounts have both increased by:
      $41,000. The interest rate does not affect this initial accounting entry, but it will be used
      for the calculation of interest expense when repayments are made in the future toward
      this loan.

92   Sprike Inc is an organization which specializes in providing their customers with athletic apparel. Today, Sprike Inc received an upfront payment for 3350 batches of athletic t-shirts which will be provided to the customer 6 months from now. The payment for each was $1600.

      A)   DR Cash $5,360,000
                  CR Unearned Revenue $5,360,000

The cash (asset) and the unearned revenue (liability) accounts have both increased by: 3350 batches of athletic t-shirts x $1,600 = $5,360,000

93   Mr. Mop provides their customers with household cleaners. Today Mr. Mop sold 23900 tons of cleaning solution which had a 30% mark-up. They had originally been bought from their suppliers for a unit cost of $2330.

      D)   DR Accounts Receivable $72,393,100
                DR Cost of Goods Sold $55,687,000
                  CR Sales $72,393,100
                  CR Inventory $55,687,000

This transaction increases the accounts receivable (asset) account, the sales (revenue) account, and the cost of goods sold (expense) account. The inventory (asset) account has decreased. 23900 tons of cleaning solution x $2,330 = $55,687,000. The 30% markup applies to the sales and accounts receivable amounts, i.e. $55,687,000 x 1.30 = $72,393,100

94   Fairway Malls is a market leader that is well-known for their brand of retail spaces in their shopping centers. Today Fairway Malls signed up for a loan with a 5% interest rate, and so the bank immediately transferred cash to the company in the amount of $94000.

      D)   DR Cash $94,000
                  CR Loan Payable $94,000

The cash (asset) and the loan payable (liability) accounts have both increased by: $94,000. The interest rate does not affect this initial accounting entry, but it will be used for the calculation of interest expense when repayments are made in the future toward this loan.

95   Comedy 253 offers their customers a wide range of live performances of stand-up comedy. Comedy 253 has just received a cash payment for the full amount that this customer owed to the company for all of their purchases to date. The outstanding balance which has now been paid was $36000.

      C)   DR Cash $36,000
                  CR Accounts Receivable $36,000

The cash (asset) account has increased, and the accounts receivable (asset) account has decreased by $36,000.

96   Jameson & Jameson is an organization which specializes in providing their customers with soap products. This December, Jameson & Jameson recognized 1 year of depreciation on equipment which had a total useful life of 10 years, and which had originally cost $260000.

      C)   DR Depreciation expense $26,000
                  CR Accumulated Depreciation $26,000

The depreciation (expense) account and the accumulated depreciation (contra-asset) accounts have both increased by: $260,000 divided by 10 years = $26,000 depreciation per year.

97   Air America is a company which offers their customers a wide selection of global flights. Air America has just received a cash payment for the full amount that this customer owed to the company for all of their purchases to date. The outstanding balance which has now been paid was $83000.

      B)   DR Cash $83,000
                CR Accounts Receivable $83,000

The cash (asset) account has increased, and the accounts receivable (asset) account has decreased by $83,000.

98   Hogtown Records sells several different types of audio services for local musicians to record their music albums. This December, Hogtown Records recognized 1 year of depreciation on equipment which had a total useful life of 10 years, and which had originally cost $210000.

      D)   DR Depreciation expense $21,000
                CR Accumulated Depreciation $21,000

The depreciation (expense) account and the accumulated depreciation (contra-asset) accounts have both increased by: $210,000 divided by 10 years = $21,000 depreciation per year.

99   Payday Now sells several different types of short-term loan arrangements. This December, Payday Now recognized 1 year of depreciation on equipment which had a total useful life of 10 years, and which had originally cost $80000.

      C)   DR Depreciation expense $8,000
                CR Accumulated Depreciation $8,000

The depreciation (expense) account and the accumulated depreciation (contra-asset) accounts have both increased by: $80,000 divided by 10 years = $8,000 depreciation per year.

100   Paytech Ltd is a privately-held corporation which focuses on their niche of premium payroll transaction processing services. This December, Paytech Ltd recognized 1 year of depreciation on equipment which had a total useful life of 10 years, and which had originally cost $120000.

      B)   DR Depreciation expense $12,000
                CR Accumulated Depreciation $12,000

The depreciation (expense) account and the accumulated depreciation (contra-asset) accounts have both increased by: $120,000 divided by 10 years = $12,000 depreciation per year.

101   McGerald's offers their customers a wide range of fast food meals. Today, McGerald's received payment upfront for 1000 large orders which will not be provided until early next year. Each order was in the amount of $1400.

      D)   DR Cash $1,400,000
                CR Unearned Revenue $1,400,000

The cash (asset) and the unearned revenue (liability) accounts have both increased by: 1000 large orders x $1,400 = $1,400,000

102   McGerald's is an organization which specializes in providing their customers with fast food meals. This week, McGerald's paid each of the 3870 staff members their bi-weekly wages, which per person had a cost of $1500.

B)   DR Wage expense $5,805,000
           CR Accounts Payable $5,805,000

The wage (expense) and the accounts payable (liability) accounts have both increased by: 3870 staff members x $1,500 = $5,805,000

103   Kola-Nut Ltd provides their customers with soft drinks. Today, Kola-Nut Ltd has paid cash to their supplier to fully pay off their account payable balance, which was $66000.

C)   DR Accounts Payable $66,000
           CR Cash $66,000

The accounts payable (liability) and cash (asset) accounts have both increased by $66,000.

104   Club Disco is a company which offers their customers a wide selection of dance venue rentals for large family gatherings. This January, Club Disco has made an advance payment to cover the next 12 months of utility bills, which have a monthly cost of $2300.

C)   DR Prepaid Expense $27,600
           CR Cash $27,600

The prepaid expense (asset) account has increased, and the cash (asset) account has decreased by: 12 months x $2,300 per month = $27,600 for the year.

105   Mount Tessory Academy provides their customers with private school education. This December, Mount Tessory Academy recognized 1 year of depreciation on equipment which had a total useful life of 10 years, and which had originally cost $140000.

B)   DR Depreciation expense $14,000
           CR Accumulated Depreciation $14,000

The depreciation (expense) account and the accumulated depreciation (contra-asset) accounts have both increased by: $140,000 divided by 10 years = $14,000 depreciation per year.

106   Toyonda offers their customers a wide range of cars. This month, Toyonda paid for 1 month of rent for their company's office space. Each month, the rent owing was $19000.

B)   DR Rent expense $19,000
           CR Accounts Payable $19,000

The rent (expense) and the accounts payable (liability) accounts are both increased by one month's worth of rent, which is $19,000.

107   LA Met Theatre Company sells several different types of live theatrical performances. Today, LA Met Theatre Company received payment upfront for 1700 large orders which will not be provided until early next year. Each order was in the amount of $1200.

D)   DR Cash $2,040,000
           CR Unearned Revenue $2,040,000

The cash (asset) and the unearned revenue (liability) accounts have both increased by: 1700 large orders x $1,200 = $2,040,000

108 LA Met Theatre Company provides their customers with live theatrical performances. This December, LA Met Theatre Company recognized 1 year of depreciation on equipment which had a total useful life of 10 years, and which had originally cost $80000.

A) DR Depreciation expense $8,000

CR Accumulated Depreciation $8,000

The depreciation (expense) account and the accumulated depreciation (contra-asset) accounts have both increased by: $80,000 divided by 10 years = $8,000 depreciation per year.

109 AC&C Ltd. is a corporation which sells cell phone plans. Today, AC&C Ltd. bought equipment which has a 5 year useful life, and which had a cost of $21000.

D) DR Equipment $21,000

CR Accounts Payable $21,000

The equipment (asset) and the accounts payable (liability) accounts have both increased by: $21,000. The useful life does not affect this original accounting entry, but it will be used to calculate depreciation of the asset in the future.

110 Comedy 253 provides their customers with live performances of stand-up comedy. This month, Comedy 253 has estimated that 30% of the accounts receivable might not end up being collectable, based on past experience. The accounts receivable will need to be adjusted from its current balance of $97000.

B) DR Bad Debt expense $29,100

CR Allowance for Doubtful Accounts $29,100

The bad debts (expense) and the allowance for doubtful accounts (contra-asset) have both increased by: 30% x $97,000 = $29,100

111 Mr. Mop is a market leader that is well-known for their brand of household cleaners. Today, Mr. Mop received an upfront payment for 1240 tons of cleaning solution which will be provided to the customer 6 months from now. The payment for each was $2600.

C) DR Cash $3,224,000

CR Unearned Revenue $3,224,000

The cash (asset) and the unearned revenue (liability) accounts have both increased by: 1240 tons of cleaning solution x $2,600 = $3,224,000

112 David & Johnson sells several different types of legal services. This week, David & Johnson paid each of the 3870 staff members their bi-weekly wages, which per person had a cost of $2700.

D) DR Wage expense $10,449,000

CR Accounts Payable $10,449,000

The wage (expense) and the accounts payable (liability) accounts have both increased by: 3870 staff members x $2,700 = $10,449,000

113 Sprike Inc is an organization which specializes in providing their customers with athletic apparel. This week, Sprike Inc purchased 3930 batches of athletic t-shirts which were placed into the warehouse, and which had a per unit cost of $2200.

D) DR Inventory $8,646,000

CR Accounts Payable $8,646,000

There was an increase in the inventory (asset) account, and also an increase in the accounts payable (liability) account. 3930 batches of athletic t-shirts x $2,200 = $8,646,000

114   Sprike Inc is an organization which specializes in providing their customers with athletic apparel. This month, Sprike Inc paid for 1 month of rent for the warehouse room, which has a monthly costs of $1700.

        B)   DR Rent expense $1,700
                CR Accounts Payable $1,700

The rent (expense) and the accounts payable (liability) accounts are both increased by one month's worth of rent, which is $1,700.

115   NBG Media Corporation sells several different types of broadcasting services for advertising agencies. NBG Media Corporation has just received a cash payment for the full amount that this customer owed to the company for all of their purchases to date. The outstanding balance which has now been paid was $86000.

        D)   DR Cash $86,000
                CR Accounts Receivable $86,000

The cash (asset) account has increased, and the accounts receivable (asset) account has decreased by $86,000.

116   Pharma Drug Company Ltd. is a privately-held corporation which focuses on their niche of premium medications. Today Pharma Drug Company Ltd. sold 17900 batches of pills which had a 30% mark-up. They had originally been bought from their suppliers for a unit cost of $2610.

        A)   DR Accounts Receivable $60,734,700
                DR Cost of Goods Sold $46,719,000
                CR Sales $60,734,700
                CR Inventory $46,719,000

This transaction increases the accounts receivable (asset) account, the sales (revenue) account, and the cost of goods sold (expense) account. The inventory (asset) account has decreased. 17900 batches of pills x $2,610 = $46,719,000. The 30% markup applies to the sales and accounts receivable amounts, i.e. $46,719,000 x 1.30 = $60,734,700

117   Grand Convention Ltd is a market leader that is well-known for their brand of banquet hall rentals for corporate meetings. This month, Grand Convention Ltd has estimated that 20% of the accounts receivable might not end up being collectable, based on past experience. The accounts receivable will need to be adjusted from its current balance of $55000.

        C)   DR Bad Debt expense $11,000
                CR Allowance for Doubtful Accounts $11,000

The bad debts (expense) and the allowance for doubtful accounts (contra-asset) have both increased by: 20% x $55,000 = $11,000

118   NBG Media Corporation is a company which offers their customers a wide selection of broadcasting services for advertising agencies. Today, NBG Media Corporation bought equipment which has a 5 year useful life, and which had a cost of $18000.

        C)   DR Equipment $18,000
                CR Accounts Payable $18,000

The equipment (asset) and the accounts payable (liability) accounts have both increased by: $18,000. The useful life does not affect this original accounting entry, but it will be used to calculate depreciation of the asset in the future.

119   NY Fitness is a market leader that is well-known for their brand of gym memberships for professional sports teams. NY Fitness has just provided 1800 large orders which had been paid for in advance last year. Each order was in the amount of $1100.

C)   DR Unearned Revenue $1,980,000
            CR Sales $1,980,000

The unearned revenue (liability) account has decreased and the and the sales (revenue) account has increased by: 1800 large orders x $1,100 = $1,980,000

120   Jameson & Jameson offers their customers a wide range of soap products. This month, Jameson & Jameson paid for 1 month of rent for the warehouse room, which has a monthly costs of $2200.

C)   DR Rent expense $2,200
            CR Accounts Payable $2,200

The rent (expense) and the accounts payable (liability) accounts are both increased by one month's worth of rent, which is $2,200.

121   David & Johnson sells several different types of legal services. This December, David & Johnson has paid each of the company's 2400 owners an annual dividend in the amount of $16000.

B)   DR Retained Earnings $38,400,000
            CR Cash $38,400,000

The retained earnings (equity) and the cash accounts have both decreased by: 2400 owners x $16,000 = $38,400,000

122   McGerald's is an organization which specializes in providing their customers with fast food meals. This month, McGerald's must amortize 1 month worth of utility bills which they had prepaid at the beginning of the year. The amount that they had paid upfront for the year was $24000.

B)   DR Utilities expense $2,000
            CR Prepaid Expense $2,000

The utilities (expense) account has increased and the prepaid expense (asset) account has decreased by: $24,000 for the year, divided by 12 months = $2,000

123   NY Fitness provides their customers with gym memberships for professional sports teams. Today, NY Fitness received payment upfront for 1900 large orders which will not be provided until early next year. Each order was in the amount of $1700.

D)   DR Cash $3,230,000
            CR Unearned Revenue $3,230,000

The cash (asset) and the unearned revenue (liability) accounts have both increased by: 1900 large orders x $1,700 = $3,230,000

124   AC&C Ltd. is a company which offers their customers a wide selection of cell phone plans. This month, AC&C Ltd. must amortize 1 month worth of utility bills which they had prepaid at the beginning of the year. The amount that they had paid upfront for the year was $44400.

B)   DR Utilities expense $3,700
            CR Prepaid Expense $3,700

The utilities (expense) account has increased and the prepaid expense (asset) account has decreased by: $44,400 for the year, divided by 12 months = $3,700

125   Club Disco is a company which offers their customers a wide selection of dance venue rentals for large family gatherings. Club Disco has just purchased a building using cash, which has an expected useful life of 30 years, and which had a total cost of $498000.

         C)   DR Building $498,000
                   CR Cash $498,000

The building (asset) account has increased, and the cash (asset) account has decreased by: $498,000. The useful life does not affect this original accounting entry, but it will be used to calculate depreciation of the asset in the future.

126   Kola-Nut Ltd sells several different types of soft drinks. This month, Kola-Nut Ltd accepted 26400 batches of soda bottles which were returned by customers. These products had been marked up by 35% and they had originally been bought at a per-unit cost of $2300.

         C)   DR Sales Returns $81,972,000
                DR Inventory $60,720,000
                   CR Accounts Receivable $81,972,000
                   CR Cost of Goods Sold $60,720,000

This transaction increases the sales returns (contra-revenue) account, and the inventory (asset) account. The accounts receivable (asset) account and the cost of goods sold (expense) account have both decreased. 26400 batches of soda bottles x $2,300 = $60,720,000. The 35% markup applies to the sales returns and accounts receivable amounts, i.e. $60,720,000 x 1.35 = $81,972,000

127   Jameson & Jameson is a corporation which sells soap products. This month, Jameson & Jameson paid for 1 month of rent for the warehouse room, which has a monthly costs of $2600.

         B)   DR Rent expense $2,600
                   CR Accounts Payable $2,600

The rent (expense) and the accounts payable (liability) accounts are both increased by one month's worth of rent, which is $2,600.

128   LA Met Theatre Company provides their customers with live theatrical performances. Today, LA Met Theatre Company bought equipment which has a 5 year useful life, and which had a cost of $12000.

         B)   DR Equipment $12,000
                   CR Accounts Payable $12,000

The equipment (asset) and the accounts payable (liability) accounts have both increased by: $12,000. The useful life does not affect this original accounting entry, but it will be used to calculate depreciation of the asset in the future.

129   McGerald's is a market leader that is well-known for their brand of fast food meals. Today McGerald's signed up for a loan with a 5% interest rate, and so the bank immediately transferred cash to the company in the amount of $89000.

         C)   DR Cash $89,000
                   CR Loan Payable $89,000

The cash (asset) and the loan payable (liability) accounts have both increased by: $89,000. The interest rate does not affect this initial accounting entry, but it will be used for the calculation of interest expense when repayments are made in the future toward this loan.

130 LA Met Theatre Company is a company which offers their customers a wide selection of live theatrical performances. This month, LA Met Theatre Company has estimated that 10% of the accounts receivable might not end up being collectable, based on past experience. The accounts receivable will need to be adjusted from its current balance of $30000.

C) DR Bad Debt expense $3,000
   CR Allowance for Doubtful Accounts $3,000

The bad debts (expense) and the allowance for doubtful accounts (contra-asset) have both increased by: 10% x $30,000 = $3,000

131 Sprike Inc is an organization which specializes in providing their customers with athletic apparel. Today, Sprike Inc received an upfront payment for 4750 batches of athletic t-shirts which will be provided to the customer 6 months from now. The payment for each was $1000.

D) DR Cash $4,750,000
   CR Unearned Revenue $4,750,000

The cash (asset) and the unearned revenue (liability) accounts have both increased by: 4750 batches of athletic t-shirts x $1,000 = $4,750,000

132 Grand Convention Ltd is a corporation which sells banquet hall rentals for corporate meetings. Today, Grand Convention Ltd has paid cash to their supplier to fully pay off their account payable balance, which was $86000.

D) DR Accounts Payable $86,000
   CR Cash $86,000

The accounts payable (liability) and cash (asset) accounts have both increased by $86,000.

133 Pharma Drug Company Ltd. is a market leader that is well-known for their brand of medications. Today, Pharma Drug Company Ltd. received an upfront payment for 4610 batches of pills which will be provided to the customer 6 months from now. The payment for each was $2000.

C) DR Cash $9,220,000
   CR Unearned Revenue $9,220,000

The cash (asset) and the unearned revenue (liability) accounts have both increased by: 4610 batches of pills x $2,000 = $9,220,000

134 Kola-Nut Ltd offers their customers a wide range of soft drinks. Today, Kola-Nut Ltd bought equipment which has a 5 year useful life, and which had a cost of $20000.

B) DR Equipment $20,000
   CR Accounts Payable $20,000

The equipment (asset) and the accounts payable (liability) accounts have both increased by: $20,000. The useful life does not affect this original accounting entry, but it will be used to calculate depreciation of the asset in the future.

135   Mr. Mop sells several different types of household cleaners. This December, Mr. Mop recognized 1 year of depreciation on a building which had a total useful life of 25 years, and which had originally been bought for $32000.
    D)   DR Depreciation expense $1,280
              CR Accumulated Depreciation $1,280
The depreciation (expense) account and the accumulated depreciation (contra-asset) accounts have both increased by: $32,000 divided by 25 years = $1,280 depreciation per year.

136   David & Johnson is an organization which specializes in providing their customers with legal services. David & Johnson has just provided 1800 large orders which had been paid for in advance last year. Each order was in the amount of $1800.
    B)   DR Unearned Revenue $3,240,000
              CR Sales $3,240,000
The unearned revenue (liability) account has decreased and the and the sales (revenue) account has increased by: 1800 large orders x $1,800 = $3,240,000

137   Fairway Malls is a corporation which sells retail spaces in their shopping centers. This December, Fairway Malls recognized 1 year of depreciation on a building which had a total useful life of 25 years, and which had originally been bought for $405000.
    D)   DR Depreciation expense $16,200
              CR Accumulated Depreciation $16,200
The depreciation (expense) account and the accumulated depreciation (contra-asset) accounts have both increased by: $405,000 divided by 25 years = $16,200 depreciation per year.

138   Jameson & Jameson is a privately-held corporation which focuses on their niche of premium soap products. This week, Jameson & Jameson purchased 1630 truckloads of bars of soap which were placed into the warehouse, and which had a per unit cost of $1600.
    D)   DR Inventory $2,608,000
              CR Accounts Payable $2,608,000
There was an increase in the inventory (asset) account, and also an increase in the accounts payable (liability) account. 1630 truckloads of bars of soap x $1,600 = $2,608,000

139   Kola-Nut Ltd is a privately-held corporation which focuses on their niche of premium soft drinks. This month, Kola-Nut Ltd accepted 9300 batches of soda bottles which were returned by customers. These products had been marked up by 35% and they had originally been bought at a per-unit cost of $2600.
    C)   DR Sales Returns $32,643,000
              DR Inventory $24,180,000
                  CR Accounts Receivable $32,643,000
                  CR Cost of Goods Sold $24,180,000
This transaction increases the sales returns (contra-revenue) account, and the inventory (asset) account. The accounts receivable (asset) account and the cost of goods sold (expense) account have both decreased. 9300 batches of soda bottles x $2,600 = $24,180,000. The 35% markup applies to the sales returns and accounts receivable amounts, i.e. $24,180,000 x 1.35 = $32,643,000

140   Jameson & Jameson is a market leader that is well-known for their brand of soap products. Today Jameson & Jameson sold 31900 truckloads of bars of soap which had a 30% mark-up. They had originally been bought from their suppliers for a unit cost of $2960.
   B) DR Accounts Receivable $122,751,200
     DR Cost of Goods Sold $94,424,000
      CR Sales $122,751,200
      CR Inventory $94,424,000
This transaction increases the accounts receivable (asset) account, the sales (revenue) account, and the cost of goods sold (expense) account. The inventory (asset) account has decreased. 31900 truckloads of bars of soap x $2,960 = $94,424,000. The 30% markup applies to the sales and accounts receivable amounts, i.e. $94,424,000 x 1.30 = $122,751,200

141   Pharma Drug Company Ltd. sells several different types of medications. Pharma Drug Company Ltd. has just received a cash payment for the full amount that this customer owed to the company for all of their purchases to date. The outstanding balance which has now been paid was $45000.
   D) DR Cash $45,000
      CR Accounts Receivable $45,000
The cash (asset) account has increased, and the accounts receivable (asset) account has decreased by $45,000.

142   Fairway Malls sells several different types of retail spaces in their shopping centers. Today, Fairway Malls bought equipment which has a 5 year useful life, and which had a cost of $23000.
   B) DR Equipment $23,000
      CR Accounts Payable $23,000
The equipment (asset) and the accounts payable (liability) accounts have both increased by: $23,000. The useful life does not affect this original accounting entry, but it will be used to calculate depreciation of the asset in the future.

143   Air America is a privately-held corporation which focuses on their niche of premium global flights. This month, Air America has estimated that 5% of the accounts receivable might not end up being collectable, based on past experience. The accounts receivable will need to be adjusted from its current balance of $52000.
   C) DR Bad Debt expense $2,600
      CR Allowance for Doubtful Accounts $2,600
The bad debts (expense) and the allowance for doubtful accounts (contra-asset) have both increased by: 5% x $52,000 = $2,600

144   NBG Media Corporation sells various broadcasting services for advertising agencies. This month, NBG Media Corporation made 1 monthly loan repayment towards their long-term note payable. The interest portion was 60% of the payment. The total amount paid in cash was $15000.

         C)   DR Interest Expense $9,000
                DR Loan Payable $6,000
                     CR Cash $15,000

The interest (expense) account has increased by $15,000 x 0.6 = $9,000. The loan payable (liability) has decreased by $15,000 x 0.4 = $6,000. The cash (asset) account has decreased by the full amount of the payment, which is $15,000

145   Toyonda is a corporation which sells cars. Today, Toyonda bought equipment which has a 5 year useful life, and which had a cost of $21000.

         D)   DR Equipment $21,000
                     CR Accounts Payable $21,000

The equipment (asset) and the accounts payable (liability) accounts have both increased by: $21,000. The useful life does not affect this original accounting entry, but it will be used to calculate depreciation of the asset in the future.

146   Mr. Mop offers their customers a wide range of household cleaners. Today, Mr. Mop bought equipment which has a 5 year useful life, and which had a cost of $12000.

         D)   DR Equipment $12,000
                     CR Accounts Payable $12,000

The equipment (asset) and the accounts payable (liability) accounts have both increased by: $12,000. The useful life does not affect this original accounting entry, but it will be used to calculate depreciation of the asset in the future.

147   Pharma Drug Company Ltd. is a privately-held corporation which focuses on their niche of premium medications. This month, Pharma Drug Company Ltd. must amortize 1 month worth of utility bills which they had prepaid at the beginning of the year. The amount that they had paid upfront for the year was $21600.

         A)   DR Utilities expense $1,800
                     CR Prepaid Expense $1,800

The utilities (expense) account has increased and the prepaid expense (asset) account has decreased by: $21,600 for the year, divided by 12 months = $1,800

148   Payday Now is a corporation which sells short-term loan arrangements. This month, Payday Now has estimated that 10% of the accounts receivable might not end up being collectable, based on past experience. The accounts receivable will need to be adjusted from its current balance of $51000.

         D)   DR Bad Debt expense $5,100
                     CR Allowance for Doubtful Accounts $5,100

The bad debts (expense) and the allowance for doubtful accounts (contra-asset) have both increased by: 10% x $51,000 = $5,100

149   Comedy 253 offers their customers a wide range of live performances of stand-up comedy. Comedy 253 has just provided 1300 large orders which had been paid for in advance last year. Each order was in the amount of $1700.

C)   DR Unearned Revenue $2,210,000
          CR Sales $2,210,000

The unearned revenue (liability) account has decreased and the and the sales (revenue) account has increased by: 1300 large orders x $1,700 = $2,210,000

150   A to Z Event Guru Ltd sells various start-to-finish event planning services for large gatherings. This month, A to Z Event Guru Ltd made 1 monthly loan repayment towards their long-term note payable. The interest portion was 60% of the payment. The total amount paid in cash was $19000.

B)   DR Interest Expense $11,400
          DR Loan Payable $7,600
              CR Cash $19,000

The interest (expense) account has increased by $19,000 x 0.6 = $11,400. The loan payable (liability) has decreased by $19,000 x 0.4 = $7,600. The cash (asset) account has decreased by the full amount of the payment, which is $19,000

151   LA Met Theatre Company is a market leader that is well-known for their brand of live theatrical performances. LA Met Theatre Company has just purchased a building using cash, which has an expected useful life of 30 years, and which had a total cost of $891000.

D)   DR Building $891,000
          CR Cash $891,000

The building (asset) account has increased, and the cash (asset) account has decreased by: $891,000. The useful life does not affect this original accounting entry, but it will be used to calculate depreciation of the asset in the future.

152   Pharma Drug Company Ltd. is a corporation which sells medications. Today, Pharma Drug Company Ltd. received an upfront payment for 4960 batches of pills which will be provided to the customer 6 months from now. The payment for each was $1000.

A)   DR Cash $4,960,000
          CR Unearned Revenue $4,960,000

The cash (asset) and the unearned revenue (liability) accounts have both increased by: 4960 batches of pills x $1,000 = $4,960,000

153   Club Disco provides their customers with dance venue rentals for large family gatherings. This year, Club Disco has provided 1500 evening rentals each of which earned revenues of $2280.

D)   DR Accounts Receivable $3,420,000
          CR Sales $3,420,000

The accounts receivable (asset) and the sales (revenue) accounts have both increased by: 1500 evening rentals x $2,280 = $3,420,000

154   AC&C Ltd. is a privately-held corporation which focuses on their niche of premium cell phone plans. AC&C Ltd. has just received a cash payment for the full amount that this customer owed to the company for all of their purchases to date. The outstanding balance which has now been paid was $29000.
       D)   DR Cash $29,000
                    CR Accounts Receivable $29,000
The cash (asset) account has increased, and the accounts receivable (asset) account has decreased by $29,000.

155   Kola-Nut Ltd sells various soft drinks. Today, Kola-Nut Ltd has paid cash to their supplier to fully pay off their account payable balance, which was $56000.
       D)   DR Accounts Payable $56,000
                    CR Cash $56,000
The accounts payable (liability) and cash (asset) accounts have both increased by $56,000.

156   Fairway Malls is an organization which specializes in providing their customers with retail spaces in their shopping centers. This month, Fairway Malls has estimated that 15% of the accounts receivable might not end up being collectable, based on past experience. The accounts receivable will need to be adjusted from its current balance of $81000.
       B)   DR Bad Debt expense $12,150
                    CR Allowance for Doubtful Accounts $12,150
The bad debts (expense) and the allowance for doubtful accounts (contra-asset) have both increased by: 15% x $81,000 = $12,150

157   Club Disco provides their customers with dance venue rentals for large family gatherings. Today, Club Disco bought equipment which has a 5 year useful life, and which had a cost of $23000.
       D)   DR Equipment $23,000
                    CR Accounts Payable $23,000
The equipment (asset) and the accounts payable (liability) accounts have both increased by: $23,000. The useful life does not affect this original accounting entry, but it will be used to calculate depreciation of the asset in the future.

158   Jameson & Jameson is a corporation which sells soap products. This month, Jameson & Jameson made 1 monthly loan repayment towards their long-term note payable. The interest portion was 60% of the payment. The total amount paid in cash was $8000.
       B)   DR Interest Expense $4,800
              DR Loan Payable $3,200
              CR Cash $8,000
The interest (expense) account has increased by $8,000 x 0.6 = $4,800. The loan payable (liability) has decreased by $8,000 x 0.4 = $3,200. The cash (asset) account has decreased by the full amount of the payment, which is $8,000

159   Cirque du Lune is a corporation which sells circus performances. Cirque du Lune has
        just received a cash payment for the full amount that this customer owed to the company
        for all of their purchases to date. The outstanding balance which has now been paid was
        $90000.
                C)   DR Cash $90,000
                            CR Accounts Receivable $90,000
        The cash (asset) account has increased, and the accounts receivable (asset) account
        has decreased by $90,000.

160   Comedy 253 is a corporation which sells live performances of stand-up comedy. This
        year, Comedy 253 has provided 1000 shows each of which earned revenues of $1580.
                C)   DR Accounts Receivable $1,580,000
                            CR Sales $1,580,000
        The accounts receivable (asset) and the sales (revenue) accounts have both increased
        by: 1000 shows x $1,580 = $1,580,000

161   Club Disco is a company which offers their customers a wide selection of dance venue
        rentals for large family gatherings. This December, Club Disco has paid each of the
        company's 1200 owners an annual dividend in the amount of $12000.
                C)   DR Retained Earnings $14,400,000
                            CR Cash $14,400,000
        The retained earnings (equity) and the cash accounts have both decreased by: 1200
        owners x $12,000 = $14,400,000

162   Cirque du Lune is a market leader that is well-known for their brand of circus
        performances. Cirque du Lune has just provided 1300 large orders which had been paid
        for in advance last year. Each order was in the amount of $1200.
                D)   DR Unearned Revenue $1,560,000
                            CR Sales $1,560,000
        The unearned revenue (liability) account has decreased and the and the sales (revenue)
        account has increased by: 1300 large orders x $1,200 = $1,560,000

163   LA Met Theatre Company provides their customers with live theatrical performances. LA
        Met Theatre Company has just purchased a building using cash, which has an expected
        useful life of 30 years, and which had a total cost of $943000.
                B)   DR Building $943,000
                            CR Cash $943,000
        The building (asset) account has increased, and the cash (asset) account has decreased
        by: $943,000. The useful life does not affect this original accounting entry, but it will be
        used to calculate depreciation of the asset in the future.

164   Sprike Inc sells various athletic apparel. Today Sprike Inc sold 30000 batches of athletic
       t-shirts which had a 30% mark-up. They had originally been bought from their suppliers
       for a unit cost of $1070.

D)   DR Accounts Receivable $41,730,000
         DR Cost of Goods Sold $32,100,000
                CR Sales $41,730,000
                CR Inventory $32,100,000

This transaction increases the accounts receivable (asset) account, the sales (revenue)
account, and the cost of goods sold (expense) account. The inventory (asset) account
has decreased. 30000 batches of athletic t-shirts x $1,070 = $32,100,000. The 30%
markup applies to the sales and accounts receivable amounts, i.e. $32,100,000 x 1.30 =
$41,730,000

165   Jameson & Jameson provides their customers with soap products. This December,
       Jameson & Jameson recognized 1 year of depreciation on a building which had a total
       useful life of 25 years, and which had originally been bought for $258000.

B)   DR Depreciation expense $10,320
                CR Accumulated Depreciation $10,320

The depreciation (expense) account and the accumulated depreciation (contra-asset)
accounts have both increased by: $258,000 divided by 25 years = $10,320 depreciation
per year.

166   A to Z Event Guru Ltd sells several different types of start-to-finish event planning
       services for large gatherings. A to Z Event Guru Ltd has just provided 2000 large orders
       which had been paid for in advance last year. Each order was in the amount of $1600.

D)   DR Unearned Revenue $3,200,000
                CR Sales $3,200,000

The unearned revenue (liability) account has decreased and the and the sales (revenue)
account has increased by: 2000 large orders x $1,600 = $3,200,000

167   A to Z Event Guru Ltd sells various start-to-finish event planning services for large
       gatherings. This year, A to Z Event Guru Ltd has provided 2100 events each of which
       earned revenues of $2140.

C)   DR Accounts Receivable $4,494,000
                CR Sales $4,494,000

The accounts receivable (asset) and the sales (revenue) accounts have both increased
by: 2100 events x $2,140 = $4,494,000

168   Air America is a market leader that is well-known for their brand of global flights. This
       December, Air America recognized 1 year of depreciation on a building which had a total
       useful life of 25 years, and which had originally been bought for $420000.

D)   DR Depreciation expense $16,800
                CR Accumulated Depreciation $16,800

The depreciation (expense) account and the accumulated depreciation (contra-asset)
accounts have both increased by: $420,000 divided by 25 years = $16,800 depreciation
per year.

169   Payday Now provides their customers with short-term loan arrangements. Payday Now has just purchased a building using cash, which has an expected useful life of 30 years, and which had a total cost of $907000.

    C)   DR Building $907,000
                CR Cash $907,000

The building (asset) account has increased, and the cash (asset) account has decreased by: $907,000. The useful life does not affect this original accounting entry, but it will be used to calculate depreciation of the asset in the future.

170   Jameson & Jameson provides their customers with soap products. This month, Jameson & Jameson paid for 1 month of rent for their company's office space. Each month, the rent owing was $23000.

    D)   DR Rent expense $23,000
                CR Accounts Payable $23,000

The rent (expense) and the accounts payable (liability) accounts are both increased by one month's worth of rent, which is $23,000.

171   Mr. Mop is a privately-held corporation which focuses on their niche of premium household cleaners. This month, Mr. Mop paid for 1 month of rent for their company's office space. Each month, the rent owing was $25000.

    C)   DR Rent expense $25,000
                CR Accounts Payable $25,000

The rent (expense) and the accounts payable (liability) accounts are both increased by one month's worth of rent, which is $25,000.

172   Mr. Mop is a privately-held corporation which focuses on their niche of premium household cleaners. Today, Mr. Mop received an upfront payment for 2470 tons of cleaning solution which will be provided to the customer 6 months from now. The payment for each was $1100.

    D)   DR Cash $2,717,000
                CR Unearned Revenue $2,717,000

The cash (asset) and the unearned revenue (liability) accounts have both increased by: 2470 tons of cleaning solution x $1,100 = $2,717,000

173   Mr. Mop is a corporation which sells household cleaners. This week, Mr. Mop purchased 1020 tons of cleaning solution which were placed into the warehouse, and which had a per unit cost of $1600.

    B)   DR Inventory $1,632,000
                CR Accounts Payable $1,632,000

There was an increase in the inventory (asset) account, and also an increase in the accounts payable (liability) account. 1020 tons of cleaning solution x $1,600 = $1,632,000

174   Sprike Inc provides their customers with athletic apparel. This month, Sprike Inc paid for 1 month of rent for the warehouse room, which has a monthly costs of $2800.

    C)   DR Rent expense $2,800
                CR Accounts Payable $2,800

The rent (expense) and the accounts payable (liability) accounts are both increased by one month's worth of rent, which is $2,800.

175   Kola-Nut Ltd is a company which offers their customers a wide selection of soft drinks. This month, Kola-Nut Ltd accepted 1700 batches of soda bottles which were returned by customers. These products had been marked up by 35% and they had originally been bought at a per-unit cost of $2800.

          B)   DR Sales Returns $6,426,000

                 DR Inventory $4,760,000

                      CR Accounts Receivable $6,426,000

                      CR Cost of Goods Sold $4,760,000

This transaction increases the sales returns (contra-revenue) account, and the inventory (asset) account. The accounts receivable (asset) account and the cost of goods sold (expense) account have both decreased. 1700 batches of soda bottles x $2,800 = $4,760,000. The 35% markup applies to the sales returns and accounts receivable amounts, i.e. $4,760,000 x 1.35 = $6,426,000

176   Payday Now is a privately-held corporation which focuses on their niche of premium short-term loan arrangements. Today, Payday Now received payment upfront for 1200 large orders which will not be provided until early next year. Each order was in the amount of $1700.

          D)   DR Cash $2,040,000

                      CR Unearned Revenue $2,040,000

The cash (asset) and the unearned revenue (liability) accounts have both increased by: 1200 large orders x $1,700 = $2,040,000

177   Mr. Mop sells several different types of household cleaners. This January, Mr. Mop has made an advance payment to cover the next 12 months of utility bills, which have a monthly cost of $1100.

          B)   DR Prepaid Expense $13,200

                      CR Cash $13,200

The prepaid expense (asset) account has increased, and the cash (asset) account has decreased by: 12 months x $1,100 per month = $13,200 for the year.

178   Cirque du Lune sells several different types of circus performances. Cirque du Lune has just provided 2100 large orders which had been paid for in advance last year. Each order was in the amount of $2500.

          D)   DR Unearned Revenue $5,250,000

                      CR Sales $5,250,000

The unearned revenue (liability) account has decreased and the and the sales (revenue) account has increased by: 2100 large orders x $2,500 = $5,250,000

179   Jameson & Jameson provides their customers with soap products. Today, Jameson & Jameson received an upfront payment for 5710 truckloads of bars of soap which will be provided to the customer 6 months from now. The payment for each was $2100.

          C)   DR Cash $11,991,000

                      CR Unearned Revenue $11,991,000

The cash (asset) and the unearned revenue (liability) accounts have both increased by: 5710 truckloads of bars of soap x $2,100 = $11,991,000

180   Paytech Ltd is a market leader that is well-known for their brand of payroll transaction processing services. This month, Paytech Ltd paid for 1 month of rent for their company's office space. Each month, the rent owing was $24000.
    B)   DR Rent expense $24,000
            CR Accounts Payable $24,000
The rent (expense) and the accounts payable (liability) accounts are both increased by one month's worth of rent, which is $24,000.

181   LA Met Theatre Company is a corporation which sells live theatrical performances. Today, LA Met Theatre Company bought equipment which has a 5 year useful life, and which had a cost of $26000.
    B)   DR Equipment $26,000
            CR Accounts Payable $26,000
The equipment (asset) and the accounts payable (liability) accounts have both increased by: $26,000. The useful life does not affect this original accounting entry, but it will be used to calculate depreciation of the asset in the future.

182   Cirque du Lune is a corporation which sells circus performances. This December, Cirque du Lune has paid each of the company's 2100 owners an annual dividend in the amount of $10000.
    D)   DR Retained Earnings $21,000,000
            CR Cash $21,000,000
The retained earnings (equity) and the cash accounts have both decreased by: 2100 owners x $10,000 = $21,000,000

183   Sprike Inc provides their customers with athletic apparel. This month, Sprike Inc accepted 26300 batches of athletic t-shirts which were returned by customers. These products had been marked up by 35% and they had originally been bought at a per-unit cost of $2600.
    D)   DR Sales Returns $92,313,000
            DR Inventory $68,380,000
            CR Accounts Receivable $92,313,000
            CR Cost of Goods Sold $68,380,000
This transaction increases the sales returns (contra-revenue) account, and the inventory (asset) account. The accounts receivable (asset) account and the cost of goods sold (expense) account have both decreased. 26300 batches of athletic t-shirts x $2,600 = $68,380,000. The 35% markup applies to the sales returns and accounts receivable amounts, i.e. $68,380,000 x 1.35 = $92,313,000

184   Payday Now is a market leader that is well-known for their brand of short-term loan arrangements. Today, Payday Now bought equipment which has a 5 year useful life, and which had a cost of $12000.
    B)   DR Equipment $12,000
            CR Accounts Payable $12,000
The equipment (asset) and the accounts payable (liability) accounts have both increased by: $12,000. The useful life does not affect this original accounting entry, but it will be used to calculate depreciation of the asset in the future.

185   Air America is a corporation which sells global flights. This December, Air America recognized 1 year of depreciation on equipment which had a total useful life of 10 years, and which had originally cost $160000.

    B)   DR Depreciation expense $16,000
            CR Accumulated Depreciation $16,000

The depreciation (expense) account and the accumulated depreciation (contra-asset) accounts have both increased by: $160,000 divided by 10 years = $16,000 depreciation per year.

186   Sprike Inc sells several different types of athletic apparel. Sprike Inc has just received a cash payment for the full amount that this customer owed to the company for all of their purchases to date. The outstanding balance which has now been paid was $19000.

    D)   DR Cash $19,000
            CR Accounts Receivable $19,000

The cash (asset) account has increased, and the accounts receivable (asset) account has decreased by $19,000.

187   Jameson & Jameson offers their customers a wide range of soap products. This week, Jameson & Jameson purchased 5200 truckloads of bars of soap which were placed into the warehouse, and which had a per unit cost of $1800.

    D)   DR Inventory $9,360,000
            CR Accounts Payable $9,360,000

There was an increase in the inventory (asset) account, and also an increase in the accounts payable (liability) account. 5200 truckloads of bars of soap x $1,800 = $9,360,000

188   LA Met Theatre Company is an organization which specializes in providing their customers with live theatrical performances. LA Met Theatre Company has just received a cash payment for the full amount that this customer owed to the company for all of their purchases to date. The outstanding balance which has now been paid was $60000.

    B)   DR Cash $60,000
            CR Accounts Receivable $60,000

The cash (asset) account has increased, and the accounts receivable (asset) account has decreased by $60,000.

189   Pharma Drug Company Ltd. is a company which offers their customers a wide selection of medications. This December, Pharma Drug Company Ltd. recognized 1 year of depreciation on a building which had a total useful life of 25 years, and which had originally been bought for $374000.

    B)   DR Depreciation expense $14,960
            CR Accumulated Depreciation $14,960

The depreciation (expense) account and the accumulated depreciation (contra-asset) accounts have both increased by: $374,000 divided by 25 years = $14,960 depreciation per year.

190   Mount Tessory Academy is a company which offers their customers a wide selection of
        private school education. This December, Mount Tessory Academy recognized 1 year of
        depreciation on a building which had a total useful life of 25 years, and which had
        originally been bought for $637000.
            D)   DR Depreciation expense $25,480
                        CR Accumulated Depreciation $25,480
        The depreciation (expense) account and the accumulated depreciation (contra-asset)
        accounts have both increased by: $637,000 divided by 25 years = $25,480 depreciation
        per year.

191   A to Z Event Guru Ltd is a privately-held corporation which focuses on their niche of
        premium start-to-finish event planning services for large gatherings. This December, A to
        Z Event Guru Ltd recognized 1 year of depreciation on a building which had a total useful
        life of 25 years, and which had originally been bought for $793000.
            D)   DR Depreciation expense $31,720
                        CR Accumulated Depreciation $31,720
        The depreciation (expense) account and the accumulated depreciation (contra-asset)
        accounts have both increased by: $793,000 divided by 25 years = $31,720 depreciation
        per year.

192   David & Johnson is an organization which specializes in providing their customers with
        legal services. Today, David & Johnson has paid cash to their supplier to fully pay off
        their account payable balance, which was $21000.
            D)   DR Accounts Payable $21,000
                        CR Cash $21,000
        The accounts payable (liability) and cash (asset) accounts have both increased by
        $21,000.

193   Hogtown Records sells various audio services for local musicians to record their music
        albums. Hogtown Records has just purchased a building using cash, which has an
        expected useful life of 30 years, and which had a total cost of $72000.
            C)   DR Building $72,000
                        CR Cash $72,000
        The building (asset) account has increased, and the cash (asset) account has decreased
        by: $72,000. The useful life does not affect this original accounting entry, but it will be
        used to calculate depreciation of the asset in the future.

194   A to Z Event Guru Ltd is a privately-held corporation which focuses on their niche of
        premium start-to-finish event planning services for large gatherings. Today, A to Z Event
        Guru Ltd has paid cash to their supplier to fully pay off their account payable balance,
        which was $94000.
            C)   DR Accounts Payable $94,000
                        CR Cash $94,000
        The accounts payable (liability) and cash (asset) accounts have both increased by
        $94,000.

241

195 Mr. Mop is an organization which specializes in providing their customers with household cleaners. This month, Mr. Mop accepted 18900 tons of cleaning solution which were returned by customers. These products had been marked up by 35% and they had originally been bought at a per-unit cost of $2700.

B) DR Sales Returns $68,890,500
DR Inventory $51,030,000
CR Accounts Receivable $68,890,500
CR Cost of Goods Sold $51,030,000

This transaction increases the sales returns (contra-revenue) account, and the inventory (asset) account. The accounts receivable (asset) account and the cost of goods sold (expense) account have both decreased. 18900 tons of cleaning solution x $2,700 = $51,030,000. The 35% markup applies to the sales returns and accounts receivable amounts, i.e. $51,030,000 x 1.35 = $68,890,500

196 Air America is a company which offers their customers a wide selection of global flights. This month, Air America must amortize 1 month worth of utility bills which they had prepaid at the beginning of the year. The amount that they had paid upfront for the year was $34800.

D) DR Utilities expense $2,900
CR Prepaid Expense $2,900

The utilities (expense) account has increased and the prepaid expense (asset) account has decreased by: $34,800 for the year, divided by 12 months = $2,900

197 Mount Tessory Academy is a company which offers their customers a wide selection of private school education. Today, Mount Tessory Academy bought equipment which has a 5 year useful life, and which had a cost of $9000.

D) DR Equipment $9,000
CR Accounts Payable $9,000

The equipment (asset) and the accounts payable (liability) accounts have both increased by: $9,000. The useful life does not affect this original accounting entry, but it will be used to calculate depreciation of the asset in the future.

198 Mr. Mop provides their customers with household cleaners. This month, Mr. Mop paid for 1 month of rent for the warehouse room, which has a monthly costs of $1800.

D) DR Rent expense $1,800
CR Accounts Payable $1,800

The rent (expense) and the accounts payable (liability) accounts are both increased by one month's worth of rent, which is $1,800.

199 Paytech Ltd is a corporation which sells payroll transaction processing services. Today, Paytech Ltd bought equipment which has a 5 year useful life, and which had a cost of $11000.

A) DR Equipment $11,000
CR Accounts Payable $11,000

The equipment (asset) and the accounts payable (liability) accounts have both increased by: $11,000. The useful life does not affect this original accounting entry, but it will be used to calculate depreciation of the asset in the future.

200   Sprike Inc offers their customers a wide range of athletic apparel. This week, Sprike Inc purchased 5750 batches of athletic t-shirts which were placed into the warehouse, and which had a per unit cost of $2600.

        B)   DR Inventory $14,950,000
                    CR Accounts Payable $14,950,000

There was an increase in the inventory (asset) account, and also an increase in the accounts payable (liability) account. 5750 batches of athletic t-shirts x $2,600 = $14,950,000

FINANCIAL ACCOUNTING NON-MULTIPLE CHOICE SOLUTIONS

1   Pharma Drug Company Ltd. sells various medications. Today, Pharma Drug Company
       Ltd. received an upfront payment for 2700 batches of pills which will be provided to the
       customer 6 months from now. The payment for each was $2000.
                DR Cash $5,400,000
                      CR Unearned Revenue $5,400,000
       The cash (asset) and the unearned revenue (liability) accounts have both increased by:
       2700 batches of pills x $2,000 = $5,400,000

2   AC&C Ltd. is a corporation which sells cell phone plans. AC&C Ltd. has just received a
       cash payment for the full amount that this customer owed to the company for all of their
       purchases to date. The outstanding balance which has now been paid was $77000.
                DR Cash $77,000
                      CR Accounts Receivable $77,000
       The cash (asset) account has increased, and the accounts receivable (asset) account
       has decreased by $77,000.

3   Sprike Inc provides their customers with athletic apparel. This month, Sprike Inc paid for
       1 month of rent for their company's office space. Each month, the rent owing was
       $10000.
                DR Rent expense $10,000
                      CR Accounts Payable $10,000
       The rent (expense) and the accounts payable (liability) accounts are both increased by
       one month's worth of rent, which is $10,000.

4   McGerald's is an organization which specializes in providing their customers with fast
       food meals. This December, McGerald's recognized 1 year of depreciation on a building
       which had a total useful life of 25 years, and which had originally been bought for
       $46000.
                DR Depreciation expense $1,840
                      CR Accumulated Depreciation $1,840
       The depreciation (expense) account and the accumulated depreciation (contra-asset)
       accounts have both increased by: $46,000 divided by 25 years = $1,840 depreciation per
       year.

5   McGerald's is a market leader that is well-known for their brand of fast food meals.
       Today, McGerald's has paid cash to their supplier to fully pay off their account payable
       balance, which was $80000.
                DR Accounts Payable $80,000
                      CR Cash $80,000
       The accounts payable (liability) and cash (asset) accounts have both increased by
       $80,000.

6   LA Met Theatre Company is an organization which specializes in providing their customers with live theatrical performances. This month, LA Met Theatre Company paid for 1 month of rent for their company's office space. Each month, the rent owing was $12000.

           DR Rent expense $12,000
                CR Accounts Payable $12,000

The rent (expense) and the accounts payable (liability) accounts are both increased by one month's worth of rent, which is $12,000.

7   Pharma Drug Company Ltd. is a privately-held corporation which focuses on their niche of premium medications. Today Pharma Drug Company Ltd. sold 12100 batches of pills which had a 30% mark-up. They had originally been bought from their suppliers for a unit cost of $1630.

           DR Accounts Receivable $25,639,900   DR Cost of Goods Sold $19,723,000
                CR Sales $25,639,900
                CR Inventory $19,723,000

This transaction increases the accounts receivable (asset) account, the sales (revenue) account, and the cost of goods sold (expense) account. The inventory (asset) account has decreased. 12100 batches of pills x $1,630 = $19,723,000. The 30% markup applies to the sales and accounts receivable amounts, i.e. $19,723,000 x 1.30 = $25,639,900

8   Air America is a market leader that is well-known for their brand of global flights. This December, Air America recognized 1 year of depreciation on equipment which had a total useful life of 10 years, and which had originally cost $170000.

           DR Depreciation expense $17,000
                CR Accumulated Depreciation $17,000

The depreciation (expense) account and the accumulated depreciation (contra-asset) accounts have both increased by: $170,000 divided by 10 years = $17,000 depreciation per year.

9   NY Fitness sells several different types of gym memberships for professional sports teams. This month, NY Fitness paid for 1 month of rent for their company's office space. Each month, the rent owing was $26000.

           DR Rent expense $26,000
                CR Accounts Payable $26,000

The rent (expense) and the accounts payable (liability) accounts are both increased by one month's worth of rent, which is $26,000.

10   NBG Media Corporation offers their customers a wide range of broadcasting services for advertising agencies. This month, NBG Media Corporation must amortize 1 month worth of utility bills which they had prepaid at the beginning of the year. The amount that they had paid upfront for the year was $45600.

           DR Utilities expense $3,800
                CR Prepaid Expense $3,800

The utilities (expense) account has increased and the prepaid expense (asset) account has decreased by: $45,600 for the year, divided by 12 months = $3,800

11   Pharma Drug Company Ltd. offers their customers a wide range of medications. This month, Pharma Drug Company Ltd. accepted 14300 batches of pills which were returned by customers. These products had been marked up by 35% and they had originally been bought at a per-unit cost of $1600.

> DR Sales Returns $30,888,000   DR Inventory $22,880,000
>   CR Accounts Receivable $30,888,000
>   CR Cost of Goods Sold $22,880,000

This transaction increases the sales returns (contra-revenue) account, and the inventory (asset) account. The accounts receivable (asset) account and the cost of goods sold (expense) account have both decreased. 14300 batches of pills x $1,600 = $22,880,000. The 35% markup applies to the sales returns and accounts receivable amounts, i.e. $22,880,000 x 1.35 = $30,888,000

12   Mr. Mop offers their customers a wide range of household cleaners. This month, Mr. Mop paid for 1 month of rent for their company's office space. Each month, the rent owing was $16000.

> DR Rent expense $16,000
>   CR Accounts Payable $16,000

The rent (expense) and the accounts payable (liability) accounts are both increased by one month's worth of rent, which is $16,000.

13   Grand Convention Ltd is a corporation which sells banquet hall rentals for corporate meetings. This year, Grand Convention Ltd has provided 2100 corporate events each of which earned revenues of $2240.

> DR Accounts Receivable $4,704,000
>   CR Sales $4,704,000

The accounts receivable (asset) and the sales (revenue) accounts have both increased by: 2100 corporate events x $2,240 = $4,704,000

14   Club Disco is a privately-held corporation which focuses on their niche of premium dance venue rentals for large family gatherings. This December, Club Disco recognized 1 year of depreciation on equipment which had a total useful life of 10 years, and which had originally cost $180000.

> DR Depreciation expense $18,000
>   CR Accumulated Depreciation $18,000

The depreciation (expense) account and the accumulated depreciation (contra-asset) accounts have both increased by: $180,000 divided by 10 years = $18,000 depreciation per year.

15   Club Disco is a corporation which sells dance venue rentals for large family gatherings. Today, Club Disco received payment upfront for 1000 large orders which will not be provided until early next year. Each order was in the amount of $1400.

> DR Cash $1,400,000
>   CR Unearned Revenue $1,400,000

The cash (asset) and the unearned revenue (liability) accounts have both increased by: 1000 large orders x $1,400 = $1,400,000

16   Kola-Nut Ltd is a corporation which sells soft drinks. This week, Kola-Nut Ltd purchased 1400 batches of soda bottles which were placed into the warehouse, and which had a per unit cost of $2800.
             DR Inventory $3,920,000
                   CR Accounts Payable $3,920,000
      There was an increase in the inventory (asset) account, and also an increase in the accounts payable (liability) account. 1400 batches of soda bottles x $2,800 = $3,920,000

17   Jameson & Jameson provides their customers with soap products. This January, Jameson & Jameson has made an advance payment to cover the next 12 months of utility bills, which have a monthly cost of $1300.
             DR Prepaid Expense $15,600
                   CR Cash $15,600
      The prepaid expense (asset) account has increased, and the cash (asset) account has decreased by: 12 months x $1,300 per month = $15,600 for the year.

18   Mr. Mop offers their customers a wide range of household cleaners. This month, Mr. Mop must amortize 1 month worth of utility bills which they had prepaid at the beginning of the year. The amount that they had paid upfront for the year was $19200.
             DR Utilities expense $1,600
                   CR Prepaid Expense $1,600
      The utilities (expense) account has increased and the prepaid expense (asset) account has decreased by: $19,200 for the year, divided by 12 months = $1,600

19   David & Johnson offers their customers a wide range of legal services. Today, David & Johnson received payment upfront for 1600 large orders which will not be provided until early next year. Each order was in the amount of $1500.
             DR Cash $2,400,000
                   CR Unearned Revenue $2,400,000
      The cash (asset) and the unearned revenue (liability) accounts have both increased by: 1600 large orders x $1,500 = $2,400,000

20   Kola-Nut Ltd provides their customers with soft drinks. This December, Kola-Nut Ltd recognized 1 year of depreciation on a building which had a total useful life of 25 years, and which had originally been bought for $215000.
             DR Depreciation expense $8,600
                   CR Accumulated Depreciation $8,600
      The depreciation (expense) account and the accumulated depreciation (contra-asset) accounts have both increased by: $215,000 divided by 25 years = $8,600 depreciation per year.

21   David & Johnson provides their customers with legal services. This month, David & Johnson paid for 1 month of rent for their company's office space. Each month, the rent owing was $25000.
             DR Rent expense $25,000
                   CR Accounts Payable $25,000
      The rent (expense) and the accounts payable (liability) accounts are both increased by one month's worth of rent, which is $25,000.

22   A to Z Event Guru Ltd sells several different types of start-to-finish event planning services for large gatherings. This December, A to Z Event Guru Ltd recognized 1 year of depreciation on a building which had a total useful life of 25 years, and which had originally been bought for $314000.
        DR Depreciation expense $12,560
                CR Accumulated Depreciation $12,560
The depreciation (expense) account and the accumulated depreciation (contra-asset) accounts have both increased by: $314,000 divided by 25 years = $12,560 depreciation per year.

23   Pharma Drug Company Ltd. is a company which offers their customers a wide selection of medications. This month, Pharma Drug Company Ltd. has estimated that 20% of the accounts receivable might not end up being collectable, based on past experience. The accounts receivable will need to be adjusted from its current balance of $102000.
        DR Bad Debt expense $20,400
                CR Allowance for Doubtful Accounts $20,400
The bad debts (expense) and the allowance for doubtful accounts (contra-asset) have both increased by: 20% x $102,000 = $20,400

24   Mount Tessory Academy is a company which offers their customers a wide selection of private school education. This December, Mount Tessory Academy recognized 1 year of depreciation on a building which had a total useful life of 25 years, and which had originally been bought for $219000.
        DR Depreciation expense $8,760
                CR Accumulated Depreciation $8,760
The depreciation (expense) account and the accumulated depreciation (contra-asset) accounts have both increased by: $219,000 divided by 25 years = $8,760 depreciation per year.

25   Fairway Malls is an organization which specializes in providing their customers with retail spaces in their shopping centers. This month, Fairway Malls paid 1 monthly loan repayment towards their long-term note payable. The interest portion was 60% of the payment. The total amount paid in cash was $26000.
        DR Interest Expense $15,600   DR Loan Payable $10,400
                CR Cash $26,000
The interest (expense) account has increased by $26,000 x 0.6 = $15,600. The loan payable (liability) has decreased by $26,000 x 0.4 = $10,400. The cash (asset) account has decreased by the full amount of the payment, which is $26,000

26   Air America offers their customers a wide range of global flights. This December, Air America has paid each of the company's 1900 owners an annual dividend in the amount of $12000.
        DR Retained Earnings $22,800,000
                CR Cash $22,800,000
The retained earnings (equity) and the cash accounts have both decreased by: 1900 owners x $12,000 = $22,800,000

248

27   Toyonda sells several different types of cars. This December, Toyonda recognized 1 year of depreciation on a building which had a total useful life of 25 years, and which had originally been bought for $385000.
         DR Depreciation expense $15,400
              CR Accumulated Depreciation $15,400
The depreciation (expense) account and the accumulated depreciation (contra-asset) accounts have both increased by: $385,000 divided by 25 years = $15,400 depreciation per year.

28   Mr. Mop sells various household cleaners. Today, Mr. Mop bought equipment which has a 5 year useful life, and which had a cost of $22000.
         DR Equipment $22,000
              CR Accounts Payable $22,000
The equipment (asset) and the accounts payable (liability) accounts have both increased by: $22,000. The useful life does not affect this original accounting entry, but it will be used to calculate depreciation of the asset in the future.

29   Kola-Nut Ltd is an organization which specializes in providing their customers with soft drinks. Today Kola-Nut Ltd signed up for a loan with a 5% interest rate, and so the bank immediately transferred cash to the company in the amount of $32000.
         DR Cash $32,000
              CR Loan Payable $32,000
The cash (asset) and the loan payable (liability) accounts have both increased by: $32,000. The interest rate does not affect this initial accounting entry, but it will be used for the calculation of interest expense when repayments are made in the future toward this loan.

30   A to Z Event Guru Ltd is a corporation which sells start-to-finish event planning services for large gatherings. Today A to Z Event Guru Ltd signed up for a loan with a 5% interest rate, and so the bank immediately transferred cash to the company in the amount of $77000.
         DR Cash $77,000
              CR Loan Payable $77,000
The cash (asset) and the loan payable (liability) accounts have both increased by: $77,000. The interest rate does not affect this initial accounting entry, but it will be used for the calculation of interest expense when repayments are made in the future toward this loan.

31   Kola-Nut Ltd is a corporation which sells soft drinks. This week, Kola-Nut Ltd purchased 4630 batches of soda bottles which were placed into the warehouse, and which had a per unit cost of $2700.
         DR Inventory $12,501,000
              CR Accounts Payable $12,501,000
There was an increase in the inventory (asset) account, and also an increase in the accounts payable (liability) account. 4630 batches of soda bottles x $2,700 = $12,501,000

32   Fairway Malls provides their customers with retail spaces in their shopping centers. This month, Fairway Malls must amortize 1 month worth of utility bills which they had prepaid at the beginning of the year. The amount that they had paid upfront for the year was $13200.
         DR Utilities expense $1,100
            CR Prepaid Expense $1,100
The utilities (expense) account has increased and the prepaid expense (asset) account has decreased by: $13,200 for the year, divided by 12 months = $1,100

33   NBG Media Corporation provides their customers with broadcasting services for advertising agencies. Today, NBG Media Corporation bought equipment which has a 5 year useful life, and which had a cost of $15000.
         DR Equipment $15,000
            CR Accounts Payable $15,000
The equipment (asset) and the accounts payable (liability) accounts have both increased by: $15,000. The useful life does not affect this original accounting entry, but it will be used to calculate depreciation of the asset in the future.

34   Pharma Drug Company Ltd. is a company which offers their customers a wide selection of medications. Today, Pharma Drug Company Ltd. received an upfront payment for 3360 batches of pills which will be provided to the customer 6 months from now. The payment for each was $2800.
         DR Cash $9,408,000
            CR Unearned Revenue $9,408,000
The cash (asset) and the unearned revenue (liability) accounts have both increased by: 3360 batches of pills x $2,800 = $9,408,000

35   NBG Media Corporation is a privately-held corporation which focuses on their niche of premium broadcasting services for advertising agencies. This December, NBG Media Corporation recognized 1 year of depreciation on a building which had a total useful life of 25 years, and which had originally been bought for $845000.
         DR Depreciation expense $33,800
            CR Accumulated Depreciation $33,800
The depreciation (expense) account and the accumulated depreciation (contra-asset) accounts have both increased by: $845,000 divided by 25 years = $33,800 depreciation per year.

36   Mr. Mop offers their customers a wide range of household cleaners. This month, Mr. Mop paid for 1 month of rent for their company's office space. Each month, the rent owing was $8000.
         DR Rent expense $8,000
            CR Accounts Payable $8,000
The rent (expense) and the accounts payable (liability) accounts are both increased by one month's worth of rent, which is $8,000.

37   Sprike Inc is a privately-held corporation which focuses on their niche of premium athletic apparel. This month, Sprike Inc paid for 1 month of rent for the warehouse room, which has a monthly costs of $2300.
>   DR Rent expense $2,300
>   CR Accounts Payable $2,300
The rent (expense) and the accounts payable (liability) accounts are both increased by one month's worth of rent, which is $2,300.

38   NY Fitness offers their customers a wide range of gym memberships for professional sports teams. This December, NY Fitness recognized 1 year of depreciation on a building which had a total useful life of 25 years, and which had originally been bought for $158000.
>   DR Depreciation expense $6,320
>   CR Accumulated Depreciation $6,320
The depreciation (expense) account and the accumulated depreciation (contra-asset) accounts have both increased by: $158,000 divided by 25 years = $6,320 depreciation per year.

39   Cirque du Lune sells several different types of circus performances. This year, Cirque du Lune has provided 2000 shows each of which earned revenues of $1360.
>   DR Accounts Receivable $2,720,000
>   CR Sales $2,720,000
The accounts receivable (asset) and the sales (revenue) accounts have both increased by: 2000 shows x $1,360 = $2,720,000

40   Mr. Mop provides their customers with household cleaners. This month, Mr. Mop paid for 1 month of rent for their company's office space. Each month, the rent owing was $8000.
>   DR Rent expense $8,000
>   CR Accounts Payable $8,000
The rent (expense) and the accounts payable (liability) accounts are both increased by one month's worth of rent, which is $8,000.

41   Jameson & Jameson offers their customers a wide range of soap products. Today Jameson & Jameson sold 41900 truckloads of bars of soap which had a 30% mark-up. They had originally been bought from their suppliers for a unit cost of $1670.
>   DR Accounts Receivable $90,964,900   DR Cost of Goods Sold $69,973,000
>   CR Sales $90,964,900
>   CR Inventory $69,973,000
This transaction increases the accounts receivable (asset) account, the sales (revenue) account, and the cost of goods sold (expense) account. The inventory (asset) account has decreased. 41900 truckloads of bars of soap x $1,670 = $69,973,000. The 30% markup applies to the sales and accounts receivable amounts, i.e. $69,973,000 x 1.30 = $90,964,900

42   Cirque du Lune is a privately-held corporation which focuses on their niche of premium circus performances. This year, Cirque du Lune has provided 1000 shows each of which earned revenues of $2910.
                 DR Accounts Receivable $2,910,000
                         CR Sales $2,910,000
      The accounts receivable (asset) and the sales (revenue) accounts have both increased by: 1000 shows x $2,910 = $2,910,000

43   Fairway Malls provides their customers with retail spaces in their shopping centers. Today Fairway Malls signed up for a loan with a 5% interest rate, and so the bank immediately transferred cash to the company in the amount of $102000.
                 DR Cash $102,000
                         CR Loan Payable $102,000
      The cash (asset) and the loan payable (liability) accounts have both increased by: $102,000. The interest rate does not affect this initial accounting entry, but it will be used for the calculation of interest expense when repayments are made in the future toward this loan.

44   Pharma Drug Company Ltd. is a company which offers their customers a wide selection of medications. This week, Pharma Drug Company Ltd. purchased 4260 batches of pills which were placed into the warehouse, and which had a per unit cost of $2200.
                 DR Inventory $9,372,000
                         CR Accounts Payable $9,372,000
      There was an increase in the inventory (asset) account, and also an increase in the accounts payable (liability) account. 4260 batches of pills x $2,200 = $9,372,000

45   AC&C Ltd. sells various cell phone plans. AC&C Ltd. has just provided 1900 large orders which had been paid for in advance last year. Each order was in the amount of $1000.
                 DR Unearned Revenue $1,900,000
                         CR Sales $1,900,000
      The unearned revenue (liability) account has decreased and the and the sales (revenue) account has increased by: 1900 large orders x $1,000 = $1,900,000

46   Mr. Mop sells various household cleaners. Today, Mr. Mop received an upfront payment for 1120 tons of cleaning solution which will be provided to the customer 6 months from now. The payment for each was $1000.
                 DR Cash $1,120,000
                         CR Unearned Revenue $1,120,000
      The cash (asset) and the unearned revenue (liability) accounts have both increased by: 1120 tons of cleaning solution x $1,000 = $1,120,000

47   Grand Convention Ltd sells several different types of banquet hall rentals for corporate meetings. Grand Convention Ltd has just purchased a building using cash, which has an expected useful life of 30 years, and which had a total cost of $424000.
                 DR Building $424,000
                         CR Cash $424,000
      The building (asset) account has increased, and the cash (asset) account has decreased by: $424,000. The useful life does not affect this original accounting entry, but it will be used to calculate depreciation of the asset in the future.

48   Jameson & Jameson is a corporation which sells soap products. This week, Jameson & Jameson purchased 1470 truckloads of bars of soap which were placed into the warehouse, and which had a per unit cost of $1400.
          DR Inventory $2,058,000
              CR Accounts Payable $2,058,000
      There was an increase in the inventory (asset) account, and also an increase in the accounts payable (liability) account. 1470 truckloads of bars of soap x $1,400 = $2,058,000

49   NY Fitness is an organization which specializes in providing their customers with gym memberships for professional sports teams. This year, NY Fitness has provided 2300 team memberships each of which earned revenues of $1690.
          DR Accounts Receivable $3,887,000
              CR Sales $3,887,000
      The accounts receivable (asset) and the sales (revenue) accounts have both increased by: 2300 team memberships x $1,690 = $3,887,000

50   Pharma Drug Company Ltd. is a privately-held corporation which focuses on their niche of premium medications. Today, Pharma Drug Company Ltd. received an upfront payment for 2260 batches of pills which will be provided to the customer 6 months from now. The payment for each was $2600.
          DR Cash $5,876,000
              CR Unearned Revenue $5,876,000
      The cash (asset) and the unearned revenue (liability) accounts have both increased by: 2260 batches of pills x $2,600 = $5,876,000

51   David & Johnson is a privately-held corporation which focuses on their niche of premium legal services. Today, David & Johnson received payment upfront for 2300 large orders which will not be provided until early next year. Each order was in the amount of $1700.
          DR Cash $3,910,000
              CR Unearned Revenue $3,910,000
      The cash (asset) and the unearned revenue (liability) accounts have both increased by: 2300 large orders x $1,700 = $3,910,000

52   AC&C Ltd. provides their customers with cell phone plans. This year, AC&C Ltd. has provided 1600 monthly cell phone service each of which earned revenues of $2800.
          DR Accounts Receivable $4,480,000
              CR Sales $4,480,000
      The accounts receivable (asset) and the sales (revenue) accounts have both increased by: 1600 monthly cell phone service x $2,800 = $4,480,000

53   NY Fitness is a market leader that is well-known for their brand of gym memberships for professional sports teams. Today, NY Fitness received payment upfront for 2300 large orders which will not be provided until early next year. Each order was in the amount of $2100.
          DR Cash $4,830,000
              CR Unearned Revenue $4,830,000
      The cash (asset) and the unearned revenue (liability) accounts have both increased by: 2300 large orders x $2,100 = $4,830,000

54   AC&C Ltd. is a market leader that is well-known for their brand of cell phone plans. Today, AC&C Ltd. has paid cash to their supplier to fully pay off their account payable balance, which was $18000.
        DR Accounts Payable $18,000
                CR Cash $18,000
The accounts payable (liability) and cash (asset) accounts have both increased by $18,000.

55   Toyonda sells various cars. This January, Toyonda has made an advance payment to cover the next 12 months of utility bills, which have a monthly cost of $2200.
        DR Prepaid Expense $26,400
                CR Cash $26,400
The prepaid expense (asset) account has increased, and the cash (asset) account has decreased by: 12 months x $2,200 per month = $26,400 for the year.

56   Pharma Drug Company Ltd. is a corporation which sells medications. This week, Pharma Drug Company Ltd. purchased 4580 batches of pills which were placed into the warehouse, and which had a per unit cost of $1100.
        DR Inventory $5,038,000
                CR Accounts Payable $5,038,000
There was an increase in the inventory (asset) account, and also an increase in the accounts payable (liability) account. 4580 batches of pills x $1,100 = $5,038,000

57   Comedy 253 offers their customers a wide range of live performances of stand-up comedy. Today, Comedy 253 bought equipment which has a 5 year useful life, and which had a cost of $18000.
        DR Equipment $18,000
                CR Accounts Payable $18,000
The equipment (asset) and the accounts payable (liability) accounts have both increased by: $18,000. The useful life does not affect this original accounting entry, but it will be used to calculate depreciation of the asset in the future.

58   Grand Convention Ltd is a market leader that is well-known for their brand of banquet hall rentals for corporate meetings. This month, Grand Convention Ltd has estimated that 15% of the accounts receivable might not end up being collectable, based on past experience. The accounts receivable will need to be adjusted from its current balance of $85000.
        DR Bad Debt expense $12,750
                CR Allowance for Doubtful Accounts $12,750
The bad debts (expense) and the allowance for doubtful accounts (contra-asset) have both increased by: 15% x $85,000 = $12,750

59   Grand Convention Ltd provides their customers with banquet hall rentals for corporate meetings. This month, Grand Convention Ltd must amortize 1 month worth of utility bills which they had prepaid at the beginning of the year. The amount that they had paid upfront for the year was $37200.
        DR Utilities expense $3,100
                CR Prepaid Expense $3,100
The utilities (expense) account has increased and the prepaid expense (asset) account has decreased by: $37,200 for the year, divided by 12 months = $3,100

60   Kola-Nut Ltd sells several different types of soft drinks. This month, Kola-Nut Ltd accepted 18400 batches of soda bottles which were returned by customers. These products had been marked up by 35% and they had originally been bought at a per-unit cost of $1300.

DR Sales Returns $32,292,000   DR Inventory $23,920,000
       CR Accounts Receivable $32,292,000
       CR Cost of Goods Sold $23,920,000

This transaction increases the sales returns (contra-revenue) account, and the inventory (asset) account. The accounts receivable (asset) account and the cost of goods sold (expense) account have both decreased. 18400 batches of soda bottles x $1,300 = $23,920,000. The 35% markup applies to the sales returns and accounts receivable amounts, i.e. $23,920,000 x 1.35 = $32,292,000

61   Cirque du Lune offers their customers a wide range of circus performances. This month, Cirque du Lune has estimated that 25% of the accounts receivable might not end up being collectable, based on past experience. The accounts receivable will need to be adjusted from its current balance of $48000.

DR Bad Debt expense $12,000
       CR Allowance for Doubtful Accounts $12,000

The bad debts (expense) and the allowance for doubtful accounts (contra-asset) have both increased by: 25% x $48,000 = $12,000

62   Club Disco is a privately-held corporation which focuses on their niche of premium dance venue rentals for large family gatherings. This December, Club Disco recognized 1 year of depreciation on equipment which had a total useful life of 10 years, and which had originally cost $180000.

DR Depreciation expense $18,000
       CR Accumulated Depreciation $18,000

The depreciation (expense) account and the accumulated depreciation (contra-asset) accounts have both increased by: $180,000 divided by 10 years = $18,000 depreciation per year.

63   Pharma Drug Company Ltd. provides their customers with medications. This month, Pharma Drug Company Ltd. has estimated that 25% of the accounts receivable might not end up being collectable, based on past experience. The accounts receivable will need to be adjusted from its current balance of $89000.

DR Bad Debt expense $22,250
       CR Allowance for Doubtful Accounts $22,250

The bad debts (expense) and the allowance for doubtful accounts (contra-asset) have both increased by: 25% x $89,000 = $22,250

64   Hogtown Records sells several different types of audio services for local musicians to record their music albums. This January, Hogtown Records has made an advance payment to cover the next 12 months of utility bills, which have a monthly cost of $1000.

DR Prepaid Expense $12,000
       CR Cash $12,000

The prepaid expense (asset) account has increased, and the cash (asset) account has decreased by: 12 months x $1,000 per month = $12,000 for the year.

65   Comedy 253 is a privately-held corporation which focuses on their niche of premium live performances of stand-up comedy. Comedy 253 has just received a cash payment for the full amount that this customer owed to the company for all of their purchases to date. The outstanding balance which has now been paid was $91000.
          DR Cash $91,000
              CR Accounts Receivable $91,000
The cash (asset) account has increased, and the accounts receivable (asset) account has decreased by $91,000.

66   Kola-Nut Ltd is a corporation which sells soft drinks. Today Kola-Nut Ltd sold 4600 batches of soda bottles which had a 30% mark-up. They had originally been bought from their suppliers for a unit cost of $2520.
          DR Accounts Receivable $15,069,600   DR Cost of Goods Sold $11,592,000
              CR Sales $15,069,600
              CR Inventory $11,592,000
This transaction increases the accounts receivable (asset) account, the sales (revenue) account, and the cost of goods sold (expense) account. The inventory (asset) account has decreased. 4600 batches of soda bottles x $2,520 = $11,592,000. The 30% markup applies to the sales and accounts receivable amounts, i.e. $11,592,000 x 1.30 = $15,069,600

67   Payday Now is a privately-held corporation which focuses on their niche of premium short-term loan arrangements. Today, Payday Now received payment upfront for 1800 large orders which will not be provided until early next year. Each order was in the amount of $2700.
          DR Cash $4,860,000
              CR Unearned Revenue $4,860,000
The cash (asset) and the unearned revenue (liability) accounts have both increased by: 1800 large orders x $2,700 = $4,860,000

68   AC&C Ltd. is a privately-held corporation which focuses on their niche of premium cell phone plans. This month, AC&C Ltd. must amortize 1 month worth of utility bills which they had prepaid at the beginning of the year. The amount that they had paid upfront for the year was $19200.
          DR Utilities expense $1,600
              CR Prepaid Expense $1,600
The utilities (expense) account has increased and the prepaid expense (asset) account has decreased by: $19,200 for the year, divided by 12 months = $1,600

69   Payday Now is a privately-held corporation which focuses on their niche of premium short-term loan arrangements. This January, Payday Now has made an advance payment to cover the next 12 months of utility bills, which have a monthly cost of $1000.
          DR Prepaid Expense $12,000
              CR Cash $12,000
The prepaid expense (asset) account has increased, and the cash (asset) account has decreased by: 12 months x $1,000 per month = $12,000 for the year.

70   NBG Media Corporation sells several different types of broadcasting services for advertising agencies. NBG Media Corporation has just received a cash payment for the full amount that this customer owed to the company for all of their purchases to date. The outstanding balance which has now been paid was $35000.
               DR Cash $35,000
                      CR Accounts Receivable $35,000
      The cash (asset) account has increased, and the accounts receivable (asset) account has decreased by $35,000.

71   Kola-Nut Ltd sells several different types of soft drinks. This month, Kola-Nut Ltd paid 1 monthly loan repayment towards their long-term note payable. The interest portion was 60% of the payment. The total amount paid in cash was $19000.
               DR Interest Expense $11,400   DR Loan Payable $7,600
                      CR Cash $19,000
      The interest (expense) account has increased by $19,000 x 0.6 = $11,400. The loan payable (liability) has decreased by $19,000 x 0.4 = $7,600. The cash (asset) account has decreased by the full amount of the payment, which is $19,000

72   Hogtown Records provides their customers with audio services for local musicians to record their music albums. This month, Hogtown Records paid for 1 month of rent for their company's office space. Each month, the rent owing was $21000.
               DR Rent expense $21,000
                      CR Accounts Payable $21,000
      The rent (expense) and the accounts payable (liability) accounts are both increased by one month's worth of rent, which is $21,000.

73   Toyonda provides their customers with cars. Today, Toyonda bought equipment which has a 5 year useful life, and which had a cost of $20000.
               DR Equipment $20,000
                      CR Accounts Payable $20,000
      The equipment (asset) and the accounts payable (liability) accounts have both increased by: $20,000. The useful life does not affect this original accounting entry, but it will be used to calculate depreciation of the asset in the future.

74   Payday Now is a corporation which sells short-term loan arrangements. This January, Payday Now has made an advance payment to cover the next 12 months of utility bills, which have a monthly cost of $1200.
               DR Prepaid Expense $14,400
                      CR Cash $14,400
      The prepaid expense (asset) account has increased, and the cash (asset) account has decreased by: 12 months x $1,200 per month = $14,400 for the year.

75   Hogtown Records is a corporation which sells audio services for local musicians to record their music albums. Hogtown Records has just purchased a building using cash, which has an expected useful life of 30 years, and which had a total cost of $469000.
               DR Building $469,000
                      CR Cash $469,000
      The building (asset) account has increased, and the cash (asset) account has decreased by: $469,000. The useful life does not affect this original accounting entry, but it will be used to calculate depreciation of the asset in the future.

76   Air America is a privately-held corporation which focuses on their niche of premium global flights. This January, Air America has made an advance payment to cover the next 12 months of utility bills, which have a monthly cost of $2700.
        DR Prepaid Expense $32,400
            CR Cash $32,400
The prepaid expense (asset) account has increased, and the cash (asset) account has decreased by: 12 months x $2,700 per month = $32,400 for the year.

77   Air America sells various global flights. This month, Air America has estimated that 10% of the accounts receivable might not end up being collectable, based on past experience. The accounts receivable will need to be adjusted from its current balance of $28000.
        DR Bad Debt expense $2,800
            CR Allowance for Doubtful Accounts $2,800
The bad debts (expense) and the allowance for doubtful accounts (contra-asset) have both increased by: 10% x $28,000 = $2,800

78   Pharma Drug Company Ltd. is a market leader that is well-known for their brand of medications. This January, Pharma Drug Company Ltd. has made an advance payment to cover the next 12 months of utility bills, which have a monthly cost of $1100.
        DR Prepaid Expense $13,200
            CR Cash $13,200
The prepaid expense (asset) account has increased, and the cash (asset) account has decreased by: 12 months x $1,100 per month = $13,200 for the year.

79   Mr. Mop sells various household cleaners. This month, Mr. Mop accepted 3000 tons of cleaning solution which were returned by customers. These products had been marked up by 35% and they had originally been bought at a per-unit cost of $2100.
        DR Sales Returns $8,505,000   DR Inventory $6,300,000
            CR Accounts Receivable $8,505,000
            CR Cost of Goods Sold $6,300,000
This transaction increases the sales returns (contra-revenue) account, and the inventory (asset) account. The accounts receivable (asset) account and the cost of goods sold (expense) account have both decreased. 3000 tons of cleaning solution x $2,100 = $6,300,000. The 35% markup applies to the sales returns and accounts receivable amounts, i.e. $6,300,000 x 1.35 = $8,505,000

80   Sprike Inc is an organization which specializes in providing their customers with athletic apparel. This month, Sprike Inc paid for 1 month of rent for the warehouse room, which has a monthly costs of $1500.
        DR Rent expense $1,500
            CR Accounts Payable $1,500
The rent (expense) and the accounts payable (liability) accounts are both increased by one month's worth of rent, which is $1,500.

81   Pharma Drug Company Ltd. is a corporation which sells medications. Today, Pharma Drug Company Ltd. received an upfront payment for 1590 batches of pills which will be provided to the customer 6 months from now. The payment for each was $2100.
        DR Cash $3,339,000
            CR Unearned Revenue $3,339,000
The cash (asset) and the unearned revenue (liability) accounts have both increased by: 1590 batches of pills x $2,100 = $3,339,000

82   Grand Convention Ltd sells several different types of banquet hall rentals for corporate meetings. This month, Grand Convention Ltd paid 1 monthly loan repayment towards their long-term note payable. The interest portion was 60% of the payment. The total amount paid in cash was $18000.
        DR Interest Expense $10,800   DR Loan Payable $7,200
            CR Cash $18,000
The interest (expense) account has increased by $18,000 x 0.6 = $10,800. The loan payable (liability) has decreased by $18,000 x 0.4 = $7,200. The cash (asset) account has decreased by the full amount of the payment, which is $18,000

83   Jameson & Jameson is a company which offers their customers a wide selection of soap products. This month, Jameson & Jameson paid for 1 month of rent for the warehouse room, which has a monthly costs of $1900.
        DR Rent expense $1,900
            CR Accounts Payable $1,900
The rent (expense) and the accounts payable (liability) accounts are both increased by one month's worth of rent, which is $1,900.

84   Payday Now is a company which offers their customers a wide selection of short-term loan arrangements. This month, Payday Now has estimated that 10% of the accounts receivable might not end up being collectable, based on past experience. The accounts receivable will need to be adjusted from its current balance of $100000.
        DR Bad Debt expense $10,000
            CR Allowance for Doubtful Accounts $10,000
The bad debts (expense) and the allowance for doubtful accounts (contra-asset) have both increased by: 10% x $100,000 = $10,000

85   Mr. Mop is an organization which specializes in providing their customers with household cleaners. This month, Mr. Mop paid for 1 month of rent for the warehouse room, which has a monthly costs of $2500.
        DR Rent expense $2,500
            CR Accounts Payable $2,500
The rent (expense) and the accounts payable (liability) accounts are both increased by one month's worth of rent, which is $2,500.

86   Air America is an organization which specializes in providing their customers with global flights. Air America has just received a cash payment for the full amount that this customer owed to the company for all of their purchases to date. The outstanding balance which has now been paid was $39000.
          DR Cash $39,000
               CR Accounts Receivable $39,000
The cash (asset) account has increased, and the accounts receivable (asset) account has decreased by $39,000.

87   Comedy 253 offers their customers a wide range of live performances of stand-up comedy. Today, Comedy 253 has paid cash to their supplier to fully pay off their account payable balance, which was $65000.
          DR Accounts Payable $65,000
               CR Cash $65,000
The accounts payable (liability) and cash (asset) accounts have both increased by $65,000.

88   AC&C Ltd. offers their customers a wide range of cell phone plans. AC&C Ltd. has just received a cash payment for the full amount that this customer owed to the company for all of their purchases to date. The outstanding balance which has now been paid was $35000.
          DR Cash $35,000
               CR Accounts Receivable $35,000
The cash (asset) account has increased, and the accounts receivable (asset) account has decreased by $35,000.

89   A to Z Event Guru Ltd offers their customers a wide range of start-to-finish event planning services for large gatherings. This December, A to Z Event Guru Ltd recognized 1 year of depreciation on equipment which had a total useful life of 10 years, and which had originally cost $110000.
          DR Depreciation expense $11,000
               CR Accumulated Depreciation $11,000
The depreciation (expense) account and the accumulated depreciation (contra-asset) accounts have both increased by: $110,000 divided by 10 years = $11,000 depreciation per year.

90   Grand Convention Ltd is a company which offers their customers a wide selection of banquet hall rentals for corporate meetings. Today Grand Convention Ltd signed up for a loan with a 5% interest rate, and so the bank immediately transferred cash to the company in the amount of $70000.
          DR Cash $70,000
               CR Loan Payable $70,000
The cash (asset) and the loan payable (liability) accounts have both increased by: $70,000. The interest rate does not affect this initial accounting entry, but it will be used for the calculation of interest expense when repayments are made in the future toward this loan.

91 Hogtown Records sells several different types of audio services for local musicians to record their music albums. This December, Hogtown Records has paid each of the company's 2400 owners an annual dividend in the amount of $8000.
DR Retained Earnings $19,200,000
CR Cash $19,200,000
The retained earnings (equity) and the cash accounts have both decreased by: 2400 owners x $8,000 = $19,200,000

92 Fairway Malls offers their customers a wide range of retail spaces in their shopping centers. This January, Fairway Malls has made an advance payment to cover the next 12 months of utility bills, which have a monthly cost of $1000.
DR Prepaid Expense $12,000
CR Cash $12,000
The prepaid expense (asset) account has increased, and the cash (asset) account has decreased by: 12 months x $1,000 per month = $12,000 for the year.

93 Fairway Malls sells various retail spaces in their shopping centers. This December, Fairway Malls recognized 1 year of depreciation on a building which had a total useful life of 25 years, and which had originally been bought for $636000.
DR Depreciation expense $25,440
CR Accumulated Depreciation $25,440
The depreciation (expense) account and the accumulated depreciation (contra-asset) accounts have both increased by: $636,000 divided by 25 years = $25,440 depreciation per year.

94 Club Disco provides their customers with dance venue rentals for large family gatherings. This month, Club Disco must amortize 1 month worth of utility bills which they had prepaid at the beginning of the year. The amount that they had paid upfront for the year was $14400.
DR Utilities expense $1,200
CR Prepaid Expense $1,200
The utilities (expense) account has increased and the prepaid expense (asset) account has decreased by: $14,400 for the year, divided by 12 months = $1,200

95 NBG Media Corporation is a corporation which sells broadcasting services for advertising agencies. This month, NBG Media Corporation paid for 1 month of rent for their company's office space. Each month, the rent owing was $11000.
DR Rent expense $11,000
CR Accounts Payable $11,000
The rent (expense) and the accounts payable (liability) accounts are both increased by one month's worth of rent, which is $11,000.

96   NY Fitness is an organization which specializes in providing their customers with gym memberships for professional sports teams. This December, NY Fitness recognized 1 year of depreciation on a building which had a total useful life of 25 years, and which had originally been bought for $587000.

          DR Depreciation expense $23,480

               CR Accumulated Depreciation $23,480

The depreciation (expense) account and the accumulated depreciation (contra-asset) accounts have both increased by: $587,000 divided by 25 years = $23,480 depreciation per year.

97   Comedy 253 is an organization which specializes in providing their customers with live performances of stand-up comedy. This month, Comedy 253 paid 1 monthly loan repayment towards their long-term note payable. The interest portion was 60% of the payment. The total amount paid in cash was $17000.

          DR Interest Expense $10,200   DR Loan Payable $6,800

               CR Cash $17,000

The interest (expense) account has increased by $17,000 x 0.6 = $10,200. The loan payable (liability) has decreased by $17,000 x 0.4 = $6,800. The cash (asset) account has decreased by the full amount of the payment, which is $17,000

98   Kola-Nut Ltd is an organization which specializes in providing their customers with soft drinks. Today, Kola-Nut Ltd received an upfront payment for 2610 batches of soda bottles which will be provided to the customer 6 months from now. The payment for each was $1100.

          DR Cash $2,871,000

               CR Unearned Revenue $2,871,000

The cash (asset) and the unearned revenue (liability) accounts have both increased by: 2610 batches of soda bottles x $1,100 = $2,871,000

99   David & Johnson is a company which offers their customers a wide selection of legal services. David & Johnson has just purchased a building using cash, which has an expected useful life of 30 years, and which had a total cost of $908000.

          DR Building $908,000

               CR Cash $908,000

The building (asset) account has increased, and the cash (asset) account has decreased by: $908,000. The useful life does not affect this original accounting entry, but it will be used to calculate depreciation of the asset in the future.

100   Mount Tessory Academy provides their customers with private school education. This year, Mount Tessory Academy has provided 2000 annual tuition memberships each of which earned revenues of $2030.

          DR Accounts Receivable $4,060,000

               CR Sales $4,060,000

The accounts receivable (asset) and the sales (revenue) accounts have both increased by: 2000 annual tuition memberships x $2,030 = $4,060,000

101   Paytech Ltd is a market leader that is well-known for their brand of payroll transaction processing services. This December, Paytech Ltd recognized 1 year of depreciation on equipment which had a total useful life of 10 years, and which had originally cost $110000.
>   DR Depreciation expense $11,000
>   CR Accumulated Depreciation $11,000
The depreciation (expense) account and the accumulated depreciation (contra-asset) accounts have both increased by: $110,000 divided by 10 years = $11,000 depreciation per year.

102   Mount Tessory Academy is a corporation which sells private school education. This December, Mount Tessory Academy has paid each of the company's 1100 owners an annual dividend in the amount of $9000.
>   DR Retained Earnings $9,900,000
>   CR Cash $9,900,000
The retained earnings (equity) and the cash accounts have both decreased by: 1100 owners x $9,000 = $9,900,000

103   Pharma Drug Company Ltd. is a company which offers their customers a wide selection of medications. Today, Pharma Drug Company Ltd. received an upfront payment for 3650 batches of pills which will be provided to the customer 6 months from now. The payment for each was $1400.
>   DR Cash $5,110,000
>   CR Unearned Revenue $5,110,000
The cash (asset) and the unearned revenue (liability) accounts have both increased by: 3650 batches of pills x $1,400 = $5,110,000

104   Sprike Inc is a corporation which sells athletic apparel. Today, Sprike Inc received an upfront payment for 1790 batches of athletic t-shirts which will be provided to the customer 6 months from now. The payment for each was $2500.
>   DR Cash $4,475,000
>   CR Unearned Revenue $4,475,000
The cash (asset) and the unearned revenue (liability) accounts have both increased by: 1790 batches of athletic t-shirts x $2,500 = $4,475,000

105   Sprike Inc sells various athletic apparel. This January, Sprike Inc has made an advance payment to cover the next 12 months of utility bills, which have a monthly cost of $1500.
>   DR Prepaid Expense $18,000
>   CR Cash $18,000
The prepaid expense (asset) account has increased, and the cash (asset) account has decreased by: 12 months x $1,500 per month = $18,000 for the year.

106   Mount Tessory Academy offers their customers a wide range of private school education. Today, Mount Tessory Academy has paid cash to their supplier to fully pay off their account payable balance, which was $96000.
>   DR Accounts Payable $96,000
>   CR Cash $96,000
The accounts payable (liability) and cash (asset) accounts have both increased by $96,000.

107   Pharma Drug Company Ltd. is a privately-held corporation which focuses on their niche of premium medications. This month, Pharma Drug Company Ltd. accepted 5900 batches of pills which were returned by customers. These products had been marked up by 35% and they had originally been bought at a per-unit cost of $1400.

           DR Sales Returns $11,151,000   DR Inventory $8,260,000
               CR Accounts Receivable $11,151,000
               CR Cost of Goods Sold $8,260,000

This transaction increases the sales returns (contra-revenue) account, and the inventory (asset) account. The accounts receivable (asset) account and the cost of goods sold (expense) account have both decreased. 5900 batches of pills x $1,400 = $8,260,000. The 35% markup applies to the sales returns and accounts receivable amounts, i.e. $8,260,000 x 1.35 = $11,151,000

108   LA Met Theatre Company is a privately-held corporation which focuses on their niche of premium live theatrical performances. Today LA Met Theatre Company signed up for a loan with a 5% interest rate, and so the bank immediately transferred cash to the company in the amount of $104000.

           DR Cash $104,000
               CR Loan Payable $104,000

The cash (asset) and the loan payable (liability) accounts have both increased by: $104,000. The interest rate does not affect this initial accounting entry, but it will be used for the calculation of interest expense when repayments are made in the future toward this loan.

109   Fairway Malls sells various retail spaces in their shopping centers. This December, Fairway Malls recognized 1 year of depreciation on equipment which had a total useful life of 10 years, and which had originally cost $210000.

           DR Depreciation expense $21,000
               CR Accumulated Depreciation $21,000

The depreciation (expense) account and the accumulated depreciation (contra-asset) accounts have both increased by: $210,000 divided by 10 years = $21,000 depreciation per year.

110   Mr. Mop is a privately-held corporation which focuses on their niche of premium household cleaners. This month, Mr. Mop paid for 1 month of rent for the warehouse room, which has a monthly costs of $1700.

           DR Rent expense $1,700
               CR Accounts Payable $1,700

The rent (expense) and the accounts payable (liability) accounts are both increased by one month's worth of rent, which is $1,700.

111   A to Z Event Guru Ltd offers their customers a wide range of start-to-finish event planning services for large gatherings. Today, A to Z Event Guru Ltd has paid cash to their supplier to fully pay off their account payable balance, which was $72000.

           DR Accounts Payable $72,000
               CR Cash $72,000

The accounts payable (liability) and cash (asset) accounts have both increased by $72,000.

112   Mr. Mop is a privately-held corporation which focuses on their niche of premium household cleaners. Today Mr. Mop sold 41300 tons of cleaning solution which had a 30% mark-up. They had originally been bought from their suppliers for a unit cost of $2960.

    DR Accounts Receivable $158,922,400   DR Cost of Goods Sold $122,248,000
        CR Sales $158,922,400
        CR Inventory $122,248,000

This transaction increases the accounts receivable (asset) account, the sales (revenue) account, and the cost of goods sold (expense) account. The inventory (asset) account has decreased. 41300 tons of cleaning solution x $2,960 = $122,248,000. The 30% markup applies to the sales and accounts receivable amounts, i.e. $122,248,000 x 1.30 = $158,922,400

113   Kola-Nut Ltd is a privately-held corporation which focuses on their niche of premium soft drinks. Today, Kola-Nut Ltd received an upfront payment for 3040 batches of soda bottles which will be provided to the customer 6 months from now. The payment for each was $1200.

    DR Cash $3,648,000
        CR Unearned Revenue $3,648,000

The cash (asset) and the unearned revenue (liability) accounts have both increased by: 3040 batches of soda bottles x $1,200 = $3,648,000

114   NY Fitness is an organization which specializes in providing their customers with gym memberships for professional sports teams. NY Fitness has just received a cash payment for the full amount that this customer owed to the company for all of their purchases to date. The outstanding balance which has now been paid was $71000.

    DR Cash $71,000
        CR Accounts Receivable $71,000

The cash (asset) account has increased, and the accounts receivable (asset) account has decreased by $71,000.

115   Fairway Malls offers their customers a wide range of retail spaces in their shopping centers. Fairway Malls has just purchased a building using cash, which has an expected useful life of 30 years, and which had a total cost of $831000.

    DR Building $831,000
        CR Cash $831,000

The building (asset) account has increased, and the cash (asset) account has decreased by: $831,000. The useful life does not affect this original accounting entry, but it will be used to calculate depreciation of the asset in the future.

116   McGerald's sells several different types of fast food meals. Today McGerald's signed up for a loan with a 5% interest rate, and so the bank immediately transferred cash to the company in the amount of $34000.

    DR Cash $34,000
        CR Loan Payable $34,000

The cash (asset) and the loan payable (liability) accounts have both increased by: $34,000. The interest rate does not affect this initial accounting entry, but it will be used for the calculation of interest expense when repayments are made in the future toward this loan.

117   Sprike Inc offers their customers a wide range of athletic apparel. Today, Sprike Inc
        bought equipment which has a 5 year useful life, and which had a cost of $15000.
                DR Equipment $15,000
                    CR Accounts Payable $15,000
        The equipment (asset) and the accounts payable (liability) accounts have both increased
        by: $15,000. The useful life does not affect this original accounting entry, but it will be
        used to calculate depreciation of the asset in the future.

118   Jameson & Jameson sells several different types of soap products. Jameson & Jameson
        has just purchased a building using cash, which has an expected useful life of 30 years,
        and which had a total cost of $912000.
                DR Building $912,000
                    CR Cash $912,000
        The building (asset) account has increased, and the cash (asset) account has decreased
        by: $912,000. The useful life does not affect this original accounting entry, but it will be
        used to calculate depreciation of the asset in the future.

119   Jameson & Jameson is a company which offers their customers a wide selection of soap
        products. This week, Jameson & Jameson purchased 4460 truckloads of bars of soap
        which were placed into the warehouse, and which had a per unit cost of $2300.
                DR Inventory $10,258,000
                    CR Accounts Payable $10,258,000
        There was an increase in the inventory (asset) account, and also an increase in the
        accounts payable (liability) account. 4460 truckloads of bars of soap x $2,300 =
        $10,258,000

120   Club Disco offers their customers a wide range of dance venue rentals for large family
        gatherings. This year, Club Disco has provided 1800 evening rentals each of which
        earned revenues of $2520.
                DR Accounts Receivable $4,536,000
                    CR Sales $4,536,000
        The accounts receivable (asset) and the sales (revenue) accounts have both increased
        by: 1800 evening rentals x $2,520 = $4,536,000

121   Pharma Drug Company Ltd. is an organization which specializes in providing their
        customers with medications. This month, Pharma Drug Company Ltd. has estimated that
        5% of the accounts receivable might not end up being collectable, based on past
        experience. The accounts receivable will need to be adjusted from its current balance of
        $77000.
                DR Bad Debt expense $3,850
                    CR Allowance for Doubtful Accounts $3,850
        The bad debts (expense) and the allowance for doubtful accounts (contra-asset) have
        both increased by: 5% x $77,000 = $3,850

122   Mr. Mop is a corporation which sells household cleaners. This week, Mr. Mop purchased 3430 tons of cleaning solution which were placed into the warehouse, and which had a per unit cost of $1900.
        DR Inventory $6,517,000
              CR Accounts Payable $6,517,000
There was an increase in the inventory (asset) account, and also an increase in the accounts payable (liability) account. 3430 tons of cleaning solution x $1,900 = $6,517,000

123   Hogtown Records sells several different types of audio services for local musicians to record their music albums. This month, Hogtown Records must amortize 1 month worth of utility bills which they had prepaid at the beginning of the year. The amount that they had paid upfront for the year was $44400.
        DR Utilities expense $3,700
              CR Prepaid Expense $3,700
The utilities (expense) account has increased and the prepaid expense (asset) account has decreased by: $44,400 for the year, divided by 12 months = $3,700

124   Kola-Nut Ltd is a corporation which sells soft drinks. Today, Kola-Nut Ltd has paid cash to their supplier to fully pay off their account payable balance, which was $64000.
        DR Accounts Payable $64,000
              CR Cash $64,000
The accounts payable (liability) and cash (asset) accounts have both increased by $64,000.

125   Jameson & Jameson provides their customers with soap products. This month, Jameson & Jameson accepted 17700 truckloads of bars of soap which were returned by customers. These products had been marked up by 35% and they had originally been bought at a per-unit cost of $1300.
        DR Sales Returns $31,063,500   DR Inventory $23,010,000
              CR Accounts Receivable $31,063,500
              CR Cost of Goods Sold $23,010,000
This transaction increases the sales returns (contra-revenue) account, and the inventory (asset) account. The accounts receivable (asset) account and the cost of goods sold (expense) account have both decreased. 17700 truckloads of bars of soap x $1,300 = $23,010,000. The 35% markup applies to the sales returns and accounts receivable amounts, i.e. $23,010,000 x 1.35 = $31,063,500

126   Mr. Mop offers their customers a wide range of household cleaners. This month, Mr. Mop must amortize 1 month worth of utility bills which they had prepaid at the beginning of the year. The amount that they had paid upfront for the year was $13200.
        DR Utilities expense $1,100
              CR Prepaid Expense $1,100
The utilities (expense) account has increased and the prepaid expense (asset) account has decreased by: $13,200 for the year, divided by 12 months = $1,100

127 Fairway Malls sells several different types of retail spaces in their shopping centers. This month, Fairway Malls has estimated that 5% of the accounts receivable might not end up being collectable, based on past experience. The accounts receivable will need to be adjusted from its current balance of $74000.

DR Bad Debt expense $3,700

CR Allowance for Doubtful Accounts $3,700

The bad debts (expense) and the allowance for doubtful accounts (contra-asset) have both increased by: 5% x $74,000 = $3,700

128 AC&C Ltd. is a company which offers their customers a wide selection of cell phone plans. This month, AC&C Ltd. paid for 1 month of rent for their company's office space. Each month, the rent owing was $18000.

DR Rent expense $18,000

CR Accounts Payable $18,000

The rent (expense) and the accounts payable (liability) accounts are both increased by one month's worth of rent, which is $18,000.

129 NBG Media Corporation offers their customers a wide range of broadcasting services for advertising agencies. This month, NBG Media Corporation paid 1 monthly loan repayment towards their long-term note payable. The interest portion was 60% of the payment. The total amount paid in cash was $26000.

DR Interest Expense $15,600   DR Loan Payable $10,400

CR Cash $26,000

The interest (expense) account has increased by $26,000 x 0.6 = $15,600. The loan payable (liability) has decreased by $26,000 x 0.4 = $10,400. The cash (asset) account has decreased by the full amount of the payment, which is $26,000

130 David & Johnson sells several different types of legal services. Today, David & Johnson received payment upfront for 2300 large orders which will not be provided until early next year. Each order was in the amount of $2100.

DR Cash $4,830,000

CR Unearned Revenue $4,830,000

The cash (asset) and the unearned revenue (liability) accounts have both increased by: 2300 large orders x $2,100 = $4,830,000

131 Club Disco sells various dance venue rentals for large family gatherings. Club Disco has just provided 1400 large orders which had been paid for in advance last year. Each order was in the amount of $2400.

DR Unearned Revenue $3,360,000

CR Sales $3,360,000

The unearned revenue (liability) account has decreased and the and the sales (revenue) account has increased by: 1400 large orders x $2,400 = $3,360,000

132 Kola-Nut Ltd sells various soft drinks. This month, Kola-Nut Ltd paid for 1 month of rent for the warehouse room, which has a monthly costs of $1200.

DR Rent expense $1,200

CR Accounts Payable $1,200

The rent (expense) and the accounts payable (liability) accounts are both increased by one month's worth of rent, which is $1,200.

133   McGerald's sells various fast food meals. This month, McGerald's has estimated that
      10% of the accounts receivable might not end up being collectable, based on past
      experience. The accounts receivable will need to be adjusted from its current balance of
      $82000.
              DR Bad Debt expense $8,200
                      CR Allowance for Doubtful Accounts $8,200
      The bad debts (expense) and the allowance for doubtful accounts (contra-asset) have
      both increased by: 10% x $82,000 = $8,200

134   Pharma Drug Company Ltd. offers their customers a wide range of medications. This
      month, Pharma Drug Company Ltd. paid 1 monthly loan repayment towards their long-
      term note payable. The interest portion was 60% of the payment. The total amount paid
      in cash was $17000.
              DR Interest Expense $10,200   DR Loan Payable $6,800
                      CR Cash $17,000
      The interest (expense) account has increased by $17,000 x 0.6 = $10,200. The loan
      payable (liability) has decreased by $17,000 x 0.4 = $6,800. The cash (asset) account
      has decreased by the full amount of the payment, which is $17,000

135   McGerald's sells various fast food meals. Today McGerald's signed up for a loan with a
      5% interest rate, and so the bank immediately transferred cash to the company in the
      amount of $27000.
              DR Cash $27,000
                      CR Loan Payable $27,000
      The cash (asset) and the loan payable (liability) accounts have both increased by:
      $27,000. The interest rate does not affect this initial accounting entry, but it will be used
      for the calculation of interest expense when repayments are made in the future toward
      this loan.

136   Mount Tessory Academy is a market leader that is well-known for their brand of private
      school education. This month, Mount Tessory Academy must amortize 1 month worth of
      utility bills which they had prepaid at the beginning of the year. The amount that they had
      paid upfront for the year was $18000.
              DR Utilities expense $1,500
                      CR Prepaid Expense $1,500
      The utilities (expense) account has increased and the prepaid expense (asset) account
      has decreased by: $18,000 for the year, divided by 12 months = $1,500

137   Comedy 253 is a privately-held corporation which focuses on their niche of premium live
      performances of stand-up comedy. Comedy 253 has just provided 1600 large orders
      which had been paid for in advance last year. Each order was in the amount of $2700.
              DR Unearned Revenue $4,320,000
                      CR Sales $4,320,000
      The unearned revenue (liability) account has decreased and the and the sales (revenue)
      account has increased by: 1600 large orders x $2,700 = $4,320,000

138   Air America is a privately-held corporation which focuses on their niche of premium global flights. This December, Air America has paid each of the company's 1500 owners an annual dividend in the amount of $16000.
         DR Retained Earnings $24,000,000
              CR Cash $24,000,000
The retained earnings (equity) and the cash accounts have both decreased by: 1500 owners x $16,000 = $24,000,000

139   Grand Convention Ltd is a privately-held corporation which focuses on their niche of premium banquet hall rentals for corporate meetings. This December, Grand Convention Ltd has paid each of the company's 1200 owners an annual dividend in the amount of $22000.
         DR Retained Earnings $26,400,000
              CR Cash $26,400,000
The retained earnings (equity) and the cash accounts have both decreased by: 1200 owners x $22,000 = $26,400,000

140   NY Fitness is a market leader that is well-known for their brand of gym memberships for professional sports teams. This month, NY Fitness must amortize 1 month worth of utility bills which they had prepaid at the beginning of the year. The amount that they had paid upfront for the year was $40800.
         DR Utilities expense $3,400
              CR Prepaid Expense $3,400
The utilities (expense) account has increased and the prepaid expense (asset) account has decreased by: $40,800 for the year, divided by 12 months = $3,400

141   Payday Now offers their customers a wide range of short-term loan arrangements. This month, Payday Now must amortize 1 month worth of utility bills which they had prepaid at the beginning of the year. The amount that they had paid upfront for the year was $13200.
         DR Utilities expense $1,100
              CR Prepaid Expense $1,100
The utilities (expense) account has increased and the prepaid expense (asset) account has decreased by: $13,200 for the year, divided by 12 months = $1,100

142   Jameson & Jameson sells various soap products. This month, Jameson & Jameson must amortize 1 month worth of utility bills which they had prepaid at the beginning of the year. The amount that they had paid upfront for the year was $39600.
         DR Utilities expense $3,300
              CR Prepaid Expense $3,300
The utilities (expense) account has increased and the prepaid expense (asset) account has decreased by: $39,600 for the year, divided by 12 months = $3,300

143   Mount Tessory Academy sells various private school education. Today Mount Tessory Academy signed up for a loan with a 5% interest rate, and so the bank immediately transferred cash to the company in the amount of $57000.

       DR Cash $57,000
            CR Loan Payable $57,000

The cash (asset) and the loan payable (liability) accounts have both increased by: $57,000. The interest rate does not affect this initial accounting entry, but it will be used for the calculation of interest expense when repayments are made in the future toward this loan.

144   LA Met Theatre Company is an organization which specializes in providing their customers with live theatrical performances. Today LA Met Theatre Company signed up for a loan with a 5% interest rate, and so the bank immediately transferred cash to the company in the amount of $37000.

       DR Cash $37,000
            CR Loan Payable $37,000

The cash (asset) and the loan payable (liability) accounts have both increased by: $37,000. The interest rate does not affect this initial accounting entry, but it will be used for the calculation of interest expense when repayments are made in the future toward this loan.

145   NY Fitness offers their customers a wide range of gym memberships for professional sports teams. This January, NY Fitness has made an advance payment to cover the next 12 months of utility bills, which have a monthly cost of $2700.

       DR Prepaid Expense $32,400
            CR Cash $32,400

The prepaid expense (asset) account has increased, and the cash (asset) account has decreased by: 12 months x $2,700 per month = $32,400 for the year.

146   LA Met Theatre Company is a market leader that is well-known for their brand of live theatrical performances. Today, LA Met Theatre Company bought equipment which has a 5 year useful life, and which had a cost of $12000.

       DR Equipment $12,000
            CR Accounts Payable $12,000

The equipment (asset) and the accounts payable (liability) accounts have both increased by: $12,000. The useful life does not affect this original accounting entry, but it will be used to calculate depreciation of the asset in the future.

147   NBG Media Corporation offers their customers a wide range of broadcasting services for advertising agencies. Today, NBG Media Corporation has paid cash to their supplier to fully pay off their account payable balance, which was $45000.

       DR Accounts Payable $45,000
            CR Cash $45,000

The accounts payable (liability) and cash (asset) accounts have both increased by $45,000.

148   Fairway Malls is a corporation which sells retail spaces in their shopping centers. Today, Fairway Malls received payment upfront for 1900 large orders which will not be provided until early next year. Each order was in the amount of $2800.
             DR Cash $5,320,000
                     CR Unearned Revenue $5,320,000
       The cash (asset) and the unearned revenue (liability) accounts have both increased by: 1900 large orders x $2,800 = $5,320,000

149   NY Fitness is a market leader that is well-known for their brand of gym memberships for professional sports teams. This January, NY Fitness has made an advance payment to cover the next 12 months of utility bills, which have a monthly cost of $1300.
             DR Prepaid Expense $15,600
                     CR Cash $15,600
       The prepaid expense (asset) account has increased, and the cash (asset) account has decreased by: 12 months x $1,300 per month = $15,600 for the year.

150   LA Met Theatre Company is a corporation which sells live theatrical performances. This December, LA Met Theatre Company recognized 1 year of depreciation on equipment which had a total useful life of 10 years, and which had originally cost $220000.
             DR Depreciation expense $22,000
                     CR Accumulated Depreciation $22,000
       The depreciation (expense) account and the accumulated depreciation (contra-asset) accounts have both increased by: $220,000 divided by 10 years = $22,000 depreciation per year.

151   Club Disco offers their customers a wide range of dance venue rentals for large family gatherings. This December, Club Disco recognized 1 year of depreciation on a building which had a total useful life of 25 years, and which had originally been bought for $437000.
             DR Depreciation expense $17,480
                     CR Accumulated Depreciation $17,480
       The depreciation (expense) account and the accumulated depreciation (contra-asset) accounts have both increased by: $437,000 divided by 25 years = $17,480 depreciation per year.

152   NY Fitness sells various gym memberships for professional sports teams. Today, NY Fitness received payment upfront for 1500 large orders which will not be provided until early next year. Each order was in the amount of $2300.
             DR Cash $3,450,000
                     CR Unearned Revenue $3,450,000
       The cash (asset) and the unearned revenue (liability) accounts have both increased by: 1500 large orders x $2,300 = $3,450,000

153   Grand Convention Ltd is a market leader that is well-known for their brand of banquet hall rentals for corporate meetings. This week, Grand Convention Ltd paid each of the 3810 staff members their bi-weekly wages, which per person had a cost of $2600.
             DR Wage expense $9,906,000
                     CR Accounts Payable $9,906,000
       The wage (expense) and the accounts payable (liability) accounts have both increased by: 3810 staff members x $2,600 = $9,906,000

154   Jameson & Jameson is a corporation which sells soap products. This month, Jameson & Jameson accepted 17000 truckloads of bars of soap which were returned by customers. These products had been marked up by 35% and they had originally been bought at a per-unit cost of $1400.
        DR Sales Returns $32,130,000   DR Inventory $23,800,000
            CR Accounts Receivable $32,130,000
            CR Cost of Goods Sold $23,800,000
This transaction increases the sales returns (contra-revenue) account, and the inventory (asset) account. The accounts receivable (asset) account and the cost of goods sold (expense) account have both decreased. 17000 truckloads of bars of soap x $1,400 = $23,800,000. The 35% markup applies to the sales returns and accounts receivable amounts, i.e. $23,800,000 x 1.35 = $32,130,000

155   Jameson & Jameson offers their customers a wide range of soap products. This December, Jameson & Jameson has paid each of the company's 1700 owners an annual dividend in the amount of $18000.
        DR Retained Earnings $30,600,000
            CR Cash $30,600,000
The retained earnings (equity) and the cash accounts have both decreased by: 1700 owners x $18,000 = $30,600,000

156   AC&C Ltd. sells several different types of cell phone plans. Today AC&C Ltd. signed up for a loan with a 5% interest rate, and so the bank immediately transferred cash to the company in the amount of $75000.
        DR Cash $75,000
            CR Loan Payable $75,000
The cash (asset) and the loan payable (liability) accounts have both increased by: $75,000. The interest rate does not affect this initial accounting entry, but it will be used for the calculation of interest expense when repayments are made in the future toward this loan.

157   Kola-Nut Ltd offers their customers a wide range of soft drinks. This month, Kola-Nut Ltd paid for 1 month of rent for the warehouse room, which has a monthly costs of $1800.
        DR Rent expense $1,800
            CR Accounts Payable $1,800
The rent (expense) and the accounts payable (liability) accounts are both increased by one month's worth of rent, which is $1,800.

158   A to Z Event Guru Ltd is a corporation which sells start-to-finish event planning services for large gatherings. This week, A to Z Event Guru Ltd paid each of the 3350 staff members their bi-weekly wages, which per person had a cost of $1300.
        DR Wage expense $4,355,000
            CR Accounts Payable $4,355,000
The wage (expense) and the accounts payable (liability) accounts have both increased by: 3350 staff members x $1,300 = $4,355,000

159   Comedy 253 provides their customers with live performances of stand-up comedy. Comedy 253 has just received a cash payment for the full amount that this customer owed to the company for all of their purchases to date. The outstanding balance which has now been paid was $15000.
         DR Cash $15,000
            CR Accounts Receivable $15,000
The cash (asset) account has increased, and the accounts receivable (asset) account has decreased by $15,000.

160   NY Fitness is an organization which specializes in providing their customers with gym memberships for professional sports teams. This month, NY Fitness paid for 1 month of rent for their company's office space. Each month, the rent owing was $12000.
         DR Rent expense $12,000
            CR Accounts Payable $12,000
The rent (expense) and the accounts payable (liability) accounts are both increased by one month's worth of rent, which is $12,000.

161   Mr. Mop is a corporation which sells household cleaners. This month, Mr. Mop accepted 20700 tons of cleaning solution which were returned by customers. These products had been marked up by 35% and they had originally been bought at a per-unit cost of $2700.
         DR Sales Returns $75,451,500   DR Inventory $55,890,000
            CR Accounts Receivable $75,451,500
            CR Cost of Goods Sold $55,890,000
This transaction increases the sales returns (contra-revenue) account, and the inventory (asset) account. The accounts receivable (asset) account and the cost of goods sold (expense) account have both decreased. 20700 tons of cleaning solution x $2,700 = $55,890,000. The 35% markup applies to the sales returns and accounts receivable amounts, i.e. $55,890,000 x 1.35 = $75,451,500

162   Jameson & Jameson is an organization which specializes in providing their customers with soap products. This month, Jameson & Jameson paid for 1 month of rent for the warehouse room, which has a monthly costs of $1200.
         DR Rent expense $1,200
            CR Accounts Payable $1,200
The rent (expense) and the accounts payable (liability) accounts are both increased by one month's worth of rent, which is $1,200.

163   LA Met Theatre Company provides their customers with live theatrical performances. This week, LA Met Theatre Company paid each of the 2150 staff members their bi-weekly wages, which per person had a cost of $2200.
         DR Wage expense $4,730,000
            CR Accounts Payable $4,730,000
The wage (expense) and the accounts payable (liability) accounts have both increased by: 2150 staff members x $2,200 = $4,730,000

164   Kola-Nut Ltd offers their customers a wide range of soft drinks. This month, Kola-Nut Ltd accepted 24900 batches of soda bottles which were returned by customers. These products had been marked up by 35% and they had originally been bought at a per-unit cost of $2100.
                DR Sales Returns $70,591,500   DR Inventory $52,290,000
                        CR Accounts Receivable $70,591,500
                        CR Cost of Goods Sold $52,290,000
        This transaction increases the sales returns (contra-revenue) account, and the inventory (asset) account. The accounts receivable (asset) account and the cost of goods sold (expense) account have both decreased. 24900 batches of soda bottles x $2,100 = $52,290,000. The 35% markup applies to the sales returns and accounts receivable amounts, i.e. $52,290,000 x 1.35 = $70,591,500

165   Comedy 253 is a company which offers their customers a wide selection of live performances of stand-up comedy. Comedy 253 has just purchased a building using cash, which has an expected useful life of 30 years, and which had a total cost of $644000.
                DR Building $644,000
                        CR Cash $644,000
        The building (asset) account has increased, and the cash (asset) account has decreased by: $644,000. The useful life does not affect this original accounting entry, but it will be used to calculate depreciation of the asset in the future.

166   Payday Now offers their customers a wide range of short-term loan arrangements. Payday Now has just provided 1000 large orders which had been paid for in advance last year. Each order was in the amount of $2000.
                DR Unearned Revenue $2,000,000
                        CR Sales $2,000,000
        The unearned revenue (liability) account has decreased and the and the sales (revenue) account has increased by: 1000 large orders x $2,000 = $2,000,000

167   Jameson & Jameson is a market leader that is well-known for their brand of soap products. This December, Jameson & Jameson recognized 1 year of depreciation on equipment which had a total useful life of 10 years, and which had originally cost $190000.
                DR Depreciation expense $19,000
                        CR Accumulated Depreciation $19,000
        The depreciation (expense) account and the accumulated depreciation (contra-asset) accounts have both increased by: $190,000 divided by 10 years = $19,000 depreciation per year.

168   Sprike Inc is a corporation which sells athletic apparel. Today, Sprike Inc received an upfront payment for 3540 batches of athletic t-shirts which will be provided to the customer 6 months from now. The payment for each was $2600.
                DR Cash $9,204,000
                        CR Unearned Revenue $9,204,000
        The cash (asset) and the unearned revenue (liability) accounts have both increased by: 3540 batches of athletic t-shirts x $2,600 = $9,204,000

169   Air America is an organization which specializes in providing their customers with global flights. This month, Air America paid 1 monthly loan repayment towards their long-term note payable. The interest portion was 60% of the payment. The total amount paid in cash was $22000.
            DR Interest Expense $13,200   DR Loan Payable $8,800
                    CR Cash $22,000
The interest (expense) account has increased by $22,000 x 0.6 = $13,200. The loan payable (liability) has decreased by $22,000 x 0.4 = $8,800. The cash (asset) account has decreased by the full amount of the payment, which is $22,000

170   Toyonda sells several different types of cars. This month, Toyonda paid 1 monthly loan repayment towards their long-term note payable. The interest portion was 60% of the payment. The total amount paid in cash was $16000.
            DR Interest Expense $9,600   DR Loan Payable $6,400
                    CR Cash $16,000
The interest (expense) account has increased by $16,000 x 0.6 = $9,600. The loan payable (liability) has decreased by $16,000 x 0.4 = $6,400. The cash (asset) account has decreased by the full amount of the payment, which is $16,000

171   Mr. Mop offers their customers a wide range of household cleaners. This month, Mr. Mop accepted 2800 tons of cleaning solution which were returned by customers. These products had been marked up by 35% and they had originally been bought at a per-unit cost of $1300.
            DR Sales Returns $4,914,000   DR Inventory $3,640,000
                    CR Accounts Receivable $4,914,000
                    CR Cost of Goods Sold $3,640,000
This transaction increases the sales returns (contra-revenue) account, and the inventory (asset) account. The accounts receivable (asset) account and the cost of goods sold (expense) account have both decreased. 2800 tons of cleaning solution x $1,300 = $3,640,000. The 35% markup applies to the sales returns and accounts receivable amounts, i.e. $3,640,000 x 1.35 = $4,914,000

172   David & Johnson is a market leader that is well-known for their brand of legal services. This month, David & Johnson paid 1 monthly loan repayment towards their long-term note payable. The interest portion was 60% of the payment. The total amount paid in cash was $13000.
            DR Interest Expense $7,800   DR Loan Payable $5,200
                    CR Cash $13,000
The interest (expense) account has increased by $13,000 x 0.6 = $7,800. The loan payable (liability) has decreased by $13,000 x 0.4 = $5,200. The cash (asset) account has decreased by the full amount of the payment, which is $13,000

173   Air America is a market leader that is well-known for their brand of global flights. This January, Air America has made an advance payment to cover the next 12 months of utility bills, which have a monthly cost of $1600.
            DR Prepaid Expense $19,200
                    CR Cash $19,200
The prepaid expense (asset) account has increased, and the cash (asset) account has decreased by: 12 months x $1,600 per month = $19,200 for the year.

174   McGerald's is a market leader that is well-known for their brand of fast food meals. McGerald's has just provided 1900 large orders which had been paid for in advance last year. Each order was in the amount of $2800.

DR Unearned Revenue $5,320,000
    CR Sales $5,320,000

The unearned revenue (liability) account has decreased and the and the sales (revenue) account has increased by: 1900 large orders x $2,800 = $5,320,000

175   Comedy 253 is an organization which specializes in providing their customers with live performances of stand-up comedy. This month, Comedy 253 must amortize 1 month worth of utility bills which they had prepaid at the beginning of the year. The amount that they had paid upfront for the year was $32400.

DR Utilities expense $2,700
    CR Prepaid Expense $2,700

The utilities (expense) account has increased and the prepaid expense (asset) account has decreased by: $32,400 for the year, divided by 12 months = $2,700

176   Mount Tessory Academy offers their customers a wide range of private school education. Today, Mount Tessory Academy has paid cash to their supplier to fully pay off their account payable balance, which was $80000.

DR Accounts Payable $80,000
    CR Cash $80,000

The accounts payable (liability) and cash (asset) accounts have both increased by $80,000.

177   Pharma Drug Company Ltd. sells various medications. This month, Pharma Drug Company Ltd. paid for 1 month of rent for the warehouse room, which has a monthly costs of $2100.

DR Rent expense $2,100
    CR Accounts Payable $2,100

The rent (expense) and the accounts payable (liability) accounts are both increased by one month's worth of rent, which is $2,100.

178   Cirque du Lune is an organization which specializes in providing their customers with circus performances. This December, Cirque du Lune recognized 1 year of depreciation on a building which had a total useful life of 25 years, and which had originally been bought for $770000.

DR Depreciation expense $30,800
    CR Accumulated Depreciation $30,800

The depreciation (expense) account and the accumulated depreciation (contra-asset) accounts have both increased by: $770,000 divided by 25 years = $30,800 depreciation per year.

179   Mr. Mop is a privately-held corporation which focuses on their niche of premium
       household cleaners. Mr. Mop has just received a cash payment for the full amount that
       this customer owed to the company for all of their purchases to date. The outstanding
       balance which has now been paid was $82000.
              DR Cash $82,000
                     CR Accounts Receivable $82,000
       The cash (asset) account has increased, and the accounts receivable (asset) account
       has decreased by $82,000.

180   Kola-Nut Ltd is an organization which specializes in providing their customers with soft
       drinks. Today, Kola-Nut Ltd received an upfront payment for 1090 batches of soda
       bottles which will be provided to the customer 6 months from now. The payment for each
       was $1900.
              DR Cash $2,071,000
                     CR Unearned Revenue $2,071,000
       The cash (asset) and the unearned revenue (liability) accounts have both increased by:
       1090 batches of soda bottles x $1,900 = $2,071,000

181   Pharma Drug Company Ltd. offers their customers a wide range of medications. This
       month, Pharma Drug Company Ltd. must amortize 1 month worth of utility bills which
       they had prepaid at the beginning of the year. The amount that they had paid upfront for
       the year was $22800.
              DR Utilities expense $1,900
                     CR Prepaid Expense $1,900
       The utilities (expense) account has increased and the prepaid expense (asset) account
       has decreased by: $22,800 for the year, divided by 12 months = $1,900

182   Jameson & Jameson is a privately-held corporation which focuses on their niche of
       premium soap products. This week, Jameson & Jameson purchased 3670 truckloads of
       bars of soap which were placed into the warehouse, and which had a per unit cost of
       $1500.
              DR Inventory $5,505,000
                     CR Accounts Payable $5,505,000
       There was an increase in the inventory (asset) account, and also an increase in the
       accounts payable (liability) account. 3670 truckloads of bars of soap x $1,500 =
       $5,505,000

183   NY Fitness is a corporation which sells gym memberships for professional sports teams.
       Today NY Fitness signed up for a loan with a 5% interest rate, and so the bank
       immediately transferred cash to the company in the amount of $42000.
              DR Cash $42,000
                     CR Loan Payable $42,000
       The cash (asset) and the loan payable (liability) accounts have both increased by:
       $42,000. The interest rate does not affect this initial accounting entry, but it will be used
       for the calculation of interest expense when repayments are made in the future toward
       this loan.

184   Kola-Nut Ltd is a company which offers their customers a wide selection of soft drinks. Today Kola-Nut Ltd signed up for a loan with a 5% interest rate, and so the bank immediately transferred cash to the company in the amount of $111000.
>> DR Cash $111,000
>>> CR Loan Payable $111,000

The cash (asset) and the loan payable (liability) accounts have both increased by: $111,000. The interest rate does not affect this initial accounting entry, but it will be used for the calculation of interest expense when repayments are made in the future toward this loan.

185   Pharma Drug Company Ltd. provides their customers with medications. Today Pharma Drug Company Ltd. signed up for a loan with a 5% interest rate, and so the bank immediately transferred cash to the company in the amount of $111000.
>> DR Cash $111,000
>>> CR Loan Payable $111,000

The cash (asset) and the loan payable (liability) accounts have both increased by: $111,000. The interest rate does not affect this initial accounting entry, but it will be used for the calculation of interest expense when repayments are made in the future toward this loan.

186   Grand Convention Ltd is a market leader that is well-known for their brand of banquet hall rentals for corporate meetings. This December, Grand Convention Ltd recognized 1 year of depreciation on equipment which had a total useful life of 10 years, and which had originally cost $110000.
>> DR Depreciation expense $11,000
>>> CR Accumulated Depreciation $11,000

The depreciation (expense) account and the accumulated depreciation (contra-asset) accounts have both increased by: $110,000 divided by 10 years = $11,000 depreciation per year.

187   Fairway Malls sells various retail spaces in their shopping centers. Today, Fairway Malls received payment upfront for 2000 large orders which will not be provided until early next year. Each order was in the amount of $2200.
>> DR Cash $4,400,000
>>> CR Unearned Revenue $4,400,000

The cash (asset) and the unearned revenue (liability) accounts have both increased by: 2000 large orders x $2,200 = $4,400,000

188   Sprike Inc provides their customers with athletic apparel. Today Sprike Inc sold 29900 batches of athletic t-shirts which had a 30% mark-up. They had originally been bought from their suppliers for a unit cost of $1190.
>> DR Accounts Receivable $46,255,300   DR Cost of Goods Sold $35,581,000
>>> CR Sales $46,255,300
>>> CR Inventory $35,581,000

This transaction increases the accounts receivable (asset) account, the sales (revenue) account, and the cost of goods sold (expense) account. The inventory (asset) account has decreased. 29900 batches of athletic t-shirts x $1,190 = $35,581,000. The 30% markup applies to the sales and accounts receivable amounts, i.e. $35,581,000 x 1.30 = $46,255,300

189   Jameson & Jameson offers their customers a wide range of soap products. This month, Jameson & Jameson paid for 1 month of rent for the warehouse room, which has a monthly costs of $2100.
                DR Rent expense $2,100
                    CR Accounts Payable $2,100
       The rent (expense) and the accounts payable (liability) accounts are both increased by one month's worth of rent, which is $2,100.

190   Kola-Nut Ltd is a privately-held corporation which focuses on their niche of premium soft drinks. This month, Kola-Nut Ltd paid for 1 month of rent for the warehouse room, which has a monthly costs of $1900.
                DR Rent expense $1,900
                    CR Accounts Payable $1,900
       The rent (expense) and the accounts payable (liability) accounts are both increased by one month's worth of rent, which is $1,900.

191   Toyonda offers their customers a wide range of cars. This January, Toyonda has made an advance payment to cover the next 12 months of utility bills, which have a monthly cost of $2200.
                DR Prepaid Expense $26,400
                    CR Cash $26,400
       The prepaid expense (asset) account has increased, and the cash (asset) account has decreased by: 12 months x $2,200 per month = $26,400 for the year.

192   Mr. Mop provides their customers with household cleaners. This week, Mr. Mop purchased 2010 tons of cleaning solution which were placed into the warehouse, and which had a per unit cost of $1200.
                DR Inventory $2,412,000
                    CR Accounts Payable $2,412,000
       There was an increase in the inventory (asset) account, and also an increase in the accounts payable (liability) account. 2010 tons of cleaning solution x $1,200 = $2,412,000

193   Toyonda is a market leader that is well-known for their brand of cars. Today, Toyonda bought equipment which has a 5 year useful life, and which had a cost of $20000.
                DR Equipment $20,000
                    CR Accounts Payable $20,000
       The equipment (asset) and the accounts payable (liability) accounts have both increased by: $20,000. The useful life does not affect this original accounting entry, but it will be used to calculate depreciation of the asset in the future.

194   Fairway Malls sells several different types of retail spaces in their shopping centers. This month, Fairway Malls has estimated that 20% of the accounts receivable might not end up being collectable, based on past experience. The accounts receivable will need to be adjusted from its current balance of $73000.
                DR Bad Debt expense $14,600
                    CR Allowance for Doubtful Accounts $14,600
       The bad debts (expense) and the allowance for doubtful accounts (contra-asset) have both increased by: 20% x $73,000 = $14,600

195   AC&C Ltd. sells various cell phone plans. This January, AC&C Ltd. has made an advance payment to cover the next 12 months of utility bills, which have a monthly cost of $1500.

        DR Prepaid Expense $18,000
            CR Cash $18,000

The prepaid expense (asset) account has increased, and the cash (asset) account has decreased by: 12 months x $1,500 per month = $18,000 for the year.

196   Kola-Nut Ltd is a corporation which sells soft drinks. Today, Kola-Nut Ltd has paid cash to their supplier to fully pay off their account payable balance, which was $57000.

        DR Accounts Payable $57,000
            CR Cash $57,000

The accounts payable (liability) and cash (asset) accounts have both increased by $57,000.

197   A to Z Event Guru Ltd is a corporation which sells start-to-finish event planning services for large gatherings. This month, A to Z Event Guru Ltd paid 1 monthly loan repayment towards their long-term note payable. The interest portion was 60% of the payment. The total amount paid in cash was $19000.

        DR Interest Expense $11,400   DR Loan Payable $7,600
            CR Cash $19,000

The interest (expense) account has increased by $19,000 x 0.6 = $11,400. The loan payable (liability) has decreased by $19,000 x 0.4 = $7,600. The cash (asset) account has decreased by the full amount of the payment, which is $19,000

198   Club Disco is an organization which specializes in providing their customers with dance venue rentals for large family gatherings. This December, Club Disco has paid each of the company's 1300 owners an annual dividend in the amount of $8000.

        DR Retained Earnings $10,400,000
            CR Cash $10,400,000

The retained earnings (equity) and the cash accounts have both decreased by: 1300 owners x $8,000 = $10,400,000

199   Cirque du Lune is a market leader that is well-known for their brand of circus performances. Today, Cirque du Lune received payment upfront for 1100 large orders which will not be provided until early next year. Each order was in the amount of $1300.

        DR Cash $1,430,000
            CR Unearned Revenue $1,430,000

The cash (asset) and the unearned revenue (liability) accounts have both increased by: 1100 large orders x $1,300 = $1,430,000

200   McGerald's sells several different types of fast food meals. Today, McGerald's received payment upfront for 1900 large orders which will not be provided until early next year. Each order was in the amount of $2400.

        DR Cash $4,560,000
            CR Unearned Revenue $4,560,000

The cash (asset) and the unearned revenue (liability) accounts have both increased by: 1900 large orders x $2,400 = $4,560,000

QUANTITATIVE ANALYSIS SOLUTUIONS

1   Annual Tax Expense
= (Net Income excluding depreciation) x Effective tax rate
= { [(Revenues) - (Cost of Sales)] - [Total Labor Costs] - [HVAC expenses] } x 32%
= { [($19,800 x 19815) + ($30,600 x 15415) + ($9,000 x 4495)] - [($600 x 19815) + ($600 x 15415) + ($200 x 4495)] - [($24 x 40 x 18) x 50 weeks + ($12 x 24 x 11) x 50 weeks + $18,000 + $8,000] - [520000] } x 32%
= $281,883,392 Monthly amount is calculated by dividing the annual amount by 12.
$281,883,392 / 12 = $23,490,283

2   Annual Cash flow
= (Net Income excluding depreciation) - Tax
= [(Revenues) - (Cost of Sales)] - [Total Labor Costs] - [Janitorial services] - Tax
= [($24,000 x 24060) + ($36,000 x 12160) + ($12,000 x 3995)] - [($1,200 x 24060) + ($1,300 x 12160) + ($400 x 3995)] - [($27 x 50 x 23) x 50 weeks + ($13 x 27 x 14) x 50 weeks + $20,000 + $9,000] - [580000] - $334,770,084
= $679,684,716 Monthly amount is calculated by dividing the annual amount by 12.
$679,684,716 / 12 = $56,640,393

3   Annual Cash flow
= (Net Income excluding depreciation) - Tax
= [(Revenues) - (Cost of Sales)] - [Total Labor Costs] - [Utilities] - Tax
= [($28,000 x 28033) + ($40,000 x 8133) + ($16,000 x 3195)] - [($3,500 x 28033) + ($3,600 x 8133) + ($900 x 3195)] - [($33 x 70 x 33) x 50 weeks + ($15 x 33 x 20) x 50 weeks + $24,000 + $11,000] - [700000] - $359,118,445
= $666,934,255 Monthly amount is calculated by dividing the annual amount by 12.
$666,934,255 / 12 = $55,577,855

4   Annual Net Income
= [(Revenues) - (Cost of Sales)] - [Total Labor Costs] - [Insurance costs] - [Depreciation]
= [($21,600 x 21670) + ($28,800 x 3370) + ($14,400 x 1595)] - [($13,900 x 21670) + ($14,000 x 3370) + ($2,700 x 1595)] - [($45 x 110 x 53) x 50 weeks + ($19 x 45 x 32) x 50 weeks + $32,000 + $15,000] - [$940,000] - [($2,350,000 / 72) + ($1,175,000 / 48)]
= $219,866,882 Monthly amount is calculated by dividing the annual amount by 12.
$219,866,882 / 12 = $18,322,240

5   Annual EBITDA
= [(Revenues) - (Cost of Sales)] - [Total Labor Costs]] - [Insurance costs]
= [($23,400 x 23424) + ($31,200 x 3591) + ($15,600 x 1728)] - [($13,900 x 23424) + ($14,000 x 3591) + ($2,700 x 1728)] - [($45 x 110 x 53) x 50 weeks + ($19 x 45 x 32) x 50 weeks + $32,000 + $15,000] - [$940,000]
= $291,111,900

6   Gross Margin
= [Gross Profit] / [Revenue]
= [($1,000 - $200) x 1071 + ($1,600 - $200) x 1771 + ($400 - $100) x 395] / [($1,000 x 1071) + ($1,600 x 1771) + ($400 x 395)]
= $3,454,700 / $4,062,600
= 85%

7   Annual Cash flow
= (Net Income excluding depreciation) - Tax
= [(Revenues) - (Cost of Sales)] - [Total Labor Costs] - [HVAC expenses] - Tax
= [($23,100 x 23164) + ($35,700 x 18014) + ($10,500 x 5245)] - [($600 x 23164) + ($600 x 18014) + ($200 x 5245)] - [($24 x 40 x 18) x 50 weeks + ($12 x 24 x 11) x 50 weeks + $18,000 + $8,000] - [520000] - $385,899,680
= $820,036,820

8   Annual EBITDA
= [(Revenues) - (Cost of Sales)] - [Total Labor Costs]] - [Janitorial services]
= [($18,000 x 18012) + ($27,000 x 9112) + ($9,000 x 2995)] - [($1,200 x 18012) + ($1,300 x 9112) + ($400 x 2995)] - [($27 x 50 x 23) x 50 weeks + ($13 x 27 x 14) x 50 weeks + $20,000 + $9,000] - [$580,000]
= $560,129,800

9   Annual Cash flow
= (Net Income excluding depreciation) - Tax
= [(Revenues) - (Cost of Sales)] - [Total Labor Costs] - [Insurance costs] - Tax
= [($36,000 x 36033) + ($48,000 x 5466) + ($24,000 x 2662)] - [($13,900 x 36033) + ($14,000 x 5466) + ($2,700 x 2662)] - [($45 x 110 x 53) x 50 weeks + ($19 x 45 x 32) x 50 weeks + $32,000 + $15,000] - [940000] - $399,126,546
= $624,274,854 Monthly amount is calculated by dividing the annual amount by 12.
$624,274,854 / 12 = $52,022,905

10   Annual Net Income
= [(Revenues) - (Cost of Sales)] - [Total Labor Costs] - [Insurance costs] - [Depreciation]
= [($18,000 x 18011) + ($24,000 x 2778) + ($12,000 x 1328)] - [($13,900 x 18011) + ($14,000 x 2778) + ($2,700 x 1328)] - [($45 x 110 x 53) x 50 weeks + ($19 x 45 x 32) x 50 weeks + $32,000 + $15,000] - [$940,000] - [($2,350,000 / 60) + ($1,175,000 / 40)]
= $98,434,458 Monthly amount is calculated by dividing the annual amount by 12.
$98,434,458 / 12 = $8,202,872

11   Annual EBITDA
= [(Revenues) - (Cost of Sales)] - [Total Labor Costs]] - [Employee assistance services]
= [($22,100 x 22140) + ($29,900 x 3878) + ($14,300 x 1783)] - [($10,400 x 22140) + ($10,600 x 3878) + ($2,200 x 1783)] - [($42 x 100 x 48) x 50 weeks + ($18 x 42 x 29) x 50 weeks + $30,000 + $14,000] - [$880,000]
= $343,357,500

12   Annual Tax Expense
= (Net Income excluding depreciation) x Effective tax rate
= { [(Revenues) - (Cost of Sales)] - [Total Labor Costs] - [Utilities] } x 36%
= { [($24,000 x 24078) + ($33,600 x 5778) + ($14,400 x 2395)] - [($5,300 x 24078) + ($5,400 x 5778) + ($1,300 x 2395)] - [($36 x 80 x 38) x 50 weeks + ($16 x 36 x 23) x 50 weeks + $26,000 + $12,000] - [760000] } x 36%
= $229,550,508 Monthly amount is calculated by dividing the annual amount by 12.
$229,550,508 / 12 = $19,129,209

13   Annual Cash flow
= (Net Income excluding depreciation) - Tax
= [(Revenues) - (Cost of Sales)] - [Total Labor Costs] - [Janitorial services] - Tax
= [($24,700 x 24768) + ($36,100 x 9193) + ($13,300 x 3320)] - [($2,200 x 24768) + ($2,200 x 9193) + ($600 x 3320)] - [($30 x 60 x 28) x 50 weeks + ($14 x 30 x 17) x 50 weeks + $22,000 + $10,000] - [640000] - $308,562,818
= $598,974,882

14   Annual Net Income
= [(Revenues) - (Cost of Sales)] - [Total Labor Costs] - [Utilities] - [Depreciation]
= [($15,000 x 15085) + ($21,000 x 3685) + ($9,000 x 1495)] - [($5,300 x 15085) + ($5,400 x 3685) + ($1,300 x 1495)] - [($36 x 80 x 38) x 50 weeks + ($16 x 36 x 23) x 50 weeks + $26,000 + $12,000] - [$760,000] - [($1,900,000 / 60) + ($950,000 / 40)]
= $208,334,183 Monthly amount is calculated by dividing the annual amount by 12.
$208,334,183 / 12 = $17,361,182

15   Annual Cash flow
= (Net Income excluding depreciation) - Tax
= [(Revenues) - (Cost of Sales)] - [Total Labor Costs] - [Janitorial services] - Tax
= [($25,200 x 25223) + ($37,800 x 12723) + ($12,600 x 4195)] - [($1,200 x 25223) + ($1,300 x 12723) + ($400 x 4195)] - [($27 x 50 x 23) x 50 weeks + ($13 x 27 x 14) x 50 weeks + $20,000 + $9,000] - [580000] - $369,109,389
= $749,403,911

16   Annual EBITDA
= [(Revenues) - (Cost of Sales)] - [Total Labor Costs]] - [HVAC expenses]
= [($16,500 x 16568) + ($25,500 x 12918) + ($7,500 x 3745)] - [($600 x 16568) + ($600 x 12918) + ($200 x 3745)] - [($24 x 40 x 18) x 50 weeks + ($12 x 24 x 11) x 50 weeks + $18,000 + $8,000] - [$520,000]
= $610,859,500

17   Annual EBITDA
= [(Revenues) - (Cost of Sales)] - [Total Labor Costs]] - [Janitorial services]
= [($16,900 x 16921) + ($24,700 x 6296) + ($9,100 x 2270)] - [($2,200 x 16921) + ($2,200 x 6296) + ($600 x 2270)] - [($30 x 60 x 28) x 50 weeks + ($14 x 30 x 17) x 50 weeks + $22,000 + $10,000] - [$640,000]
= $406,144,700

18 Annual Net Income
= [(Revenues) - (Cost of Sales)] - [Total Labor Costs] - [Utilities] - [Depreciation]
= [($15,400 x 15470) + ($22,000 x 4570) + ($8,800 x 1755)] - [($3,500 x 15470) + ($3,600 x 4570) + ($900 x 1755)] - [($33 x 70 x 33) x 50 weeks + ($15 x 33 x 20) x 50 weeks + $24,000 + $11,000] - [$700,000] - [($1,750,000 / 66) + ($875,000 / 44)]
= $276,957,598

19 Annual Net Income
= [(Revenues) - (Cost of Sales)] - [Total Labor Costs] - [Janitorial services] - [Depreciation]
= [($13,000 x 13082) + ($19,000 x 4932) + ($7,000 x 1745)] - [($2,200 x 13082) + ($2,200 x 4932) + ($600 x 1745)] - [($30 x 60 x 28) x 50 weeks + ($14 x 30 x 17) x 50 weeks + $22,000 + $10,000] - [$640,000] - [($1,600,000 / 60) + ($800,000 / 40)]
= $231,715,533 Monthly amount is calculated by dividing the annual amount by 12.
$231,715,533 / 12 = $19,309,628

20 Annual Cash flow
= (Net Income excluding depreciation) - Tax
= [(Revenues) - (Cost of Sales)] - [Total Labor Costs] - [Insurance costs] - Tax
= [($37,800 x 37807) + ($50,400 x 5707) + ($25,200 x 2795)] - [($13,900 x 37807) + ($14,000 x 5707) + ($2,700 x 2795)] - [($45 x 110 x 53) x 50 weeks + ($19 x 45 x 32) x 50 weeks + $32,000 + $15,000] - [940000] - $451,907,469
= $706,829,631

21 Annual Cash flow
= (Net Income excluding depreciation) - Tax
= [(Revenues) - (Cost of Sales)] - [Total Labor Costs] - [Insurance costs] - Tax
= [($34,200 x 34291) + ($45,600 x 5258) + ($22,800 x 2528)] - [($13,900 x 34291) + ($14,000 x 5258) + ($2,700 x 2528)] - [($45 x 110 x 53) x 50 weeks + ($19 x 45 x 32) x 50 weeks + $32,000 + $15,000] - [940000] - $350,064,156
= $547,536,244

22 Annual Net Income
= [(Revenues) - (Cost of Sales)] - [Total Labor Costs] - [HVAC expenses] - [Depreciation]
= [($12,000 x 12007) + ($19,200 x 19307) + ($4,800 x 4795)] - [($200 x 12007) + ($200 x 19307) + ($100 x 4795)] - [($21 x 30 x 13) x 50 weeks + ($11 x 21 x 8) x 50 weeks + $16,000 + $7,000] - [$460,000] - [($1,150,000 / 72) + ($575,000 / 48)]
= $530,039,249 Monthly amount is calculated by dividing the annual amount by 12.
$530,039,249 / 12 = $44,169,937

23 Annual Cash flow
= (Net Income excluding depreciation) - Tax
= [(Revenues) - (Cost of Sales)] - [Total Labor Costs] - [HVAC expenses] - Tax
= [($23,100 x 23154) + ($35,700 x 18004) + ($10,500 x 5245)] - [($600 x 23154) + ($600 x 18004) + ($200 x 5245)] - [($24 x 40 x 18) x 50 weeks + ($12 x 24 x 11) x 50 weeks + $18,000 + $8,000] - [520000] - $385,715,360
= $819,645,140

24 Annual Tax Expense
= (Net Income excluding depreciation) x Effective tax rate
= { [(Revenues) - (Cost of Sales)] - [Total Labor Costs] - [Janitorial services] } x 34%
= { [($22,100 x 22163) + ($32,300 x 8238) + ($11,900 x 2970)] - [($2,200 x 22163) + ($2,200 x 8238) + ($600 x 2970)] - [($30 x 60 x 28) x 50 weeks + ($14 x 30 x 17) x 50 weeks + $22,000 + $10,000] - [640000] } x 34%
= $244,466,630

25 Annual EBITDA
= [(Revenues) - (Cost of Sales)] - [Total Labor Costs]] - [Insurance costs]
= [($26,600 x 26659) + ($35,000 x 3659) + ($18,200 x 1815)] - [($18,000 x 26659) + ($18,200 x 3659) + ($3,300 x 1815)] - [($48 x 120 x 58) x 50 weeks + ($20 x 48 x 35) x 50 weeks + $34,000 + $16,000] - [$1,000,000]
= $298,348,100 Monthly amount is calculated by dividing the annual amount by 12.
$298,348,100 / 12 = $24,862,342

26 Annual Cash flow
= (Net Income excluding depreciation) - Tax
= [(Revenues) - (Cost of Sales)] - [Total Labor Costs] - [Utilities] - Tax
= [($31,500 x 31580) + ($44,100 x 7530) + ($18,900 x 3145)] - [($5,300 x 31580) + ($5,400 x 7530) + ($1,300 x 3145)] - [($36 x 80 x 38) x 50 weeks + ($16 x 36 x 23) x 50 weeks + $26,000 + $12,000] - [760000] - $420,201,576
= $747,025,024

27 Annual Net Income
= [(Revenues) - (Cost of Sales)] - [Total Labor Costs] - [Utilities] - [Depreciation]
= [($18,000 x 18076) + ($25,200 x 4376) + ($10,800 x 1795)] - [($5,300 x 18076) + ($5,400 x 4376) + ($1,300 x 1795)] - [($36 x 80 x 38) x 50 weeks + ($16 x 36 x 23) x 50 weeks + $26,000 + $12,000] - [$760,000] - [($1,900,000 / 72) + ($950,000 / 48)]
= $326,283,919 Monthly amount is calculated by dividing the annual amount by 12.
$326,283,919 / 12 = $27,190,327

28 Gross Margin
= [Gross Profit] / [Revenue]
= [($3,900 - $2,200) x 3907 + ($5,700 - $2,200) x 1532 + ($2,100 - $600) x 520] / [($3,900 x 3907) + ($5,700 x 1532) + ($2,100 x 520)]
= $12,783,900 / $25,061,700
= 51%

29 Annual Net Income
= [(Revenues) - (Cost of Sales)] - [Total Labor Costs] - [Employee assistance services] - [Depreciation]
= [($16,000 x 16091) + ($22,000 x 3334) + ($10,000 x 1424)] - [($7,600 x 16091) + ($7,700 x 3334) + ($1,700 x 1424)] - [($39 x 90 x 43) x 50 weeks + ($17 x 39 x 26) x 50 weeks + $28,000 + $13,000] - [$820,000] - [($2,050,000 / 60) + ($1,025,000 / 40)]
= $185,330,608 Monthly amount is calculated by dividing the annual amount by 12.
$185,330,608 / 12 = $15,444,217

30   Annual EBITDA
= [(Revenues) - (Cost of Sales)] - [Total Labor Costs]] - [HVAC expenses]
= [($13,000 x 13028) + ($20,800 x 20928) + ($5,200 x 5195)] - [($200 x 13028) + ($200 x 20928) + ($100 x 5195)] - [($21 x 30 x 13) x 50 weeks + ($11 x 21 x 8) x 50 weeks + $16,000 + $7,000] - [$460,000]
= $623,384,800

31   Annual Cash flow
= (Net Income excluding depreciation) - Tax
= [(Revenues) - (Cost of Sales)] - [Total Labor Costs] - [Insurance costs] - Tax
= [($34,200 x 34225) + ($45,600 x 5192) + ($22,800 x 2528)] - [($13,900 x 34225) + ($14,000 x 5192) + ($2,700 x 2528)] - [($45 x 110 x 53) x 50 weeks + ($19 x 45 x 32) x 50 weeks + $32,000 + $15,000] - [940000] - $348,728,250
= $545,446,750

32   Annual Cash flow
= (Net Income excluding depreciation) - Tax
= [(Revenues) - (Cost of Sales)] - [Total Labor Costs] - [HVAC expenses] - Tax
= [($23,100 x 23170) + ($35,700 x 18020) + ($10,500 x 5245)] - [($600 x 23170) + ($600 x 18020) + ($200 x 5245)] - [($24 x 40 x 18) x 50 weeks + ($12 x 24 x 11) x 50 weeks + $18,000 + $8,000] - [520000] - $386,010,272
= $820,271,828

33   Annual Net Income
= [(Revenues) - (Cost of Sales)] - [Total Labor Costs] - [Insurance costs] - [Depreciation]
= [($20,900 x 20955) + ($27,500 x 2905) + ($14,300 x 1425)] - [($18,000 x 20955) + ($18,200 x 2905) + ($3,300 x 1425)] - [($48 x 120 x 58) x 50 weeks + ($20 x 48 x 35) x 50 weeks + $34,000 + $16,000] - [$1,000,000] - [($2,500,000 / 66) + ($1,250,000 / 44)]
= $83,960,712

34   Annual EBITDA
= [(Revenues) - (Cost of Sales)] - [Total Labor Costs]] - [Utilities]
= [($22,500 x 22592) + ($31,500 x 5442) + ($13,500 x 2245)] - [($5,300 x 22592) + ($5,400 x 5442) + ($1,300 x 2245)] - [($36 x 80 x 38) x 50 weeks + ($16 x 36 x 23) x 50 weeks + $26,000 + $12,000] - [$760,000]
= $551,075,200

35   Annual Tax Expense
= (Net Income excluding depreciation) x Effective tax rate
= { [(Revenues) - (Cost of Sales)] - [Total Labor Costs] - [Janitorial services] } x 34%
= { [($22,100 x 22103) + ($32,300 x 8178) + ($11,900 x 2970)] - [($2,200 x 22103) + ($2,200 x 8178) + ($600 x 2970)] - [($30 x 60 x 28) x 50 weeks + ($14 x 30 x 17) x 50 weeks + $22,000 + $10,000] - [640000] } x 34%
= $243,446,630

287

36   Annual EBITDA
= [(Revenues) - (Cost of Sales)] - [Total Labor Costs]] - [HVAC expenses]
= [($15,000 x 15052) + ($24,000 x 24152) + ($6,000 x 5995)] - [($200 x 15052) + ($200 x 24152) + ($100 x 5995)] - [($21 x 30 x 13) x 50 weeks + ($11 x 21 x 8) x 50 weeks + $16,000 + $7,000] - [$460,000]
= $831,972,800

37   Annual Net Income
= [(Revenues) - (Cost of Sales)] - [Total Labor Costs] - [Utilities] - [Depreciation]
= [($14,000 x 14091) + ($20,000 x 4191) + ($8,000 x 1595)] - [($3,500 x 14091) + ($3,600 x 4191) + ($900 x 1595)] - [($33 x 70 x 33) x 50 weeks + ($15 x 33 x 20) x 50 weeks + $24,000 + $11,000] - [$700,000] - [($1,750,000 / 60) + ($875,000 / 40)]
= $222,919,858 Monthly amount is calculated by dividing the annual amount by 12.
$222,919,858 / 12   = $18,576,655

38   Annual EBITDA
= [(Revenues) - (Cost of Sales)] - [Total Labor Costs]] - [Employee assistance services]
= [($24,000 x 24088) + ($33,000 x 4902) + ($15,000 x 2138)] - [($7,600 x 24088) + ($7,700 x 4902) + ($1,700 x 2138)] - [($39 x 90 x 43) x 50 weeks + ($17 x 39 x 26) x 50 weeks + $28,000 + $13,000] - [$820,000]
= $538,229,800

39   Annual Tax Expense
= (Net Income excluding depreciation) x Effective tax rate
= { [(Revenues) - (Cost of Sales)] - [Total Labor Costs] - [Insurance costs] } x 40%
= { [($32,300 x 32379) + ($42,500 x 4429) + ($22,100 x 2205)] - [($18,000 x 32379) + ($18,200 x 4429) + ($3,300 x 2205)] - [($48 x 120 x 58) x 50 weeks + ($20 x 48 x 35) x 50 weeks + $34,000 + $16,000] - [1000000] } x 40%
= $237,065,760

40   Annual Net Income
= [(Revenues) - (Cost of Sales)] - [Total Labor Costs] - [Employee assistance services] - [Depreciation]
= [($20,400 x 20430) + ($27,600 x 3580) + ($13,200 x 1645)] - [($10,400 x 20430) + ($10,600 x 3580) + ($2,200 x 1645)] - [($42 x 100 x 48) x 50 weeks + ($18 x 42 x 29) x 50 weeks + $30,000 + $14,000] - [$880,000] - [($2,200,000 / 72) + ($1,100,000 / 48)]
= $271,101,328 Monthly amount is calculated by dividing the annual amount by 12.
$271,101,328 / 12   = $22,591,777

41   Annual Cash flow
= (Net Income excluding depreciation) - Tax
= [(Revenues) - (Cost of Sales)] - [Total Labor Costs] - [Utilities] - Tax
= [($26,600 x 26699) + ($38,000 x 7799) + ($15,200 x 3035)] - [($3,500 x 26699) + ($3,600 x 7799) + ($900 x 3035)] - [($33 x 70 x 33) x 50 weeks + ($15 x 33 x 20) x 50 weeks + $24,000 + $11,000] - [700000] - $323,187,025
= $600,204,475

42   Annual Cash flow
= (Net Income excluding depreciation) - Tax
= [(Revenues) - (Cost of Sales)] - [Total Labor Costs] - [Employee assistance services] - Tax
= [($30,400 x 30449) + ($41,800 x 6120) + ($19,000 x 2709)] - [($7,600 x 30449) + ($7,700 x 6120) + ($1,700 x 2709)] - [($39 x 90 x 43) x 50 weeks + ($17 x 39 x 26) x 50 weeks + $28,000 + $13,000] - [820000] - $347,994,435
= $592,531,065

43   Annual Net Income
= [(Revenues) - (Cost of Sales)] - [Total Labor Costs] - [HVAC expenses] - [Depreciation]
= [($12,000 x 12064) + ($19,200 x 19364) + ($4,800 x 4795)] - [($200 x 12064) + ($200 x 19364) + ($100 x 4795)] - [($21 x 30 x 13) x 50 weeks + ($11 x 21 x 8) x 50 weeks + $16,000 + $7,000] - [$460,000] - [($1,150,000 / 72) + ($575,000 / 48)]
= $531,794,849 Monthly amount is calculated by dividing the annual amount by 12. $531,794,849 / 12 = $44,316,237

44   Annual Tax Expense
= (Net Income excluding depreciation) x Effective tax rate
= { [(Revenues) - (Cost of Sales)] - [Total Labor Costs] - [Utilities] } x 36%
= { [($24,000 x 24067) + ($33,600 x 5767) + ($14,400 x 2395)] - [($5,300 x 24067) + ($5,400 x 5767) + ($1,300 x 2395)] - [($36 x 80 x 38) x 50 weeks + ($16 x 36 x 23) x 50 weeks + $26,000 + $12,000] - [760000] } x 36%
= $229,364,784 Monthly amount is calculated by dividing the annual amount by 12. $229,364,784 / 12 = $19,113,732

45   Annual Net Income
= [(Revenues) - (Cost of Sales)] - [Total Labor Costs] - [Janitorial services] - [Depreciation]
= [($15,600 x 15689) + ($22,800 x 5889) + ($8,400 x 2095)] - [($2,200 x 15689) + ($2,200 x 5889) + ($600 x 2095)] - [($30 x 60 x 28) x 50 weeks + ($14 x 30 x 17) x 50 weeks + $22,000 + $10,000] - [$640,000] - [($1,600,000 / 72) + ($800,000 / 48)]
= $344,299,111 Monthly amount is calculated by dividing the annual amount by 12. $344,299,111 / 12 = $28,691,593

46   Annual EBITDA
= [(Revenues) - (Cost of Sales)] - [Total Labor Costs]] - [Janitorial services]
= [($16,900 x 16972) + ($24,700 x 6347) + ($9,100 x 2270)] - [($2,200 x 16972) + ($2,200 x 6347) + ($600 x 2270)] - [($30 x 60 x 28) x 50 weeks + ($14 x 30 x 17) x 50 weeks + $22,000 + $10,000] - [$640,000]
= $408,041,900

47   Annual Cash flow
= (Net Income excluding depreciation) - Tax
= [(Revenues) - (Cost of Sales)] - [Total Labor Costs] - [HVAC expenses] - Tax
= [($23,100 x 23106) + ($35,700 x 17956) + ($10,500 x 5245)] - [($600 x 23106) + ($600 x 17956) + ($200 x 5245)] - [($24 x 40 x 18) x 50 weeks + ($12 x 24 x 11) x 50 weeks + $18,000 + $8,000] - [520000] - $384,830,624
= $817,765,076

48 Annual Cash flow
= (Net Income excluding depreciation) - Tax
= [(Revenues) - (Cost of Sales)] - [Total Labor Costs] - [HVAC expenses] - Tax
= [($21,000 x 21025) + ($33,600 x 33725) + ($8,400 x 8395)] - [($200 x 21025) + ($200 x 33725) + ($100 x 8395)] - [($21 x 30 x 13) x 50 weeks + ($11 x 21 x 8) x 50 weeks + $16,000 + $7,000] - [460000] - $506,052,866
= $1,126,375,734

49 Annual Net Income
= [(Revenues) - (Cost of Sales)] - [Total Labor Costs] - [Utilities] - [Depreciation]
= [($16,800 x 16887) + ($24,000 x 4987) + ($9,600 x 1915)] - [($3,500 x 16887) + ($3,600 x 4987) + ($900 x 1915)] - [($33 x 70 x 33) x 50 weeks + ($15 x 33 x 20) x 50 weeks + $24,000 + $11,000] - [$700,000] - [($1,750,000 / 72) + ($875,000 / 48)]
= $337,908,365 Monthly amount is calculated by dividing the annual amount by 12. $337,908,365 / 12   = $28,159,030

50 Annual Net Income
= [(Revenues) - (Cost of Sales)] - [Total Labor Costs] - [Utilities] - [Depreciation]
= [($18,000 x 18054) + ($25,200 x 4354) + ($10,800 x 1795)] - [($5,300 x 18054) + ($5,400 x 4354) + ($1,300 x 1795)] - [($36 x 80 x 38) x 50 weeks + ($16 x 36 x 23) x 50 weeks + $26,000 + $12,000] - [$760,000] - [($1,900,000 / 72) + ($950,000 / 48)]
= $325,568,919 Monthly amount is calculated by dividing the annual amount by 12. $325,568,919 / 12   = $27,130,743

51 Annual Cash flow
= (Net Income excluding depreciation) - Tax
= [(Revenues) - (Cost of Sales)] - [Total Labor Costs] - [Janitorial services] - Tax
= [($24,700 x 24726) + ($36,100 x 9151) + ($13,300 x 3320)] - [($2,200 x 24726) + ($2,200 x 9151) + ($600 x 3320)] - [($30 x 60 x 28) x 50 weeks + ($14 x 30 x 17) x 50 weeks + $22,000 + $10,000] - [640000] - $307,757,426
= $597,411,474

52 Annual Net Income
= [(Revenues) - (Cost of Sales)] - [Total Labor Costs] - [Utilities] - [Depreciation]
= [($16,500 x 16589) + ($23,100 x 4039) + ($9,900 x 1645)] - [($5,300 x 16589) + ($5,400 x 4039) + ($1,300 x 1645)] - [($36 x 80 x 38) x 50 weeks + ($16 x 36 x 23) x 50 weeks + $26,000 + $12,000] - [$760,000] - [($1,900,000 / 66) + ($950,000 / 44)]
= $264,451,321

53 Annual Cash flow
= (Net Income excluding depreciation) - Tax
= [(Revenues) - (Cost of Sales)] - [Total Labor Costs] - [HVAC expenses] - Tax
= [($22,000 x 22046) + ($34,000 x 17146) + ($10,000 x 4995)] - [($600 x 22046) + ($600 x 17146) + ($200 x 4995)] - [($24 x 40 x 18) x 50 weeks + ($12 x 24 x 11) x 50 weeks + $18,000 + $8,000] - [520000] - $349,389,888
= $742,453,512 Monthly amount is calculated by dividing the annual amount by 12. $742,453,512 / 12   = $61,871,126

54   Annual Cash flow
= (Net Income excluding depreciation) - Tax
= [(Revenues) - (Cost of Sales)] - [Total Labor Costs] - [Insurance costs] - Tax
= [($34,200 x 34273) + ($45,600 x 5240) + ($22,800 x 2528)] - [($13,900 x 34273) +
($14,000 x 5240) + ($2,700 x 2528)] - [($45 x 110 x 53) x 50 weeks + ($19 x 45 x 32
) x 50 weeks + $32,000 + $15,000] - [940000] - $349,699,818
= $546,966,382

55   Annual Net Income
= [(Revenues) - (Cost of Sales)] - [Total Labor Costs] - [Janitorial services] -
[Depreciation]
= [($14,300 x 14396) + ($20,900 x 5421) + ($7,700 x 1920)] - [($2,200 x 14396) + (
$2,200 x 5421) + ($600 x 1920)] - [($30 x 60 x 28) x 50 weeks + ($14 x 30 x 17) x 50
weeks + $22,000 + $10,000] - [$640,000] - [($1,600,000 / 66) + ($800,000 / 44)]
= $285,604,876

56   Gross Margin
= [Gross Profit] / [Revenue]
= [($3,600 - $1,200) x 3648 + ($5,400 - $1,300) x 1948 + ($1,800 - $400) x 595] / [
($3,600 x 3648) + ($5,400 x 1948) + ($1,800 x 595)]
= $17,575,000 / $24,723,000
= 71%

57   Annual Net Income
= [(Revenues) - (Cost of Sales)] - [Total Labor Costs] - [Employee assistance services] -
[Depreciation]
= [($17,600 x 17657) + ($24,200 x 3614) + ($11,000 x 1566)] - [($7,600 x 17657) + (
$7,700 x 3614) + ($1,700 x 1566)] - [($39 x 90 x 43) x 50 weeks + ($17 x 39 x 26) x
50 weeks + $28,000 + $13,000] - [$820,000] - [($2,050,000 / 66) + ($1,025,000 / 44)]
= $241,441,044

58   Annual Tax Expense
= (Net Income excluding depreciation) x Effective tax rate
= { [(Revenues) - (Cost of Sales)] - [Total Labor Costs] - [HVAC expenses] } x 31%
= { [($16,000 x 16005) + ($25,600 x 25705) + ($6,400 x 6395)] - [($200 x 16005) + (
$200 x 25705) + ($100 x 6395)] - [($21 x 30 x 13) x 50 weeks + ($11 x 21 x 8) x 50
weeks + $16,000 + $7,000] - [460000] } x 31%
= $292,977,776 Monthly amount is calculated by dividing the annual amount by 12.
$292,977,776 / 12 = $24,414,815

59   Annual Cash flow
= (Net Income excluding depreciation) - Tax
= [(Revenues) - (Cost of Sales)] - [Total Labor Costs] - [Employee assistance services]
- Tax
= [($34,000 x 34049) + ($46,000 x 5899) + ($22,000 x 2745)] - [($10,400 x 34049) +
($10,600 x 5899) + ($2,200 x 2745)] - [($42 x 100 x 48) x 50 weeks + ($18 x 42 x 29
) x 50 weeks + $30,000 + $14,000] - [880000] - $400,760,084
= $653,871,716 Monthly amount is calculated by dividing the annual amount by 12.
$653,871,716 / 12 = $54,489,310

60	Annual Tax Expense
= (Net Income excluding depreciation) x Effective tax rate
= { [(Revenues) - (Cost of Sales)] - [Total Labor Costs] - [Insurance costs] } x 40%
= { [($34,200 x 34291) + ($45,000 x 4691) + ($23,400 x 2335)] - [($18,000 x 34291)
+ ($18,200 x 4691) + ($3,300 x 2335)] - [($48 x 120 x 58) x 50 weeks + ($20 x 48 x
35) x 50 weeks + $34,000 + $16,000] - [1000000] } x 40%
= $283,493,000 Monthly amount is calculated by dividing the annual amount by 12.
$283,493,000 / 12 = $23,624,417

61	Gross Margin
= [Gross Profit] / [Revenue]
= [($2,000 - $200) x 2042 + ($3,200 - $200) x 3342 + ($800 - $100) x 795] / [($2,000
x 2042) + ($3,200 x 3342) + ($800 x 795)]
= $14,258,100 / $15,414,400
= 92%

62	Annual Net Income
= [(Revenues) - (Cost of Sales)] - [Total Labor Costs] - [Utilities] - [Depreciation]
= [($14,000 x 14020) + ($20,000 x 4120) + ($8,000 x 1595)] - [($3,500 x 14020) + (
$3,600 x 4120) + ($900 x 1595)] - [($33 x 70 x 33) x 50 weeks + ($15 x 33 x 20) x 50
weeks + $24,000 + $11,000] - [$700,000] - [($1,750,000 / 60) + ($875,000 / 40)]
= $221,009,958 Monthly amount is calculated by dividing the annual amount by 12.
$221,009,958 / 12 = $18,417,497

63	Annual Net Income
= [(Revenues) - (Cost of Sales)] - [Total Labor Costs] - [Utilities] - [Depreciation]
= [($18,000 x 18091) + ($25,200 x 4391) + ($10,800 x 1795)] - [($5,300 x 18091) + (
$5,400 x 4391) + ($1,300 x 1795)] - [($36 x 80 x 38) x 50 weeks + ($16 x 36 x 23) x
50 weeks + $26,000 + $12,000] - [$760,000] - [($1,900,000 / 72) + ($950,000 / 48)]
= $326,771,419 Monthly amount is calculated by dividing the annual amount by 12.
$326,771,419 / 12 = $27,230,952

64	Annual Net Income
= [(Revenues) - (Cost of Sales)] - [Total Labor Costs] - [Utilities] - [Depreciation]
= [($16,500 x 16566) + ($23,100 x 4016) + ($9,900 x 1645)] - [($5,300 x 16566) + (
$5,400 x 4016) + ($1,300 x 1645)] - [($36 x 80 x 38) x 50 weeks + ($16 x 36 x 23) x
50 weeks + $26,000 + $12,000] - [$760,000] - [($1,900,000 / 66) + ($950,000 / 44)]
= $263,786,621

65	Annual Tax Expense
= (Net Income excluding depreciation) x Effective tax rate
= { [(Revenues) - (Cost of Sales)] - [Total Labor Costs] - [HVAC expenses] } x 32%
= { [($17,600 x 17676) + ($27,200 x 13776) + ($8,000 x 3995)] - [($600 x 17676) + (
$600 x 13776) + ($200 x 3995)] - [($24 x 40 x 18) x 50 weeks + ($12 x 24 x 11) x 50
weeks + $18,000 + $8,000] - [520000] } x 32%
= $222,888,384 Monthly amount is calculated by dividing the annual amount by 12.
$222,888,384 / 12 = $18,574,032

66   Annual Tax Expense
= (Net Income excluding depreciation) x Effective tax rate
= { [(Revenues) - (Cost of Sales)] - [Total Labor Costs] - [Utilities] } x 35%
= { [($25,200 x 25256) + ($36,000 x 7356) + ($14,400 x 2875)] - [($3,500 x 25256) + ($3,600 x 7356) + ($900 x 2875)] - [($33 x 70 x 33) x 50 weeks + ($15 x 33 x 20) x 50 weeks + $24,000 + $11,000] - [700000] } x 35%
= $287,056,210 Monthly amount is calculated by dividing the annual amount by 12.
$287,056,210 / 12 = $23,921,351

67   Annual EBITDA
= [(Revenues) - (Cost of Sales)] - [Total Labor Costs]] - [Utilities]
= [($19,500 x 19537) + ($27,300 x 4687) + ($11,700 x 1945)] - [($5,300 x 19537) + ($5,400 x 4687) + ($1,300 x 1945)] - [($36 x 80 x 38) x 50 weeks + ($16 x 36 x 23) x 50 weeks + $26,000 + $12,000] - [$760,000]
= $393,366,300

68   Annual Cash flow
= (Net Income excluding depreciation) - Tax
= [(Revenues) - (Cost of Sales)] - [Total Labor Costs] - [HVAC expenses] - Tax
= [($22,000 x 22002) + ($34,000 x 17102) + ($10,000 x 4995)] - [($600 x 22002) + ($600 x 17102) + ($200 x 4995)] - [($24 x 40 x 18) x 50 weeks + ($12 x 24 x 11) x 50 weeks + $18,000 + $8,000] - [520000] - $348,618,304
= $740,813,896 Monthly amount is calculated by dividing the annual amount by 12.
$740,813,896 / 12 = $61,734,491

69   Annual Net Income
= [(Revenues) - (Cost of Sales)] - [Total Labor Costs] - [Janitorial services] - [Depreciation]
= [($14,400 x 14425) + ($21,600 x 7325) + ($7,200 x 2395)] - [($1,200 x 14425) + ($1,300 x 7325) + ($400 x 2395)] - [($27 x 50 x 23) x 50 weeks + ($13 x 27 x 14) x 50 weeks + $20,000 + $9,000] - [$580,000] - [($1,450,000 / 72) + ($725,000 / 48)]
= $352,951,057 Monthly amount is calculated by dividing the annual amount by 12.
$352,951,057 / 12 = $29,412,588

70   Gross Margin
= [Gross Profit] / [Revenue]
= [($3,900 - $2,200) x 3991 + ($5,700 - $2,200) x 1616 + ($2,100 - $600) x 520] / [($3,900 x 3991) + ($5,700 x 1616) + ($2,100 x 520)]
= $13,220,700 / $25,868,100
= 51%

71   Annual Net Income
= [(Revenues) - (Cost of Sales)] - [Total Labor Costs] - [Utilities] - [Depreciation]
= [($18,000 x 18028) + ($25,200 x 4328) + ($10,800 x 1795)] - [($5,300 x 18028) + ($5,400 x 4328) + ($1,300 x 1795)] - [($36 x 80 x 38) x 50 weeks + ($16 x 36 x 23) x 50 weeks + $26,000 + $12,000] - [$760,000] - [($1,900,000 / 72) + ($950,000 / 48)]
= $324,723,919 Monthly amount is calculated by dividing the annual amount by 12.
$324,723,919 / 12 = $27,060,327

72   Annual Tax Expense
= (Net Income excluding depreciation) x Effective tax rate
= { [(Revenues) - (Cost of Sales)] - [Total Labor Costs] - [HVAC expenses] } x 32%
= { [($18,700 x 18729) + ($28,900 x 14579) + ($8,500 x 4245)] - [($600 x 18729) + ($600 x 14579) + ($200 x 4245)] - [($24 x 40 x 18) x 50 weeks + ($12 x 24 x 11) x 50 weeks + $18,000 + $8,000] - [520000] } x 32%
= $251,278,624

73   Annual Net Income
= [(Revenues) - (Cost of Sales)] - [Total Labor Costs] - [Janitorial services] - [Depreciation]
= [($12,000 x 12020) + ($18,000 x 6120) + ($6,000 x 1995)] - [($1,200 x 12020) + ($1,300 x 6120) + ($400 x 1995)] - [($27 x 50 x 23) x 50 weeks + ($13 x 27 x 14) x 50 weeks + $20,000 + $9,000] - [$580,000] - [($1,450,000 / 60) + ($725,000 / 40)]
= $240,742,508 Monthly amount is calculated by dividing the annual amount by 12. $240,742,508 / 12 = $20,061,876

74   Annual Cash flow
= (Net Income excluding depreciation) - Tax
= [(Revenues) - (Cost of Sales)] - [Total Labor Costs] - [Janitorial services] - Tax
= [($26,000 x 26075) + ($38,000 x 9675) + ($14,000 x 3495)] - [($2,200 x 26075) + ($2,200 x 9675) + ($600 x 3495)] - [($30 x 60 x 28) x 50 weeks + ($14 x 30 x 17) x 50 weeks + $22,000 + $10,000] - [640000] - $343,479,560
= $666,754,440 Monthly amount is calculated by dividing the annual amount by 12. $666,754,440 / 12 = $55,562,870

75   Annual EBITDA
= [(Revenues) - (Cost of Sales)] - [Total Labor Costs]] - [Janitorial services]
= [($16,900 x 16985) + ($24,700 x 6360) + ($9,100 x 2270)] - [($2,200 x 16985) + ($2,200 x 6360) + ($600 x 2270)] - [($30 x 60 x 28) x 50 weeks + ($14 x 30 x 17) x 50 weeks + $22,000 + $10,000] - [$640,000]
= $408,525,500

76   Annual EBITDA
= [(Revenues) - (Cost of Sales)] - [Total Labor Costs]] - [Employee assistance services]
= [($24,000 x 24036) + ($33,000 x 4850) + ($15,000 x 2138)] - [($7,600 x 24036) + ($7,700 x 4850) + ($1,700 x 2138)] - [($39 x 90 x 43) x 50 weeks + ($17 x 39 x 26) x 50 weeks + $28,000 + $13,000] - [$820,000]
= $536,061,400

77   Annual Cash flow
= (Net Income excluding depreciation) - Tax
= [(Revenues) - (Cost of Sales)] - [Total Labor Costs] - [Insurance costs] - Tax
= [($34,200 x 34278) + ($45,600 x 5245) + ($22,800 x 2528)] - [($13,900 x 34278) + ($14,000 x 5245) + ($2,700 x 2528)] - [($45 x 110 x 53) x 50 weeks + ($19 x 45 x 32) x 50 weeks + $32,000 + $15,000] - [940000] - $349,801,023
= $547,124,677

78   Annual EBITDA
= [(Revenues) - (Cost of Sales)] - [Total Labor Costs]] - [Insurance costs]
= [($26,600 x 26634) + ($35,000 x 3634) + ($18,200 x 1815)] - [($18,000 x 26634) +
($18,200 x 3634) + ($3,300 x 1815)] - [($48 x 120 x 58) x 50 weeks + ($20 x 48 x 35
) x 50 weeks + $34,000 + $16,000] - [$1,000,000]
= $297,713,100 Monthly amount is calculated by dividing the annual amount by 12.
$297,713,100 / 12 = $24,809,425

79   Annual EBITDA
= [(Revenues) - (Cost of Sales)] - [Total Labor Costs]] - [Insurance costs]
= [($26,600 x 26656) + ($35,000 x 3656) + ($18,200 x 1815)] - [($18,000 x 26656) +
($18,200 x 3656) + ($3,300 x 1815)] - [($48 x 120 x 58) x 50 weeks + ($20 x 48 x 35
) x 50 weeks + $34,000 + $16,000] - [$1,000,000]
= $298,271,900 Monthly amount is calculated by dividing the annual amount by 12.
$298,271,900 / 12 = $24,855,992

80   Annual Tax Expense
= (Net Income excluding depreciation) x Effective tax rate
= { [(Revenues) - (Cost of Sales)] - [Total Labor Costs] - [Employee assistance services]
} x 38%
= { [($30,600 x 30627) + ($41,400 x 5302) + ($19,800 x 2470)] - [($10,400 x 30627)
+ ($10,600 x 5302) + ($2,200 x 2470)] - [($42 x 100 x 48) x 50 weeks + ($18 x 42 x
29) x 50 weeks + $30,000 + $14,000] - [880000] } x 38%
= $309,068,744 Monthly amount is calculated by dividing the annual amount by 12.
$309,068,744 / 12 = $25,755,729

81   Annual Net Income
= [(Revenues) - (Cost of Sales)] - [Total Labor Costs] - [Janitorial services] -
[Depreciation]
= [($12,000 x 12066) + ($18,000 x 6166) + ($6,000 x 1995)] - [($1,200 x 12066) + (
$1,300 x 6166) + ($400 x 1995)] - [($27 x 50 x 23) x 50 weeks + ($13 x 27 x 14) x 50
weeks + $20,000 + $9,000] - [$580,000] - [($1,450,000 / 60) + ($725,000 / 40)]
= $242,007,508 Monthly amount is calculated by dividing the annual amount by 12.
$242,007,508 / 12 = $20,167,292

82   Annual Net Income
= [(Revenues) - (Cost of Sales)] - [Total Labor Costs] - [Employee assistance services] -
[Depreciation]
= [($17,000 x 17076) + ($23,000 x 3051) + ($11,000 x 1370)] - [($10,400 x 17076) +
($10,600 x 3051) + ($2,200 x 1370)] - [($42 x 100 x 48) x 50 weeks + ($18 x 42 x 29
) x 50 weeks + $30,000 + $14,000] - [$880,000] - [($2,200,000 / 60) + ($1,100,000 / 40
)]
= $150,425,633 Monthly amount is calculated by dividing the annual amount by 12.
$150,425,633 / 12 = $12,535,469

83   Annual Net Income
= [(Revenues) - (Cost of Sales)] - [Total Labor Costs] - [Utilities] - [Depreciation]
= [($16,500 x 16556) + ($23,100 x 4006) + ($9,900 x 1645)] - [($5,300 x 16556) + ($5,400 x 4006) + ($1,300 x 1645)] - [($36 x 80 x 38) x 50 weeks + ($16 x 36 x 23) x 50 weeks + $26,000 + $12,000] - [$760,000] - [($1,900,000 / 66) + ($950,000 / 44)]
= $263,497,621

84   Annual EBITDA
= [(Revenues) - (Cost of Sales)] - [Total Labor Costs]] - [Janitorial services]
= [($19,500 x 19597) + ($28,500 x 7322) + ($10,500 x 2620)] - [($2,200 x 19597) + ($2,200 x 7322) + ($600 x 2620)] - [($30 x 60 x 28) x 50 weeks + ($14 x 30 x 17) x 50 weeks + $22,000 + $10,000] - [$640,000]
= $553,985,700

85   Annual Cash flow
= (Net Income excluding depreciation) - Tax
= [(Revenues) - (Cost of Sales)] - [Total Labor Costs] - [Utilities] - Tax
= [($30,000 x 30090) + ($42,000 x 7190) + ($18,000 x 2995)] - [($5,300 x 30090) + ($5,400 x 7190) + ($1,300 x 2995)] - [($36 x 80 x 38) x 50 weeks + ($16 x 36 x 23) x 50 weeks + $26,000 + $12,000] - [760000] - $377,805,996
= $671,655,104 Monthly amount is calculated by dividing the annual amount by 12.
$671,655,104 / 12   = $55,971,259

86   Gross Margin
= [Gross Profit] / [Revenue]
= [($2,400 - $1,200) x 2442 + ($3,600 - $1,300) x 1342 + ($1,200 - $400) x 395] / [($2,400 x 2442) + ($3,600 x 1342) + ($1,200 x 395)]
= $6,333,000 / $11,166,000
= 57%

87   Annual EBITDA
= [(Revenues) - (Cost of Sales)] - [Total Labor Costs]] - [Utilities]
= [($19,500 x 19541) + ($27,300 x 4691) + ($11,700 x 1945)] - [($5,300 x 19541) + ($5,400 x 4691) + ($1,300 x 1945)] - [($36 x 80 x 38) x 50 weeks + ($16 x 36 x 23) x 50 weeks + $26,000 + $12,000] - [$760,000]
= $393,510,700

88   Annual EBITDA
= [(Revenues) - (Cost of Sales)] - [Total Labor Costs]] - [Insurance costs]
= [($27,000 x 27056) + ($36,000 x 4156) + ($18,000 x 1995)] - [($13,900 x 27056) + ($14,000 x 4156) + ($2,700 x 1995)] - [($45 x 110 x 53) x 50 weeks + ($19 x 45 x 32) x 50 weeks + $32,000 + $15,000] - [$940,000]
= $460,916,600

89 Annual Cash flow
= (Net Income excluding depreciation) - Tax
= [(Revenues) - (Cost of Sales)] - [Total Labor Costs] - [Employee assistance services]
- Tax
= [($35,700 x 35741) + ($48,300 x 6179) + ($23,100 x 2883)] - [($10,400 x 35741) +
($10,600 x 6179) + ($2,200 x 2883)] - [($42 x 100 x 48) x 50 weeks + ($18 x 42 x 29
) x 50 weeks + $30,000 + $14,000] - [880000] - $450,433,038
= $734,917,062

90 Annual Tax Expense
= (Net Income excluding depreciation) x Effective tax rate
= { [(Revenues) - (Cost of Sales)] - [Total Labor Costs] - [Utilities] } x 35%
= { [($22,400 x 22491) + ($32,000 x 6591) + ($12,800 x 2555)] - [($3,500 x 22491) +
($3,600 x 6591) + ($900 x 2555)] - [($33 x 70 x 33) x 50 weeks + ($15 x 33 x 20) x
50 weeks + $24,000 + $11,000] - [700000] } x 35%
= $223,169,555 Monthly amount is calculated by dividing the annual amount by 12.
$223,169,555 / 12 = $18,597,463

91 Annual Cash flow
= (Net Income excluding depreciation) - Tax
= [(Revenues) - (Cost of Sales)] - [Total Labor Costs] - [Utilities] - Tax
= [($26,600 x 26626) + ($38,000 x 7726) + ($15,200 x 3035)] - [($3,500 x 26626) + (
$3,600 x 7726) + ($900 x 3035)] - [($33 x 70 x 33) x 50 weeks + ($15 x 33 x 20) x 50
weeks + $24,000 + $11,000] - [700000] - $321,717,900
= $597,476,100

92 Annual EBITDA
= [(Revenues) - (Cost of Sales)] - [Total Labor Costs]] - [Employee assistance services]
= [($20,800 x 20891) + ($28,600 x 4277) + ($13,000 x 1852)] - [($7,600 x 20891) + (
$7,700 x 4277) + ($1,700 x 1852)] - [($39 x 90 x 43) x 50 weeks + ($17 x 39 x 26) x
50 weeks + $28,000 + $13,000] - [$820,000]
= $376,808,700

93 Annual Net Income
= [(Revenues) - (Cost of Sales)] - [Total Labor Costs] - [Employee assistance services] -
[Depreciation]
= [($17,000 x 17028) + ($23,000 x 3003) + ($11,000 x 1370)] - [($10,400 x 17028) +
($10,600 x 3003) + ($2,200 x 1370)] - [($42 x 100 x 48) x 50 weeks + ($18 x 42 x 29
) x 50 weeks + $30,000 + $14,000] - [$880,000] - [($2,200,000 / 60) + ($1,100,000 / 40
)]
= $149,513,633 Monthly amount is calculated by dividing the annual amount by 12.
$149,513,633 / 12 = $12,459,469

94 Annual Cash flow
= (Net Income excluding depreciation) - Tax
= [(Revenues) - (Cost of Sales)] - [Total Labor Costs] - [HVAC expenses] - Tax
= [($20,900 x 20993) + ($32,300 x 16343) + ($9,500 x 4745)] - [($600 x 20993) + (
$600 x 16343) + ($200 x 4745)] - [($24 x 40 x 18) x 50 weeks + ($12 x 24 x 11) x 50
weeks + $18,000 + $8,000] - [520000] - $315,773,152
= $671,017,948

297

95 Annual Cash flow
= (Net Income excluding depreciation) - Tax
= [(Revenues) - (Cost of Sales)] - [Total Labor Costs] - [HVAC expenses] - Tax
= [($21,000 x 21079) + ($33,600 x 33779) + ($8,400 x 8395)] - [($200 x 21079) + ($200 x 33779) + ($100 x 8395)] - [($21 x 30 x 13) x 50 weeks + ($11 x 21 x 8) x 50 weeks + $16,000 + $7,000] - [460000] - $506,960,174
= $1,128,395,226

96 Annual Cash flow
= (Net Income excluding depreciation) - Tax
= [(Revenues) - (Cost of Sales)] - [Total Labor Costs] - [Insurance costs] - Tax
= [($36,000 x 36095) + ($48,000 x 5528) + ($24,000 x 2662)] - [($13,900 x 36095) + ($14,000 x 5528) + ($2,700 x 2662)] - [($45 x 110 x 53) x 50 weeks + ($19 x 45 x 32) x 50 weeks + $32,000 + $15,000] - [940000] - $400,483,044
= $626,396,556 Monthly amount is calculated by dividing the annual amount by 12.
$626,396,556 / 12 = $52,199,713

97 Gross Margin
= [Gross Profit] / [Revenue]
= [($2,000 - $200) x 2059 + ($3,200 - $200) x 3359 + ($800 - $100) x 795] / [($2,000 x 2059) + ($3,200 x 3359) + ($800 x 795)]
= $14,339,700 / $15,502,800
= 92%

98 Annual EBITDA
= [(Revenues) - (Cost of Sales)] - [Total Labor Costs]] - [Employee assistance services]
= [($22,100 x 22107) + ($29,900 x 3845) + ($14,300 x 1783)] - [($10,400 x 22107) + ($10,600 x 3845) + ($2,200 x 1783)] - [($42 x 100 x 48) x 50 weeks + ($18 x 42 x 29) x 50 weeks + $30,000 + $14,000] - [$880,000]
= $342,334,500

99 Annual Net Income
= [(Revenues) - (Cost of Sales)] - [Total Labor Costs] - [Utilities] - [Depreciation]
= [($16,800 x 16803) + ($24,000 x 4903) + ($9,600 x 1915)] - [($3,500 x 16803) + ($3,600 x 4903) + ($900 x 1915)] - [($33 x 70 x 33) x 50 weeks + ($15 x 33 x 20) x 50 weeks + $24,000 + $11,000] - [$700,000] - [($1,750,000 / 72) + ($875,000 / 48)]
= $335,077,565 Monthly amount is calculated by dividing the annual amount by 12.
$335,077,565 / 12 = $27,923,130

100 Annual Net Income
= [(Revenues) - (Cost of Sales)] - [Total Labor Costs] - [HVAC expenses] - [Depreciation]
= [($13,200 x 13206) + ($20,400 x 10306) + ($6,000 x 2995)] - [($600 x 13206) + ($600 x 10306) + ($200 x 2995)] - [($24 x 40 x 18) x 50 weeks + ($12 x 24 x 11) x 50 weeks + $18,000 + $8,000] - [$520,000] - [($1,300,000 / 72) + ($650,000 / 48)]
= $386,225,403 Monthly amount is calculated by dividing the annual amount by 12.
$386,225,403 / 12 = $32,185,450

101   Annual EBITDA
= [(Revenues) - (Cost of Sales)] - [Total Labor Costs]] - [HVAC expenses]
= [($15,000 x 15066) + ($24,000 x 24166) + ($6,000 x 5995)] - [($200 x 15066) + ($200 x 24166) + ($100 x 5995)] - [($21 x 30 x 13) x 50 weeks + ($11 x 21 x 8) x 50 weeks + $16,000 + $7,000] - [$460,000]
= $832,513,200

102   Annual Tax Expense
= (Net Income excluding depreciation) x Effective tax rate
= { [(Revenues) - (Cost of Sales)] - [Total Labor Costs] - [Janitorial services] } x 34%
= { [($23,400 x 23476) + ($34,200 x 8726) + ($12,600 x 3145)] - [($2,200 x 23476) + ($2,200 x 8726) + ($600 x 3145)] - [($30 x 60 x 28) x 50 weeks + ($14 x 30 x 17) x 50 weeks + $22,000 + $10,000] - [640000] } x 34%
= $275,778,828 Monthly amount is calculated by dividing the annual amount by 12.
$275,778,828 / 12 = $22,981,569

103   Annual Net Income
= [(Revenues) - (Cost of Sales)] - [Total Labor Costs] - [Janitorial services] - [Depreciation]
= [($14,300 x 14355) + ($20,900 x 5380) + ($7,700 x 1920)] - [($2,200 x 14355) + ($2,200 x 5380) + ($600 x 1920)] - [($30 x 60 x 28) x 50 weeks + ($14 x 30 x 17) x 50 weeks + $22,000 + $10,000] - [$640,000] - [($1,600,000 / 66) + ($800,000 / 44)]
= $284,342,076

104   Annual Cash flow
= (Net Income excluding depreciation) - Tax
= [(Revenues) - (Cost of Sales)] - [Total Labor Costs] - [Employee assistance services] - Tax
= [($34,000 x 34022) + ($46,000 x 5872) + ($22,000 x 2745)] - [($10,400 x 34022) + ($10,600 x 5872) + ($2,200 x 2745)] - [($42 x 100 x 48) x 50 weeks + ($18 x 42 x 29) x 50 weeks + $30,000 + $14,000] - [880000] - $400,154,744
= $652,884,056 Monthly amount is calculated by dividing the annual amount by 12.
$652,884,056 / 12 = $54,407,005

105   Annual Tax Expense
= (Net Income excluding depreciation) x Effective tax rate
= { [(Revenues) - (Cost of Sales)] - [Total Labor Costs] - [Employee assistance services] } x 38%
= { [($27,200 x 27269) + ($36,800 x 4769) + ($17,600 x 2195)] - [($10,400 x 27269) + ($10,600 x 4769) + ($2,200 x 2195)] - [($42 x 100 x 48) x 50 weeks + ($18 x 42 x 29) x 50 weeks + $30,000 + $14,000] - [880000] } x 38%
= $229,812,524 Monthly amount is calculated by dividing the annual amount by 12.
$229,812,524 / 12 = $19,151,044

106   Annual Tax Expense
= (Net Income excluding depreciation) x Effective tax rate
= { [(Revenues) - (Cost of Sales)] - [Total Labor Costs] - [Utilities] } x 35%
= { [($23,800 x 23816) + ($34,000 x 6916) + ($13,600 x 2715)] - [($3,500 x 23816) + ($3,600 x 6916) + ($900 x 2715)] - [($33 x 70 x 33) x 50 weeks + ($15 x 33 x 20) x 50 weeks + $24,000 + $11,000] - [700000] } x 35%
= $253,102,570

107   Annual EBITDA
= [(Revenues) - (Cost of Sales)] - [Total Labor Costs]] - [Employee assistance services]
= [($20,800 x 20818) + ($28,600 x 4204) + ($13,000 x 1852)] - [($7,600 x 20818) + ($7,700 x 4204) + ($1,700 x 1852)] - [($39 x 90 x 43) x 50 weeks + ($17 x 39 x 26) x 50 weeks + $28,000 + $13,000] - [$820,000]
= $374,319,400

108   Annual EBITDA
= [(Revenues) - (Cost of Sales)] - [Total Labor Costs]] - [Janitorial services]
= [($15,600 x 15644) + ($23,400 x 7944) + ($7,800 x 2595)] - [($1,200 x 15644) + ($1,300 x 7944) + ($400 x 2595)] - [($27 x 50 x 23) x 50 weeks + ($13 x 27 x 14) x 50 weeks + $20,000 + $9,000] - [$580,000]
= $417,631,800

109   Annual Tax Expense
= (Net Income excluding depreciation) x Effective tax rate
= { [(Revenues) - (Cost of Sales)] - [Total Labor Costs] - [Janitorial services] } x 33%
= { [($20,400 x 20489) + ($30,600 x 10389) + ($10,200 x 3395)] - [($1,200 x 20489) + ($1,300 x 10389) + ($400 x 3395)] - [($27 x 50 x 23) x 50 weeks + ($13 x 27 x 14) x 50 weeks + $20,000 + $9,000] - [580000] } x 33%
= $240,454,599

110   Annual EBITDA
= [(Revenues) - (Cost of Sales)] - [Total Labor Costs]] - [Janitorial services]
= [($18,200 x 18255) + ($26,600 x 6805) + ($9,800 x 2445)] - [($2,200 x 18255) + ($2,200 x 6805) + ($600 x 2445)] - [($30 x 60 x 28) x 50 weeks + ($14 x 30 x 17) x 50 weeks + $22,000 + $10,000] - [$640,000]
= $477,067,000 Monthly amount is calculated by dividing the annual amount by 12.
$477,067,000 / 12   = $39,755,583

111   Annual Cash flow
= (Net Income excluding depreciation) - Tax
= [(Revenues) - (Cost of Sales)] - [Total Labor Costs] - [Utilities] - Tax
= [($29,400 x 29453) + ($42,000 x 8553) + ($16,800 x 3355)] - [($3,500 x 29453) + ($3,600 x 8553) + ($900 x 3355)] - [($33 x 70 x 33) x 50 weeks + ($15 x 33 x 20) x 50 weeks + $24,000 + $11,000] - [700000] - $398,849,815
= $740,721,085

112   Annual Tax Expense

= (Net Income excluding depreciation) x Effective tax rate

= { [(Revenues) - (Cost of Sales)] - [Total Labor Costs] - [Janitorial services] } x 34%

= { [($20,800 x 20877) + ($30,400 x 7777) + ($11,200 x 2795)] - [($2,200 x 20877) + ($2,200 x 7777) + ($600 x 2795)] - [($30 x 60 x 28) x 50 weeks + ($14 x 30 x 17) x 50 weeks + $22,000 + $10,000] - [640000] } x 34%

= $215,458,544   Monthly amount is calculated by dividing the annual amount by 12.

$215,458,544 / 12   = $17,954,879

113   Annual Cash flow

= (Net Income excluding depreciation) - Tax

= [(Revenues) - (Cost of Sales)] - [Total Labor Costs] - [Janitorial services] - Tax

= [($25,200 x 25255) + ($37,800 x 12755) + ($12,600 x 4195)] - [($1,200 x 25255) + ($1,300 x 12755) + ($400 x 4195)] - [($27 x 50 x 23) x 50 weeks + ($13 x 27 x 14) x 50 weeks + $20,000 + $9,000] - [580000] - $369,748,269

= $750,701,031

114   Annual Cash flow

= (Net Income excluding depreciation) - Tax

= [(Revenues) - (Cost of Sales)] - [Total Labor Costs] - [Utilities] - Tax

= [($30,000 x 30042) + ($42,000 x 7142) + ($18,000 x 2995)] - [($5,300 x 30042) + ($5,400 x 7142) + ($1,300 x 2995)] - [($36 x 80 x 38) x 50 weeks + ($16 x 36 x 23) x 50 weeks + $26,000 + $12,000] - [760000] - $376,746,732

= $669,771,968   Monthly amount is calculated by dividing the annual amount by 12.

$669,771,968 / 12   = $55,814,331

115   Annual EBITDA

= [(Revenues) - (Cost of Sales)] - [Total Labor Costs]] - [Insurance costs]

= [($25,200 x 25289) + ($33,600 x 3922) + ($16,800 x 1862)] - [($13,900 x 25289) + ($14,000 x 3922) + ($2,700 x 1862)] - [($45 x 110 x 53) x 50 weeks + ($19 x 45 x 32) x 50 weeks + $32,000 + $15,000] - [$940,000]

= $373,418,600   Monthly amount is calculated by dividing the annual amount by 12.

$373,418,600 / 12   = $31,118,217

116   Annual Cash flow

= (Net Income excluding depreciation) - Tax

= [(Revenues) - (Cost of Sales)] - [Total Labor Costs] - [Employee assistance services] - Tax

= [($35,700 x 35748) + ($48,300 x 6186) + ($23,100 x 2883)] - [($10,400 x 35748) + ($10,600 x 6186) + ($2,200 x 2883)] - [($42 x 100 x 48) x 50 weeks + ($18 x 42 x 29) x 50 weeks + $30,000 + $14,000] - [880000] - $450,600,618

= $735,190,482

117   Annual EBITDA

= [(Revenues) - (Cost of Sales)] - [Total Labor Costs]] - [Utilities]

= [($19,600 x 19685) + ($28,000 x 5785) + ($11,200 x 2235)] - [($3,500 x 19685) + ($3,600 x 5785) + ($900 x 2235)] - [($33 x 70 x 33) x 50 weeks + ($15 x 33 x 20) x 50 weeks + $24,000 + $11,000] - [$700,000]

= $476,061,500   Monthly amount is calculated by dividing the annual amount by 12.

$476,061,500 / 12   = $39,671,792

118 Annual Tax Expense
= (Net Income excluding depreciation) x Effective tax rate
= { [(Revenues) - (Cost of Sales)] - [Total Labor Costs] - [Insurance costs] } x 39%
= { [($28,800 x 28881) + ($38,400 x 4448) + ($19,200 x 2128)] - [($13,900 x 28881)
+ ($14,000 x 4448) + ($2,700 x 2128)] - [($45 x 110 x 53) x 50 weeks + ($19 x 45 x
32) x 50 weeks + $32,000 + $15,000] - [940000] } x 39%
= $217,814,064 Monthly amount is calculated by dividing the annual amount by 12.
$217,814,064 / 12 = $18,151,172

119 Gross Margin
= [Gross Profit] / [Revenue]
= [($3,300 - $600) x 3376 + ($5,100 - $600) x 2726 + ($1,500 - $200) x 745] / [
($3,300 x 3376) + ($5,100 x 2726) + ($1,500 x 745)]
= $22,350,700 / $26,160,900
= 85%

120 Annual Cash flow
= (Net Income excluding depreciation) - Tax
= [(Revenues) - (Cost of Sales)] - [Total Labor Costs] - [Utilities] - Tax
= [($28,500 x 28586) + ($39,900 x 6836) + ($17,100 x 2845)] - [($5,300 x 28586) + (
$5,400 x 6836) + ($1,300 x 2845)] - [($36 x 80 x 38) x 50 weeks + ($16 x 36 x 23) x
50 weeks + $26,000 + $12,000] - [760000] - $337,340,088
= $599,715,712

121 Annual Tax Expense
= (Net Income excluding depreciation) x Effective tax rate
= { [(Revenues) - (Cost of Sales)] - [Total Labor Costs] - [Employee assistance services]
} x 38%
= { [($30,600 x 30697) + ($41,400 x 5372) + ($19,800 x 2470)] - [($10,400 x 30697)
+ ($10,600 x 5372) + ($2,200 x 2470)] - [($42 x 100 x 48) x 50 weeks + ($18 x 42 x
29) x 50 weeks + $30,000 + $14,000] - [880000] } x 38%
= $310,425,344 Monthly amount is calculated by dividing the annual amount by 12.
$310,425,344 / 12 = $25,868,779

122 Annual Tax Expense
= (Net Income excluding depreciation) x Effective tax rate
= { [(Revenues) - (Cost of Sales)] - [Total Labor Costs] - [Employee assistance services]
} x 37%
= { [($25,600 x 25638) + ($35,200 x 5167) + ($16,000 x 2281)] - [($7,600 x 25638) +
($7,700 x 5167) + ($1,700 x 2281)] - [($39 x 90 x 43) x 50 weeks + ($17 x 39 x 26) x
50 weeks + $28,000 + $13,000] - [820000] } x 37%
= $231,962,398 Monthly amount is calculated by dividing the annual amount by 12.
$231,962,398 / 12 = $19,330,200

123   Annual Net Income
= [(Revenues) - (Cost of Sales)] - [Total Labor Costs] - [Janitorial services] - [Depreciation]
= [($13,000 x 13094) + ($19,000 x 4944) + ($7,000 x 1745)] - [($2,200 x 13094) + ($2,200 x 4944) + ($600 x 1745)] - [($30 x 60 x 28) x 50 weeks + ($14 x 30 x 17) x 50 weeks + $22,000 + $10,000] - [$640,000] - [($1,600,000 / 60) + ($800,000 / 40)]
= $232,046,733 Monthly amount is calculated by dividing the annual amount by 12.
$232,046,733 / 12 = $19,337,228

124   Annual EBITDA
= [(Revenues) - (Cost of Sales)] - [Total Labor Costs]] - [Janitorial services]
= [($16,900 x 16936) + ($24,700 x 6311) + ($9,100 x 2270)] - [($2,200 x 16936) + ($2,200 x 6311) + ($600 x 2270)] - [($30 x 60 x 28) x 50 weeks + ($14 x 30 x 17) x 50 weeks + $22,000 + $10,000] - [$640,000]
= $406,702,700

125   Annual Tax Expense
= (Net Income excluding depreciation) x Effective tax rate
= { [(Revenues) - (Cost of Sales)] - [Total Labor Costs] - [HVAC expenses] } x 32%
= { [($17,600 x 17692) + ($27,200 x 13792) + ($8,000 x 3995)] - [($600 x 17692) + ($600 x 13792) + ($200 x 3995)] - [($24 x 40 x 18) x 50 weeks + ($12 x 24 x 11) x 50 weeks + $18,000 + $8,000] - [520000] } x 32%
= $223,111,616 Monthly amount is calculated by dividing the annual amount by 12.
$223,111,616 / 12 = $18,592,635

126   Annual Cash flow
= (Net Income excluding depreciation) - Tax
= [(Revenues) - (Cost of Sales)] - [Total Labor Costs] - [HVAC expenses] - Tax
= [($23,100 x 23133) + ($35,700 x 17983) + ($10,500 x 5245)] - [($600 x 23133) + ($600 x 17983) + ($200 x 5245)] - [($24 x 40 x 18) x 50 weeks + ($12 x 24 x 11) x 50 weeks + $18,000 + $8,000] - [520000] - $385,328,288
= $818,822,612

127   Annual Tax Expense
= (Net Income excluding depreciation) x Effective tax rate
= { [(Revenues) - (Cost of Sales)] - [Total Labor Costs] - [Employee assistance services] } x 37%
= { [($28,800 x 28875) + ($39,600 x 5832) + ($18,000 x 2566)] - [($7,600 x 28875) + ($7,700 x 5832) + ($1,700 x 2566)] - [($39 x 90 x 43) x 50 weeks + ($17 x 39 x 26) x 50 weeks + $28,000 + $13,000] - [820000] } x 37%
= $307,376,464 Monthly amount is calculated by dividing the annual amount by 12.
$307,376,464 / 12 = $25,614,705

128   Annual Net Income
= [(Revenues) - (Cost of Sales)] - [Total Labor Costs] - [HVAC expenses] - [Depreciation]
= [($11,000 x 11042) + ($17,000 x 8642) + ($5,000 x 2495)] - [($600 x 11042) + ($600 x 8642) + ($200 x 2495)] - [($24 x 40 x 18) x 50 weeks + ($12 x 24 x 11) x 50 weeks + $18,000 + $8,000] - [$520,000] - [($1,300,000 / 60) + ($650,000 / 40)]
= $266,935,283 Monthly amount is calculated by dividing the annual amount by 12.
$266,935,283 / 12 = $22,244,607

129 Annual EBITDA
= [(Revenues) - (Cost of Sales)] - [Total Labor Costs]] - [Employee assistance services]
= [($22,100 x 22145) + ($29,900 x 3883) + ($14,300 x 1783)] - [($10,400 x 22145) + ($10,600 x 3883) + ($2,200 x 1783)] - [($42 x 100 x 48) x 50 weeks + ($18 x 42 x 29) x 50 weeks + $30,000 + $14,000] - [$880,000]
= $343,512,500

130 Annual Cash flow
= (Net Income excluding depreciation) - Tax
= [(Revenues) - (Cost of Sales)] - [Total Labor Costs] - [Employee assistance services] - Tax
= [($32,300 x 32349) + ($43,700 x 5612) + ($20,900 x 2608)] - [($10,400 x 32349) + ($10,600 x 5612) + ($2,200 x 2608)] - [($42 x 100 x 48) x 50 weeks + ($18 x 42 x 29) x 50 weeks + $30,000 + $14,000] - [880000] - $353,730,486
= $577,139,214

131 Annual Net Income
= [(Revenues) - (Cost of Sales)] - [Total Labor Costs] - [Janitorial services] - [Depreciation]
= [($13,200 x 13261) + ($19,800 x 6761) + ($6,600 x 2195)] - [($1,200 x 13261) + ($1,300 x 6761) + ($400 x 2195)] - [($27 x 50 x 23) x 50 weeks + ($13 x 27 x 14) x 50 weeks + $20,000 + $9,000] - [$580,000] - [($1,450,000 / 66) + ($725,000 / 44)]
= $295,373,853

132 Annual Tax Expense
= (Net Income excluding depreciation) x Effective tax rate
= { [(Revenues) - (Cost of Sales)] - [Total Labor Costs] - [Employee assistance services] } x 37%
= { [($25,600 x 25640) + ($35,200 x 5169) + ($16,000 x 2281)] - [($7,600 x 25640) + ($7,700 x 5169) + ($1,700 x 2281)] - [($39 x 90 x 43) x 50 weeks + ($17 x 39 x 26) x 50 weeks + $28,000 + $13,000] - [820000] } x 37%
= $231,996,068 Monthly amount is calculated by dividing the annual amount by 12.
$231,996,068 / 12   = $19,333,006

133 Annual EBITDA
= [(Revenues) - (Cost of Sales)] - [Total Labor Costs]] - [Utilities]
= [($21,000 x 21047) + ($30,000 x 6147) + ($12,000 x 2395)] - [($3,500 x 21047) + ($3,600 x 6147) + ($900 x 2395)] - [($33 x 70 x 33) x 50 weeks + ($15 x 33 x 20) x 50 weeks + $24,000 + $11,000] - [$700,000]
= $552,146,300

134 Annual Net Income
= [(Revenues) - (Cost of Sales)] - [Total Labor Costs] - [Employee assistance services] - [Depreciation]
= [($17,600 x 17613) + ($24,200 x 3570) + ($11,000 x 1566)] - [($7,600 x 17613) + ($7,700 x 3570) + ($1,700 x 1566)] - [($39 x 90 x 43) x 50 weeks + ($17 x 39 x 26) x 50 weeks + $28,000 + $13,000] - [$820,000] - [($2,050,000 / 66) + ($1,025,000 / 44)]
= $240,275,044

135 Annual Cash flow
= (Net Income excluding depreciation) - Tax
= [(Revenues) - (Cost of Sales)] - [Total Labor Costs] - [Utilities] - Tax
= [($30,000 x 30018) + ($42,000 x 7118) + ($18,000 x 2995)] - [($5,300 x 30018) + ($5,400 x 7118) + ($1,300 x 2995)] - [($36 x 80 x 38) x 50 weeks + ($16 x 36 x 23) x 50 weeks + $26,000 + $12,000] - [760000] - $376,217,100
= $668,830,400 Monthly amount is calculated by dividing the annual amount by 12.
$668,830,400 / 12 = $55,735,867

136 Annual EBITDA
= [(Revenues) - (Cost of Sales)] - [Total Labor Costs]] - [Utilities]
= [($21,000 x 21078) + ($30,000 x 6178) + ($12,000 x 2395)] - [($3,500 x 21078) + ($3,600 x 6178) + ($900 x 2395)] - [($33 x 70 x 33) x 50 weeks + ($15 x 33 x 20) x 50 weeks + $24,000 + $11,000] - [$700,000]
= $553,507,200

137 Annual EBITDA
= [(Revenues) - (Cost of Sales)] - [Total Labor Costs]] - [Insurance costs]
= [($26,600 x 26605) + ($35,000 x 3605) + ($18,200 x 1815)] - [($18,000 x 26605) + ($18,200 x 3605) + ($3,300 x 1815)] - [($48 x 120 x 58) x 50 weeks + ($20 x 48 x 35) x 50 weeks + $34,000 + $16,000] - [$1,000,000]
= $296,976,500 Monthly amount is calculated by dividing the annual amount by 12.
$296,976,500 / 12 = $24,748,042

138 Annual Net Income
= [(Revenues) - (Cost of Sales)] - [Total Labor Costs] - [Employee assistance services] - [Depreciation]
= [($18,700 x 18772) + ($25,300 x 3335) + ($12,100 x 1508)] - [($10,400 x 18772) + ($10,600 x 3335) + ($2,200 x 1508)] - [($42 x 100 x 48) x 50 weeks + ($18 x 42 x 29) x 50 weeks + $30,000 + $14,000] - [$880,000] - [($2,200,000 / 66) + ($1,100,000 / 44)]
= $207,602,767

139 Annual Cash flow
= (Net Income excluding depreciation) - Tax
= [(Revenues) - (Cost of Sales)] - [Total Labor Costs] - [Janitorial services] - Tax
= [($24,000 x 24040) + ($36,000 x 12140) + ($12,000 x 3995)] - [($1,200 x 24040) + ($1,300 x 12140) + ($400 x 3995)] - [($27 x 50 x 23) x 50 weeks + ($13 x 27 x 14) x 50 weeks + $20,000 + $9,000] - [580000] - $334,390,584
= $678,914,216 Monthly amount is calculated by dividing the annual amount by 12.
$678,914,216 / 12 = $56,576,185

140 Annual Net Income
= [(Revenues) - (Cost of Sales)] - [Total Labor Costs] - [Janitorial services] - [Depreciation]
= [($12,000 x 12057) + ($18,000 x 6157) + ($6,000 x 1995)] - [($1,200 x 12057) + ($1,300 x 6157) + ($400 x 1995)] - [($27 x 50 x 23) x 50 weeks + ($13 x 27 x 14) x 50 weeks + $20,000 + $9,000] - [$580,000] - [($1,450,000 / 60) + ($725,000 / 40)]
= $241,760,008 Monthly amount is calculated by dividing the annual amount by 12.
$241,760,008 / 12 = $20,146,667

141 Annual Cash flow
= (Net Income excluding depreciation) - Tax
= [(Revenues) - (Cost of Sales)] - [Total Labor Costs] - [Janitorial services] - Tax
= [($25,200 x 25263) + ($37,800 x 12763) + ($12,600 x 4195)] - [($1,200 x 25263) +
($1,300 x 12763) + ($400 x 4195)] - [($27 x 50 x 23) x 50 weeks + ($13 x 27 x 14) x
50 weeks + $20,000 + $9,000] - [580000] - $369,907,989
= $751,025,311

142 Annual EBITDA
= [(Revenues) - (Cost of Sales)] - [Total Labor Costs]] - [Janitorial services]
= [($16,900 x 16967) + ($24,700 x 6342) + ($9,100 x 2270)] - [($2,200 x 16967) + (
$2,200 x 6342) + ($600 x 2270)] - [($30 x 60 x 28) x 50 weeks + ($14 x 30 x 17) x 50
weeks + $22,000 + $10,000] - [$640,000]
= $407,855,900

143 Annual Tax Expense
= (Net Income excluding depreciation) x Effective tax rate
= { [(Revenues) - (Cost of Sales)] - [Total Labor Costs] - [Insurance costs] } x 39%
= { [($30,600 x 30653) + ($40,800 x 4686) + ($20,400 x 2262)] - [($13,900 x 30653)
+ ($14,000 x 4686) + ($2,700 x 2262)] - [($45 x 110 x 53) x 50 weeks + ($19 x 45 x
32) x 50 weeks + $32,000 + $15,000] - [940000] } x 39%
= $258,201,372

144 Annual Cash flow
= (Net Income excluding depreciation) - Tax
= [(Revenues) - (Cost of Sales)] - [Total Labor Costs] - [Utilities] - Tax
= [($30,000 x 30027) + ($42,000 x 7127) + ($18,000 x 2995)] - [($5,300 x 30027) + (
$5,400 x 7127) + ($1,300 x 2995)] - [($36 x 80 x 38) x 50 weeks + ($16 x 36 x 23) x
50 weeks + $26,000 + $12,000] - [760000] - $376,415,712
= $669,183,488 Monthly amount is calculated by dividing the annual amount by 12.
$669,183,488 / 12 = $55,765,291

145 Annual Tax Expense
= (Net Income excluding depreciation) x Effective tax rate
= { [(Revenues) - (Cost of Sales)] - [Total Labor Costs] - [Employee assistance services]
} x 37%
= { [($28,800 x 28843) + ($39,600 x 5800) + ($18,000 x 2566)] - [($7,600 x 28843) +
($7,700 x 5800) + ($1,700 x 2566)] - [($39 x 90 x 43) x 50 weeks + ($17 x 39 x 26) x
50 weeks + $28,000 + $13,000] - [820000] } x 37%
= $306,747,760 Monthly amount is calculated by dividing the annual amount by 12.
$306,747,760 / 12 = $25,562,313

146 Annual Tax Expense
= (Net Income excluding depreciation) x Effective tax rate
= { [(Revenues) - (Cost of Sales)] - [Total Labor Costs] - [HVAC expenses] } x 31%
= { [($16,000 x 16033) + ($25,600 x 25733) + ($6,400 x 6395)] - [($200 x 16033) + (
$200 x 25733) + ($100 x 6395)] - [($21 x 30 x 13) x 50 weeks + ($11 x 21 x 8) x 50
weeks + $16,000 + $7,000] - [460000] } x 31%
= $293,335,392 Monthly amount is calculated by dividing the annual amount by 12.
$293,335,392 / 12 = $24,444,616

147 Annual EBITDA
= [(Revenues) - (Cost of Sales)] - [Total Labor Costs]] - [Utilities]
= [($21,000 x 21072) + ($29,400 x 5072) + ($12,600 x 2095)] - [($5,300 x 21072) + ($5,400 x 5072) + ($1,300 x 2095)] - [($36 x 80 x 38) x 50 weeks + ($16 x 36 x 23) x 50 weeks + $26,000 + $12,000] - [$760,000]
= $469,299,500 Monthly amount is calculated by dividing the annual amount by 12.
$469,299,500 / 12 = $39,108,292

148 Annual Net Income
= [(Revenues) - (Cost of Sales)] - [Total Labor Costs] - [Janitorial services] - [Depreciation]
= [($13,200 x 13248) + ($19,800 x 6748) + ($6,600 x 2195)] - [($1,200 x 13248) + ($1,300 x 6748) + ($400 x 2195)] - [($27 x 50 x 23) x 50 weeks + ($13 x 27 x 14) x 50 weeks + $20,000 + $9,000] - [$580,000] - [($1,450,000 / 66) + ($725,000 / 44)]
= $294,977,353

149 Annual Net Income
= [(Revenues) - (Cost of Sales)] - [Total Labor Costs] - [Employee assistance services] - [Depreciation]
= [($17,000 x 17034) + ($23,000 x 3009) + ($11,000 x 1370)] - [($10,400 x 17034) + ($10,600 x 3009) + ($2,200 x 1370)] - [($42 x 100 x 48) x 50 weeks + ($18 x 42 x 29) x 50 weeks + $30,000 + $14,000] - [$880,000] - [($2,200,000 / 60) + ($1,100,000 / 40)]
= $149,627,633 Monthly amount is calculated by dividing the annual amount by 12.
$149,627,633 / 12 = $12,468,969

150 Annual Cash flow
= (Net Income excluding depreciation) - Tax
= [(Revenues) - (Cost of Sales)] - [Total Labor Costs] - [Janitorial services] - Tax
= [($27,300 x 27392) + ($39,900 x 10167) + ($14,700 x 3670)] - [($2,200 x 27392) + ($2,200 x 10167) + ($600 x 3670)] - [($30 x 60 x 28) x 50 weeks + ($14 x 30 x 17) x 50 weeks + $22,000 + $10,000] - [640000] - $380,471,254
= $738,561,846

151 Annual EBITDA
= [(Revenues) - (Cost of Sales)] - [Total Labor Costs]] - [Employee assistance services]
= [($20,800 x 20814) + ($28,600 x 4200) + ($13,000 x 1852)] - [($7,600 x 20814) + ($7,700 x 4200) + ($1,700 x 1852)] - [($39 x 90 x 43) x 50 weeks + ($17 x 39 x 26) x 50 weeks + $28,000 + $13,000] - [$820,000]
= $374,183,000

152 Gross Margin
= [Gross Profit] / [Revenue]
= [($4,200 - $3,500) x 4225 + ($6,000 - $3,600) x 1325 + ($2,400 - $900) x 475] / [($4,200 x 4225) + ($6,000 x 1325) + ($2,400 x 475)]
= $6,850,000 / $26,835,000
= 26%

153 Annual Cash flow
= (Net Income excluding depreciation) - Tax
= [(Revenues) - (Cost of Sales)] - [Total Labor Costs] - [Janitorial services] - Tax
= [($22,800 x 22805) + ($34,200 x 11505) + ($11,400 x 3795)] - [($1,200 x 22805) +
($1,300 x 11505) + ($400 x 3795)] - [($27 x 50 x 23) x 50 weeks + ($13 x 27 x 14) x
50 weeks + $20,000 + $9,000] - [580000] - $300,445,299
= $609,995,001

154 Annual Net Income
= [(Revenues) - (Cost of Sales)] - [Total Labor Costs] - [Janitorial services] -
[Depreciation]
= [($15,600 x 15682) + ($22,800 x 5882) + ($8,400 x 2095)] - [($2,200 x 15682) + (
$2,200 x 5882) + ($600 x 2095)] - [($30 x 60 x 28) x 50 weeks + ($14 x 30 x 17) x 50
weeks + $22,000 + $10,000] - [$640,000] - [($1,600,000 / 72) + ($800,000 / 48)]
= $344,061,111 Monthly amount is calculated by dividing the annual amount by 12.
$344,061,111 / 12   = $28,671,759

155 Annual EBITDA
= [(Revenues) - (Cost of Sales)] - [Total Labor Costs]] - [Utilities]
= [($22,500 x 22511) + ($31,500 x 5361) + ($13,500 x 2245)] - [($5,300 x 22511) + (
$5,400 x 5361) + ($1,300 x 2245)] - [($36 x 80 x 38) x 50 weeks + ($16 x 36 x 23) x
50 weeks + $26,000 + $12,000] - [$760,000]
= $547,567,900

156 Annual Cash flow
= (Net Income excluding depreciation) - Tax
= [(Revenues) - (Cost of Sales)] - [Total Labor Costs] - [Janitorial services] - Tax
= [($27,300 x 27356) + ($39,900 x 10131) + ($14,700 x 3670)] - [($2,200 x 27356) +
($2,200 x 10131) + ($600 x 3670)] - [($30 x 60 x 28) x 50 weeks + ($14 x 30 x 17) x
50 weeks + $22,000 + $10,000] - [640000] - $379,702,582
= $737,069,718

157 Annual Tax Expense
= (Net Income excluding depreciation) x Effective tax rate
= { [(Revenues) - (Cost of Sales)] - [Total Labor Costs] - [HVAC expenses] } x 31%
= { [($16,000 x 16095) + ($25,600 x 25795) + ($6,400 x 6395)] - [($200 x 16095) + (
$200 x 25795) + ($100 x 6395)] - [($21 x 30 x 13) x 50 weeks + ($11 x 21 x 8) x 50
weeks + $16,000 + $7,000] - [460000] } x 31%
= $294,127,256 Monthly amount is calculated by dividing the annual amount by 12.
$294,127,256 / 12   = $24,510,605

158 Annual EBITDA
= [(Revenues) - (Cost of Sales)] - [Total Labor Costs]] - [Janitorial services]
= [($18,000 x 18019) + ($27,000 x 9119) + ($9,000 x 2995)] - [($1,200 x 18019) + (
$1,300 x 9119) + ($400 x 2995)] - [($27 x 50 x 23) x 50 weeks + ($13 x 27 x 14) x 50
weeks + $20,000 + $9,000] - [$580,000]
= $560,427,300

159 Annual Net Income
= [(Revenues) - (Cost of Sales)] - [Total Labor Costs] - [HVAC expenses] - [Depreciation]
= [($12,100 x 12170) + ($18,700 x 9520) + ($5,500 x 2745)] - [($600 x 12170) + ($600 x 9520) + ($200 x 2745)] - [($24 x 40 x 18) x 50 weeks + ($12 x 24 x 11) x 50 weeks + $18,000 + $8,000] - [$520,000] - [($1,300,000 / 66) + ($650,000 / 44)]
= $325,212,630

160 Annual Net Income
= [(Revenues) - (Cost of Sales)] - [Total Labor Costs] - [Insurance costs] - [Depreciation]
= [($19,800 x 19840) + ($26,400 x 3073) + ($13,200 x 1462)] - [($13,900 x 19840) + ($14,000 x 3073) + ($2,700 x 1462)] - [($45 x 110 x 53) x 50 weeks + ($19 x 45 x 32) x 50 weeks + $32,000 + $15,000] - [$940,000] - [($2,350,000 / 66) + ($1,175,000 / 44)]
= $154,977,389

161 Annual Net Income
= [(Revenues) - (Cost of Sales)] - [Total Labor Costs] - [Employee assistance services] - [Depreciation]
= [($18,700 x 18750) + ($25,300 x 3313) + ($12,100 x 1508)] - [($10,400 x 18750) + ($10,600 x 3313) + ($2,200 x 1508)] - [($42 x 100 x 48) x 50 weeks + ($18 x 42 x 29) x 50 weeks + $30,000 + $14,000] - [$880,000] - [($2,200,000 / 66) + ($1,100,000 / 44)]
= $207,096,767

162 Annual Tax Expense
= (Net Income excluding depreciation) x Effective tax rate
= { [(Revenues) - (Cost of Sales)] - [Total Labor Costs] - [Janitorial services] } x 34%
= { [($20,800 x 20872) + ($30,400 x 7772) + ($11,200 x 2795)] - [($2,200 x 20872) + ($2,200 x 7772) + ($600 x 2795)] - [($30 x 60 x 28) x 50 weeks + ($14 x 30 x 17) x 50 weeks + $22,000 + $10,000] - [640000] } x 34%
= $215,378,984 Monthly amount is calculated by dividing the annual amount by 12.
$215,378,984 / 12 = $17,948,249

163 Annual Cash flow
= (Net Income excluding depreciation) - Tax
= [(Revenues) - (Cost of Sales)] - [Total Labor Costs] - [Employee assistance services] - Tax
= [($34,000 x 34046) + ($46,000 x 5896) + ($22,000 x 2745)] - [($10,400 x 34046) + ($10,600 x 5896) + ($2,200 x 2745)] - [($42 x 100 x 48) x 50 weeks + ($18 x 42 x 29) x 50 weeks + $30,000 + $14,000] - [880000] - $400,692,824
= $653,761,976 Monthly amount is calculated by dividing the annual amount by 12.
$653,761,976 / 12 = $54,480,165

164 Annual EBITDA
= [(Revenues) - (Cost of Sales)] - [Total Labor Costs]] - [Utilities]
= [($19,500 x 19588) + ($27,300 x 4738) + ($11,700 x 1945)] - [($5,300 x 19588) + ($5,400 x 4738) + ($1,300 x 1945)] - [($36 x 80 x 38) x 50 weeks + ($16 x 36 x 23) x 50 weeks + $26,000 + $12,000] - [$760,000]
= $395,207,400

165   Annual Cash flow
      = (Net Income excluding depreciation) - Tax
      = [(Revenues) - (Cost of Sales)] - [Total Labor Costs] - [Utilities] - Tax
      = [($29,400 x 29497) + ($42,000 x 8597) + ($16,800 x 3355)] - [($3,500 x 29497) + (
      $3,600 x 8597) + ($900 x 3355)] - [($33 x 70 x 33) x 50 weeks + ($15 x 33 x 20) x 50
      weeks + $24,000 + $11,000] - [700000] - $399,840,035
      = $742,560,065

166   Annual Cash flow
      = (Net Income excluding depreciation) - Tax
      = [(Revenues) - (Cost of Sales)] - [Total Labor Costs] - [HVAC expenses] - Tax
      = [($22,000 x 22023) + ($34,000 x 17123) + ($10,000 x 4995)] - [($600 x 22023) + (
      $600 x 17123) + ($200 x 4995)] - [($24 x 40 x 18) x 50 weeks + ($12 x 24 x 11) x 50
      weeks + $18,000 + $8,000] - [520000] - $348,986,560
      = $741,596,440 Monthly amount is calculated by dividing the annual amount by 12.
      $741,596,440 / 12   = $61,799,703

167   Annual Net Income
      = [(Revenues) - (Cost of Sales)] - [Total Labor Costs] - [Insurance costs] - [Depreciation]
      = [($22,800 x 22854) + ($30,000 x 3154) + ($15,600 x 1555)] - [($18,000 x 22854) +
      ($18,200 x 3154) + ($3,300 x 1555)] - [($48 x 120 x 58) x 50 weeks + ($20 x 48 x 35
) x 50 weeks + $34,000 + $16,000] - [$1,000,000] - [($2,500,000 / 72) + ($1,250,000 /
      48)]
      = $146,548,136 Monthly amount is calculated by dividing the annual amount by 12.
      $146,548,136 / 12   = $12,212,345

168   Annual Cash flow
      = (Net Income excluding depreciation) - Tax
      = [(Revenues) - (Cost of Sales)] - [Total Labor Costs] - [Janitorial services] - Tax
      = [($26,000 x 26013) + ($38,000 x 9613) + ($14,000 x 3495)] - [($2,200 x 26013) + (
      $2,200 x 9613) + ($600 x 3495)] - [($30 x 60 x 28) x 50 weeks + ($14 x 30 x 17) x 50
      weeks + $22,000 + $10,000] - [640000] - $342,223,192
      = $664,315,608 Monthly amount is calculated by dividing the annual amount by 12.
      $664,315,608 / 12   = $55,359,634

169   Annual Tax Expense
      = (Net Income excluding depreciation) x Effective tax rate
      = { [(Revenues) - (Cost of Sales)] - [Total Labor Costs] - [Janitorial services] } x 34%
      = { [($22,100 x 22154) + ($32,300 x 8229) + ($11,900 x 2970)] - [($2,200 x 22154) +
      ($2,200 x 8229) + ($600 x 2970)] - [($30 x 60 x 28) x 50 weeks + ($14 x 30 x 17) x
      50 weeks + $22,000 + $10,000] - [640000] } x 34%
      = $244,313,630

170   Annual Net Income
      = [(Revenues) - (Cost of Sales)] - [Total Labor Costs] - [Utilities] - [Depreciation]
      = [($18,000 x 18003) + ($25,200 x 4303) + ($10,800 x 1795)] - [($5,300 x 18003) + (
      $5,400 x 4303) + ($1,300 x 1795)] - [($36 x 80 x 38) x 50 weeks + ($16 x 36 x 23) x
      50 weeks + $26,000 + $12,000] - [$760,000] - [($1,900,000 / 72) + ($950,000 / 48)]
      = $323,911,419 Monthly amount is calculated by dividing the annual amount by 12.
      $323,911,419 / 12   = $26,992,618

171 Gross Margin
= [Gross Profit] / [Revenue]
= [($1,000 - $200) x 1021 + ($1,600 - $200) x 1721 + ($400 - $100) x 395] / [($1,000 x 1021) + ($1,600 x 1721) + ($400 x 395)]
= $3,344,700 / $3,932,600
= 85%

172 Annual Cash flow
= (Net Income excluding depreciation) - Tax
= [(Revenues) - (Cost of Sales)] - [Total Labor Costs] - [Janitorial services] - Tax
= [($22,800 x 22803) + ($34,200 x 11503) + ($11,400 x 3795)] - [($1,200 x 22803) + ($1,300 x 11503) + ($400 x 3795)] - [($27 x 50 x 23) x 50 weeks + ($13 x 27 x 14) x 50 weeks + $20,000 + $9,000] - [580000] - $300,409,329
= $609,921,971

173 Annual EBITDA
= [(Revenues) - (Cost of Sales)] - [Total Labor Costs]] - [Insurance costs]
= [($27,000 x 27038) + ($36,000 x 4138) + ($18,000 x 1995)] - [($13,900 x 27038) + ($14,000 x 4138) + ($2,700 x 1995)] - [($45 x 110 x 53) x 50 weeks + ($19 x 45 x 32) x 50 weeks + $32,000 + $15,000] - [$940,000]
= $460,284,800

174 Annual Net Income
= [(Revenues) - (Cost of Sales)] - [Total Labor Costs] - [HVAC expenses] - [Depreciation]
= [($11,000 x 11090) + ($17,600 x 17790) + ($4,400 x 4395)] - [($200 x 11090) + ($200 x 17790) + ($100 x 4395)] - [($21 x 30 x 13) x 50 weeks + ($11 x 21 x 8) x 50 weeks + $16,000 + $7,000] - [$460,000] - [($1,150,000 / 66) + ($575,000 / 44)]
= $447,201,108

175 Annual Net Income
= [(Revenues) - (Cost of Sales)] - [Total Labor Costs] - [Utilities] - [Depreciation]
= [($15,400 x 15496) + ($22,000 x 4596) + ($8,800 x 1755)] - [($3,500 x 15496) + ($3,600 x 4596) + ($900 x 1755)] - [($33 x 70 x 33) x 50 weeks + ($15 x 33 x 20) x 50 weeks + $24,000 + $11,000] - [$700,000] - [($1,750,000 / 66) + ($875,000 / 44)]
= $277,745,398

176 Annual Tax Expense
= (Net Income excluding depreciation) x Effective tax rate
= { [(Revenues) - (Cost of Sales)] - [Total Labor Costs] - [Insurance costs] } x 39%
= { [($30,600 x 30697) + ($40,800 x 4730) + ($20,400 x 2262)] - [($13,900 x 30697) + ($14,000 x 4730) + ($2,700 x 2262)] - [($45 x 110 x 53) x 50 weeks + ($19 x 45 x 32) x 50 weeks + $32,000 + $15,000] - [940000] } x 39%
= $258,947,832

177 Annual Net Income
= [(Revenues) - (Cost of Sales)] - [Total Labor Costs] - [Utilities] - [Depreciation]
= [($14,000 x 14034) + ($20,000 x 4134) + ($8,000 x 1595)] - [($3,500 x 14034) + ($3,600 x 4134) + ($900 x 1595)] - [($33 x 70 x 33) x 50 weeks + ($15 x 33 x 20) x 50 weeks + $24,000 + $11,000] - [$700,000] - [($1,750,000 / 60) + ($875,000 / 40)]
= $221,386,558 Monthly amount is calculated by dividing the annual amount by 12.
$221,386,558 / 12 = $18,448,880

178 Annual Cash flow
= (Net Income excluding depreciation) - Tax
= [(Revenues) - (Cost of Sales)] - [Total Labor Costs] - [Employee assistance services] - Tax
= [($32,000 x 32015) + ($44,000 x 6401) + ($20,000 x 2852)] - [($7,600 x 32015) + ($7,700 x 6401) + ($1,700 x 2852)] - [($39 x 90 x 43) x 50 weeks + ($17 x 39 x 26) x 50 weeks + $28,000 + $13,000] - [820000] - $390,884,465
= $665,560,035 Monthly amount is calculated by dividing the annual amount by 12.
$665,560,035 / 12 = $55,463,336

179 Annual EBITDA
= [(Revenues) - (Cost of Sales)] - [Total Labor Costs]] - [HVAC expenses]
= [($16,500 x 16523) + ($25,500 x 12873) + ($7,500 x 3745)] - [($600 x 16523) + ($600 x 12873) + ($200 x 3745)] - [($24 x 40 x 18) x 50 weeks + ($12 x 24 x 11) x 50 weeks + $18,000 + $8,000] - [$520,000]
= $609,023,500

180 Annual Net Income
= [(Revenues) - (Cost of Sales)] - [Total Labor Costs] - [Utilities] - [Depreciation]
= [($16,800 x 16855) + ($24,000 x 4955) + ($9,600 x 1915)] - [($3,500 x 16855) + ($3,600 x 4955) + ($900 x 1915)] - [($33 x 70 x 33) x 50 weeks + ($15 x 33 x 20) x 50 weeks + $24,000 + $11,000] - [$700,000] - [($1,750,000 / 72) + ($875,000 / 48)]
= $336,829,965 Monthly amount is calculated by dividing the annual amount by 12.
$336,829,965 / 12 = $28,069,164

181 Annual Tax Expense
= (Net Income excluding depreciation) x Effective tax rate
= { [(Revenues) - (Cost of Sales)] - [Total Labor Costs] - [Insurance costs] } x 40%
= { [($30,400 x 30475) + ($40,000 x 4175) + ($20,800 x 2075)] - [($18,000 x 30475) + ($18,200 x 4175) + ($3,300 x 2075)] - [($48 x 120 x 58) x 50 weeks + ($20 x 48 x 35) x 50 weeks + $34,000 + $16,000] - [1000000] } x 40%
= $194,313,400 Monthly amount is calculated by dividing the annual amount by 12.
$194,313,400 / 12 = $16,192,783

182 Gross Margin
= [Gross Profit] / [Revenue]
= [($2,200 - $600) x 2226 + ($3,400 - $600) x 1826 + ($1,000 - $200) x 495] / [($2,200 x 2226) + ($3,400 x 1826) + ($1,000 x 495)]
= $9,070,400 / $11,600,600
= 78%

183   Annual EBITDA
= [(Revenues) - (Cost of Sales)] - [Total Labor Costs]] - [Employee assistance services]
= [($24,000 x 24061) + ($33,000 x 4875) + ($15,000 x 2138)] - [($7,600 x 24061) + ($7,700 x 4875) + ($1,700 x 2138)] - [($39 x 90 x 43) x 50 weeks + ($17 x 39 x 26) x 50 weeks + $28,000 + $13,000] - [$820,000]
= $537,103,900

184   Annual Tax Expense
= (Net Income excluding depreciation) x Effective tax rate
= { [(Revenues) - (Cost of Sales)] - [Total Labor Costs] - [HVAC expenses] } x 32%
= { [($18,700 x 18744) + ($28,900 x 14594) + ($8,500 x 4245)] - [($600 x 18744) + ($600 x 14594) + ($200 x 4245)] - [($24 x 40 x 18) x 50 weeks + ($12 x 24 x 11) x 50 weeks + $18,000 + $8,000] - [520000] } x 32%
= $251,501,344

185   Annual Net Income
= [(Revenues) - (Cost of Sales)] - [Total Labor Costs] - [Utilities] - [Depreciation]
= [($16,500 x 16557) + ($23,100 x 4007) + ($9,900 x 1645)] - [($5,300 x 16557) + ($5,400 x 4007) + ($1,300 x 1645)] - [($36 x 80 x 38) x 50 weeks + ($16 x 36 x 23) x 50 weeks + $26,000 + $12,000] - [$760,000] - [($1,900,000 / 66) + ($950,000 / 44)]
= $263,526,521

186   Annual Cash flow
= (Net Income excluding depreciation) - Tax
= [(Revenues) - (Cost of Sales)] - [Total Labor Costs] - [Employee assistance services] - Tax
= [($32,300 x 32359) + ($43,700 x 5622) + ($20,900 x 2608)] - [($10,400 x 32359) + ($10,600 x 5622) + ($2,200 x 2608)] - [($42 x 100 x 48) x 50 weeks + ($18 x 42 x 29) x 50 weeks + $30,000 + $14,000] - [880000] - $353,939,486
= $577,480,214

187   Annual Tax Expense
= (Net Income excluding depreciation) x Effective tax rate
= { [(Revenues) - (Cost of Sales)] - [Total Labor Costs] - [Janitorial services] } x 34%
= { [($20,800 x 20861) + ($30,400 x 7761) + ($11,200 x 2795)] - [($2,200 x 20861) + ($2,200 x 7761) + ($600 x 2795)] - [($30 x 60 x 28) x 50 weeks + ($14 x 30 x 17) x 50 weeks + $22,000 + $10,000] - [640000] } x 34%
= $215,203,952 Monthly amount is calculated by dividing the annual amount by 12.
$215,203,952 / 12   = $17,933,663

188   Annual Cash flow
= (Net Income excluding depreciation) - Tax
= [(Revenues) - (Cost of Sales)] - [Total Labor Costs] - [Insurance costs] - Tax
= [($37,800 x 37848) + ($50,400 x 5748) + ($25,200 x 2795)] - [($13,900 x 37848) + ($14,000 x 5748) + ($2,700 x 2795)] - [($45 x 110 x 53) x 50 weeks + ($19 x 45 x 32) x 50 weeks + $32,000 + $15,000] - [940000] - $452,871,666
= $708,337,734

189 Annual Cash flow
= (Net Income excluding depreciation) - Tax
= [(Revenues) - (Cost of Sales)] - [Total Labor Costs] - [Janitorial services] - Tax
= [($26,000 x 26034) + ($38,000 x 9634) + ($14,000 x 3495)] - [($2,200 x 26034) + ($2,200 x 9634) + ($600 x 3495)] - [($30 x 60 x 28) x 50 weeks + ($14 x 30 x 17) x 50 weeks + $22,000 + $10,000] - [640000] - $342,648,736
= $665,141,664 Monthly amount is calculated by dividing the annual amount by 12.
$665,141,664 / 12 = $55,428,472

190 Annual EBITDA
= [(Revenues) - (Cost of Sales)] - [Total Labor Costs]] - [Janitorial services]
= [($18,200 x 18210) + ($26,600 x 6760) + ($9,800 x 2445)] - [($2,200 x 18210) + ($2,200 x 6760) + ($600 x 2445)] - [($30 x 60 x 28) x 50 weeks + ($14 x 30 x 17) x 50 weeks + $22,000 + $10,000] - [$640,000]
= $475,249,000 Monthly amount is calculated by dividing the annual amount by 12.
$475,249,000 / 12 = $39,604,083

191 Annual EBITDA
= [(Revenues) - (Cost of Sales)] - [Total Labor Costs]] - [Employee assistance services]
= [($22,400 x 22440) + ($30,800 x 4540) + ($14,000 x 1995)] - [($7,600 x 22440) + ($7,700 x 4540) + ($1,700 x 1995)] - [($39 x 90 x 43) x 50 weeks + ($17 x 39 x 26) x 50 weeks + $28,000 + $13,000] - [$820,000]
= $452,255,100 Monthly amount is calculated by dividing the annual amount by 12.
$452,255,100 / 12 = $37,687,925

192 Gross Margin
= [Gross Profit] / [Revenue]
= [($3,300 - $600) x 3379 + ($5,100 - $600) x 2729 + ($1,500 - $200) x 745] / [($3,300 x 3379) + ($5,100 x 2729) + ($1,500 x 745)]
= $22,372,300 / $26,186,100
= 85%

193 Annual Net Income
= [(Revenues) - (Cost of Sales)] - [Total Labor Costs] - [HVAC expenses] - [Depreciation]
= [($11,000 x 11096) + ($17,000 x 8696) + ($5,000 x 2495)] - [($600 x 11096) + ($600 x 8696) + ($200 x 2495)] - [($24 x 40 x 18) x 50 weeks + ($12 x 24 x 11) x 50 weeks + $18,000 + $8,000] - [$520,000] - [($1,300,000 / 60) + ($650,000 / 40)]
= $268,382,483 Monthly amount is calculated by dividing the annual amount by 12.
$268,382,483 / 12 = $22,365,207

194 Annual Cash flow
= (Net Income excluding depreciation) - Tax
= [(Revenues) - (Cost of Sales)] - [Total Labor Costs] - [Janitorial services] - Tax
= [($25,200 x 25257) + ($37,800 x 12757) + ($12,600 x 4195)] - [($1,200 x 25257) + ($1,300 x 12757) + ($400 x 4195)] - [($27 x 50 x 23) x 50 weeks + ($13 x 27 x 14) x 50 weeks + $20,000 + $9,000] - [580000] - $369,788,199
= $750,782,101

195 Annual Tax Expense
= (Net Income excluding depreciation) x Effective tax rate
= { [(Revenues) - (Cost of Sales)] - [Total Labor Costs] - [HVAC expenses] } x 32%
= { [($19,800 x 19872) + ($30,600 x 15472) + ($9,000 x 4495)] - [($600 x 19872) + ($600 x 15472) + ($200 x 4495)] - [($24 x 40 x 18) x 50 weeks + ($12 x 24 x 11) x 50 weeks + $18,000 + $8,000] - [520000] } x 32%
= $282,780,800 Monthly amount is calculated by dividing the annual amount by 12.
$282,780,800 / 12 = $23,565,067

196 Annual Cash flow
= (Net Income excluding depreciation) - Tax
= [(Revenues) - (Cost of Sales)] - [Total Labor Costs] - [HVAC expenses] - Tax
= [($22,000 x 22034) + ($34,000 x 17134) + ($10,000 x 4995)] - [($600 x 22034) + ($600 x 17134) + ($200 x 4995)] - [($24 x 40 x 18) x 50 weeks + ($12 x 24 x 11) x 50 weeks + $18,000 + $8,000] - [520000] - $349,179,456
= $742,006,344 Monthly amount is calculated by dividing the annual amount by 12.
$742,006,344 / 12 = $61,833,862

197 Annual EBITDA
= [(Revenues) - (Cost of Sales)] - [Total Labor Costs]] - [Employee assistance services]
= [($23,800 x 23805) + ($32,200 x 4130) + ($15,400 x 1920)] - [($10,400 x 23805) + ($10,600 x 4130) + ($2,200 x 1920)] - [($42 x 100 x 48) x 50 weeks + ($18 x 42 x 29) x 50 weeks + $30,000 + $14,000] - [$880,000]
= $421,438,800 Monthly amount is calculated by dividing the annual amount by 12.
$421,438,800 / 12 = $35,119,900

198 Annual Net Income
= [(Revenues) - (Cost of Sales)] - [Total Labor Costs] - [Utilities] - [Depreciation]
= [($15,400 x 15414) + ($22,000 x 4514) + ($8,800 x 1755)] - [($3,500 x 15414) + ($3,600 x 4514) + ($900 x 1755)] - [($33 x 70 x 33) x 50 weeks + ($15 x 33 x 20) x 50 weeks + $24,000 + $11,000] - [$700,000] - [($1,750,000 / 66) + ($875,000 / 44)]
= $275,260,798

199 Annual Cash flow
= (Net Income excluding depreciation) - Tax
= [(Revenues) - (Cost of Sales)] - [Total Labor Costs] - [Utilities] - Tax
= [($29,400 x 29491) + ($42,000 x 8591) + ($16,800 x 3355)] - [($3,500 x 29491) + ($3,600 x 8591) + ($900 x 3355)] - [($33 x 70 x 33) x 50 weeks + ($15 x 33 x 20) x 50 weeks + $24,000 + $11,000] - [700000] - $399,705,005
= $742,309,295

200 Annual Net Income
= [(Revenues) - (Cost of Sales)] - [Total Labor Costs] - [Insurance costs] - [Depreciation]
= [($21,600 x 21677) + ($28,800 x 3377) + ($14,400 x 1595)] - [($13,900 x 21677) + ($14,000 x 3377) + ($2,700 x 1595)] - [($45 x 110 x 53) x 50 weeks + ($19 x 45 x 32) x 50 weeks + $32,000 + $15,000] - [$940,000] - [($2,350,000 / 72) + ($1,175,000 / 48)]
= $220,024,382 Monthly amount is calculated by dividing the annual amount by 12.
$220,024,382 / 12 = $18,335,365

AUDIT SOLUTIONS

1   C: Valuation

2   C: The audit client has increased the headcount of the accounting department in the past year.. The elimination of understaffing can decrease the potential for accounting errors, and so this decreases inherent risk.

3   A: Vouch a sample of purchase orders and invoices from the first and last month of the fiscal year.

4   A: If inherent risk is high, control risk is low and audit risk is medium, then detection risk is medium. $0.11 / (0.66 \times 0.33) = 0.5$

5   B: If inherent risk is low, control risk is low and detection risk is medium, then audit risk is low. $0.33 \times 0.33 \times 0.5 = 0.05$

6   B: If inherent risk is high, control risk is medium and detection risk is high, then audit risk is high. $0.66 \times 0.5 \times 0.66 = 0.22$

7   D: Perform an inventory count and indicate which items have been in stock for longer than one year

8   C: Audit risk is equal to inherent risk multiplied by control risk multiplied by detection risk. In order for audit risk to remain unchanged when control risk has increased, detection risk can be lowered through the use of additional substantive testing.

9   C: Accuracy

10   A: Perform an inventory count and compare results to a list of inventory

11   B: The financial institution has begun to invest in derivative investments which involve complex contractual arrangements.. The acquisition of assets that involve complex accounting regulations increases the company's inherent risk, since relatively few accountants are familiar with these assets and since specialists will be required.

12   A: If inherent risk is medium, control risk is medium and audit risk is medium, then detection risk is medium. $0.13 / (0.5 \times 0.5) = 0.5$

13   B: The company has experienced a decrease in accounts receivable, which used to require significant estimations in order to quantify the amounts that were collectible.. The elimination of assets that are valued using professional judgment and management estimations decreases the company's inherent risk.

14   B: Existence

15   C: The media organization has sold all of its largest license agreements and goodwill assets. . By eliminating intangible assets which can create difficulties in valuation, inherent risk is decreased.

16   B: If inherent risk is low, control risk is medium and audit risk is low, then detection risk is low. $0.05 / (0.33 \times 0.5) = 0.33$

17 C: If inherent risk is medium, control risk is low and audit risk is low, then detection risk is low. 0.05 / (0.5 x 0.33) = 0.33

18 A: If inherent risk is medium, control risk is high and detection risk is low, then audit risk is medium. 0.5 x 0.66 x 0.33 = 0.11

19 A: If control risk increases, then this will cause detection risk to decrease. Substantive testing is increased when internal controls are found to be not reliable. This means that detection risk is reduced. Detection risk is calculated as audit risk divided by the product of control risk and inherent risk.

20 B: If inherent risk is high, control risk is low and audit risk is medium-high, then detection risk is high. 0.14 / (0.66 x 0.33) = 0.66

21 B: Rights

22 B: Check the price that would be incurred to obtain a similar asset from the market

23 C: If inherent risk is low, control risk is high and detection risk is low, then audit risk is medium-low. 0.33 x 0.66 x 0.33 = 0.07

24 D: Cut-off

25 B: If inherent risk is low, control risk is medium and detection risk is low, then audit risk is low. 0.33 x 0.5 x 0.33 = 0.05

26 B: During internal control testing, several major control weaknesses that were noted during last year's audit have been mitigated by adding additional internal controls.. Control risk has decreased, and so the auditors will place more reliance on internal controls. This will result in less substantive testing, which increases detection risk.

27 C: Rights

28 D: Perform a reasonability analysis.

29 B: Perform an inventory count on items that were selected from a list of inventory

30 A: During internal control testing, several major control weaknesses were discovered by the internal audit team.. Control risk has increased, and so substantive testing will increase, which reduces detection risk.

31 C: Vouch accounting records to the underlying third party documentation

32 C: If inherent risk is low, control risk is medium and audit risk is medium-low, then detection risk is medium. 0.08 / (0.33 x 0.5) = 0.5

33 B: Send confirmations to the organizations to whom the outstanding balances are owing

34 B: If inherent risk is medium, control risk is high and audit risk is medium, then detection risk is low. 0.11 / (0.5 x 0.66) = 0.33

35   C: If inherent risk is medium, control risk is low and detection risk is low, then audit risk is low. 0.5 x 0.33 x 0.33 = 0.05

36   A: The media organization has purchased smaller media agencies which includes the purchase of very costly licenses and goodwill assets. . The acquisition of intangible assets can create difficulties in valuation, and so this increases the inherent risk.

37   C: Accuracy

38   B: If inherent risk is high, control risk is high and audit risk is medium-high, then detection risk is low. 0.14 / (0.66 x 0.66) = 0.33

39   C: If inherent risk is medium, control risk is high and detection risk is high, then audit risk is high. 0.5 x 0.66 x 0.66 = 0.22

40   C: The company's information system which was fully implemented two years ago has continued to be used in the past year.. Since the information system has been well established, the control risk is low, and so the auditors are able to increase their reliance on internal controls.

41   B: If inherent risk is high, control risk is medium and detection risk is medium, then audit risk is medium-high. 0.66 x 0.5 x 0.5 = 0.17

42   B: Existence

43   C: Completeness

44   B: Within the past year, the level of debt that is owed by the organization has remained low, which is consistent with prior years.. Low levels of debt can be an indication that management is free from bias, and so this decreases inherent risk.

45   D: Audit risk is equal to inherent risk multiplied by control risk multiplied by detection risk. In order for audit risk to remain unchanged when control risk has decreased, detection risk can be raised through the use of less substantive testing and more control testing.

46   B: Valuation

47   A: The internal audit reports reveal that mitigating controls have been added and have succeeded in preventing theft of company assets for the past three years. . The prevention and reduction of illegal acts are an indication that the company's inherent risk has decreased.

48   B: The company has experienced an increase in accounts receivable, which involves estimations to quantify the amounts that are likely to be collectible.. The acquisition of assets that are valued using professional judgment and management estimations increases the company's inherent risk.

49   C: If inherent risk is low, control risk is low and detection risk is low, then audit risk is low. 0.33 x 0.33 x 0.33 = 0.04

50   B: If inherent risk is high, control risk is low and detection risk is high, then audit risk is medium-high. 0.66 x 0.33 x 0.66 = 0.14

51   C: If inherent risk is high, control risk is medium and audit risk is medium, then detection risk is low. 0.11 / (0.66 x 0.5) = 0.33

52   C: Accuracy

53   C: The audit client has reduced the headcount in the accounting department in the past year.. Understaffing can increase the potential for accounting errors, and so this increases inherent risk.

54   A: If inherent risk is medium, control risk is medium and audit risk is medium-low, then detection risk is low. 0.08 / (0.5 x 0.5) = 0.33

55   B: Audit risk is equal to inherent risk multiplied by control risk multiplied by detection risk. In order for audit risk to remain unchanged when inherent risk has increased, detection risk can be lowered through the use of additional substantive testing.

56   B: Send confirmations to customers that have balances owing

57   D: Perform a reasonability analysis by comparing the accounting records to the bank account, and by reconciling the cash flow.

58   A: The economy is currently experiencing a downturn, however this audit client is exhibiting record high profits.. If a company is prospering while the industry is not performing well, this is an indication of increased inherent risk.

59   A: Audit risk is equal to inherent risk multiplied by control risk multiplied by detection risk. In order for audit risk to remain unchanged when inherent risk has decreased, detection risk can be raised through the use of less substantive testing and more control testing.

60   B: Send confirmations to the organizations to whom the outstanding balances are owing

61   B: If inherent risk is low, control risk is high and audit risk is medium-high, then detection risk is high. 0.14 / (0.33 x 0.66) = 0.66

62   A: If control risk increases, then this will cause substantive testing to increase. Substantive testing is increased when internal controls are found to be not reliable.

63   C: Management has decided to cancel the profit sharing plan which paid a bonus to staff members based on the company's performance. The discontinuation of a profit sharing compensation package has the potential to reduce management bias, and so this decreases the company's inherent risk.

64   C: Transactions that comprise the final balance are checked against the originating documents

65   A: Perform analytics by calculating if Inventory Turnover has increased or decreased

66   D: Rights

67 B: The company's information system has been changed in the past year. Control risk has increased, and so substantive testing will increase, which reduces detection risk. This reduction in detection risk offsets the increase in control risk, which results in no change to the audit risk.

68 C: If inherent risk is medium, control risk is high and audit risk is medium-high, then detection risk is medium. $0.17 / (0.5 \times 0.66) = 0.5$

69 B: If inherent risk is high, control risk is high and audit risk is high, then detection risk is medium. $0.22 / (0.66 \times 0.66) = 0.5$

70 B: Perform analytics by calculating if Day Sales Inventory has increased or decreased

71 B: Completeness

72 B: Check third party documentation to verify that the amount is owing.

73 B: If inherent risk is low, control risk is medium and audit risk is medium, then detection risk is high. $0.11 / (0.33 \times 0.5) = 0.66$

74 A: If substantive testing increases, then this will cause detection risk to decrease. Substantive testing increases when control risk has been deemed to be high. This means that detection risk is reduced. Detection risk is calculated as audit risk divided by the product of control risk and inherent risk.

75 B: If inherent risk is medium, control risk is medium and detection risk is low, then audit risk is medium-low. $0.5 \times 0.5 \times 0.33 = 0.08$

76 B: If inherent risk is medium, control risk is medium and detection risk is high, then audit risk is medium-high. $0.5 \times 0.5 \times 0.66 = 0.17$

77 A: If inherent risk is medium, control risk is low and audit risk is medium, then detection risk is high. $0.11 / (0.5 \times 0.33) = 0.66$

78 B: If inherent risk is medium, control risk is low and detection risk is medium, then audit risk is medium-low. $0.5 \times 0.33 \times 0.5 = 0.08$

79 C: Within the past year, the level of debt that is owed by the organization has increased significantly.. Major increases in debt creates a management bias, and so this increases inherent risk.

80 B: During internal control testing, several major control weaknesses that were noted during last year's audit have been mitigated by adding additional internal controls.. Since the internal control weaknesses were rectified, the control risk has decreased, and so the auditors are able to increase their reliance on internal controls.

81 B: If inherent risk is high, control risk is low and detection risk is medium, then audit risk is medium. $0.66 \times 0.33 \times 0.5 = 0.11$

82 D: Perform substantive analytics by calculating the number of units that were sold and multiplying by the average per unit sales price for each category of products that are sold.

83 B: If inherent risk decreases, then this will cause audit risk to decrease. Audit risk is equal to inherent risk multiplied by control risk multiplied by detection risk.

84 B: If inherent risk is low, control risk is high and detection risk is high, then audit risk is medium-high. 0.33 x 0.66 x 0.66 = 0.14

85 B: Management has decided to begin paying a bonus to staff members based on the company's performance. The introduction of a profit sharing compensation package has the potential to create management bias, and so this increases the company's inherent risk.

86 D: Valuation

87 C: If inherent risk is low, control risk is high and audit risk is medium-low, then detection risk is low. 0.07 / (0.33 x 0.66) = 0.33

88 D: Completeness

89 B: The economy is currently experiencing a downturn, and this audit client has been affected, as noted by the decrease in net income.. If a company is performing consistently with industry benchmarks, this is an indication of decreased inherent risk.

90 C: Existence

91 A: If inherent risk is medium, control risk is medium and detection risk is medium, then audit risk is medium. 0.5 x 0.5 x 0.5 = 0.13

92 C: During internal control testing, several major control weaknesses were discovered by the internal audit team.. Since the internal controls were found to be insufficient, the control risk is high, and so the auditors are unable to rely on its internal controls.

93 A: Test a sample of customer transactions to see if they appear in the billing system

94 C: Vouch accounting records to the underlying third party purchase order and invoice

95 B: The company's information system has been changed in the past year. Since the information system is new, the control risk is high, and so the auditors are unable to rely on its internal controls.

96 B: If inherent risk is high, control risk is low and detection risk is low, then audit risk is medium-low. 0.66 x 0.33 x 0.33 = 0.07

97 A: In the past year, the audit client finished repaying a contractual debt arrangement which required that their debt was to be repaid in full if certain key financial performance ratios were not maintained. . A company that has eliminated its obligations to maintaining financial performance ratios has reduced management bias, and so this decreases inherent risk.

98 C: If inherent risk is low, control risk is low and audit risk is medium-low, then detection risk is high. 0.07 / (0.33 x 0.33) = 0.66

99 B: Completeness

100 C: If control risk decreases, then this will cause detection risk to increase. Substantive testing is decreased when internal controls are considered to be reliable. This means that detection risk is higher since there will be an increase in control testing. Detection risk is calculated as audit risk divided by the product of control risk and inherent risk.

101 D: Valuation

102 C: If inherent risk is high, control risk is medium and audit risk is high, then detection risk is high. 0.22 / (0.66 x 0.5) = 0.66

103 B: Existence

104 D: Observe that inventory is not moved and double-counted during inventory count

105 C: In the past year, the audit client has signed a contractual agreement which requires that their debt must be repaid in full if certain key financial performance ratios are not maintained. . A company that is contractually obligated to maintain financial performance ratios creates a management bias, and so this increases inherent risk.

106 C: Vouch accounting records to the underlying third party documentation

107 A: Rights

108 D: If control risk decreases, then this will cause substantive testing to decrease. Substantive testing is decreased when internal controls are considered to be reliable.

109 A: Vouch the accounting records by physically locating and examining the assets that are recorded in the ledger.

110 C: The internal audit reports reveal that some employees were found to have stolen company assets in the past year. . Illegal acts are an indication that the company's inherent risk has increased.

111 B: Cut-off

112 C: If inherent risk is low, control risk is low and audit risk is low, then detection risk is low. 0.04 / (0.33 x 0.33) = 0.33

113 A: If inherent risk is medium, control risk is low and audit risk is medium-low, then detection risk is medium. 0.08 / (0.5 x 0.33) = 0.5

114 D: Occurrence

115 B: Send confirmations to customers that have balances owing

116 A: Accuracy

117 B: Vouch a sample of customer transactions from the first and last month of the fiscal year.

118 B: Valuation

119   B: If inherent risk is high, control risk is low and audit risk is medium-low, then detection risk is low. 0.07 / (0.66 x 0.33) = 0.33

120   A: If inherent risk is low, control risk is medium and detection risk is high, then audit risk is medium. 0.33 x 0.5 x 0.66 = 0.11

121   D: Vouch a sample of the accounting records to the third-party delivery documents.

122   B: If inherent risk is low, control risk is low and detection risk is high, then audit risk is medium-low. 0.33 x 0.33 x 0.66 = 0.07

123   C: Completeness

124   C: Perform reasonability checks using substantive analytics

125   C: Completeness

126   C: Perform an inventory count on items that are held on consignment

127   C: If inherent risk is medium, control risk is low and detection risk is high, then audit risk is medium. 0.5 x 0.33 x 0.66 = 0.11

128   C: If inherent risk is low, control risk is high and audit risk is medium, then detection risk is medium. 0.11 / (0.33 x 0.66) = 0.5

129   B: The client has added discontinued their line of diamonds from their collections of fashion accessories. . The elimination of assets which have a tendency to be misappropriated will decrease the inherent risk.

130   C: If inherent risk is medium, control risk is high and audit risk is high, then detection risk is high. 0.22 / (0.5 x 0.66) = 0.66

131   C: If inherent risk is low, control risk is low and audit risk is low, then detection risk is medium. 0.05 / (0.33 x 0.33) = 0.5

132   C: Existence

133   D: If inherent risk increases, then this will cause audit risk to increase. Audit risk is equal to inherent risk multiplied by control risk multiplied by detection risk.

134   C: If inherent risk is low, control risk is medium and detection risk is medium, then audit risk is medium-low. 0.33 x 0.5 x 0.5 = 0.08

135   C: If inherent risk is high, control risk is medium and detection risk is low, then audit risk is medium. 0.66 x 0.5 x 0.33 = 0.11

136   A: The financial institution has sold all of its in derivative investments which had been arranged with complex contractual arrangements.. The elimination of assets that involve complex accounting regulations decreases the company's inherent risk, since the accounting records will be more straight-forward and since it will no longer be necessary to involve specialists.

137 A: If inherent risk is medium, control risk is medium and audit risk is medium-high, then detection risk is high. $0.17 / (0.5 \times 0.5) = 0.66$

138 C: The company's information system which was fully implemented two years ago has continued to be used in the past year.. Control risk has decreased, and so the auditors will place more reliance on internal controls. This will result in less substantive testing, which increases detection risk.

139 A: The company's information system which was fully implemented two years ago has continued to be used in the past year.. Control risk has decreased, and so the auditors will place more reliance on internal controls. This will result in less substantive testing, which increases detection risk. This increase in detection risk offsets the decrease in control risk, which results in no change to the audit risk.

140 B: If inherent risk is high, control risk is high and detection risk is medium, then audit risk is high. $0.66 \times 0.66 \times 0.5 = 0.22$

141 B: Upon accepting a new client, the auditor has contacted the previous auditors and found that the client had no disagreements with the auditors.. The absence of major disagreements with the previous auditors are an indication that the company's inherent risk has decreased.

142 B: Completeness

143 A: If inherent risk is high, control risk is medium and audit risk is medium-high, then detection risk is medium. $0.17 / (0.66 \times 0.5) = 0.5$

144 B: If inherent risk is high, control risk is high and audit risk is high, then detection risk is high. $0.29 / (0.66 \times 0.66) = 0.66$

145 C: Vouch accounting records to the underlying third party purchase order and invoice

146 A: Occurrence

147 B: Upon accepting a new client, the auditor has contacted the previous auditors and found that the client had significant disagreements with the auditors, which lead the client to seek out a different audit firm.. Major disagreements with the previous auditors are an indication that the company's inherent risk has increased.

148 B: The client has added genuine diamonds to their collections of fashion accessories. . The acquisition of assets which have a tendency to be misappropriated will increase the inherent risk.

149 C: If substantive testing decreases, then this will cause detection risk to increase. Substantive testing decreases when control risk has been deemed to be low. This means that detection risk is higher since there will be an increase in control testing. Detection risk is calculated as audit risk divided by the product of control risk and inherent risk.

150 B: If inherent risk is high, control risk is high and detection risk is low, then audit risk is medium-high. $0.66 \times 0.66 \times 0.33 = 0.14$

CASE #1 SOLUTION:

General Journal Entries:

Date: 01/05
      DR Inventory $1356364
            CR Accounts Payable $1356364

Date: 01/08
      DR Accounts Receivable $4069092
            CR Service Revenue $4069092

Date: 01/10
      DR Accounts Receivable $1627636.8
            CR Sales Revenue $1627636.8
      DR Cost of Goods Sold $1356364
            CR Inventory $1356364

Date: 01/24
      DR Sales Returns $32552.74
            CR Accounts Receivable $32552.74
      DR Inventory $27127.28
            CR Cost of Goods Sold $27127.28

Date: 02/01
      DR Rent Expense $339091
            CR Accounts Payable $339091

Date: 02/05
      DR Inventory $1627636.8
            CR Accounts Payable $1627636.8

Date: 02/08
      DR Accounts Receivable $4069092
            CR Service Revenue $4069092

Date: 02/10
      DR Accounts Receivable $2278691.52
            CR Sales Revenue $2278691.52
      DR Cost of Goods Sold $1627636.8
            CR Inventory $1627636.8

Date: 02/15
      DR Salaries Expense $813818.4
            CR Accounts Payable $813818.4

Date: 02/24
      DR Sales Returns $45573.83
            CR Accounts Receivable $45573.83
      DR Inventory $37978.192
            CR Cost of Goods Sold $37978.192

Date: 02/27
    DR Bad Debt Expense $598319.29
        CR Allowance for Doubtful Accounts $598319.29

Date: 02/30
    DR Salaries Expense $813818.4
        CR Accounts Payable $813818.4

Date: 03/01
    DR Rent Expense $339091
        CR Accounts Payable $339091

Date: 03/05
    DR Inventory $2034546
        CR Accounts Payable $2034546

Date: 03/08
    DR Accounts Receivable $4069092
        CR Service Revenue $4069092

Date: 03/10
    DR Accounts Receivable $2848364.4
        CR Sales Revenue $2848364.4
    DR Cost of Goods Sold $2034546
        CR Inventory $2034546

Date: 03/15
    DR Salaries Expense $813818.4
        CR Accounts Payable $813818.4

Date: 03/24
    DR Sales Returns $56967.29
        CR Accounts Receivable $56967.29
    DR Inventory $47472.74
        CR Cost of Goods Sold $47472.74

Date: 03/26
    DR Accounts Payable $8138184
        CR Cash $8138184

Date: 03/27
    DR Bad Debt Expense $941343.74
        CR Allowance for Doubtful Accounts $941343.74

Date: 03/28
    DR Cash $17885531.12
        CR Accounts Receivable $17885531.12

Date: 03/29
    DR Allowance for Doubtful Accounts $1539663.03
        CR Accounts Receivable $1539663.03

Date: 03/30
        DR Salaries Expense $813818.4
            CR Accounts Payable $813818.4

Date: 04/01
        DR Rent Expense $339091
            CR Accounts Payable $339091

Date: 04/05
        DR Inventory $2441455.2
            CR Accounts Payable $2441455.2

Date: 04/06
        DR Equipment $8138184
            CR Accounts Payable $8138184

Date: 04/08
        DR Accounts Receivable $4069092
            CR Service Revenue $4069092

Date: 04/10
        DR Accounts Receivable $3418037.28
            CR Sales Revenue $3418037.28
        DR Cost of Goods Sold $2441455.2
            CR Inventory $2441455.2

Date: 04/15
        DR Salaries Expense $813818.4
            CR Accounts Payable $813818.4

Date: 04/24
        DR Sales Returns $68360.75
            CR Accounts Receivable $68360.75
        DR Inventory $56967.288
            CR Cost of Goods Sold $56967.288

Date: 04/26
        DR Accounts Payable $12546367
            CR Cash $12546367

Date: 04/27
        DR Bad Debt Expense $341022.46
            CR Allowance for Doubtful Accounts $341022.46

Date: 04/28
        DR Cash $6479426.78
            CR Accounts Receivable $6479426.78

Date: 04/29
        DR Allowance for Doubtful Accounts $341022.46
            CR Accounts Receivable $341022.46

Date: 04/30
     DR Salaries Expense $813818.4
       CR Accounts Payable $813818.4

Date: 05/01
     DR Rent Expense $339091
       CR Accounts Payable $339091

Date: 05/05
     DR Inventory $2848364.4
       CR Accounts Payable $2848364.4

Date: 05/06
     DR Depreciation Expense $135636.4
       CR Accum Deprn Eqmt $135636.4

Date: 05/08
     DR Accounts Receivable $4069092
       CR Service Revenue $4069092

Date: 05/10
     DR Accounts Receivable $3987710.16
       CR Sales Revenue $3987710.16
     DR Cost of Goods Sold $2848364.4
       CR Inventory $2848364.4

Date: 05/15
     DR Salaries Expense $813818.4
       CR Accounts Payable $813818.4

Date: 05/24
     DR Sales Returns $79754.2
       CR Accounts Receivable $79754.2
     DR Inventory $66461.836
       CR Cost of Goods Sold $66461.836

Date: 05/26
     DR Accounts Payable $4815092.2
       CR Cash $4815092.2

Date: 05/27
     DR Bad Debt Expense $398852.4
       CR Allowance for Doubtful Accounts $398852.4

Date: 05/28
     DR Cash $7578195.56
       CR Accounts Receivable $7578195.56

Date: 05/29
     DR Allowance for Doubtful Accounts $398852.4
       CR Accounts Receivable $398852.4

Date: 05/30
      DR Salaries Expense $813818.4
           CR Accounts Payable $813818.4

Date: 06/01
      DR Rent Expense $339091
           CR Accounts Payable $339091

Date: 06/03
      DR Cash $101727300
           CR Business Loan $101727300

Date: 06/04
      DR Building $101727300
           CR Cash $101727300

Date: 06/05
      DR Inventory $3255273.6
           CR Accounts Payable $3255273.6

Date: 06/06
      DR Depreciation Expense $135636.4
           CR Accum Deprn Eqmt $135636.4

Date: 06/08
      DR Accounts Receivable $4069092
           CR Service Revenue $4069092

Date: 06/10
      DR Accounts Receivable $4557383.04
           CR Sales Revenue $4557383.04
      DR Cost of Goods Sold $3255273.6
           CR Inventory $3255273.6

Date: 06/15
      DR Salaries Expense $813818.4
           CR Accounts Payable $813818.4

Date: 06/24
      DR Sales Returns $91147.66
           CR Accounts Receivable $91147.66
      DR Inventory $75956.384
           CR Cost of Goods Sold $75956.384

Date: 06/26
      DR Accounts Payable $5222001.4
           CR Cash $5222001.4

Date: 06/27
      DR Bad Debt Expense $426766.37
           CR Allowance for Doubtful Accounts $426766.37

Date: 06/28
  DR Cash $8108561.01
    CR Accounts Receivable $8108561.01

Date: 06/29
  DR Allowance for Doubtful Accounts $426766.37
    CR Accounts Receivable $426766.37

Date: 06/30
  DR Salaries Expense $813818.4
    CR Accounts Payable $813818.4

Date: 07/01
  DR Cash $20345460
    CR Owner's Equity $20345460

Date: 07/02
  DR Interest Expense $423863.75
    CR Cash $423863.75

Date: 07/03
  DR Business Loan $1495855.9
    CR Cash $1495855.9

Date: 07/04
  DR Depreciation Expense $423863.75
    CR Accum Deprn Bldg $423863.75

Date: 07/05
  DR Inventory $3662182.8
    CR Accounts Payable $3662182.8

Date: 07/06
  DR Depreciation Expense $135636.4
    CR Accum Deprn Eqmt $135636.4

Date: 07/08
  DR Accounts Receivable $4069092
    CR Service Revenue $4069092

Date: 07/10
  DR Accounts Receivable $5127055.92
    CR Sales Revenue $5127055.92
  DR Cost of Goods Sold $3662182.8
    CR Inventory $3662182.8

Date: 07/15
  DR Salaries Expense $813818.4
    CR Accounts Payable $813818.4

Date: 07/24
    DR Sales Returns $102541.12
        CR Accounts Receivable $102541.12
    DR Inventory $85450.932
        CR Cost of Goods Sold $85450.932

Date: 07/26
    DR Accounts Payable $5289819.6
        CR Cash $5289819.6

Date: 07/27
    DR Bad Debt Expense $454680.34
        CR Allowance for Doubtful Accounts $454680.34

Date: 07/28
    DR Cash $8638926.46
        CR Accounts Receivable $8638926.46

Date: 07/29
    DR Allowance for Doubtful Accounts $454680.34
        CR Accounts Receivable $454680.34

Date: 07/30
    DR Salaries Expense $813818.4
        CR Accounts Payable $813818.4

Date: 08/02
    DR Interest Expense $417631.02
        CR Cash $417631.02

Date: 08/03
    DR Business Loan $1502088.63
        CR Cash $1502088.63

Date: 08/04
    DR Depreciation Expense $423863.75
        CR Accum Deprn Bldg $423863.75

Date: 08/05
    DR Inventory $4069092
        CR Accounts Payable $4069092

Date: 08/06
    DR Depreciation Expense $135636.4
        CR Accum Deprn Eqmt $135636.4

Date: 08/08
    DR Accounts Receivable $4069092
        CR Service Revenue $4069092

Date: 08/10
      DR Accounts Receivable $5696728.8
          CR Sales Revenue $5696728.8
      DR Cost of Goods Sold $4069092
          CR Inventory $4069092

Date: 08/11
      DR Prepaid Expense $4882910.4
          CR Accounts Payable $4882910.4

Date: 08/15
      DR Salaries Expense $813818.4
          CR Accounts Payable $813818.4

Date: 08/24
      DR Sales Returns $113934.58
          CR Accounts Receivable $113934.58
      DR Inventory $94945.48
          CR Cost of Goods Sold $94945.48

Date: 08/26
      DR Accounts Payable $10579639.2
          CR Cash $10579639.2

Date: 08/27
      DR Bad Debt Expense $482594.31
          CR Allowance for Doubtful Accounts $482594.31

Date: 08/28
      DR Cash $9169291.91
          CR Accounts Receivable $9169291.91

Date: 08/29
      DR Allowance for Doubtful Accounts $482594.31
          CR Accounts Receivable $482594.31

Date: 08/30
      DR Salaries Expense $813818.4
          CR Accounts Payable $813818.4

Date: 09/02
      DR Interest Expense $411372.31
          CR Cash $411372.31

Date: 09/03
      DR Business Loan $1508347.33
          CR Cash $1508347.33

Date: 09/04
      DR Depreciation Expense $423863.75
          CR Accum Deprn Bldg $423863.75

Date: 09/05
    DR Inventory $4476001.2
        CR Accounts Payable $4476001.2

Date: 09/06
    DR Depreciation Expense $135636.4
        CR Accum Deprn Eqmt $135636.4

Date: 09/08
    DR Accounts Receivable $4069092
        CR Service Revenue $4069092

Date: 09/10
    DR Accounts Receivable $6266401.68
        CR Sales Revenue $6266401.68
    DR Cost of Goods Sold $4476001.2
        CR Inventory $4476001.2

Date: 09/11
    DR Insurance Expense $406909.2
        CR Prepaid Expense $406909.2

Date: 09/15
    DR Salaries Expense $813818.4
        CR Accounts Payable $813818.4

Date: 09/24
    DR Sales Returns $125328.03
        CR Accounts Receivable $125328.03
    DR Inventory $104440.028
        CR Cost of Goods Sold $104440.028

Date: 09/26
    DR Accounts Payable $6103638
        CR Cash $6103638

Date: 09/27
    DR Bad Debt Expense $510508.28
        CR Allowance for Doubtful Accounts $510508.28

Date: 09/28
    DR Cash $9699657.37
        CR Accounts Receivable $9699657.37

Date: 09/29
    DR Allowance for Doubtful Accounts $510508.28
        CR Accounts Receivable $510508.28

Date: 09/30
    DR Salaries Expense $813818.4
        CR Accounts Payable $813818.4

Date: 10/02
        DR Interest Expense $405087.53
            CR Cash $405087.53

Date: 10/03
        DR Business Loan $1514632.11
            CR Cash $1514632.11

Date: 10/04
        DR Depreciation Expense $423863.75
            CR Accum Deprn Bldg $423863.75

Date: 10/05
        DR Inventory $4882910.4
            CR Accounts Payable $4882910.4

Date: 10/06
        DR Depreciation Expense $135636.4
            CR Accum Deprn Eqmt $135636.4

Date: 10/08
        DR Accounts Receivable $4069092
            CR Service Revenue $4069092

Date: 10/10
        DR Accounts Receivable $6836074.56
            CR Sales Revenue $6836074.56
        DR Cost of Goods Sold $4882910.4
            CR Inventory $4882910.4

Date: 10/11
        DR Insurance Expense $406909.2
            CR Prepaid Expense $406909.2

Date: 10/13
        DR Cash $16276368
            CR Unearned Revenue $16276368

Date: 10/15
        DR Salaries Expense $813818.4
            CR Accounts Payable $813818.4

Date: 10/24
        DR Sales Returns $136721.49
            CR Accounts Receivable $136721.49
        DR Inventory $113934.576
            CR Cost of Goods Sold $113934.576

Date: 10/26
        DR Accounts Payable $6510547.2
            CR Cash $6510547.2

334

Date: 10/27
    DR Bad Debt Expense $538422.25
        CR Allowance for Doubtful Accounts $538422.25

Date: 10/28
    DR Cash $10230022.82
        CR Accounts Receivable $10230022.82

Date: 10/29
    DR Allowance for Doubtful Accounts $538422.25
        CR Accounts Receivable $538422.25

Date: 10/30
    DR Salaries Expense $813818.4
        CR Accounts Payable $813818.4

Date: 11/02
    DR Interest Expense $398776.57
        CR Cash $398776.57

Date: 11/03
    DR Business Loan $1520943.08
        CR Cash $1520943.08

Date: 11/04
    DR Depreciation Expense $423863.75
        CR Accum Deprn Bldg $423863.75

Date: 11/05
    DR Inventory $5289819.6
        CR Accounts Payable $5289819.6

Date: 11/06
    DR Depreciation Expense $135636.4
        CR Accum Deprn Eqmt $135636.4

Date: 11/08
    DR Accounts Receivable $4069092
        CR Service Revenue $4069092

Date: 11/10
    DR Accounts Receivable $7405747.44
        CR Sales Revenue $7405747.44
    DR Cost of Goods Sold $5289819.6
        CR Inventory $5289819.6

Date: 11/11
    DR Insurance Expense $406909.2
        CR Prepaid Expense $406909.2

Date: 11/13
DR Unearned Revenue $16276368
    CR Service Revenue $16276368

Date: 11/15
DR Salaries Expense $813818.4
    CR Accounts Payable $813818.4

Date: 11/20
DR Retained Earnings $4069092
    CR Cash $4069092

Date: 11/24
DR Sales Returns $148114.95
    CR Accounts Receivable $148114.95
DR Inventory $123429.124
    CR Cost of Goods Sold $123429.124

Date: 11/26
DR Accounts Payable $6917456.4
    CR Cash $6917456.4

Date: 11/27
DR Bad Debt Expense $566336.22
    CR Allowance for Doubtful Accounts $566336.22

Date: 11/28
DR Cash $10760388.27
    CR Accounts Receivable $10760388.27

Date: 11/29
DR Allowance for Doubtful Accounts $566336.22
    CR Accounts Receivable $566336.22

Date: 11/30
DR Salaries Expense $813818.4
    CR Accounts Payable $813818.4

Date: 12/02
DR Interest Expense $392439.3
    CR Cash $392439.3

Date: 12/03
DR Business Loan $1527280.34
    CR Cash $1527280.34

Date: 12/04
DR Depreciation Expense $423863.75
    CR Accum Deprn Bldg $423863.75

Date: 12/05
        DR Inventory $5696728.8
                CR Accounts Payable $5696728.8

Date: 12/06
        DR Depreciation Expense $135636.4
                CR Accum Deprn Eqmt $135636.4

Date: 12/08
        DR Accounts Receivable $4069092
                CR Service Revenue $4069092

Date: 12/10
        DR Accounts Receivable $7975420.32
                CR Sales Revenue $7975420.32
        DR Cost of Goods Sold $5696728.8
                CR Inventory $5696728.8

Date: 12/11
        DR Insurance Expense $406909.2
                CR Prepaid Expense $406909.2

Date: 12/15
        DR Salaries Expense $813818.4
                CR Accounts Payable $813818.4

Date: 12/24
        DR Sales Returns $159508.41
                CR Accounts Receivable $159508.41
        DR Inventory $132923.672
                CR Cost of Goods Sold $132923.672

Date: 12/26
        DR Accounts Payable $7324365.6
                CR Cash $7324365.6

Date: 12/27
        DR Bad Debt Expense $594250.2
                CR Allowance for Doubtful Accounts $594250.2

Date: 12/28
        DR Cash $11290753.71
                CR Accounts Receivable $11290753.71

Date: 12/29
        DR Allowance for Doubtful Accounts $594250.2
                CR Accounts Receivable $594250.2

Date: 12/30
        DR Salaries Expense $813818.4
                CR Accounts Payable $813818.4

Date: 12/31
DR Revenue $121970218.87
    CR Retained Earnings $121970218.87
DR Retained Earnings $73830923.908
    CR Expense $73830923.908

GENERAL LEDGER:

Cash

03/26	(8,138,184.00)	
03/28	17,885,531.12	
04/26	(12,546,367.00)	
04/28	6,479,426.78	
05/26	(4,815,092.20)	
05/28	7,578,195.56	
06/03	101,727,300.00	
06/04	(101,727,300.00)	
06/26	(5,222,001.40)	
06/28	8,108,561.01	
07/01	20,345,460.00	
07/02	(423,863.75)	
07/03	(1,495,855.90)	
07/26	(5,289,819.60)	
07/28	8,638,926.46	
08/02	(417,631.02)	
08/03	(1,502,088.63)	
08/26	(10,579,639.20)	
08/28	9,169,291.91	
09/02	(411,372.31)	
09/03	(1,508,347.33)	
09/26	(6,103,638.00)	
09/28	9,699,657.37	
10/02	(405,087.53)	
10/03	(1,514,632.11)	
10/13	16,276,368.00	
10/26	(6,510,547.20)	
10/28	10,230,022.82	
11/02	(398,776.57)	
11/03	(1,520,943.08)	
11/20	(4,069,092.00)	
11/26	(6,917,456.40)	
11/28	10,760,388.27	
12/02	(392,439.30)	
12/03	(1,527,280.34)	
12/26	(7,324,365.60)	
12/28	11,290,753.71	
12/31 BALANCE	47,428,062.54	

Accounts Receivable

01/08	4,069,092.00	
01/10	1,627,636.80	
01/24	(32,552.74)	
02/08	4,069,092.00	
02/10	2,278,691.52	
02/24	(45,573.83)	
03/08	4,069,092.00	
03/10	2,848,364.40	
03/24	(56,967.29)	
03/28	(17,885,531.12)	
03/29	(1,539,663.03)	
04/08	4,069,092.00	
04/10	3,418,037.28	
04/24	(68,360.75)	
04/28	(6,479,426.78)	
04/29	(341,022.46)	
05/08	4,069,092.00	
05/10	3,987,710.16	
05/24	(79,754.20)	
05/28	(7,578,195.56)	
05/29	(398,852.40)	
06/08	4,069,092.00	
06/10	4,557,383.04	
06/24	(91,147.66)	
06/28	(8,108,561.01)	
06/29	(426,766.37)	
07/08	4,069,092.00	
07/10	5,127,055.92	
07/24	(102,541.12)	
07/28	(8,638,926.46)	
07/29	(454,680.34)	
08/08	4,069,092.00	
08/10	5,696,728.80	
08/24	(113,934.58)	
08/28	(9,169,291.91)	
08/29	(482,594.31)	
09/08	4,069,092.00	
09/10	6,266,401.68	
09/24	(125,328.03)	
09/28	(9,699,657.37)	
09/29	(510,508.28)	
10/08	4,069,092.00	
10/10	6,836,074.56	
10/24	(136,721.49)	
10/28	(10,230,022.82)	
10/29	(538,422.25)	
11/08	4,069,092.00	
11/10	7,405,747.44	
11/24	(148,114.95)	

```
11/28          (10,760,388.27)
11/29          (566,336.22)
12/08          4,069,092.00
12/10          7,975,420.32
12/24          (159,508.41)
12/28          (11,290,753.71)
12/29          (594,250.20)
12/31 BALANCE      0.00
```

Allowance for Doubtful Accounts

```
02/27          (598,319.29)
03/27          (941,343.74)
03/29          1,539,663.03
04/27          (341,022.46)
04/29          341,022.46
05/27          (398,852.40)
05/29          398,852.40
06/27          (426,766.37)
06/29          426,766.37
07/27          (454,680.34)
07/29          454,680.34
08/27          (482,594.31)
08/29          482,594.31
09/27          (510,508.28)
09/29          510,508.28
10/27          (538,422.25)
10/29          538,422.25
11/27          (566,336.22)
11/29          566,336.22
12/27          (594,250.20)
12/29          594,250.20
12/31 BALANCE      0.00
```

Inventory

01/05	1,356,364.00	
01/10	(1,356,364.00)	
01/24	27,127.28	
02/05	1,627,636.80	
02/10	(1,627,636.80)	
02/24	37,978.19	
03/05	2,034,546.00	
03/10	(2,034,546.00)	
03/24	47,472.74	
04/05	2,441,455.20	
04/10	(2,441,455.20)	
04/24	56,967.29	
05/05	2,848,364.40	
05/10	(2,848,364.40)	
05/24	66,461.84	
06/05	3,255,273.60	
06/10	(3,255,273.60)	
06/24	75,956.38	
07/05	3,662,182.80	
07/10	(3,662,182.80)	
07/24	85,450.93	
08/05	4,069,092.00	
08/10	(4,069,092.00)	
08/24	94,945.48	
09/05	4,476,001.20	
09/10	(4,476,001.20)	
09/24	104,440.03	
10/05	4,882,910.40	
10/10	(4,882,910.40)	
10/24	113,934.58	
11/05	5,289,819.60	
11/10	(5,289,819.60)	
11/24	123,429.12	
12/31 BALANCE	834,163.86	

Equipment

04/06	8,138,184.00	
12/31 BALANCE	8,138,184.00	

Accum Deprn Eqmt

05/06	(135,636.40)	
06/06	(135,636.40)	
07/06	(135,636.40)	
08/06	(135,636.40)	
09/06	(135,636.40)	
10/06	(135,636.40)	
11/06	(135,636.40)	
12/06	(135,636.40)	
12/31 BALANCE	(1,085,091.20)	

Building
        06/04   101,727,300.00
        12/31 BALANCE   101,727,300.00

Accum Deprn Bldg
        07/04   (423,863.75)
        08/04   (423,863.75)
        09/04   (423,863.75)
        10/04   (423,863.75)
        11/04   (423,863.75)
        12/04   (423,863.75)
        12/31 BALANCE   (2,543,182.50)

Prepaid Expense
        08/11   4,882,910.40
        09/11   (406,909.20)
        10/11   (406,909.20)
        11/11   (406,909.20)
        12/11   (406,909.20)
        12/31 BALANCE   3,255,273.60

Accounts Payable

Date	Amount
01/05	(1,356,364.00)
02/01	(339,091.00)
02/05	(1,627,636.80)
02/15	(813,818.40)
02/30	(813,818.40)
03/01	(339,091.00)
03/05	(2,034,546.00)
03/15	(813,818.40)
03/26	8,138,184.00
03/30	(813,818.40)
04/01	(339,091.00)
04/05	(2,441,455.20)
04/06	(8,138,184.00)
04/15	(813,818.40)
04/26	12,546,367.00
04/30	(813,818.40)
05/01	(339,091.00)
05/05	(2,848,364.40)
05/15	(813,818.40)
05/26	4,815,092.20
05/30	(813,818.40)
06/01	(339,091.00)
06/05	(3,255,273.60)
06/15	(813,818.40)
06/26	5,222,001.40
06/30	(813,818.40)
07/05	(3,662,182.80)
07/15	(813,818.40)
07/26	5,289,819.60
07/30	(813,818.40)
08/05	(4,069,092.00)
08/11	(4,882,910.40)
08/15	(813,818.40)
08/26	10,579,639.20
08/30	(813,818.40)
09/05	(4,476,001.20)
09/15	(813,818.40)
09/26	6,103,638.00
09/30	(813,818.40)
10/05	(4,882,910.40)
10/15	(813,818.40)
10/26	6,510,547.20
10/30	(813,818.40)
11/05	(5,289,819.60)
11/15	(813,818.40)
11/26	6,917,456.40
11/30	(813,818.40)
12/05	(5,696,728.80)
12/15	(813,818.40)

```
         12/26      7,324,365.60
         12/31 BALANCE    0.00

Business Loan
         06/03      (101,727,300.00)
         07/03      1,495,855.90
         08/03      1,502,088.63
         09/03      1,508,347.33
         10/03      1,514,632.11
         11/03      1,520,943.08
         12/03      1,527,280.34
         12/31 BALANCE    (92,658,152.61)

Unearned Revenue
         10/13      (16,276,368.00)
         11/13      16,276,368.00
         12/31 BALANCE    0.00

Retained Earnings
         11/20      4,069,092.00
         12/31      (48,139,294.96)
         12/31 BALANCE    (44,070,202.96)

Owner's Equity
         07/01      (20,345,460.00)
         12/31 BALANCE    (20,345,460.00)


         Service Revenue
         01/08      (4,069,092.00)
         02/08      (4,069,092.00)
         03/08      (4,069,092.00)
         04/08      (4,069,092.00)
         05/08      (4,069,092.00)
         06/08      (4,069,092.00)
         07/08      (4,069,092.00)
         08/08      (4,069,092.00)
         09/08      (4,069,092.00)
         10/08      (4,069,092.00)
         11/08      (4,069,092.00)
         11/13      (16,276,368.00)
         12/08      (4,069,092.00)
         12/31      65,105,472.00
         12/31 BALANCE    0.00
```

Sales Revenue

01/10	(1,627,636.80)
02/10	(2,278,691.52)
03/10	(2,848,364.40)
04/10	(3,418,037.28)
05/10	(3,987,710.16)
06/10	(4,557,383.04)
07/10	(5,127,055.92)
08/10	(5,696,728.80)
09/10	(6,266,401.68)
10/10	(6,836,074.56)
11/10	(7,405,747.44)
12/10	(7,975,420.32)
12/31	58,025,251.92
12/31 BALANCE	0.00

Sales Returns

01/24	32,552.74
02/24	45,573.83
03/24	56,967.29
04/24	68,360.75
05/24	79,754.20
06/24	91,147.66
07/24	102,541.12
08/24	113,934.58
09/24	125,328.03
10/24	136,721.49
11/24	148,114.95
12/24	159,508.41
12/31	(1,160,505.05)
12/31 BALANCE	0.00

Cost of Goods Sold

Date	Amount
01/10	1,356,364.00
01/24	(27,127.28)
02/10	1,627,636.80
02/24	(37,978.19)
03/10	2,034,546.00
03/24	(47,472.74)
04/10	2,441,455.20
04/24	(56,967.29)
05/10	2,848,364.40
05/24	(66,461.84)
06/10	3,255,273.60
06/24	(75,956.38)
07/10	3,662,182.80
07/24	(85,450.93)
08/10	4,069,092.00
08/24	(94,945.48)
09/10	4,476,001.20
09/24	(104,440.03)
10/10	4,882,910.40
10/24	(113,934.58)
11/10	5,289,819.60
11/24	(123,429.12)
12/10	5,696,728.80
12/24	(132,923.67)
12/31	(40,673,287.27)
12/31 BALANCE	0.00

Salaries Expense

02/15	813,818.40	
02/30	813,818.40	
03/15	813,818.40	
03/30	813,818.40	
04/15	813,818.40	
04/30	813,818.40	
05/15	813,818.40	
05/30	813,818.40	
06/15	813,818.40	
06/30	813,818.40	
07/15	813,818.40	
07/30	813,818.40	
08/15	813,818.40	
08/30	813,818.40	
09/15	813,818.40	
09/30	813,818.40	
10/15	813,818.40	
10/30	813,818.40	
11/15	813,818.40	
11/30	813,818.40	
12/15	813,818.40	
12/30	813,818.40	
12/31	(17,904,004.80)	
12/31 BALANCE	0.00	

Rent Expense

02/01	339,091.00	
03/01	339,091.00	
04/01	339,091.00	
05/01	339,091.00	
06/01	339,091.00	
12/31	(1,695,455.00)	
12/31 BALANCE	0.00	

Bad Debt Expense

02/27	598,319.29	
03/27	941,343.74	
04/27	341,022.46	
05/27	398,852.40	
06/27	426,766.37	
07/27	454,680.34	
08/27	482,594.31	
09/27	510,508.28	
10/27	538,422.25	
11/27	566,336.22	
12/27	594,250.20	
12/31	(5,853,095.86)	
12/31 BALANCE	0.00	

Depreciation Expense

05/06	135,636.40	
06/06	135,636.40	
07/04	423,863.75	
07/06	135,636.40	
08/04	423,863.75	
08/06	135,636.40	
09/04	423,863.75	
09/06	135,636.40	
10/04	423,863.75	
10/06	135,636.40	
11/04	423,863.75	
11/06	135,636.40	
12/04	423,863.75	
12/06	135,636.40	
12/31	(3,628,273.70)	
12/31 BALANCE	0.00	

Insurance Expense

09/11	406,909.20	
10/11	406,909.20	
11/11	406,909.20	
12/11	406,909.20	
12/31	(1,627,636.80)	
12/31 BALANCE	0.00	

Interest Expense

07/02	423,863.75	
08/02	417,631.02	
09/02	411,372.31	
10/02	405,087.53	
11/02	398,776.57	
12/02	392,439.30	
12/31	(2,449,170.48)	
12/31 BALANCE	0.00	

TRIAL BALANCE BEFORE AND AFTER CLOSING ENTRY:

Cash	47,428,062.54	47,428,062.54
Accounts Receivable	0.00	0.00
Allowance for Doubtful Accounts	0.00	0.00
Inventory	967,087.53	967,087.53
Equipment	8,138,184.00	8,138,184.00
Accum Deprn Eqmt	(1,085,091.20)	(1,085,091.20)
Building	101,727,300.00	101,727,300.00
Accum Deprn Bldg	(2,543,182.50)	(2,543,182.50)
Prepaid Expense	3,255,273.60	3,255,273.60
Accounts Payable	(813,818.40)	(813,818.40)
Business Loan	(92,658,152.61)	(92,658,152.61)
Unearned Revenue	0.00	0.00
Retained Earnings	0.00	(44,070,202.96)
Owner's Equity	(20,345,460.00)	(20,345,460.00)
Service Revenue	(65,105,472.00)	0.00
Sales Revenue	(58,025,251.92)	0.00
Sales Returns	1,160,505.05	0.00
Cost of Goods Sold	40,673,287.27	0.00
Salaries Expense	17,904,004.80	0.00
Rent Expense	1,695,455.00	0.00
Bad Debt Expense	5,853,095.86	0.00
Depreciation Expense	3,628,273.70	0.00
Insurance Expense	1,627,636.80	0.00
Interest Expense	2,449,170.48	0.00

FINANCIAL STATEMENTS

Balance Sheet (Dec 31)

ASSETS

Cash	47,428,062.54
Accounts Receivable	0.00
Inventory	967,087.53
Prepaids	3,255,273.60
Property Plant & Equipment	109,865,484.00
Accumulated Depreciation Expense	(3,628,273.70)
Net Property Plant & Equipment	106,237,210.30
Total Assets	157,887,633.97

LIABILITIES

Accounts Payable	813,818.40
Loans	92,658,152.61
Total Liabilities	93,471,971.01

SHAREHOLDER'S EQUITY

Owner's Equity	20,345,460.00
Retained Earnings	44,070,202.96
Total Shareholder's Equity	64,415,662.96
Total Liabilities & Shareholder's Equity	157,887,633.97

Income Statement (Jan 1 to Dec 31)

REVENUE

Services	65,105,472.00
Sales	58,025,251.92
Sales Returns	(1,160,505.05)
Total Revenue	121,970,218.87

EXPENSES

Cost of Goods Sold	40,673,287.27
Salaries Expense	17,904,004.80
Rent Expense	1,695,455.00
Bad Debts	5,853,095.86
Depreciation Expense	3,628,273.70
Insurance	1,627,636.80
Interest	2,449,170.48
Total Expenses	73,830,923.91
Net Income	48,139,294.96

Statement of Retained Earnings (Jan 1 to Dec 31)

Opening Balance	0.00
Net Income	48,139,294.96
Dividends Paid	(4,069,092.00)
Closing Balance	44,070,202.96

Statement of Cash Flows (Jan 1 to Dec31)

Beginning Cash Balance	0.00
Operating Activities	
Net Income	48,139,294.96
Depreciation Expense	3,628,273.70
Increase in Prepaid Expenses	(3,255,273.60)
Increase in Accounts Payable	813,818.40
Increase in Inventory	(967,087.53)
Investment Activities	
PPE Purchases	(109,865,484.00)
Financing Activities	
Bank Loan	101,727,300.00
Bank Loan repayment of principal	(9,069,147.39)
Owner Investment	20,345,460.00
Dividend Paid to Owner	(4,069,092.00)
Net Cash Flows	47,428,062.54
Ending Cash Balance	47,428,062.54

CASE #2 SOLUTION:

General Journal Entries:

Date: 01/05
      DR Inventory $1532691
           CR Accounts Payable $1532691

Date: 01/08
      DR Accounts Receivable $4598073
           CR Service Revenue $4598073

Date: 01/10
      DR Accounts Receivable $1839229.2
           CR Sales Revenue $1839229.2
      DR Cost of Goods Sold $1532691
           CR Inventory $1532691

Date: 01/24
      DR Sales Returns $36784.58
           CR Accounts Receivable $36784.58
      DR Inventory $30653.82
           CR Cost of Goods Sold $30653.82

Date: 02/01
      DR Rent Expense $383172.75
           CR Accounts Payable $383172.75

Date: 02/05
      DR Inventory $1839229.2
           CR Accounts Payable $1839229.2

Date: 02/08
      DR Accounts Receivable $4598073
           CR Service Revenue $4598073

Date: 02/10
      DR Accounts Receivable $2574920.88
           CR Sales Revenue $2574920.88
      DR Cost of Goods Sold $1839229.2
           CR Inventory $1839229.2

Date: 02/15
      DR Salaries Expense $919614.6
           CR Accounts Payable $919614.6

Date: 02/24
      DR Sales Returns $51498.42
           CR Accounts Receivable $51498.42
      DR Inventory $42915.348
           CR Cost of Goods Sold $42915.348

Date: 02/27
      DR Bad Debt Expense $676100.65
          CR Allowance for Doubtful Accounts $676100.65

Date: 02/30
      DR Salaries Expense $919614.6
          CR Accounts Payable $919614.6

Date: 03/01
      DR Rent Expense $383172.75
          CR Accounts Payable $383172.75

Date: 03/05
      DR Inventory $2299036.5
          CR Accounts Payable $2299036.5

Date: 03/08
      DR Accounts Receivable $4598073
          CR Service Revenue $4598073

Date: 03/10
      DR Accounts Receivable $3218651.1
          CR Sales Revenue $3218651.1
      DR Cost of Goods Sold $2299036.5
          CR Inventory $2299036.5

Date: 03/15
      DR Salaries Expense $919614.6
          CR Accounts Payable $919614.6

Date: 03/24
      DR Sales Returns $64373.02
          CR Accounts Receivable $64373.02
      DR Inventory $53644.185
          CR Cost of Goods Sold $53644.185

Date: 03/26
      DR Accounts Payable $9196146
          CR Cash $9196146

Date: 03/27
      DR Bad Debt Expense $1063718.21
          CR Allowance for Doubtful Accounts $1063718.21

Date: 03/28
      DR Cash $20210645.95
          CR Accounts Receivable $20210645.95

Date: 03/29
      DR Allowance for Doubtful Accounts $1739818.86
          CR Accounts Receivable $1739818.86

Date: 03/30
  DR Salaries Expense $919614.6
    CR Accounts Payable $919614.6

Date: 04/01
  DR Rent Expense $383172.75
    CR Accounts Payable $383172.75

Date: 04/05
  DR Inventory $2758843.8
    CR Accounts Payable $2758843.8

Date: 04/06
  DR Equipment $9196146
    CR Accounts Payable $9196146

Date: 04/08
  DR Accounts Receivable $4598073
    CR Service Revenue $4598073

Date: 04/10
  DR Accounts Receivable $3862381.32
    CR Sales Revenue $3862381.32
  DR Cost of Goods Sold $2758843.8
    CR Inventory $2758843.8

Date: 04/15
  DR Salaries Expense $919614.6
    CR Accounts Payable $919614.6

Date: 04/24
  DR Sales Returns $77247.63
    CR Accounts Receivable $77247.63
  DR Inventory $64373.022
    CR Cost of Goods Sold $64373.022

Date: 04/26
  DR Accounts Payable $14177391.75
    CR Cash $14177391.75

Date: 04/27
  DR Bad Debt Expense $385355.3
    CR Allowance for Doubtful Accounts $385355.3

Date: 04/28
  DR Cash $7321750.74
    CR Accounts Receivable $7321750.74

Date: 04/29
  DR Allowance for Doubtful Accounts $385355.3
    CR Accounts Receivable $385355.3

Date: 04/30
  DR Salaries Expense $919614.6
      CR Accounts Payable $919614.6

Date: 05/01
  DR Rent Expense $383172.75
      CR Accounts Payable $383172.75

Date: 05/05
  DR Inventory $3218651.1
      CR Accounts Payable $3218651.1

Date: 05/06
  DR Depreciation Expense $153269.1
      CR Accum Deprn Eqmt $153269.1

Date: 05/08
  DR Accounts Receivable $4598073
      CR Service Revenue $4598073

Date: 05/10
  DR Accounts Receivable $4506111.54
      CR Sales Revenue $4506111.54
  DR Cost of Goods Sold $3218651.1
      CR Inventory $3218651.1

Date: 05/15
  DR Salaries Expense $919614.6
      CR Accounts Payable $919614.6

Date: 05/24
  DR Sales Returns $90122.23
      CR Accounts Receivable $90122.23
  DR Inventory $75101.859
      CR Cost of Goods Sold $75101.859

Date: 05/26
  DR Accounts Payable $5441053.05
      CR Cash $5441053.05

Date: 05/27
  DR Bad Debt Expense $450703.12
      CR Allowance for Doubtful Accounts $450703.12

Date: 05/28
  DR Cash $8563359.19
      CR Accounts Receivable $8563359.19

Date: 05/29
  DR Allowance for Doubtful Accounts $450703.12
      CR Accounts Receivable $450703.12

Date: 05/30
  DR Salaries Expense $919614.6
    CR Accounts Payable $919614.6

Date: 06/01
  DR Rent Expense $383172.75
    CR Accounts Payable $383172.75

Date: 06/03
  DR Cash $114951825
    CR Business Loan $114951825

Date: 06/04
  DR Building $114951825
    CR Cash $114951825

Date: 06/05
  DR Inventory $3678458.4
    CR Accounts Payable $3678458.4

Date: 06/06
  DR Depreciation Expense $153269.1
    CR Accum Deprn Eqmt $153269.1

Date: 06/08
  DR Accounts Receivable $4598073
    CR Service Revenue $4598073

Date: 06/10
  DR Accounts Receivable $5149841.76
    CR Sales Revenue $5149841.76
  DR Cost of Goods Sold $3678458.4
    CR Inventory $3678458.4

Date: 06/15
  DR Salaries Expense $919614.6
    CR Accounts Payable $919614.6

Date: 06/24
  DR Sales Returns $102996.84
    CR Accounts Receivable $102996.84
  DR Inventory $85830.696
    CR Cost of Goods Sold $85830.696

Date: 06/26
  DR Accounts Payable $5900860.35
    CR Cash $5900860.35

Date: 06/27
  DR Bad Debt Expense $482245.9
    CR Allowance for Doubtful Accounts $482245.9

Date: 06/28
        DR Cash $9162672.02
            CR Accounts Receivable $9162672.02

Date: 06/29
        DR Allowance for Doubtful Accounts $482245.9
            CR Accounts Receivable $482245.9

Date: 06/30
        DR Salaries Expense $919614.6
            CR Accounts Payable $919614.6

Date: 07/01
        DR Cash $22990365
            CR Owner's Equity $22990365

Date: 07/02
        DR Interest Expense $478965.94
            CR Cash $478965.94

Date: 07/03
        DR Business Loan $1690316.81
            CR Cash $1690316.81

Date: 07/04
        DR Depreciation Expense $478965.94
            CR Accum Deprn Bldg $478965.94

Date: 07/05
        DR Inventory $4138265.7
            CR Accounts Payable $4138265.7

Date: 07/06
        DR Depreciation Expense $153269.1
            CR Accum Deprn Eqmt $153269.1

Date: 07/08
        DR Accounts Receivable $4598073
            CR Service Revenue $4598073

Date: 07/10
        DR Accounts Receivable $5793571.98
            CR Sales Revenue $5793571.98
        DR Cost of Goods Sold $4138265.7
            CR Inventory $4138265.7

Date: 07/15
        DR Salaries Expense $919614.6
            CR Accounts Payable $919614.6

Date: 07/24
        DR Sales Returns $115871.44
             CR Accounts Receivable $115871.44
        DR Inventory $96559.533
             CR Cost of Goods Sold $96559.533

Date: 07/26
        DR Accounts Payable $5977494.9
             CR Cash $5977494.9

Date: 07/27
        DR Bad Debt Expense $513788.68
             CR Allowance for Doubtful Accounts $513788.68

Date: 07/28
        DR Cash $9761984.86
             CR Accounts Receivable $9761984.86

Date: 07/29
        DR Allowance for Doubtful Accounts $513788.68
             CR Accounts Receivable $513788.68

Date: 07/30
        DR Salaries Expense $919614.6
             CR Accounts Payable $919614.6

Date: 08/02
        DR Interest Expense $471922.95
             CR Cash $471922.95

Date: 08/03
        DR Business Loan $1697359.8
             CR Cash $1697359.8

Date: 08/04
        DR Depreciation Expense $478965.94
             CR Accum Deprn Bldg $478965.94

Date: 08/05
        DR Inventory $4598073
             CR Accounts Payable $4598073

Date: 08/06
        DR Depreciation Expense $153269.1
             CR Accum Deprn Eqmt $153269.1

Date: 08/08
        DR Accounts Receivable $4598073
             CR Service Revenue $4598073

Date: 08/10
     DR Accounts Receivable $6437302.2
         CR Sales Revenue $6437302.2
     DR Cost of Goods Sold $4598073
         CR Inventory $4598073

Date: 08/11
     DR Prepaid Expense $5517687.6
         CR Accounts Payable $5517687.6

Date: 08/15
     DR Salaries Expense $919614.6
         CR Accounts Payable $919614.6

Date: 08/24
     DR Sales Returns $128746.04
         CR Accounts Receivable $128746.04
     DR Inventory $107288.37
         CR Cost of Goods Sold $107288.37

Date: 08/26
     DR Accounts Payable $11954989.8
         CR Cash $11954989.8

Date: 08/27
     DR Bad Debt Expense $545331.46
         CR Allowance for Doubtful Accounts $545331.46

Date: 08/28
     DR Cash $10361297.7
         CR Accounts Receivable $10361297.7

Date: 08/29
     DR Allowance for Doubtful Accounts $545331.46
         CR Accounts Receivable $545331.46

Date: 08/30
     DR Salaries Expense $919614.6
         CR Accounts Payable $919614.6

Date: 09/02
     DR Interest Expense $464850.62
         CR Cash $464850.62

Date: 09/03
     DR Business Loan $1704432.13
         CR Cash $1704432.13

Date: 09/04
     DR Depreciation Expense $478965.94
         CR Accum Deprn Bldg $478965.94

Date: 09/05
      DR Inventory $5057880.3
            CR Accounts Payable $5057880.3

Date: 09/06
      DR Depreciation Expense $153269.1
            CR Accum Deprn Eqmt $153269.1

Date: 09/08
      DR Accounts Receivable $4598073
            CR Service Revenue $4598073

Date: 09/10
      DR Accounts Receivable $7081032.42
            CR Sales Revenue $7081032.42
      DR Cost of Goods Sold $5057880.3
            CR Inventory $5057880.3

Date: 09/11
      DR Insurance Expense $459807.3
            CR Prepaid Expense $459807.3

Date: 09/15
      DR Salaries Expense $919614.6
            CR Accounts Payable $919614.6

Date: 09/24
      DR Sales Returns $141620.65
            CR Accounts Receivable $141620.65
      DR Inventory $118017.207
            CR Cost of Goods Sold $118017.207

Date: 09/26
      DR Accounts Payable $6897109.5
            CR Cash $6897109.5

Date: 09/27
      DR Bad Debt Expense $576874.24
            CR Allowance for Doubtful Accounts $576874.24

Date: 09/28
      DR Cash $10960610.53
            CR Accounts Receivable $10960610.53

Date: 09/29
      DR Allowance for Doubtful Accounts $576874.24
            CR Accounts Receivable $576874.24

Date: 09/30
      DR Salaries Expense $919614.6
            CR Accounts Payable $919614.6

Date: 10/02
        DR Interest Expense $457748.82
            CR Cash $457748.82

Date: 10/03
        DR Business Loan $1711533.93
            CR Cash $1711533.93

Date: 10/04
        DR Depreciation Expense $478965.94
            CR Accum Deprn Bldg $478965.94

Date: 10/05
        DR Inventory $5517687.6
            CR Accounts Payable $5517687.6

Date: 10/06
        DR Depreciation Expense $153269.1
            CR Accum Deprn Eqmt $153269.1

Date: 10/08
        DR Accounts Receivable $4598073
            CR Service Revenue $4598073

Date: 10/10
        DR Accounts Receivable $7724762.64
            CR Sales Revenue $7724762.64
        DR Cost of Goods Sold $5517687.6
            CR Inventory $5517687.6

Date: 10/11
        DR Insurance Expense $459807.3
            CR Prepaid Expense $459807.3

Date: 10/13
        DR Cash $18392292
            CR Unearned Revenue $18392292

Date: 10/15
        DR Salaries Expense $919614.6
            CR Accounts Payable $919614.6

Date: 10/24
        DR Sales Returns $154495.25
            CR Accounts Receivable $154495.25
        DR Inventory $128746.044
            CR Cost of Goods Sold $128746.044

Date: 10/26
        DR Accounts Payable $7356916.8
            CR Cash $7356916.8

Date: 10/27
DR Bad Debt Expense $608417.02
CR Allowance for Doubtful Accounts $608417.02

Date: 10/28
DR Cash $11559923.37
CR Accounts Receivable $11559923.37

Date: 10/29
DR Allowance for Doubtful Accounts $608417.02
CR Accounts Receivable $608417.02

Date: 10/30
DR Salaries Expense $919614.6
CR Accounts Payable $919614.6

Date: 11/02
DR Interest Expense $450617.43
CR Cash $450617.43

Date: 11/03
DR Business Loan $1718665.32
CR Cash $1718665.32

Date: 11/04
DR Depreciation Expense $478965.94
CR Accum Deprn Bldg $478965.94

Date: 11/05
DR Inventory $5977494.9
CR Accounts Payable $5977494.9

Date: 11/06
DR Depreciation Expense $153269.1
CR Accum Deprn Eqmt $153269.1

Date: 11/08
DR Accounts Receivable $4598073
CR Service Revenue $4598073

Date: 11/10
DR Accounts Receivable $8368492.86
CR Sales Revenue $8368492.86
DR Cost of Goods Sold $5977494.9
CR Inventory $5977494.9

Date: 11/11
DR Insurance Expense $459807.3
CR Prepaid Expense $459807.3

Date: 11/13
> DR Unearned Revenue $18392292
>> CR Service Revenue $18392292

Date: 11/15
> DR Salaries Expense $919614.6
>> CR Accounts Payable $919614.6

Date: 11/20
> DR Retained Earnings $4598073
>> CR Cash $4598073

Date: 11/24
> DR Sales Returns $167369.86
>> CR Accounts Receivable $167369.86
> DR Inventory $139474.881
>> CR Cost of Goods Sold $139474.881

Date: 11/26
> DR Accounts Payable $7816724.1
>> CR Cash $7816724.1

Date: 11/27
> DR Bad Debt Expense $639959.8
>> CR Allowance for Doubtful Accounts $639959.8

Date: 11/28
> DR Cash $12159236.2
>> CR Accounts Receivable $12159236.2

Date: 11/29
> DR Allowance for Doubtful Accounts $639959.8
>> CR Accounts Receivable $639959.8

Date: 11/30
> DR Salaries Expense $919614.6
>> CR Accounts Payable $919614.6

Date: 12/02
> DR Interest Expense $443456.32
>> CR Cash $443456.32

Date: 12/03
> DR Business Loan $1725826.43
>> CR Cash $1725826.43

Date: 12/04
> DR Depreciation Expense $478965.94
>> CR Accum Deprn Bldg $478965.94

Date: 12/05
    DR Inventory $6437302.2
        CR Accounts Payable $6437302.2

Date: 12/06
    DR Depreciation Expense $153269.1
        CR Accum Deprn Eqmt $153269.1

Date: 12/08
    DR Accounts Receivable $4598073
        CR Service Revenue $4598073

Date: 12/10
    DR Accounts Receivable $9012223.08
        CR Sales Revenue $9012223.08
    DR Cost of Goods Sold $6437302.2
        CR Inventory $6437302.2

Date: 12/11
    DR Insurance Expense $459807.3
        CR Prepaid Expense $459807.3

Date: 12/15
    DR Salaries Expense $919614.6
        CR Accounts Payable $919614.6

Date: 12/24
    DR Sales Returns $180244.46
        CR Accounts Receivable $180244.46
    DR Inventory $150203.718
        CR Cost of Goods Sold $150203.718

Date: 12/26
    DR Accounts Payable $8276531.4
        CR Cash $8276531.4

Date: 12/27
    DR Bad Debt Expense $671502.58
        CR Allowance for Doubtful Accounts $671502.58

Date: 12/28
    DR Cash $12758549.04
        CR Accounts Receivable $12758549.04

Date: 12/29
    DR Allowance for Doubtful Accounts $671502.58
        CR Accounts Receivable $671502.58

Date: 12/30
    DR Salaries Expense $919614.6
        CR Accounts Payable $919614.6

Date: 12/31
  DR Revenue $137826318.56
    CR Retained Earnings $137826318.56
  DR Retained Earnings $83428926.647
    CR Expense $83428926.647

GENERAL LEDGER:

Cash

Date	Amount
03/26	(9,196,146.00)
03/28	20,210,645.95
04/26	(14,177,391.75)
04/28	7,321,750.74
05/26	(5,441,053.05)
05/28	8,563,359.19
06/03	114,951,825.00
06/04	(114,951,825.00)
06/26	(5,900,860.35)
06/28	9,162,672.02
07/01	22,990,365.00
07/02	(478,965.94)
07/03	(1,690,316.81)
07/26	(5,977,494.90)
07/28	9,761,984.86
08/02	(471,922.95)
08/03	(1,697,359.80)
08/26	(11,954,989.80)
08/28	10,361,297.70
09/02	(464,850.62)
09/03	(1,704,432.13)
09/26	(6,897,109.50)
09/28	10,960,610.53
10/02	(457,748.82)
10/03	(1,711,533.93)
10/13	18,392,292.00
10/26	(7,356,916.80)
10/28	11,559,923.37
11/02	(450,617.43)
11/03	(1,718,665.32)
11/20	(4,598,073.00)
11/26	(7,816,724.10)
11/28	12,159,236.20

12/02	(443,456.32)	
12/03	(1,725,826.43)	
12/26	(8,276,531.40)	
12/28	12,758,549.04	
12/31 BALANCE		53,593,699.45

Accounts Receivable

01/08	4,598,073.00
01/10	1,839,229.20
01/24	(36,784.58)
02/08	4,598,073.00
02/10	2,574,920.88
02/24	(51,498.42)
03/08	4,598,073.00
03/10	3,218,651.10
03/24	(64,373.02)
03/28	(20,210,645.95)
03/29	(1,739,818.86)
04/08	4,598,073.00
04/10	3,862,381.32
04/24	(77,247.63)
04/28	(7,321,750.74)
04/29	(385,355.30)
05/08	4,598,073.00
05/10	4,506,111.54
05/24	(90,122.23)
05/28	(8,563,359.19)
05/29	(450,703.12)
06/08	4,598,073.00
06/10	5,149,841.76
06/24	(102,996.84)
06/28	(9,162,672.02)
06/29	(482,245.90)
07/08	4,598,073.00
07/10	5,793,571.98
07/24	(115,871.44)
07/28	(9,761,984.86)
07/29	(513,788.68)
08/08	4,598,073.00
08/10	6,437,302.20
08/24	(128,746.04)
08/28	(10,361,297.70)
08/29	(545,331.46)
09/08	4,598,073.00
09/10	7,081,032.42
09/24	(141,620.65)
09/28	(10,960,610.53)
09/29	(576,874.24)
10/08	4,598,073.00

```
10/10    7,724,762.64
10/24    (154,495.25)
10/28    (11,559,923.37)
10/29    (608,417.02)
11/08    4,598,073.00
11/10    8,368,492.86
11/24    (167,369.86)
11/28    (12,159,236.20)
11/29    (639,959.80)
12/08    4,598,073.00
12/10    9,012,223.08
12/24    (180,244.46)
12/28    (12,758,549.04)
12/29    (671,502.58)
12/31 BALANCE          0.00
```

Allowance for Doubtful Accounts

```
02/27    (676,100.65)
03/27    (1,063,718.21)
03/29    1,739,818.86
04/27    (385,355.30)
04/29    385,355.30
05/27    (450,703.12)
05/29    450,703.12
06/27    (482,245.90)
06/29    482,245.90
07/27    (513,788.68)
07/29    513,788.68
08/27    (545,331.46)
08/29    545,331.46
09/27    (576,874.24)
09/29    576,874.24
10/27    (608,417.02)
10/29    608,417.02
11/27    (639,959.80)
11/29    639,959.80
12/27    (671,502.58)
12/29    671,502.58
12/31 BALANCE          0.00
```

Inventory

```
01/05    1,532,691.00
01/10    (1,532,691.00)
01/24    30,653.82
02/05    1,839,229.20
02/10    (1,839,229.20)
02/24    42,915.35
03/05    2,299,036.50
03/10    (2,299,036.50)
03/24    53,644.19
```

```
04/05    2,758,843.80
04/10    (2,758,843.80)
04/24    64,373.02
05/05    3,218,651.10
05/10    (3,218,651.10)
05/24    75,101.86
06/05    3,678,458.40
06/10    (3,678,458.40)
06/24    85,830.70
07/05    4,138,265.70
07/10    (4,138,265.70)
07/24    96,559.53
08/05    4,598,073.00
08/10    (4,598,073.00)
08/24    107,288.37
09/05    5,057,880.30
09/10    (5,057,880.30)
09/24    118,017.21
10/05    5,517,687.60
10/10    (5,517,687.60)
10/24    128,746.04
11/05    5,977,494.90
11/10    (5,977,494.90)
11/24    139,474.88
12/31 BALANCE        942,604.97
```

Equipment
```
04/06    9,196,146.00
12/31 BALANCE        9,196,146.00
```

Accum Deprn Eqmt
```
05/06    (153,269.10)
06/06    (153,269.10)
07/06    (153,269.10)
08/06    (153,269.10)
09/06    (153,269.10)
10/06    (153,269.10)
11/06    (153,269.10)
12/06    (153,269.10)
12/31 BALANCE        (1,226,152.80)
```

Building
```
06/04    114,951,825.00        12/31 BALANCE        114,951,825.00
```

Accum Deprn Bldg
```
07/04    (478,965.94)
08/04    (478,965.94)
09/04    (478,965.94)
10/04    (478,965.94)
11/04    (478,965.94)
```

```
12/04   (478,965.94)
12/31 BALANCE       (2,873,795.64)

Prepaid Expense
       08/11   5,517,687.60
       09/11   (459,807.30)
       10/11   (459,807.30)
       11/11   (459,807.30)
       12/11   (459,807.30)
       12/31 BALANCE       3,678,458.40

Accounts Payable
       01/05   (1,532,691.00)
       02/01   (383,172.75)
       02/05   (1,839,229.20)
       02/15   (919,614.60)
       02/30   (919,614.60)
       03/01   (383,172.75)
       03/05   (2,299,036.50)
       03/15   (919,614.60)
       03/26   9,196,146.00
       03/30   (919,614.60)
       04/01   (383,172.75)
       04/05   (2,758,843.80)
       04/06   (9,196,146.00)
       04/15   (919,614.60)
       04/26   14,177,391.75
       04/30   (919,614.60)
       05/01   (383,172.75)
       05/05   (3,218,651.10)
       05/15   (919,614.60)
       05/26   5,441,053.05
       05/30   (919,614.60)
       06/01   (383,172.75)
       06/05   (3,678,458.40)
       06/15   (919,614.60)
       06/26   5,900,860.35
       06/30   (919,614.60)
       07/05   (4,138,265.70)
       07/15   (919,614.60)
       07/26   5,977,494.90
       07/30   (919,614.60)
       08/05   (4,598,073.00)
       08/11   (5,517,687.60)
       08/15   (919,614.60)
       08/26   11,954,989.80
       08/30   (919,614.60)
       09/05   (5,057,880.30)
       09/15   (919,614.60)
       09/26   6,897,109.50
```

```
09/30    (919,614.60)
10/05    (5,517,687.60)
10/15    (919,614.60)
10/26    7,356,916.80
10/30    (919,614.60)
11/05    (5,977,494.90)
11/15    (919,614.60)
11/26    7,816,724.10
11/30    (919,614.60)
12/05    (6,437,302.20)
12/15    (919,614.60)
12/26    8,276,531.40
12/31 BALANCE        0.00
```

Business Loan
```
06/03    (114,951,825.00)
07/03    1,690,316.81
08/03    1,697,359.80
09/03    1,704,432.13
10/03    1,711,533.93
11/03    1,718,665.32
12/03    1,725,826.43
12/31 BALANCE        (104,703,690.58)
```

Unearned Revenue
```
10/13    (18,392,292.00)
11/13    18,392,292.00
12/31 BALANCE        0.00
```

Retained Earnings
```
11/20    4,598,073.00
12/31    (54,397,391.91)
12/31 BALANCE        (49,799,318.91)
```

Owner's Equity
```
07/01    (22,990,365.00)
12/31 BALANCE        (22,990,365.00)
```

Service Revenue
```
01/08    (4,598,073.00)
02/08    (4,598,073.00)
03/08    (4,598,073.00)
04/08    (4,598,073.00)
05/08    (4,598,073.00)
06/08    (4,598,073.00)
07/08    (4,598,073.00)
08/08    (4,598,073.00)
09/08    (4,598,073.00)
10/08    (4,598,073.00)
11/08    (4,598,073.00)
```

```
11/13    (18,392,292.00)
12/08    (4,598,073.00)
12/31    73,569,168.00
12/31 BALANCE          0.00
```

Sales Revenue
```
01/10    (1,839,229.20)
02/10    (2,574,920.88)
03/10    (3,218,651.10)
04/10    (3,862,381.32)
05/10    (4,506,111.54)
06/10    (5,149,841.76)
07/10    (5,793,571.98)
08/10    (6,437,302.20)
09/10    (7,081,032.42)
10/10    (7,724,762.64)
11/10    (8,368,492.86)
12/10    (9,012,223.08)
12/31    65,568,520.98
12/31 BALANCE          0.00
```

Sales Returns
```
01/24    36,784.58
02/24    51,498.42
03/24    64,373.02
04/24    77,247.63
05/24    90,122.23
06/24    102,996.84
07/24    115,871.44
08/24    128,746.04
09/24    141,620.65
10/24    154,495.25
11/24    167,369.86
12/24    180,244.46
12/31    (1,311,370.42)
12/31 BALANCE          0.00
```

Cost of Goods Sold
```
01/10    1,532,691.00
01/24    (30,653.82)
02/10    1,839,229.20
02/24    (42,915.35)
03/10    2,299,036.50
03/24    (53,644.19)
04/10    2,758,843.80
04/24    (64,373.02)
05/10    3,218,651.10
05/24    (75,101.86)
06/10    3,678,458.40
06/24    (85,830.70)
```

```
07/10    4,138,265.70
07/24    (96,559.53)
08/10    4,598,073.00
08/24    (107,288.37)
09/10    5,057,880.30
09/24    (118,017.21)
10/10    5,517,687.60
10/24    (128,746.04)
11/10    5,977,494.90
11/24    (139,474.88)
12/10    6,437,302.20
12/24    (150,203.72)
12/31    (45,960,805.02)
12/31 BALANCE        (0.01)
```

Salaries Expense
```
02/15    919,614.60
02/30    919,614.60
03/15    919,614.60
03/30    919,614.60
04/15    919,614.60
04/30    919,614.60
05/15    919,614.60
05/30    919,614.60
06/15    919,614.60
06/30    919,614.60
07/15    919,614.60
07/30    919,614.60
08/15    919,614.60
08/30    919,614.60
09/15    919,614.60
09/30    919,614.60
10/15    919,614.60
10/30    919,614.60
11/15    919,614.60
11/30    919,614.60
12/15    919,614.60
12/30    919,614.60
12/31    (20,231,521.20)
12/31 BALANCE        0.00
```

Rent Expense
```
02/01    383,172.75
03/01    383,172.75
04/01    383,172.75
05/01    383,172.75
06/01    383,172.75
12/31    (1,915,863.75)
12/31 BALANCE        0.00
```

Bad Debt Expense
```
       02/27   676,100.65
       03/27   1,063,718.21
       04/27   385,355.30
       05/27   450,703.12
       06/27   482,245.90
       07/27   513,788.68
       08/27   545,331.46
       09/27   576,874.24
       10/27   608,417.02
       11/27   639,959.80
       12/27   671,502.58
       12/31   (6,613,996.96)
       12/31 BALANCE        0.00
```

Depreciation Expense
```
       05/06   153,269.10
       06/06   153,269.10
       07/04   478,965.94
       07/06   153,269.10
       08/04   478,965.94
       08/06   153,269.10
       09/04   478,965.94
       09/06   153,269.10
       10/04   478,965.94
       10/06   153,269.10
       11/04   478,965.94
       11/06   153,269.10
       12/04   478,965.94
       12/06   153,269.10
       12/31   (4,099,948.44)
       12/31 BALANCE        0.00
```

Insurance Expense
```
       09/11   459,807.30
       10/11   459,807.30
       11/11   459,807.30
       12/11   459,807.30
       12/31   (1,839,229.20)
       12/31 BALANCE        0.00
```

Interest Expense
```
       07/02   478,965.94
       08/02   471,922.95
       09/02   464,850.62
       10/02   457,748.82
       11/02   450,617.43
       12/02   443,456.32
       12/31   (2,767,562.08)
       12/31 BALANCE        0.00
```

TRIAL BALANCE BEFORE AND AFTER CLOSING ENTRY:

Cash	53,593,699.45	53,593,699.45
Accounts Receivable	0.00	0.00
Allowance for Doubtful Accounts	0.00	0.00
Inventory	1,092,808.68	1,092,808.68
Equipment	9,196,146.00	9,196,146.00
Accum Deprn Eqmt	(1,226,152.80)	(1,226,152.80)
Building	114,951,825.00	114,951,825.00
Accum Deprn Bldg	(2,873,795.64)	(2,873,795.64)
Prepaid Expense	3,678,458.40	3,678,458.40
Accounts Payable	(919,614.60)	(919,614.60)
Business Loan	(104,703,690.58)	(104,703,690.58)
Unearned Revenue	0.00	0.00
Retained Earnings	0.00	(49,799,318.91)
Owner's Equity	(22,990,365.00)	(22,990,365.00)
Service Revenue	(73,569,168.00)	0.00
Sales Revenue	(65,568,520.98)	0.00
Sales Returns	1,311,370.42	0.00
Cost of Goods Sold	45,960,805.02	0.00
Salaries Expense	20,231,521.20	0.00
Rent Expense	1,915,863.75	0.00
Bad Debt Expense	6,613,996.96	0.00
Depreciation Expense	4,099,948.44	0.00
Insurance Expense	1,839,229.20	0.00
Interest Expense	2,767,562.08	0.00

FINANCIAL STATEMENTS

Balance Sheet (Dec 31)

ASSETS
Cash   53,593,699.45
Accounts Receivable   0.00
Inventory   1,092,808.68
Prepaids   3,678,458.40
Property Plant & Equipment   124,147,971.00
Accumulated Depreciation Expense   (4,099,948.44)
Net Property Plant & Equipment 120,048,022.56
Total Assets   178,412,989.09

LIABILITIES
Accounts Payable   919,614.60
Loans   104,703,690.58
Total Liabilities 105,623,305.18

SHAREHOLDER'S EQUITY
Owner's Equity 22,990,365.00
Retained Earnings   49,799,318.91
Total Shareholder's Equity   72,789,683.91

Total Liabilities & Shareholder's Equity   178,412,989.09

Income Statement (Jan 1 to Dec 31)

REVENUE
Services   73,569,168.00
Sales   65,568,520.98
Sales Returns   (1,311,370.42)
Total Revenue   137,826,318.56

EXPENSES
Cost of Goods Sold   45,960,805.02
Salaries Expense   20,231,521.20
Rent Expense   1,915,863.75
Bad Debts   6,613,996.96
Depreciation Expense   4,099,948.44
Insurance   1,839,229.20
Interest 2,767,562.08
Total Expenses 83,428,926.65

Net Income   54,397,391.91

Statement of Retained Earnings (Jan 1 to Dec 31)

Opening Balance   0.00
Net Income   54,397,391.91
Dividends Paid (4,598,073.00)
Closing Balance   49,799,318.91

Statement of Cash Flows (Jan 1 to Dec31)

 Beginning Cash Balance   0.00

Operating Activities
Net Income   54,397,391.91
Depreciation Expense   4,099,948.44
Increase in Prepaid Expenses   (3,678,458.40)
Increase in Accounts Payable   919,614.60
Increase in Inventory   (1,092,808.68)

Investment Activities
PPE Purchases (124,147,971.00)

Financing Activities
Bank Loan   114,951,825.00
Bank Loan repayment of principal   (10,248,134.42)
Owner Investment   22,990,365.00
Dividend Paid to Owner (4,598,073.00)

 Net Cash Flows   53,593,699.45

Ending Cash Balance   53,593,699.45

CASE #3 SOLUTION:

General Journal Entries:

Date: 01/05
      DR Inventory $1731941
          CR Accounts Payable $1731941

Date: 01/08
      DR Accounts Receivable $5195823
          CR Service Revenue $5195823

Date: 01/10
      DR Accounts Receivable $2078329.2
          CR Sales Revenue $2078329.2
      DR Cost of Goods Sold $1731941
          CR Inventory $1731941

Date: 01/24
      DR Sales Returns $41566.58
          CR Accounts Receivable $41566.58
      DR Inventory $34638.82
          CR Cost of Goods Sold $34638.82

Date: 02/01
      DR Rent Expense $432985.25
          CR Accounts Payable $432985.25

Date: 02/05
      DR Inventory $2078329.2
          CR Accounts Payable $2078329.2

Date: 02/08
      DR Accounts Receivable $5195823
          CR Service Revenue $5195823

Date: 02/10
      DR Accounts Receivable $2909660.88
          CR Sales Revenue $2909660.88
      DR Cost of Goods Sold $2078329.2
          CR Inventory $2078329.2

Date: 02/15
      DR Salaries Expense $1039164.6
          CR Accounts Payable $1039164.6

Date: 02/24
      DR Sales Returns $58193.22
          CR Accounts Receivable $58193.22
      DR Inventory $48494.3479999999
          CR Cost of Goods Sold $48494.3479999999

Date: 02/27
    DR Bad Debt Expense $763993.81
        CR Allowance for Doubtful Accounts $763993.81

Date: 02/30
    DR Salaries Expense $1039164.6
        CR Accounts Payable $1039164.6

Date: 03/01
    DR Rent Expense $432985.25
        CR Accounts Payable $432985.25

Date: 03/05
    DR Inventory $2597911.5
        CR Accounts Payable $2597911.5

Date: 03/08
    DR Accounts Receivable $5195823
        CR Service Revenue $5195823

Date: 03/10
    DR Accounts Receivable $3637076.1
        CR Sales Revenue $3637076.1
    DR Cost of Goods Sold $2597911.5
        CR Inventory $2597911.5

Date: 03/15
    DR Salaries Expense $1039164.6
        CR Accounts Payable $1039164.6

Date: 03/24
    DR Sales Returns $72741.52
        CR Accounts Receivable $72741.52
    DR Inventory $60617.935
        CR Cost of Goods Sold $60617.935

Date: 03/26
    DR Accounts Payable $10391646
        CR Cash $10391646

Date: 03/27
    DR Bad Debt Expense $1202001.69
        CR Allowance for Doubtful Accounts $1202001.69

Date: 03/28
    DR Cash $22838032.17
        CR Accounts Receivable $22838032.17

Date: 03/29
    DR Allowance for Doubtful Accounts $1965995.5
        CR Accounts Receivable $1965995.5

Date: 03/30
>   DR Salaries Expense $1039164.6
>   CR Accounts Payable $1039164.6

Date: 04/01
>   DR Rent Expense $432985.25
>   CR Accounts Payable $432985.25

Date: 04/05
>   DR Inventory $3117493.8
>   CR Accounts Payable $3117493.8

Date: 04/06
>   DR Equipment $10391646
>   CR Accounts Payable $10391646

Date: 04/08
>   DR Accounts Receivable $5195823
>   CR Service Revenue $5195823

Date: 04/10
>   DR Accounts Receivable $4364491.32
>   CR Sales Revenue $4364491.32
>   DR Cost of Goods Sold $3117493.8
>   CR Inventory $3117493.8

Date: 04/15
>   DR Salaries Expense $1039164.6
>   CR Accounts Payable $1039164.6

Date: 04/24
>   DR Sales Returns $87289.83
>   CR Accounts Receivable $87289.83
>   DR Inventory $72741.522
>   CR Cost of Goods Sold $72741.522

Date: 04/26
>   DR Accounts Payable $16020454.25
>   CR Cash $16020454.25

Date: 04/27
>   DR Bad Debt Expense $435451.53
>   CR Allowance for Doubtful Accounts $435451.53

Date: 04/28
>   DR Cash $8273579.15
>   CR Accounts Receivable $8273579.15

Date: 04/29
>   DR Allowance for Doubtful Accounts $435451.53
>   CR Accounts Receivable $435451.53

Date: 04/30
DR Salaries Expense $1039164.6
    CR Accounts Payable $1039164.6

Date: 05/01
DR Rent Expense $432985.25
    CR Accounts Payable $432985.25

Date: 05/05
DR Inventory $3637076.1
    CR Accounts Payable $3637076.1

Date: 05/06
DR Depreciation Expense $173194.1
    CR Accum Deprn Eqmt $173194.1

Date: 05/08
DR Accounts Receivable $5195823
    CR Service Revenue $5195823

Date: 05/10
DR Accounts Receivable $5091906.54
    CR Sales Revenue $5091906.54
DR Cost of Goods Sold $3637076.1
    CR Inventory $3637076.1

Date: 05/15
DR Salaries Expense $1039164.6
    CR Accounts Payable $1039164.6

Date: 05/24
DR Sales Returns $101838.13
    CR Accounts Receivable $101838.13
DR Inventory $84865.109
    CR Cost of Goods Sold $84865.109

Date: 05/26
DR Accounts Payable $6148390.55
    CR Cash $6148390.55

Date: 05/27
DR Bad Debt Expense $509294.57
    CR Allowance for Doubtful Accounts $509294.57

Date: 05/28
DR Cash $9676596.84
    CR Accounts Receivable $9676596.84

Date: 05/29
DR Allowance for Doubtful Accounts $509294.57
    CR Accounts Receivable $509294.57

Date: 05/30
        DR Salaries Expense $1039164.6
                CR Accounts Payable $1039164.6

Date: 06/01
        DR Rent Expense $432985.25
                CR Accounts Payable $432985.25

Date: 06/03
        DR Cash $129895575
                CR Business Loan $129895575

Date: 06/04
        DR Building $129895575
                CR Cash $129895575

Date: 06/05
        DR Inventory $4156658.4
                CR Accounts Payable $4156658.4

Date: 06/06
        DR Depreciation Expense $173194.1
                CR Accum Deprn Eqmt $173194.1

Date: 06/08
        DR Accounts Receivable $5195823
                CR Service Revenue $5195823

Date: 06/10
        DR Accounts Receivable $5819321.76
                CR Sales Revenue $5819321.76
        DR Cost of Goods Sold $4156658.4
                CR Inventory $4156658.4

Date: 06/15
        DR Salaries Expense $1039164.6
                CR Accounts Payable $1039164.6

Date: 06/24
        DR Sales Returns $116386.44
                CR Accounts Receivable $116386.44
        DR Inventory $96988.696
                CR Cost of Goods Sold $96988.696

Date: 06/26
        DR Accounts Payable $6667972.85
                CR Cash $6667972.85

Date: 06/27
        DR Bad Debt Expense $544937.92
                CR Allowance for Doubtful Accounts $544937.92

Date: 06/28
    DR Cash $10353820.4
        CR Accounts Receivable $10353820.4

Date: 06/29
    DR Allowance for Doubtful Accounts $544937.92
        CR Accounts Receivable $544937.92

Date: 06/30
    DR Salaries Expense $1039164.6
        CR Accounts Payable $1039164.6

Date: 07/01
    DR Cash $25979115
        CR Owner's Equity $25979115

Date: 07/02
    DR Interest Expense $541231.56
        CR Cash $541231.56

Date: 07/03
    DR Business Loan $1910058.18
        CR Cash $1910058.18

Date: 07/04
    DR Depreciation Expense $541231.56
        CR Accum Deprn Bldg $541231.56

Date: 07/05
    DR Inventory $4676240.7
        CR Accounts Payable $4676240.7

Date: 07/06
    DR Depreciation Expense $173194.1
        CR Accum Deprn Eqmt $173194.1

Date: 07/08
    DR Accounts Receivable $5195823
        CR Service Revenue $5195823

Date: 07/10
    DR Accounts Receivable $6546736.98
        CR Sales Revenue $6546736.98
    DR Cost of Goods Sold $4676240.7
        CR Inventory $4676240.7

Date: 07/15
    DR Salaries Expense $1039164.6
        CR Accounts Payable $1039164.6

Date: 07/24
        DR Sales Returns $130934.74
                CR Accounts Receivable $130934.74
        DR Inventory $109112.283
                CR Cost of Goods Sold $109112.283

Date: 07/26
        DR Accounts Payable $6754569.9
                CR Cash $6754569.9

Date: 07/27
        DR Bad Debt Expense $580581.26
                CR Allowance for Doubtful Accounts $580581.26

Date: 07/28
        DR Cash $11031043.98
                CR Accounts Receivable $11031043.98

Date: 07/29
        DR Allowance for Doubtful Accounts $580581.26
                CR Accounts Receivable $580581.26

Date: 07/30
        DR Salaries Expense $1039164.6
                CR Accounts Payable $1039164.6

Date: 08/02
        DR Interest Expense $533272.99
                CR Cash $533272.99

Date: 08/03
        DR Business Loan $1918016.76
                CR Cash $1918016.76

Date: 08/04
        DR Depreciation Expense $541231.56
                CR Accum Deprn Bldg $541231.56

Date: 08/05
        DR Inventory $5195823
                CR Accounts Payable $5195823

Date: 08/06
        DR Depreciation Expense $173194.1
                CR Accum Deprn Eqmt $173194.1

Date: 08/08
        DR Accounts Receivable $5195823
                CR Service Revenue $5195823

Date: 08/10
DR Accounts Receivable $7274152.2
    CR Sales Revenue $7274152.2
DR Cost of Goods Sold $5195823
    CR Inventory $5195823

Date: 08/11
DR Prepaid Expense $6234987.6
    CR Accounts Payable $6234987.6

Date: 08/15
DR Salaries Expense $1039164.6
    CR Accounts Payable $1039164.6

Date: 08/24
DR Sales Returns $145483.04
    CR Accounts Receivable $145483.04
DR Inventory $121235.87
    CR Cost of Goods Sold $121235.87

Date: 08/26
DR Accounts Payable $13509139.8
    CR Cash $13509139.8

Date: 08/27
DR Bad Debt Expense $616224.61
    CR Allowance for Doubtful Accounts $616224.61

Date: 08/28
DR Cash $11708267.55
    CR Accounts Receivable $11708267.55

Date: 08/29
DR Allowance for Doubtful Accounts $616224.61
    CR Accounts Receivable $616224.61

Date: 08/30
DR Salaries Expense $1039164.6
    CR Accounts Payable $1039164.6

Date: 09/02
DR Interest Expense $525281.25
    CR Cash $525281.25

Date: 09/03
DR Business Loan $1926008.49
    CR Cash $1926008.49

Date: 09/04
DR Depreciation Expense $541231.56
    CR Accum Deprn Bldg $541231.56

Date: 09/05
  DR Inventory $5715405.3
        CR Accounts Payable $5715405.3

Date: 09/06
  DR Depreciation Expense $173194.1
        CR Accum Deprn Eqmt $173194.1

Date: 09/08
  DR Accounts Receivable $5195823
        CR Service Revenue $5195823

Date: 09/10
  DR Accounts Receivable $8001567.42
        CR Sales Revenue $8001567.42
  DR Cost of Goods Sold $5715405.3
        CR Inventory $5715405.3

Date: 09/11
  DR Insurance Expense $519582.3
        CR Prepaid Expense $519582.3

Date: 09/15
  DR Salaries Expense $1039164.6
        CR Accounts Payable $1039164.6

Date: 09/24
  DR Sales Returns $160031.35
        CR Accounts Receivable $160031.35
  DR Inventory $133359.457
        CR Cost of Goods Sold $133359.457

Date: 09/26
  DR Accounts Payable $7793734.5
        CR Cash $7793734.5

Date: 09/27
  DR Bad Debt Expense $651867.95
        CR Allowance for Doubtful Accounts $651867.95

Date: 09/28
  DR Cash $12385491.12
        CR Accounts Receivable $12385491.12

Date: 09/29
  DR Allowance for Doubtful Accounts $651867.95
        CR Accounts Receivable $651867.95

Date: 09/30
  DR Salaries Expense $1039164.6
        CR Accounts Payable $1039164.6

387

Date: 10/02
        DR Interest Expense $517256.21
            CR Cash $517256.21

Date: 10/03
        DR Business Loan $1934033.53
            CR Cash $1934033.53

Date: 10/04
        DR Depreciation Expense $541231.56
            CR Accum Deprn Bldg $541231.56

Date: 10/05
        DR Inventory $6234987.6
            CR Accounts Payable $6234987.6

Date: 10/06
        DR Depreciation Expense $173194.1
            CR Accum Deprn Eqmt $173194.1

Date: 10/08
        DR Accounts Receivable $5195823
            CR Service Revenue $5195823

Date: 10/10
        DR Accounts Receivable $8728982.64
            CR Sales Revenue $8728982.64
        DR Cost of Goods Sold $6234987.6
            CR Inventory $6234987.6

Date: 10/11
        DR Insurance Expense $519582.3
            CR Prepaid Expense $519582.3

Date: 10/13
        DR Cash $20783292
            CR Unearned Revenue $20783292

Date: 10/15
        DR Salaries Expense $1039164.6
            CR Accounts Payable $1039164.6

Date: 10/24
        DR Sales Returns $174579.65
            CR Accounts Receivable $174579.65
        DR Inventory $145483.044
            CR Cost of Goods Sold $145483.044

Date: 10/26
        DR Accounts Payable $8313316.8
            CR Cash $8313316.8

Date: 10/27
      DR Bad Debt Expense $687511.3
            CR Allowance for Doubtful Accounts $687511.3

Date: 10/28
      DR Cash $13062714.69
            CR Accounts Receivable $13062714.69

Date: 10/29
      DR Allowance for Doubtful Accounts $687511.3
            CR Accounts Receivable $687511.3

Date: 10/30
      DR Salaries Expense $1039164.6
            CR Accounts Payable $1039164.6

Date: 11/02
      DR Interest Expense $509197.74
            CR Cash $509197.74

Date: 11/03
      DR Business Loan $1942092
            CR Cash $1942092

Date: 11/04
      DR Depreciation Expense $541231.56
            CR Accum Deprn Bldg $541231.56

Date: 11/05
      DR Inventory $6754569.9
            CR Accounts Payable $6754569.9

Date: 11/06
      DR Depreciation Expense $173194.1
            CR Accum Deprn Eqmt $173194.1

Date: 11/08
      DR Accounts Receivable $5195823
            CR Service Revenue $5195823

Date: 11/10
      DR Accounts Receivable $9456397.86
            CR Sales Revenue $9456397.86
      DR Cost of Goods Sold $6754569.9
            CR Inventory $6754569.9

Date: 11/11
      DR Insurance Expense $519582.3
            CR Prepaid Expense $519582.3

Date: 11/13
DR Unearned Revenue $20783292
    CR Service Revenue $20783292

Date: 11/15
DR Salaries Expense $1039164.6
    CR Accounts Payable $1039164.6

Date: 11/20
DR Retained Earnings $5195823
    CR Cash $5195823

Date: 11/24
DR Sales Returns $189127.96
    CR Accounts Receivable $189127.96
DR Inventory $157606.631
    CR Cost of Goods Sold $157606.631

Date: 11/26
DR Accounts Payable $8832899.1
    CR Cash $8832899.1

Date: 11/27
DR Bad Debt Expense $723154.65
    CR Allowance for Doubtful Accounts $723154.65

Date: 11/28
DR Cash $13739938.26
    CR Accounts Receivable $13739938.26

Date: 11/29
DR Allowance for Doubtful Accounts $723154.65
    CR Accounts Receivable $723154.65

Date: 11/30
DR Salaries Expense $1039164.6
    CR Accounts Payable $1039164.6

Date: 12/02
DR Interest Expense $501105.69
    CR Cash $501105.69

Date: 12/03
DR Business Loan $1950184.05
    CR Cash $1950184.05

Date: 12/04
DR Depreciation Expense $541231.56
    CR Accum Deprn Bldg $541231.56

Date: 12/05
        DR Inventory $7274152.2
              CR Accounts Payable $7274152.2

Date: 12/06
        DR Depreciation Expense $173194.1
              CR Accum Deprn Eqmt $173194.1

Date: 12/08
        DR Accounts Receivable $5195823
              CR Service Revenue $5195823

Date: 12/10
        DR Accounts Receivable $10183813.08
              CR Sales Revenue $10183813.08
        DR Cost of Goods Sold $7274152.2
              CR Inventory $7274152.2

Date: 12/11
        DR Insurance Expense $519582.3
              CR Prepaid Expense $519582.3

Date: 12/15
        DR Salaries Expense $1039164.6
              CR Accounts Payable $1039164.6

Date: 12/24
        DR Sales Returns $203676.26
              CR Accounts Receivable $203676.26
        DR Inventory $169730.218
              CR Cost of Goods Sold $169730.218

Date: 12/26
        DR Accounts Payable $9352481.4
              CR Cash $9352481.4

Date: 12/27
        DR Bad Debt Expense $758797.99
              CR Allowance for Doubtful Accounts $758797.99

Date: 12/28
        DR Cash $14417161.82
              CR Accounts Receivable $14417161.82

Date: 12/29
        DR Allowance for Doubtful Accounts $758797.99
              CR Accounts Receivable $758797.99

Date: 12/30
        DR Salaries Expense $1039164.6
              CR Accounts Payable $1039164.6

Date: 12/31
        DR Revenue $155743755.26
             CR Retained Earnings $155743755.26
        DR Retained Earnings $94274696.297
             CR Expense $94274696.297

GENERAL LEDGER:

Cash

03/26	(10,391,646.00)
03/28	22,838,032.17
04/26	(16,020,454.25)
04/28	8,273,579.15
05/26	(6,148,390.55)
05/28	9,676,596.84
06/03	129,895,575.00
06/04	(129,895,575.00)
06/26	(6,667,972.85)
06/28	10,353,820.40
07/01	25,979,115.00
07/02	(541,231.56)
07/03	(1,910,058.18)
07/26	(6,754,569.90)
07/28	11,031,043.98
08/02	(533,272.99)
08/03	(1,918,016.76)
08/26	(13,509,139.80)
08/28	11,708,267.55
09/02	(525,281.25)
09/03	(1,926,008.49)
09/26	(7,793,734.50)
09/28	12,385,491.12
10/02	(517,256.21)
10/03	(1,934,033.53)
10/13	20,783,292.00
10/26	(8,313,316.80)
10/28	13,062,714.69
11/02	(509,197.74)
11/03	(1,942,092.00)
11/20	(5,195,823.00)
11/26	(8,832,899.10)
11/28	13,739,938.26
12/02	(501,105.69)
12/03	(1,950,184.05)
12/26	(9,352,481.40)
12/28	14,417,161.82
12/31 BALANCE	60,560,886.38

Accounts Receivable

01/08	5,195,823.00
01/10	2,078,329.20
01/24	(41,566.58)
02/08	5,195,823.00
02/10	2,909,660.88
02/24	(58,193.22)
03/08	5,195,823.00
03/10	3,637,076.10
03/24	(72,741.52)
03/28	(22,838,032.17)
03/29	(1,965,995.50)
04/08	5,195,823.00
04/10	4,364,491.32
04/24	(87,289.83)
04/28	(8,273,579.15)
04/29	(435,451.53)
05/08	5,195,823.00
05/10	5,091,906.54
05/24	(101,838.13)
05/28	(9,676,596.84)
05/29	(509,294.57)
06/08	5,195,823.00
06/10	5,819,321.76
06/24	(116,386.44)
06/28	(10,353,820.40)
06/29	(544,937.92)
07/08	5,195,823.00
07/10	6,546,736.98
07/24	(130,934.74)
07/28	(11,031,043.98)
07/29	(580,581.26)
08/08	5,195,823.00
08/10	7,274,152.20
08/24	(145,483.04)
08/28	(11,708,267.55)
08/29	(616,224.61)
09/08	5,195,823.00
09/10	8,001,567.42
09/24	(160,031.35)
09/28	(12,385,491.12)
09/29	(651,867.95)
10/08	5,195,823.00
10/10	8,728,982.64
10/24	(174,579.65)
10/28	(13,062,714.69)
10/29	(687,511.30)
11/08	5,195,823.00
11/10	9,456,397.86
11/24	(189,127.96)

```
11/28              (13,739,938.26)
11/29              (723,154.65)
12/08              5,195,823.00
12/10              10,183,813.08
12/24              (203,676.26)
12/28              (14,417,161.82)
12/29              (758,797.99)
12/31 BALANCE          (0.00)
```

Allowance for Doubtful Accounts

```
02/27              (763,993.81)
03/27              (1,202,001.69)
03/29              1,965,995.50
04/27              (435,451.53)
04/29              435,451.53
05/27              (509,294.57)
05/29              509,294.57
06/27              (544,937.92)
06/29              544,937.92
07/27              (580,581.26)
07/29              580,581.26
08/27              (616,224.61)
08/29              616,224.61
09/27              (651,867.95)
09/29              651,867.95
10/27              (687,511.30)
10/29              687,511.30
11/27              (723,154.65)
11/29              723,154.65
12/27              (758,797.99)
12/29              758,797.99
12/31 BALANCE          0.00
```

Inventory

01/05	1,731,941.00	
01/10	(1,731,941.00)	
01/24	34,638.82	
02/05	2,078,329.20	
02/10	(2,078,329.20)	
02/24	48,494.35	
03/05	2,597,911.50	
03/10	(2,597,911.50)	
03/24	60,617.94	
04/05	3,117,493.80	
04/10	(3,117,493.80)	
04/24	72,741.52	
05/05	3,637,076.10	
05/10	(3,637,076.10)	
05/24	84,865.11	
06/05	4,156,658.40	
06/10	(4,156,658.40)	
06/24	96,988.70	
07/05	4,676,240.70	
07/10	(4,676,240.70)	
07/24	109,112.28	
08/05	5,195,823.00	
08/10	(5,195,823.00)	
08/24	121,235.87	
09/05	5,715,405.30	
09/10	(5,715,405.30)	
09/24	133,359.46	
10/05	6,234,987.60	
10/10	(6,234,987.60)	
10/24	145,483.04	
11/05	6,754,569.90	
11/10	(6,754,569.90)	
11/24	157,606.63	
12/31 BALANCE	1,065,143.72	

Equipment

04/06	10,391,646.00	
12/31 BALANCE	10,391,646.00	

Accum Deprn Eqmt

05/06	(173,194.10)	
06/06	(173,194.10)	
07/06	(173,194.10)	
08/06	(173,194.10)	
09/06	(173,194.10)	
10/06	(173,194.10)	
11/06	(173,194.10)	
12/06	(173,194.10)	
12/31 BALANCE	(1,385,552.80)	

Building

06/04		129,895,575.00
12/31 BALANCE		129,895,575.00

Accum Deprn Bldg

07/04		(541,231.56)
08/04		(541,231.56)
09/04		(541,231.56)
10/04		(541,231.56)
11/04		(541,231.56)
12/04		(541,231.56)
12/31 BALANCE		(3,247,389.36)

Prepaid Expense

08/11		6,234,987.60
09/11		(519,582.30)
10/11		(519,582.30)
11/11		(519,582.30)
12/11		(519,582.30)
12/31 BALANCE		4,156,658.40

Accounts Payable

Date	Amount
01/05	(1,731,941.00)
02/01	(432,985.25)
02/05	(2,078,329.20)
02/15	(1,039,164.60)
02/30	(1,039,164.60)
03/01	(432,985.25)
03/05	(2,597,911.50)
03/15	(1,039,164.60)
03/26	10,391,646.00
03/30	(1,039,164.60)
04/01	(432,985.25)
04/05	(3,117,493.80)
04/06	(10,391,646.00)
04/15	(1,039,164.60)
04/26	16,020,454.25
04/30	(1,039,164.60)
05/01	(432,985.25)
05/05	(3,637,076.10)
05/15	(1,039,164.60)
05/26	6,148,390.55
05/30	(1,039,164.60)
06/01	(432,985.25)
06/05	(4,156,658.40)
06/15	(1,039,164.60)
06/26	6,667,972.85
06/30	(1,039,164.60)
07/05	(4,676,240.70)
07/15	(1,039,164.60)
07/26	6,754,569.90
07/30	(1,039,164.60)
08/05	(5,195,823.00)
08/11	(6,234,987.60)
08/15	(1,039,164.60)
08/26	13,509,139.80
08/30	(1,039,164.60)
09/05	(5,715,405.30)
09/15	(1,039,164.60)
09/26	7,793,734.50
09/30	(1,039,164.60)
10/05	(6,234,987.60)
10/15	(1,039,164.60)
10/26	8,313,316.80
10/30	(1,039,164.60)
11/05	(6,754,569.90)
11/15	(1,039,164.60)
11/26	8,832,899.10
11/30	(1,039,164.60)
12/05	(7,274,152.20)
12/15	(1,039,164.60)

```
                    12/26              9,352,481.40
                    12/31 BALANCE          0.00

Business Loan
                    06/03           (129,895,575.00)
                    07/03            1,910,058.18
                    08/03            1,918,016.76
                    09/03            1,926,008.49
                    10/03            1,934,033.53
                    11/03            1,942,092.00
                    12/03            1,950,184.05
                    12/31 BALANCE    (118,315,181.99)

Unearned Revenue
                    10/13           (20,783,292.00)
                    11/13            20,783,292.00
                    12/31 BALANCE          0.00

Retained Earnings
                    11/20            5,195,823.00
                    12/31           (61,469,058.96)
                    12/31 BALANCE    (56,273,235.96)

Owner's Equity
                    07/01           (25,979,115.00)
                    12/31 BALANCE    (25,979,115.00)


                    Service Revenue
                    01/08            (5,195,823.00)
                    02/08            (5,195,823.00)
                    03/08            (5,195,823.00)
                    04/08            (5,195,823.00)
                    05/08            (5,195,823.00)
                    06/08            (5,195,823.00)
                    07/08            (5,195,823.00)
                    08/08            (5,195,823.00)
                    09/08            (5,195,823.00)
                    10/08            (5,195,823.00)
                    11/08            (5,195,823.00)
                    11/13           (20,783,292.00)
                    12/08            (5,195,823.00)
                    12/31            83,133,168.00
                    12/31 BALANCE          0.00
```

Sales Revenue

01/10	(2,078,329.20)
02/10	(2,909,660.88)
03/10	(3,637,076.10)
04/10	(4,364,491.32)
05/10	(5,091,906.54)
06/10	(5,819,321.76)
07/10	(6,546,736.98)
08/10	(7,274,152.20)
09/10	(8,001,567.42)
10/10	(8,728,982.64)
11/10	(9,456,397.86)
12/10	(10,183,813.08)
12/31	74,092,435.98
12/31 BALANCE	0.00

Sales Returns

01/24	41,566.58
02/24	58,193.22
03/24	72,741.52
04/24	87,289.83
05/24	101,838.13
06/24	116,386.44
07/24	130,934.74
08/24	145,483.04
09/24	160,031.35
10/24	174,579.65
11/24	189,127.96
12/24	203,676.26
12/31	(1,481,848.72)
12/31 BALANCE	0.00

Cost of Goods Sold

Date	Amount
01/10	1,731,941.00
01/24	(34,638.82)
02/10	2,078,329.20
02/24	(48,494.35)
03/10	2,597,911.50
03/24	(60,617.94)
04/10	3,117,493.80
04/24	(72,741.52)
05/10	3,637,076.10
05/24	(84,865.11)
06/10	4,156,658.40
06/24	(96,988.70)
07/10	4,676,240.70
07/24	(109,112.28)
08/10	5,195,823.00
08/24	(121,235.87)
09/10	5,715,405.30
09/24	(133,359.46)
10/10	6,234,987.60
10/24	(145,483.04)
11/10	6,754,569.90
11/24	(157,606.63)
12/10	7,274,152.20
12/24	(169,730.22)
12/31	(51,935,714.77)
12/31 BALANCE	(0.01)

Salaries Expense

	02/15	1,039,164.60
	02/30	1,039,164.60
	03/15	1,039,164.60
	03/30	1,039,164.60
	04/15	1,039,164.60
	04/30	1,039,164.60
	05/15	1,039,164.60
	05/30	1,039,164.60
	06/15	1,039,164.60
	06/30	1,039,164.60
	07/15	1,039,164.60
	07/30	1,039,164.60
	08/15	1,039,164.60
	08/30	1,039,164.60
	09/15	1,039,164.60
	09/30	1,039,164.60
	10/15	1,039,164.60
	10/30	1,039,164.60
	11/15	1,039,164.60
	11/30	1,039,164.60
	12/15	1,039,164.60
	12/30	1,039,164.60
	12/31	(22,861,621.20)
	12/31 BALANCE	0.00

Rent Expense

	02/01	432,985.25
	03/01	432,985.25
	04/01	432,985.25
	05/01	432,985.25
	06/01	432,985.25
	12/31	(2,164,926.25)
	12/31 BALANCE	0.00

Bad Debt Expense

	02/27	763,993.81
	03/27	1,202,001.69
	04/27	435,451.53
	05/27	509,294.57
	06/27	544,937.92
	07/27	580,581.26
	08/27	616,224.61
	09/27	651,867.95
	10/27	687,511.30
	11/27	723,154.65
	12/27	758,797.99
	12/31	(7,473,817.28)
	12/31 BALANCE	0.00

Depreciation Expense

05/06	173,194.10	
06/06	173,194.10	
07/04	541,231.56	
07/06	173,194.10	
08/04	541,231.56	
08/06	173,194.10	
09/04	541,231.56	
09/06	173,194.10	
10/04	541,231.56	
10/06	173,194.10	
11/04	541,231.56	
11/06	173,194.10	
12/04	541,231.56	
12/06	173,194.10	
12/31	(4,632,942.16)	
12/31 BALANCE		0.00

Insurance Expense

09/11	519,582.30	
10/11	519,582.30	
11/11	519,582.30	
12/11	519,582.30	
12/31	(2,078,329.20)	
12/31 BALANCE		0.00

Interest Expense

07/02	541,231.56	
08/02	533,272.99	
09/02	525,281.25	
10/02	517,256.21	
11/02	509,197.74	
12/02	501,105.69	
12/31	(3,127,345.44)	
12/31 BALANCE		0.00

TRIAL BALANCE BEFORE AND AFTER CLOSING ENTRY:

Cash	60,560,886.38	60,560,886.38
Accounts Receivable	(0.00)	(0.00)
Allowance for Doubtful Accounts	0.00	0.00
Inventory	1,234,873.93	1,234,873.93
Equipment	10,391,646.00	10,391,646.00
Accum Deprn Eqmt	(1,385,552.80)	(1,385,552.80)
Building	129,895,575.00	129,895,575.00
Accum Deprn Bldg	(3,247,389.36)	(3,247,389.36)
Prepaid Expense	4,156,658.40	4,156,658.40
Accounts Payable	(1,039,164.60)	(1,039,164.60)
Business Loan	(118,315,181.99)	(118,315,181.99)
Unearned Revenue	0.00	0.00
Retained Earnings	0.00	(56,273,235.96)
Owner's Equity	(25,979,115.00)	(25,979,115.00)
Service Revenue	(83,133,168.00)	0.00
Sales Revenue	(74,092,435.98)	0.00
Sales Returns	1,481,848.72	0.00
Cost of Goods Sold	51,935,714.77	0.00
Salaries Expense	22,861,621.20	0.00
Rent Expense	2,164,926.25	0.00
Bad Debt Expense	7,473,817.28	0.00
Depreciation Expense	4,632,942.16	0.00
Insurance Expense	2,078,329.20	0.00
Interest Expense	3,127,345.44	0.00

FINANCIAL STATEMENTS

Balance Sheet (Dec 31)

ASSETS
Cash	60,560,886.38
Accounts Receivable	(0.00)
Inventory	1,234,873.93
Prepaids	4,156,658.40
Property Plant & Equipment	140,287,221.00
Accumulated Depreciation Expense	(4,632,942.16)
Net Property Plant & Equipment	135,654,278.84
Total Assets	201,606,697.55

LIABILITIES
Accounts Payable	1,039,164.60
Loans	118,315,181.99
Total Liabilities	119,354,346.59

SHAREHOLDER'S EQUITY
Owner's Equity	25,979,115.00
Retained Earnings	56,273,235.96
Total Shareholder's Equity	82,252,350.96

Total Liabilities & Shareholder's Equity	201,606,697.55

Income Statement (Jan 1 to Dec 31)

REVENUE
Services	83,133,168.00
Sales	74,092,435.98
Sales Returns	(1,481,848.72)
Total Revenue	155,743,755.26

EXPENSES
Cost of Goods Sold	51,935,714.77
Salaries Expense	22,861,621.20
Rent Expense	2,164,926.25
Bad Debts	7,473,817.28
Depreciation Expense	4,632,942.16
Insurance	2,078,329.20
Interest	3,127,345.44
Total Expenses	94,274,696.30

Net Income	61,469,058.96

Statement of Retained Earnings (Jan 1 to Dec 31)

Opening Balance	0.00
Net Income	61,469,058.96
Dividends Paid	(5,195,823.00)
Closing Balance	56,273,235.96

Statement of Cash Flows (Jan 1 to Dec31)

Beginning Cash Balance	0.00
Operating Activities	
Net Income	61,469,058.96
Depreciation Expense	4,632,942.16
Increase in Prepaid Expenses	(4,156,658.40)
Increase in Accounts Payable	1,039,164.60
Increase in Inventory	(1,234,873.93)
Investment Activities	
PPE Purchases	(140,287,221.00)
Financing Activities	
Bank Loan	129,895,575.00
Bank Loan repayment of principal	(11,580,393.01)
Owner Investment	25,979,115.00
Dividend Paid to Owner	(5,195,823.00)
Net Cash Flows	60,560,886.38
Ending Cash Balance	60,560,886.38

CASE #4 SOLUTION:

General Journal Entries:

Date: 01/05
    DR Inventory $1957093
        CR Accounts Payable $1957093

Date: 01/08
    DR Accounts Receivable $5871279
        CR Service Revenue $5871279

Date: 01/10
    DR Accounts Receivable $2348511.6
        CR Sales Revenue $2348511.6
    DR Cost of Goods Sold $1957093
        CR Inventory $1957093

Date: 01/24
    DR Sales Returns $46970.23
        CR Accounts Receivable $46970.23
    DR Inventory $39141.86
        CR Cost of Goods Sold $39141.86

Date: 02/01
    DR Rent Expense $489273.25
        CR Accounts Payable $489273.25

Date: 02/05
    DR Inventory $2348511.6
        CR Accounts Payable $2348511.6

Date: 02/08
    DR Accounts Receivable $5871279
        CR Service Revenue $5871279

Date: 02/10
    DR Accounts Receivable $3287916.24
        CR Sales Revenue $3287916.24
    DR Cost of Goods Sold $2348511.6
        CR Inventory $2348511.6

Date: 02/15
    DR Salaries Expense $1174255.8
        CR Accounts Payable $1174255.8

Date: 02/24
    DR Sales Returns $65758.32
        CR Accounts Receivable $65758.32
    DR Inventory $54798.604
        CR Cost of Goods Sold $54798.604

Date: 02/27
　　DR Bad Debt Expense $863312.86
　　　　CR Allowance for Doubtful Accounts $863312.86

Date: 02/30
　　DR Salaries Expense $1174255.8
　　　　CR Accounts Payable $1174255.8

Date: 03/01
　　DR Rent Expense $489273.25
　　　　CR Accounts Payable $489273.25

Date: 03/05
　　DR Inventory $2935639.5
　　　　CR Accounts Payable $2935639.5

Date: 03/08
　　DR Accounts Receivable $5871279
　　　　CR Service Revenue $5871279

Date: 03/10
　　DR Accounts Receivable $4109895.3
　　　　CR Sales Revenue $4109895.3
　　DR Cost of Goods Sold $2935639.5
　　　　CR Inventory $2935639.5

Date: 03/15
　　DR Salaries Expense $1174255.8
　　　　CR Accounts Payable $1174255.8

Date: 03/24
　　DR Sales Returns $82197.91
　　　　CR Accounts Receivable $82197.91
　　DR Inventory $68498.255
　　　　CR Cost of Goods Sold $68498.255

Date: 03/26
　　DR Accounts Payable $11742558
　　　　CR Cash $11742558

Date: 03/27
　　DR Bad Debt Expense $1358261.68
　　　　CR Allowance for Doubtful Accounts $1358261.68

Date: 03/28
　　DR Cash $25806972
　　　　CR Accounts Receivable $25806972

Date: 03/29
　　DR Allowance for Doubtful Accounts $2221574.54
　　　　CR Accounts Receivable $2221574.54

Date: 03/30
  DR Salaries Expense $1174255.8
    CR Accounts Payable $1174255.8

Date: 04/01
  DR Rent Expense $489273.25
    CR Accounts Payable $489273.25

Date: 04/05
  DR Inventory $3522767.4
    CR Accounts Payable $3522767.4

Date: 04/06
  DR Equipment $11742558
    CR Accounts Payable $11742558

Date: 04/08
  DR Accounts Receivable $5871279
    CR Service Revenue $5871279

Date: 04/10
  DR Accounts Receivable $4931874.36
    CR Sales Revenue $4931874.36
  DR Cost of Goods Sold $3522767.4
    CR Inventory $3522767.4

Date: 04/15
  DR Salaries Expense $1174255.8
    CR Accounts Payable $1174255.8

Date: 04/24
  DR Sales Returns $98637.49
    CR Accounts Receivable $98637.49
  DR Inventory $82197.906
    CR Cost of Goods Sold $82197.906

Date: 04/26
  DR Accounts Payable $18103110.25
    CR Cash $18103110.25

Date: 04/27
  DR Bad Debt Expense $492060.15
    CR Allowance for Doubtful Accounts $492060.15

Date: 04/28
  DR Cash $9349142.86
    CR Accounts Receivable $9349142.86

Date: 04/29
  DR Allowance for Doubtful Accounts $492060.15
    CR Accounts Receivable $492060.15

Date: 04/30
    DR Salaries Expense $1174255.8
        CR Accounts Payable $1174255.8

Date: 05/01
    DR Rent Expense $489273.25
        CR Accounts Payable $489273.25

Date: 05/05
    DR Inventory $4109895.3
        CR Accounts Payable $4109895.3

Date: 05/06
    DR Depreciation Expense $195709.3
        CR Accum Deprn Eqmt $195709.3

Date: 05/08
    DR Accounts Receivable $5871279
        CR Service Revenue $5871279

Date: 05/10
    DR Accounts Receivable $5753853.42
        CR Sales Revenue $5753853.42
    DR Cost of Goods Sold $4109895.3
        CR Inventory $4109895.3

Date: 05/15
    DR Salaries Expense $1174255.8
        CR Accounts Payable $1174255.8

Date: 05/24
    DR Sales Returns $115077.07
        CR Accounts Receivable $115077.07
    DR Inventory $95897.557
        CR Cost of Goods Sold $95897.557

Date: 05/26
    DR Accounts Payable $6947680.15
        CR Cash $6947680.15

Date: 05/27
    DR Bad Debt Expense $575502.77
        CR Allowance for Doubtful Accounts $575502.77

Date: 05/28
    DR Cash $10934552.58
        CR Accounts Receivable $10934552.58

Date: 05/29
    DR Allowance for Doubtful Accounts $575502.77
        CR Accounts Receivable $575502.77

Date: 05/30
        DR Salaries Expense $1174255.8
            CR Accounts Payable $1174255.8

Date: 06/01
        DR Rent Expense $489273.25
            CR Accounts Payable $489273.25

Date: 06/03
        DR Cash $146781975
            CR Business Loan $146781975

Date: 06/04
        DR Building $146781975
            CR Cash $146781975

Date: 06/05
        DR Inventory $4697023.2
            CR Accounts Payable $4697023.2

Date: 06/06
        DR Depreciation Expense $195709.3
            CR Accum Deprn Eqmt $195709.3

Date: 06/08
        DR Accounts Receivable $5871279
            CR Service Revenue $5871279

Date: 06/10
        DR Accounts Receivable $6575832.48
            CR Sales Revenue $6575832.48
        DR Cost of Goods Sold $4697023.2
            CR Inventory $4697023.2

Date: 06/15
        DR Salaries Expense $1174255.8
            CR Accounts Payable $1174255.8

Date: 06/24
        DR Sales Returns $131516.65
            CR Accounts Receivable $131516.65
        DR Inventory $109597.208
            CR Cost of Goods Sold $109597.208

Date: 06/26
        DR Accounts Payable $7534808.05
            CR Cash $7534808.05

Date: 06/27
        DR Bad Debt Expense $615779.74
            CR Allowance for Doubtful Accounts $615779.74

Date: 06/28
  DR Cash $11699815.09
    CR Accounts Receivable $11699815.09

Date: 06/29
  DR Allowance for Doubtful Accounts $615779.74
    CR Accounts Receivable $615779.74

Date: 06/30
  DR Salaries Expense $1174255.8
    CR Accounts Payable $1174255.8

Date: 07/01
  DR Cash $29356395
    CR Owner's Equity $29356395

Date: 07/02
  DR Interest Expense $611591.56
    CR Cash $611591.56

Date: 07/03
  DR Business Loan $2158365.38
    CR Cash $2158365.38

Date: 07/04
  DR Depreciation Expense $611591.56
    CR Accum Deprn Bldg $611591.56

Date: 07/05
  DR Inventory $5284151.1
    CR Accounts Payable $5284151.1

Date: 07/06
  DR Depreciation Expense $195709.3
    CR Accum Deprn Eqmt $195709.3

Date: 07/08
  DR Accounts Receivable $5871279
    CR Service Revenue $5871279

Date: 07/10
  DR Accounts Receivable $7397811.54
    CR Sales Revenue $7397811.54
  DR Cost of Goods Sold $5284151.1
    CR Inventory $5284151.1

Date: 07/15
  DR Salaries Expense $1174255.8
    CR Accounts Payable $1174255.8

Date: 07/24
DR Sales Returns $147956.23
CR Accounts Receivable $147956.23
DR Inventory $123296.859
CR Cost of Goods Sold $123296.859

Date: 07/26
DR Accounts Payable $7632662.7
CR Cash $7632662.7

Date: 07/27
DR Bad Debt Expense $656056.72
CR Allowance for Doubtful Accounts $656056.72

Date: 07/28
DR Cash $12465077.59
CR Accounts Receivable $12465077.59

Date: 07/29
DR Allowance for Doubtful Accounts $656056.72
CR Accounts Receivable $656056.72

Date: 07/30
DR Salaries Expense $1174255.8
CR Accounts Payable $1174255.8

Date: 08/02
DR Interest Expense $602598.37
CR Cash $602598.37

Date: 08/03
DR Business Loan $2167358.57
CR Cash $2167358.57

Date: 08/04
DR Depreciation Expense $611591.56
CR Accum Deprn Bldg $611591.56

Date: 08/05
DR Inventory $5871279
CR Accounts Payable $5871279

Date: 08/06
DR Depreciation Expense $195709.3
CR Accum Deprn Eqmt $195709.3

Date: 08/08
DR Accounts Receivable $5871279
CR Service Revenue $5871279

Date: 08/10
        DR Accounts Receivable $8219790.6
            CR Sales Revenue $8219790.6
        DR Cost of Goods Sold $5871279
            CR Inventory $5871279

Date: 08/11
        DR Prepaid Expense $7045534.8
            CR Accounts Payable $7045534.8

Date: 08/15
        DR Salaries Expense $1174255.8
            CR Accounts Payable $1174255.8

Date: 08/24
        DR Sales Returns $164395.81
            CR Accounts Receivable $164395.81
        DR Inventory $136996.51
            CR Cost of Goods Sold $136996.51

Date: 08/26
        DR Accounts Payable $15265325.4
            CR Cash $15265325.4

Date: 08/27
        DR Bad Debt Expense $696333.69
            CR Allowance for Doubtful Accounts $696333.69

Date: 08/28
        DR Cash $13230340.1
            CR Accounts Receivable $13230340.1

Date: 08/29
        DR Allowance for Doubtful Accounts $696333.69
            CR Accounts Receivable $696333.69

Date: 08/30
        DR Salaries Expense $1174255.8
            CR Accounts Payable $1174255.8

Date: 09/02
        DR Interest Expense $593567.71
            CR Cash $593567.71

Date: 09/03
        DR Business Loan $2176389.23
            CR Cash $2176389.23

Date: 09/04
        DR Depreciation Expense $611591.56
            CR Accum Deprn Bldg $611591.56

Date: 09/05
  DR Inventory $6458406.9
    CR Accounts Payable $6458406.9

Date: 09/06
  DR Depreciation Expense $195709.3
    CR Accum Deprn Eqmt $195709.3

Date: 09/08
  DR Accounts Receivable $5871279
    CR Service Revenue $5871279

Date: 09/10
  DR Accounts Receivable $9041769.66
    CR Sales Revenue $9041769.66
  DR Cost of Goods Sold $6458406.9
    CR Inventory $6458406.9

Date: 09/11
  DR Insurance Expense $587127.9
    CR Prepaid Expense $587127.9

Date: 09/15
  DR Salaries Expense $1174255.8
    CR Accounts Payable $1174255.8

Date: 09/24
  DR Sales Returns $180835.39
    CR Accounts Receivable $180835.39
  DR Inventory $150696.161
    CR Cost of Goods Sold $150696.161

Date: 09/26
  DR Accounts Payable $8806918.5
    CR Cash $8806918.5

Date: 09/27
  DR Bad Debt Expense $736610.66
    CR Allowance for Doubtful Accounts $736610.66

Date: 09/28
  DR Cash $13995602.61
    CR Accounts Receivable $13995602.61

Date: 09/29
  DR Allowance for Doubtful Accounts $736610.66
    CR Accounts Receivable $736610.66

Date: 09/30
  DR Salaries Expense $1174255.8
    CR Accounts Payable $1174255.8

Date: 10/02
      DR Interest Expense $584499.42
           CR Cash $584499.42

Date: 10/03
      DR Business Loan $2185457.52
           CR Cash $2185457.52

Date: 10/04
      DR Depreciation Expense $611591.56
           CR Accum Deprn Bldg $611591.56

Date: 10/05
      DR Inventory $7045534.8
           CR Accounts Payable $7045534.8

Date: 10/06
      DR Depreciation Expense $195709.3
           CR Accum Deprn Eqmt $195709.3

Date: 10/08
      DR Accounts Receivable $5871279
           CR Service Revenue $5871279

Date: 10/10
      DR Accounts Receivable $9863748.72
           CR Sales Revenue $9863748.72
      DR Cost of Goods Sold $7045534.8
           CR Inventory $7045534.8

Date: 10/11
      DR Insurance Expense $587127.9
           CR Prepaid Expense $587127.9

Date: 10/13
      DR Cash $23485116
           CR Unearned Revenue $23485116

Date: 10/15
      DR Salaries Expense $1174255.8
           CR Accounts Payable $1174255.8

Date: 10/24
      DR Sales Returns $197274.97
           CR Accounts Receivable $197274.97
      DR Inventory $164395.812
           CR Cost of Goods Sold $164395.812

Date: 10/26
      DR Accounts Payable $9394046.4
           CR Cash $9394046.4

Date: 10/27
        DR Bad Debt Expense $776887.64
                CR Allowance for Doubtful Accounts $776887.64

Date: 10/28
        DR Cash $14760865.11
                CR Accounts Receivable $14760865.11

Date: 10/29
        DR Allowance for Doubtful Accounts $776887.64
                CR Accounts Receivable $776887.64

Date: 10/30
        DR Salaries Expense $1174255.8
                CR Accounts Payable $1174255.8

Date: 11/02
        DR Interest Expense $575393.35
                CR Cash $575393.35

Date: 11/03
        DR Business Loan $2194563.59
                CR Cash $2194563.59

Date: 11/04
        DR Depreciation Expense $611591.56
                CR Accum Deprn Bldg $611591.56

Date: 11/05
        DR Inventory $7632662.7
                CR Accounts Payable $7632662.7

Date: 11/06
        DR Depreciation Expense $195709.3
                CR Accum Deprn Eqmt $195709.3

Date: 11/08
        DR Accounts Receivable $5871279
                CR Service Revenue $5871279

Date: 11/10
        DR Accounts Receivable $10685727.78
                CR Sales Revenue $10685727.78
        DR Cost of Goods Sold $7632662.7
                CR Inventory $7632662.7

Date: 11/11
        DR Insurance Expense $587127.9
                CR Prepaid Expense $587127.9

Date: 11/13
>   DR Unearned Revenue $23485116
>   CR Service Revenue $23485116

Date: 11/15
>   DR Salaries Expense $1174255.8
>   CR Accounts Payable $1174255.8

Date: 11/20
>   DR Retained Earnings $5871279
>   CR Cash $5871279

Date: 11/24
>   DR Sales Returns $213714.56
>   CR Accounts Receivable $213714.56
>   DR Inventory $178095.463
>   CR Cost of Goods Sold $178095.463

Date: 11/26
>   DR Accounts Payable $9981174.3
>   CR Cash $9981174.3

Date: 11/27
>   DR Bad Debt Expense $817164.61
>   CR Allowance for Doubtful Accounts $817164.61

Date: 11/28
>   DR Cash $15526127.61
>   CR Accounts Receivable $15526127.61

Date: 11/29
>   DR Allowance for Doubtful Accounts $817164.61
>   CR Accounts Receivable $817164.61

Date: 11/30
>   DR Salaries Expense $1174255.8
>   CR Accounts Payable $1174255.8

Date: 12/02
>   DR Interest Expense $566249.34
>   CR Cash $566249.34

Date: 12/03
>   DR Business Loan $2203707.61
>   CR Cash $2203707.61

Date: 12/04
>   DR Depreciation Expense $611591.56
>   CR Accum Deprn Bldg $611591.56

Date: 12/05
       DR Inventory $8219790.6
            CR Accounts Payable $8219790.6

Date: 12/06
       DR Depreciation Expense $195709.3
            CR Accum Deprn Eqmt $195709.3

Date: 12/08
       DR Accounts Receivable $5871279
            CR Service Revenue $5871279

Date: 12/10
       DR Accounts Receivable $11507706.84
            CR Sales Revenue $11507706.84
       DR Cost of Goods Sold $8219790.6
            CR Inventory $8219790.6

Date: 12/11
       DR Insurance Expense $587127.9
            CR Prepaid Expense $587127.9

Date: 12/15
       DR Salaries Expense $1174255.8
            CR Accounts Payable $1174255.8

Date: 12/24
       DR Sales Returns $230154.14
            CR Accounts Receivable $230154.14
       DR Inventory $191795.114
            CR Cost of Goods Sold $191795.114

Date: 12/26
       DR Accounts Payable $10568302.2
            CR Cash $10568302.2

Date: 12/27
       DR Bad Debt Expense $857441.59
            CR Allowance for Doubtful Accounts $857441.59

Date: 12/28
       DR Cash $16291390.12
            CR Accounts Receivable $16291390.12

Date: 12/29
       DR Allowance for Doubtful Accounts $857441.59
            CR Accounts Receivable $857441.59

Date: 12/30
       DR Salaries Expense $1174255.8
            CR Accounts Payable $1174255.8

Date: 12/31
      DR Revenue $175990413.77
           CR Retained Earnings $175990413.77
      DR Retained Earnings $106530388.861
           CR Expense $106530388.861

GENERAL LEDGER:

Cash

Date	Amount
03/26	(11,742,558.00)
03/28	25,806,972.00
04/26	(18,103,110.25)
04/28	9,349,142.86
05/26	(6,947,680.15)
05/28	10,934,552.58
06/03	146,781,975.00
06/04	(146,781,975.00)
06/26	(7,534,808.05)
06/28	11,699,815.09
07/01	29,356,395.00
07/02	(611,591.56)
07/03	(2,158,365.38)
07/26	(7,632,662.70)
07/28	12,465,077.59
08/02	(602,598.37)
08/03	(2,167,358.57)
08/26	(15,265,325.40)
08/28	13,230,340.10
09/02	(593,567.71)
09/03	(2,176,389.23)
09/26	(8,806,918.50)
09/28	13,995,602.61
10/02	(584,499.42)
10/03	(2,185,457.52)
10/13	23,485,116.00
10/26	(9,394,046.40)
10/28	14,760,865.11
11/02	(575,393.35)
11/03	(2,194,563.59)
11/20	(5,871,279.00)
11/26	(9,981,174.30)
11/28	15,526,127.61
12/02	(566,249.34)
12/03	(2,203,707.61)
12/26	(10,568,302.20)
12/28	16,291,390.12
12/31 BALANCE	68,433,790.07

Accounts Receivable

01/08	5,871,279.00
01/10	2,348,511.60
01/24	(46,970.23)
02/08	5,871,279.00
02/10	3,287,916.24
02/24	(65,758.32)
03/08	5,871,279.00
03/10	4,109,895.30
03/24	(82,197.91)
03/28	(25,806,972.00)
03/29	(2,221,574.54)
04/08	5,871,279.00
04/10	4,931,874.36
04/24	(98,637.49)
04/28	(9,349,142.86)
04/29	(492,060.15)
05/08	5,871,279.00
05/10	5,753,853.42
05/24	(115,077.07)
05/28	(10,934,552.58)
05/29	(575,502.77)
06/08	5,871,279.00
06/10	6,575,832.48
06/24	(131,516.65)
06/28	(11,699,815.09)
06/29	(615,779.74)
07/08	5,871,279.00
07/10	7,397,811.54
07/24	(147,956.23)
07/28	(12,465,077.59)
07/29	(656,056.72)
08/08	5,871,279.00
08/10	8,219,790.60
08/24	(164,395.81)
08/28	(13,230,340.10)
08/29	(696,333.69)
09/08	5,871,279.00
09/10	9,041,769.66
09/24	(180,835.39)
09/28	(13,995,602.61)
09/29	(736,610.66)
10/08	5,871,279.00
10/10	9,863,748.72
10/24	(197,274.97)
10/28	(14,760,865.11)
10/29	(776,887.64)
11/08	5,871,279.00
11/10	10,685,727.78
11/24	(213,714.56)

11/28	(15,526,127.61)	
11/29	(817,164.61)	
12/08	5,871,279.00	
12/10	11,507,706.84	
12/24	(230,154.14)	
12/28	(16,291,390.12)	
12/29	(857,441.59)	
12/31 BALANCE	(0.01)	

Allowance for Doubtful Accounts

02/27	(863,312.86)	
03/27	(1,358,261.68)	
03/29	2,221,574.54	
04/27	(492,060.15)	
04/29	492,060.15	
05/27	(575,502.77)	
05/29	575,502.77	
06/27	(615,779.74)	
06/29	615,779.74	
07/27	(656,056.72)	
07/29	656,056.72	
08/27	(696,333.69)	
08/29	696,333.69	
09/27	(736,610.66)	
09/29	736,610.66	
10/27	(776,887.64)	
10/29	776,887.64	
11/27	(817,164.61)	
11/29	817,164.61	
12/27	(857,441.59)	
12/29	857,441.59	
12/31 BALANCE	0.00	

Inventory

Date	Amount
01/05	1,957,093.00
01/10	(1,957,093.00)
01/24	39,141.86
02/05	2,348,511.60
02/10	(2,348,511.60)
02/24	54,798.60
03/05	2,935,639.50
03/10	(2,935,639.50)
03/24	68,498.26
04/05	3,522,767.40
04/10	(3,522,767.40)
04/24	82,197.91
05/05	4,109,895.30
05/10	(4,109,895.30)
05/24	95,897.56
06/05	4,697,023.20
06/10	(4,697,023.20)
06/24	109,597.21
07/05	5,284,151.10
07/10	(5,284,151.10)
07/24	123,296.86
08/05	5,871,279.00
08/10	(5,871,279.00)
08/24	136,996.51
09/05	6,458,406.90
09/10	(6,458,406.90)
09/24	150,696.16
10/05	7,045,534.80
10/10	(7,045,534.80)
10/24	164,395.81
11/05	7,632,662.70
11/10	(7,632,662.70)
11/24	178,095.46
12/31 BALANCE	1,203,612.20

Equipment

Date	Amount
04/06	11,742,558.00
12/31 BALANCE	11,742,558.00

Accum Deprn Eqmt

Date	Amount
05/06	(195,709.30)
06/06	(195,709.30)
07/06	(195,709.30)
08/06	(195,709.30)
09/06	(195,709.30)
10/06	(195,709.30)
11/06	(195,709.30)
12/06	(195,709.30)
12/31 BALANCE	(1,565,674.40)

Building
06/04		146,781,975.00
12/31 BALANCE		146,781,975.00

Accum Deprn Bldg
07/04		(611,591.56)
08/04		(611,591.56)
09/04		(611,591.56)
10/04		(611,591.56)
11/04		(611,591.56)
12/04		(611,591.56)
12/31 BALANCE		(3,669,549.36)

Prepaid Expense
08/11		7,045,534.80
09/11		(587,127.90)
10/11		(587,127.90)
11/11		(587,127.90)
12/11		(587,127.90)
12/31 BALANCE		4,697,023.20

Accounts Payable

01/05	(1,957,093.00)
02/01	(489,273.25)
02/05	(2,348,511.60)
02/15	(1,174,255.80)
02/30	(1,174,255.80)
03/01	(489,273.25)
03/05	(2,935,639.50)
03/15	(1,174,255.80)
03/26	11,742,558.00
03/30	(1,174,255.80)
04/01	(489,273.25)
04/05	(3,522,767.40)
04/06	(11,742,558.00)
04/15	(1,174,255.80)
04/26	18,103,110.25
04/30	(1,174,255.80)
05/01	(489,273.25)
05/05	(4,109,895.30)
05/15	(1,174,255.80)
05/26	6,947,680.15
05/30	(1,174,255.80)
06/01	(489,273.25)
06/05	(4,697,023.20)
06/15	(1,174,255.80)
06/26	7,534,808.05
06/30	(1,174,255.80)
07/05	(5,284,151.10)
07/15	(1,174,255.80)
07/26	7,632,662.70
07/30	(1,174,255.80)
08/05	(5,871,279.00)
08/11	(7,045,534.80)
08/15	(1,174,255.80)
08/26	15,265,325.40
08/30	(1,174,255.80)
09/05	(6,458,406.90)
09/15	(1,174,255.80)
09/26	8,806,918.50
09/30	(1,174,255.80)
10/05	(7,045,534.80)
10/15	(1,174,255.80)
10/26	9,394,046.40
10/30	(1,174,255.80)
11/05	(7,632,662.70)
11/15	(1,174,255.80)
11/26	9,981,174.30
11/30	(1,174,255.80)
12/05	(8,219,790.60)
12/15	(1,174,255.80)

12/26   10,568,302.20
12/31 BALANCE   0.00

Business Loan
06/03   (146,781,975.00)
07/03   2,158,365.38
08/03   2,167,358.57
09/03   2,176,389.23
10/03   2,185,457.52
11/03   2,194,563.59
12/03   2,203,707.61
12/31 BALANCE   (133,696,133.10)

Unearned Revenue
10/13   (23,485,116.00)
11/13   23,485,116.00
12/31 BALANCE   0.00

Retained Earnings
11/20   5,871,279.00
12/31   (69,460,024.91)
12/31 BALANCE   (63,588,745.91)

Owner's Equity
07/01   (29,356,395.00)
12/31 BALANCE   (29,356,395.00)

Service Revenue
01/08   (5,871,279.00)
02/08   (5,871,279.00)
03/08   (5,871,279.00)
04/08   (5,871,279.00)
05/08   (5,871,279.00)
06/08   (5,871,279.00)
07/08   (5,871,279.00)
08/08   (5,871,279.00)
09/08   (5,871,279.00)
10/08   (5,871,279.00)
11/08   (5,871,279.00)
11/13   (23,485,116.00)
12/08   (5,871,279.00)
12/31   93,940,464.00
12/31 BALANCE   0.00

427

Sales Revenue

01/10	(2,348,511.60)
02/10	(3,287,916.24)
03/10	(4,109,895.30)
04/10	(4,931,874.36)
05/10	(5,753,853.42)
06/10	(6,575,832.48)
07/10	(7,397,811.54)
08/10	(8,219,790.60)
09/10	(9,041,769.66)
10/10	(9,863,748.72)
11/10	(10,685,727.78)
12/10	(11,507,706.84)
12/31	83,724,438.54
12/31 BALANCE	0.00

Sales Returns

01/24	46,970.23
02/24	65,758.32
03/24	82,197.91
04/24	98,637.49
05/24	115,077.07
06/24	131,516.65
07/24	147,956.23
08/24	164,395.81
09/24	180,835.39
10/24	197,274.97
11/24	213,714.56
12/24	230,154.14
12/31	(1,674,488.77)
12/31 BALANCE	0.00

Cost of Goods Sold

Date	Amount
01/10	1,957,093.00
01/24	(39,141.86)
02/10	2,348,511.60
02/24	(54,798.60)
03/10	2,935,639.50
03/24	(68,498.26)
04/10	3,522,767.40
04/24	(82,197.91)
05/10	4,109,895.30
05/24	(95,897.56)
06/10	4,697,023.20
06/24	(109,597.21)
07/10	5,284,151.10
07/24	(123,296.86)
08/10	5,871,279.00
08/24	(136,996.51)
09/10	6,458,406.90
09/24	(150,696.16)
10/10	7,045,534.80
10/24	(164,395.81)
11/10	7,632,662.70
11/24	(178,095.46)
12/10	8,219,790.60
12/24	(191,795.11)
12/31	(58,687,347.79)
12/31 BALANCE	0.00

Salaries Expense

	02/15	1,174,255.80
	02/30	1,174,255.80
	03/15	1,174,255.80
	03/30	1,174,255.80
	04/15	1,174,255.80
	04/30	1,174,255.80
	05/15	1,174,255.80
	05/30	1,174,255.80
	06/15	1,174,255.80
	06/30	1,174,255.80
	07/15	1,174,255.80
	07/30	1,174,255.80
	08/15	1,174,255.80
	08/30	1,174,255.80
	09/15	1,174,255.80
	09/30	1,174,255.80
	10/15	1,174,255.80
	10/30	1,174,255.80
	11/15	1,174,255.80
	11/30	1,174,255.80
	12/15	1,174,255.80
	12/30	1,174,255.80
	12/31	(25,833,627.60)
	12/31 BALANCE	0.00

Rent Expense

	02/01	489,273.25
	03/01	489,273.25
	04/01	489,273.25
	05/01	489,273.25
	06/01	489,273.25
	12/31	(2,446,366.25)
	12/31 BALANCE	0.00

Bad Debt Expense

	02/27	863,312.86
	03/27	1,358,261.68
	04/27	492,060.15
	05/27	575,502.77
	06/27	615,779.74
	07/27	656,056.72
	08/27	696,333.69
	09/27	736,610.66
	10/27	776,887.64
	11/27	817,164.61
	12/27	857,441.59
	12/31	(8,445,412.11)
	12/31 BALANCE	0.00

430

Depreciation Expense

05/06		195,709.30
06/06		195,709.30
07/04		611,591.56
07/06		195,709.30
08/04		611,591.56
08/06		195,709.30
09/04		611,591.56
09/06		195,709.30
10/04		611,591.56
10/06		195,709.30
11/04		611,591.56
11/06		195,709.30
12/04		611,591.56
12/06		195,709.30
12/31		(5,235,223.76)
12/31	BALANCE	0.00

Insurance Expense

09/11		587,127.90
10/11		587,127.90
11/11		587,127.90
12/11		587,127.90
12/31		(2,348,511.60)
12/31	BALANCE	0.00

Interest Expense

07/02		611,591.56
08/02		602,598.37
09/02		593,567.71
10/02		584,499.42
11/02		575,393.35
12/02		566,249.34
12/31		(3,533,899.75)
12/31	BALANCE	0.00

TRIAL BALANCE BEFORE AND AFTER CLOSING ENTRY:

Cash	68,433,790.07	68,433,790.07
Accounts Receivable	(0.01)	(0.01)
Allowance for Doubtful Accounts	0.00	0.00
Inventory	1,395,407.31	1,395,407.31
Equipment	11,742,558.00	11,742,558.00
Accum Deprn Eqmt	(1,565,674.40)	(1,565,674.40)
Building	146,781,975.00	146,781,975.00
Accum Deprn Bldg	(3,669,549.36)	(3,669,549.36)
Prepaid Expense	4,697,023.20	4,697,023.20
Accounts Payable	(1,174,255.80)	(1,174,255.80)
Business Loan	(133,696,133.10)	(133,696,133.10)
Unearned Revenue	0.00	0.00
Retained Earnings	0.00	(63,588,745.91)
Owner's Equity	(29,356,395.00)	(29,356,395.00)
Service Revenue	(93,940,464.00)	0.00
Sales Revenue	(83,724,438.54)	0.00
Sales Returns	1,674,488.77	0.00
Cost of Goods Sold	58,687,347.79	0.00
Salaries Expense	25,833,627.60	0.00
Rent Expense	2,446,366.25	0.00
Bad Debt Expense	8,445,412.11	0.00
Depreciation Expense	5,235,223.76	0.00
Insurance Expense	2,348,511.60	0.00
Interest Expense	3,533,899.75	0.00

FINANCIAL STATEMENTS

Balance Sheet (Dec 31)

ASSETS
Cash	68,433,790.07
Accounts Receivable	(0.01)
Inventory	1,395,407.31
Prepaids	4,697,023.20
Property Plant & Equipment	158,524,533.00
Accumulated Depreciation Expense	(5,235,223.76)
Net Property Plant & Equipment	153,289,309.24
Total Assets	227,815,529.81

LIABILITIES
Accounts Payable	1,174,255.80
Loans	133,696,133.10
Total Liabilities	134,870,388.90

SHAREHOLDER'S EQUITY
Owner's Equity	29,356,395.00
Retained Earnings	63,588,745.91
Total Shareholder's Equity	92,945,140.91
Total Liabilities & Shareholder's Equity	227,815,529.81

Income Statement (Jan 1 to Dec 31)

REVENUE
Services	93,940,464.00
Sales	83,724,438.54
Sales Returns	(1,674,488.77)
Total Revenue	175,990,413.77

EXPENSES
Cost of Goods Sold	58,687,347.79
Salaries Expense	25,833,627.60
Rent Expense	2,446,366.25
Bad Debts	8,445,412.11
Depreciation Expense	5,235,223.76
Insurance	2,348,511.60
Interest	3,533,899.75
Total Expenses	106,530,388.86
Net Income	69,460,024.91

Statement of Retained Earnings (Jan 1 to Dec 31)

Opening Balance	0.00
Net Income	69,460,024.91
Dividends Paid	(5,871,279.00)
Closing Balance	63,588,745.91

Statement of Cash Flows (Jan 1 to Dec31)

Beginning Cash Balance	0.00
Operating Activities	
Net Income	69,460,024.91
Depreciation Expense	5,235,223.76
Increase in Prepaid Expenses	(4,697,023.20)
Increase in Accounts Payable	1,174,255.80
Increase in Inventory	(1,395,407.31)
Investment Activities	
PPE Purchases	(158,524,533.00)
Financing Activities	
Bank Loan	146,781,975.00
Bank Loan repayment of principal	(13,085,841.90)
Owner Investment	29,356,395.00
Dividend Paid to Owner	(5,871,279.00)
Net Cash Flows	68,433,790.06
Ending Cash Balance	68,433,790.06

CASE #5 SOLUTION:

General Journal Entries:

Date: 01/05
      DR Inventory $2211515
          CR Accounts Payable $2211515

Date: 01/08
      DR Accounts Receivable $6634545
          CR Service Revenue $6634545

Date: 01/10
      DR Accounts Receivable $2653818
          CR Sales Revenue $2653818
      DR Cost of Goods Sold $2211515
          CR Inventory $2211515

Date: 01/24
      DR Sales Returns $53076.36
          CR Accounts Receivable $53076.36
      DR Inventory $44230.3
          CR Cost of Goods Sold $44230.3

Date: 02/01
      DR Rent Expense $552878.75
          CR Accounts Payable $552878.75

Date: 02/05
      DR Inventory $2653818
          CR Accounts Payable $2653818

Date: 02/08
      DR Accounts Receivable $6634545
          CR Service Revenue $6634545

Date: 02/10
      DR Accounts Receivable $3715345.2
          CR Sales Revenue $3715345.2
      DR Cost of Goods Sold $2653818
          CR Inventory $2653818

Date: 02/15
      DR Salaries Expense $1326909
          CR Accounts Payable $1326909

Date: 02/24
      DR Sales Returns $74306.9
          CR Accounts Receivable $74306.9
      DR Inventory $61922.42
          CR Cost of Goods Sold $61922.42

Date: 02/27
>   DR Bad Debt Expense $975543.5
>   CR Allowance for Doubtful Accounts $975543.5

Date: 02/30
>   DR Salaries Expense $1326909
>   CR Accounts Payable $1326909

Date: 03/01
>   DR Rent Expense $552878.75
>   CR Accounts Payable $552878.75

Date: 03/05
>   DR Inventory $3317272.5
>   CR Accounts Payable $3317272.5

Date: 03/08
>   DR Accounts Receivable $6634545
>   CR Service Revenue $6634545

Date: 03/10
>   DR Accounts Receivable $4644181.5
>   CR Sales Revenue $4644181.5
>   DR Cost of Goods Sold $3317272.5
>   CR Inventory $3317272.5

Date: 03/15
>   DR Salaries Expense $1326909
>   CR Accounts Payable $1326909

Date: 03/24
>   DR Sales Returns $92883.63
>   CR Accounts Receivable $92883.63
>   DR Inventory $77403.025
>   CR Cost of Goods Sold $77403.025

Date: 03/26
>   DR Accounts Payable $13269090
>   CR Cash $13269090

Date: 03/27
>   DR Bad Debt Expense $1534835.64
>   CR Allowance for Doubtful Accounts $1534835.64

Date: 03/28
>   DR Cash $29161877.17
>   CR Accounts Receivable $29161877.17

Date: 03/29
>   DR Allowance for Doubtful Accounts $2510379.14
>   CR Accounts Receivable $2510379.14

Date: 03/30
          DR Salaries Expense $1326909
               CR Accounts Payable $1326909

Date: 04/01
          DR Rent Expense $552878.75
               CR Accounts Payable $552878.75

Date: 04/05
          DR Inventory $3980727
               CR Accounts Payable $3980727

Date: 04/06
          DR Equipment $13269090
               CR Accounts Payable $13269090

Date: 04/08
          DR Accounts Receivable $6634545
               CR Service Revenue $6634545

Date: 04/10
          DR Accounts Receivable $5573017.8
               CR Sales Revenue $5573017.8
          DR Cost of Goods Sold $3980727
               CR Inventory $3980727

Date: 04/15
          DR Salaries Expense $1326909
               CR Accounts Payable $1326909

Date: 04/24
          DR Sales Returns $111460.36
               CR Accounts Receivable $111460.36
          DR Inventory $92883.63
               CR Cost of Goods Sold $92883.63

Date: 04/26
          DR Accounts Payable $20456513.75
               CR Cash $20456513.75

Date: 04/27
          DR Bad Debt Expense $556027.95
               CR Allowance for Doubtful Accounts $556027.95

Date: 04/28
          DR Cash $10564530.99
               CR Accounts Receivable $10564530.99

Date: 04/29
          DR Allowance for Doubtful Accounts $556027.95
               CR Accounts Receivable $556027.95

Date: 04/30
DR Salaries Expense $1326909
    CR Accounts Payable $1326909

Date: 05/01
DR Rent Expense $552878.75
    CR Accounts Payable $552878.75

Date: 05/05
DR Inventory $4644181.5
    CR Accounts Payable $4644181.5

Date: 05/06
DR Depreciation Expense $221151.5
    CR Accum Deprn Eqmt $221151.5

Date: 05/08
DR Accounts Receivable $6634545
    CR Service Revenue $6634545

Date: 05/10
DR Accounts Receivable $6501854.1
    CR Sales Revenue $6501854.1
DR Cost of Goods Sold $4644181.5
    CR Inventory $4644181.5

Date: 05/15
DR Salaries Expense $1326909
    CR Accounts Payable $1326909

Date: 05/24
DR Sales Returns $130037.08
    CR Accounts Receivable $130037.08
DR Inventory $108364.235
    CR Cost of Goods Sold $108364.235

Date: 05/26
DR Accounts Payable $7850878.25
    CR Cash $7850878.25

Date: 05/27
DR Bad Debt Expense $650318.1
    CR Allowance for Doubtful Accounts $650318.1

Date: 05/28
DR Cash $12356043.92
    CR Accounts Receivable $12356043.92

Date: 05/29
DR Allowance for Doubtful Accounts $650318.1
    CR Accounts Receivable $650318.1

Date: 05/30
DR Salaries Expense $1326909
    CR Accounts Payable $1326909

Date: 06/01
DR Rent Expense $552878.75
    CR Accounts Payable $552878.75

Date: 06/03
DR Cash $165863625
    CR Business Loan $165863625

Date: 06/04
DR Building $165863625
    CR Cash $165863625

Date: 06/05
DR Inventory $5307636
    CR Accounts Payable $5307636

Date: 06/06
DR Depreciation Expense $221151.5
    CR Accum Deprn Eqmt $221151.5

Date: 06/08
DR Accounts Receivable $6634545
    CR Service Revenue $6634545

Date: 06/10
DR Accounts Receivable $7430690.4
    CR Sales Revenue $7430690.4
DR Cost of Goods Sold $5307636
    CR Inventory $5307636

Date: 06/15
DR Salaries Expense $1326909
    CR Accounts Payable $1326909

Date: 06/24
DR Sales Returns $148613.81
    CR Accounts Receivable $148613.81
DR Inventory $123844.84
    CR Cost of Goods Sold $123844.84

Date: 06/26
DR Accounts Payable $8514332.75
    CR Cash $8514332.75

Date: 06/27
DR Bad Debt Expense $695831.08
    CR Allowance for Doubtful Accounts $695831.08

Date: 06/28
  DR Cash $13220790.51
    CR Accounts Receivable $13220790.51

Date: 06/29
  DR Allowance for Doubtful Accounts $695831.08
    CR Accounts Receivable $695831.08

Date: 06/30
  DR Salaries Expense $1326909
    CR Accounts Payable $1326909

Date: 07/01
  DR Cash $33172725
    CR Owner's Equity $33172725

Date: 07/02
  DR Interest Expense $691098.44
    CR Cash $691098.44

Date: 07/03
  DR Business Loan $2438952.78
    CR Cash $2438952.78

Date: 07/04
  DR Depreciation Expense $691098.44
    CR Accum Deprn Bldg $691098.44

Date: 07/05
  DR Inventory $5971090.5
    CR Accounts Payable $5971090.5

Date: 07/06
  DR Depreciation Expense $221151.5
    CR Accum Deprn Eqmt $221151.5

Date: 07/08
  DR Accounts Receivable $6634545
    CR Service Revenue $6634545

Date: 07/10
  DR Accounts Receivable $8359526.7
    CR Sales Revenue $8359526.7
  DR Cost of Goods Sold $5971090.5
    CR Inventory $5971090.5

Date: 07/15
  DR Salaries Expense $1326909
    CR Accounts Payable $1326909

Date: 07/24
DR Sales Returns $167190.53
CR Accounts Receivable $167190.53
DR Inventory $139325.445
CR Cost of Goods Sold $139325.445

Date: 07/26
DR Accounts Payable $8624908.5
CR Cash $8624908.5

Date: 07/27
DR Bad Debt Expense $741344.06
CR Allowance for Doubtful Accounts $741344.06

Date: 07/28
DR Cash $14085537.11
CR Accounts Receivable $14085537.11

Date: 07/29
DR Allowance for Doubtful Accounts $741344.06
CR Accounts Receivable $741344.06

Date: 07/30
DR Salaries Expense $1326909
CR Accounts Payable $1326909

Date: 08/02
DR Interest Expense $680936.13
CR Cash $680936.13

Date: 08/03
DR Business Loan $2449115.09
CR Cash $2449115.09

Date: 08/04
DR Depreciation Expense $691098.44
CR Accum Deprn Bldg $691098.44

Date: 08/05
DR Inventory $6634545
CR Accounts Payable $6634545

Date: 08/06
DR Depreciation Expense $221151.5
CR Accum Deprn Eqmt $221151.5

Date: 08/08
DR Accounts Receivable $6634545
CR Service Revenue $6634545

Date: 08/10
        DR Accounts Receivable $9288363
             CR Sales Revenue $9288363
        DR Cost of Goods Sold $6634545
             CR Inventory $6634545

Date: 08/11
        DR Prepaid Expense $7961454
             CR Accounts Payable $7961454

Date: 08/15
        DR Salaries Expense $1326909
             CR Accounts Payable $1326909

Date: 08/24
        DR Sales Returns $185767.26
             CR Accounts Receivable $185767.26
        DR Inventory $154806.05
             CR Cost of Goods Sold $154806.05

Date: 08/26
        DR Accounts Payable $17249817
             CR Cash $17249817

Date: 08/27
        DR Bad Debt Expense $786857.04
             CR Allowance for Doubtful Accounts $786857.04

Date: 08/28
        DR Cash $14950283.7
             CR Accounts Receivable $14950283.7

Date: 08/29
        DR Allowance for Doubtful Accounts $786857.04
             CR Accounts Receivable $786857.04

Date: 08/30
        DR Salaries Expense $1326909
             CR Accounts Payable $1326909

Date: 09/02
        DR Interest Expense $670731.49
             CR Cash $670731.49

Date: 09/03
        DR Business Loan $2459319.73
             CR Cash $2459319.73

Date: 09/04
        DR Depreciation Expense $691098.44
             CR Accum Deprn Bldg $691098.44

Date: 09/05
        DR Inventory $7297999.5
              CR Accounts Payable $7297999.5

Date: 09/06
        DR Depreciation Expense $221151.5
              CR Accum Deprn Eqmt $221151.5

Date: 09/08
        DR Accounts Receivable $6634545
              CR Service Revenue $6634545

Date: 09/10
        DR Accounts Receivable $10217199.3
              CR Sales Revenue $10217199.3
        DR Cost of Goods Sold $7297999.5
              CR Inventory $7297999.5

Date: 09/11
        DR Insurance Expense $663454.5
              CR Prepaid Expense $663454.5

Date: 09/15
        DR Salaries Expense $1326909
              CR Accounts Payable $1326909

Date: 09/24
        DR Sales Returns $204343.99
              CR Accounts Receivable $204343.99
        DR Inventory $170286.655
              CR Cost of Goods Sold $170286.655

Date: 09/26
        DR Accounts Payable $9951817.5
              CR Cash $9951817.5

Date: 09/27
        DR Bad Debt Expense $832370.02
              CR Allowance for Doubtful Accounts $832370.02

Date: 09/28
        DR Cash $15815030.29
              CR Accounts Receivable $15815030.29

Date: 09/29
        DR Allowance for Doubtful Accounts $832370.02
              CR Accounts Receivable $832370.02

Date: 09/30
        DR Salaries Expense $1326909
              CR Accounts Payable $1326909

Date: 10/02
        DR Interest Expense $660484.32
            CR Cash $660484.32

Date: 10/03
        DR Business Loan $2469566.9
            CR Cash $2469566.9

Date: 10/04
        DR Depreciation Expense $691098.44
            CR Accum Deprn Bldg $691098.44

Date: 10/05
        DR Inventory $7961454
            CR Accounts Payable $7961454

Date: 10/06
        DR Depreciation Expense $221151.5
            CR Accum Deprn Eqmt $221151.5

Date: 10/08
        DR Accounts Receivable $6634545
            CR Service Revenue $6634545

Date: 10/10
        DR Accounts Receivable $11146035.6
            CR Sales Revenue $11146035.6
        DR Cost of Goods Sold $7961454
            CR Inventory $7961454

Date: 10/11
        DR Insurance Expense $663454.5
            CR Prepaid Expense $663454.5

Date: 10/13
        DR Cash $26538180
            CR Unearned Revenue $26538180

Date: 10/15
        DR Salaries Expense $1326909
            CR Accounts Payable $1326909

Date: 10/24
        DR Sales Returns $222920.71
            CR Accounts Receivable $222920.71
        DR Inventory $185767.26
            CR Cost of Goods Sold $185767.26

Date: 10/26
        DR Accounts Payable $10615272
            CR Cash $10615272

Date: 10/27
DR Bad Debt Expense $877882.99
    CR Allowance for Doubtful Accounts $877882.99

Date: 10/28
DR Cash $16679776.9
    CR Accounts Receivable $16679776.9

Date: 10/29
DR Allowance for Doubtful Accounts $877882.99
    CR Accounts Receivable $877882.99

Date: 10/30
DR Salaries Expense $1326909
    CR Accounts Payable $1326909

Date: 11/02
DR Interest Expense $650194.46
    CR Cash $650194.46

Date: 11/03
DR Business Loan $2479856.76
    CR Cash $2479856.76

Date: 11/04
DR Depreciation Expense $691098.44
    CR Accum Deprn Bldg $691098.44

Date: 11/05
DR Inventory $8624908.5
    CR Accounts Payable $8624908.5

Date: 11/06
DR Depreciation Expense $221151.5
    CR Accum Deprn Eqmt $221151.5

Date: 11/08
DR Accounts Receivable $6634545
    CR Service Revenue $6634545

Date: 11/10
DR Accounts Receivable $12074871.9
    CR Sales Revenue $12074871.9
DR Cost of Goods Sold $8624908.5
    CR Inventory $8624908.5

Date: 11/11
DR Insurance Expense $663454.5
    CR Prepaid Expense $663454.5

Date: 11/13
    DR Unearned Revenue $26538180
        CR Service Revenue $26538180

Date: 11/15
    DR Salaries Expense $1326909
        CR Accounts Payable $1326909

Date: 11/20
    DR Retained Earnings $6634545
        CR Cash $6634545

Date: 11/24
    DR Sales Returns $241497.44
        CR Accounts Receivable $241497.44
    DR Inventory $201247.865
        CR Cost of Goods Sold $201247.865

Date: 11/26
    DR Accounts Payable $11278726.5
        CR Cash $11278726.5

Date: 11/27
    DR Bad Debt Expense $923395.97
        CR Allowance for Doubtful Accounts $923395.97

Date: 11/28
    DR Cash $17544523.49
        CR Accounts Receivable $17544523.49

Date: 11/29
    DR Allowance for Doubtful Accounts $923395.97
        CR Accounts Receivable $923395.97

Date: 11/30
    DR Salaries Expense $1326909
        CR Accounts Payable $1326909

Date: 12/02
    DR Interest Expense $639861.72
        CR Cash $639861.72

Date: 12/03
    DR Business Loan $2490189.5
        CR Cash $2490189.5

Date: 12/04
    DR Depreciation Expense $691098.44
        CR Accum Deprn Bldg $691098.44

Date: 12/05
        DR Inventory $9288363
              CR Accounts Payable $9288363

Date: 12/06
        DR Depreciation Expense $221151.5
              CR Accum Deprn Eqmt $221151.5

Date: 12/08
        DR Accounts Receivable $6634545
              CR Service Revenue $6634545

Date: 12/10
        DR Accounts Receivable $13003708.2
              CR Sales Revenue $13003708.2
        DR Cost of Goods Sold $9288363
              CR Inventory $9288363

Date: 12/11
        DR Insurance Expense $663454.5
              CR Prepaid Expense $663454.5

Date: 12/15
        DR Salaries Expense $1326909
              CR Accounts Payable $1326909

Date: 12/24
        DR Sales Returns $260074.16
              CR Accounts Receivable $260074.16
        DR Inventory $216728.47
              CR Cost of Goods Sold $216728.47

Date: 12/26
        DR Accounts Payable $11942181
              CR Cash $11942181

Date: 12/27
        DR Bad Debt Expense $968908.95
              CR Allowance for Doubtful Accounts $968908.95

Date: 12/28
        DR Cash $18409270.09
              CR Accounts Receivable $18409270.09

Date: 12/29
        DR Allowance for Doubtful Accounts $968908.95
              CR Accounts Receivable $968908.95

Date: 12/30
        DR Salaries Expense $1326909
              CR Accounts Payable $1326909

Date: 12/31
DR Revenue $198869159.47
CR Retained Earnings $198869159.47
DR Retained Earnings $120379334.555
CR Expense $120379334.555

GENERAL LEDGER:

Cash

03/26	(13,269,090.00)
03/28	29,161,877.17
04/26	(20,456,513.75)
04/28	10,564,530.99
05/26	(7,850,878.25)
05/28	12,356,043.92
06/03	165,863,625.00
06/04	(165,863,625.00)
06/26	(8,514,332.75)
06/28	13,220,790.51
07/01	33,172,725.00
07/02	(691,098.44)
07/03	(2,438,952.78)
07/26	(8,624,908.50)
07/28	14,085,537.11
08/02	(680,936.13)
08/03	(2,449,115.09)
08/26	(17,249,817.00)
08/28	14,950,283.70
09/02	(670,731.49)
09/03	(2,459,319.73)
09/26	(9,951,817.50)
09/28	15,815,030.29
10/02	(660,484.32)
10/03	(2,469,566.90)
10/13	26,538,180.00
10/26	(10,615,272.00)
10/28	16,679,776.90
11/02	(650,194.46)
11/03	(2,479,856.76)
11/20	(6,634,545.00)
11/26	(11,278,726.50)
11/28	17,544,523.49
12/02	(639,861.72)
12/03	(2,490,189.50)
12/26	(11,942,181.00)
12/28	18,409,270.09
12/31 BALANCE	77,330,179.60

Accounts Receivable

01/08	6,634,545.00	
01/10	2,653,818.00	
01/24	(53,076.36)	
02/08	6,634,545.00	
02/10	3,715,345.20	
02/24	(74,306.90)	
03/08	6,634,545.00	
03/10	4,644,181.50	
03/24	(92,883.63)	
03/28	(29,161,877.17)	
03/29	(2,510,379.14)	
04/08	6,634,545.00	
04/10	5,573,017.80	
04/24	(111,460.36)	
04/28	(10,564,530.99)	
04/29	(556,027.95)	
05/08	6,634,545.00	
05/10	6,501,854.10	
05/24	(130,037.08)	
05/28	(12,356,043.92)	
05/29	(650,318.10)	
06/08	6,634,545.00	
06/10	7,430,690.40	
06/24	(148,613.81)	
06/28	(13,220,790.51)	
06/29	(695,831.08)	
07/08	6,634,545.00	
07/10	8,359,526.70	
07/24	(167,190.53)	
07/28	(14,085,537.11)	
07/29	(741,344.06)	
08/08	6,634,545.00	
08/10	9,288,363.00	
08/24	(185,767.26)	
08/28	(14,950,283.70)	
08/29	(786,857.04)	
09/08	6,634,545.00	
09/10	10,217,199.30	
09/24	(204,343.99)	
09/28	(15,815,030.29)	
09/29	(832,370.02)	
10/08	6,634,545.00	
10/10	11,146,035.60	
10/24	(222,920.71)	
10/28	(16,679,776.90)	
10/29	(877,882.99)	
11/08	6,634,545.00	
11/10	12,074,871.90	
11/24	(241,497.44)	

11/28	(17,544,523.49)
11/29	(923,395.97)
12/08	6,634,545.00
12/10	13,003,708.20
12/24	(260,074.16)
12/28	(18,409,270.09)
12/29	(968,908.95)
12/31 BALANCE	0.00

Allowance for Doubtful Accounts

02/27	(975,543.50)
03/27	(1,534,835.64)
03/29	2,510,379.14
04/27	(556,027.95)
04/29	556,027.95
05/27	(650,318.10)
05/29	650,318.10
06/27	(695,831.08)
06/29	695,831.08
07/27	(741,344.06)
07/29	741,344.06
08/27	(786,857.04)
08/29	786,857.04
09/27	(832,370.02)
09/29	832,370.02
10/27	(877,882.99)
10/29	877,882.99
11/27	(923,395.97)
11/29	923,395.97
12/27	(968,908.95)
12/29	968,908.95
12/31 BALANCE	0.00

Inventory

	01/05	2,211,515.00
	01/10	(2,211,515.00)
	01/24	44,230.30
	02/05	2,653,818.00
	02/10	(2,653,818.00)
	02/24	61,922.42
	03/05	3,317,272.50
	03/10	(3,317,272.50)
	03/24	77,403.03
	04/05	3,980,727.00
	04/10	(3,980,727.00)
	04/24	92,883.63
	05/05	4,644,181.50
	05/10	(4,644,181.50)
	05/24	108,364.24
	06/05	5,307,636.00
	06/10	(5,307,636.00)
	06/24	123,844.84
	07/05	5,971,090.50
	07/10	(5,971,090.50)
	07/24	139,325.45
	08/05	6,634,545.00
	08/10	(6,634,545.00)
	08/24	154,806.05
	09/05	7,297,999.50
	09/10	(7,297,999.50)
	09/24	170,286.66
	10/05	7,961,454.00
	10/10	(7,961,454.00)
	10/24	185,767.26
	11/05	8,624,908.50
	11/10	(8,624,908.50)
	11/24	201,247.87
	12/31 BALANCE	1,360,081.75

Equipment

	04/06	13,269,090.00
	12/31 BALANCE	13,269,090.00

Accum Deprn Eqmt

	05/06	(221,151.50)
	06/06	(221,151.50)
	07/06	(221,151.50)
	08/06	(221,151.50)
	09/06	(221,151.50)
	10/06	(221,151.50)
	11/06	(221,151.50)
	12/06	(221,151.50)
	12/31 BALANCE	(1,769,212.00)

Building
| | 06/04 | 165,863,625.00 |
| | 12/31 BALANCE | 165,863,625.00 |

Accum Deprn Bldg
	07/04	(691,098.44)
	08/04	(691,098.44)
	09/04	(691,098.44)
	10/04	(691,098.44)
	11/04	(691,098.44)
	12/04	(691,098.44)
	12/31 BALANCE	(4,146,590.64)

Prepaid Expense
	08/11	7,961,454.00
	09/11	(663,454.50)
	10/11	(663,454.50)
	11/11	(663,454.50)
	12/11	(663,454.50)
	12/31 BALANCE	5,307,636.00

Accounts Payable

01/05	(2,211,515.00)
02/01	(552,878.75)
02/05	(2,653,818.00)
02/15	(1,326,909.00)
02/30	(1,326,909.00)
03/01	(552,878.75)
03/05	(3,317,272.50)
03/15	(1,326,909.00)
03/26	13,269,090.00
03/30	(1,326,909.00)
04/01	(552,878.75)
04/05	(3,980,727.00)
04/06	(13,269,090.00)
04/15	(1,326,909.00)
04/26	20,456,513.75
04/30	(1,326,909.00)
05/01	(552,878.75)
05/05	(4,644,181.50)
05/15	(1,326,909.00)
05/26	7,850,878.25
05/30	(1,326,909.00)
06/01	(552,878.75)
06/05	(5,307,636.00)
06/15	(1,326,909.00)
06/26	8,514,332.75
06/30	(1,326,909.00)
07/05	(5,971,090.50)
07/15	(1,326,909.00)
07/26	8,624,908.50
07/30	(1,326,909.00)
08/05	(6,634,545.00)
08/11	(7,961,454.00)
08/15	(1,326,909.00)
08/26	17,249,817.00
08/30	(1,326,909.00)
09/05	(7,297,999.50)
09/15	(1,326,909.00)
09/26	9,951,817.50
09/30	(1,326,909.00)
10/05	(7,961,454.00)
10/15	(1,326,909.00)
10/26	10,615,272.00
10/30	(1,326,909.00)
11/05	(8,624,908.50)
11/15	(1,326,909.00)
11/26	11,278,726.50
11/30	(1,326,909.00)
12/05	(9,288,363.00)
12/15	(1,326,909.00)

```
12/26              11,942,181.00
12/31 BALANCE         0.00

Business Loan
        06/03         (165,863,625.00)
        07/03          2,438,952.78
        08/03          2,449,115.09
        09/03          2,459,319.73
        10/03          2,469,566.90
        11/03          2,479,856.76
        12/03          2,490,189.50
        12/31 BALANCE    (151,076,624.24)

Unearned Revenue
        10/13         (26,538,180.00)
        11/13          26,538,180.00
        12/31 BALANCE       0.00

Retained Earnings
        11/20          6,634,545.00
        12/31         (78,489,824.92)
        12/31 BALANCE    (71,855,279.92)

Owner's Equity
        07/01         (33,172,725.00)
        12/31 BALANCE    (33,172,725.00)


Service Revenue
        01/08          (6,634,545.00)
        02/08          (6,634,545.00)
        03/08          (6,634,545.00)
        04/08          (6,634,545.00)
        05/08          (6,634,545.00)
        06/08          (6,634,545.00)
        07/08          (6,634,545.00)
        08/08          (6,634,545.00)
        09/08          (6,634,545.00)
        10/08          (6,634,545.00)
        11/08          (6,634,545.00)
        11/13         (26,538,180.00)
        12/08          (6,634,545.00)
        12/31         106,152,720.00
        12/31 BALANCE       0.00
```

Sales Revenue

01/10	(2,653,818.00)
02/10	(3,715,345.20)
03/10	(4,644,181.50)
04/10	(5,573,017.80)
05/10	(6,501,854.10)
06/10	(7,430,690.40)
07/10	(8,359,526.70)
08/10	(9,288,363.00)
09/10	(10,217,199.30)
10/10	(11,146,035.60)
11/10	(12,074,871.90)
12/10	(13,003,708.20)
12/31	94,608,611.70
12/31 BALANCE	0.00

Sales Returns

01/24	53,076.36
02/24	74,306.90
03/24	92,883.63
04/24	111,460.36
05/24	130,037.08
06/24	148,613.81
07/24	167,190.53
08/24	185,767.26
09/24	204,343.99
10/24	222,920.71
11/24	241,497.44
12/24	260,074.16
12/31	(1,892,172.23)
12/31 BALANCE	0.00

Cost of Goods Sold

Date	Amount
01/10	2,211,515.00
01/24	(44,230.30)
02/10	2,653,818.00
02/24	(61,922.42)
03/10	3,317,272.50
03/24	(77,403.03)
04/10	3,980,727.00
04/24	(92,883.63)
05/10	4,644,181.50
05/24	(108,364.24)
06/10	5,307,636.00
06/24	(123,844.84)
07/10	5,971,090.50
07/24	(139,325.45)
08/10	6,634,545.00
08/24	(154,806.05)
09/10	7,297,999.50
09/24	(170,286.66)
10/10	7,961,454.00
10/24	(185,767.26)
11/10	8,624,908.50
11/24	(201,247.87)
12/10	9,288,363.00
12/24	(216,728.47)
12/31	(66,316,700.31)
12/31 BALANCE	(0.03)

Salaries Expense

	02/15	1,326,909.00
	02/30	1,326,909.00
	03/15	1,326,909.00
	03/30	1,326,909.00
	04/15	1,326,909.00
	04/30	1,326,909.00
	05/15	1,326,909.00
	05/30	1,326,909.00
	06/15	1,326,909.00
	06/30	1,326,909.00
	07/15	1,326,909.00
	07/30	1,326,909.00
	08/15	1,326,909.00
	08/30	1,326,909.00
	09/15	1,326,909.00
	09/30	1,326,909.00
	10/15	1,326,909.00
	10/30	1,326,909.00
	11/15	1,326,909.00
	11/30	1,326,909.00
	12/15	1,326,909.00
	12/30	1,326,909.00
	12/31	(29,191,998.00)
	12/31 BALANCE	0.00

Rent Expense

	02/01	552,878.75
	03/01	552,878.75
	04/01	552,878.75
	05/01	552,878.75
	06/01	552,878.75
	12/31	(2,764,393.75)
	12/31 BALANCE	0.00

Bad Debt Expense

	02/27	975,543.50
	03/27	1,534,835.64
	04/27	556,027.95
	05/27	650,318.10
	06/27	695,831.08
	07/27	741,344.06
	08/27	786,857.04
	09/27	832,370.02
	10/27	877,882.99
	11/27	923,395.97
	12/27	968,908.95
	12/31	(9,543,315.30)
	12/31 BALANCE	0.00

Depreciation Expense

Date	Amount
05/06	221,151.50
06/06	221,151.50
07/04	691,098.44
07/06	221,151.50
08/04	691,098.44
08/06	221,151.50
09/04	691,098.44
09/06	221,151.50
10/04	691,098.44
10/06	221,151.50
11/04	691,098.44
11/06	221,151.50
12/04	691,098.44
12/06	221,151.50
12/31	(5,915,802.64)
12/31 BALANCE	0.00

Insurance Expense

Date	Amount
09/11	663,454.50
10/11	663,454.50
11/11	663,454.50
12/11	663,454.50
12/31	(2,653,818.00)
12/31 BALANCE	0.00

Interest Expense

Date	Amount
07/02	691,098.44
08/02	680,936.13
09/02	670,731.49
10/02	660,484.32
11/02	650,194.46
12/02	639,861.72
12/31	(3,993,306.56)
12/31 BALANCE	0.00

TRIAL BALANCE BEFORE AND AFTER CLOSING ENTRY:

Cash	77,330,179.60	77,330,179.60
Accounts Receivable	0.00	0.00
Allowance for Doubtful Accounts	0.00	0.00
Inventory	1,576,810.20	1,576,810.20
Equipment	13,269,090.00	13,269,090.00
Accum Deprn Eqmt	(1,769,212.00)	(1,769,212.00)
Building	165,863,625.00	165,863,625.00
Accum Deprn Bldg	(4,146,590.64)	(4,146,590.64)
Prepaid Expense	5,307,636.00	5,307,636.00
Accounts Payable	(1,326,909.00)	(1,326,909.00)
Business Loan	(151,076,624.24)	(151,076,624.24)
Unearned Revenue	0.00	0.00
Retained Earnings	0.00	(71,855,279.92)
Owner's Equity	(33,172,725.00)	(33,172,725.00)
Service Revenue	(106,152,720.00)	0.00
Sales Revenue	(94,608,611.70)	0.00
Sales Returns	1,892,172.23	0.00
Cost of Goods Sold	66,316,700.31	0.00
Salaries Expense	29,191,998.00	0.00
Rent Expense	2,764,393.75	0.00
Bad Debt Expense	9,543,315.30	0.00
Depreciation Expense	5,915,802.64	0.00
Insurance Expense	2,653,818.00	0.00
Interest Expense	3,993,306.56	0.00

FINANCIAL STATEMENTS

Balance Sheet (Dec 31)

ASSETS
Cash	77,330,179.60
Accounts Receivable	0.00
Inventory	1,576,810.20
Prepaids	5,307,636.00
Property Plant & Equipment	179,132,715.00
Accumulated Depreciation Expense	(5,915,802.64)
Net Property Plant & Equipment	173,216,912.36
Total Assets	257,431,538.16

LIABILITIES
Accounts Payable	1,326,909.00
Loans	151,076,624.24
Total Liabilities	152,403,533.24

SHAREHOLDER'S EQUITY
Owner's Equity	33,172,725.00
Retained Earnings	71,855,279.92
Total Shareholder's Equity	105,028,004.92

Total Liabilities & Shareholder's Equity	257,431,538.16

Income Statement (Jan 1 to Dec 31)

REVENUE
Services	106,152,720.00
Sales	94,608,611.70
Sales Returns	(1,892,172.23)
Total Revenue	198,869,159.47

EXPENSES
Cost of Goods Sold	66,316,700.31
Salaries Expense	29,191,998.00
Rent Expense	2,764,393.75
Bad Debts	9,543,315.30
Depreciation Expense	5,915,802.64
Insurance	2,653,818.00
Interest	3,993,306.56
Total Expenses	120,379,334.56

Net Income	78,489,824.92

Statement of Retained Earnings (Jan 1 to Dec 31)

Opening Balance	0.00
Net Income	78,489,824.92
Dividends Paid	(6,634,545.00)
Closing Balance	71,855,279.92

Statement of Cash Flows (Jan 1 to Dec31)

Beginning Cash Balance	0.00
Operating Activities	
Net Income	78,489,824.92
Depreciation Expense	5,915,802.64
Increase in Prepaid Expenses	(5,307,636.00)
Increase in Accounts Payable	1,326,909.00
Increase in Inventory	(1,576,810.20)
Investment Activities	
PPE Purchases	(179,132,715.00)
Financing Activities	
Bank Loan	165,863,625.00
Bank Loan repayment of principal	(14,787,000.76)
Owner Investment	33,172,725.00
Dividend Paid to Owner	(6,634,545.00)
Net Cash Flows	77,330,179.60
Ending Cash Balance	77,330,179.60

APPENDIX A: Sample Audit Risk Categorization Table

Inherent Risk, Control Risk, and Detection Risk
Low   33%
Medium 50%
High   66%

Audit Risk
Low   4-5%
medium-low   7-8%
medium 11-13%
medium-high   14-17%
high   >22%

Take a look at these comprehensive books on Amazon!
Paperback and ebook formats are both available
Introductory Accounting Double Entry Exercises (Expanded Edition):
40 Full Cycle Accounting Cases with Complete Solutions
Introductory Accounting Double Entry Exercises:
20 Full Cycle Accounting Cases with Complete Solutions

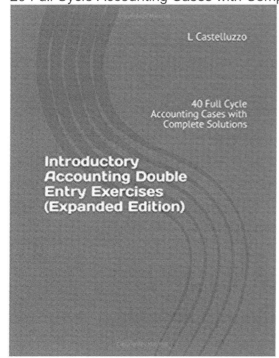
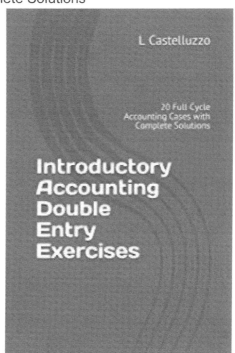

Financial accounting and managerial accounting exercises are also available, as well as audit, and case writing.

Introductory Accounting Exercise Workbook Combo Edition:

755 Practice Questions and Business Cases Pertaining to Financial Accounting, Management Accounting and Financial Audit

Financial Audit Exercise Workbook:

156 Multiple Choice Practice Questions with Solutions

Introductory Double Entry Accounting Practice Workbook:

1000 Questions with Solutions

Introductory Double Entry Accounting Workbook:

800 Multiple Choice Questions with Solutions and Explanations

Introductory Quantitative Analysis Workbook: Management Decision Making:

1000 Mini Business Cases with Questions and Full Solutions

Introduction to Case Writing for Accountants:

23 Business Cases Pertaining to Financial Accounting, Key Performance Indicators and Audit

14805088R00282